Les Demoiselles d'Avignon *by Pablo Picasso (1907). Picasso's unconventional treatment of five prostitutes from Avignon Street in Barcelona made this a controversial painting and ushered in the new style of Cubism.*

THE

GREAT

IDEAS

TODAY

ENCYCLOPÆDIA BRITANNICA, INC.

CHICAGO

AUCKLAND

LONDON • MADRID

MANILA • PARIS

ROME • SEOUL • SYDNEY

TOKYO • TORONTO

The Teacher by St. Augustine, is reprinted from *Fathers of the
Church,* vol. 59, pp. 7–61, with permission of The Catholic University
of America Press.
Copyright © 1968.

Library of Congress Number: 61-65561
International Standard Book Number: 0-85229-658-4
International Standard Serial Number: 0072-7288

A NOTE ON REFERENCE STYLE

In the following pages, passages in *Great Books of the Western World* are referred to by the initials "*GBWW*," followed by a roman numeral (indicating the first edition of 1952 [I] or the second edition of 1990 [II]) with volume and page number. Thus, "*GBWW* I: 5, 100; II: 4, 112" refers to a passage from Sophocles' *Oedipus the King,* which is on page 100 in Volume 5 of the first edition, and on page 112 in Volume 4 of the second edition. Sometimes only one reference will be given, since the contents of the first and second editions differ. Also note that passages quoted in an article may differ from the translation of that passage in either the first or second edition, since newer translations of some works are included in the second edition.

Gateway to the Great Books is referred to by the initials "*GGB*," followed by volume and page number. Thus, "*GGB* 10, 39–57" refers to pages 39 through 57 of Volume 10 of *Gateway to the Great Books,* which is James's essay, "The Will to Believe."

The Great Ideas Today is referred to by the initials "*GIT*," followed by the year and page number. Thus, "*GIT* 1968, 210" refers to page 210 of the 1968 edition of *The Great Ideas Today.*

CONTENTS

Preface

The way of ideas in the world—something of that sort can be said to be the common concern of contributors to this year's volume, or most of them. It is the preoccupation, certainly, of Laurence Berns, a longtime student of political affairs, who in surveying the political situation of the United States at the present time, finds a loss of memory, or perhaps it is only understanding, of the political ideas from which the nation was conceived and its government created—ideas, without which, we do not realize who as a people we really are and how we can take care of ourselves, or should. We will not succeed in either undertaking until we recover these ideas, Mr. Berns tells us, and we cannot hope to do that until we establish a much better system of education than the one we now have. This is the heart of the matter, in his view. Without such an education, which the founders assumed, we cannot tell what to demand of those who govern us, who might be startled if we seemed to know what was good for us.

Would education have altered the economic policies of the American government in the Caribbean after the end of World War II, of which Thomas K. Simpson writes under the title of "Good Housekeeping," this being what Aristotle meant by the term "economics" in the first place? We cannot be sure. We can doubt if it would have been allowed to overcome propaganda, supposing that had been thought necessary to employ in one interest or another—supposing we had been sufficiently concerned to seek its enlightenment in the first place. So much of our education *is* propaganda, we may reflect, designed as it is to serve our cause, or hinder the causes of others, that it could hardly have helped us to see what we as a nation were doing in that part of the world unless we had thought to see through it. But ideas—of justice, of reason, of revolution—were in any case the things to be discovered, and these are the business of education to put before us.

What plagues us nowadays in these matters is doubt of ideas themselves. Why this has come over us is not easy to say. It is believed to stem from the failure of certain ideas, or ideologies, to sustain themselves in the late twentieth century, but this is odd if true, seeing that *those* ideas were overcome, as we believe, by ideas of a superior kind, mainly freedom, which we professed for fifty years and then suddenly abandoned: liberty— or liberalism, which might not have been called *our* ideology—is now thought to be a bad idea by those who formerly were insistent that it should prevail.

At the same time, a kind of nihilism has overtaken us whereby we not only doubt ideas, but are positively hostile to them—the idea of government is a case in point—and distrust their protagonists, so far as they have any. The name—one name—for this attitude is postmodernism, and it has so many facets that we are likely to despair of understanding it unless someone comes along to enlighten us. Fortunately, such a person—Alex

Callinicos, of the University of York, who has written a substantial book on the subject—has provided an article for this issue of the annual which is instructive, though it cannot be said to be encouraging except as to indicate the poverty of the views he exposes, which seem unlikely to last, for that reason.

The critical faculties we need to counter this state of affairs are what the liberal arts were once conceived to provide. How that was so, and how it might be so now, are indicated by Otto Bird's essay on the subject, a master work by the former editor of *The Great Ideas Today,* who with clarity and command recalls the tradition that underlies both our annual and the *Great Books* themselves. His article is an education in itself, and one that all who think to profess the liberal arts will find they have been taught by.

Teaching is the concern also of George Anastaplo's essay this year, which begins with a consideration of St. Augustine's work on that subject and then goes on to the difficult question raised famously by Plato's "Meno" of whether virtue—or as we like now to say, morality—can be taught. Mr. Anastaplo, who says something also in his essay of Aquinas, intended originally to treat of modern teachers as well, among them Leo Strauss; but it is clear we will have to wait for that.

In the meantime we have a second essay by Cynthia L. Rutz on Shakespeare—here, "The Merchant of Venice"—and fairy tales. This is not the academic exercise it may seem. Ms. Rutz is the kind of teacher and scholar who discovers ideas wherever they exist, and they exist—she convinces us—not only in Shakespeare, where we would expect to find them, but in fairy tales, where we might not. Thus, she shows us another way to read a play we thought we had finished with.

Augustine's work, "The Teacher," itself appears among the "Additions to the Great Books Library" this year. It is not easy reading, but it illustrates some of what Professor Anastaplo says about teaching and also what Mr. Bird tells us of the liberal arts. Augustine himself was a master of those arts—in fact he wrote a treatise on each of them, though only the one on Music survives—and his very much more expanded account of teaching will be found, as Mr. Bird indicates, in *On Christian Doctrine* (*GBWW* I: 18, 621–98; II: 16, 699–784).

Other reprints this year are more recent; indeed they must be, being that they are all American. One—much the longest—is by Margaret Fuller, the contemporary of Ralph Waldo Emerson who considered herself his intellectual superior and said so. She had certainly read much (so had he, though he wore it lightly) and taught him things he would not otherwise have known; but she wrote without grace and was besides prolix, so that she has not had equal fame until now, when we care more about what she cared about, which was the condition of women. "Woman in the Nineteenth Century" shows all her faults as a writer and all her virtues, too, these being a strong mind of great seriousness which made the case for gender equality so well that nothing seems necessary to add, though it has had to be repeated frequently, and must, in our time.

Included as well is Thoreau's "A Plea for John Brown," which makes the case that Antigone made over two millennia ago for law higher than the civil one—this to be reflected upon, perhaps, by those who have read the essays by Mr. Berns and Mr. Simpson in the earlier pages of this volume—and Hawthorne's tale called "My Kinsman, Major Molineux." The implications of this last are not social, for all that Hawthorne seems to have thought they might be, but theological—and psychological, too, since whatever the story means, it calls up the devil and the sinful heart, for what we can make of them.

Books on which our contributors have ventured to comment this year will be found—that is, their comments will be found—at the end of the volume. The selections have been made in the belief that the titles, or at least their subjects, will be of particular interest to *GIT* readers, who otherwise may not have been aware of their publication. One is a book of photographs by Diane Arbus, and it is here because it extends the idea of man—of the human—to regions we must be prepared to enter, however painful they are. But have we not done so, if we have read the Greek tragedies, or Dante's *Comedy,* or the works of Freud—of which these pictures may be taken, in at least some part, as illustrations?

CURRENT DEVELOPMENTS

IN THE

ARTS AND SCIENCES

Teaching, Nature, and the Moral Virtues

George Anastaplo

I. On Plato's *Meno* and the *Republic*

> Some suppose that people become good by nature, some that it is by habit, and some that it is by teaching. Now then it is clear that what is from nature does not belong to those things that are in our power, but that it belongs to those who are truly fortunate through some divine cause. Argument and teaching, I am afraid, are not effective with all, but what is needed is for the soul of the hearer to be cultivated before by habits so as both to enjoy and to hate nobly...To hit upon the right training for virtue from youth on is difficult if one has not been brought up under the right kind of laws.
>
> —Aristotle[1]

i.

A classic discussion, as well as a series of illustrations of teaching may be found in Plato's *Meno*.[2] It opens with an inquiry put to Socrates as to how virtue is acquired by human beings. The point of departure in this dialogue is a question about whether virtue is teachable. The inquiry develops (or, from the acquisitive Meno's point of view, degenerates?) into an inquiry as to what virtue is and what it means to teach or to learn. The dialogue concludes with the revelation (or is it a teaching?) that those men who are generally recognized as virtuous, such as the leading statesmen of Athens for at least two generations, became what they were because of divine dispensation, not because anyone had taught them to be good.

Thus it is reported, in textbooks and elsewhere, that Plato concluded in the *Meno* that virtue cannot be taught, that it comes to human beings in a mysterious way attributable to divinity. Does Plato want this conclusion taught?[3] Is this good for a city to believe? If virtue depends on divine dispensation, what does vice depend on? Does it, too, depend somehow on divine allocations, or is vice what men are "naturally" inclined to when there is no divine provision for virtue?

ii.

(Overleaf) The School of Athens *by Raphael, 1508–11. Perhaps the most famous of Raphael's frescos, it shows Plato and Aristotle surrounded by philosophers from various historic periods.*

We recall, however, that the same Plato argues in the *Republic* that a properly ordered city could produce virtuous citizens, including rulers, generation after generation. The role of the gods is muted in that dialogue, however much divine intervention may help to account for the opportunity that philosophers have to shape and govern a city.[4]

The *Republic* ends with the Myth of Er, which somehow accounts for the lives that human beings lead, lives chosen by them a thousand or so years after their preceding lives had consigned them to the millennium of rewards or purgations that serve as prelude to their next stint of life on earth. But, it seems, however much one's earlier life affects the life one chooses for oneself "this time around," little if anything is remembered of one's previous life. The waters of Lethe see to that.[5]

This account in the *Republic* is somewhat at variance with what we seem to be told by the *Meno,* where human learning is put emphatically in terms of recollecting. According to the *Meno,* there is neither teaching nor learning but rather a recalling of what we have known before, if not even "always."[6] The spirit here is quite different from that evident in the *Republic,* where systematic teaching and habituation, for those properly equipped and prepared, are arranged for by astute rulers. So different an approach to the development of virtuous citizens and rulers, elaborated in such a massive work as the *Republic,* obliges us to reconsider what the *Meno* seems to say.

iii.

We return to Meno's opening speech (as set forth in a standard translation of this Platonic dialogue):

> Can you tell me, Socrates, whether virtue is acquired by teaching or by practice; or if neither by teaching nor practice, then whether it comes to man by nature, or in what other way? (*GBWW* I: 7, 174; II: 6, 174)

We notice that Meno has an array of possible answers to his question which, it turns out, he has evidently heard proposed in discussions of these matters in Thessaly: teaching, practice, nature, and some "'other way."[7] We also notice that Meno assumes that these ways are to be considered as alternatives. Perhaps this, too, reflects the discussions he has heard elsewhere. This assumption may be important, if not decisive, for the course that this conversation follows.

Socrates' immediate response to Meno's opening speech (again, as set forth in a standard translation) emphasizes critical disclaimers:

> O Meno, there was a time when the Thessalians were famous among the other Hellenes only for their riches and their riding; but now, if I am not mistaken, they are equally famous for their wisdom, especially at Larisa, which is the native city of your friend Aristippus. And this is Gorgias' doing; for when he came there, the follower of Aleuadae, among them your admirer Aristippus, and the other chiefs of the Thessalians, fell in love with his wisdom. And he has taught you the habit of answering questions in a grand and bold style, which becomes those who know, and is the style in which he himself answers all comers; and any Hellene who likes may ask him anything. How different is our lot, my dear Meno. Here at Athens there is a dearth of the commodity, and all wisdom seems to have emigrated from us to you. I am certain that if you were to ask any

An engraving of Plato (428 B.C.?–348/347). "According to [Plato's] *Meno,* there is neither teaching nor learning but rather a recalling of what we have known before…"

Athenian whether virtue was natural or acquired, he would laugh in your face, and say: "Stranger, you have far too good an opinion of me, if you think that I can answer your question. For I literally do not know what virtue is, and much less whether it is acquired by teaching or not." And I myself, Meno, living as I do in this region of poverty, am as poor as the rest of the world; and I confess with shame that I know literally nothing about virtue; and when I do not know [what something is, how could I know what sort of thing it is]? How, if I knew nothing at all of Meno, could I tell if he was fair, or the opposite of fair; rich and noble, or the reverse of rich and noble? Do you think that I could?[8] *(GBWW* I: 7, 174; II: 6, 174)

This response is disappointing to Meno, who had hoped to acquire from Socrates an answer, perhaps even a novel argument, to take north with him. This is how Meno understands what Socrates has just said about his lack of knowledge concerning virtue:

But are you in earnest, Socrates, in saying that you do not know what virtue is? And am I to carry back this report of you to Thessaly?

An engraving of Socrates (470 B.C.?– 399?) by Bartolozzi Kaufmann (1782). The Meno "opens with an inquiry put to Socrates as to how virtue is acquired by human beings."

Thus, what is decisive for Meno here is that Socrates has presented himself as not knowing what virtue is. And yet, we not only suspect that Socrates knows more about virtue than he admits, but we also see him talk again and again in this dialogue as if he has a reliable enough grasp of what virtue is to make the observations and arguments that he does make.

iv.

We must consider again what Socrates does say in his first speech. That he cannot be taken completely at face value there is suggested by what he predicts about all Athenians professing themselves to be as ignorant as Socrates says he is about what virtue is. Whatever suspicions we have about this are reinforced by how a prominent politician, Anytus, conducts himself when he joins the conversation in the *Meno. He* certainly does not profess ignorance of such matters.[9]

We return to Meno's opening speech, which has him asking (in a more precise translation of the dialogue):

Can you tell me, Socrates, whether virtue is teachable? Or is it not teachable, but to be acquired by practice? Or is it to be acquired by neither practice nor by learning, but does it come to human beings by nature or in some other way?

The illustration with which Socrates ends his own opening speech (provided here, too, in a more precise translation) is instructive:

> Does it seem to you to be possible that someone who has no cognizance at all of who Meno is could know whether he is fair, or rich, or well-born, or the opposites of these?

We notice that the attributes of Meno are put in the alternative by Socrates (fair or rich or well-born or their opposites), just as had been Meno's list of the ways that virtue is acquired (teaching or practice or nature or in some other way). Yet we are shown in the course of the dialogue that Meno himself is indeed fair *and* rich, *and* well-born (in the conventional sense of these terms), not "the opposites of these." Should virtue, then, be understood to be acquired by human beings through a combination of teaching and practice for those who are naturally equipped to be receptive? This would be consistent with the illustrations used later by Socrates about the young men trained in horsemanship, gymnastics, and the like. We would expect there, also, a combination of elements for the emergence of the best horsemen and gymnasts.

Meno, we recall, had a fourth way for acquiring virtue: "some other way." It is that, it can be said, which happens to leave a place in his scheme of things for the divine dispensation finally resorted to in this dialogue. We see that Socrates, as well, has a fourth element in his inventory (of Meno's attributes): "the opposites of these." Is there a sense in which divine dispensation should be considered somehow critically different from, if not the opposite of, the three modes that Meno had listed? Also, is there a sense in which Meno's being fair, rich, and well-born depends upon something other than, if not the opposite of, these? That is, does Meno merely appear to be fair, rich, and well-born?

v.

When we return to the *Republic* we notice a reliance upon knowledgeable leaders who identify the various natural capacities among the young and who thereafter provide the appropriate teaching and practice required to produce virtuous citizens in the service of the city. Even in ordinary cities, good men and women arise, and we can see upon examining those situations the combination of nature, teaching, and practice needed to that end. But in the ordinary city chance—or, if one prefers, divine intervention—seems to have much more to do with whether the youngsters who are naturally equipped for virtue happen to be provided the required teaching and habituation.

Perhaps more important, at least for us on this occasion, than the lessons offered as to how virtue is acquired are the lessons about teaching itself. Socrates both says and does not say what we have found him to indicate in his opening speech in the *Meno*. Or rather, Meno does not recognize that Socrates in his opening speech indicates what we have found him to indicate. What Socrates indicates, albeit quietly, very much affects how the rest of this dialogue should be read. We can see that however much may be offered by a would-be teacher, it is not likely to register with a student unless he is both disposed and prepared to receive it. In this sense, it can be said, teaching as a sovereign activity is not possible—and this opens the way to the "recollection" made so much of in the *Meno* and in textbook accounts of that dialogue. But does not talk about recollection become an inspired or poetic way of talking about that which is natural to the reasoning capacity of human beings?

vi.

The development of virtuous human beings depends, in part, on circumstances. It is useful, as one reads the *Meno,* to be aware of differences between Anytus' Athens and Aristippus' Thessaly. Troublesome inquiries into virtue can be expected in democratic Athens, just as successful efforts on behalf of horsemanship can be expected in oligarchic Thessaly.

The Socrates of the *Meno* resorts to divine dispensation only after it becomes clear that the limitations of Meno and Anytus make it impossible for him to develop an account of any systematic training for virtue which works from a reliable definition of virtue and from a dispassionate recognition of natural differences among men. Would the fierce democrat, Anytus, be tamed only if he could be induced to believe that there are vital differences between those who know, such as Socrates, and those who do not; just as the unscrupulous oligarch Meno would be restrained only if he

Plato's school in Bithynia. Known as the "Academy," Plato founded the school around 387. The Academy's main focus was philosophical and scientific teaching and research.

could be induced to believe that there are powerful gods who truly prefer just men to those who look out for themselves alone?

Meno's limitations are reflected in his assumption that virtue must come by only one of the three or four ways he proposes in his acquisitively abrupt opening speech. As we have seen, it is indicated in the dialogue, beginning with the way an anything-but-abrupt Socrates ends his first response to Meno, that virtue may come by a *combination* of the alternatives listed disjunctively by Meno. That is, the virtues can be expected to develop in a human being naturally receptive to them only after the establishment of proper habits prepares one to be taught. Whether those naturally receptive to virtue have the opportunity to be habituated and taught properly may depend upon the gods, or upon chance.[10]

Meno, whatever *his* nature, will not practice. This is evident throughout the dialogue. The habits he has already acquired have become second nature to him. Meno's "instinctive" avoidance of practice may be confirmed in a late restatement by him of his opening inquiry, after Socrates has several times tried to discipline him: he drops "practice" from the alternatives he now lists (*GBWW* I: 7, 183; II: 67, 183).[11] Indeed, Meno can be recognized as a man devoted to "freedom"—to the tyrannical desire to have power himself, while not being subject at all to the power or standards of another.[12]

vii.

Meno's general position can be said to have been made explicit, in the first book of Plato's *Republic,* by Polemarchus and Thrasymachus. Both of them are more receptive to serious arguments than Meno can ever be.[13] The groundwork is laid there for the elaboration in the *Republic* of a system of education, for teachers and students alike, which makes the development of virtuous men and women far more likely than it is apt to be in the ordinary city.

We turn now to two texts from St. Augustine that start, in a sense, from Platonic doctrines about teaching and learning. Even so, those doctrines are called into question by Augustine, who makes far more than Plato probably did of the divine-dispensation solution offered in the *Meno*.

Also implicitly called into question in the Augustinian account of things is the status of nature in human affairs, a subject to which we shall return (in Part III of this article) after Augustine has had his say. That will be a return, in effect, to the Socratic/Platonic/Aristotelian mode of thought about these matters.

II. On Augustine's *De Magistro* and *Confessions*

Thinking then whence it could arise that in those ancient times the peoples were greater lovers of liberty than in these, I believe it arose from that same cause that now makes men less strong, which I believe to be the

difference in our education from that of the ancient, founded on the difference of our religion from that of the ancient. For our religion, having
shown us the truth and the true way, makes us esteem less the honor of the
world. Whence the Gentiles [that is, the ancients], esteeming it much, and
having placed that as the highest good, were more ferocious in their
actions....They lacked neither pomp nor magnificence in ceremonies, but
they conjoined to [these] the action of sacrifice full of blood and ferocity,
killing multitudes of animals—which aspect being terrible, made men
similar to it. The ancient religion, besides this, did not beatify anyone but
men full of worldly glory; such as were captains of armies and princes of
republics. Our religion has glorified humble and contemplative men more
than the active. It has then placed the highest good in humility, abasement,
and in the disparagement of human things; the other placed it in greatness
of soul, in the strength of the body and in all those things that are fitted to
make men most strong. And if our religion asks that you have strength in
you, it wants that you be apt more to suffer than to do a forceful thing.
This mode of life, then, seems to have rendered the world weak, and given
it as a prey to wicked men who have been able securely to manipulate it,
seeing how the universality [of men] in order to go to Paradise think more
of enduring their beatings than of avenging them.

—Niccolò Machiavelli [14]

i.

Augustine himself seems to have adapted the ostensible teaching of the
Meno to his purposes, insisting in effect that there can be no effective
teaching of the most important things. That is, there can be no teaching and
learning unless they are keyed to something within us.

This insistence may be seen in such passages as the following in Augustine's *De Magistro* dialogue (14:45):

> But when teachers have made use of words to explain all those branches of
> learning which they profess to be teaching, including even those dealing
> with virtue and wisdom, then those who are known as pupils reflect within
> themselves whether what has been said is true, contemplating, that is, that
> inner truth according to their capacity.[15] (*GIT* 1997, 296)

It is said that we bring things "to light from some sort of hidden abode by
means of our inquiry and discussion" (8:21), that "reason's own law [is]
implanted in our minds" (8:24), and that "we use our reason to consult that
inner truth for the things that we understand" (12:39).

An echo here from the *Meno* (or, more likely, from the Neoplatonists,
such as Plotinus, studied by Augustine), is the calling forth of that which
has been instilled in the human soul. "Teaching," then, consists of simulat-
ing that which lies dormant in each of us. This brings to mind the recollection argument in the *Meno* but without the unchristian reincarnation-of-the-
soul conjectures nominally relied upon both in the *Meno* and in the tenth
book of the *Republic*.

Another echo of the *Meno* in *De Magistro* brings to mind Socrates' "divine dispensation" argument.[16] Augustine suggests that all serious teaching and learning, indeed all being itself, depend for us upon Jesus Christ—as may be seen in such passages as the following (11:38):

> But as for all those things which we "understand," it is not the outward sound of [a] speaker's words that we consult, but the truth which presides over the mind itself from within, though we may have been led to consult it because of the [speaker's] words. Now He who is consulted and who is said to "dwell in the inner man,"[17] He it is who teaches us, namely, Christ, that is to say, "the unchangeable Power of God and everlasting wisdom."[18] This is the Wisdom which every rational soul does indeed consult, but it reveals itself to each according to his capacity to grasp it by reason of the good or evil disposition of his will. (*GIT* 1997, 291–92)

Elsewhere, Jesus is recognized as "the greatest Teacher of all" (1:2).[19] It is also said of Jesus that "He alone teaches who made use of external words to remind us that He dwells within us" (14:46). It is said as well that "we should not call any man on earth a teacher, seeing that there is One in heaven who is the Teacher of all."[20] Years later, Augustine recalled that he had "composed a book called *The Teacher* [*De Magistro*] where, after some discussion and inquiry, we find that it is God alone who teaches men knowledge, all of which is also in accord with what is written in the Gospel: 'One is your teacher, Christ.'"[21]

This sort of thing may in a roundabout way anticipate, perhaps even influence, certain questionable modern developments. The Augustinian approach accustomed Westerners to believe both that human understanding would be severely limited if not impossible and that existence including ethical choices would be meaningless without the benefit of divine revelation. The more that Augustine and his successors succeeded in establishing this and related doctrines, including an emphasis upon the role of *conscience,* the more vulnerable Westerners have become to nihilism wherever Biblical faith loses its authority. That faith, with its heightening of personal expectations, had undermined the ancient reliance among pagans upon

Saint Augustine by Sandro Botticelli. According to Augustine, "there can be no effective teaching of the most important things. That is, there can be no teaching and learning unless they are keyed to something within us."

reason and nature. Also troubling are implications of the observation that the virtues are, according to Augustine, "rather vices than virtues so long as there is no reference to God in the matter."[22]

The nihilistic mischief implicit in the Augustinian approach to being and knowing may be noticed in the following profession of faith with respect to the God of Biblical revelation by a twentieth century theologian:

> We are wholly caused by God. So is everything else. Therefore without God everything is literally inexplicable, not only in the sense that men cannot find the explanation, but that there isn't one. Therefore, again, apart from the knowledge of God, man really is doomed to live in a meaningless universe, and he can but grow weary of the effort to live a meaningful life in a context that has no meaning. Not knowing God, he does not know what he is; equally he does not know what he is here for, where he is supposed to be going, how to go there.[23]

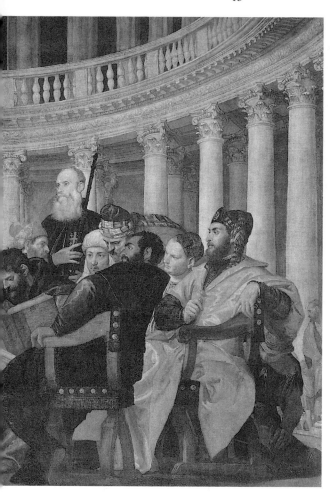

Christ Among the Doctors in the Temple *by Paolo Veronese, 1558–60. It is said of Jesus that* "we should not call any man on earth a teacher, seeing that there is One in heaven who is the Teacher of all."

On the other hand, Thomas Aquinas, in the ways he relies upon Aristotle, repeatedly testifies to the opinion that, however limited the pagan philosophers may have been by their lack of access to Biblical revelation, it does not make sense to insist that "without [knowledge of the God of the Bible] everything is literally inexplicable." Of course, Thomas considers significant gaps to remain in pagan philosophy; but then he also considers the Biblical divinity, especially in its Trinitarian form, to be a mystery, and ultimately inexplicable.[24]

In *De Magistro,* Augustine examines the limitations of teaching with the aid of his talented son, Adeodatus ("Gift of God"). The reliance in that dialogue upon a divine agency, which can seem to some *pro forma,* is magnified and intensified in Augustine's *Confessions,* where there are, as in his *De Magistro,* pioneering investigations of language and signs (a subject discussed by Otto Bird elsewhere in this volume). The primacy, if not also the comprehensiveness, of divine agency in human affairs may be seen in the line from Virgil's *Aeneid* (2:659; *GBWW* I: 13, 142; II: 12, 115) that is used in *De Magistro* to examine the use of words as signs (2:3): "If it please the gods that nothing remains of so great a city." The pagan poet, it would seem, sensed the sovereignty of the divine in the governance of the world even if only in the form of "the gods."[25]

ii.

In *De Magistro,* both Augustine and his son are relied upon as characters with a loving relation to one another, for the dialogue unfolds before our eyes through their exchanges. In reading an autobiographical exercise such as Augustine's *Confessions,* which has provided for many readers a ready access to Christian piety, the personality (as we say nowadays) of the author naturally matters even more. An artist and his creations tend to be governed by the established art form to which he dedicates himself. That hardly appears to be the case in the *Confessions,* however, where the narrator attempts to reveal the most intimate things about himself, perhaps creating in the process a new art form.

The status or intrinsic worth of the revelations relied upon by Augustine is critical—not only the general biblical revelation, upon which Christianity builds, but even more the revelations personal to him, such as they are. What is the evidence for such revelations? What is the significance of that evidence? Whatever the status may be of revelation in general, one is obliged to wonder about the amount and kind of evidence required by this narrator, for that throws light upon both his state of mind and his conclusions.

It does not suffice, I believe, merely to conclude that some believe this, while others believe that. We cannot begin to understand gifted innovators such as Augustine until we make a judgment, if only a provisional judgment, about the intrinsic plausibility of the things they advance. We sometimes have to begin hypothetically by asking, If they believe this, then what follows? But we should be clear that this *is* what we are doing—and we should also be clear about what the hypothesized conditions or beliefs are.[26]

We must in any event proceed cautiously in dealing with such a work as Augustine's *Confessions.* It can cause difficulty in a community, to say nothing of acute and unproductive discomfort, to reduce discussion of such matters to contending professions of faith by various readers. Still, may we not all benefit from efforts to clarify the presuppositions, and to suggest the consequences, of the particular articles of faith (if faith it is) under consideration?

iii.

The account in the *Confessions* is personal to Augustine. Yet it seems archetypically Christian.[27] This may help to explain its influence over the centuries, dramatizing as it does the pattern for the typical Christian confession. Does it strike a responsive chord in many in the West because it has helped shape the kind of soul which would be receptive to such an account?

One is driven to wonder—one may be intended to wonder—about Augustine personally. He is, perhaps of all the authors of the great books available to us in the Western World, the one who is most likely to be considered by many readers a fit subject himself for psychological analysis. Augustine, among the pre-modern authors of stature to whom we happen to have access, may have anticipated most of all the psychological insights of the moderns, at least to the extent of making much both of the not-so-innocent desires of children and of the pervasive guilt of adolescence and of the adolescent in the adult.[28] There is a sense in which the Augustine of the *Confessions* never "grew up"—but then, he might have added in his maturity (as he had indicated in his youthful *De Magistro*), that all men are necessarily childlike before the true God.

Certainly, the modern student of psychology finds intriguing Augustine's sexually-linked sense of sin (a residue perhaps of his early Manichaeism), his relations with his mother, and his intimacy with male comrades.[29] His father does not figure much in his account; it is his widowed mother who is very much interested in his spiritual salvation, the mother who had opposed an early marriage by him.[30] It is perhaps not irrelevant to notice the appeal, for Augustine and his most intimate male companion, Alypius, of the monasteries they learn about just before they take together the decisive steps toward explicit conversion to Christianity.[31]

The passion with which Augustine speaks about what is happening to him suggests that it may be difficult for him to understand what is going on, especially in such a crisis as that which led to the final stage of his conversion. Is a sufficient cause reported for his conversion? Relatively little is said in the *Confessions* in support of the divinity of Jesus or, for that matter, with respect to what the basis is of the authority of the scriptures that he quotes so abundantly.[32] Much is assumed from the outset with respect to these matters, so much that the modern reader may be tempted to conclude that the critical decision—the major affirmation of faith—was made by Augustine long before the dramatic conversion described in the *Confessions* was completed.

Here is Augustine's famous account of the turning point in his life—the decisive conversion-inducing episode in Milan at a time, for him, of considerable spiritual agitation (VIII, 12):

> I probed the hidden depths of my soul and wrung its pitiful secrets from it, and when I mustered them all before the eyes of my heart, a great storm broke within me, bringing with it a great deluge of tears. I stood up and left Alypius so that I might weep and cry to my heart's content, for it occurred to me that tears were best shed in solitude. I moved away far enough to avoid being embarrassed even by his presence. He must have realized what my feelings were, for I suppose I had said something and he had known from the sound of my voice that I was ready to burst into tears.

So I stood up and left him where we had been sitting, utterly bewildered. Somehow I flung myself down beneath a fig tree and gave way to the tears which now streamed from my eyes, the sacrifice that is acceptable to you. I had much to say to you, my God, not in these very words but in this strain: *Lord, will you never be content? Must we always taste your vengeance? Forget the long record of our sins.*[33] For I felt that I was still the captive of my sins, and in my misery I kept crying "How long shall I go on saying 'tomorrow, tomorrow'? Why not now? Why not make an end of my ugly sins at this moment?"

I was asking myself these questions, weeping all the while with the most bitter sorrow in my heart, when all at once I heard the singsong voice of a child in a nearby house. Whether it was the voice of a boy or a girl I cannot say, but again and again it repeated the refrain "Take it and read, take it and read." ["*Tolle lege, tolle lege.*"] At this I looked up, thinking hard whether there was any kind of game in which children used to chant words like these, but I could not remember ever hearing them before. I stemmed my flood of tears and stood up, telling myself that this could only be a divine command to open my book of Scripture and read the first passage on which my eyes should fall. For I had heard the story of Antony, and I remembered how he had happened to go into a church while the Gospel was being read and had taken it as a counsel addressed to himself when he heard the words *Go home and sell all that belongs to you. Give it to the poor, and so the treasure you have shall be in heaven; then come back and follow me.*[34] By this divine pronouncement he had at once been converted to you.

So I hurried back to the place where Alypius was sitting, for when I stood up to move away I had put down the book containing Paul's Epistles. I seized it and opened it, and in silence I read the first passage on which my eyes fell: *Not in revelling and drunkenness, not in lust and wantonness, not in quarrels and rivalries. Rather, arm yourselves with the Lord Jesus Christ; spend no more thought on nature and nature's appetites.*[35] I had no wish to read more and no need to do so. For in an instant, as I came to the end of the sentence, it was as though the light of confidence flooded into my heart and all the darkness of doubt was dispelled.

This account continues with a provision for Augustine's friend, beginning thereby Augustine's decades-long career as a Christian missionary (VIII, 12):

I marked the place with my finger or by some other sign and closed the book. My looks now were quite calm as I told Alypius what had happened to me. He too told me what he had been feeling, which of course I did not know. He asked to see what I had read. I showed it to him and he read on beyond the text which I had read. I did not know what followed, but it was this: *Find room among you for a man of over-delicate conscience.*[36] Alypius applied this to himself and told me so. This admonition was enough to give him strength, and without suffering the distress of hesitation he made his resolution and took this good purpose to himself. And it very well suited his moral character, which had long been far, far better than my own.

Augustine with his mother, Monica. She played a dominant role in Augustine's life and was "very much interested in his spiritual salvation."

Then we went in and told my mother, who was overjoyed. When we went on to describe how it had all happened, she was jubilant with triumph and glorified you, *who are powerful enough, and more than powerful enough, to carry out your purpose beyond all our hopes and dreams.*[37] For she saw that you had granted her far more than she used to ask in her tearful prayers and plaintive lamentations. You converted me to yourself, so that I no longer desired a wife or placed any hope in this world but stood firmly upon the rule of faith, where you had shown me to her in a dream so many years before. And you *turned her sadness into rejoicing,*[38] into joy far fuller than her dearest wish, far sweeter and more chaste than any she had hoped to find in children begotten of my flesh. (*GBWW* I: 16, 60–61; II: 18, 76–77)[39]

We are encouraged by Augustine to try to make sense of these things. He himself tried to do so with respect to the voice he had heard say, "Take it and read, take it and read." He considered, for instance, whether he knew of any children's game which included these particular words.[40]

We follow in Augustine's footsteps, therefore, when we subject this episode to analysis, albeit an analysis somewhat more extended than he himself was moved to resort to in his *Confessions.*

iv.

What really moves Augustine in this episode in the year 386?[41] What moves him to convert? And, not an unrelated question, what moves him to write his confessions?[42]

One key issue, as Augustine presents his early life, is that of celibacy. He indicates this in various ways both before and after his conversion, as well as in the Biblical verse upon which he draws during the conversion episode. He is torn between his longstanding indulgences in sexual gratification and his opinion that salvation, insofar as Christianity provides it, depends for him upon a sincere repudiation of his sexual interests. He is obviously a man of strong passions, someone who could, as a young man, pray, "Give me chastity and continence, but not yet" (*Confessions*, VII, 7: *GBWW* I: 18, 47; II: 16, 59).[43]

Particularly significant is Augustine's repeated use of such terms as "unchaste love."[44] They indicate what estrangement from the will of God means, even where sexual conduct is a secondary concern.[45] This seems to be the locus of the basic misconduct, the root of all evil, the sin in light of which all other sinfulness may be graphically seen. Thus Augustine speaks elsewhere of the lusts of the flesh, of the eyes, and of ambition.[46] His often extravagant language about love (a precursor of the modern preoccupation with eroticism) suggests that a form of hedonistically inclined materialism is fundamental for him: all human activity is seen in terms of desire, with the *love* of God as the rarified form of a longing that is corrupted in carnal lust. Related to this is his defining *virtue* as rightly ordered love.[47] It is revealing that Augustine could say of the materialistic Epicurus, "In my judgement [he] would have won all the honours, were it not that I believed that the soul lived on after death and received the reward or punishment which it deserved. Epicurus had refused to believe this."[48]

What, then, moves Augustine to convert when he does? He reports afterwards that his lungs had been giving out, which necessitated that he reconsider his career as a public speaker and as a teacher of public speaking.[49] Perhaps more significant, however, is that he had been obliged, evidently for the sake of the respectable marriage urged upon him by his mother, to give up a much-beloved mistress with whom he had lived for some time.[50] It is obvious that the woman had taken the enforced separation hard—and one cannot rule out, on Augustine's part, either guilt or resentment (or both). It is almost as if he says (to his mother?) about his mistress that if he cannot any longer have *her,* he will not have anyone else.

Or is it that he himself wants to abandon a faithful mistress, a woman to whom he had pledged himself and with whom he had had a son years before (the son who distinguishes himself in the *De Magistro* dialogue)? Is he troubled, that is, by his infidelity, an infidelity promoted by family ambition?[51]

v.

These speculations must take second place to further consideration of the critical conversion episode itself, the kind of episode that in certain kinds of men may be more revealing than the narrator himself suspects. What is Augustine taught here—and how? We are invited to speculate about the role of divine intervention in such matters.

What, for example, are we to make of the child's voice that Augustine hears? For one thing, it may be less important, really, than the voice of a visitor, Ponticianus (his countryman from North Africa) who happened to tell Augustine and Alypius about an Egyptian monk, Antony, and about other inspiring things.[52] But the childish voice[53] that Augustine hears is somehow more dramatic and invites special attention. This voice seems to be, in this entire account of Augustine's life, the only miraculous event (in the ordinary sense of "miracle") that Augustine himself encounters. He anticipates this by saying, "[God] had pity on our misery and came to our aid in a wonderful way that we could not understand" (*Confessions*, VI, 12; *GBWW* I :18, 41–42; II: 16, 52).[54] One problem we have is whether this is indeed a mysterious and wonderful working out of things. We may be equipped, if not to pass judgment on this, at least (as in many such cases) to clarify the problem.

Consider how the fateful voice is reported. Even though it is regarded as having come from another house, no one else is reported to have heard it. A highly distraught Augustine has moved a little way from Alypius into the garden; he even prostrates himself beneath a tree.[55] This voice comes to him almost like a dream. Elsewhere Augustine speaks of God or others speaking to him, but nowhere else, it should at once be added, with the suggestion that the speaking is audible to his outer ear. It is, in one sense, inconvenient that Alypius did not also hear the voice.[56]

Augustine assumes that others have visions and dreams derived from God. His mother is especially gifted in this respect.[57] He recognizes, however, that these signs have to be interpreted; he seems also to recognize that people can be mistaken about such matters.[58] Does he not recognize as well that he may not have here a conventional miracle, however important the episode was for him? At various points during this episode, before he heard the voice, Augustine had almost broken down and surrendered to God. Did his state of mind make likely the resolution we do see? Augustine might even grant this, especially since he attributes to God the overall governance of his life, not just a sleight-of-hand trick here and there.[59]

Of course, it can be suspected that Augustine "knew" one way or another, perhaps without being conscious of it, just where to turn to in the

Epistles of St. Paul that he had been studying, and to which the voice directed him.[60] This could be readily explained by his familiarity with the text, a familiarity exploited in this instance by what he knew to be his deep-lying conflict with respect to the consequences of a genuine conversion. Augustine's experience could be explained as readily thus as by the assumption that some divine agency guided his opening of the book. One might even suspect it would be inevitable that whatever Augustine happened upon which confirmed what his psyche was being driven toward would be reinforced after the fact by the recollection of whatever moved him to look around him or to open a book or to go where he did.[61]

What seems clearly to have guided Augustine to open the book was what Ponticianus had just told Alypius and him about Antony, the Egyptian monk. That is, Augustine can be seen as having patterned himself upon Antony (and Alypius in turn upon Antony and Augustine).[62] That Antony was successful enough to have his century-old life celebrated in a foreign land could have stimulated someone such as Augustine (again, without his necessarily being conscious of it) to imitate and even to surpass him. Augustine is, after all, a man whose oratorial talents and accomplishments reflected his lifelong desire to be celebrated and to influence men at large. He contributes, by his confessions, to the promulgation of *his* Antony-like story.

Antony had heard, we are only now told, a particularly relevant verse of Scripture being read when he came into a church; Augustine, in a moment of crisis, hears a voice directing him in turn to read; and Alypius then takes his lead from Augustine, reading on in Scripture from the point Augustine had stopped (VIII, 12). [Did at least Alypius know what followed?] Augustine's episode appears to be the most spectacular of the three—unless we are to assume that he probably "knew" from the outset what passage he was turning to—or that he later remembered only those parts of the episode which so fit together as to appeal to his sense of God's providence.

Each of the three revelations (Antony's, Augustine's, and Alypius') seems to be attuned to the circumstances and passions of the man to whom it is initially directed. (Antony had evidently been a man of some means.) On the other hand, if an injunction to give up his wealth had turned up for Augustine upon consulting Scripture, it could no doubt have been interpreted by him as appropriate, especially since he not only had long taught for considerable money but also had accumulated much learning.[63] Augustine's attachment to sexual satisfaction and to his accomplishments in public speaking make the Biblical verse "selected" particularly appropriate—and hence particularly effective for him. He is prepared for just such a renunciation as is called for: that, after all, seemed to have been what his extended impassioned struggle had been about. Thus he can say (VIII, 12), "I had no wish to read more and no need to do so." Augustine and Alypius now do, with one following the other into the service of the Church, what in the story told by Ponticianus two other people had done who happened upon a life of Antony. In these matters, we have noticed, imitation is critical.[64] Perhaps for this reason as well, public confession is important in that it provides models to others by which to guide their own passionate inclinations.

Augustine is far more impassioned in this scene than is Alypius. This difference may account, in part, for Augustine's greater effectiveness in dealing, in his own time and for centuries thereafter, with multitudes. His turmoil of soul, in part at the thought of what he was obliged or prepared (if not eager) to give up, finds a ready response in the storm-tossed souls of others—in desperate souls which are far more receptive to turmoil and its resolution than to the precise form in which that resolution happens to be put. It probably has not mattered to most of Augustine's readers whether he actually heard a voice on this occasion. Nor may it have mattered to Augustine himself. What did matter, as we noticed also in *De Magistro,* were the things in himself that he was somehow moved to recognize, to accept, and to renounce. He had had to accept these things in order to be able to renounce them and to rise above them, even as he used them.[65]

vi.

Augustine had not been content to rest with the engaging Platonists he had studied. Although he thought them far better than the Manicheans, they lacked a place in their scheme of things for Christ and the Incarnation, for confession, and hence for salvation.[66] Flesh and spirit are seen by Augustine to be in contention,[67] with Christ providing the basis for reconciliation. This is a reconciliation which sees divinity taking humble human form—and hence providing human beings with a model of humility, unlike the posturings of the proud philosophers.

Augustine can see himself as "sordid...deformed and squalid...tainted with ulcers and sores."[68] Is there, the philosopher might ask, something questionable about such self-disparagement, just as there is about any considerable concern with the body—with its inevitable maladies, with the painful prospect of eventually having to renounce the pleasures we can have from time to time, and even with the celebration of such renunciation? Is there not something immoderate, if not the risk of bad taste, in the introspection and self-abasement indulged on such occasions? In short, is there not, underlying this kind of exercise, too much concern with one's personal fate and hence with the accidents of *self?* To such questions, rooted in the classical sense of restraint, Augustine might reply, as he does in *The City of God,* that any old woman is superior in her Christian faith to all of the learned philosophers among the pagans.[69] One consequence of the kind of assessment he makes is likely to be a depreciation of prudence.

Any considerable concern with the bodily element, if only to repudiate it, is likely to be a concern with the personal, with the self, with a salvation of the individual soul which is somehow keyed to the body. This kind of concern encourages—does it not?—an openness to a personal God, to a divinity which can appear at least as interested in the individuality of a man, properly purged, as the man himself usually is.[70] Such legitimated self-centeredness, which testifies to the mercy and providence of God, also makes confession appropriate, if not even necessary. One's personal experiences very much matter. In this, too, Augustine may be distinctively modern, perhaps even the first of the moderns.

Augustine may be modern also in his recognition that he is tired of living and yet afraid of dying.[71] We return to the philosophical response to Augustine's troubled account of human existence. Is there in the passion story of the *Confessions,* along with the self-centeredness we have noticed, too much disparagement of oneself? Or, put another way, what should be made of the descriptions in the *Confessions* of the greedy infant at his mother's breast[72] or of Augustine's notorious pear-theft experience?[73] One suspects that these, too, are aspects of an undue concern for the body and its gratification. Augustine recognizes that all this relates to a fleeting set of pleasures—and that worries him.

One may even say that what is wrong with Augustine, who is about forty-five at the time he is writing the *Confessions,* is not the series of faults he describes but rather that he should consider them to *be* faults, or, at least that he should consider them to be as bad as he evidently does. Does he make too much of petty inclinations and base passions? Does he fail to make enough of nature, that nature (*eros* and all) which he dismisses as delusive and unreliable? Is it unnatural for him to treat nature as he does?[74] Or, to put this inquiry still another way, is nobility somehow lost sight of in Augustine's work, except as seen in that remarkable contempt of death which is often promoted by the Christian faith?[75]

vii.

With questions such as these we have returned to an issue with which we began our examination of the *Confessions* (and which we also noticed in our discussion of the *Meno*). Is it possible to study such a work without attempting to assess what happens to have been believed and reported by its gifted author about the role of the divine in human affairs? We can attempt to assess what has moved many readers of the *Confessions* and how its author's desire thus to move readers may be understood.

A full understanding of Augustine's desire may depend upon a further assessment of a mind capable of the subtle disquisitions upon the opening verses of *Genesis* to which he turns in the closing books of his *Confessions.* This exposition of *Genesis* by Augustine follows his account of the thirty-three-year-long journey to his conversion and of his relations with his mother, who died not long after his conversion, as did his recently baptized son. Augustine's personal life ends, so to speak, with his union with Christ. After that, he devotes himself to an account of how he as a Christian came to be, and how he developed. Perhaps it is as an aid to understanding his own coming-to-be that Augustine investigates, in his instructive discourses upon *Genesis,* how all things have come to be.[76]

Even more instructive may be what we can learn from the *Confessions* about the use that can be made of philosophy by Christian partisans—by conscientious women and men profoundly devoted to Biblical stories and to the passions and institutions legitimated and nurtured by those stories.[77] Also instructive is the status of nature in post-pagan times, not least with respect to ethical matters. That status has been called into question, sometimes inadvertently, by Christianity, perhaps depriving human beings of that guidance by which, with the aid of reason, they might conduct themselves without revelation. It is an awareness of nature (but not "a fallen nature") which makes philosophy possible. And it was to nature that thoughtful human beings have looked whenever they did not have the benefit of a reliable revelation. It could also be said that it is nature that guides the implementation, if not the identification and even the reformulation, of the sounder revelations upon which the more astute leaders rely in shaping their communities.[78]

What, then, is the relation between nature and virtue, aside from the problem of what natural elements are needed for effective training in virtue? Can virtue (moral as well as intellectual) be considered grounded in nature, something that reasoning beings may have reliable access to independent of divine revelation? Thus, we are, in a roundabout way, back both to Meno's opening question to Socrates in Plato's dialogue and to an underlying concern in Augustine's *De Magistro*.

III. On Nature and the Moral Virtues

All good men whom I know have taught me that we do not commit a grievous error if we make it our purpose to be as good as possible.

—Leo Strauss[79]

i.

Are the moral virtues grounded in nature? The common understanding of the three terms I have just used—*moral virtues, nature,* and *grounded*—suffices for our immediate purpose. It is on the basis of that understanding that our question is first likely to engage us.[80]

This question is an ancient one. But it may be dramatized by modern science—and by our contemporary doubts, related perhaps to the effects of science, about the knowability and the authority of nature, at least with respect to human affairs.[81] The question with which we start here is likely to generate many other questions whenever a serious effort is made to clarify the issues by which one may be confronted upon delving into these matters. Thus, the question of the relation between nature and the moral virtues is central to this entire article.

Nature, as it has long been understood, is consistent with the notion of the eternity, in one form or another, of the physical universe.[82] This notion is reinforced, or made more plausible, by the vast extent of time and space that modern science lays out before us.

Related to this notion of the eternity of the universe, for all practical purposes, is the evidence offered us for the accidental origins of the human

race, as well as of all other species here on earth. The substantial anatomical correspondence between several other species and the human species is now taken for granted by most biologists. We notice in passing that we do not consider the other species of animals known to us to have much if anything to do with the moral virtues, however much what they do, or "have to do," may be grounded in nature.*

The more that is made of evolution, the more likely it seems to the modern scientist that the origins of the human species depended upon fortuitous combinations of matter. (This tendency is reinforced by the radically materialistic bent, at least up to now, of modern science.) These material combinations, about which disciplines such as physics and chemistry have much to say, make it possible if not likely that our passions and appetites, with which the moral virtues are very much concerned, are in large part due to physical causes.

These currently pervasive opinions suggest to some that there may be other forms of life elsewhere in the vast reaches of the universe, even as cautions are heard about the exceedingly rare combination of material factors that permits life to emerge and sustain itself here.[83] But may there not be forms of life that we can do little more than imagine, if even that? Those who believe in angels, for example, cannot tell us much, if anything, about the "chemistry" of those living yet bodiless beings.

Thus, the possibility of life elsewhere in the universe—aside, of course, from what has long been believed to be found in such "places" as Hades, the Inferno, Purgatory, Paradise, and the Elysian Fields—is no longer dismissed as merely fanciful or rejected outright. That is, it is said, the vastness of the universe, in both time and space, makes other life possible if not even likely, here and there. What is not said as often is that that very vastness makes physical contact between those loci of life virtually impossible, assuming that the speed of light is indeed the upper limit of the speed of all matter in motion, (and hence of the transmission of information?) in the universe.[84]

What do such scientific findings and speculations tend to do to the traditional reliance upon that divine revelation which ministers to the guidance and care of one particular set of immortal souls, those of the human species on earth? The significance not only of individual human souls but also of the human species itself becomes harder to take seriously now that our scientists tell us about billions upon billions of galaxies, among which even our galaxy, let alone our solar system, can seem inconsequential.

What difference does it make, and to whom, how other rational beings conduct themselves, especially in circumstances where we are not immediately or personally concerned? This is related to questions about the goodness or enduring worth of personal conduct that no one else ever knows about. Another way of putting it is to wonder whether a study of nature may help our theoretical understanding, as distinguished from our practical

Atlas Major, by Joan Blaeu, c. 17th century. "What do such scientific findings and specu-lations...do to the tradi-tional reliance upon that di-vine revela-tion which ministers to the guidance and care of one particular set of immor-tal souls...?"

*See, however, Quinton on de Waal, in this issue of GIT.

judgment, leading to the possibility that the only reliable grasp of things by the reason of human beings may be intellectual, not moral.

What difference does it make now, or ever, what was thought, said, or done by the immeasurable multitudes of persons we can be sure lived on the earth itself if not elsewhere also, at various times in the past? What, if anything, does the vast expansion of the human perspective of time and space witnessed in the twentieth century do to our ability and willingness to regard the moral virtues as grounded in nature—that is, as matters to be taken seriously by the dispassionate observer? May not the movements of distant and often long-gone stars and planets be easier to understand, if not ultimately more interesting?

ii.

Let us come back down to earth by considering our question about the grounding of the moral virtues from a much more limited, even prosaic, perspective, however much that perspective may be influenced by the remarkable cosmological speculations of our day.

What should or does guide us in what we do? To some extent—at times, to a considerable extent—we are moved by familiar pleasures and pains. Related to this is the desire for self-preservation, or at least by the desire to avoid an early or a painful death. This can be keyed to personal advantage or to communal advantage, or to both.

If a species does not have an intense, sometimes all-consuming, desire for self-preservation, it probably would not either have emerged into self-replicating life or have been able to perpetuate itself very long thereafter. A pain/pleasure guidance related to this desire is seen in nonhuman forms of life as well—and it has many benefits, as well as creating problems. Biologists find it useful to approach instinctive conduct as if it were purposive, serving thereby the overall interests of a species if not also of individual members of the species.

Arguments are rarely needed to persuade the typical human being to seek and increase pleasures or to avoid and reduce pains in their lives.[85] Arguments are much more likely to be needed to encourage, if not even to require, someone to forego certain pleasures and to undergo certain pains. Most human beings learn early in life that some immediate pleasures can bring on severe pains, or can deprive us of other pleasures. It is in the arguments related to these matters that morality, as ordinarily understood, comes to view.

The enjoyment of pleasure, if not also the avoidance of pain, has been said to be seen in its most satisfying if not also in its most enduring form (at least on earth) in the activity of the genuine philosopher. Other kinds of activities are regarded by many as more enjoyable. But, it can be argued, only those who have had some experience of the range of activities to which human beings have always been drawn can reliably rank them with a view to what they may contribute to the most effective use of one's talents and hence to a general satisfaction with one's life.

The most serious alternative, if not opposition, to philosophy, at least among worldly pursuits, is offered by a political life and its ambitions and rewards. But the pleasure available to a few in politics is too dependent upon others to be reliable—and for this, and other reasons, it may be illusory.[86]

Many more would look to bodily gratifications, and especially sexuality, as the source of the most intense, all-engrossing pleasures. But this sort of pleasure is notoriously brief—and all too often it does not deliver what it promises. Even so, there is a *knowing* element in sexuality which beguiles us, and which is probably related to the long-recognized role of *eros* in philosophy. In addition, sexuality can help us learn what knowing is, including a self-confident knowing of ourselves.[87]

In any event, philosophy is critical to the ability to make sure that one's soul is in proper condition. It can help one know oneself well enough to make allowances for one's limitations and circumstances, thereby making it more likely that one will act as one should.

The ranking of the principal human pursuits, by those who have experienced enough of each to be able to judge among them, extends also to the subjects investigated by the inquiring mind. It comes to be observed that there is something intrinsic to various subjects, with some perceivable as higher and others as lower. Both the crossword-puzzler and the cosmologist work with "wholes" (as well as with holes)—but is it not obvious to most of us which pursuit is intrinsically higher?

Nature provides, or at least seems to provide, guidance as to what it means to know, as to what is most worth knowing, and as to the premises

An illustration of a philosophy lesson from the Ovid Moralise, *14th century.* "The enjoyment of pleasure…has been said to be seen in its most satisfying…form…in the activity of the genuine philosopher."

and forms of reasoning needed for learning and knowing. Someone such as Augustine would argue that the supernatural is also vital here, that its "personal" intervention may be not only instructive but even essential if there is to be reliable understanding.

iii.

We have reminded ourselves of the pleasures and pains or limitations of the body and also of the mind. We can now turn directly (however tentatively) to the critical question of the status of, or the grounding for, the moral virtues. Is there a sense of moral goodness that is not keyed to, or is not in the service primarily of, either personal or communal interests and advantages as ordinarily understood? We might well ask, as *the* test for exercising the virtues for their own sake, what basis there may be among us for personal self-sacrifice.

If nature is at work here, the human being may be inclined or directed toward morality (self-sacrificing or otherwise) without appreciating how or why this is so. This would be seen, for example, among those who have never discovered or thought much about *nature,* whether there is any such order of existence outside what we attribute to biology. Our question may appear then as largely theoretical. But the way we answer it may affect how morality, or the rules dependent upon and serving morality, should be regarded. Care must be taken not to subvert the hold upon a people of the established morality of their time and place, a morality that does tend to be respected on the highest level as worth practicing for itself alone. The "realistic" opinions here of a few may eventually have profound consequences.

This development can become acute if there should be an undermining of conventions and tradition, or the old way, with respect to morality by modern science. This may be related to the long-recognized tension between the pursuit of the common good (or justice) and the quest for truth (or the noble).[88]

Be that as it may, is there something about morality that provides pleasure in somewhat the way that there are physical pleasures, whether personal or shared, and intellectual pleasures, whether in the form of theology or of philosophy? Is there even something about morality that provides an attraction, generating something other than pleasure, which is superior to pleasure in whatever form? We seem in some way pleased to think that we are in accord with things, where we like to believe we have arrived at a certain fitness. This may be what Immanuel Kant was reaching for in his reflections on *duty.*[89]

The pleasure related to the exercise of the moral virtues may be more complicated than either the pleasures of the soul or those of the body. Are not the pleasures associated with the moral virtues sometimes less "single-minded" than those other pleasures—and hence, in a sense, more vulnerable? It can be difficult to sustain a combination of "thought" with "feeling."[90]

iv.

To recapitulate: there are pleasures of the body that may be enjoyed with little or no thinking required. This may be observed in all kinds of living things as well as in what happens to and with our bodies as we sleep. The mind may be very much required for, as well as involved in, the more interesting of the bodily pleasures. Still, it is body-driven.

There are also pleasures which are experienced by the incorporeal soul (for example, in heaven), and which one can anticipate somewhat here on Earth, forgetting in moments of ecstasy one's body, time, place, or other circumstances. Certain intellectual virtues may guide the use of the mind on such occasions.

What, if any, basis is there, then, for morality in nature. A digression may be of some use as we refine this question further. Aside from the question of whether morality is grounded in nature, there is the question which I can do little more than allude to here of whether nature herself should be obeyed, assuming that nature makes her guidance known.

Does not nature make us feel that we should obey her? But is it right or necessary that we should obey? Should we do so only because nature moves us to do so? If we cannot help acting one way rather than another in a particular situation, where is the moral element in that action? Still, one should take care here (whatever Kant may seem to tell us about these matters) not to disparage a proper habituation and its consequences.

Enough, at least for the moment, for this digression. What if any basis is there for morality in nature? There is a natural basis for morality in the sense that nature provides us physical equipment, parts of the soul, and perhaps inclinations and instincts which make us open to moral considerations and guidance.

This openness seems to be largely confined on earth to human beings among the living things we know by direct observation. Nature permits human beings to use moral teachings, including the curbing of various pleasures, to serve various ends. Human beings can also clarify the principles on the basis of which they act as no other animal can. This suggests that there is something intrinsic to human beings which makes them open to moral teachings, whatever the sources of morality. But what does nature herself say about those sources?

An inquiry as to the sources of morality is related to what the standards and rules are and to why we should observe those standards and obey those rules. We have anticipated what is sometimes said, even by quite respectable students of this subject. Morality, it is said, is exclusively instrumental or ministerial; it is not something worth having, exercising, or honoring for its own sake, but only, if at all, for its consequences.

Less of a problem, in a sense, is the radical nihilist for whom not even philosophy means much if anything. Such a nihilist is both harder and easier to deal with here. We put him to one side as virtually impossible to argue with, addressing instead those who recognize a grounding in nature for philosophy, or the intellectual virtues, but not for the moral virtues.

This position may be one consequence of the modern insistence upon an unprecedented standard of certainty in all subjects of inquiry. Is moral discourse incapable of appearing precise and hence certain enough for modern tastes? We have not been concerned here with whether the moral virtues should be ranked as high as, if not higher than, the intellectual or philosophic virtues, but rather with whether the moral virtues have any grounding in nature as something worth having for their own sake. [91]

Much can be said for the proposition that the moral virtues indeed are largely instrumental and properly so, especially since most, if not all, of the virtues depend upon conventions or have obvious practical consequences. No matter what the sources, impulses, or motivation involved, conventions and consequences are often critical in determining how one should act. For example, several virtues depend upon how property is dealt with: what *is* property and what may be done with it very much depend upon ever-changing laws.[92]

Those who argue for the exclusively instrumental character of the moral virtues sometimes refer to obviously thoughtful people who are said to endorse this argument. But when one happens to observe such men and women close up, what does one see? They feel obliged to pronounce moral judgments, sometimes about ancient or long-past events or actors, some-times about twentieth century events (such as what the Nazis did in their death camps), and sometimes about individuals they know personally. These people can pronounce moral judgments in such a way as not to seem to regard morality as merely instrumental. A genuine moral feeling, as if grounded in nature, is expressed, sometimes spontaneously.[93]

Besides, when we consider someone such as Socrates, for whom the life of the inquiring mind seemed most worthy of the human being, we remember that he was prepared on more than one occasion to risk his life, and hence the opportunity to continue philosophizing here on earth, for the sake of moral rectitude.[94] This kind of self-sacrificing response, in defiance of the city's "teaching" of the moment, seems to be an endorsement of the moral virtues for their own sake, something that the moral skeptics of our time cannot easily explain away.

Furthermore, there is a problem in regarding the intellectual virtues as grounded in nature, but not the moral virtues. Do not the philosopher's honesty and willingness to run risks in pursuit of the truth seem to have some of the characteristics of the moral virtues?[95] In addition, if the intellectual virtues do depend, as Socrates argued, upon an erotic element, what guides that element? Is it guided in the interest of nature-grounded philosophy—and, if so, does nature indirectly shape the erotic? The erotic, I have suggested, may connect the realm of the intellectual virtues to the realm of the moral virtues.

It has been argued that we cannot see certain actions if we do not grasp and take seriously the moral element in those actions.[96] But how seriously can the moral virtues be taken if they are regarded as merely instrumental? Consider as well, the *noble,* that which seems to be worth having and savoring for its own sake. Is it what makes it easier for us to see, for example, that it is better that a man should be treated unjustly than that he be unjust himself?

v.

However all this may be, there are difficulties, if not risks, in considering morality as exclusively instrumental, especially if this opinion becomes widely accepted. For one thing, morality cannot be effectively instrumental if it is believed to be merely instrumental. We may want morality to be regarded as more than instrumental because we sense that it is important, that it is vulnerable, and that it is most effective when it is regarded as grounded in nature (or, to somewhat the same effect, in divine revelation).

Our deepest concerns here may reflect an instinctive, or natural, opening in us to morality. To recognize what we have said about the appeal of the moral virtues is to recognize some grounding in nature for them. This recognition may be required if there is to be an effective response to the challenges posed by Polemarchus and Thrasymachus in Book I of Plato's *Republic (GBWW I: 7, 295–310; II: 6, 295–310),* by Glaucon and Adeimantus in Book II (*GBWW* I: 7, 310–24; 6, 310–24), and by Polus and Callicles in Plato's *Gorgias (GBWW I: 7, 252–94; II: 6, 252–94).* Those vigorous challenges suggest that "everyone knows" that if one can "get away with" injustice, with no one else ever knowing of it, one may seem to have the best of two worlds: others are thus encouraged to be respectful of justice (which contributes to your security) while you enjoy things that would not otherwise be available to you.

"Be realistic," we are told by those who believe they know what it is that truly moves people. But may there not be a naturally moral component to facing up to the truth? Those who regard the intellectual virtues as grounded in nature probably rely somewhat upon the moral virtues in the conduct and assessment of the inquiries which the intellectual virtues require and glory in. Furthermore, do not the challenges posed by Polemarchus, Thrasymachus and the others somehow draw upon something natural in us? Intellectual honesty is invoked or relied upon by Socrates' challengers, as if that is something we should all respect.

If the moral virtues are not grounded in nature, then they are at best only instrumental, borrowing their dignity from the activity they may happen to serve. Thus, morality would be grounded in nature, but only indirectly, in that it is in the service of natural desires (whether of the body or of the mind, if not of the community as well in forming a city). Thus, also, the moral virtues would have no intrinsic dignity.

If morality is indeed only something to be *used,* does not that tend to make the will paramount? An insistence upon the decisiveness of the will in human, if not also in divine, affairs is perhaps distinctively modern. Critical here seems to be the opinion that man makes everything, including his "values."[97] This opinion is reinforced by the growing popular awareness, partly because of modern science and technology, of the remarkable variety of ways of human life around the world.

vi.

What does the variety of conventions show, that variety which seems so much a manifestation of chance in human life and which is made so much of by "realists"? However varied these conventions may be, do not their similarities suggest that there may be something natural at work here?

First, there is the very fact that almost all, if not all, communities have moral guides, as if they are intrinsic to human beings or at least to their associations. Both this fact and the variety of ways have long been evident, as may be seen in the various works of Homer, Herodotus, Livy, Lucretius, and the Bible.

Second, there is a remarkable compatibility among the many moral codes around the world, even for peoples who were not in touch with each other during their formative stages centuries, if not millennia, ago. Critical details of a code here or there may depend upon chance circumstances. But we can usually see the sense of most rules in the circumstances in which we find them. Thus, there is sometimes available an indication of what the basis was, in a particular community, of the determination to adopt the moral code relied upon, a basis which includes elements that we can recognize as defensible if not even as praiseworthy. This can help us get to the roots of a moral code.[98]

Third, there is the prevalence of the notion that one *should* be virtuous, whatever the specifics of the morality of a time or place may be. When a convention is questioned, this is usually done on the basis of moral standards that are generally accepted. We can be troubled by someone who casually disregards the long-established morals of his time and place, even when we have serious reservations about the political regime under which he lives.

Often, we have noticed the moral code of a people is rooted in some form of divine revelation. Which revelation governs where may be largely a matter of chance (except, it should be conceded, for the true revelation). No doubt, acceptance of revelation may be in part due to ignorance and fear, reinforced by glimpses of the abyss. But there may also be a natural appetite for revelation—or for that which revelation provides, a comprehensive view of the whole reinforced by divine authority. It may be related to that natural desire-to-know of which Aristotle spoke.[99]

A caution is in order here, a caution already noticed in our discussion of Augustine. Care must be taken in making use of divine revelation, or of any other expression of an authoritative will, to support rules of conduct, lest that use, if deemed indispensable, undermine the grounding of morality in nature. Besides, is not nature useful in shaping us, including our religious organizations and other communities day in and day out? Care must be taken, that is, lest religion come to be regarded as little more than a super-convention, not itself consistent with nature.

And if, as happens in the course of centuries to all but perhaps the true religion, purported revelations here and there come to be questioned (or worn out) and replaced, what becomes of the status of morality? One problem here is suggested by the tendency in some quarters today to see a public promotion of morality as a way of surreptitiously foisting revealed, as distinguished from natural, religion upon the citizen body.

Nature may express herself through the believer, even when the believer no longer considers nature sufficient as

A course in theology, 15th century. "[P]hilosophy is critical to the ability to make sure that one's soul is in proper condition."

a guide. (There has long been talk in the Western World of "a fallen nature.") Does the believer, like the modern realist, tend to undermine reliance upon nature? We return again to Augustine here. Does not the believer tend to believe that, without revelation, life is ultimately meaningless and hopeless, as well as immediately fragile? He does not recognize any natural basis of morality—or perhaps the intrinsic goodness even of the rational life. It is in this direction that nihilism may lie.

Does the believer, like the modern scientist, also make too much of the tenuousness of the human species absent divine providence? What is the significance of the fact, if fact it is, that everything we have and can know, and even the very possibility of knowing, is temporary and provisional, with all the things that we depend upon (including memory) doomed to deterioration and annihilation? Yet if matter/energy is eternal, is not the potential always "here" for "us" to appear again and again? That is, is there not something natural about our very being, including our aspirations, however fortuitous any particular appearance and form of a species and its yearnings may be?

vii.

We should not conclude this part of our inquiry without noticing the question of what the basis is of the choice of a code when rules of conduct are offered as divine commands, or as super-conventions.

If a "divine" code is contrived by human beings, there may be either delusion or deliberate deception at work there. In either case, the moral soundness or worth of the enterprise can be suspected—unless there is a noble lie involved, which may be salutary in its effect as well as in its intention. Even the invention by human beings of gods may reveal a divine spark or urge in our species, something that is naturally there in both the prophet (or poet) and his audience.

If a moral code is truly from God, there is still the question of how God chooses what He does. It need not be—indeed, probably should not be—considered as arbitrary.[100] Why should that to which God looks in framing a moral code be considered different from that which nature, in its perfection, also offers for our guidance?

If divine intervention is put to one side, what does a finite earthly existence, with no reliable prospect of immortal life, do to our sense of the meaningfulness of life here? It may depend partly upon whether the prevalent appetite for immortal life and salvation is not natural but rather cultivated, and if so how.[101]

We have moved from asking whether morality is good in itself to whether human life, with nothing following personally after death, is good in itself. These may be related questions. Have not human beings usually had the sense that existence is a good thing if not burdened by great calamities and pains?[102] If we are naturally attracted to human life, should we not also be naturally drawn to the moral code that evidently makes human life work well and be well? If this is instrumentality, it is on a very

high level which dignifies the moral virtues, virtually making them worth practicing for their own sake.

Any kind of inquiry into the natural basis for morality could well inspire us to wonder whether there is something immoral in raising questions about the natural basis for morality, unless perhaps one insists at the same time upon the divine basis of morality. If there *is* a natural basis for morality, is there something wrong morally or intellectually or both with those who explicitly deny, and perhaps thereby subvert reliance upon, such a basis?

We can wonder, furthermore, whether there is something deeply wrong with those who are not simply open to the good. Do some intellectuals "allow" their speculative appetites to overcome their moral sensibilities when they consider, or at least talk about, these matters? A comment by John Van Doren (Executive Editor of *The Great Ideas Today*) on the arguments I have developed here offers a salutary corrective to contemporary skepticism.

The Discourse: A Chat *by Sir Lawrence Alma-Tedema.* "Ultimately critical here may be the question whether there is *an idea of the good* that guides ... serious inquiry and thought."

I am not sure it can be *proved* that the moral virtues are grounded in nature, but the evidence of our persistent and spontaneous response to injustice, say, powerfully suggests that they are. This response may not be everywhere the same, or as strong, but that is only to acknowledge that cultural beliefs and convictions can affect it. I think it can be found usually, however skewed, even in such cases. There exists a pervasive human sense of "ought," to some end or ends which is defied only with embarrassment or bravado, both of which are forms of recognition—or if they are not, we say men are acting inhumanly. To say nothing of the fact that if the moral virtues were not grounded in nature there would be no way to teach them, that is, awaken us to them, except as rote lessons. Some of our moralists would be willing to settle for this, to be sure.[103]

Ultimately critical here may be the question whether there is *an idea of the good* that guides all actions as well as all serious inquiry and thought. We recall the opening passages of the *Nicomachean Ethics* and the *Politics* of Aristotle, with their insistence that every pursuit is thought to aim at some good. If Aristotle is correct in what he thus says again and again, does not that reveal a natural opening in human beings to the good—and hence to the moral virtues? The virtues, if seen in this way, may not be exclusively instrumental, however useful they may indeed be.

Even our pleasures and pains continually teach us, or illustrate for us, the idea of the good. Is not that idea vital to the philosophic inquiry which as we have noticed some concede to be grounded in nature, reinforcing thereby that enduring sense of rightness which moral choices naturally seem to us to rest upon and to serve?

At the very least, then, there may be nothing wrong, depending of course upon how one goes about it, in affirming, or reaffirming, the natural basis for a sensible morality.[104]

1. Aristotle, *Nicomachean Ethics,* bk. 10, chap. 9 (Laurence Berns translation) (*GBWW* I: 9, 434–36; II: 8, 434–36). See Plato, *Meno* 70A, 89A–C, 99B–100C (*GBWW* I: 7, 174, 184, 189–90; II: 6, 174, 184, 189–90.) Another manuscript has "cultivated before by training character" for "cultivated before by habits."

2. *See,* on Plato's *Meno,* Jacob Klein, *A Commentary on Plato's "Meno"* (Chapel Hill: North Carolina University Press, 1965). *See also,* Anastaplo, *Human Being and Citizen: Essays on Virtue, Freedom, and the Common Good* (Chicago: Swallow Press, 1975), p. 74; Anastaplo, book review, *Review of Metaphysics,* vol. 32, p. 773, (1979). In the last paragraph of this book review "It is not true" should be "Is it not true."

3. *See* Plato, *Meno* 99C–100C (*GBWW* I: 7, 189–90; II: 6, 189–90).

4. *See,* on Plato's *Republic,* Leo Strauss, *The City and Man* (Chicago: Rand McNally & Co., 1964), pp. 50f. *See also,* Anastaplo, *The Constitutionalist: Notes on the First Amendment* (Dallas: Southern Methodist University Press, 1971), pp. 274–81; Anastaplo, *The Amendments to the Constitution: A Commentary* (Baltimore: John Hopkins University Press, 1995), pp. 107–24; Anastaplo, *The Thinker as Artist: From Homer to Plato & Aristotle* (Athens, Ohio: Ohio University Press, 1997), p. 303–17; Harry V. Jaffa, *Original Intent and the Framers of the Constitution* (Washington, D.C.: Regnery Gateway, 1994), pp. 199f, 353f.; note 16 below.

5. *See* Plato, *The Republic* 621A–B (*GBWW* I: 7, 440–41; II: 6, 440–41). *Compare* Plato, *Apology of Socrates* 40C sq. (*GBWW* I: 7, 211; II: 6, 211).

6. This recalling seems to encompass other things besides the virtues, such as geometry. *See*, on the place of mathematics in education, Plato, *The Republic*, e.g., 522–26, 526 sq. (*GBWW* I: 7, 391–94; II: 7, 391–94).

7. These discussions continue and may be heard, among us, in debates about welfare programs, illegitimacy rates, prenatal care, Head Start, "family values," neighborhood policing, and capital punishment. *See*, e.g., Judith Stacey, "The New Family Values Crusaders," *Nation*, July 25, 1994, p. 119. *See also*, the opening scene of Shakespeare, *As You Like It* (*GBWW* I: 26, 597–99; II: 24, 597–99); note 104 below.

8. *See*, on Gorgias, Plato, *Gorgias* (*GBWW* I: 7, 252–94; II: 6, 252–94); Anastaplo, *The Thinker as Artist*, pp. 264–78. *See also*, note 49 below.

9. Anytus may have been the principal accuser of Socrates. *See* Plato, *Apology* 29C, 30B (*GBWW* I: 7, 206–7; II: 6, 206–7). *See*, on the trial of Socrates, Anastaplo, *Human Being and Citizen*, pp. 8, 203. *See*, on what Socrates does know, Anastaplo, "Freedom of Speech and the First Amendment: Explorations," *Texas Tech Law Review*, vol. 21, p. 1945 (1990).

10. *See* Anastaplo, *Human Being and Citizen*, p. v (Dedication).

11. *See* Plato, *Meno* 86C–D.

12. *See*, on tyranny, Aristotle, *Politics* 1310 a 39 sq. (*GBWW* I: 9, 512; II: 8, 512). Leo Strauss, *On Tyranny* (Glencoe, Illinois: The Free Press, 1963). *See also*, Anastaplo, *Human Being and Citizen*, p. 3; Anastaplo, *The Artist as Thinker: From Shakespeare to Joyce* (Athens, Ohio: Ohio University Press, 1983), p. 331; Anastaplo, *The American Moralist: On Law, Ethics, and Government* (Athens, Ohio: Ohio University Press, 1992), pp. 37, 51, 144, 161, 501, 508, 555.

13. *See*, e.g., Plato, *The Republic* 498C–D (*GBWW* I: 7, 381; II: 6, 381).

14. Niccolò Machiavelli, *Discourses on the First Decade of Titus Livy*, II, 2 (Leo Paul S. de Alvarez translation). *See*, on Machiavelli and the Church, Anastaplo, *The American Moralist*, p. 516.

15. Augustine, who was born in 354, wrote the *De Magistro* in 386; he wrote the *Confessions* in 397–400. *See* note 41 below. The translation of *De Magistro* (*The Teacher*) drawn upon here is by Robert P. Russell (first published in 1968 by the Catholic University of America Press). It may be found among the *Additions to the Great Books Library* in this volume of *GIT*. The citations in the text of sections *I* and *II* of part two of this article are, by chapter and section, to the *De Magistro*.

16. Also brought to mind is the doctrine of the ideas developed in Plato's *Republic*. *See* Anastaplo, *The Thinker as Artist*, pp. 303-17. *See also*, note 4 above.

17. See *Ephesians* 3:14–17.

18. *See* 1 *Corinthians* 1:23–24.

19. *See*, for discussion of early Christian thinkers, Anastaplo, "Rome, Law, and Civilization: Explorations," *Loyola University of New Orleans Law Review*, vol. 39, p. 47f (1993); note 60 below. *See*, on Julian the Apostate, ibid., p. 83. *See*, on St. Paul, ibid., pp. 32f, 39f. *See*, on the trial of Jesus, Anastaplo, "On Trial: Explorations," *Loyola University of Chicago Law Journal*, vol. 22, p. 882 (1991). *See also*, note 27 below.

20. See *Matthew* 23:9.

21. *See* Augustine, *Retractions*, 1: 12. *See also*, Augustine, *Confessions*, IX, 6 (*GBWW* I: 16, 67; II: 18, 82). All citations in the text of this article to the *Confessions* (*GBWW* I; 16, 1–125; II: 18, 1–159) are to the R. S. Pine-Coffin translation.

22. *Syntopicon*, 2: 780. *See*, on conscience, Anastaplo, *Human Being and Citizen*, p. 324; Anastaplo, *The American Moralist*, p. 607. *See also*, notes 90 and 91 below.

23. F. J. Sheed, *Theology and Sanity* (New York: Sheed & Ward, 1946), p. 333. *See also*, ibid., pp. 4–11, 31–36, 40f, 77, 99f, 170, 174, 320, 330. Is not Pascal an important influence in the way these sentiments are expressed? *See also*, Augustine, *Confessions*,

VII, 11 (*GBWW* I: 18, 49; II: 16, 61); Anastaplo, "An Introduction to Buddhist Thought," (*GIT* 1992, 246, n. 57).

24. Thomas Aquinas, too, wrote a *De Magistro*. It has been available as a Great Books Foundation pamphlet. Augustine, if persuaded that his Christian faith was not sound, might have decided that nothing else he "knew" was reliable. How would Thomas Aquinas have responded in like circumstances? *See* note 99 below.

25. *See also,* Augustine, *De Magistro.* The Virgilian line examined in this dialogue is, *Si nihil ex tanta superis placet urbe relingui.* The minute examination word by word of this line, which seems to show the pagans recognizing divine omnipotence, does not get to the gods in this dialogue. Is the intriguing character of such recognition by a pagan author reflected in Augustine's having chosen first to examine this line and then to hold off from examining it fully here? I draw, for my discussion hereafter of Augustine's *Confessions,* on Anastaplo, "Rome, Law, and Civilization," p. 53f.

26. *See* Anastaplo, "On Freedom: Explorations," *Oklahoma City University Law Review,* vol. 17, pp. 465, 666 (1992); Anastaplo, "Lessons for the Student of Law: The Oklahoma Lectures," *Oklahoma City University Law Review,* vol. 20, pp. 17, 187 (1995); Anastaplo, "The O. J. Simpson Case Revisited," *Loyola University of Chicago Law Journal,* vol. 28 p. 464 (1997).

27. Christian thought (as we have come to know it) may be better seen in someone such as Augustine than in Jesus himself, if only because Jesus (insofar as he was human) was raised as a Jew with relatively little exposure to the philosophical tradition of the Greeks that figures so prominently in Christianity. But *see* Jaffa, *Original Intent and the Framers of the Constitution,* pp. 181f, 345f. The *Encyclopædia Britannica* article by John Bornaby on Augustine opens with this useful introduction to his life and work:

> Saint Augustine (in Latin, Augustinus), bishop of Hippo in Roman Africa from 396 to 430, and the dominant personality of the Western Church of his time, is generally recognized as having been the greatest thinker of Christian antiquity. His mind was the crucible in which the religion of the New Testament was most completely fused with the Platonic tradition of Greek philosophy; and it was also the means by which the product of this fusion was transmitted to the Christendoms of medieval Roman Catholicism and Renaissance Protestantism.

> This unique significance would have belonged to Augustine had he never written the famous *Confessions,* in which at the age of about 45 he told the story of his own restless youth and of the stormy voyage that had ended, as he believed, 12 years before he put it in writing, in the haven of the Catholic Church. It is easy to forget that the real work of Augustine's life did not begin until the last scene of the *Confessions* was already receding for him into a remembered past. Moreover, the *Confessions* themselves are not so much autobiography as they are devotional outpourings of penitence and thanksgiving. Augustine's conscientious memory generally can be trusted for the facts: his reflections upon them are those of the bishop on his knees.

Ernest L. Fortin has provided us an instructive introduction to the political thought of Augustine:

> St. Augustine is the first author to deal more or less comprehensively with the subject of civil society in the light of the new situation created by the emergence of revealed religion and its encounter with philosophy in the Greco-Roman world. As a Roman he inherited and restated for his own time the political philosophy inaugurated by Plato and adapted to the Latin world by Cicero, and as a Christian he modified that philosophy to suit the requirements of the faith. He thus appears if not as the originator at least as the foremost exponent in ancient

times of a new tradition of political thought characterized by its attempt to fuse or reconcile elements derived from two originally independent and hitherto unrelated sources, the Bible and classical philosophy. Augustine writes first and foremost as a theologian and not as a philosopher.

Fortin, "St. Augustine (354–430)," in Leo Strauss and Joseph Cropsey, eds., *History of Political Philosophy* (Chicago: Rand McNally & Company, 1972; 2d ed.), p. 151. *See* Anastaplo, "An Introduction to Buddhist Thought," (*GIT* 1992, 246 n. 57). *See* as well, note 19 above, note 66 below.

28. *See,* e.g., *Confessions,* I, 6 (*GBWW* I: 16, 2–3; II: 18, 2–3).

29. *See,* e.g., *Confessions,* III, 8; VI, 10, 12 (*GBWW* I: 16, 17, 40, 41–42; II: 18, 21–22, 50–51, 52). *See,* on Manichaeism, note 66 below.

30. Augustine's father had died by the time of Augustine's conversion, having himself been baptized as a Christian on his deathbed.

31. See *Confessions,* VIII, 6 (*GBWW* I: 16, 56–57; II: 18, 71–72). Augustine has become known as the father of Western monasticism. *See* Anastaplo, "An Introduction to Buddhist Thought," (*GIT* 1992, 240 n. 3; 246, 56).

32. *See,* e.g., *Confessions,* VII, 18, 19 (*GBWW* I; 16, 50–51, 544–45, 557–60; II: 18, 600, 616, 629–32). *Compare,* e.g., Augustine, *The City of God,* XX, 1, 17, 29, 30.

33. See *Psalms* 6:4 (6:3), *Psalms* 78:5, 8 (79:5, 8). Christians could come to see such Old Testament passages as anticipations of their faith. *See* note 76 below.

34. See *Matthew* 19:21.

35. See *Romans* 13: 13–14. *See also,* note 74 below. Augustine does not quote the entire passage, which begins, "Let us pass our time honorably, as by the light of the day, not in revelling and drunkenness, etc." A better translation of *Roman* 13:14 is, "But put ye on the Lord Jesus Christ, and make not provision for the flesh, to fulfill the lusts thereof." *Nature* is *not* in the Greek text, whatever the inclination of Augustine may have been to reduce *nature* to *lust. See* the text at note 46 below; also, note 61 below. *See,* on conscience, note 22 above.

36. See *Romans* 14:1. Another translation of these words is, "Him that is weak in the faith receive." The passage continues, "but not to doubtful disputations." Why did the sometimes polemical Augustine omit this? *See* note 61 below.

37. See *Ephesians* 3:20.

38. See *Psalms* 29:12 (30:11).

39. *Confessions,* VIII, 12. *See,* for the appeals of continence to a much moved but yet resisting Augustine, ibid., VIII, 11, (*GBWW* I: 16, 60; II: 18, 75–76).

40. Is this an echo of the "take and eat" heard during the Eucharist?

41. This episode, in Milan, is in the summer of 386. Augustine had been born in a Roman province in North Africa in 354. He died in 430, at Hippo in North Africa, where he had been a bishop of the Roman Catholic Church for thirty-five years.

42. *See,* on Augustine and Descartes, Anastaplo, *The American Moralist,* p. 87. *See* also Anastaplo, "An Introduction to Buddhist Thought," (*GIT,* 1992, 247, n. 63). Jean-Jacques Rousseau, for better or for worse, seems to be in the confessional tradition inaugurated by Augustine. *See* note 76 below.

43. Representative Barney Frank quoted this prayer by Augustine when he chided his republican colleagues for voting for a term limitation constitutional amendment that would *not* take effect immediately upon ratification for sitting members of Congress. *See* Adam Clymer, "Measure on Term Limits," *New York Times,* Feb. 5, 1997, p. A8. *See also,* Anastaplo, "An Introduction to Buddhist Thought," (*GIT* 1992, 245 n. 47).

44. *See,* e.g., *Confessions,* V, 6 (*GBWW* I: 16, 29–30; II: 18, 37). Augustine reports that he early fell in love with the idea of love. *See* ibid., III, i. Are Catullus and Ovid more in his background here than Sappho and Plato's *Symposium?* (*See,* for Sappho and Plato on love, philosophy, and the divine, Anastaplo, *The Thinker as Artist,* pp. 45, 171.

45. *See*, e.g., *Confessions*, I, 13; II, 6; V, 12 (*GBWW* I: 16, 6, 11–12, 33; II: 18, 7–8; 14–15; 41–42).

46. See *Confessions*, X, 30 (*GBWW* I: 16, 81–82; II: 18, 103). *See also*, note 35 above.

47. See *The City of God*, XV, 22 (*GBWW* I: 16, 416; II: 18, 476). *See*, on *eros* and philosophy, section *ii* of part three of this article. *See also*, Plato, *Symposium* (*GBWW* I: 7, 149–73; II: 6, 149–73); Anastaplo, *The Thinker as Artist*, p. 171.

48. *Confessions*, VI, 16 (*GBWW* I: 16, 42; II: 18, 53). *See* Francis Bacon, *The Essayes or Counsels, Civil and Moral*, Essay No. XVI, "Of Atheism," Essay No. XVII, "Of Superstition."

49. See *Confessions*, IX, 2, 5 (*GBWW* I: 16, 62, 651; II: 18, 78–79, 82). How much did chance have to play in the course that Augustine's career took here? Someone such as Gorgias may have been Augustine's mentor in public speaking. *See*, on the influence of Cicero, *Confessions*, III, 4 (*GBWW* I: 16, 14–15; II: 18). *See also*, note 8 above.

50. See *Confessions*, IV, 2; VI, 15 (*GBWW* I: 16, 19–20, 42; II: 18, 24–25, 53). The effect of his conversion on his impending marriage is mentioned by Augustine immediately after his account of the conversion. Was a conversion the way out that he had, perhaps unknown to himself, been seeking?

51. Evidently, the woman with whom Augustine had been living for some time was of a lower class and hence not suitable for marriage to someone of his status and family ambitions. He found another woman for himself after giving up the woman he had had and before he could be married two years later. (The age of his prospective bride evidently required that he wait. Perhaps also he was troubled at the prospect of marrying in his mid-thirties someone two decades younger. *See* Anastaplo, "An Introduction to Islamic Thought," (*GIT*, 1989, 278 n. 95).

52. See *Confessions*, VIII, 6 (*GBWW* I: 16, 56–7; II: 18, 71–2). Is there not something refreshingly naive about how Augustine describes the influences upon him? Central to what happens to him seems to be a powerful inclination toward "salvation" on his part (an urge to which his remarkably persistent mother had probably contributed), much more so than any arguments he may have been exposed to. We, after all, can be exposed to the arguments he was exposed to without being moved to his resolution. Are we "entitled" also to the kind of "miracles" that he and others have had to be moved by? *See*, e.g., note 60 below. Only if we too are prepared for and open to the miraculous? *See* Augustine, *The City of God*, XXII, 8 (*GBWW* I: 16, 591–98; II: 18, 666–74).

53. The gender of the providential speaker could not be determined by Augustine. Does he leave open the possibility that it was an angel? *See* note 59 below.

54. Does Augustine believe he understands enough to know that much of this *is* God's doing? On these questions Maimonides and Machiavelli can be instructive.

55. Does the emphasis upon the tree take us back to the Garden of Eden and another fateful tree? *See*, on John Milton's *Paradise Lost*, Anastaplo, "Individualism, Professional Ethics, and the Sense of Community: From Runnymede to a London Telephone Booth," *Loyola University of Chicago Law Journal*, vol. 28, p. 320, Appendix (1997). *See also*, Anastaplo, "On Trial," pp. 767–84.

56. *See*, for other "voices," *Confessions*, X, 27, 31; XI, 6; XII, 11, 15 (*GBWW* I: 16, 81, 82–83, 91, 102, 103–4; II: 18, 102, 103–5, 115, 129, 130–32).

57. *See*, e.g., *Confessions*, III, 11, 12; VI, 1 (*GBWW* I: 16, 18, 19, 34–35; II: 18, 23, 23–24, 43–44). *Compare* note 58 below.

58. *See*, e.g., *Confessions*, XI, 13 (*GBWW* I: 16, 92–93; II: 18, 117). Augustine insists that Biblical stories, too, must be properly interpreted. *See*, on the voices of Joan of Arc, Anastaplo, "On Trial," p. 919f.

59. Augustine is not concerned to investigate whether what had seemed a miracle was indeed so. *See*, on what leads to sudden enlightenment, W. Theodore de Bary, ed., *The Buddhist Tradition in India, China, and Japan* (New York: Vintage Books, 1969),

p. 360. *See,* on Socrates' voice, Anastaplo, *Human Being and Citizen,* pp. 10–11, 27–28. *See also,* note 77 below.

60. Does Augustine imitate St. Paul to some extent, the man whose epistles he *is* reading? Did anyone else both see and hear what Saul did at that fateful moment for Christianity on the road to Damascus? See *Acts of the Apostles,* 9:3–8, 22:5–12, 26:12–14. *See,* on St. Paul, note 19 above. *See also,* Anastaplo, "An Introduction to Buddhist Thought," (*GIT,* 1992, 243 n. 36).

61. The "dynamics" of what is at work here may be related to what we now know as "Freudian slips." How does Augustine "know" that it is a book that he is instructed to read—and, if a book, which one? *See* notes 35 and 36 above, note 63 below.

62. This Antony was born, it seems, a century before Augustine. Was the verse picked for Augustine to read chosen partly with Alypius in mind? Alypius could thus be spiritually allied with Augustine on the highest authority. *See* note 29 above.

63. Herodotus and Thucydides instruct us how oracles and other divine signs can be adapted to the circumstances. So does the Socrates of Plato's *Apology.*

64. See *Confessions,* VIII, 6 (*GBWW* I: 16, 56–57; II: 18, 71–72). I have commented, in part one of this article, upon the instructive imitation of Meno by Socrates in his opening speech in Plato's *Meno.*

65. If this is self-seeking, it is on a scale not imagined by Meno. Nor would Meno have considered this an acquisition of virtue by Augustine. Would Socrates, on the other hand, have considered Augustine's new form of virtue to be grounded in his passions whatever the role of divine dispensation in its emergence?

66. *See,* e.g., *Confessions,* III, 4; V, 10, 14; VII, 9, 20, 21. (*GBWW* I: 16, 14–15, 32–33, 34, 47–48, 51–52; II: 18, 40–41, 42–43, 60–61, 65–66) There is much more drawn from the Platonists in *The City of God.* But *see* Fortin, "St. Augustine," p. 155 (emphasis added):

Augustine regarded Plato as the greatest of the pagan philosophers and as the philosopher whose thought most clearly approximated that of Christianity. He even goes so far as to speak of him as the philosopher who would have become a Christian if he had lived in Christian times. However, his primary source of information concerning Plato's political philosophy is not Plato himself, to whose dialogues he had only limited access, but Cicero's Roman *and stocized* version of that philosophy as it is found in Cicero's [works].

See also, note 27 above. The *Encyclopædia Britannica* article on Augustine includes this description of Manichaeism:

The Manichaean system as propagated in the Western Roman Empire was a materialistic dualism that accounted for the creation of the world as the product of a conflict between light and dark substances and for the soul of man as an element of the light entangled in the dark. Manichaeism claimed to be the true Christianity, preaching Christ as the Redeemer who enables the imprisoned particles of light to escape and return to their own region. In the Manichaean Church the higher order of "elect" adhered to a strict regimen of asceticism and celibacy, all physical generation being held to serve the realm of darkness.

67. *See,* e.g., *Confessions,* VIII, 6 (*GBWW* I: 16, 56–57; II: 18, 71–72).

68. *Confessions,* VIII, 7 (*GBWW* I: 16, 57–58; II: 18, 72–73). Although there is an emphasis on humility in the rabbinic tradition of the Jews and some self-abnegation, that is not so in the Hebrew Bible. Individual sages do not say much about themselves. Moses *is* said to be humble, but he may not look that way to us. He can doubt his worthiness as the agent of God, but he can put down a rebellion with confident vigor. Radical self-abnegation seems to come, in the West, with Christianity. Is it anticipated

by the *Book of Job*? Still, some might question the depth of Augustine's self-abnegation, considering how he deliberately celebrates it as a critical part of his rhetorical appeal to others in like circumstances. *See* note 76 below. *See also,* Anastaplo, "An Introduction to Buddhist Thought,'' (*GIT,* 1992, 246 n. 57).

69. *See,* e.g., *The City of God,* X, 11, 18; XXII, 5 (*GBWW* I: 16, 305–6, 310, 589–90; II: 18, 356–57, 361–62, 663–64). *See also,* Fortin, "St. Augustine," pp. 164–65, 169; Anastaplo, *Human Being and Citizen,* pp. 87–96. Consider as well the criticism voiced by Maimonides in his *Guide* about Elisha ben Abuyah. *See also,* note 90 below, Anastaplo, "An Introduction to Buddhist Thought," (*GIT,* 1992, 247 n. 60). *See,* on the self, note 90 below.

70. Consider the tension between an insistence upon self-abnegation and a reliance upon a personal and caring God. *See* the discussion of "privacy" and "individuality" in Anastaplo, "The Public Interest in Privacy: On Becoming and Being Human," *DePaul Law Review,* vol. 26, p. 767 (1977).

71. *See,* e.g., *Confessions,* IV, 6; VII, 5 (*GBWW* I: 16, 21–22, 45–47; II: 18, 27, 56–57). Augustine tries to make sense of the world and of man's place in it. It is his concern to make sense of things, rather than a fear of death and of what is to become of him that can be said to dominate his inquiries. Most men do not concern themselves thus in their thoughts, but such a concern is reflected in many men's activities. *See* Anastaplo, "An Introduction to Buddhist Thought," (*GIT,* 192, 242 n. 32, 245 n. 50). *See also,* note 76 below and the text at note 87 below.

72. *See,* e.g., *Confessions,* I, 7 (*GBWW* I: 16, 3–4; II: 18, 4–5). See also, *The City of God,* XXI, 16 (*GBWW* I: 16, 573–74; II: 18, 646–47).

73. See *Confessions,* II, 4–10 (*GBWW* I: 16, 10–13; II: 18, 13–16).

74. *See,* on man's fallen nature and the limitations of philosophy, Fortin, "St. Augustine," pp. 158–59. *See also,* Anastaplo, *The American Moralist,* pp. 345–48.

75. Contempt of death may be seen also among the philosophers. *See,* on the four types of disturbances of the mind, *Confessions,* X, 14 sq. (*GBWW* I: 16, 76–77; II: 18, 96–97).

76. Was Augustine, because of the significance of "33" in Christendom, particularly receptive to conversion when it did happen? I personally find the last three books of the *Confessions* more interesting than the first ten books with their personal revelations. But in this preference I recognize I am in the minority of readers. Augustine seems to appeal to most readers because he gives them the impression that they really "know" him—and hence know themselves better than they otherwise would. *See* notes 42 and 71 above.

77. Augustine may have been moderated somewhat in his heroic attempts at self-abnegation by the philosophical tradition which Christianity inherited, in however diluted a form, along with the Greek language of the New Testament. *See,* on how the Church was obliged to take more than it wanted of classical antiquity with the Latin language, Machiavelli, *Discourses,* II, 5. *See,* on the Christian use of philosophy, the discussion of Soren Kierkegaard in Anastaplo, "On Trial," pp. 854–73. "Christianity, as Augustine understands it, does indeed provide a solution to the problem of human society, but the solution is not one that is attained or attainable in and through human society. Like that of the classical philosophers, albeit in a different way, it remains essentially transpolitical." Fortin, "St. Augustine," p. 179. Despite the passions that Augustine describes and exhibits, is it not prudent to allow for Augustine's having known, by and large, precisely what he was doing? Certainly, his remarkable, and surely not simply accidental, success has to be reckoned with. *See* notes 52 and 59, above. *See also,* Anastaplo, "An Introduction to Buddhist Thought," (*GIT,* 1992, 246 n. 56). [I am not sure that the classical philosophers should be described as "essentially transpolitical." *See* note 79 below.]

78. *See,* on prophecy as "the political name for political science," Anastaplo, "An Introduction to Confucian Thought," (*GIT* 1984, 159 n. 38).

79. *See* Hugh S. Moorhead, ed., *The Meaning of Life* (Chicago: Chicago Review Press, 1988), p. 188 (a quotation of April 8, 1953). *See also,* ibid., p. 18; note 93 below. *See,* on "natural valuations," note 102 below. A 1995 version of the remarks in Part III of this article has been published in Anastaplo, *Campus Hate-Speech Codes and Twentieth Century Atrocities* (Lewiston, New York: Edwin Mellen Press, 1997), p. 103. The considerable changes since 1995 have been influenced by suggestions from Clifford A. Bates, Jr., Laurence Berns, Keith Cleveland, Christopher A. Colmo, Thomas Engeman, Harry V. Jaffa, and John Van Doren.

80. *See,* on nature and natural right, Leo Strauss, *Natural Right and History* (Chicago: University of Chicago Press, 1953); Yves R. Simon, *The Definition of Moral Virtue,* ed. Yukan Kuic (New York: Fordham University Press, 1986); Anastaplo, *Human Being and Citizen,* pp. 46f, 74f; Anastaplo, *The American Moralist,* p. 616; Anastaplo, "Natural Law or Natural Right?" *Loyola University of New Orleans Law Review,* vol. 38, p. 915 (1993). *See also,* note 93 below.

81. *See,* e.g., Anastaplo, *The American Moralist,* p. 83. The most recent dramatic announcement by our scientists, with profound implications for the nature of nature, is the report that a mammal has been cloned. *See* Gina Kolata, "Scientist Reports First Cloning Ever of Adult Mammal," *New York Times,* Feb. 23, 1997, p. 1; Michael Specter and Gina Kolata, "After Decades and Many Missteps, Cloning Success," *New York Times,* March 3, 1997 p. A1. Roman Catholic theologians argue, however, that the sould for a cloned human being would still have to be provided by God.

82. Augustine, like Moses Maimonides, considered this a challenge to the Faith.

83. Speculations, in recent scientific literature, about what is called the Anthropic Principle spell out such cautions. *See* Anastaplo, book review, *(GIT* 1997, p. 448).

84. Still, it may be instructive to consider here how long it takes for any change in the gravitational pull of a body to be felt elsewhere. *See* Anastaplo, "Lessons for the Student of Law: The Oklahoma Lectures," p. 187.

85. A few severely inhibited people may have to be encouraged to let themselves enjoy, now and then, the physical pleasures legitimatly available to them. *See* note 104 below.

86. *See,* on the limitations of even Alexander the Great, Anastaplo, *The Constitutionalist,* pp. 31–32. *Compare* ibid., pp. 436–38.

87. *See,* e.g., Shakespeare, *Julius Caesar,* I, ii, 51–62 (*GBWW* I: 26, 569–70; II: 24, 569–70); *Antony and Cleopatra,* I, iii, 35. (*GBWW* I: 27, 315; II: 25, 36) See also notes 71 and 76, above.

88. *See* Anastaplo, *The Thinker as Artist,* p. 182.

89. *See* Anastaplo, *The American Moralist,* p. 27. *See also,* ibid., p. 582. Are the attractions of Heaven, as conventionally understood, based upon familiar pleasures of various kinds—and upon the avoidance of familiar pains? *See* note 101, below. *See also,* Aristotle, *Nicomachean Ethics* 1099a12, 1104b4–9, 1153b10–19 (*GBWW* I: 9, 344, 349–50, 404–5; II: 8, 344, 349–50, 404–5).

90. If neither the body nor the soul of the human being can exist separately, is the soul directed in its conduct by nature (if only because of the body, which "everyone" recognizes is constantly shaped by nature)? Similar to this relation may be that between "individual" and "society." *See,* on the relation of "self" to "soul," Anastaplo, *Human Being and Citizen,* p. 87; Anastaplo, *Campus Hate-Speech Codes and Twentieth Century Atrocities,* p. 87f.

91. Augustine seems to have regarded the moral virtues, guided by the conscience, as more solid than the intellectual virtues. *See* note 22, above. Thinkers such as Descartes, Hobbes, and Spinoza looked to mathematics for models of certainty for their inquiries even into human things.

92. Aristotle, for one, was aware of the variability of justice. But if there is a best regime, itself grounded in nature, would justice be as variable there as he recognizes it to

be in the everyday world? Be that as it may, the decent human being respects others' opinions to a considerable extent, avoiding as much as possible being thought "offensive." *See*, on "the best regime" in Aristotle's *Politics*, Harry V. Jaffa, "Aristotle (384–322 B.C.)," in Strauss and Cropsey, eds., *History of Political Philosophy*, p. 64.

93. *See*, e.g., Anastaplo, "Lessons for the Student of the Law," p. 179; Strauss, *Natural Right and History*, p. x. *See also*, the text at note 79 above.

94. *See*, e.g., Plato *Apology* 32 A-E. (*GBWW* I: 7, 207; II: 6, 207) *See also*, note 9 above.

95. Thomas Aquinas, however, spoke of prudence as the only intellectual virtue which includes the moral virtues. See Anastaplo, "On Freedom," pp. 681–82.

96. *See* Anastaplo, *The Artist as Thinker*, p. 1f.

97. In American law, this opinion may be seen developed in the writings of Oliver Wendell Holmes, Jr., and in cases such as *Erie Railroad Company* v. *Tompkins*, 304 U.S. 64 (1938). *See* Anastaplo, *The Constitution of 1787: A Commentary* (Baltimore: Johns Hopkins University Press, 1989), pp. 128–37; William T. Braithwaite, "The Common Law and the Judicial Power: An Introduction to *Swift-Erie*," in John A. Murley, Robert L. Stone, and William T. Braithwaite, eds., *Law and Philosophy: The Practice of Theory* (Athens, Ohio: Ohio University Press, 1992), p. 774.

98. *See* the seven introductions to non-Western thought I have prepared for *The Great Ideas Today:* Confucian (1984), Hindu (1985), Mesopotamian (1986), Islamic (1989), Buddhist (1992), North American Indian (1993), and African (1995). Related to these introductions are two other articles by me in *The Great Ideas Today:* on the Parliaments of the World's Religions (1994); on *Robert's Rules of Order* (1996).

99. It may also be related to the Aristotalian notion that a well-formed moral character seems itself to be a way of knowing what otherwise might not be known. I have, throughout these remarks, set aside Kant's argument that if morality is grounded in nature, then it cannot be *known* to be good in itself. (He wants to establish that the moral law is simply good in itself.) I sense that he may not be an altogether reliable ally for the Aristotalian in these matters, especially if the Kantian doctrine should tend to leave *good intentions* as sovereign in moral matters. *See* note 24 above.

100. *See*, e.g., Thomas Aquinas, *On Truth*, Q. 23, A 6, c. (quoted in Anastaplo, *The American Moralist*, p. 139).

101. Few if any, it can be said, want immorality in the form of an eternally unchanging life. Would not such a life be too dependent upon a soul's memories for its "activities' and pleasure? *See* note 89, above. Consider the implications of the newspaper story about the French woman who is said to be the world's oldest person. The story concludes, "Though blind, virtually deaf and confined to a wheelchair, she retains a good appetite and has her hair done once a week." "World's Oldest Person Celebrates 122nd With Cake," *Chicago Tribune*, Feb. 22, 1997, sec. 1, p. 15.

102. *See* Aristotle, *Politics* 1278b25–26 (*GBWW* I: 9, 476; II: 8, 476); Anastaplo, *The American Moralist*, pp. 596–601. *See also*, Leo Strauss, *The Political Philosophy of Hobbes* (Chicago: University of Chicago Press, 1952; Phoenix edition, 1963), pp. 124–25. *See*, on "the truth hidden [for Plato] in the natural valuations," ibid., p. 163.

103. *See*, for the perspective from which this comment is made, John Van Doren, "Poetic Justice," (*GIT* 1996, 260–75). *See also*, Anastaplo, "The O. J. Simpson Case Revisited," *Loyola University of Chicago Law Journal*, vol. 28, p. 503.

104. *See*, for cautions with respect to moral crusades, Anastaplo, *The American Moralist*, p. 327; Anastaplo, book review, (*GIT* 1996, 464); Anastaplo, "Did Anyone 'In Charge' Know What He Was Doing? The Thirty Years' War of the Twentieth Century," in *A Weekend With the Great War*, Steven Weingartner, ed., (Shippensburg, PA.: White Mane Publishing Co., 1997), p. 2; note 7, above. *See*, on the good, the true, and the beautiful, Anastaplo, *The Artist as Thinker*, p. 275; note 16 above.

George Anastaplo is a professor of law at Loyola University of Chicago, lecturer in the liberal arts at the University of Chicago, and professor *emeritus* of political science and philosophy at Dominican University. Professor Anastaplo is widely known as an author and lecturer on law and public morality, especially in constitutional matters.

Among his books are *The Constitutionalist: Notes on the First Amendment* (1971), *The Artist as Thinker: From Shakespeare to Joyce* (1983), and *The American Moralist: Essays on Law, Ethics, and Government* (1992). A recent book, *The Amendments to the Constitution* (1995), includes a commentary on the Emancipation Proclamation and a defense of affirmative action programs. This is a companion volume to *The Constitution of 1787* (1989). Both of these commentaries have as a foundation Professor Anastaplo's book *Human Being and Citizen: Essays on Virtue, Freedom, and the Common Good* (1975). His latest book is *The Thinker as Artist: From Homer to Plato and Aristotle* (1997).

Professor Anastaplo has been honored by the publication of a *festschrift*, *Law and Philosophy: The Practice of Theory* (1992). In addition, the 1997 volume of the *Political Science Reviewer* includes six articles about his scholarship.

The Liberal Arts of

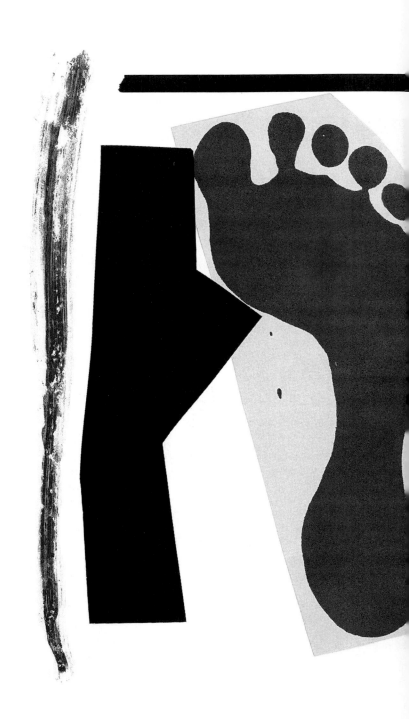

Words and Numbers

Otto Bird

Illustrations by Ivan Chermayeff

A spectre is haunting the world, Karl Marx declared in the opening words of the *Communist Manifesto,* "the spectre of Communism" (*GBWW* I: 50, 419; II: 50, 419). That particular threat has been exorcised in the West, at least temporally, but many others still remain. One of the worst of these and the most debilitating in its effects is the loss of the basic arts of learning—the arts of words and of numbers. This lack is glaringly apparent in the failure of our schools, especially at the elementary and secondary level from which students are graduated without having acquired these basic arts. Nor are their teachers without blame for this failure, since many of them know nothing of the long tradition of the liberal arts, while those who do know something of it reject it as obsolete and "without relevance" to our present situation.

Even if it is admitted that such arts *are* relevant, like reading, some might argue that there is not the need for them now, in the day of the computer, that there once was. Why go through the pain and difficulty of acquiring the arts of language if linguistic usage can always be "looked up?" We all need *some* language, but do we not learn to speak one merely by growing up in a society? As for the mathematical arts, can't they be forgotten, since any operation with numbers can now be performed on a calculator?

Given this situation, we can see that there is another spectre that haunts us—the spectre of ignorance and illiteracy. And if we undertake to exorcise *it,* we shall see that the tradition of great books holds a position of power. For among the qualities that entitle a book to be called great is the fact that it is the product and result of great art. Before we consider the significance of this fact we must first meet and destroy a mistaken and superficial criticism that has arisen recently with regard to the so-called "canon" of great books. This error consists in the claim that all books and especially great books are bound ineradicably to the language and culture of their origin. According to this charge, *Great Books of the Western World* are great only in the West. But this is false. There are many different kinds of books, and not all of them are related in the same way to the culture in which they are produced.

Books of science, mathematics, and logic speak truths that are world-wide in their scope and not at all bound only to the West, and they are so received, studied, and understood throughout the world.

The charge of relativity is somewhat more true of works in philosophy, especially of those in moral and political philosophy. Even here, however, the relativity is not absolute since there are goods that are universal, such as happiness, which all human beings seek, however they define it, and which everything else they do, or acquire, is acknowledged as a means to.

The reading and judgment of imaginative literature is the one that is most closely bound to its culture and dependent upon it. This is so mainly because of its close dependence upon the language in which it was written. It is difficult, almost impossible, to appreciate the beauty and greatness of Virgil's *Georgics* when it is read in translation and not in its original Latin. This is less so, say, of Shakespeare and Racine, since the characters, actions, and situations in their dramas can evoke more or less comparable responses whether read in translation or not. Yet something of the same difficulty remains as in the appreciation of Virgil. The English reader who knows no French has greater difficulty in recognizing the greatness of Racine's theater than a French reader. The same holds for the French reader of Shakespeare who knows no English.

Yet, however much a work of imaginative literature may depend upon the original language in which it was written, that dependence is not complete. In any language one poem or novel may be better than another: better in that it meets more fully the standards of the form it expresses as well as the conventions of that form. *The Iliad, The Aeneid, The Divine Comedy, Paradise Lost,* and *Faust,* each written in a different language, are each preeminently great as an achievement of their own language and culture. But more than that, and what is more important, each is also great as a poetic structure of the epic.

Even in books of religion and theology, where reading and judgment depend still more upon the beliefs of the reader, there remain objective standards of judgment, as was demonstrated by Mortimer Adler in his recent book entitled *The Plurality of Religions and the Unity of Truth.* Thus the charge of cultural dependency and relativity made against great books has little more justification than the claim, which is also made, that each reader constructs his own private text of a book without any objective dependence whatsoever upon the one that he is given, his task being to "deconstruct" it for his own uses.

Great books and the arts

The great books in any case have much to say about the basic arts of learning. This is part of what gives them their stature. The earliest formulation of a complete curriculum of studies is to be found in the dialogue of Plato entitled *The Republic* (*GBWW* I: 7, 295–441; II: 6, 295–441). Although its main purpose concerns the education of the philosopher-king, the ruler of the ideal state, it begins with a consideration of the elementary training needed for a person to become literate. In Book II, Socrates has a discussion with Glaucon and Adeimantus, brothers of Plato, about the education called by the Greeks *paideia.* For this, the traditional system is recommended consisting of "gymnastic for the body, and music for the soul" (*GBWW* I: 7, 320; II: 6, 320). "Music" includes not only songs, measures, and tunes, but also stories and other literature aiming at such a control over words as to obtain "beauty of style and harmony and grace and good rhythm" that is consonant with, if not actually productive of, "the true simplicity of a rightly and nobly ordered mind and character" (*GBWW* I: 7, 333; II: 6, 333).

The teacher responsible for this early stage of education in ancient Athens was the *grammatistes,* or teacher of *grammata* (letters), hence of reading and writing. For centuries thereafter, even up to modern times, the place in which this teaching occurred was called a grammar school. The arts taught and learned there were arts of words, music having lost its place. For Socrates, and presumably for Plato as well, *paideia* had a strong moral and even a religious basis.

Training of the intellect, especially as centered upon abstract thinking, follows after that of *paideia*. Discussion of this program, which occurs in Book VII of *The Republic,* calls for an extensive course of mathematical studies: arithmetic, geometry, solid as well as plane; also astronomy, and the mathematical study of harmony. Although these disciplines have practical applications, Plato says they should be focused not upon those, but upon the problems of understanding that arise from them, so that in struggling to solve such problems the intellect may advance toward a vision of true being, what we might call the nature of things. Thus the mathematical arts are not to be pursued for their own sake but are to be used as a means leading to the place where "all these studies reach the point of inter-communion and connection with one another, and come to be considered in their mutual affinities" (*GBWW* I: 7, 396–7; II: 6, 396–7).

The two groups of arts that have just been distinguished came to be codified, as it were, during Greek and Latin antiquity into three arts of words, consisting of grammar, rhetoric, and logic, and four arts of mathematics, namely geometry, arithmetic, astronomy, and music—the arts that came to be known in the Middle Ages respectively as the trivium and the quadrivium, or the three-fold and the four-fold way.

They are to be found enumerated, analyzed, and recommended in the educational program that Augustine drew up for the training of the Christian teacher in the work entitled *On Christian Doctrine*. He calls them *liberales disciplinas* ("liberal instruction" in *GBWW* I: 18, 655; II: 16, 738). The vast difference in the way in which Plato and Augustine think of the supreme truth leads to the different priorities that they assign to the arts. Augustine, the Christian theologian, holds that the simplest and most efficacious, and in fact the only sure way to God lies through the revelation that He has given through the sacred scriptures. Consequently, the most important arts of learning are those that enable us to read and understand the meaning of the words of the Bible, and not, as for Plato, the mathematical arts culminating in philosophy. Accordingly, Augustine places a much greater emphasis upon language and reading than Plato does. Thus he is credited with developing the first detailed theory of reading, as Brian Stock has shown in *Augustine The Reader: Meditation, Self-knowledge, and the Ethics of Interpretation.*

Reading the Bible poses special problems. Augustine is writing in Latin, but the Bible is written in Hebrew, Aramaic, and Greek. Hence the problem of translation must be faced, which calls for knowledge of the originals (*GBWW* I: 18, 641; II: 16, 722). Since the teacher must present and communicate his understanding of the text, he will need the arts of dialectic or logic, and also of rhetoric (*GBWW* I: 18, 653–4; II: 16, 736); indeed the whole of Book IV in *On Christian Doctrine* is devoted to an analysis of the use of rhetoric in the scriptures. Knowledge of numbers is also required, but in this case Augustine is an exegete of his day, since he only wants that art in order to give an allegorical interpretation of the numerical references to be found in the biblical text. Astronomy gets barely a passing mention, since it is said to be too closely allied with superstitious astrology. Knowledge of music is needed, however, not only for understanding the literal references that occur, but also for their allegorical significance, as in the case of numbers (*GBWW* I: 18, 645; II: 16, 727).

Almost contemporary with Augustine and from a North African writer Martianus Capella, who is not a Christian but a pagan, there is a curious compendium of the arts entitled after its long introduction *On the Marriage of Mercury and Philology and the Seven Liberal Arts*. The heavenly marriage described at length in the first two books is written in a late Latin so turgid and fantastically overblown, ripe with neologisms, that it has been described as perhaps the most difficult ever written. The seven arts, represented as maidens of great beauty and erudition, are dowry gifts of Mercury to his bride, Philology, and each of them is allotted a separate book-length speech in which to expound her art in the following order: grammar, dialectic (or logic), rhetoric, geometry (although the discussion is almost entirely devoted to geography), arithmetic, astronomy, and music (or harmony). Despite the fact that a modern reader finds the allegory of the marriage tediously fantastic and the exposition of the arts extremely elementary, the book enjoyed an immense success in the Middle Ages and contributed greatly to the analysis and understanding of the basic arts of learning, the trivium and the quadrivium.

The nature of a sign

The reason for dividing these arts into two distinct groups seems clear enough. Grammar, logic, and rhetoric are all concerned with words and the arts required for operating with them so that they can function well and effectively to accomplish their purposes. Geometry, arithmetic, astronomy, and music (understood as the numerical study of proportions) are all mathematical arts for controlling the ways of magnitudes and multitudes. Trivium and quadrivium thus have different and distinct subject matters as well as different methods of dealing with them.

At first it might appear that the difference here corresponds to the distinction Augustine makes at the beginning of his *Christian Doctrine,* where he declares that "all instruction is either about things or about signs" (*GBWW* I: 18, 624; II: 16, 704). Figures, numbers, moving planets, and stars, as well as sounding numbers, are all things. Words, speeches, and arguments are all signs. Once it is asked, however, how these matters are dealt with by their respective arts, it must be acknowledged that mathematical as well as verbal arts depend upon and operate through the use of signs. Mathematics in the course of its history has developed its own specialized notation, and this is considerably more abstract than our common language of words. But that notation is still a complex of signs no less than is our native tongue. Hence it is to the notion of a sign that we must look if we would find what is common to both trivium and quadrivium.

Augustine provides the essential definition with which to start. "A sign," he writes, "is a thing which, over and above the impression it makes on the senses, causes something else to come into the mind as a consequence of itself" (*GBWW* I: 18, 636; II: 16, 717). This definition is quite general, as is indicated by the examples that he offers: the footprint of an animal, the smoke of a fire, the voice of a person that shows his feelings. These are all instances of occurrences in the natural world and can be observed among animals as well as humans. Our social world also possesses signs, although these are conventional and not natural as are the previous ones: the motions and tones of voice of actors; the flags, standards, and signals of the military; and most important of all, the words of human language and the sacraments of religion. Such examples make manifest that Augustine is offering a general notion of a sign. Yet the definition that he gives is not completely general. For it restricts a sign to a thing that makes an impression upon the senses. There are many signs that function without making any sensible impression. The concept of a three-sided plane figure is two-dimensional and as such conceivable but not sensible, as is the idea of justice or that of a purely spiritual being. The definition accordingly should be revised to state that a sign is that which makes known something other than itself. Even this is still too restrictive in that it defines a sign as actually signifying. For a sign remains a sign when only potentially and not actually signifying, as being capable of making something other than itself to be known.

A closer look at the notion of a sign will reveal that it constitutes a triadic relation. Read again Augustine's description of a sign at work: "when we see a footprint, we conclude that an animal whose footprint this is has passed by" (*GBWW* I: 18, 636–37; 16, 717). In this case there is

1. The footprint itself, say, as an impression visible in the earth.
2. The animal whose foot made the print.
3. Showing that an animal has passed by.

Yet this third item is not the only indication that the footprint is capable of providing. It also shows that the animal was heavy enough to leave its imprint; that the earth was soft enough to take an imprint, or how long ago it was made (a very long time ago if it is fossilized); and that the animal that made it was a primitive cheetah. All of these are possible significations that the sign is capable of providing. All three elements have to be present to constitute a sign as such, i.e., one that represents something other than itself as knowable, and for ease of reference we need names for each of them.

The first element, the footprint in the example, is often called the sign. This is inaccurate, since for the fully constituted sign all three elements have to be distinguished. Hence this first element is better termed the *sign-vehicle*.

The second element, the animal in the above case, is the object that is represented by the sign-vehicle. It can therefore be named the *sign-object.*

The third element is the most difficult as being the most complex of the three. How the sign functions, what it makes known, depends upon the context in which it is functioning. While the sign-vehicle and the sign-object remain the same, the third element, as we have seen, may be either that an animal has passed by, that it was heavy, that the earth was soft, that the imprint was made a long time ago, or that it was made by a primitive cheetah. This third element has been named the *interpretant,* or, more simply, the *sign use,* after the coinage of Charles Sanders Peirce (1839–1914), father of the modern theory of semiotics. His major work on the subject, though unfinished, was entitled *A System of Logic, Considered as Semiotic.*

It must be emphasized that, so far, the only thing we have been discussing is the sign itself. Let us say a potential or virtual sign is one that is capable of signifying and hence containing within itself all three necessary elements. When actually functioning as a sign, the sign represents the animal as one that has passed by, or one of the other sign-uses noted. Outside and beyond the sign proper there is on the side of the sign-object the animal that made the footprint, whereas on the side of the sign-use there is the knower who interprets the footprint as showing that an animal has passed by. Thus the triadic relationship established by the sign leads through the sign-object to its external correlate and through the sign-use to its knowers interpreting the sign.

Enough about the nature of a sign. Our interest here is not in the general theory of signs, i.e., in semiotics, but in what it can reveal about the arts of learning. How can the triadic relation of the sign indicate that there are three fundamental arts of language? To discover the reason, we need a somewhat more complicated example of language at work. For this purpose consider the following sentence:

> And soon, mechanically, weary after a dull day with the prospect of a depressing morrow, I raised to my lips a spoonful of the tea in which I had soaked a morsel of the cake.

This consists of some 35 separate words strung along the page forming a sentence well enough to make sense in English. Each one of the printed marks is a sign-vehicle with its own sign-object and sign-use. But the sentence as a whole also constitutes a single sign, however complex, the entire string of printed marks composing its sign-vehicle. The sign-object presented is that of a person in a certain emotional condition taking a spoonful of tea in which a piece of cake had been soaked. The sign-use that determines how that object is to be taken is specified by the context in which the sentence occurs, namely the fact that it is found toward the end of the initial section in volume one of an English translation of *The Remembrance of Things Past* by French novelist Marcel Proust, who lived from 1871 to 1922. A portion of the multi-volume work can be found in *GBWW* II: 59, 281–408.

For the sentence to function actually as a sign, to signify and be understood, the reader has to have command of the English language just as Proust, to write this one, had to know French. For this to occur requires the acquisition of a vocabulary along with the ability to combine its variously functioning elements so as to obtain its intended effect. In this case the various grammatical elements have to be combined so as to depict a particular action of a character in a novel. The words proceed one after another, presenting their objects so as to offer a unified picture of a possibility that is fictional rather than the report of an actual historic event. It is the claim of the tradition of the liberal arts that to bring about such an achievement successfully at least three distinct and different arts are necessary: the trivium of grammar, logic, and rhetoric.

The art and discipline of grammar

Grammar, as already noted, takes its name from the Greek word for a written letter (*gramma*) and as a discipline, consists of the study of reading and writing. It enjoyed a special and privileged place in a society where literacy was limited to a few and where the language of learning as well as of literature differed from the spoken vernacular, as it did in ancient Greece and Rome. Learning one's letters included not only learning the formal and basic structure of the language or "grammar" in the narrow sense, but also acquaintance with the literature that provided models of excellence in the written form. In this latter respect grammar was based upon a course in great books.

Our set of *Great Books of the Western World* contains no work devoted to grammar in the narrow sense. Among the dialogues of Plato, however, the one entitled *Cratylus,* deals with problems of language and provides among other matters a classification of words, many etymologies of Greek words, and even the beginning of a linguistics and a philosophy of language (*GBWW* I: 7, 85–114; II: 6, 85–114) .

The dialogue presents a discussion of Socrates with his friends about the question, "Is language at its root a work of nature, or convention, or both?" This is a question, it might be noted, that is still with us and one that is hotly debated. The linguist Noam Chomsky and his followers claim that speech is produced naturally by humans much as a cobweb is by a spider, while their opponents deny that claim and maintain that any particular language is entirely the work of convention by a human society.

Scholars of Plato do not well know what to make of *Cratylus* and disagree widely about its value, some even thinking it to be a huge joke. This is especially true of the lengthy section that deals with the etymologies of more than a hundred words, many of them being fantastic, even ridiculous. Yet when Socrates comes to recommend the best method for investigating the elements of language, he envisions a scientific study of language, including a grammar and a linguistic. He claims that in seeking for the primary forms of language we must begin by differentiating words and syllables and distinguishing vowels, consonants, and mutes in various classes; showing how letters are used to make syllables and how these combine into nouns and verbs to "arrive at language, large and fair and whole; and as the painter made a figure, even so shall we make speech by the art of the namer or the rhetorician, or by some other art" (*GBWW* I: 7, 106; II: 6, 106).

Traditionally, models of excellent writing for the study of grammar have been taken from great books of imaginative literature. In classical antiquity these consisted for the most part of works of poetry; prose writings were reserved for the discipline of rhetoric. Hence, the study of the elements of reading and writing also included an introduction to literary criticism.

The first treatise on this subject that, in addition, sketches an outline of a general theory of fine art, is the *Poetics* of Aristotle. Its program is set forth in the beginning sentence:

I propose to speak not only of the art in general but also of its species and their respective capacities; of the structure of plot required for a good poem; of the number and nature of the constituent parts of a poem; and likewise of any other matters in the same line of inquiry. (*GBWW* I: 9, 681; II: 8, 681)

As Aristotle develops his theory of art as imitation, it becomes clear that he is analyzing not just poetry as tragedy and comedy in verse, but also music, dancing, painting, and sculpture, i.e., the fine arts.

For Aristotle, all art falls within the realm of making (*poiesis*) as distinct from the two realms of knowing, and doing, these two being respectively that of theoretical knowing and that of moral and political action. Art (*techné*) as a quality or faculty possessed by the maker is defined as "a productive (*poietiké*) habit with true reason that

is concerned with coming into being, i.e., with contriving and considering how something may come into being which is capable of either being or not being, and whose origin is in the maker and not in the thing made; for art is concerned neither with things that are, or come into being, by necessity, nor with things that do so in accordance with nature (since these have their origin in themselves). [*GBWW* I: 9, 388; II: 8, 388]

Such an idea of art is distinct and also extremely broad. As concerned with making and the makeable, it includes the fine arts of the beautiful as well as the useful arts, and also the liberal arts of the trivium and the quadrivium. Written words, spoken words, rational arguments, political speeches, geometrical and numerical constructions—all are things that are made, produced by one who possesses the art and skill of their making.

Grammar, too, is an art. It is a quality and faculty of the mind, one that is possessed by its teacher and one that its students endeavor to acquire by making, analyzing, and criticizing. By and of itself, however, it is not sufficient to accomplish fully and well the work of language. This requires still other verbal arts.

The art and discipline of logic

Merely to be able to form a sentence in accord with the syntax and vocabulary of one's language is not enough to assure that it is working well. The objects presented through the sign-vehicles must be connected together in such a way that they can achieve the end intended. In its most formal aspect the ability to so connect is trained by the art of logic. The name comes from the Greek *logos* that can mean either word or reason, but here it is used to mean reason, so that logic is primarily the art of reasoning. It is by putting reasons together that one obtains the simplest form of argument, the syllogism. This is defined by Aristotle, the father of logic, in the *Prior Analytics* as discourse [*logos*] in which, certain things being stated, something other than what is stated follows of necessity from their being so. I mean by the last phrase that they produce the consequence, and by this, that no further term is required from without in order to make the consequence necessary. (*GBWW* I: 8, 39; II: 7, 39)

Thus if a maker is an artist, and a person is a maker, then that person is an artist, and this is so as logically necessary. Its truth, of course, is dependent upon art being something that is made. Since grammatical and logical products of words are constructures, i.e., makings, we are also engaged in showing that their producers, all persons using them, are as such, indeed artists.

Aristotle deserves this patronym since he wrote the first great book covering the entire subject matter of logic. Known as the *Organon,* the tool or instrument of knowing, it consists of six separate treatises, as follows:

> *Categories,* dealing with terms
> *On Interpretation,* concerning the proposition
> *Prior Analytics,* treating the syllogism in general
> *Posterior Analytics,* on the methodology of scientific reasoning
> *Topics,* on the resources for probable reasoning
> *On Sophistical Refutations,* dealing with fallacies

That Aristotle was aware and proud of his originality in this work appears from one of the few remarks he made about his own work. It occurs at the end of his treatise on fallacies, but it can be read as applying to the whole *Organon:*

> Of this inquiry... it was not the case that part of the work had been thoroughly done before, while part had not. Nothing existed at all.... on the subject of reasoning we had nothing else of an earlier date to speak of at all, but were kept at work for a long time in experimental researches. (*GBWW* I: 8, 253; II: 7, 253)

The art and discipline of rhetoric

For a full and excellent use of language more is needed than the ability to put words and reasons together, of course. Language can be used to teach, to move, and to delight as to aim, respectively, at the true, the good, and the beautiful. Such different ends and purposes demand different means for their accomplishment—different arrangements of words and reasons, different styles. A valid syllogistic argument may fail completely to inspire a person with the courage to face a difficult situation, although a moving speech can do so, and yet neither of these may delight like a poem or song. To have the skill to bring about such different effects a special and distinct skill is needed, one that can control the element in the functioning of a sign that is the sign-use. This traditionally is the task that has been assigned to the art of rhetoric.

In its beginnings in ancient Greece and Rome, rhetoric was conceived specifically as the training of the public speaker or orator to prepare him for the deliberations of the public assemblies and courts. Among the Romans the exemplary model of this activity and position was Cicero, who was also known for his writings upon rhetoric. But teaching of the art and the preparation of manuals for it had begun long before his time among the Sophists of ancient Greece. Some of their representative figures appear in the dialogues of Plato, especially in the *Georgics* (*GBWW* I: 7, 252–94; II: 6, 252–94) and *Phaedrus* (*GBWW* I: 7, 115–41; II: 6, 115–41), both concerned with rhetoric. But the first systematic treatise on the whole of the art we owe to Aristotle.

In the *Rhetoric* Aristotle defines the art as "the faculty of observing in any given case the available means of persuasion" (*GBWW* I: 9, 595; II: 8, 595). In this concern it differs from other disciplines, each of which is concerned with a particular subject matter, as grammar is with a language, logic with reasoning, arithmetic with number. Rhetoric, however, treats of "the means of persuasion on almost any subject presented to us." Three

different kinds of means are distinguished according to the kind of audience to be persuaded:

1. Political which aims at establishing "the expediency or harmfulness of a proposed course of action."
2. Forensic which considers "the justice or injustice of some action" at law.
3. Epideictic which concerns the praise or dispraise of a person as worthy of praise or the reverse.

There are three elements in a persuasive speech: the subject, the speaker, and the person addressed. Accordingly, the artist in rhetoric has to study the effective means of each element. Regarding the subject, the need is to produce arguments so persuasive as to establish the case. But this by itself cannot assure success. That depends also upon the response of the audience, which is also influenced in part by the character of the speaker. Hence, both speaker and audience must be considered so as to establish the credibility of the speaker and dispose the character of the audience favorably to the end that it may be convinced—or as we say in judicial trials, to obtain a conviction.

Aristotle's *Rhetoric* is divided accordingly into a discussion of argumentation on the one hand and an analysis of the various kinds of character on the other, as well as of the emotions useful for achieving conviction. These two elements constitute the part of the art known as invention (i.e., of arguments) and occupy the first two books of the treatise. The other two parts, on style and arrangement, are the subject of the third and final book.

Augustine in his work *On Christian Doctrine* offers an example of rhetorical analysis based on the ancient art, although he is addressing the question of the arts that a Christian teacher should possess. Here, the aim, he writes, is "to put the hearer into a friendly, or attentive, or teachable frame of mind," and this can be achieved by "[speaking] briefly, clearly, and plausibly... to awe, to melt, to enliven, and to rouse" (*GBWW* I: 18, 675–6; II: 16, 759–60). Three different aims are to be distinguished and Cicero is quoted to the effect that "an eloquent man must speak so as to teach, to delight, and to persuade.... To teach is a necessity, to delight is a beauty, to persuade is a triumph" (*GBWW* I: 18, 683; II: 16, 768). To achieve these ends he should be able, again in the words of Cicero, "[to] say little things in a subdued style, moderate things in a temperate style, and great things in a majestic style" (*GBWW* I: 18, 686; II: 16, 771).

Augustine maintains that the best way of acquiring these rhetorical skills consists in studying and imitating not manuals of the art, but the best models. Given his audience, he holds up for imitation the writers of the sacred scriptures as models, and he quotes extensively from the Epistles of St. Paul to illustrate how *he* utilizes all three of the styles just mentioned to obtain the results he wants.

Public speaking to achieve its end successfully certainly requires ability and skill, and rhetoric must be adapted to that purpose. Yet the art is not restricted to that alone. The central concern of rhetoric is with the means of achieving an effect through signs, and language is capable of many other effects besides that of persuasion to some action. Scientists frequently dismiss rhetoric claiming that they have no need of its tricks. Yet in composing an exposition of their discoveries, they have to make decisions that are rhetorical even though they may not be aware of it. Euclid, for example, ended the first book of the *Elements* with the Pythagorean theorem and its converse, although he could have proved it several theorems earlier had he chosen to (*GBWW* I: 11, 28–9; II: 10, 28–9). Newton likewise had to decide that the best form in which to present his *Principia* was that of an axiomatic system, just as Euclid had done (*GBWW* I: 32, 5–368; II: 34, 5–368). Galileo, on the other hand, although he could have presented his discoveries axiomatically, chose instead the dialogue form as indicated by the title of his *Dialogues Concerning the Two Sciences* (*GBWW* I: 28, 129–260; II: 26, 129–260).

All of the above are works of exposition, not works of argumentative persuasion. Euclid and Newton are free of that entirely. There is some in Galileo's work, and he well may have selected the dialogue form as a means of attacking his Aristotelian opponent in order to persuade the reader to accept his theory instead; yet as expository writing, the work consists mostly of mathematical demonstrations. Like Euclid and Newton, it shows rhetoric at work.

Scientific exposition and practical persuasion are but two of the general ways of organizing verbal material. Besides these two there are also the organizing forms proper to the narration of events in history and the novel, to the description of objects observed, and to the compositions of poetry and the drama. The use of language to produce the effects proper to such various functions is the task of rhetoric, and has been such since its beginnings in ancient Greece and Rome. The continuing utility and value of that tradition has been effectively shown by Edward P. J. Corbett in his *Classical Rhetoric for the Modern Student* (New York, Oxford University Press, 1965).

We have now completed our consideration of the trivium, but before leaving it entirely, we should emphasize the special character of our concern. For this purpose it is useful to apply the distinction that Augustine draws between signs that are of human institution (i.e., conventional) and those that are not, being natural. Thus language is natural for human beings, but the fact that it is English is of human institution. That it is oral is natural; that it is written is not. So too for logic. As Augustine writes, "the validity of logical sequences is not a thing devised by men, but it is observed and noted by them that they may be able to learn and teach it; for it exists eternally in the reason of things, and has its origin with God" (*GBWW* I: 18, 652; II: 16, 735). The same claim can be made of the art of rhetoric: "Nor is it owing to an arrangement [*institutum est*] among men that the expression of affection conciliates the hearer, or that a narrative, when it is short and clear, is effective, and that variety arrests men's attention without wearying them" (*GBWW* I: 18, 653; II: 16, 736).

Thus, the origin of all three branches of the trivium lies in human nature. They are capable of finding expression without the study of the human arts that have been devised to cultivate and improve their use. Our natural faculties as well as the human arts we use to express them of their use can also be made the object of scientific investigation and result in the sciences of linguistics, mathematical logic, and communication theory. These sciences have all made tremendous advances since their first beginnings in antiquity, and as much would certainly be admitted by those responsible for their initiation.

In sum, there are three distinctive aspects that can be noted in the functioning of language: It is natural in respect of its basis and origin in human nature, artistic in respect of the skill involved in making it function well, and scientific in respect of the knowledge of the elements, principles, and causes of both its natural and artistic functioning.

That great progress has been made in these aspects of language can only be said with confidence of the third, the scientific. At the level of nature the use of speech is acquired by every normal human person, and with it the ability to signify, to reason, and to persuade. Some are better than others in achieving their effects; they demonstrate more skill in exercising the arts of language, of the trivium. Yet in the works they have produced over time there is little evidence of any great progress being made since the arts were developed and defined. After twenty centuries and more we do not write, reason, or plead any better, if as well, as Plato, Aristotle, Homer, Virgil, Cicero, or Augustine. The contrast between art and science in these matters corresponds to that between studies that are permanent and those that are progressive. Nowhere is the contrast more glaring than when we turn from the linguistic arts of the trivium to consider the mathematical arts of the quadrivium.

The ancient quadrivium

In Greek and Roman antiquity as well as in the Middle Ages, as has already been noted, the quadrivium comprised the mathematical arts and sciences of arithmetic, geometry, "music," and astronomy. The rationale for maintaining that only these four are truly basic is given by Nicomachus in his *Introduction to Arithmetic,* written about 100 A.D. (*GBWW* I: 11, 811–48; II: 10, 599–636). The first distinction separates the continuous from the discrete: "[the] unified and continuous, for example, an animal, the universe, a tree ... properly and peculiarly called 'magnitudes' [and the] discontinuous, in a side-by-side arrangement, and, as it were, in heaps ... called 'multitudes,' a flock, for instance, a people, a heap, a chorus." Both the continuous and the discrete are species of quantity and as such can be considered in two different ways, yielding a second distinction: "one kind is viewed by itself, having no relation to anything else, as 'even,' 'odd,' ... and the other is relative to something else and is conceived of together with its relationship to another thing, like 'double,' 'greater,'

'smaller,' 'half,' 'one and one-half times.'" From this distinction we obtain two sciences for investigating discrete multitudes: arithmetic for the study of absolute number and music for the study of relative numbers expressing harmonic intervals.

For the study of continuous magnitude we need a third distinction: That between what is "in a state of rest and stability" and that which is "in motion and revolution." Accordingly, we obtain Geometry as the study dealing with magnitude at rest and Astronomy with magnitude in motion (*GBWW* I: 11, 811–12; II: 10, 599–600).

As displayed in a diagram, the quadrivium appears thus:

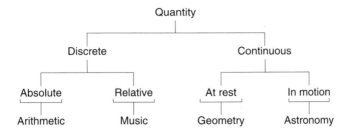

Besides identifying the four sciences, Nicomachus also establishes a priority among them. He claims that arithmetic "is superior and takes the place of origin and root and, as it were, of mother to the others." It enjoys this primacy "inasmuch as it abolishes other sciences with itself, but is not abolished together with them." Geometry as well as astronomy depend upon number to define their figures, as a triangle is a *three*-sided figure. The same is true of music considered as the study of harmonic ratios expressed as ratios of numbers. Two tones an octave apart are in vibrations related as the ratio of 2:1. Yet arithmetic itself is independent of all the others and in the investigation of the absolute can be studied by and for itself.

In this claim about the primacy of arithmetic, Nicomachus proved to be prophetic of the future history of mathematics. As we shall see in some detail, the dominant theme especially in the modern period has been the arithmetization of all mathematics based upon the generalization of number.

Our set of *Great Books* contains representatives for all of the ancient quadrivium. For arithmetic there is not only the *Introduction* of Nicomachus, but also Books VII–IX of Euclid (*GBWW* I: 11, 127–90; II: 10, 127–90). Mathematically, a vast gulf separates the two. Euclid's work is a scientific treatise, Nicomachus's is an elementary text. Compare the two, for example, on the method for determining whether two unequal numbers are prime to one another, i.e., the rule for finding the greatest common divisor. Nicomachus accomplishes this entirely in words, and prolixly, without using a single numerical sign and also without proof (*GBWW* I: 11, 819; II: 10, 607). Euclid, on the other hand, in a single proposition, the first in his arithmetical books (*GBWW* I: 11, 128; II: 10, 128), shows how numbers represented by lines can be true variables standing for any whole number—far more comprehensive than Nicomachus who, in giving examples always cites specific numbers and thus never attains complete generality.

For what we now call elementary geometry, Euclid supplies the classical text: plane geometry in Books I–VI, solid in Books XI–XIII. Books V and X consider the properties of ratios and thus provide the basis for the study of harmonic relations which constitutes the ancient mathematics of music.

For astronomy there is the *Almagist* of Ptolemy, the standard text on the subject until the advent of *On the Revolutions of the Heavenly Spheres* by Copernicus, along with Kepler's *Epitome of Copernican Astronomy,* all included in *GBWW* I: 16; II: 15.

The reform of the quadrivium

The basic linguistic arts of the trivium remain the same as they were in classical antiquity and differ now only in being acquired and practiced in various languages other than Greek and Latin. The elementary mathematical arts, however, stand in an entirely different relation in respect of time. For them, time has resulted in great changes, so much so that an ancient

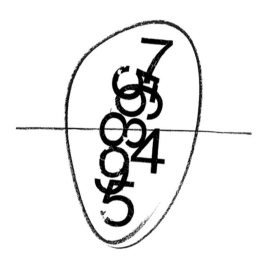

expert in the quadrivium would fail to recognize how even the simplest arithmetic is done today. All of mathematics beginning at the simplest level has been arithmetized, an achievement such a student would have thought impossible.

This truly historic accomplishment has been carried through by successive extensions or generalization of the number system so as to free the basic arithmetical operations from any restriction whatsoever. These operations consist of addition, subtraction, multiplication, division, and the extraction of roots. But if we possess only the natural integers, i.e., whole numbers, there are certain cases in which some of these operations cannot be performed, namely subtraction, division, and the extraction of roots. If we want to get rid of such restrictions and become free to perform all operations in any case whatsoever, we will have to get beyond the system of whole numbers.

Before we can even begin such a work there is an initial step to take, however. We need a notation for numbers that is simple, perspicuous, and easy to work with. The ancients used letters as the names of numbers, with the result that the relationship between numbers was entirely opaque. Compare, for example, the following notations:

	five	fifty	five hundred	five thousand
Roman	V	L	D	I
Arabic	5	50	500	5000

The Arabic numerals as well as the English words indicate that a five is present in all four numbers, whereas the Roman numerals indicate no sameness whatsoever. Of course, to show the relation here in numerals, a symbol for zero in a decimal system of numeration is needed, and that also was missing in the ancient quadrivium.

The addition of zero to the system of natural whole numbers, the integers, also indicates immediately the result of subtracting a number from itself, namely $a-a=0$, where a stands for any number. It should be noted that the use of letters here to stand for numbers differs radically from the ancient use. In antiquity, letters as notations for numbers always indicated a specific number, as L=50. But now the letters stand for any number. They are truly variables.

Looking further at the operation of subtraction, we note that limiting ourselves to whole numbers, cases arise in which that operation becomes impossible. It is possible only if the subtrahend is smaller than the minuend: Two can be subtracted from three, but not three from two. To overcome this limitation we have to extend the number system beyond that of the integers alone. To do so, consider a straight line extending in one direction from a zero-point and also in the opposite direction from that same point. Then mark off and number points from zero in both directions, thus

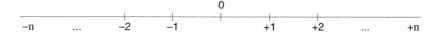

The numbers extending indefinitely to the right of the zero-origin are called positive and are represented by a plus sign before the numeral; to the left they are negative and represented by a minus sign before the numeral. Our number system has now been extended beyond the integers to include negative and positive numbers. To be completely literal we should indicate the sign of numbers when operating with them and thus for their addition write $(+3) + (+1) = +4$. As Whitehead points out in his *Introduction to Mathematics* (*GBWW* II: 56, 143), however, it would be pedantic to include these signs when there is no danger of confusion, since $3+1=4$ holds for both positive and negative numbers.

With this extension of the number system there is no longer a limitation upon subtraction. We can say that $2-3=-1$. As represented on the number line, we start at +2 and move 3 steps to the left, arriving at −1. Hence the extension to negative numbers also entails changed definitions for the basic arithmetical operations.

Division, like subtraction, lies under a restriction when it deals only with integers. For it is then possible only if the dividend is greater than the divisor. Four is divisible by two, whereas two is not divisible by four. Of course in this case there is still a definite relation between the numbers. A line two feet long is related to one four feet long in the ratio of 2:4. Hence, such pairs of numbers came to be called rational, although now we are more apt to call them fractions and write them thus, $\frac{2}{4}$. Here the denominator indicates a division into four parts while the numerator calls for taking two of them. In effect division is now possible even when the dividend is less than the divisor, and our number system has undergone another extension so as to include rational numbers or fractions, negative as well as positive, as well as the integers.

Another extension is needed when we come to the operation of the extracting of roots. To see why, it is clearer and simpler to begin with a geometrical example, thus: Construct a right-angles triangle with sides a and b each equal to one and draw the hypotenuse c. Euclid in *Elements* I.47 (Book One, Proposition 47) proves that the square on the hypotenuse is equal to the sum of the squares on the other two sides, i.e., $c^2 = a^2 + b^2$. (*GBWW* I: 11, 28–29; II: 10, 28–29). Given that a and b each equal one, we have $1^2 + 1^2 = c^2$, or $c^2 = 2$, and $c = \sqrt{2}$. Now we know that c, the hypotenuse of the triangle, is a perfectly definite length. But what is the number $\sqrt{2}$? We know what it is not, for it can be proven that it cannot be expressed as a ratio of two integers. Hence, it must be irrational (meaning not that it contradicts reason, but that it cannot be a ratio of two whole numbers). We have come to a number that is beyond the integers, the positive and negative numbers, as well as the rational numbers—namely, to the irrationals. Expressed numerically, the length of the hypotenuse equals an unending decimal 1.414…and is located somewhere on the number line between 1.414 and 1.415, since $(1.414)^2 = 1.999$, and $(1.415)^2 = 2.002$. And we have perceived in the hypotenuse a length that is incommensurable, i.e., one not measurable by integral units.

The ancients saw a mystery in this fact of incommensurability, and there is a story that the Pythagorean who first revealed it was put to death for profanation, since, for one who believed that everything consists of whole numbers, it was blasphemy to declare that the incommensurable existed as something that was not. Plato made no such condemnation and said that it was disgraceful not to be able to think about the incommensurable—that it made one more of a pig than a man (*GBWW* I: 7, 729; II: 6, 729).

Modern mathematics sees the difference as that which separates the continuous and the discontinuous, the hypotenuse as a line and the number as 1.414; and more than that, the possibility of describing if not defining the continuous in terms of the discontinuous. For as we have seen, the line $c = \sqrt{2}$ can be located on the number line somewhere between 1.414 and 1.415. The definition given by Whitehead accordingly reads as follows:

> A function $f(x)$ is 'continuous' at a value a of its argument, when in the neighborhood of a its values approximate to $f(a)$ (i.e., to its value at a) within *every* standard of approximation. (*GBWW* II: 56, 164)

This is to say, in terms of our example, that the hypotenuse, which is a continuous line, can be equated with $\sqrt{2}$, which is a discontinuous number, because there is no limit to how close we can get to this on the number line, even if we can never quite reach it.

There remains still another restriction upon the extraction of roots that has to be eliminated. It appears when we are dealing with negative numbers. Consider the equation $x^2 - 1 = 0$ where $x^2 = 1$, so that x can be both +1 and −1. But what about the equation $x^2 + 1 = 0$ where $x^2 = -1$? We must allow two possibilities: $x = +\sqrt{-1}$ which squared yields $x^2 + 1$ and $x = -\sqrt{-1}$ which squared also gives $x^2 = 1$. Yet we still do not have a positive or negative number that multiplied by itself results in a negative number. Hence to have a meaning for $\sqrt{-1}$ the number system has to be extended to include this new value, giving us what has been called an imaginary number and is represented by i.

The number system we now have as a result of these various extensions consists of the integers (positive and negative numbers), the fractions, and the irrationals, and constitutes the class of real numbers ('real' as providing the numbers capable of measuring the real world). The imaginary number i is known as a complex unity and added to the real numbers establishes the realm of complex numbers.

With the successive extension of the set of numbers, we have, with one exception, overcome any restriction upon the basic arithmetical operations of addition, subtraction, multiplication, division, and the extraction of roots. The one exception is division by zero, which by definition is said to be meaningless. We will have more to say about this when we come to consider calculus.

Arithmetizing geometry

The basic distinction underlying the ancient quadrivium, as noted above, was that between the continuous and the discontinuous. These were conceived of as radically different, requiring different kinds of mathematics— geometry in the one case and arithmetic in the other. The overthrow of that distinction effectively destroys the old quadrivium and demands a reconsideration of the basics of elementary mathematics.

The accomplishment of this feat was mainly the work of René Descartes, by his invention of analytical or coordinate geometry. As he boasts toward the end of the book in which he presents his discovery,

> in the method I use all problems which present themselves to geometers reduce to a single type, namely, to the question of finding the values of the roots of an equation. (*Geometry, GBWW* I: 31, 347; II: 28, 575)

Indeed, this revolutionary work gets under way in the very first paragraph with the claim that geometric problems can be solved by means of the arithmetic operations of addition, subtraction, multiplication, division, and the extraction of roots (*GBWW* I: 31, 295; II: 28, 523).

As an example of this operation, consider the simple one that Whitehead gives in his *Introduction to Mathematics* (*GBWW* II: 56, 154–55). This shows how an equation of numbers can define a straight line, and how numbers can determine points. For this we need a surface on which to locate points by means of measuring with numbers. Thus, as is illustrated on page 68, we draw two straight lines intersecting at right angles so as to

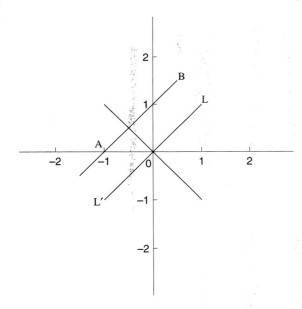

form four quadrants about the zero point of origin, marked with 0. The horizontal line represents the x-axis measured in positive numbers to the right of zero and negative numbers to the left. The vertical line provides the y-axis with positive numbers above the x-axis, negative below it. Accordingly, the quadrants designate the locus of points measured along the two axes as respectively $(+x,+y)$, $(+x,-y)$, $(-x,-y)$, $(-x,+y)$.

Take now the simple equation $ax+by=c$, where a, b, c stand for any numbers provided they remain constant during the life of the equation, whereas x and y represent numbers that can vary and take any value. Let us now see what happens when values are assigned to the constants. Let $c=0$ while both a and $b=1$, so that we have the case $y-x=0$. By assigning values that solve the equation we also obtain a method to locate points within our system of coordinates. When $x=0$ and $y=0$ the equation is satisfied, and we locate a point zero on the x-axis as well as on the y-axis coinciding thus with the origin 0. Now let both x and $y=1$, which meets the condition set in the equation and yields another point within the quadrants at 1 on the positive x-axis and up to 1 on the positive y-axis, and since two points serve to establish a line, we draw the line LOL′ passing through the origin. The equation $y + x = 0$ will plot a line at right angles to this one, passing through the origin from the second to the fourth quadrant.

Try now the equation $y-x = 1$. Then, when $y = 0$ and $x = -1$, we can locate a point at 0 on the y-axis and -1 on the x-axis, and mark it A on the diagram. Now for the second point let $y = 1$ up on the y-axis and 0 on the x-axis marked B. Connecting the two we have the line AB parallel to line LOL′, but one step removed.

In all three cases of the equation $y-x = c$ we have obtained straight lines. In fact, an equation of the form $ax-by = 0$ gives a straight one through the origin of the coordinates. More generally still, the equation $ax+by = c$ is a statement about numbers (although as variables and constants) and hence is an arithmetic one, and yet it also determines a straight line which is a geometric thing. What now is the relation between geometry and arithmetic?

In geometry a straight line as defined by Euclid is "a line which lies evenly with the points on itself" (Book I, def. 4, *GBWW* I: 11, 1; II: 10, 11). If we did not already know the meaning of "straight," this definition might well leave one still in ignorance. Plato defined it as "that of which the center intercepts the view of the extremes" and apparently imagines sight-

ing along the line from either end and in neither case being able to see the other end (in *Parmenides, GBWW* I: 7, 492; II: 6, 492). Euclid may be trying to remove the appeal to sight by trusting that "evenly" will do the same thing; but without including the reference to sighting, it is not of much help.

The coordinate definition also refers to points, but in a much clearer way, since it provides a formula for locating the points establishing a straight line. The method can also be generalized so that various kinds of lines can be distinguished by the form of the equations that define them. Thus the equation $x^2+y^2-4 = 0$ determines a circle with its center at the origin 0 and a radius of 2 units. In general a quadratic equation (i.e., one having variables raised to the second power) defines a conic section, as Whitehead shows in Chapter 10 of his *Introduction.*

Hence it would appear that analytic geometry has bridged the gap that separates geometry from arithmetic, magnitude from multitude. Whitehead claims that

> The fundamental ideas of geometry are exactly the same as those of algebra; except that algebra deals with numbers and geometry with lines, angles, areas, and other geometrical entities. (*GBWW* II: 56, 184)

Yet he also insists that "the 'spaciness' of space and the 'numerosity' of numbers are essentially different things and must be directly apprehended." Here, however, he is speaking of our experience of the two, i.e., as a philosopher. Speaking as a mathematician engaged in doing mathematics, he claims that it is a mistake to think that this difference has to be taken into account, since "the 'spaciness' of space does not enter into our geometric *reasoning* at all" (*GBWW* II: 56, 184).

Putting this conclusion into the terms of our history, the fundamental distinction underlying the ancient quadrivium has been done away with. When we come to see how mathematics deals with the continuous, the primacy indeed supremacy of discrete multitude becomes even more apparent.

The problem of zero

Let us begin with the example from pure mathematics that Whitehead uses (ibid., p. 180). Take the function x^2 and note how rapidly it increases as the values of its progression increase:

x	1	2	3	4	...	n
x^2	1	4	9	16	...	n^2

If x now increases by an increment amounting to h, x^2 then increases to $(x+h)^2$, and the total increment equals $(x + h)^2 - x^2$. Hence the average increase during the interval amounts to $\frac{(x+h)^2-x^2}{h}$. Performing the indicated operations, $\frac{(x^2 + 2hx + h^2) - x^2}{h}$, and dividing through by x^2 and then by h, we find that the average increase during the interval from x to $(x + h)$ is equal to $2x+h$, the value of which depends on the size of the interval h. If now we want to know the rate of increase at the value x, we let the value of h decrease more and more, and, as it does so, it approaches zero; and with that the problem of zero arises.

The example just analyzed is an algebraic formulation of a problem that Newton treats geometrically in Book II of his *Mathematical Principles of Natural Philosophy* (*GBWW* I: 34, 168; II: 32, 168). Regarding the diminishing moments just noted, he writes that they are to be considered to be doing so "as it were by a continual motion or flux," and are not to be looked upon as "finite particles as such," but as "just nascent principles of finite magnitudes." Commenting upon this procedure, Whitehead claims that "Newton would have phrased the question by saying that, as h approaches zero, in the limit $2x + h$ becomes $2x$…and it is tempting to seek simplicity by saying…that h is zero" (*GBWW* II: 56, 181).

Among the early readers of Newton there were those who criticized that very claim. Anglo-Irish philosopher Bishop George Berkeley was a famous objector. In a work entitled *The Analyst,* published in 1734, he attacked the above "Lemma" by asserting in effect that if h is destroyed so is $2x$, and thereby dismissed "any need of considering quantities either infinitely great or infinitely small," and branded as "shocking to good sense…that a finite quantity divided by nothing is infinite" (in James R. Newman, editor, *The World of Mathematics,* vol. I, 293).

But if it is nonsensical to think of dividing by zero, we are confronted by the problem: How are we to understand that h is allowed to continually diminish and can we treat it as if it *were* zero? The answer is provided by the concept of a limit, a concept that was not developed until the middle of the 19th century, two centuries after calculus had been operating with fluxions and the infinitely little.

A concrete case may help to clarify the problem. The law of falling bodies has the form of an x^2 function. As discovered and formulated by Galileo, it reads as follows:

> The spaces described by a body falling from rest with a uniformly accelerated motion are to each other as the squares of the time intervals employed in traversing these distances. (*Two New Sciences, GBWW* I: 28, 206; II: 26, 206)

Suppose then that someone drops a stone from a tower 100 feet tall, as Galileo did, according to a story. During the first second of time ($t = 1$) it is observed to have fallen a distance of 16 feet ($D = 16\ t^2$) and is 84 feet above the Earth. During the next second ($t = 2$) the stone falls $16 \times 2^2 = 64$ feet and is now 36 feet above the ground. Thus we have two intervals: one in
distance, $D_2 - D_1$ or $84 - 36 = 48$,
and in time, $t_2 - t_1 = 1$.
By comparing the two we can calculate the speed at which the stone is

falling, since speed or velocity (V) is the ratio of distance to time i.e., $V = \frac{D}{t}$ or $\frac{48}{1}$ or 48 feet per second as the speed.

However, this number indicates only the average speed at which the stone is falling. If we want greater accuracy, we need to diminish the time interval of one second, and we now face the same situation we had above in finding the change of x^2 as its argument x increases by the increment h to $(x+h)$, except that now our variables represent time (t). Letting dt stand for the temporal increment by which the interval is to be contracted the equation becomes $\frac{(t^2 + dt)^2 - t^2}{dt^2}$ and this works out to $2t - dt$. Since $t = 16$, as the increment diminishes it approaches zero, and the velocity approaches 2×16, or 32; and we have found that the velocity of the falling stone at any instant is 32 ft./sec.

That the velocity is approaching 32 appears from the velocities at different moments of its fall:

When the time interval = 1,	V = 48 ft./sec.
t = .05	V = 40
t = .01	V = 33.6
t = .001	V = 32.016
t = .0001	V = 32.0016

That velocity of 32 ft./sec. holds for any instant during the fall, including the final one when the stone reaches earth. At that point the distance interval does equal zero, a fact to which Newton refers by claiming that the vanishing increments do not cancel out all the other quantities: the motion of the stone is zero as it ends, the speed at impact being 32 ft./sec. (*GBWW* I: 34, 31; II: 32, 31). The increment dt is named the differential, and operating with it is the work of the differential calculus.

We are now in a position to see how the concept of a limit overcomes the difficulty of appearing to divide by zero. Consider again the equation which began the discussion about zero. We were analyzing the behavior of the increment h in the equation $\frac{(x + h)^2 - x^2}{h}$ giving $\frac{2hx + h^2}{h}$ and $\frac{h(2x + h)}{h}$. In this we can divide through with any value of h except when $h = 0$. Decreasing the size of that interval, we approach ever more closely the value $2x$, as appears when we let $x = 1$ and decrease h:

at $h = 0.5$ we have	$\frac{0.5(2 + 0.5)}{0.5}$	= 2.5
$h = 0.1$	" "	= 2.1
$h = 0.001$	" "	= 2.001
$h = 0.000001$ "	" "	= 2.000001

The interval h in this example represents a standard of approximation. Hence the expression that $2x + h = 2x$ at the value $h = 0$ is equivalent to saying that the limit of $\frac{h(2x + h)}{h}$ is $2x$ at $h = 0$, meaning thereby that within the neighborhood of $h = 0$, $2x + h$ approaches the value $2x$ within any standard of approximation whatsoever (*GBWW* II: 56, 173–74).

With this limit concept we are in effect defining the *continuous* in terms of the *discrete,* as may be seen from the definition of a continuous function given above. A geometric illustration can be given by determining the numerical value of $x^2 = 2$ where $x = \sqrt{2}$. As already noted, geometrically this is a definite line, the hypotenuse of a right-angled triangle with sides each equal to 1. Representing numbers as points along a line, we can superimpose that hypotenuse upon the line. Yet there is no whole number or fraction that corresponds to that length, which is equal to the unending decimal 1.414.... However, by the use of the limit concept that end point can be defined. For within the neighborhood of the number 2 it is possible to locate an interval within which $\sqrt{2}$ lies within any standard of approximation. The $\sqrt{2}$ is the limit between the points on the number line $(1.414)^2 = 1.9993$ and $(1.4145)^2 = 2.0002$ and this lies within an interval of 0.0009.

A new quadrivium

Here at the end of relating what the development of mathematics has done to the ancient quadrivium we well might ask just what has been accomplished? It has been the story, as we have seen, of the arithmetization of mathematics achieved by successive extensions of the system of numbers so as to eliminate any restrictions upon the basic operations of arithmetic. First had to come a perspicuous notation for the whole or natural numbers including zero through the adoption of Arabic numbers, thereby establishing the *lingua franca* for all of mathematics throughout the world. The existing restrictions that came from operating only with the integers could then be lifted. The invention of negative numbers liberated the operation of subtraction; of rational numbers or fractions, that upon division; of irrational and imaginary numbers, that upon the extraction of roots. With this greatly extended system of numbers the invention of analytic geometry liberated geometry from its bondage to magnitude by accomplishing its work with equations of variables and constants representing numbers. The invention of the calculus overcame the restriction against division by zero, or what appeared to be such, by the conception of a mathematical limit.

If *now* we were to identify four branches that constitute the very foundation of elementary mathematics, what would they be? Arithmetic and geometry would certainly come first as providing basic understanding of multitude and magnitude, of numerosity and spaciness. Algebra would come next, studied graphically so as to include coordinate geometry. All would be capped by calculus with the means that it offers for the study of motion and change. With these four we have a modern version of the old quadrivium.

The arts that liberate

The development of the mathematic arts can be taken as a paradigm for the effective working of all the arts, of the arts of words as well as of numbers, of trivium as well as of quadrivium. The mathematic arts progressed by freeing themselves from the restraints that prevented their free and full operation. So on the more general level all the arts of learning liberate us for a freer and fuller intellectual activity.

The first identification of the liberal as differentiated from other arts emphasized their relation to freedom. Thus, Aristotle in his discussion of education in the eighth book of the *Politics* distinguishes arts that are liberal from those that are illiberal. The illiberal consists of "any occupation, art, or science, which makes the body or soul or mind of the freeman less fit for the practice or exercise of virtue," and he characterizes such as vulgar, menial, and servile (*GBWW* I: 9, 542; II: 8, 542). It may be charged that Aristotle here betrays his prejudice as a member of a slave-owning society in which all menial and heavy physical work was performed by slaves, and that this may be true as a sociological statement. But there is more to it. Under it, and implied, is the observation that there are activities that hinder, obstruct, even prevent the full and free activity of the mind. Long, heavy, back-breaking labor is certainly not conducive to lofty and abstract thought. So, too, an activity that is concerned solely with producing one particular effect has to that extent a limiting effect. The cabinet-maker engages in constructing one particular table. The geometer considers the properties of any and all triangles, none of which is material. The difference is that between the particular individual and the universal, that between the here-and-now and that which transcends both space and time.

This is what Aristotle means by the distinction between the liberal and illiberal, and it goes beyond any sociological bias it may or may not reveal to indicate and emphasize a difference with respect to the freedom and extension of the mind. The one contributes something to our existence; the other defines it.

The liberal arts, freeing and liberating the mind, release us from restrictions of time and place and enable us to converse across the times of the ages and the places of the world. Aristotle and Euclid more than two thousand years ago in Athens were able to teach only a few individuals. Yet through the arts of language and mathematics their books are able to reach, continue to teach, any one, any place, any time. To profit from their teaching, i.e., to learn, we require the same liberal arts they were masters of, and, in learning, we can also increase our own mastery.

Otto Bird was executive editor of *The Great Ideas Today* from 1964 to 1970 and its consulting editor until 1988. Since 1981 he has contributed pieces of his own to "Reconsiderations of Great Books and Ideas."

His connection with the *Great Books of the Western World* set goes back to 1947, when for three years he worked as associate editor of *The Syntopicon*. Trained as a philosopher with particular interest in logic and medieval thought, he became subsequently a member of the faculty at the University of Notre Dame, where he founded and directed the general program of liberal studies from 1959 to 1963, and where he was a university professor from 1970 until his retirement in 1976.

In addition to essays and reviews, Mr. Bird has written *Syllogistic Logic and its Extensions* (1964), *The Idea of Justice* (1967), and *Cultures in Conflict: An Essay in the Philosophy of the Humanities* (1976). He was also a major contributor to the *Propædia,* or *Outline of Knowledge,* of the fifteenth edition of the *Encyclopædia Britannica*. In 1991, Mr. Bird published his autobiography, *Seeking a Center: My Life as a "Great Bookie."*

2

RECONSIDERATIONS

OF GREAT BOOKS AND IDEAS

Our Political Situation: Good Government, Self-government, and American Democracy

Laurence Berns

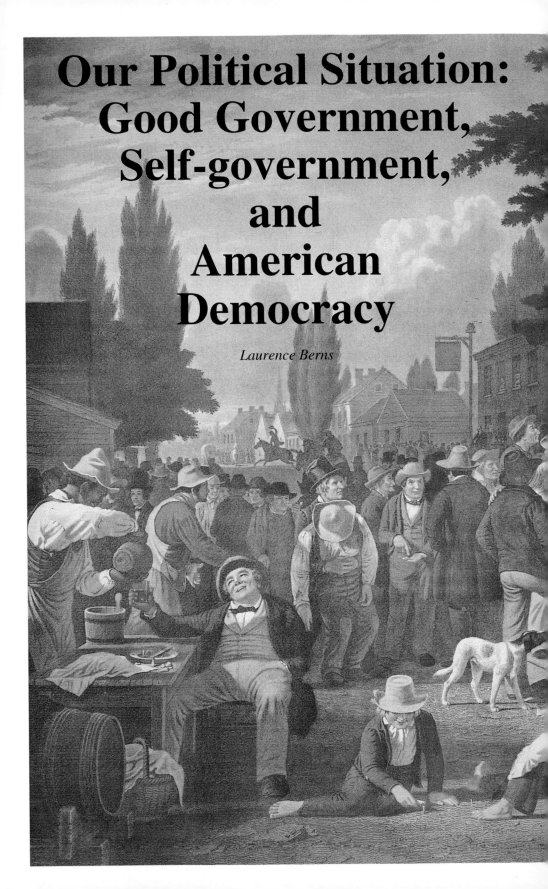

Two things I ask of thee; deny them not to me before I die:
Remove vanity and false words far from me: give me neither poverty nor
riches; feed me with food needful for me:
Lest I be full, and deny thee, and say, Who is the Lord?
Or lest I be poor and steal, and profane the name of my God.
                                                      —*Proverbs,* 30:7–9

…ignorance is the curse of God,
Knowledge the wing wherewith we fly to Heaven…
            —Shakespeare, *Second Part of King Henry VI,* Act IV, scene vii
                                        (*GBWW* I: 26, 62; II: 24, 62)

I n 1988, as part of her husband's campaign for the Democratic Party's
nomination for president, Tipper Gore (the wife of the Vice President)
visited a southern inner city, mostly black, elementary school class. She
explained to the very young students that she was trying to help her
husband, and if he were elected she would become the first lady of the
United States. She then turned to a young black girl, a first or second
grader, and asked: "Wouldn't you like to be first lady?" "No, ma'am,"
came the unexpected reply. "What *would* you like to be?" Mrs. Gore
asked. The reply was, "I'd like to be president, ma'am."

On Nov. 8, 1995, after much speculation by the general public, Gen.
Colin Powell (former chairman of the U.S. Joint Chiefs of Staff) announced that he would not seek the presidency in 1996. He concluded his
remarks by observing:

> In one generation, we have moved from denying a black man service at a
> lunch counter to elevating one to the highest military office in the nation
> and to being a serious contender for the presidency. This is a magnificent
> country, and I am proud to be one of its sons.

These two stories, hardly conceivable before the Civil Rights movement, indicate something of what has been done toward removing what
many regard as the greatest stain on the American political record. More to
the point of this paper, they indicate that apparently the *promise* of American politics, of American democracy, has not lost its luster, despite widely
publicized misgivings about its directions and coherence. It might make
sense for us here to discuss the promise before the misgivings, the standards before the lapses from the standards. The survey within these pages
of some selected elements of the American political tradition is not undertaken for purposes of "background." The English philosopher Francis Bacon once made the observation that conceit of plenty is the greatest cause
of want. The illusion of great progress in matters psychological, social, and
political has, it will be argued here, led to a serious failure to appreciate the
subtlety and depth of the political thought of the American founders.
Important misgivings about the American way of politics, some justified,
some unjustified, will be traced to this failure.

(Overleaf)
The County
Elections *by*
George Caleb
Bingham
(1851).
"Under
representative
democracy
the primary
relations be-
tween people
and govern-
ment are de-
termined by
elections."

Equality, deliberation, and merit

The great watchword of American politics en-
shrined in *The Declaration of Independence* asserts "that all men are created equal." One of the
first things to notice, perhaps, in this phrase is
the theological word "created." In his *Essay
Concerning Civil Government* (*GBWW* I: 35,
25–81; II: 33, 25–81), which inspired some of
the language of the Declaration, the English philosopher John Locke declares "That all men are
by nature equal" [section 54]. The two traditions,
natural right and biblical, are conflated in the very
first sentence of the Declaration, where the ensuing
rights are derived from "the Laws of Nature and of
Nature's God." The most discussed word of the key
phrase is, of course, the word "equal." In what sense does the
Declaration assert that all men are equal? One of the most authoritative
interpreters of the Declaration and 16th president of the United States,
Abraham Lincoln, commented:

John Locke, by Herman Verelst. "In his Essay Concerning Civil Government *...which inspired some of the language of the Declara-tion... John Locke de-clares 'That all men are by nature equal.'"*

> I think the authors of that notable instrument intended to include *all* men,
> but they did not intend to declare all men equal *in all respects.* They did
> not mean to say all were equal in color, size, intellect, moral develop-
> ments, or social capacity. They defined with tolerable distinctness, in what
> respects they did consider all men created equal—equal in "certain in-
> alienable rights, among which are life, liberty, and the pursuit of
> happiness."[1]

Locke, as previously cited, states what I believe Lincoln had in mind:

> Though I have said… *"That all men are by Nature equal,"* I cannot be
> supposed to understand all sorts of "Equality." Age or Virtue may give
> men a just precedency. *Excellency of Parts and Merit* may place others
> above the Common level…and yet all this consists with the equality which
> all men are in respect of Jurisdiction of Dominion one over another, which
> was the *Equality* I there spoke of…being that *equal Right* that every man
> hath to his *Natural Freedom,* without being subjected to the Will or
> Authority of any other Man.[2] (*GBWW* I: 35, 36; II: 33, 36)

In the language of *The Declaration of Independence,* governments derive
"their just powers from the consent of the governed."

Thomas Jefferson, in the context of a discussion of natural talents, observed of people that "whatever be their degree of talent it is no measure of
their rights. Because Sir Isaac Newton was superior to others in understanding, he was not therefore lord of the person or property of others."[3] A
properly constituted government, properly administered, Jefferson, Locke,
and Lincoln seem to imply, would protect and secure those natural rights

naturally due to each and every human being simply by virtue of their being human beings.

Again, Jefferson, Locke, and Lincoln seem to find no inconsistency between this universal equality of rights and clear differences of rank in abilities to exercise and administer government. (Inequalities of capacity for self-government, implicit in laws for parental jurisdiction and criminal incarceration, would seem to be obvious, though they are rarely discussed as such.) In fact, Jefferson argues, inequalities in capacity to govern must be carefully considered with a view to that excellence in governing that is required for "the instruction, the trusts, and government of society...May we not even say, that that form of government is the best which provides the most effectually for a pure selection of these natural aristoi [i.e., best] into the offices of government?"[4] The Declaration's principle of equality is, then, not only not inconsistent with, but even requires, a coordinate principle of excellence. Publius, the Federalist, reminds us,

Abraham Lincoln by John Wesley Jarvis (1861). Lincoln, the sixteenth president (1861–65) was "one of the most authoritative interpreters of the Declaration [of Independence]."

> As there is a degree of depravity in mankind which requires a certain degree of circumspection and distrust, so there are other qualities in human nature which justify a certain portion of esteem and confidence. Republican government presupposes the existence of these qualities in a higher degree than any other form.[5] (GBWW I: 43, 174; II: 40, 174)

Democratic political practice itself attests to the necessary presence of a principle of excellence, of merit, insofar as democratic political practice depends upon free elections. Free elections presuppose inequalities of ability, or merit, to fulfill the offices for which the elections are held; they also presuppose capacities in the voters roughly to discern those inequalities. If we were to adopt the classical Greek definition of democracy as simply "rule of the many," while the selection of governors on the basis of alleged merits and demerits, or "virtues" and "vices," were defined as *aristocracy,* then free elections would have to be regarded as aristocratic institutions. Alternatively, to the extent that the rights to vote and to be a candidate are fairly widespread with no property qualifications, elections could be regarded as democratic, but insofar as *merit* is contested, they would be regarded as aristocratic, i.e., every election asks voters to decide who is the better candidate; as a whole, therefore, the institution of free elections would be a mixed institution, democratic and aristocratic. Democratic political practice, then, as we Americans speak of it, rests on at least two fundamental coordinate principles: a basic equality of God-given or natural rights and a coordinate principle of excellence or merit. When we normally speak of democracy, we also tend to mean good government.

Perhaps the most unequivocal expression of the fundamentally democratic character of the American polity is to be found in the Preamble to the Constitution which declares that "We the People of the United States…do ordain and establish this Constitution for the United States of America."[6] We pride ourselves as living under a rule of law more than a rule of men; but laws, at least human laws, are laid down by men: The fundamental framework of American laws, *The Constitution,* is ordained and established by the authority of "We the People.…"

It is not to be expected that all the people will always, or even often, agree on what is to be done. Large numbers of those who constituted the people that ratified the Constitution opposed its ratification.[7] So, in fact, democratic rule means the rule of the majority or a plurality of the people. Is a measure or a decision right and good, then, if it is desired or approved of by a majority or plurality of the people? Once one asks the question this way, the answer seems obvious,[8] despite the current scientistic demagoguery that seems to equate rightness and goodness with high standing in public opinion polls.

Jefferson again is helpful here, "All, too, will bear in mind this sacred principle, that though the will of the majority is in all cases to prevail, that will to be rightful must be reasonable.…"[9] That is a consummation devoutly to be wished, but it might not be altogether reasonable to expect perfect reasonability in political affairs. Lincoln offers us a less exacting but perhaps more reasonable standard: "A majority, held in restraint by

Thomas Jefferson, third president of the United States (1801–09). Jefferson argued that "excellence in governing…is required for 'the instruction, the trusts, and government of society.'"

constitutional checks, and limitations, and always changing easily, with *deliberate* changes of popular opinion and sentiments, is the only true sovereign of a free people."[10] Lincoln's use of the word "deliberate" here was most deliberate.[11] Near the end of the speech, addressing all, but aiming especially at southerners and his opposition, he said:

> My countrymen, one and all, think calmly and *well,* upon this whole subject. Nothing valuable can be lost by taking time. If there be an object to *hurry* any of you, in hot haste, to a step which you would never take *deliberately,* that object will be frustrated by taking time; but no good object can be frustrated by it.[12]

Lincoln seems to have had *The Federalist,* No. 63, in mind:

> such an institution [a well-constructed Senate] may be sometimes necessary as a defence to the people against their own temporary errors and delusions. As the cool and *deliberate sense of the community* ought, in all governments, and actually will, in all free[13] governments, ultimately prevail over the views of its rulers; so there are particular moments in public affairs when the people, stimulated by some irregular passion, or some illicit advantage, or misled by the artful misrepresentations of interested men, may call for measures which they themselves will afterwards be the most ready to lament and condemn. (*GBWW* I: 43, 192; II: 40, 192)

or *The Federalist,* No. 71:

> The republican principle demands that the *deliberate sense of the community* should govern the conduct of those to whom they intrust the management of their affairs; but it does not require an unqualified complaisance to every sudden breeze of passion, or to every transient impulse which the people may receive from the arts of men, who flatter their prejudices to betray their interests.[14]

The people, then, that are entitled to ordain and establish constitutions, entitled to rule, are the people insofar as they are a free, deliberate and thoughtful people.

There is, however, more than one way to see that the American political system, the American rule of law, is tied to the possibility of general reasonable and deliberate *discussion* of political matters.

The First Amendment's right to "freedom of speech" seems to have been first conceived as an extension to the population as a whole of the freedom of speech and debate of legislators in their legislature: that is, parliamentary immunities are extended to a self-governing citizenry, not as a general license to "freedom of expression," but in order to enable them to fulfill their functions as citizens in discussion and debate about the public business. The right is restricted, the speech to be protected is political *speech*.[15]

At the time of the American Revolution, Justice Joseph Story tells us, in all the Colonies

> the common law of England, as far as it was applicable to their situation, was made the basis of their jurisprudence...the first revolutionary Conti-

Scene at the signing of the constitution of the United States, Sept. 17, 1787, by Howard Chandler Christy (1940). "Perhaps the most unequivocal expression... of the American polity is to be found in the Preamble to the Constitution."

nental Congress, in 1774, unanimously resolved, that the respective Colonies are entitled to the common law...the common law can hardly be affirmed to have been exactly the same in all the Colonies. Each Colony selected for itself, and judged for itself, what was most consonant to its institutions...in its actual application, the common law became the guardian of their civil and political rights; it protected their infant liberties; it watched over their maturer growth; it expanded with their wants; it nourished in them that spirit of independence, which checked the first approaches of arbitrary power...[16]

The traditional understanding of the common law is that it is a law of principles, of rational principles applied rationally and diversely, by adjustment to the different circumstances of different communities and times.[17] It is made manifest primarily through the decisions of judges, through judicial precedent, in contrast to expressly legislated statute law, although in practice statutes modifying common law judicial rulings can also be regarded as part of the common law.

> The common law is a way of applying, case-by-case, the enduring standards of the community, and in such a way as to bring the community along, even as reforms are being made....[C]ommon-law judges discover the law; they do not simply make it. Reason looks to nature (instead of will looking to desire) in declaring the rule that is to be followed.[18]

Our theme, thus far, has been the centrality of general, public, deliberate discussion for American political life, at least as it is conceived with a view toward "the better angels of our nature." We have found this theme implicit in a number of American foundational documents and institutions: *The Declaration of Independence, The Federalist,* The First Amendment and the common law. Both the last and the first of these "instruments" evince a reliance on traditions of natural law or natural rights.[19]

Natural right—natural law

Generally speaking, natural right and natural law refer to those ethical or moral precepts that can be drawn from the study of human nature, which includes the study of political society. It could be argued that this approach simply spells out the logical presuppositions about human nature implicit in any rational discussion of good and bad, or right and wrong; or conversely, what is implicit about good and bad practice, right and wrong practice, in any rational discussion of human nature.

> Are the safeguards for individual liberty [in the Constitution of 1787, as amended in 1791] good because adopted or adopted because good? Are the 13th, 14th, and 15th amendments to the Constitution good because adopted, or adopted because good? If the answer to both questions is that they were adopted because good, then their goodness must rest upon principles antecedent to their adoption. Knowledge of that goodness must

then form part of the knowledge of the original intention of those who framed and ratified them. In this sense, the natural law and the positive law are, to use Aristotle's phrase, as inseparable as the concavity and the convexity of a curved line.[20]

The natural right, natural law approach tends to mean in practice that discussions of good and bad, right and wrong, are anchored in down-to-earth facts and reasoning which are understood to be accessible, potentially, to every rational person. Rational discussion, not preaching, intimidation, or propaganda is the method by which it aims at arriving at and communicating its conclusions. Goals are to be traced back to, and derived from, natural powers, not from mere desire, from will, from utopian or wishful thinking. The natural right, natural law approach militates against unreasonable expectations, including the unreasonable expectation that this doctrine, unlike any other doctrine, will never be abused by partisan passion. Disagreements both about the facts and the conclusions drawn from them are to be expected.

The pursuit of this kind of knowledge requires certain disciplines and a certain kind of approach rather different from other rational disciplines and especially different from those paradigmatic rational disciplines, mathematics and mathematical physics. One difficulty concerns subject matter; the danger here, especially for the mathematically trained, is misplaced exactitude, the error that goes along with the lack of that "connoisseurship of the pedestrian" that the study of human affairs requires.[21] The other difficulty, perhaps more important, concerns the investigator, the engagement of passion and interest: in articulating what is good and bad for human beings in general, one cannot avoid implicitly calling one's own character, one's own inmost being, before the bar of one's standards. Self-righteousness and self-justification are always temptations. If the subject matter should be inherently controversial, learning to live with disagreement and controversy is required. More generally, there is need for a special discipline for learning how to counter the manifold ways our other desires have for frustrating the desire for truth.[22]

The most important political conclusions that can be drawn from natural law and natural right reasoning are those that concern the purposes of government. Implicit in any determination of the purposes of government is the right or duty to alter or abolish any government that does not measure up to those purposes. Statements about the purposes of government clarify the proper limits and scope of government. The *Declaration of Independence,* our most authoritative statement on the purposes of government, uses elements from all three of the major traditions of natural right and natural law: 1) the ancient or classical notion of natural right based on the idea of an impersonal, but end-directed, nature; 2) the medieval notion of natural law that understands classical purposive nature as a promulgation by the God of the Bible or of the Koran; and 3) the modern notion of natural right, conceived so as to be compatible with modern mathematical physics.[23]

Political deliberation and the media

While the language of our political principles is, for the most part, the language of natural and God-given right, for most ordinary political conversation one need not reach so far. Our national political conversation takes place on a number of more or less interconnected levels: The scholarly level of books, journal articles, conventions, conferences, lectures and discussions by and often between academic, think-tank, and foundation research professionals; extensive publication of public information by governmental agencies; issue-oriented books and political biography by journalists and political operatives; interest group advocacy; political party organizations; newspaper reporting, commentary and editorializing; and radio and television advertising, talk shows, public-interest programs, news reporting and editorializing. The discussion of our next topic, the *conditions* of rational, deliberate, political discussion in America, must, therefore, be highly selective. We must concern ourselves primarily with those developments that have most to do with shaping the opinions and attitudes of ordinary citizens, of the ultimate authorities in a system that depends upon free elections. It would be a mistake, however, to ignore the enormous proliferation of high-level literature and information on political,

An early political cartoon entitled Midsummer Madness. A Hot But Hopeless Chase After The Presidential Butterfly.

social, and economic policy pouring out of academic and public policy foundation presses. One practical problem would seem to be to bring this more carefully thought-out opinion and information to bear more directly on the political decision-making process itself, partly by making it more available, with suitable transformations, to policy makers, to public opinion leaders, or to mass audiences. This is being done on some scale by congressional committee hearings, rare news programs like *The NewsHour with Jim Lehrer* (formerly *The McNeill-Lehrer NewsHour*) and C-Span.[24]

The two media which seem to have most influence in shaping the general tone of American political discourse are, of course, newspapers and television. The media operators, those who provide the rest of us with the information we require, have a professional interest in being well informed; they are, in general, more intellectual than most of those they inform. They are, whether they know it or not, important shapers of public opinion. The more a government depends upon public opinion, the more these shapers of public opinion earn their quasi-governing sobriquet "The Fourth Estate."[25]

One of the more decisive ways the media shape public policy is their selection of what is or is not newsworthy. This influence is particularly conspicuous in matters of foreign and military policy. Deplorable events can happen in places like Bosnia, Somalia, or Zaire without producing any strong interest in American governmental circles to do something about them. After a certain diet of vivid pictures of extreme human suffering and outrage, as television can present them, public feeling can build up in such a way as to create an *interest* in elected officials to do something about the situation, even where sound policy might require not taking action.

Sentiment, or feeling, may be an indispensable element for all action, but there are obvious problems with allowing it to become the controlling or deciding factor in action. The desire to produce a sensational show more often than not overrules the citizens' aim to provide the less excited conditions for rational debate and deliberation about politics. The professional bias for theatricality within the media, especially in television, may do even more damage than political biases of the usual kind.

One complaint about the media is that of all the major players in our political "game," they are the least accountable for the consequences of their actions. Elected officials are accountable to the electorate; judges, where not elected, are held to higher standards of "good behavior;"[26] but the most decisive standard that seems to be controlling the media is the number of readers or viewers they can attract, a standard that seems to foster sensationalism and theater rather than rational debate and deliberation. This criticism applies more particularly to commercial television: there are a good number of newspapers (and even some few public affairs television shows) that seem to aim at acquiring not just more readers, but more better-informed readers. Robert McNeill has suggested that the impossibility, or great difficulty, of remedying this structural defect of commercial television news was a primary consideration for him and for Jim Lehrer in the shaping of their *NewsHour* on PBS. Much the same, I would

Jim Lehrer interviews a guest on his PBS news show, The NewsHour with Jim Lehrer.

assume, is behind the creation of the invaluable C-Span stations which are only available, however, through subscription television. The growing influence of those two institutions might be taken as a sign that the problems they were meant to remedy are receiving increasing recognition.

The problem we have been approaching is the corruption of the American political process itself.

The spirit of advertising and the corruption of the political process

In 1956 John Schneider published an unfortunately prophetic novel, *The Golden Kazoo.* The story is about how an American presidential election is taken over by ad men and run in strict accordance with advertising principles. The two greatest geniuses of American advertising are locked in battle to determine who shall be president. The ultimate victor (the candidates themselves are rather inconsequential) at some point in the book states what he calls, if memory serves, The First Law of the Adman, namely: *There is a little bit of the high-brow in some people, but there's a lot of the low-brow in everybody.* The practical conclusion, plainly, is: If you are interested in numbers, aim low. The 1996 presidential campaign exhibited the growing, some say dominant, influence of advertising in our political life. The spirit of advertising fosters a certain kind of egalitarianism, egalitarianism on the lowest common denominator of human motivation.

The most pervasive presence of advertising is, of course, in our commercial life. The most legitimate function claimed by advertisers is to provide
viewers and listeners with information about what is available for purchase. Yet advertisers never present us with information about what might
be defective, questionable, or problematic about the things they present for
our consideration, excepting references to competing products. We suspect
that we get no more information from advertising than is required to induce
us to buy what they are selling.

It is a commonplace of good sense, as well as ethical theory, that a
means should be appropriate or proportionate to the end it serves.[27] One of
the major perversities in modern advertising, it might be thought, is the
prodigious artfulness, imagination, disciplined thought, exquisite economy
and adjustment of means—especially in major network, prime-time television—that goes into the selling of all kinds of products, even the most
trivial. A discriminating viewer, a man of my acquaintance, whose professional life has been devoted to study of the means by which the fine arts
achieve their effects, has noted that there is nothing on television which for
sheer artfulness matches advertising. Can the souls of those using their
higher powers to produce this stuff be satisfied by the high monetary
rewards they reap? Great artistic powers would seem to have been made
for the elevation, perhaps even exaltation, of the human spirit: Do—
should—these powerful artisans of advertising feel that their talents are
being prostituted?

An economic argument could be made for commercial advertising that
cannot be made for political advertising: higher productivity depends on
increasing and extending mass production, mass production requires mass
markets, advertising has the task of producing and maintaining those markets. This argument does not, perhaps, directly address the problem of
prostituted talents. Recent fact (as well as economic arguments) seems to
support the notion that free markets are most conducive to the expansion of
production. It also seems to be fairly generally accepted, however, that
such creation of markets can be restricted, limited, and even in some cases
eliminated for reasons of health, e.g., alcohol, tobacco, and narcotics. Such
restrictions in the name of what could be called moral health, e.g., auto-
matic and regular censorship of movies, were in the past more generally
accepted than they seem to be today. The idea of moral "health" and
"sickness," however, seems to have been eclipsed for many intellectuals by
a certain notion of "autonomy."[28] Older, more robust, autonomy doctrines
(like Kant's, or that of the American Founders) keyed autonomy to a fairly
high level of virtue. From this point of view, moral restrictions on expression, or not to mince words, reasonable censorship,[29] can be made *in the
name of* autonomy.[30] By contrast, the new autonomy doctrine of contemporary intellectuals, coupled with so-called "value neutrality," might seem to
be more pathological than liberating. "Autonomy" so-called, without or
contrary to virtue, would then more aptly be called license. The rights of
the individual in these "sound" older notions are not in conflict with community standards, but, on the contrary, are conceived as dependent upon

"[T]he more the spirit of advertising pervades our political life, the more the spirit of propaganda replaces deliberative rhetoric…"

the maintenance of a decent moral tone in society. Throughout most of American history it seems to have been taken for granted, by thoughtful non-believers as well as believers, that society's moral tone is not set only by the law, but also by thriving religious institutions.[31]

Why then this concern about advertising? Everyone knows what is corrupting our political process: huge campaign expenditures that force conscientious legislators to spend far too much of their time in the dispiriting activity of raising money, far too much reliance on public opinion polls and talk about the "horse race," attack campaigning and journalism, the decline of political civility, "the demoralizing happenstance found in the primary system we now have,"[32] rampant demagoguery, and so on.

The argument here is that the spirit of advertising, that is so pervasive an influence in our non-political life, has now dangerously insinuated itself into our political life. It is very hard to sort out cause and effect in these matters, but the growing skill of advertisers seems to be matched by their growing success: the feeling also grows that viewers owe it to themselves, as if by natural right to gratify the desires that advertisers' products cater to. Those feelings seem to serve the purposes of both of our competing major political factions: "liberals" feed on the resentments of "deprivation," while "conservatives" extol the natural rightness of more and more acquisition. To the extent that the advertisers form national character, it may become more difficult to insist that we be treated with the dignities befitting free men and women.

Central to this paper as a whole is the presupposition that every political arrangement presupposes certain qualities of character in the populace that is to live under, or in accordance with, that arrangement. Free government based on enlightened consent may not survive if the feeling becomes widespread that its citizens are unworthy of such government and are incapable of making it work. More bluntly and grimly put, when people cease to place limits upon themselves, it becomes natural to begin to think about imposing limits on them from above. The less grim alternative is that they, and that is, we, be educated in such a way that placing limits upon ourselves becomes "second nature," i.e., habitual. The crisis, or at least alarming developments, in American education, especially "higher educa-tion" that go along with the increasing influence of the spirit of advertising will be discussed in the final section of this paper.

What is wrong with advertising? If, as I will argue, advertising is a species of propaganda, the question appears less problematic. What is wrong with propaganda?

Propaganda, as distinct from rheto-ric, aims at moving the rational animal primarily by animal feeling, rather than by those feelings derivative from and associated with what we call evi-dence. Rhetoric, which aims at per-suasion, of course appeals to feeling, but not in separation from evidence purporting to establish the rightness of the speaker's cause. Disparagers of rhetoric speak of "verbal manipula-tion"; if it were merely manipulation with no appeal to the hearers' capacity

FARMER GARFIELD
Cutting a Swath to the White House.

for independent judgment, it would be what I am calling propaganda. In so far as the persuasion concerns doing or forbearing from something, rhetoric could be called practical reasoning.[33]

The line between rhetoric and propaganda is not always easy to draw: part of the drama in Robert Penn Warren's *All the King's Men,* especially in the excellent film starring Broderick Crawford, consists in the transfor-mation of Willy Stark's reformist rhetoric into something else. One of the things that makes what is portrayed in that film appear to be impressively natural is the difficulty in locating just when that transformation takes place. Cross burnings by the KKK might be examples of fairly pure propa-ganda; also the way Stokely Carmichael (as he was called when I observed

A Currier & Ives poster from 1880 shows James A. Garfield, the Republican candidate for president.

him in action extolling "black power") placed strong, good-looking young men on stage with him and in the aisles who stared coldly, if not menacingly, at the spectators as he spoke. The passion meant to be evoked was clearly fear, as if to say, "You don't want to be against this man, it might not even be safe to be against this man." The Reverend Louis Farrakhan uses the same technique.[34]

In sum, the more the spirit of advertising pervades our political life, the more the spirit of propaganda replaces deliberative rhetoric and the "deliberate sense of the community" as the chief determinant of our political ways, the more we treat each other as objects of manipulation rather than as fellow citizens, the more we betray that grand heritage that took justifiable pride in the notion that

> it seems to have been reserved to the people of this country, by their conduct and example, to decide the important question, whether societies of men are really capable or not of establishing good government from reflection and choice, or whether they are forever destined to depend for their political constitutions on accident and force.[35] (*GBWW* I: 43, 29; II: 40, 29)

What kind of people's will?

The will of the people, according to this argument, that is constituted the ultimate authority in the American political scheme of things is not the mere will, but the people's thoughtful and deliberate, i.e., its rational, will. During the recent general elections, at the same time that the people as thoughtful and deliberate beings were being insulted by the onslaught of political advertising, they were rhetorically addressed and flattered as some mystical repository of political wisdom and virtue. Much was made of that originally retail marketing device, the focus group, where small groups of people with little serious interest in, or information about, politics, sat around with some well-known media interviewer and were made to feel that their usually uninformed and self-interested, often prejudiced, opinions were

Senator John F. Kennedy and Vice President Richard M. Nixon during the televised debates of the 1960 presidential campaign. The debates were a major factor in the election—over 85 million Americans watched them.

terribly important. The degree to which they were taken seriously, even by some normally competent commentators, reveals a growing insensitivity to the difference between political salesmanship and genuine political discussion.

Politically interested high school and college students often join and take part in well-organized debating teams and contests, and they are sometimes given the illuminating assignment of arguing for positions they personally disapprove. They learn how to research political materials, how to marshal evidence and how to deal with (even to appreciate) rational and rhetorical opposition in a civilized manner. There is no paucity of skilled debaters in our population and in the halls of government. How then are we to account for these miserable exchanges of sound bites that we have been calling presidential debates?

The answer, it seems to me, is simple and obvious: no large *mass* audience would listen to a substantive, intellectually demanding debate of normal length; that is, no audience corrupted by the expectations for entertainment fostered by the spirit of advertising, sitcoms, and sports events.

There is, of course, a very large number of politically interested people who would be perfectly capable of following a substantive debate of something like normal debate length. That "very large number" of the politically interested, a kind of natural political leadership, should, it seems to me, have their needs and interests attended to, but I doubt if that number could ever equal the audience size that prime-time advertising on the major networks normally reaches. Are there in every society, including democracies, substantial numbers of people whose nature is such as to preclude a serious interest in politics? If so, can they be educated, especially by appeals to their own self-interest, to be different? Or does nature have nothing to do with the problem? Is it rather a consequence of the "education," or conditioning, or habituation, engendered by the mass media? Or both factors?

In August 1858 in rural Illinois, general literacy was far more rare than it is today all over the country. Nevertheless, Lincoln and Douglas, in their famous debates in the race for the U.S. Senate agreed on the following plan:

> ...we shall alternately open and close the discussion. I will speak at Ottawa *one hour,* you can reply, occupying *an hour and a half,* and I will then follow for *half an hour.* We will alternate in like manner in each successive place.[36]

The Chicago newspaper, the *Press and Tribune,* of Aug. 26, 1858, reported:

> From sunrise till high noon on Saturday [August 21], Ottawa was deluged in dust. The first of the seven great debates which Douglas had consented to hold with Lincoln, had started La Salle, Will, Kendall, Grudy, Kankakee, Cook and other surrounding counties, in unwonted commotion. Be-

Abraham Lincoln and Stephen A. Douglas met for a series of seven debates, each three hours long. It was estimated that twelve thousand people were in attendance at the one held on Aug. 26, 1858.

fore breakfast Ottawa was beleaguered with a multiplying host from all points of the compass. At eight o'clock the streets and avenues leading from the country were so enveloped with dust that the town resembled a vast smokehouse. Teams, trains and processions poured in from every direction... Both candidates arrived in Ottawa about noon... At one o'clock the crowd commenced pouring into the public square....The whole number of persons present could not have been less than twelve thousand.

The editor of the debates then adds, "At 2:30, with the sun scorching the standing spectators, Douglas opened the debate."[37]

Assuming human nature has not changed in 138 years, how are we to account for the change in political interest and attentiveness? Perhaps if our general opportunities for entertainment were reduced to those of rural Illinois in the 1850's, we could experience a rebirth of general public spiritedness and attentiveness. Not a very practical solution. A more sober interpretation of the events, however, suggests that Lincoln and Douglas's twelve thousand, for all their down-to-earth boisterousness, were a fairly select crowd. The slavery, popular sovereignty, and states' rights issues discussed were fundamental and dramatic. And the speakers…! But nevertheless this twelve thousand stood in the scorching sun for three hours to hear and watch a political debate!

Could we not have presidential debates without moderators, but with timekeepers, where each candidate speaks for 20 to 30 minutes, then each responds for fifteen minutes, and then each has 5 minutes to pose questions for the other with 10 minutes for each to respond? Perhaps not, if we insist on reaching mass audiences and are not content with reaching those merely large numbers of reasonably informed and politically interested people. Adlai Stevenson is said to have had this exchange with an enthusiastic supporter of his candidacy for the presidency, "Governor Stevenson, you have the vote of every thinking person." His reply to her was, "Madam, that's not enough, I need a majority." The spirits of political advertising, political propagandizing, and calls for "direct democracy," tend in unwitting cooperation to raise the same flawed standard: Adhering to the mere will of the people rather than to their deliberate and thoughtful will.[38]

The movement for more direct democracy, and the growing reliance on propagandistic political advertising both hold out the prospect of by-passing the cumbersome, compromising, deliberative, and negotiating processes of representative government; practices bringing the people more directly into the process are brought forward like direct mail campaigns[39] (with their phony questionnaires), referenda, "ballot initiatives," and primaries in place of conventions.[40] If this analysis is correct, what these movements may be moving us towards is that degenerate form of democracy called variously plebiscitary democracy, totalitarian democracy, or more simply, demagogic despotism. The specter of direct electronic democracy making representative systems "redundant," touted by technocrats whose human understanding seems to be inversely proportional to their technical proficiency, deserves a sentence of its own.[41] The premise of this movement, again, is that the mere will of the people is to be served, rather than their thoughtful and deliberate will. When we look for examples of this kind of thing in other times and places, we find it associated with names like Vladimir Lenin, Benito Mussolini, Adolf Hitler, Juan Perón, Mao Zedong, Kim Il-sung, Fidel Castro. The appeals of such leaders to their peoples usually cease or change their character after they gain accession to power; the techniques of direct "democracy" then become occasional instruments to rally their respective populations.

In modern times, however, as this list of names indicates, demagoguery has taken a new turn, with the rise of what could be called the ideological demagogue. The ideological demagogue adds a certain fanatic intellectuality, a kind of secular spirit of prophecy, to the character of the straight or natural demagogue. The skilled natural demagogue has a dramatic flair for divining and arousing the passions of large crowds of people and for mimicking the qualities of genuine statesmanship. What distinguishes him or her from the natural orator, or equally skilled statesman, is his or her overpowering ambition to be by hook or crook at the head of an adoring crowd.[42] Ambition "within reasonable bounds"[43] is not to be disparaged: the Chorus in Oedipus prays "that god may never abolish the eager ambition that keeps the city noble."[44] (*GBWW* I: 5, 107; II: 4, 123) The ambitious statesman knows that the love of glory or honor is a selfish passion, but one that obtains its object most securely through public service, service to the long-range good of society. The ideological demagogue hides his own ambition from himself and stifles normal human feeling in order to steel himself to fulfill the destiny imposed upon him by "History." It is ironic how in the loose usage of today's political marketplace the word ideology, which was first intended to oppose and replace philosophy, has come to be used as almost synonymous with philosophy.[45]

The problem of democracy

"Democracy," Churchill once said, "is the worst form of government, except for all the others." For all its superiority to "all the others," for all its considerable virtues, democracy is problematic. The Founders of the United States addressed themselves to the problems and virtues of democracy with a subtlety that is nowadays too little appreciated and insufficiently studied.[46] One of those considerable virtues, according to Hamilton, is "the tendency of the Free Government to interest the passions of the community in its favour, [and to] beget public spirit and public confidence."[47] In the ratification debates James Wilson expounded upon the advantages and disadvantages of monarchy, aristocracy, and democracy:[48]

> The advantages of democracy are, liberty, equality, cautious and salutary laws, public spirit, frugality, peace, *opportunities of exciting and producing abilities of the best citizens.*[49] Its disadvantages are, dissensions, the delay and disclosure of public counsels, the imbecility [weakness] of public measures, retarded by the necessity of a numerous consent.

Wilson's paragraph on democracy follows two on monarchy and aristocracy. It is clear that, according to Wilson, the democracy worked out in the Constitution was contrived to avoid the disadvantages of the other forms, to mitigate the usual disadvantages of democracy, and to obtain, as much as is possible within a democratic framework, the advantages of the two other forms. The Convention proposed a constitution wherein "all authority is derived from the people," a government that "[i]n its principle it is purely democratical. But that principle is applied in different forms, in order to obtain the advantages, and exclude the inconveniences, of the simple modes of government."[50]

Democracy in its political dimension (as distinguished from its guarantees of individual rights) aims at providing all citizens with the opportunity to participate in the processes of government, either as governors or as electors of governors. It cannot ensure that all citizens will participate in those processes thoughtfully and deliberately; nor can it abolish demagoguery, the endemic vice of democratic leadership. Unruly passion in the people and demagoguery usually go together, the latter often determines the direction of the former. Even more usually, both elements shape one another; the demagogue flatters, arouses, or exploits the people's unreasonable passions (frequently envy and anger) in order to get him or herself at the head of things. The causes of both the demagoguery and the unruly passions of the people, according to the non-utopian traditions of both ancients and moderns, lie deep in human nature and are not likely to be eliminated.

Then how can they be opposed? By devising institutions and creating conditions that can counteract and frustrate their operation. There is a theatrical element in all political life. At rare times it provides high and edifying drama: The Gettysburg Address, Lincoln's Second Inaugural, Churchill's "Blood, Sweat and Tears" speech, De Gaulle's remarkable invocations of the almost palpable spirit of France; Shakespeare's use of Henry the Vth's St. Crispian's Day Speech, and Antony's fateful speech at Caesar's funeral.

More often, the theatrical element provides commonplace pomp and required political ceremony. Frequently, however, it sets the stage for the low dramas of demagoguery.[51] In democracies the political audience is larger and the problem of demagogic theatricality more acute: a key problem for democracies is to prevent democracy from degenerating through demagogic theatocracy into despotism and tyranny. Television obviously magnifies the dangers by enormously enlarging the theater's audience. In direct democracies there is little or no way to counteract the blandishments of demagoguery.

> A common passion or interest will, in almost every case, be felt by a majority of the whole; a communication and concert result from the form of government itself; and there is nothing to check the inducements to sacrifice the weaker party or an obnoxious individual. Hence it is that such democracies have ever been spectacles of turbulence and contention; have ever been found incompatible with personal security or the rights of property; and have in general been as short in their lives as they have been violent in their deaths.[52] (*GBWW* I: 43, 51; II: 40, 51)

The fundamental, but certainly not total or foolproof, solution to the problem of democratic demagoguery (there may not be any total solution) is the institution of a system of representation, or representative democracy:

> …a government in which the scheme of representation takes place, opens a different prospect, and promises the cure for which we are seeking…the delegation of the government…to a small number of citizens elected by the rest…. The effect…is…to refine and enlarge the public views, by passing them through the medium of a chosen body of citizens, whose wisdom may best discern the true interest of their country, and whose patriotism and love of justice will be least likely to sacrifice it to tempo-

rary or partial considerations. Under such a regulation, it may well happen that the public voice, pronounced by the representatives of the people, will be more consonant to the public good than if pronounced by the people themselves, convened for the purpose.[53]

The best merely institutional solution, Madison knows, cannot be a cure-all. He goes on to say:

> On the other hand, the effect may be inverted. Men of factious tempers, of local prejudices, or of sinister designs, may, by intrigue, by corruption, or by other means, first obtain the suffrages, and then betray the interests, of the people. (GBWW I: 43, 51–52; II: 40, 51–52)

Wilson, at first, seems more optimistic. In a democracy, he says, there

James A. Madison was the fourth president of the United States (1809–17). He collaborated with Alexander Hamilton and John Jay in the publication of The Federalist Papers.

can be no disorder in the community but may here receive a radical cure. If the error be in the legislature, it may be corrected by the constitution;[54] if in the constitution, it may be corrected by the people. There is a remedy, therefore, for every distemper of government, if the people are not wanting to themselves; if they are wanting to themselves, there is no remedy.

An illustration of how the Constitution works to mitigate disadvantages of democracy and to incorporate advantages of aristocracy while keeping everything within an ultimately democratic framework might be useful. The original scheme for choosing presidential electors (the "Electoral College") is a nice contrivance for all the people to participate in a process that enables a more thoughtful, deliberate, and better informed part of the people to make the final decision; or, to follow the usual abstraction, for the will of all the people to turn the power of decision over to one of its more thoughtful and better informed parts.

> It was desirable that the sense of the people should operate in the choice of the person to whom so important a trust was to be confided. This end will be answered by committing the right of making it, not to any pre-established body, but to men *chosen by the people* for the special purpose, and at the particular conjuncture.
> It was equally desirable that the immediate election should be made by men *most capable of analysing the qualities adapted to the station, and acting under circumstances favorable to deliberation....* A small number of persons, selected by their fellow-citizens from the general mass, will be most likely to possess the *information and discernment* requisite to such complicated investigations.

It was also peculiarly desirable to afford as little opportunity as possible to tumult and disorder.... The choice of *several,* to form *an intermediate body of electors,* will be much less apt to convulse the community...than the choice of *one* who was himself to be the final object of the public wishes. And as the electors chosen in each State are to assemble and vote in the State in which they are chosen, this *detached and divided situation* will expose them much less to heats and ferments, which might be communicated from them to the people, than if they were all to be convened at one time in one place.

...And they have excluded from eligibility to this trust, all those who from situation might be suspected of too great devotion to the President in office. No senator, representative, or other person holding a place of trust or profit under the United States can be of the numbers of the electors.[55] (*GBWW* I: 43, 205–6; II: 40, 205–6)

The overall structure of the government of the United States perhaps most visibly illustrates how aristocratic and monarchic advantages are combined under a democratic aegis. The House of Representatives is obviously the most democratic branch, because of its short tenure, that is, the frequency (every two years) with which it must go back to the people for election. The Senate can be thought of as more aristocratic because of its longer tenure (six years), that is, the relative infrequency of its elections, and because its members are not apportioned according to population.[56] Before the Seventeenth Amendment [1913] one could also say because they are not elected by the people directly, but by State legislatures (Article I, Section 3, of the Constitution). The Supreme Court is obviously the most aristocratic branch: Life-time appointment "during good Behaviour" with the approval of the Senate, no elections. The term of the president (four years) is the mean between the House's and the Senate's, suggesting a guard against both democratic and aristocratic extremes. The ceremonial and educative functions of the presidency suggest both aristocracy and monarchy; the monarchic side is also implicit in the evident need for secrecy, dispatch, special information, and room for maneuver in foreign and military affairs, the latter, of course, being the special responsibility of the Commander-in-Chief of the armed forces.[57] But funding for all activities of all branches depends upon legislation that must originate in the most democratic branch, the House of Representatives (Article I, Section 7).

"In defect of better motives"
Preventing the abuse of government

If what is said about the Devil being a fallen angel be true, it may be too optimistic to assert that

> If men were angels, no government would be necessary. If angels were to govern men, neither external nor internal controls on government would be necessary. In framing a government which is to be administered by men over men, the great difficulty lies in this: you must first *enable* the

government to control the governed; and in the next place *oblige* it to control itself. A dependence on the people is, no doubt, the primary control on the government; but experience has taught mankind the necessity of auxiliary precautions.[58] (*GBWW* I: 43, 163; II: 40, 163)

In other words, the American Founders did their best to foster reflection, choice, thoughtfulness, and deliberation in their democracy. But it will not do to look on government from the point of view of the "better angels of our nature" alone; the American revolution was, in the words of Martin Diamond, a "revolution of sober expectations." The Founders' most urgent concern was to remedy, prevent, and mitigate the abuse of government that non-angelic human nature made well-nigh inevitable. Government works better when enlightened statesmen are at the helm, but we cannot rely on this, for "Enlightened statesmen will not always be at the helm."[59] (*GBWW* I: 43, 51; II: 40, 51)

The powers of government are to be separated, blended, and balanced so as to function efficiently when guided by deliberation,[60] but to check and block one another when ordinary less enlightened motives of action come into play, or when there is insufficient consensus as to what constitutes the common good. The fact that America is a "compound republic," that is, compounded of separate State governments, themselves subdivided into distinct and separate departments, and the national or general ("Federal") government, also subdivided, doubles the effect of separation of powers and doubles the "security [it provides] to the rights of the people. The different governments will control each other, at the same time that each will be controlled by itself."[61] (*GBWW* I: 43, 164; II: 40, 164) In other words, the Founders anticipated that a good deal of the political and legislative processes of America would be characterized not simply by deliberation, but by contention, competition, and negotiation between regional and other kinds of interest groups.

The high-minded among us must beware of becoming too disgusted with this process, for, as the classic treatise on republican and democratic faction, *Federalist* Number 10, reminds us, the only sure way to eliminate faction would be to eliminate the liberty which provides it and liberty's blessings with their life-breath. The most volatile and dangerous of contending "interests" are those formed from various and unequal distributions of property and from differences of religion. Enlarging the sphere of the extended republic, comprehending a larger variety of economic interests and religious denominations, reduces the dangers of despotic domination from any one or few "interested combinations…In a free government the security for civil rights must be the same as that for religious rights. It consists in the one case in the multiplicity of interests, and in the other in the multiplicity of sects."[62] (*GBWW* I: 43, 164; II: 40, 164) To return to the main point, under the Constitution these political processes of contention are checked, limited, and controlled.

The Federalist, "Publius,"[63] did not confine himself merely to institutional analysis,

[T]he great security against a gradual concentration of the several powers in the same department, consists in giving to those who administer each department the necessary constitutional means and personal motives to resist encroachments of the others.... Ambition must be made to counteract ambition. The interest of the man must be connected with the constitutional rights of the place.... This policy of supplying, by opposite and rival interests, the defect of better motives, might be traced through the whole system of human affairs, private as well as public.... to divide and arrange the several offices in such a manner as that each may be a check on the other-that the private interest of every individual may be a sentinel over the public rights. These inventions of prudence cannot be less requisite in the distribution of the supreme powers of the State.[64]

In more than one place Madison remarks that in a democratic republic the power of the people, more concretely, of the majority, is the supreme power and therefore the first place where the dangers of abuse of power are to be looked for. Under a scheme wherein the presidency was not popularly elected and was much more restricted in scope than the modern presidency, the branch closest to the people and more likely to encroach on the others was thought to be the legislature. It is remarkable how infrequently the judiciary, "the least dangerous" branch, is mentioned in such discussions. That seems to suggest that either judicial review of acts of Congress was not contemplated, or that the judiciary was expected to restrain itself from dealing with political questions, inherently controversial questions, questions that were meant to be worked out through political and legislative competition, deliberation, and negotiation.

Elections

Under representative democracy the primary relations between people and government are determined by elections. For us now, thinking about elections means thinking about parties. This is one area, however, where the Framers provide no direct guidance, although one might argue that the future existence of parties could have been deduced from the arguments of *Federalist* 10 and 51.

In 1792 the conflict between the ideas and economic interests personified by Hamilton and Jefferson began to crystallize in the form of political parties. To the framers of the Constitution, this was a sinister turn of events: far from supposing that political parties were essential to the proper functioning of republican government, they regarded them as a source of weakness and division.[65] "If we mean to support the Liberty and Independence which it has cost us so much blood and treasure to establish," Washington said in 1790, "we must drive far away the daemon of party spirit and local reproach."[66]

Alarmed by the spread of Jacobinism and party spirit in America, Hamilton proposed the formation of a "Christian Constitutional Society" to promote the election of fit men to office and to perform other useful and charitable services. But,

> His supporters would not support his plan. Bayard, Hamilton's devoted follower…told him that the government of the United States was too free for any fixing of public opinion: the exertions of good men would be wasted if they made the attempt systematically to form the minds of the citizens, a task impossible to perform, but the exertions of good men would not be wasted if they performed the task of preventing the infinite evils to which the country was exposed by the selfish and ambitious intrigues of demagogues.[67]

Whatever may have been in the minds of the Founders, parties now seem to be a fact of life in electoral politics: Thus, for us at the present time, the important distinction may be between different kinds of parties. Election laws, then are critical for representative democracy to work efficiently. Three considerations come to the fore: 1) frequency of elections, or from the point of view of government, terms of office; 2) mode of representation: Should representatives be responsible to parties, to special sets of opinion-holders, or to local districts, definite sets of citizens determined by the localities they live in? 3) qualifications of electors and candidates.

In a 1948 New York election, voters line up before the polling booths. "[P]opular control over government through elections is the chief preventative of the abuse of government...."

Elections that are too frequent do not allow governments enough time to put their policies into practice and to test them. Too much time is given to the divisive arts of getting into office ("just politics") as distinct from governing. Respect for law itself is likely to decline when laws are changed too rapidly, so that following them is not given enough time to become habitual, and they come to be perceived as primarily serving the narrow and partisan purposes of their makers rather than the long range interests of the community as a whole.[68]

On the other hand, popular control over government through elections is the chief preventive of the abuse of government, and also the most practical way of keeping

broad communal concerns before the minds of governors. When majority rule becomes traditional and many or most constitutional rights secure some minority against the will of the majority, it becomes easy to disparage majority rule in favor of minority rights. It becomes easy to forget that governmental power is required to provide those securities; "and the quality, extent, and durability of such security will depend very much upon who holds…sovereign power and on what terms. Majority rule and minority rights, as Lincoln perceived, are interlocking parts of one structure of freedom."[69]

There is no simple answer to the question of how frequent elections should be. Frequency should perhaps vary in accordance with the capacities and expectations of both voters and governors. The Constitution, as we have seen, finesses the problem by dividing powers of government, and in a rather artful scheme provides different terms for different powers.

Lyndon B. Johnson during his 1948 Senate campaign. He became president after the assassination of John F. Kennedy. "The leader of broad coalitions should have the capacity to rise above ordinary partisanship..."

We have already noted how in presidential elections under the old party convention system, party leaders were forced to become aware of the opinions and pressures facing their counterparts across the country: how they learned to moderate and modify their views so as to arrive at candidates and policies capable of providing national leadership. Its replacement, the primary system, usually carried on before the great bulk of the population has concentrated on making its decision, caters to more extreme voters, party partisans, single-issue voters, and regional interests. During the general election, however, this fragmentation of the electorate is partly remedied and moderated, thanks to the Electoral College with its winner-take-all system within each state, that directs attention to the swing votes in the middle, thus contributing to statewide consensus.

The second consideration, mode of representation, concerns itself with the question whether one should aim as much as possible at representing every shade of opinion with systems of proportional representation, or is it better to have something like the American system, with its broad compromising coalitions?

Since these differences look to different qualities of leadership, they bring our third consideration into view, qualifications of electors and candidates. The most important qualification from the proportional representation point of view seems to be the ability to articulate and present the party's special opinions most clearly. From this point of view the alternatives set out in the previous paragraph appear to constitute a choice between "ideological" (doctrinal) purity and expediency. On the other hand, for the qualities of leadership emphasized by the American system, I can think of no higher model than Lincoln.[70] The leader of broad coalitions should have the capacity to rise above ordinary partisanship, as well as the capacity to find the common ground held by different interests and partisans. Most important, he or she should have the capacity to distinguish fundamental from non-fundamental principles, compromisable from uncompromisable issues, basic rights and wrongs from lesser rights and wrongs, resolvable conflicts from unresolvable conflicts. What from the point of view of the political puritan looks like mediocrity is for the Lincolnian a mutually refining mixture of justice, moderation, prudence, and courage.[71]

The electorate corresponding to such leadership should be sufficiently enlightened to live with compromises and sufficiently virtuous to make good use of their considerable liberties.

Such enlightenment, clearly, requires education, an education that is capable of exploring and comprehending the principles underlying our political institutions, that is capable of raising the questions about human nature, about nature in general and about divinity, to which those principles are answers. Such an education could help to expose those misunderstandings of liberty and rights which lead to behavior that offends or violates our natures as ethical and political animals.

Education

It has been a commonplace of common sense as well as of political philosophy, at least since Plato's *Republic* and Aristotle's *Politics,* that no polity can survive unless its citizens are educated in the principles of that polity. "Education" is here meant in its broadest sense, from the formation of habit in children, the formation of taste, to what we call higher education. Who are the educators of America? It would be nice to be able to say those who could be defined by the primacy that learning, teaching, and self-improvement have for their lives, those who might be called by the classical philosophers, and by people who have been influenced by them, like Thomas Jefferson, the natural aristocracy.[72] To speak more descriptively, however, educators in the broad sense include, of course, elementary school, high school, and college and university teachers, artists, writers, editors, parents, clergy, operatives of the mass media, the "communications industry," government officials in their educative capacities, in fact, just about everyone—heads of businesses, of departments, sports and acting celebrities—has become, in our over-theatricalized jargon, a "role model" for others. If this argument has any merit, the political ills we fly from have more than a little to do with the ills—I hope remediable—of modern education.

The political association is perhaps first of all an association of citizens, but it is also an association of families. The social pathologies connected with the depreciation of domestic virtue ("family values"), crime, illegitimacy, and the exploitation of sex and gratuitous violence on television have been receiving increased and deserved attention.[73] We need, it seems to me, some kind of rehabilitation of the sense of shame, or, at the very least, a careful look at the problem of shame, especially the connection between the private sense of shame and the principal political virtue, justice.

At the beginning of Book II of Plato's *Republic,* the great dialogue on Justice, two bold young men, Glaucon and Adeimantus, challenge Socrates to prove that it is better to be just than to be unjust. For the proof to be conclusive, the best possible case for the life of injustice must be made and refuted. They would like to approve justice because it is good, not merely call it good because some authority approves it. Both parties to the argument agree about where to look for the standard of goodness. They look to what holds true everywhere with the same force, to nature, not to any arbitrary human enactment or opinion. For most men, because they are weak, the praisers of injustice say, the evil from suffering injustice outweighs the good they could get from committing it.[74] Therefore, although they would really prefer to commit injustice, out of fear and self-interest they make a compact with one another neither to commit nor suffer it, but to adhere to the law of society. Justice then is only a poor conventional substitute for the life which is attractive by nature, the life of injustice.

How do we learn whether what the praisers of injustice say is true? Glaucon bids us to make a mental experiment: imagine both the just and the unjust man with complete license and power to do whatever they want. You would then see both led by natural desire to the same conduct. As Glaucon puts it, every nature naturally pursues its own selfish advantage as good. Law or convention alone, that which has power only because some coercive authority ordered it, not nature, which determines impersonally what is intrinsically attractive, leads us to appear to be concerned with others and to pay honor to justice. To illustrate this thesis Glaucon tells the following story: a certain shepherd, an ancestor of the Gyges that Herodotus tells about, found a ring that enabled him to become invisible. When he turned the stone to the inside of his hand he became invisible; when he turned it outside again he became visible. What did the shepherd do, what would anyone do who possessed such a ring? He contrived to have himself sent as a messenger to the king. Once at court he seduced the king's wife and with her help killed the king and seized control of the kingdom.

How, according to the story, is one to go about finding what the great guide, nature, has set down as good for human beings? It is as if what is social hides what is natural. Invisibility removes all public pressures, all social pressures, and allows one to test whether an action is good or bad in itself, regardless what other people say, think, or do about it. People cannot make us feel ashamed about what they have no way of knowing. Something that is against nature, or by nature bad, carries its own punishment along with itself, like gluttony or alcoholism. Something that is by nature good carries its own reward along with itself, like health. What about injustice? Is it really bad, or is getting caught at it what is really bad? What about justice? Is it really good, or only appearing to be just that is good?

Many influential modern thinkers have followed the Glauconian[75] way of uncovering nature, and some have tried to reinstate civil society on the basis of the radical individualism it presupposes through social contract theory.[76]

To restate the lesson of the story: When any human being becomes invisible and is removed from public scrutiny and fear of public opinion, his or her nature asserts itself and reveals human beings to be fundamentally selfish, asocial, and unjust. But, let us reflect, what does the shepherd with the magic ring do when he gets to the court? He seduces the queen, definitely a social act. He conspires with her to kill the king—also social. He makes himself king; kings require subjects; this too is social and political. Nevertheless, Glaucon might answer, do not all these so-called social acts serve anti-social and purely selfish purposes? To address the story's fundamental premise, however, what if Glaucon's shepherd was the kind of man that by nature needed to have others watching him in order to live well? If justice is a social or political virtue, perhaps it can exist only in the open where people can both see and understand each other's mutual needs and characters. Quite simply, we are not by nature invisible, we are in many ways by nature visible to one another. Furthermore, there is a capacity, which we share with other primates,[77] that links us naturally with our fellows, sympathetic imagination, the ability to imagine oneself in another's position and thereby to anticipate and to appreciate how the other might respond or react to one's own behavior. Sympathetic imagination, for Adam Smith, lies at the basis of what he calls moral sentiment;[78] it is rather obviously connected with the sense of shame.

Shame is that remarkable feeling that is both intimately private and intimately social at the same time: one's relations with oneself are intimately connected to one's relations to others, especially those others one respects, admires, and loves.[79] (Shame is possible even when one is alone with oneself in one's thoughts, since the sympathetic imagination also allows one to look upon oneself as an other.) With a view to one's behavior in relation to oneself, shame is an important natural predisposition for the virtue moderation, or to use the political language of classical psychology, self-government;[80] with a view to one's behavior in relation to others it is an important natural predisposition for the social and political virtue of justice. Yet, for all its amiability, being overgenerous to humanity may be a political mistake; Plato, I believe, did not want us to reject Glaucon's argument altogether, but rather to see it as insufficient. The mainstay of ordinary day-to-day justice is the penal law: there are quite a few people who need the help of the fear of punishment both to control themselves and to keep themselves from injuring their fellows. It is hardly higher education, but the educative functions of the penal law are not inconsiderable. One might say that to the extent that we are kept decent and law-abiding by the fear of punishment, we are *subjects* of government; to the extent that we keep ourselves decent and law-abiding with the help of the sense of shame, because we think and feel that it is right so to do, we are self-governing *citizens*.

Human beings, Aristotle suggests, are in-between beings, in-between beasts and gods. Tensions and confusions between the two poles of our natures are the very stuff of comedy, especially when the bestial and bodily shows through what purports to be an ascent to the celestial, or when the merely conventional side of the shameful gets taken for the natural. On the other hand, sophisticates who simply disparage the conventional might not be sophisticated enough. We seem to be *by nature* convention-making animals.[81] "Don't eat with your hands," children are or should be told. "Use your fork." What would be wrong (abstracting from questions of efficiency) with even dispensing with hands and feeding mouth to meat directly? Why plates? All those things that connect us more directly to the other, "lower," animals are natural subjects for comedy and for shame. Through our conventions we show off the "human difference."[82] Being laughed at makes one feel ashamed, not being laughed with; but there too one must be careful: the "beggar for laughs," the buffoon, begins to take on the odor of the stuff he dishes out, especially when he fails to discriminate sufficiently between the offensively ribald and the simply funny.

Sex, which has been a traditional subject for comedy for millennia, is also closely connected with shame. What is the difference between the bawdy of Aristophanes and Shakespeare and pornography?[83] One difference, surely, is that pornography arouses lust; the bawdy does not. What is wrong with lust? In Sonnet 129 Shakespeare tells us that

> The expense of spirit in a waste of shame
> Is lust in action; and till action, lust
> Is perjured, murderous, bloody, full of blame...
> (*GBWW* I: 27, 606; II: 25, 606)

Why is lust *perjured*? Is it not because it presents itself in a garb that decent feeling senses is appropriate only for love? That somehow love's absence is felt through shame? "Shame protects love against desire without love.... When sexual intercourse is merely the satisfaction of a sexual urge, shame insists upon the co-presence of its lack. Without love the partner becomes an observer. The more mutual the love the less it knows either shame or shamelessness."[84]

In many languages there are two words for shame: *aidôs-aischunê, pudeur-honte, Scham-Schande, pudore-vergogna.* The first in each set is that fear of disgrace before people one respects, admires or loves, it can merge with awe and reverence: it predisposes its possessor to avoid shameful acts. The other set designates the guilty disgrace felt after being caught in a shameful act. The Greek word for it, *aischunê,* is related to the word for ugly. The connection of this second kind of shame with the justice rendered by the penal law has already been discussed; the connection of the first meaning with justice is more interesting.

No political society exists without some way of distributing the advantages and disadvantages, the rewards and punishments, entailed in living together. Some ranking of the values of goods exchanged and distributed gets worked out. Implicit in those rankings are rankings of the activities productive of the goods and, most importantly, rankings of the human beings who receive the distributions and produce the goods. Some such order, called distributive justice by Aristotle, is operative in every political community, even where there might be no explicit talk about the idea of justice. The contribution of the imagination to the order of distributive justice in setting out what is to be revered and what regarded as shameful has been expressed by Kurt Riezler, my guide through much of this section, as follows:

> Every society sets up an image of man, clear or unclear, distinct or blurred. This image is formulated in theoretical terms. It is represented in remembered or idealized images of exemplary individuals who are revered as great. Usually a change in the guiding image of a society can be recognized only indirectly in the change of heroes, hero worship, and the mode of idealization. Apart from these guiding images a society sets up some negative images, images of human ways it disparages, detests, abhors. These negative images are usually more distinct than the positive; naturally so, since it is easier to make clear what man should not be. Yet even they indicate the positive, though only indirectly.[85]

"It has been a commonplace of common sense as well as of political philosophy… that no polity can survive unless its citizen's are educated in the principles of that polity."

Since the criminal and civil law serve to promote and rectify violations of the order of distributive justice, the framers of these guiding images

FIRE DRILL
STAIRCASE II² E⁶⁷ F
OUTER CT. TURN
.EFT ⁰⁺ B. 12 ST.
IGHT ⁰⁺ B. 12 ST.

LEARNING MY WAY TO
CITIZENSHIP

could be thought of as legislators in the most fundamental sense of that word.[86]

* * * * *

From the question of the formation of taste in a free society, we turn to higher education, the education of those who are more likely to be forming the tastes of the rest of us.

The situation described in the earlier parts of this paper, "our political situation," tends to support George Anastaplo's observation that

> the prudence and eloquence of the Founding Period in this Country drew upon intellectual and spiritual capital that was not adequately preserved by the education and training of the decades that followed. Lincoln and his colleagues had, by the middle of the nineteenth century, "used up" much of what remained of that intellectual capital, except as it continued to be incorporated in the plays of Shakespeare and in the Bible. A failure in sustaining our roots may be seen in what has become of both Biblical influences and classical education among us.[87]

The health of our polity, I have argued, requires a citizenry educated in the principles of that polity. To be educated in principles is not simply to have read about them in some history or text book or to be only vaguely aware of them; it means, again, to have studied and lived with the questions those principles are answers to, in this case questions about freedom, about excellence, democracy, right, reason, passion, nature, human nature, divinity, the kinds of questions raised by the books that the Framers and the educators of the Framers read: classical Greek and Roman literature, the classic books of ancient, medieval, and modern political and moral philosophy, the classic historians, the Bible, medieval and modern theologians, Dante, Cervantes, Shakespeare, Milton, the basic founding documents, The Federalist, Madison's *Notes*, and so on. The education I refer to, education for free men and women, has a name: liberal education. It has a core and requires a core curriculum.

We do not support this kind of education because it was approved by the American Framers, but rather argue that it was approved by the Framers because it is good. If we are free to the extent that we can live and act thoughtfully and deliberately, we want an education that can most fully prepare us so to live and so to act. We grow up and form our habits of speaking, feeling, and thinking within a definite already formed context of thinking, feeling, and speaking, very generally speaking, within the context of Western Civilization. Those among us, who think that they are transcending Western Civilization by arguing against it, don't seem to realize that by so doing they brand themselves as Westerners, that is, members of that rare civilization, formed by the Bible and rational science and philosophy, that allows for the rational examination and criticism of its own principles. Freely to approve, or freely to reject, those principles first of all require understanding them; they require an education in those great books, those great works of art, and those great deeds that founded and formed those principles. If aspects of that founding were not great, or high, but low, that too should be studied, but here, and especially now, a caveat is in order:

> It is safer to try to understand the low in the light of the high than the high in the light of the low. In doing the latter one necessarily distorts the high, whereas in doing the former one does not deprive the low of the freedom to reveal itself fully as what it is.[88]

Liberal education requires a liberal mode of study and teaching. That means the principles cannot be learned as a catalogue of doctrines. This civilization exists in a tension, an argument, a discussion between alternative fundamental principles: different understandings of nature, differences about whether access is gained to the principles through reason or through divine revelation, or through both, etc. Again, one approaches the principles by raising the questions the principles are answers to, and at some point later by raising the questions posed to one's text by the most important alternatives to it. The best way to open a class on these matters may be, not to provide a historical introduction, but to try to put the question the book attempts to answer directly to the students for their discussion, or to select some key or puzzling passage, read it, and ask what the author was getting at. Foundational books usually supply most of the context they require. They sometimes presuppose reading their predecessors: Plato and Aristotle expect readers to be familiar with Homer; Aquinas expects them to be familiar with Aristotle and the Bible; Machiavelli, Hobbes, Locke, raise fundamental questions about all those previous works and authors, and so on. This problem can be handled simply by reading the texts in rough chronological order.

If the books are not read and discussed *in their own terms,* they will not begin to be understood. If they are read in terms of the currently fashionable doctrine that everything written, said, or thought is primarily "ideological," that is, merely an expression of the writer and thinker's class, gender, and political interests, what one gains is some understanding of ideology theory, not an understanding of those books that are based on very different principles. Little is to be gained from any reading that does not, at least, question the dogmatic skepticism that we, modern or "postmodern" men and women, cannot learn in a way that is important for our own lives from thinkers of the past, that no thinker can do any more than represent the thought of his or her own historical situation. (The Bible, incidentally, when read liberally, that is on its own terms, holds its own quite well with modern students as a book whose claims must be taken seriously.)

The fundamental and growing dependency of human life in modern times on science, or its product, technology, pervades our thinking as well as our practical lives. Trying to understand how this great power shapes our thinking as well as our practice is an indispensable part of a liberal education, if liberal education aims at clarifying the principles by which we think, feel, and act. Once again, the best way to study these matters is not primarily to study the works of people who write *about* science, textbook writers, but, as much as possible, to study original books and papers and to discover for oneself the truths these works contain.[89]

Some representative authors are Euclid, Ptolomey, Apollonius (of Perga), Archimedes, Copernicus, Galileo, Descartes, Leibniz, Huygens, Newton, Pascal, Dalton, Lavoisier, Faraday, Oersted, Ampère, Maxwell, Lobachevski, Gauss, Einstein, Bohr, De Broglie, Schrödinger, Heisenberg, Dedekind, Hilbert, Harvey, Schwann, Roux, Driesch, Darwin, Mendel, Spemann, Jacob and Monod, and so on.

There is no better way to come to understand that the older ethical, political, and theological works have not, as is often facilely uncritically assumed, been refuted by modern science than to study modern science. Students of such a program will not fall prey to simplistic textbook definitions of scientific method. They will know that science is not a catalogue of infallible truths, but rather a fascinating field of arguable hypotheses, ingenious experiments, and open questions. Science and mathematics in such programs are to be taught as liberal arts, that is, in addition to having the students acquire the necessary technical competence, the works are talked about seriously and carefully, they are analyzed, compared, and questioned.

How is this practicable? It does require an almost all-required program. I have been describing a program I know fairly well, one I have lived with and taught in for more than thirty-five years, the Great Books Program of St. John's College of Annapolis and Santa Fe. It works pretty well, most students love it, or at least like it, very much.

At any rate, this is the kind of education available in present-day America that comes closest to the education that nourished the American Founders. There is certainly no guarantee that it will turn out statesmen, philosophers, or American patriots, but there is a good chance of its turning out citizens with some grasp of what the American Founders were trying to do, and with some appreciation of the subtlety and depth of understanding with which they did it. The long-range remedy for the ills, here explored, plaguing the American polity, it seems to me, lies in such a revamping of American education. If it happens, it will not happen overnight. To prepare for it requires work: long, hard, but highly gratifying, work.

1. *The Collected Works of Abraham Lincoln,* Roy P. Basler, ed. (New Brunswick, N. J.; Rutgers University Press, 1953), vol. II, pp. 405–6. Speech at Springfield, Ill., June 26, 1857.

2. *Essay Concerning Civil Government,* section 54.

3. Letter to Henri Gregoire, Feb. 25, 1809, *Thomas Jefferson: Writings*, ed., Merrill D. Peterson, (New York: The Library of America, 1984), p. 1202.

4. Letter to John Adams, Oct. 28, 1813, ibid., p. 1306.

5. Alexander Hamilton, John Jay, James Madison, *The Federalist,* No. 55.

6. The Preamble is carefully analyzed and explicated in George Anastaplo, *The Constitution of 1787: A Commentary* (Baltimore and London: The Johns Hopkins University Press, 1989), Lecture 2, pp. 13–25.

7. *See* Herbert J. Storing, *What the Anti-Federalists Were For* (Chicago: University of Chicago Press, 1981), and Jonathan Elliott, ed., *The Debates in the Several State*

Conventions on the Adoption of the Federal Constitution, 5 vols. (Philadelphia: J. B. Lippincott Co., 1863–91).

8. This is not to deny that sometimes it is more important to get a divisive issue settled and decided than to see that it is decided rightly.

9. In his First Inaugural Address, March 4, 1801, Writings, op. cit., pp. 492–93.

10. Basler, op. cit., vol. IV, p. 268, The First Inaugural Address, March 4, 1861, emphasis added.

11. The sentence quoted is from Lincoln's final text. This was a change from the "First Edition" version: "A constitutional majority is the only true sovereign of a free people." *See* Basler, op. cit., vol. IV, pp. 256–57 and p. 268.

12. Ibid., pp. 270–71, emphasis in the original.

13. The freedom of the people, then, according to this sentence, consists not simply in their having their will, but essentially in the clear-headed and deliberate exercise of that will.

14. Emphasis supplied. Evidently by 1838, if not earlier, Lincoln had studied *The Federalist* rather carefully: *Compare* Lincoln, *Works,* vol. I, pp. 114–15 with *The Federalist,* No. 49, the sixth and seventh paragraphs.

15. George Anastaplo, *The Constitutionalist: Notes on the First Amendment,* (Dallas: Southern Methodist University Press, 1971), chap. V. Legislatures by rules of relevance and decorum do abridge that kind of speech and behavior that would defeat the possibility of arriving at any reasonable legislation. Anastaplo faces that problem by arguing that Americans have always been at their best when extending, and at their worst when restricting, the limits of toleration for that abuse. The states, he argues, as a last resort, are, and perhaps should be, left free by the Constitution, in those rare circumstances calling for it, to abridge political speech, but, he also argues, the First Amendment does not prohibit the Congress "from regulating State abridgments of freedom of speech or of the press." *The Amendments to the Constitution: A Commentary* (Baltimore and London: The Johns Hopkins University Press, 1995), p. 54. On the fundamental differences between constitutional freedom of speech and of the press and what is now called freedom of expression, *see* pp. 52–56.

16. Joseph Story, LL. D., *A Familiar Exposition of the Constitution of the United States,* (New York: Harper & Brothers, 1859), pp. 20–22.

17. Blackstone speaks of *maxims,* "established customs...rules and maxims" and "that what is not reason is not law." William Blackstone, *Commentaries on the Laws of England,* A Facsimile of the First Edition of 1765–69, (Chicago & London: The University of Chicago Press, 1979), vol. I, pp. 68–74.

18. Anastaplo, op. cit., note 6 above, p. 138, *see also,* pp. 3–5, 124–139. *See also,* Steven H. Gifis, *Law Dictionary* (New York: Barron's Educational Series, Inc., 1984), p. 81.

19. We have here been speaking of the traditional notion of the common law. The reader should be made aware that since 1938 and the case, *Erie Railroad Co.* v. *Tompkins,* the Supreme Court has been following a very different understanding of what constitutes the common law. For students of philosophy and history this difference is quite interesting: for strikingly different practical consequences follow from very clear philosophic differences. Justice Brandeis in *Erie* explicitly follows the Hobbesian positivist views of Justice Oliver Wendell Holmes, Jr., that law is the "will of the sovereign." [Thomas Hobbes, *Leviathan,* chap. 26 (*GBWW* I: 23, 130–38; II: 21, 130–38)] Since the common law is declared primarily through the decisions of local judges, if there is a common law under this understanding, it is *made* by these judges acting as sovereigns. In effect *Erie* declares that in questions of common law the decisions of State courts rule: there is no over-arching general or Federal common law jurisdiction. Cases involving conflicts between State rules are then to be decided in terms of which State's ruling is authoritative in the case. The ruling opinion that *Erie* overrules is the 1842 opinion, of the same Justice Story we have cited, in the case of *Swift* v. *Tyson.* The understanding of law governing this traditional understanding is that law is "an ordinance of reason for the common good" [Thomas Aquinas, *Summa Theologiæ,* I–II, Q. 90, A. 4 (*GBWW* I: 20, 208; II: 18, 208)]. The *Swift* opinion, which was authoritative for almost one hundred years, declared a Federal jurisdiction under the Supreme Court based on "general reasoning and legal analogies" to decide cases such as this (commercial cases). The techni-

cal aspects of the cases and the arguments for both sides, and more importantly, the presuppositions of those arguments, are stated with great clarity in William T. Braithwaite, "The Common Law and the Judicial Power: An Introduction to Swift-Erie and the Problem of Transcendental versus Positive Law," *Law and Philosophy: The Practice of Theory: Essays in Honor of George Anastaplo* (Athens: Ohio University Press, 1992), vol. II, pp. 774–818, edited by John A. Murley, Robert L. Stone, and William T. Braithwaite; *see also,* in the same volumes, Laurence Berns, "Xenophon's Alcibiades and Pericles on the Question of Law, with Applications to the Polity of the United States," vol. I, pp. 464–77.

20. Harry V. Jaffa, *Personal Correspondence.* Cf. Plato, *Euthyphro,* 10aff. (*GBWW* I: 7, 195; II: 6, 195).

21. This problem did not require the rise of modern mathematical physics to become visible: *see* Aristotle, *Politics,* vol. II, chap. 8, 1267b 23–1269a 29 (*GBWW* I: 9, 463–64; II: 8, 463–64); Thomas Aquinas, *Summa Theologiæ,* I-II, Q. 97, A. 2, ad 1 (*GBWW* I: 20, 236–37; II: 18, 236–37); Francis Bacon, *Valerius Terminus,* chap. 26. (I owe the phrase quoted to Harvey Flaumenhaft of St. John's College.)

22. Cf. Plato, *Laws,* 731e–732a (*GBWW* I: 7, 688–89; II: 6, 688–89).

23. Cf. Laurence Berns, "The Relation Between Philosophy and Religion: Reflections on Leo Strauss's Suggestion Concerning the Source and Sources of Modern Philosophy," *Interpretation: A Journal of Political Philosophy,* Fall 1991, pp. 43–60.

24. The future significance of the enormous amount of information, opinion, and discussion available on public computer networks, the Internet, is not easy to predict. Will it remain the preserve of a minority of computer competent proficients, or become a major medium of American political "discussion"? What should its legal status be? Should legal regulation be kept to a minimum, allowing market forces to predominate? Should it be regulated as a common carrier like telephone and rail lines? Should its enterprises be regulated as managers of public assets, trustees for the public with public service requirements like substantial time for serious political discussion: electoral opposition, controversial public policy, educational, safety and medical programs? These same questions have been raised as well about television and radio. The right balance of regulations in these matters, it seems to this writer, is not likely to be achieved until the Supreme Court returns from a First Amendment policy that licenses so called freedom of expression to the more sober original policy of guaranteeing that freedom of speech that is required for more or less reasonable deliberation over public affairs. Cf. Doris A. Graber, "The 'New' Media and Politics: What Does the Future Hold?", *PS: Political Science & Politics* (The American Political Science Association: March 1996), pp. 33–36.

25. Like the "legislator" of Rousseau's…*Social Contract* (II.7), [though far less sublime], they contribute to shaping the governing constitution, despite the fact that they have no official position within it. (*GBWW* I: 38, 400–2; II: 35, 400–2) During the Vietnam War, barely articulate privates, corporals, and sergeants were assigned to read official reports to reporters. They were unequipped to deal with reporters' critical questions and tended to confirm intellectual biases about the crudity of the military mind. In the Persian Gulf War, the media and the public were briefed by highly articulate captains, majors, colonels, and generals whose impressive intelligence and civility provided reassuring evidence of the high caliber of military leadership. That leadership had obviously absorbed some important lessons about the power of the press between those wars.

26. *The Constitution of the United States,* Art. 3, Sect. 1 (*GBWW* I: 43, 15; II: 40, 15).

27. In a class on Kant's *Foundations of a Metaphysics of Morals,* to a request for an example of a "hypothetical imperative," Leo Strauss responded: "If you want to open a can, do not use a hand grenade."

28. Those intellectuals have often included five Justices of the Supreme Court. Cf. especially *Planned Parenthood of Southeastern Pennsylvania* v. *Casey,* 505 U.S. 833 (1992), section II of the opinion of the Court, and the recent tendency of the Court to strike down morally focused local regulations. "Moral autonomy…the natural child of the modern doctrine of natural rights," according to Robert Licht, is "[t]he central idea that animates the natural aristocracy of our time." "On the Three Parties in America," *Political Parties in the Eighties,* Robert A. Goldwin, ed., (Washington, D.C.: American Enterprise Institute for Public Policy Research, 1980), p. 87ff. *See* the same author's

"Respect Is Not a Right: Secular Orthodoxy and the Liberty of Conscience," *Crisis,* vol. 11, no. 7, July–August 1993, pp. 41–47.

29. *See* the article "Censorship," *Encyclopædia Britannica,* Fifteenth Edition (beginning with the 1985 printing), vol. 15, pp. 604–11. The best censorship is obviously self-censorship, the control of the less creditable side of one's self by a better side. (In a society of saints, perhaps, such control might not be necessary.) The better sides of the self have many names; a few traditional ones are understanding, conscience, reason. "In the case of freedom," Yves Simon argues, common sense provides evidence at least equally convincing as philosophic argument: "many persons, without having gone to schools of philosophy or any school, consider it obvious that a man cannot be held responsible for acts committed in sleep, early childhood, delirium, insanity, and more generally, in a state in which the reason is not in actual use. The argument which bears out this conviction can be summed up as follows: the actual exercise of the reason is a necessary condition of the actual possession of freedom." *Freedom of Choice,* Peter Wolff, ed. (New York: Fordham University Press, 1969), p. 91. For those who might argue that "now we know" that reason means only scientific reason and that scientific reason cannot substantiate "value judgments," we have suggested that in these matters (moral and political matters), the scientific model might rather be, not mathematical physics, but medicine, with a controlling distinction like that between health and sickness.

30. "Autonomy" is derived from Ancient Greek *autonomia,* which means self-legislation, self-regulation. The use of the word seems to be fashionable among those who regard themselves as going beyond traditional notions of freedom or liberty. On the other hand, "autonomy" does distinguish itself from notions of freedom or liberty, conceived only negatively, "freedom *from.*" The word "liberty" has perhaps frequently been associated with the idea of "liberation from." The words "free" and "freedom" have for millennia been associated with negative and positive meanings, freedom from oppressive or discreditable physical, political, or psychic conditions and positively, the possession of creditable powers of self-direction. Cf., for example, Aristotle, *Metaphysics,* 1075a 18–25 (*GBWW* I: 8, 605–6; II: 7, 605–6) and *Politics,* 1337b 4–11. (*GBWW* I: 9, 542; II: 8, 542) *See also,* note 13 above and its accompanying text.

31. Cf. George Washington, "Farewell Address"; Benjamin Franklin, Letter to Thomas Paine. (The letter was first published with no addressee designated.) Jared Sparks, ed. Franklin's *Works* (Boston: Hilliard, Gray and Company, 1840), vol. X, p. 36, argues plausibly that it was directed to Paine. In The Library of America edition, (New York: 1987), it appears on pp. 748–49; de Tocqueville, *Democracy in America,* vol. II, bk. 2, chap. 15 (*GBWW* II: 44, 291–94).

32. Op. cit., note 6 above, p. 106.

33. Cf. *Aristotle on Political Reasoning: a Commentary on the "Rhetoric,"* by Larry Arnhart (DeKalb: Northern Illinois University Press, 1981). Consider the traditional three forms of rhetoric: 1) deliberative, 2) forensic, the rhetoric of the law courts, and 3) epideictic, or display rhetoric, set orations; in a society influenced by Biblical religion this third type comes close to preaching or giving sermons.

34. The proffered reason for the presence of such men is bodyguard protection. Bodyguards, however, need not be so unusually conspicuous: they are obviously there as much or more for intimidation. In classical times having a conspicuously sizable bodyguard was the usual sign of a tyrant. Then too it also served for purposes of intimidation. In modern times the Nazis were most famous for artful political propaganda. Leni Riefenstahl's films, *Triumph of the Will* and *Olympia* (on the 1936 Berlin Olympics) are still worth study. Both rhetoric and propaganda would seem to be coeval with human life. The word propaganda seems first to have been used in religious contexts, referring to the propagation of the faith, instilling a conviction that was regarded as outside the sphere of operation of reason (but not, according to Thomas Aquinas, in contradiction with reason). How should one address unruly children before their reasoning powers are developed? Dr. Benjamin Spock, writing some twenty years after his notable book on child care first appeared, was concerned that in earlier editions he may have misled parents to follow overly permissive lines: with young children, he advised, it is sometimes necessary to make yourself sound like the voice of Zeus.

35. *The Federalist,* No. 1. Without underestimating the dangerously trivializing effects of the spirit of advertising, one can also see apparently counteracting trends in our

national life, e.g., the growing numbers of those seeking and gaining access to institutions of higher education, the apparently still growing religious revival. We return to these topics in later sections of this paper.

36. Paul M. Angle, *Created Equal? The Complete Lincoln-Douglas Debates of 1858* (Chicago: The University of Chicago Press, 1958), p. 88. Emphasis added.

37. Ibid., pp. 102–3.

38. One of the few national journalists who have tried to think through this portentous development is Georgie Anne Geyer, "Direct Democracy Demons," *The Washington Times,* Feb. 9, 1996, p. A 19. Along with expanded opportunities for "teletronic" democracy, "information age campaigning," come even more expanded opportunities for teletronic demagoguery.

39. In order to raise the tremendous amounts of money required for political advertising. The corruption of the political process by a seemingly unending pursuit of campaign money and the rise of political advertising are obviously connected. By declaring electoral campaign money giving to be included in the increasingly sewer-like boundaries of "free expression" the Supreme Court (in *Buckley* v. *Valeo* [1976]) has made it possible for sophistic opponents of legislation limiting campaign spending to argue that such legislation violates our free speech protection.

40. When presidential candidates were chosen in party conventions rather than in primaries, one could observe how party leaders from all over the country were forced to become aware of and familiar with the pressures and opinions governing their counterparts from different areas; they learned to modify and moderate their own preferences and objectives with a view to arriving at candidates and policies that could provide effective national leadership. The convention system put more of an emphasis on common goods and national unity, the primary system fosters special and regional interest politics. One rather deep student of the earlier party system (Austin Ranney) suggested that party "bosses" often, even usually, took a professional interest in choosing good candidates; their judgments might even be compared favorably with that of the average primary voter.

41. Cf. note 38, above. I have not made a scientific survey, but a number of the supporters of Mr. Perot I have talked to seemed to be on the whole rather decent people, who apparently deplore the controversy, compromise, and delay inherent in any deliberative process: "They talk and talk and never get anything *done.*" Robert A. Goldwin, in connection with the constitutional ratification conventions, observes: "The complexity of the representative system… as opposed to direct democracy, also had the advantage of taking much time. Quick decisions were avoided, which made deliberation and conciliation possible and likely… there are benefits in the complexity of constitutional procedures and the time they allow for citizens to understand the issues, compose the differences among competing individuals, and make their decisions." *From Parchment to Power: How James Madison Used the Bill of Rights to Save the Constitution,* (Washington D.C.: AEI Press, 1997), p. 52.

42. Classical sources for the study of natural demagoguery include Thucydides, *History of the Peloponnesian War,* vol. III. 36–50 (*GBWW* I: 6, 424–29; II: 5, 424–29), Plutarch (*GBWW* I: 14; II: 13), Shakespeare's Roman Plays, and especially *Second Part of King Henry VI,* Act IV, scenes ii–x, the story of Jack Cade (*GBWW* I: 26, 57–64; II: 24, 57–64).

43. Abraham Lincoln, Letter to General Joseph Hooker, 1/26/1863, vol. VI, p. 78.

44. *Oedipus Tyrannus,* vol. II, pp. 880–81, Cf. *The Federalist,* No. 72. (*GBWW* I: 43, 216–18; II: 40, 216–18).

45. I have tried to deal with the question of ideology in the context of a discussion of "Historicist Liberalism" in "Speculations on Liberal and Illiberal Politics," *The Review of Politics* (Notre Dame, Ind.: April 1978), vol. 40, no. 2, pp. 233–42.

46. The two most important texts are the records of the Federal Convention of 1787, especially Madison's *Notes* (*see* next note) and *The Federalist.* Madison's *Notes* recording a strictly closed meeting exhibit a remarkable freedom of discussion. Like intelligent human beings everywhere the delegates had a variety of different opinions on most fundamental questions. In *The Federalist,* on the other hand, which was published to garner support for the proposed Constitution the disagreements leading up to the final result were deemphasized.

47. *The Records of the Federal Convention of 1787,* ed. Max Farrand (New Haven and London: Yale University Press, 1966), vol. I, p. 145. The extraordinary confluence of private interest and civic virtue in America through relatively unfettered voluntary association is one of the great themes of Alexis de Tocqueville's *Democracy in America,* vol. 1, chap. V, especially toward the end (*GBWW* II: 44, 28–48).

48. *See* J. Elliott, ed., op. cit., note 7 above, vol. 2, p. 434ff. Wilson was one of the chief draftsmen of the Constitution, especially through his work on the Committee on Detail, and an original member of the Supreme Court.

49. The words here italicized are another expression of what I have earlier spoken of as the principle of excellence coordinate with the Declaration's principle of equality.

50. Op. cit., note 48 above. The paragraphs on monarchy and aristocracy are as follows: "The advantages of a *monarchy* are, strength, despatch, secrecy, unity of counsel. Its disadvantages are, tyranny, expense, ignorance of the situation and wants of the people, insecurity, unnecessary wars, evils attending elections or successions.

The advantages of *aristocracy* are, wisdom, arising from experience and education. Its disadvantages are, dissensions among themselves, oppression to the lower orders." Further comment on those passages can be found in Berns, op. cit., end of note 19 above, pp. 472–75.

51. I have been concentrating here primarily on political theatricality, which should include the sometimes educating, frequently distorting, even vicious, theatricality of televised congressional committee hearings. The growing problem of judicial theatricality, however, should be noted, the problems connected with the televising of trials. To think that an awareness that what they are doing is being observed, by hundreds of thousands, sometimes millions, of people is not going to have a possibly damaging distracting effect on attorneys, witnesses, judges, and jurors is at best quite obtuse. Supreme Court Justice David Souter has testified convincingly before a congressional judicial affairs committee about how when serving on the televised Supreme Court of New Hampshire he was led to hold back potentially revealing questions when he thought of how they were bound to be misunderstood or misused by members of the television audience. Center stage is hardly the best location for conducting a search in pursuit of contested, complicated, and frequently disguised truths.

52. *The Federalist,* No. 10.

53. Ibid. In *Federalist,* No. 10 Madison uses the term republic to convey what Wilson included under the term democracy. He (Madison) there uses the term democracy to refer to "a pure democracy, by which I mean a society consisting of a small number of citizens, who assemble and administer the government in person." Wilson speaks of "a republic or democracy, where the people at large *retain* the supreme power, and act either collectively or by representation."

54. This is probably not to be construed, as is customary today, as implying a constitutional power in the Supreme Court to review acts of Congress. The Supreme Court, then, was intended to be supreme, *as a Court,* supervising all lower courts in both constitutional and common law questions. (Cf. note 19 above.) Each branch of government was thought to have powers to resist encroachment on its own special jurisdiction. Wilson apparently accepted the notion that governmentally speaking the legislature is supreme, but the constitution determines the limits of legislative power, and the people, in accordance with constitutional amendment provisions, can amend the constitution. Cf. the records of the constitutional convention for July 21, and William Winslow Crosskey, *Politics and the Constitution in the History of the United States* (Chicago & London: The University of Chicago Press, 1953), vol. II, pp. 1014–16. But cf. John Agresto, *The Supreme Court and Constitutional Democracy* (Ithaca and London: Cornell University Press, 1984), p. 59 ff. and note, pp. 124–25; and Farrand, op. cit., note 47 above, vol. III, pp. 240–41.

55. *The Federalist,* No. 68, emphasis added.

56. Assigning Senators according to States, two each, regardless of population, is known as the Constitutional Convention's "Great Compromise." It was hotly debated, small States insisted that their "liberties" would be swallowed up by large State power, if there were not one branch of the legislature that represented States, as States, not as populations. Madison and Wilson and others opposed to the measure conceded only when it appeared that the Convention itself would break up if they did not concede. It

might be thought of as a concession by the reigning equality principle to the principle of liberty, a concession by the spirit of national unity to the spirit of regional diversity.

57. Cf. note 50 above. The Framers evidently were wary of that natural idolatry (the "divinity" that "doth hedge a king") that vaguely associates ceremonial heads of state with more than human powers. Something of that sort may still persist in modern America, as the following may indicate: Some two or three weeks after Lyndon Johnson of Texas (and an occasional 10-gallon hat wearer) won the presidency in 1964 an item in the back pages of the newspaper revealed that since the election the only two manufacturers of 10-gallon hats in the country, despite shifting to 24 hours a day production lines, could not keep up with the sudden post-election demand. Cf. Max Lerner, *Wounded Titans*, (New York: Arcade Publishing Inc., 1996) ed., Robert Schmuhl, especially pp. 13–30.

58. *The Federalist,* No. 51, Emphasis supplied.

59. *The Federalist,* No. 10.

60. Deliberation is a process of reasoning about, or "weighing," alternative actions, measures, and means with a view to how well they serve the common goods of those reasoning about them.

61. *The Federalist,* No. 51.

62. Ibid. Madison knew, according to Robert Goldwin, that the wrong kind of multiplication lead to violent disunity. Multiplicity "works for freedom only in the context of a stable society suffused with a vigorous national unity." Op. cit., note 41 above, pp. 72-74.

63. Publius was the authors' pseudonym for all the papers of *The Federalist.* It referred to Publius Valerius Publicola, known to readers of Plutarch as a saviour of the Roman republic. *See* Martin Diamond in *History of Political Philosophy,* eds. Leo Strauss and Joseph Cropsey, 3rd Edition (Chicago and London: The University of Chicago Press, 1987), pp. 660–61.

64. *The Federalist,* No. 51. In the last sentence, note the plural "powers."

65. The word party derives from the Latin *partire,* to divide.

66. John C. Miller, *The Federalist Era, 1789–1801* (New York: Harper Brothers, 1960), p. 99. In a note said to have been written about 1821, Madison remarks, "No free country has ever been without parties, which are a natural offspring of Freedom." His use of the term party corresponds more to what now would be called major interest groups, major political divisions of the population. Farrand, vol. III, p. 452.

67. Harvey Flaumenhaft, *The Effective Republic: Administration and Constitution in the Thought of Alexander Hamilton* (Durham and London: Duke University Press, 1992), p. 201, *see also,* 302–05.

68. The American system deals with this problem rather ingeniously: The fixed Constitution provides a stable legislative structure and focus for respect, even reverence, while legislation under the Constitution can change as rapidly as changed conditions call for changes.

69. Don E. Fehrenbacher, *Lincoln in Text and Context* (Stanford: Stanford University Press, 1987), p. 142. *See above,* the quote marked by note 10. For the rationale behind the framing of the Bill of Rights, *see* Goldwin, op.cit., note 41 above; and George Anastaplo, *The Amendments to the Constitution,* cited in note 15 above, pp. 33–46 and pp. 315–29 (Documents).

70. Cf. Fehrenbacher, op. cit., previous note, pp. 44–62, 87–88, 105–111, 126–128, 285–286; and Anastaplo, "The Emancipation Proclamation of 1862–1863" in *The Amendments to the Constitution...,* cited in note 15 above, pp. 135–167.

71. Cf. *Oration by Frederick Douglass delivered on the occasion of the unveiling of the Freedmen's Monument in memory of Abraham Lincoln,* in Lincoln Park, Washington, D.C., April 14, 1876: Lincoln's "great mission was to accomplish two things: first, to save his country from dismemberment and ruin; and, second, to free his country from the great crime of slavery. To do one or the other, or both, he must have the earnest sympathy and the powerful cooperation of his loyal fellow-countrymen. Without this primary and essential condition to success his efforts must have been in vain and utterly fruitless. Had he put the abolition of slavery before the salvation of the Union, he would have inevitably driven from him a powerful class of the American people and rendered resistance to rebellion impossible. Viewed from the genuine abolition ground, Mr.

Lincoln seemed tardy, cold, dull, and indifferent; but measuring him by the sentiment of his country, a sentiment he was bound as a statesman to consult, he was swift, zealous, radical, and determined." *What Country Have I? Political Writings by Black Americans*, ed., Herbert J. Storing, (New York: St. Martin's Press, 1970), pp. 52–53.

72. *See* the text marked by note 4 above.

73. *See*, for example, *The Index of Leading Cultural Indicators: Facts and Figures on the State of American Society*, compiled by William J. Bennett (New York: Simon & Schuster, 1994). It seems to me to have been insufficiently noted how the failure by government to eliminate or adequately reduce violent crime has led to a certain internal militarization of American society: I refer to the very great proliferation of evidently needed private security forces.

74. James Wilson makes an argument very close to Glaucon's to clarify the end aimed at by the Constitutional Convention, not in praise of injustice, but with a view to the liberty, perfection, and happiness of humanity. He calls a state of society without government or "civil restraint" a state of nature: "in a state of nature, any one individual may act uncontrolled by others; but it is equally true that, in such a state, every other individual may act uncontrolled by him. Amidst this universal independence, the dissensions and animosities between interfering members of the society would be numerous and ungovernable. The consequence would be, that each member, in such a natural state, would enjoy less liberty, and suffer more interruption, than he would in a regulated society. Hence the universal introduction of governments of some kind or other into the social state. The liberty of every member is increased by this introduction; for each gains more by the limitation of the freedom of every other member, than he loses by the limitation of his own. The result is, that civil government is necessary to the perfection and happiness of man." J. Elliott, ed., op. cit., note 48 above, p. 426.

75. Lest I be accused of maligning Glaucon: The reader should be reminded that Glaucon says that he develops this argument so thoroughly only so that it might be more decisively refuted by Socrates.

76. Cf. *History of Political Philosophy*, cited in note 63, Laurence Berns, "Thomas Hobbes" and Robert A. Goldwin, "John Locke."

77. Frans de Waal, *Chimpanzee Politics: Power and Sex among Apes*, (New York: Harper & Row, 1984), p. 133; Jane Goodall, *In the Shadow of Man*, (New York: Dell Publishing Co., 1971), pp. 96–97, 109–110.

78. See *The Theory of Moral Sentiments*, eds., D. D. Raphael and A. L. Macfie, Glasgow Edition (Indianapolis: Liberty Classics, 1982), pp. 9–26; David Hume, *A Treatise of Human Nature*, eds. L. A. Selby-Bigge and P. H. Nidditch (Oxford: Oxford University Press, 1978), 2.1.11; and Laurence Berns, "Aristotle and Adam Smith on Justice: Cooperation between Ancients and Moderns?", *Review of Metaphysics*, vol. 48 (September 1994), pp. 71–90.

79. Kurt Riezler, *Man: Mutable and Immutable: the Fundamental Structure of Social Life* (Chicago: Henry Regnery Co., 1950), pp. 226–34.

80. Cf. notes 29 and 30 above.

81. Cf. Laurence Berns, "Rational Animal—Political Animal: Nature and Convention in Human Speech and Politics," *Essays in Honor of Jacob Klein* (Annapolis: St. John's College Press, 1976), pp. 29–35; and Gisela Berns, "*Nomos and Physis* (An Interpretation of Euripedes' *Hippolytos*),"*Hermes*, 101, No. 2 (1973), pp. 165–87.

82. These questions and much more are explored in *The Hungry Soul: Eating and the Perfecting of Our Nature*, Leon R. Kass, M.D., (New York: The Free Press, 1994).

83. The fundamental misapprehension behind obscenity and pornography would seem to be a confusion between the properly private and the properly public. We now have the prospect of obscenity cloaking itself in the garb of liberation. Though by natural necessity still much used, the arts of silence seem to have lost respectability: Francis Bacon could speak of "that penetration of judgment as he can discern what things are to be laid open, and what to be secreted, and what to be shewed at half lights, and to whom, and when, (which indeed are arts of state and arts of life....)" *Essays or Counsels, Civil and Moral*, Essay VI.

84. Op. cit., note 79 above, p. 231.

85. Ibid., p. 229.

86. Cf. Plato, *Laws*, beginning (*GBWW* I: 7, 640; II: 6, 640); Machiavelli,

Discourses..., Book I, chap. 11; Rousseau, *Social Contract,* Book II, chap. 7 (*GBWW* I: 38, 400–2; II: 35, 400–2); Montesquieu, *The Spirit of the Laws,* Book XXIX, chap. XIX (*GBWW* I: 38, 269; II: 35, 269); Lincoln, op. cit., note 1 above, and Speech on "The Perpetuation of Our Political Institutions," Jan. 27, 1838.

87. *The Amendments to the Constitution...,* cited in note 15 above, p. 112.

88. Leo Strauss, *Spinoza's Critique of Religion* (New York: Schocken Books, 1965), p. 2. Cf. Goldwin, op.cit., note 41, above: "these highly principled, honorable, and public-spirited lawgivers were also clever, resourceful, skillful, experienced, and practical politicians, who were not above using questionable means to accomplish noble ends," p. 6.

89. Many scientific books and papers presuppose a fairly high degree of technical and mathematical sophistication. Here manuals written by specialist colleagues can help non-specialist teachers and students over technical and theoretical difficulties. In the senior year at St. John's College, for example, in studying Einstein's Special Relativity paper, after working through the meaning of a certain calculus formula, one reads, "from this it follows that," and then comes another formula. The non-specialist has no idea how that "follows," but in a manual written by a specialist colleague, for non-specialists, with one or two pages of calculus formulas it is shown how indeed that "follows." Elementary calculus is required. Elementary calculus is studied by *all* students in the junior year. Mathematics at St. John's begins in the freshman year with a six or seven months study of Euclid's *Elements.* It is taught as a liberal art, that is, it is liberally discussed. Mathematically talented students come to understand that it is part of their job to join their teachers in helping the less mathematically talented to understand. Many students who regarded mathematics as inaccessible for them, when it is taught liberally and thoughtfully, come not only to understand it, but to enjoy it. All students go through four years of the same mathematics program, and three years of the same laboratory (physics, elementary chemistry, and biology) science program.

A series of books for general readers, with aims similar to the program we are describing, is being published by Rutgers University Press, under the editorship of Harvey M. Flaumenhaft (of St. John's College): *Masterworks of Discovery: Guided Studies of Great Texts in Science.* The Series Editor's foreword presents the case for science as a liberal art as follows: "We often take for granted the terms, the premises, and the methods that prevail in our time and place. We take for granted, as the starting points for our own thinking, the outcome of a process of thinking by our predecessors.

...Questions are asked, and answers are given. These answers in turn provoke new questions, with their own answers. The new questions are built from the answers that were given to the old questions, but the old questions are now no longer asked. Foundations get covered over by what is built upon them.

Progress thus can lead to a kind of forgetfulness, making us less thoughtful in some ways than the people whom we go beyond.... The purpose of the series is to foster the reading of classic texts in science,... so that readers will become more thoughtful by attending to the thinking that is out of sight but still at work in the achievements it has generated.

To be thoughtful human beings—to be thoughtful about what it is that makes us human—we need to read the record of the thinking that has shaped the world around us, and still shapes our minds as well. Scientific thinking is a fundamental part of this record.... Only by actively taking part in discovery—only by engaging in its rediscovery ourselves—can we avoid both blind reaction against the scientific enterprise and blind submission to it.

When we combine the scientific quest for the roots of things with the humanistic endeavor to make the dead letter come alive in a thoughtful mind, then the past becomes a living source of wisdom that prepares us for the future—a more solid source of wisdom than vague attempts at being "interdisciplinary," which all too often merely provide an excuse for avoiding the study of scientific thought itself. The love of wisdom in its wholeness requires exploration of the sources of the things we take for granted— and this includes the thinking that has sorted out the various disciplines, making demarcations between fields as well as envisioning what is to be done within them." *Newton's Optical Writings: A Guided Study,* Dennis L. Sepper, (New Jersey: Rutgers University Press, 1994), pp. ix and x.

Laurence Berns has been teaching at St. John's College, Annapolis, Maryland since 1960. Among his writings on ethics, political philosophy, and literature are "Gratitude, Nature and Piety in *King Lear*," (*Interpretation*, Autumn, 1972); "Rational Animal—Political Animal: Nature and Concention in Human Speech and Politics," (*Essays in Honor of Jacob Klein*, St. John's College Press, Annapolis, 1976) and "The Relation Between Philosophy and Religion: Reflections on Leo Strauss's Suggestion Concerning the Source and Sources of Modern Philosophy," (*Interpretation*, Fall, 1991). He is currently engaged in a translation of Aristotle's *Politics* into English.

Good Housekeeping: The Real Economics of the Caribbean

Thomas K. Simpson

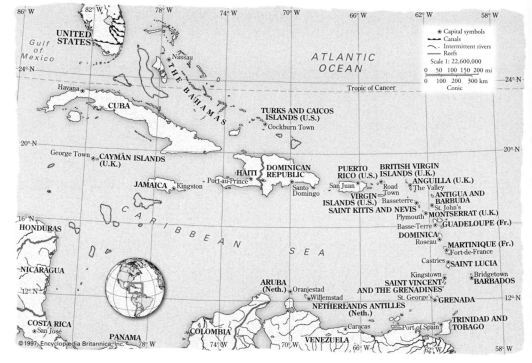

Introduction

T he present investigation begins with a reference to Aristotle, from the early pages of Marx's *Capital*. It comes in a footnote, which we may imagine to have been rescued from the fading of popular interest in the body of the work, placed in a bottle, carefully corked, and now perhaps found washed up on the shore of some quiet cove in the Caribbean. The faded text, with some omissions, can be made out as follows:

> Aristotle opposes *Œconomic* to *Chrematistic*. He starts from the former. So far as it is the art of gaining a livelihood, it is limited to procuring those articles that are necessary to existence and useful either to a household or the state. "True wealth consists of such values in use; for the quantity of possessions of this kind, capable of making life pleasant, is not unlimited. There is, however, a second mode of acquiring things, to which we may by preference and with correctness give the name of *"Chrematistics,"* and in this case there appear to be no limits to riches and possessions....[1]

(Overleaf) Uncertain anticipation and then joyous welcome are seen in the faces of a Cuban crowd before and after their first glimpse of Cuba's new leader Fidel Castro.

Marx, who was a classicist, has been a bit free in this translation; we might go further and interpolate our own suggestion concerning the word *economics* itself. The modern term is pure Greek: it speaks of the *nomos,* the rule or order, of the *oikos,* the home or household. It is thus the art of household-management, or as we might say more simply, *good housekeeping.* Aristotle does make it quite explicit that this *good housekeeping* applies to the *koinonia,* the *community,* at both the domestic and the political level. Marx's note goes on to pick up Aristotle's distinction of a true art, which works toward an end, as opposed to a mere surrogate which in this sense is not an art at all, but is preoccupied with itself and thus has lost any sense of goal:

> Œconomic, not Chrematistic, has a limit...the object of the former is something different from money, of the latter the augmentation of money....By confounding these two forms....some people have been led to look upon the preservation and increase of money *alld infinitum* as the end and aim of Œconomic."[2]

Marx is interested in what is Aristotle's essential point: true *reason* works always with a purpose, with the aim of achieving a good. In this sense the real economics is rational, and employs money only as a means. An impostor such as economics—when it is misunderstood as the art of money-making—confuses means with ends, works frenetically and irrationally to compound the means itself, and forgets that the goal was to have been the achievement of those things that are good and useful to human life.

For Marx, the insight reflected in this footnote was the seed of his critique of capitalism, and of a search to recover in the modern world the concept of a rational society.[3] For us, it will be enough to take this cast-up fragment as a hint and, proceeding from this cove that we have happened upon, to roam throughout the Caribbean in a search for Aristotle's treasure, the human good. This paper will, then, be an investigation of the "economics" of the Caribbean—taking the concept of *economics* in its proper sense as *good housekeeping,* that in the end, money as a mere means to what is useful and good, cancels out.

Karl Marx (1818–83) was the author of Das Kapital *(1867–94), which was known as "the Bible of the working class."*

The Caribbean is an appropriate choice for this inquiry, since its islands, like those of Aristotle's Aegean, constitute societies separate and compact enough to be regarded as the *communities* of our definition. Further, since they have typically gained independence since World War II, each object of our study has set out on a course of good housekeeping, defining human goals and laboring mightily to achieve them through a process which the modern sense of history has colored with the term, *development.* Half a century has given these projects time to ripen so that we may now, with our borrowed Aristotelian insight, review the record and ask how these courses of development have, or have not, proved adequate to their human goals.

We need not be complicated about this question of the human good. Aristotle has put it in terms of what is useful, and we will be on the right track if we think first of simple matters, such as food, housing, health, and education. We will have trouble getting beyond a concern for just these elements. These things, however, are in turn useful only insofar as they support lives which are fundamentally human and good, releasing heirs to the traditions of slavery and conquest from such indignities into a domain of human autonomy and freedom. The economics we will be looking for, our *good housekeeping,* is a rational art whose purpose is to pave the way for what we may speak of as authentic human freedom. We need hardly add that it is not on behalf of the few, but for those whom Aristotle calls the democratic "many," that we apply this criterion of implemented human freedom.

Virtually every island has its fascinating story, so our choice of ports of call during this journey in thought must seem somewhat arbitrary. There will be just a few, but we will visit them in an order that reflects the approaches they have taken in these recent decades to the process of development; each represents a development model, and these models form an approximate spectrum of alternatives. At one extreme lies the Puerto Rican model in which everything is done to encourage modern industry and investment and, from that point of view we will find that Puerto Rico presents an image of success; our criteria are, however, some-what different. We go next to Trinidad and Tobago where the Puerto Rican model was followed, but with greater restraint, and where every effort was being made to modulate its outcome toward democratic human objectives. Jamaica, our next port of call, for a period under Michael Manley consciously chose a "third way"—neither throwing open the doors to the free reign of capital in the manner of Puerto Rico, nor falling into the extremes of socialism. We will watch the process by which the efforts of this "third way" were undone.

Finally, we will defy all U.S. State Department bans against free travel and visit the island of Cuba, that realm which has dared to defy, it would seem, the general opinion of the whole Western world and the gathered momentum of history as well, to raise an unwelcome question. Cuba has carefully read that note out of Marx's bottle and has undertaken to ignore laws of the marketplace and ask whether economics might not be shaped rationally and directly to serve the needs of the many. At this writing, Cuba and its economic policies are in deep retreat, and a chorus of commentators would be confident that by the time this essay is read, the Cuba which pursued such an ardent question for more than three decades will have been driven to abandon their economic experiment. It sounds a bit harsh to say that, for our purposes, the outcome one way or the other will not matter. Our very difficult assignment will be to somehow contrive to disembark on that island too, at a time when the revolution was still taking its shape, and to look at the Cuban experiment from the Cuban point of view—something that is seldom done in proper Western commentary. We will be guaranteed safe passage back, but for a time we must try to see what sense has been given to *economics* in Cuba, where a curious effort has been made to achieve *good housekeeping* and implemented freedom, not for market forces or the corporations, nor for the most fortunate or cleverest few, but for everybody.

Who knows how we will fare? This will be something of an adventure, a kind of investigative piracy sharing the arrogance of Odysseus with his determination to "see men's cities, and know their minds." Presumably, in a successful outcome we will better know our own—both our cities and our minds. Embarking, then, in Pirates Cove, we journey first to Puerto Rico.

A spectrum of planning

Puerto Rico: Investment by invitation[4]

Modern Puerto Rico is in a sense a child of the New Deal—of that era of Franklin Delano Roosevelt and the "Brain Trust" in which it was widely believed that the forces of modern capitalism could be shaped with a sense of rational purpose to achieve a level of human life which other systems could not reach, but which capitalism itself could not achieve without serious planning and social guidance. If capitalism in its pure "free market" form represents, in terms of our note from Aristotle, the power of unleashed chrematism, then Roosevelt's concept was of capitalism entrained to the purposes of good human housekeeping—an effort to join the power of capitalism with rational planning for a common social good. Perhaps the outstanding exemplar of this concept, inspiring to many who grew up in that era of a happier social prospect, was the Tennessee Valley Authority, described by its director, David Lillienthal in a landmark work of its time, *TVA: Democracy on the March.*[5] Here the many components bearing on the economy of that valley were brought together in their interdependence in a process of joint planning to develop the geographic region as a whole. Though it was despised as "socialist" by many whose toes it stepped on, it demonstrated that reason could, even in the complex conditions of the modern world, bring disparate forces together to work in common toward a highly practical image of the human good. Might the TVA not serve as a

Below, left to right is the nominated governor Rexford Tugwell, Senate President Luis Muñoz Marín, and former governor Guy J. Swope.

The interior of a sugar mill. For decades, Puerto Rico's 'Operation Bootstraps' "would utilize the promise of American capitalism to transform Puerto Rico into a modern society..."

provisional image of real Aristotelian *economics* in a contemporary context?

It was apparently Eleanor Roosevelt to whom the project of transforming the economy of Puerto Rico was first brought, by Luis Muñoz Marín, leader of a new mode of social thought in Puerto Rico. He said of the new generation for whom he spoke:

> It wants to fight hunger...with social justice, operating within an economy that shall be as far as possible planned and autonomous...It wants to diversify crops, plant food...It wants to foster industrial development...It wants to give dignity and purpose to political action.[6]

The challenge was taken up by Franklin Roosevelt, and entrusted to one of the principal architects of the programs of the New Deal, Rexford Tugwell. For five years, as governor of the island, Tugwell worked to challenge the sugar barons of the old guard in Puerto Rico. His program emerged from the ferment of World War II to become the first stage of the spectacular industrial development of the island, now often put forward as a showpiece of American success in utilizing modern capitalism to achieve deliberate and transforming social goals—America's answer to the challenge of socialism and Latin-American political unrest.[7] Over the years, however, the program has been transformed into something very nearly the opposite of that planning concept which moved Muñoz and Tugwell—from a vision of real economics, to an orgy of corporate chrematistics.

At the time at which all this attention was first being turned to it, Puerto Rico presented the image of the old way in the Caribbean—a sugar economy, in the hands primarily of a few large American corporations and practicing labor-intensive agricultural methods which belonged to an earlier era.[8] The laborers who harvested the sugar crop had work, rough and low-paid as it was, for less than half the year, surviving for the balance of the year at primitive levels of rural life. Though its political status has been given a succession of formulations and Puerto Ricans have gained American citizenship, it was then and remains in essence a colony of the United States, ruled by Congress, in which it does not have voting rights.

The project which became known as "Operation Bootstraps" was a dedicated effort to begin a process which would ultimately change all this. It would utilize the promise of American capitalism to transform Puerto Rico into a modern society, combining individual dignity and political freedom, with access to good jobs in modern industries, to health, education, and housing, and to a standard of living comparable to that on the mainland. The original strategy was to do this by inviting private investment on terms which would ensure its contribution to these goals. The island inherently had a number of features which would indeed induce investment—an attractive climate, an abundant source of cheap and willing labor, proximity to the United States, a colonial status which minimized trade complications and, it must be added, the presence of extensive United States military installations which could help ensure against any risk of political unrest. To these would now be added a number of altogether new inducements, including tax and tariff concessions and infrastructural support on the part of the government—not only the customary provision for roads and services, but construction of buildings in industrial enclaves into which new industries could move without cost. During his governorship, Tugwell vetoed the tax concessions, but they became law under his successor, and as we shall see, special tax concessions have remained the centerpiece of Puerto Rico's industrial development since that time. It was supposed initially that although special subsidies and concessions would be required to lure the first investments, over time, surplus accumulated from the success of these initial industries would fund the establishment of further enterprises and development would become self-sustaining: the project was, in effect, to demonstrate the feasibility of "bootstraps" development.

With this expectation, the island government offered tax exemption to new industries for a limited period of years. New industries did in fact arrive in impressive numbers, mostly labor-intensive garment and assembly operations drawn not only by the tax advantages, but by the abundance of labor available at wages much lower than those in the United States. The United States Congress soon thereafter enacted a special provision in the Internal Revenue Code, later expanded to become what is now famous as "Section 936," which excused United States corporations from federal income tax on income earned in production on the island. In language which was intended to direct earnings toward the development of the island's economy, it required that such earnings not be repatriated, but be held in Puerto Rico—or within the possessions of the United States.

With the addition of this federal tax advantage, what was becoming the "Puerto Rican model" appeared to be working very well.[9] As the new industries sprang up, the old sugar economy declined rapidly, and rural agricultural workers migrated in large numbers to the cities. It was noticed, however, that though new industrial jobs were being created, their numbers were not nearly large enough to compensate for the massive loss of work in agriculture. From that time to the present, unemployment has run very high on the island and would be completely unmanageable if the migration to the capital, San Juan, had not been followed by an equal flow to the United States; at one point it was estimated that some two million Puerto Ricans were living in the United States, while the island population itself was only three and one half million.

It was becoming evident that the "bootstraps" model was inherently flawed. Not only had it lost all touch with the social planning envisioned in the era of Tugwell and Muñoz, but the tax privileges, intended to be temporary, were getting out of hand. Under threats by the corporations that they would not otherwise remain, the time limitations of the original exemptions from Puerto Rican taxes had to be extended; the consequence was that the Puerto Rican economy was continuing to bear financial burdens which would normally have been supported by taxes on productive industry. Further, the earnings which the corporations were required under

Section 936 to *retain* on the island were in fact effecting an escape. Two provisions of the federal code opened gaps which were not so much loopholes as gateways. First, there was no positive requirement for the actual reinvestment of earnings—they could be retained in liquid form, in *any* U.S. possession, and thus be transferred to Guam, from which outpost they could slip smoothly into the labyrinth of the global banking system. Further, accumulated earnings could be repatriated whenever the corporation ceased operations in Puerto Rico; the result was a wave of plant closures, some real and others merely nominal, as routine devices for extracting wealth.

The effect of this was devastating: it meant that the very large profits of operation in Puerto Rico, far higher than those of mainland counterparts, could be siphoned from the island. From the point of view of international exchange, it had the effect of leaving a corresponding gap in the balance between island and mainland which could only be made up by borrowing on the part of the Puerto Rican state, resulting in a debt burden which by the present time has become enormous.[10]

It was this extraordinary profit opportunity, now undisguised chrematism, which was on the one hand the driving force that made the model run with great vigor, yet on the other doomed it to fail in its intended long-term effects. What was occurring was a munificent *subsidy* on the part of the taxpayers of the United States to the corporations investing in Puerto Rico. Far from the "bootstraps" operation it still appeared in the world's eyes, it was in fact a state-subsidized bonanza for the corporations involved. On the island, the citizens of Puerto Rico found themselves subsidizing services provided to the corporations free of taxes. There seems to be, in fact, two models: the "bootstraps" model which appears on the surface, and behind it another, more realistic model which involves different forces and portends different outcomes: economic on the face, chrematistic in the working core.

We need not trace in detail the succession of events which constitute the dramatic evolution of the Puerto Rican model, having especially to do with the duality of the island's relation to the United States. On the one hand, mainland labor standards, labor unions, and minimum wage legislation gradually reached the island, erasing that advantage of "cheap and willing labor" which labor-intensive industry had enjoyed. There was as a consequence in a second phase of Operation Bootstraps a massive shift to large-scale, capital-intensive industry; some 100 of the "Fortune 500" corporations now operate in Puerto Rico. On the other hand, federal entitlement programs apply to the island as well: with its very high levels of unemployment and poverty, programs such as food stamps now play a very large part in supporting the island's population. In 1990, it was reported that where average family wage and salary income was $14,190, government transfer income contributed an additional $6,102, or 43% of the original wages and salaries, a strong clue to the island's dependence on the mainland.[11] Cumulative federal support to Puerto Rico had at one point amounted to $52 billion. What we may think of as the "deep" model underlying the "bootstraps" facade, therefore, emerges as a massive corporate subsidy program; both direct, in terms of tax concessions to the corporations themselves, and indirect, in mainland taxes which subsidize the enormous social costs on the island not borne by their corporate visitors.[12]

Striking examples of this phenomenon are the General Electric Corporation (which at one reading had some 17 plants in Puerto Rico) and Union Carbide (with 27)—representatives of two of the principal industries burgeoning on the island; electrical equipment and chemicals. Puerto Rico was becoming an arena for the conduct of very large business. Where in 1960 Operation Bootstraps was proud to have lured investments of less than $700 million, by 1976 the figure had exceeded $7 billion.[13] It was not the island, but the trick of the tax code that mattered: farming the special IRS provisions, manufacturers of electrical machinery have been able to achieve returns on investment of over 26% in Puerto Rico, as opposed to 13% on the mainland; in an extreme example, those in primary metals matched 46% on the island against 10% at home, while overall the average rate was 17% on the island as compared with 13% at home.[14] These numbers, multipliers to the profit rates of great industries, mean little to most of us; but to the true connoisseur of chrematistics they are gems finer than the treasures of the fumbling Puerto Rican pirates of an earlier era. To shift the metaphor, we are uncovering a Mississippi River of money flowing, not into, but through, Puerto Rico.

Those who marvel at the abandonment of such traditional mainland home sites as General Electric's in Schenectady, New York, need puzzle no longer: the bottom of this syllogism is that, unbeknownst to themselves, the citizens of Schenectady have been paying GE to go away! The Puerto Rican opportunity has functioned as an immense program of subsidies—not to the island, but to the corporations which have occupied it, on the part of the mainland taxpayer. The effect has not implausibly been characterized as "corporate welfare," altogether outclassing the common human variety.[15]

Here, from another point of view, is a piece of chrematistic thermodynamics: a purely monetary heat-engine running to transfer funds out of the pockets of American taxpayers and into certain corporate coffers; but those "coffers" are merely other pockets, so the whole circuit is completed on the mainland, with the excursion to Puerto Rico largely incidental. We realize, trying to navigate the Caribbean, that we have hit on an astonishing discovery concerning the mainland itself. This whole engine runs to pump money uphill and enlarge the ever-increasing gap in American society between the wealthy and the poor: exchanging, we might say, honest workshops for bankers' trade towers, or classic rowboats for large plastic yachts. Meanwhile, Puerto Rico, despite the fact that it is endowed now with large inflows of government support from the mainland, remains a social disaster: what was a stable, if meagre, mode of rural existence at the outset of the program has developed into one further, tragic instance of modern urban poverty, marked by high levels of drug use, social stress, and crime.

At the outset of the Puerto Rican experiment, the intent had been to demonstrate that we could as a society reason together to guide the economic forces of the modern world to ends which by common agreement would serve humanity well. That, we observed earlier, would have been real economics. The chrematistic inducements employed to energize the process, however, ultimately burned through and destroyed the operation. In reflecting on the destructive effect of the crucial tax inducements, we should remember how different the final model is from the original conception; Rexford Tugwell as governor, sensing what the outcome of the corporate tax exemptions might be, had refused to let that particular camel into the tent.

Trinidad and Tobago: Occupying the commanding heights[16]

Trinidad gained its political independence from England in 1962, at a time in which it was still possible to believe that the "Puerto Rican model" was a promising paradigm for good housekeeping in the Caribbean. The first prime minister of the newly independent Trinidad and Tobago was Eric Williams, a black scholar who was an Oxford graduate and at the time he was called to political office, on the faculty of Howard University in Washington, D.C. Williams shared many of the convictions which underlay the original planning for Puerto Rico, and was convinced that modern economic forces could be shaped under skillful direction to achieve the liberation of a people long subject to oppression, such as those of Trinidad.

Eric Williams led Trinidad and Tobago to independence in 1962 and became its first prime minister (1962–81).

Williams had written a book, *Capitalism and Slavery,* now a classic of economic history, in which he looked broad and deep at the structure of the slave trade and the origins there of great fortunes which in the succeeding era laid the foundations of the industrial revolution.[17] He thus had a keen eye for such powerful movements in the history of society, and was remarkably prepared to take a leading personal role in this arena in guiding the course of a newly independent Caribbean state. He would continue to do so as Prime Minister of Trinidad and Tobago until the end of his life, and in the process to wrestle with forces far too large to master, or even perhaps to comprehend.

Williams himself emphasized the difficulty of recognizing the historic forces at work in one's own time; he had written in *Capitalism and Slavery:*

These economic changes are gradual, imperceptible, but they have an irresistible cumulative effect. Men, pursuing their interests, are rarely aware of the ultimate results of their activity.

With the voice of an Elijah, he brought this historical insight to bear on the British colonial rule which he had known intimately from the point of view of the oppressed:

> An outworn interest, whose bankruptcy smells to heaven in historical perspective, can exercise an obstructionist and disruptive effect which can only be explained by the powerful services it had previously rendered and the entrenchment previously gained...

> We have to guard not only against these old prejudices but also against the new which are being constantly created. *No age is exempt.*[18]

In speaking of new prejudices, he may be anticipating in effect a new economic domain, successor in turn to the industrial era which had emerged from the colonial, and which he understood. With it would come a new judgmental spirit which, as we shall see, fell upon his own efforts on behalf of Trinidad. He himself was to meet defeat at the hands of subtle forces and new prejudices of a global economy, just beginning to take shape, which was passing in turn beyond the industrial age of which he had written.

The population of modern Trinidad consists in large part of the inheritors of two successive waves of sugar-plantation labor: first, the slaves imported from black Africa, and following them, indentured laborers imported from India to take the places of the emancipated slaves, who, once liberated, refused to return obediently to their chains. Under generations of British control, Trinidad had conformed to a colonial plantation paradigm: a vast and easy flow of wealth from the sugar fields to owners who for the most part remained in England; and a colonial political administration well devised to keep unrest under control and the system in reliable stability. Careful analysis today suggests that the deep structure of this social syntax may have survived Williams' efforts to break free from it, and that the old plantation paradigm flourishes today in a new historic form which, though more subtle, is by the same token even more severely binding.[19] It is striking that *Capitalism and Slavery* seems to warn of just such a possibility.

"Massa Day Done"

In a ringing address not long after his return to Trinidad, Williams not only attacked his immediate political opposition, a conservative party representing the interests of the old plantation system, but cast a wider net, to speak of liberation from the very concept of domination itself.[20] Condemning all such subjection of one group to another with an emotion-charged term out of the tradition of Black suppression, *massa,* he proclaimed— explicitly on behalf of both the East Indian and Black workers of Trinidad—"Massa Day Done!" For Williams, the other face of this resounding negation was a clear, positive prospect. In the historic terms we have already sensed in *Capitalism and Slavery,* he perceived a powerful new economic force at work in the world which he believed he could tap on behalf of Trinidad, working with modern industrial capitalism to place his people in power in a productive, modern society.

Here is indeed a brave attempt at good housekeeping in practice: a clear plan for an industrialized Trinidad, and an informed grasp of the practical means by which this goal may be reached. The plan is essentially that of Puerto Rico—to make the society attractive to the direct foreign investment necessary to effect this transformation—while avoiding the pitfalls associated with Puerto Rico's close binding to the United States. Trinidad would be in a position to strike deals freely with industrial capital, at the same time remaining its own political master. In this truly "liberal" spirit Williams expressed nothing but contempt for concepts of socialism emerging in Cuba, and was unwilling as well to compromise Trinidad's new autonomy by cooperating with plans for Caribbean regional organization. Trinidad would plot its own course.

Trinidad had the advantage shared by many Caribbean societies of natural resources valued in the world market; in Trinidad's case, these were chiefly petroleum and natural gas. Good planning would utilize these to the best advantage to attract capital and establish industries in Trinidad which would provide work and income for an awakened economy. Texaco, third largest of the American multinational petroleum corporations, owned a major refinery in Trinidad; with a daily capacity of some 350,000 barrels, it was in fact the largest American refinery operating outside of the United States. Though there were others, this would also remain the largest petroleum operation in Trinidad.[21] Between Texaco and Trinidad, nevertheless, there was a fatal mismatch. With respect to the fortunes of Trinidad, Texaco loomed very large indeed; but in the worldwide perspective of the multinational giant, the operation on the island played a merely incidental role. Trinidad was essentially a location of convenience for Texaco; it was no more than a way-station; geographically convenient for the processing of oil from the Middle East. This had been the real purpose of the refinery from the outset, as its products went directly to supply Texaco's own extensive marketing structure in the United States.

Trinidad could place a tariff on the oil as it passed through, and it could collect a percentage on the far smaller quantity of oil which was extracted in Trinidad. The income from several operations of this kind, termed "rents" by the economists, gave the island a source of income extremely important to it, constituting a crucial economic key to autonomy in the management of its affairs. In terms of good housekeeping, however, what further significance would these petroleum operations have for the island's economy? The number of workers required to operate a modern refinery is very small, so the direct impact on Williams' primary interest in finding good work for the unemployed citizens of Trinidad was minimal. Technical, professional, and managerial personnel were brought, of necessity, from the United States; even later, when in the course of time university graduates in these fields began to emerge in Trinidad, it was observed that a large proportion were emigrating in a dismaying "brain drain." Materials for the refinery operation came from the mainland, and on the whole the "linkage" to the island's economy was slight.[22]

Williams' plan had been to build on this industry, by encouraging foreign investment in new enterprises that would utilize the petroleum fuels or the petroleum products. He would at the same time use the government's own income from petroleum as leverage to build industrial enclaves and basic infrastructure improvements to attract further investment. He pursued such a strategy intelligently and actively; yet after a decade of faltering development it was necessary to admit its utter failure to satisfy the high hopes he had raised among the people of Trinidad. The contradiction between these very hopes and his limited accomplishment was leading to increasing unrest. Ultimately, in 1970, when a "Black Power" movement was sweeping the Caribbean, the flash point was reached and an outbreak occurred in Trinidad which scholars now judge to have been a serious attempt at outright revolution.[23]

Why had Williams' program failed? Essentially, Trinidad had no handles adequate to turn the wheels required to transform its economy. In negotiations, Trinidad could be no match for Texaco, which not only vastly surpassed the island in resources but on a world scale was pursuing strategies of its own inscrutable to Trinidad and involving only a passing interest in the fortunes of any small Caribbean island. The new industries which indeed did get underway tended, like the oil industry, to employ relatively

In 1970 the "Black Power" movement swept through the Caribbean. Here, Port of Spain police remove signs from a protest.

few people, and when the crucial hard-currency earnings balance was struck were found to be spending more abroad for the inputs they required than they brought in through sales, draining Trinidad's crucial foreign exchange reserves. For Puerto Rico, for each developing nation its reserves of "hard currency," exchangeable for dollars, is critical, since development requires capital items and materials which must be purchased abroad.

Overall, Williams was unable to compete with greater opportunities for gain that investors were finding elsewhere, as indeed we have seen in the case of Puerto Rico; the limited investment he was able to lure did not begin to address Trinidad's problems. Tens of thousands of those citizens who had responded enthusiastically to his "Massa Day" speech were still waiting to be put to good work, and when they revolted in 1970, Eric Williams found the old tables reversed; he was himself now on the side of the oppressor, using his rhetorical skills to quell hopes and suppress revolutionary ferment exactly as had those predecessors whom he so openly despised. The mood was not good as Williams after 1970 formulated plans for a new, more aggressive attack on the problem of development.

Occupying the commanding heights

Previously, the role of Trinidad's government in initiating foreign investment had been focused on provision of infrastructure. Now, convinced that this would be insufficient, Williams was determined that government must play a more forceful role, using its income from petroleum to assume ownership itself in certain major enterprises in a strategy which he characterized as "occupying the commanding heights" of industry. In his mind, this was nationalism, by no means to be confused with socialism. Its intent was to initiate economic progress where private sources were slow to move, activating private investment but not substituting for it in the long run. The government would invest in state-owned industries designed to set labor to work, and in particular, to weave the petroleum resource into the general economy. It would itself use petroleum feedstocks to make fertilizer and petrochemicals, or utilize oil and natural gas as fuel in plants for the manufacture of basic steel forms to support manufactures, or cement to support a local construction industry. The overall vision was to convert government petroleum earnings into state ownership in critical new industries, and thus to stimulate progress toward a vital and truly autonomous Trinidad.

At first, fortune smiled on Williams' new program, for it was shortly after the launching of these bold enterprises that the OPEC initiative caused oil prices to soar, and with them, the government's income from these rents. Suddenly, immense sums became available in hard currency to equip new factories, which sprang up rapidly. Furthermore, the directors of these new corporations found themselves in a position to command credit in the European market, and soon began to tap this beguiling resource as well. There was a sudden, undeniable sense that Trinidad was swimming in cash, that was finding its way by many innovative channels into consumer

pockets: expenditures for such items as travel abroad and consumer dura-
bles began to soar.

A certain atmosphere of irresponsibility inevitably contributed to inefficient and inept management at many of the new enterprises; balance-sheet
discipline was relaxed in the face of all-too-easily acquired support from
government coffers. It must at the same time be acknowledged, however,
that there was good reason to expect management to be awkward and
technology insecure in these early days: with breathtaking speed, Trinida-
dians were taking on responsibilities for which they had had little preparation. Allowance would need to be made for a long and erratic learning
curve, during which the new endeavors might be forgiven if their efforts
were awkward.

It should also be remembered that these endeavors were serving a double
purpose: in chrematistic terms, to pave the way for a thriving capitalism,
and thus to succeed by market analysts' measures, and at the same time, in
terms of good housekeeping, to provide steady work at new, higher levels,
and to begin a transformation of the lives of the people of Trinidad. Some
financial compromises, by way, for example, of price subsidies, and some
latitude and "inefficiency" in terms of labor costs for extra hirings, would
be expected if the second objective were to be achieved. Prices charged for
electricity could plausibly be subsidized as a service to both consumers and
the new industries, with the utility allowed to run at a loss covered by
government funding as a matter of sound social policy. Both Trinidad's
economy and society were being turned around together, and in a very
short time.

That time proved shorter than the situation demanded, for prices in the
oil market soon plunged as suddenly as they had risen. Further, Texaco for
reasons of its own was abandoning Trinidad, and with it would go a large
portion of the funds to support the government's efforts, no matter what the
price of oil. Trinidad, it soon developed, was to suffer the effects of a
gigantomachy—open combat among multinationals in the great global
marketplace. Texaco, foiled in 1984 in a desperate effort to take over Getty
Oil Corporation for the sake of its petroleum sources, lost an overwhelming
lawsuit in a New York courtroom and was struck down by a judgment
against it of more than ten billion dollars.

As a consequence, Texaco, third largest of the American petroleum
majors, filed for bankruptcy and ended up in receivership.[24] In the ensuing
reorganization it shed the Trinidad refinery, which no longer suited its
global plans. As a result, Trinidad has been left with ownership of the cast-
off refinery, which it essentially continues to run at a loss rather than
abandon as scrap. The entire episode suggests that when a nation such as
Trinidad and Tobago enters the realm of the new global marketplace, it is
matched against entities far beyond its power to influence, pursuing hectic
strategies unrelated to its welfare.

In Trinidad, fledgling industries, unable to show profits, still required
subsidies the government could now no longer afford; a foreign debt had
already been incurred on which interest payments constituted a new bur-

den. Labor and consumer expectations which had once been encouraged now had to be quelled, while major construction projects would remain unfinished for years. We recall that Eric Williams had once written of economic changes which are "gradual, imperceptible..." but with "an irresistible cumulative effect," warning that "No age is exempt." The emergence of the post-war global economy has been such a change, now peopled with authoritarian corporations beyond the scale of nations and indifferent to their fortunes. Williams may have found himself defeated by such a new, dimly perceived yet seemingly irresistible birth, and we may in turn do well to learn what we can from his experience.

How to read a World Bank Report

Following Williams' death in 1981, reportedly in disillusionment and despair, successive governments turned away from his bold efforts to use the government of independent Trinidad and Tobago to "mount the commanding heights" of the economy or to employ government planning and initiatives. In 1983, a physician, in the form of the World Bank, was summoned to Trinidad's bedside and four years later in 1987, the Bank issued a thoroughgoing diagnosis of Trinidad's economic pathology, with firm suggestions for corrective procedures. Trinidad has since that time became a subscriber to the Bank's financial policies, and has thus been swept into the stream of the new global economy as a small but fully conforming participant.

The Bank's 1987 report was by implication deeply critical of the economic policies implemented by Williams and his government.[25] To be sure, a World Bank Report is the work of undoubted experts, who have taken the time to examine the workings of an economy in scrupulous detail; its findings in this report must therefore carry great weight. It is indeed an excellent corrective to ill-founded or idealistic speculations, for these world bankers are by definition masters of their business! On the other hand, it is essential to ask, what *is* their business, in relation to the purposes of an independent Trinidad? The World Bank, as is well known, serves as the anteroom for the international bankers of the world; it does not itself move the majority of aid funding, but its stamp of approval is critical for any nation in obtaining credit, whether from the International Monetary Fund or from private bankers the world over. Banking is a business, and it would not be controversial to assert that the purpose of the banking business is to make money; Trinidad appears here as an applicant for loan endorsement, and the function of the Bank's experts is to examine it as a prospective customer—as an opportunity for banks to make money—or insofar as it is not yet creditworthy, to advise it concerning courses of action by which it may become so.

The analogy to the physician is helpful, for the Bank has a genuine and highly professional interest in the patient's health. But this is veterinary medicine: the Bank is in the position of the shepherd, expertly appraising the sheep. The shepherd is inherently uninterested in the liberation of sheep; his interest is in mutton and wool.

Overall, the Report criticizes Trinidad for its "dependency" on oil revenues, which it observes with undoubted truth to be unstable and unreliable, and whose rise and subsequent fall account for the "plummeting" and "tailspin" of Trinidad's fortunes, landing it in the plight for which the Bank chides it. There is a strong moral tone in this; reproach is heavy in the Bank's prose. We can hardly repress the thought that Kuwait and Saudi Arabia are hardly reproached for their similar dependence on the same volatile commodity, nor Rockefeller or Mellon, family pillars of the very banks the World Bank serves. It is not in truth a moral issue; money can be made off of volatile substances. What the Bank does not like is the fact that access to oil revenues short-circuits Trinidad's dependence on the world banking system. Insofar as Trinidad continues to be able to finance its own needs from its own source, the banks get nothing out of it. "Dependence" on oil revenues is "independence" of the banking system.

Trinidad's old economic plan is further scolded for encouraging what the economists call "import substitution," instead of production for the global marketplace, and a number of its recommendations are aimed at reversing this policy. "Import substitution," however, is inverted rhetoric for building an integrated economy at home. Local steel and local cement, in Williams' plan, could be employed in local construction; if this is done with low-priced gas or subsidized electricity, that may create a loss to the gas account and cause the utility to show a deficit and be branded as "inefficient"; but it becomes a positive entry in a kind of social accounting which is never obvious to observers, and it means productive work for the engineers and architects of Trinidad. To reread this report from the point of view of the people of Trinidad, we seem called upon to perform a topological trick: interchanging means and ends. We may accept the report's columns but turn them, like a jacket, inside-out—in the process, transforming chrematistics into economics.

The Bank demands that the government tighten its belt and the belts of all its component industries and those of its citizens as well, by cutting wages and lowering what may be called the *social wage*—the basket of services and life-supporting provisions which include health, affordable housing, inexpensive fuel, electricity and transportation costs, and access to secondary and higher education. The Bank would have all these cut back, wages reduced, health services and education charged for, consumer prices raised. Taxes on investments and corporations as well as rents on the oil stream, which had supported this new prospect for Trinidad, would be cut so as to encourage greater investment by foreign entrepreneurs. Finally, by securing what the Bank regards as the essential right to repatriation of earnings, the forces of the global economy would be guaranteed the unrestricted right to extract all profits earned, and keep the people of Trinidad, like those of Puerto Rico, in their designated places. We can see the sense in which the commentator we alluded to earlier proposed that the deep structure of the old plantation system remain in place, latent behind a new facade.[26]

Carnival in Trinidad

There was good cause for celebration when U.S. Secretary of State, Warren Christopher, made a historic stopover in Port of Spain in the spring of 1996. For nearly a decade, governments of Trinidad had carefully followed the path laid out for them by the World Bank and the results were indeed impressive. The secretary was able to join the recently elected Prime Minister Basdeo Panday in contemplating a dazzling array of victories for American corporations in Trinidad, which had become in recent years the most fully industrialized nation in the Caribbean, second only to Canada as a target for American investment. The secretary, completing a five-nation itinerary of "democratic" nations granted favor by the United States, a list which included such dubious entries as Chile and El Salvador, remarked:

> Democratic governments and open markets are bringing stability and prosperity to those countries. Now this extraordinary progress extends to the Caribbean—and nowhere is it more apparent than here in Trinidad and Tobago. The success that we see here in meeting the challenges of a multiethnic democracy and the *economic reform* that has *lifted your people* is a very stirring thing to watch ... Trinidad's economy, already the fastest growing in the Eastern Caribbean, is a *very strong magnet* for foreign investment. Our delegation and the prime minister will inaugurate new investments by the United States that will reinforce our role as the country's leading investor.[27]

The prime minister, in response, expressed the deep gratitude of his people for the benefactions of the United States, his deferential rhetoric acknowledging the lofty judgment in the secretary's choice of the word *reform*. At a ceremony the next day, the American ambassador added without exaggeration that "the Trinidad and Tobago business directory really reads like the Who's Who of corporate America." One of the enterprises being celebrated was an impressive installation designed to load Trinidad's natural gas supplies, after suitable liquefaction, onto boats for delivery direct to Boston.

There remains only the question whether this fulfillment of the bankers' dream really has "lifted" the people of Trinidad and Tobago in whatever way it may be that the secretary had in mind. Some things indeed had gone up: poverty and crime have increased, and unemployment, which was high enough in 1987 to draw the passing notice of the World Bank, has reached new levels.[28] The cost of basic goods and services has likewise risen, but the secretary would be disappointed to learn that other things of immediate concern to the people have gone down. Per capita income and the real wages are notably lower; indeed one cause of a general fall in the social wage is the attainment of a principal objective set forth by the World Bank: the government's budget is now in balance, making Trinidad an exemplar of an attractive banking customer. Indeed, while social services are drastically reduced, and daily caloric and protein intakes had fallen by 12 and

The World Bank "criticize[d] Trinidad for its 'dependency' on oil revenues, which it observe[d] with undoubted truth to be unstable and unreliable…"

22% respectively during one five-year interval in this period of adjustment,[29] payments to the world's banks have been most strictly attended to: the total amount extracted by the banks as debt service on foreign loans in 1995 was $444,000,000. The World Bank's plan for optimum operation of the steel industry, according to the projections contained in their report, was to contrive a flow of profits more than 70% greater than total wages and salaries by the year 1991. By contrast, over the period from 1980 to 1992, expenditures on health services were actually reduced 62%.[30]

It is not important for our purposes to multiply evidence of this pattern, which the Secretary finds so uplifting to the people. The *chrematistic* indicators are all cause for satisfaction. But when low rents for natural gas resources and low taxes and minimal interference with "open trade" have done their work in attracting investment "partnership," those other, less-celebrated indices of the state of good housekeeping fall into disarray.

The scolding tone of the World Bank's Report and the moral reproach in the secretary's choice of the term *reform*—a word now on every commentator's lips, as if deviation from the rule of free-market economics were thought to be some form of decadence—suggests that we are meeting here the lofty judgments of a new, pervasive prejudice, in effect just the new colonialism of the sort which Eric Williams originally predicted the world might inherit, unnoticing, from an older order.

Jamaica and the "third path"[31]

Once again, we consider a Caribbean society striving to attain a freedom which at last seemed within its grasp following World War II. This time we turn to Jamaica, which for a while followed a development model distinct from either of the two we have discussed thus far. There are many fundamental similarities between Jamaica and the others: each entered the modern world out of an inheritance of enforced labor in the fields of sugar plantations, and for each, the first half of the twentieth century was spent in a mode of political and economic tutelage of a colonial system. In Jamaica, the population today consists principally of more or less direct descendants of African slaves, so that in a sense Jamaica poses our question of real economics in pure form: with such a solid picture of gross servitude in their past, what kind of life are these free people able to look forward to today? It does not take long to discover that though it is a land of music with a life often vibrant in spirit, in elementary terms of the provision of the means of existence, or of equal access to the opportunities of the modern world, it has been a life of poverty, stark depravation, and injustice. How are the people of Jamaica to achieve that freedom which their legal emancipation so long ago promised to them?

I suspect the question is not quite clear, but a bit abstract. Let me sharpen it by quoting from a recent report which describes conditions that remain today, despite the efforts described in this section:

> ... downtown Kingston resembles Beirut ... with burned-out shells of abandoned buildings and dense smoke curling up from the sooty coal yards where the sufferers turn scarce hardwood into cooking fuel. There are a half-million people sweltering in shanties and tenement yards without toilets, waiting for the cholera epidemic that public-health officials know will soon come ... [32]

I refrain from quoting further, the account becomes too graphic. We are speaking of the inheritance of the West Indian slavery, which a scholar, carefully weighing the numbers, has concluded could only be described by the word *genocide*.[33] This is not being recalled here as a moral issue—our moral memories are written in water—but other memories, those of property, are of iron. Not often is a dollar of an inheritance overlooked, and though the great fortunes of the Jamaican buccaneers or the sugar planters may disperse, they are seldom unaccounted for. It is the other side of that coin that is our present concern: those who were torn from Africa to be transported as chattel on the slavers and sold on the auction block without possessions. When they died in the fields they left that same nothing to their descendants—and that *nothing* remains the Jamaican people's inheritance today. It is that legacy of sheer want, unalleviated by any significant opportunities to earn and save from then until now, that haunts the slums of Kingston today. There were no reparations to accompany emancipation.[34] So when we turn to look at a development model for Jamaica, it is this human outcry, not a formula out of the economics texts, which must trouble our thoughts.

Even under slavery Jamaican labor had always been restive; in the early decades of this century a tense equilibrium had been established between new generations of independent black workers and unyielding plantation managers. In more recent decades a fighting spirit out of the tradition of

British labor had found root in Kingston under the leadership of Norman Manley, combining a drive for genuine freedom with a vision, that of democratic socialism, of a better way to run a society for the benefit of the majority rather than the few. It was Manley's son, Michael, elected as prime minister in 1972, who reintroduced onto the contemporary scene the prospect of a social-democratic "third path" for Jamaica. It would be socialist in the sense that the state would own and run a number of the primary means of production, but limited in that throughout the remainder of society, private ownership of the means of production, governed by the profit motive, would continue. The political system would become fully "democratic," not only in the formal sense of free speech and equal electoral rights, but in the stronger, more difficult yet crucial sense of assuring true access to education and opportunity. By contrast with the Puerto Rican model of capitalist development by open invitation, or Trinidad's failed effort at a more restrained version of that model, we now track the fortunes of Manley's middle path, his "third way" of democratic socialism. Jamaica, attempting a middle course internationally as well, led a growing non-aligned movement in an attempt to avoid entrapment by either of the two competing alliances of the Cold War, that of the Western powers, or that of the Soviet bloc.

Manley's first dramatic moves to implement these plans, two years after taking office, aimed to gain for Jamaica greater participation in its bauxite industry.[35] Bauxite, which had been discovered in Jamaica in 1950, is the primary ore from which aluminum is extracted. Aluminum itself had come into its own for military purposes during the war, and with conversion to peace it had taken its place as the miracle metal of the future. All six of the vast, vertically-integrated transnational corporations dominating the industry (the "Six Sisters" of aluminum, among them the American firms ALCOA, Kaiser, and Reynolds, and the Canadian ALCAN) were operating in Jamaica.

In the production of aluminum, pure aluminum oxide, or *alumina,* is first extracted from the bauxite ore; aluminum is then extracted electrolytically from alumina with the expenditure of large quantities of electrical energy; aluminum production therefore centers on sources of massive hydroelectric power. Jamaica was involved with the first two phases, but not the third. The original ore is obtained in Jamaica relatively easily through open-pit mining, with the result that extraction of the bauxite represents an even smaller fraction of the total value of resulting aluminum products than does the primary extraction phase in most other such in-

dustries. It was important to Manley, therefore, not only to gain for Jamaica greater economic participation in this first phase, but to go on to develop further the higher-level refining of alumina within Jamaica in order to gain fuller participation in the value-stream originating with Jamaican ore.

The manner in which Jamaica took command of the industry is significant as spelling out the principle of the "middle road"—it nationalized the

Above, Michael Manley, prime minister of Jamaica from 1972–80 and 1989–92. Below, "In Jamaica, the population today consists principally of more or less direct descendants of African slaves..."

mines, but at the same time, in a spirit of cooperation with the corporations, leased the same properties back to be operated by their original owners for a period of forty years. The rate for this lease was set at a reasonable percentage of the purchase price, which had itself been set at a generous level in order to obviate complaints from the corporations. This was a procedure meant to be neither confiscatory nor a challenge to the concept of private industry—it merely asserted the principle that the ore belonged to those Jamaican people, who had a right to lay claim to a fuller share of its value and a voice in decisions about modes of its use; but it attested as well, in a spirit reminiscent of the dreams of Tugwell and Muñoz for Puerto Rico, to a willingness to work with the corporations in the joint development of the resource, with an eye to social goals as well as to private profit.

Bauxite, the primary ore from which aluminum is extracted, has been Jamaica's main mineral industry since the early 1950s.

Manley's initiative was greeted with unanimous protest on the part of the corporations. And just as had Trinidad with the petroleum industry, Jamaica found itself at a complete disadvantage in any contest with the massive resources of the transnational corporations with which it was called upon to deal. Not only was the total income of the government of Jamaica on the order of 3% of that of just three of these corporations, but, though Jamaica at the time supplied some 18.8% of the world's bauxite resources, aluminum is widely distributed over the Earth's surface, and the corporations could, as they were soon to demonstrate, turn freely to other sources whenever Jamaica's mode of operation did not suit them.[36]

As is the general rule in the relation of underdeveloped countries to their own resources, Jamaica was without expertise or experience in the aluminum industry. Out of this recognition was born the Jamaica Bauxite Institute, one of the first findings of which was that the nation's bauxite reserves had been grossly underreported by the corporations. There were other Caribbean producers in a similar position—in particular, Guyana and Suriname (at the time third and fifth in the world's production, as Jamaica was second)—and on the principle that only through combination would the small nations be able to stand up to the corporations, Manley took the lead in forming an International Bauxite Association, a producers' association which might insist on a larger share of the industry's immense economic flows to the countries in which the resource originates. Manley's effort with the Association failed, however, since Guyana refused to join, and Australia, the world's largest producer, identified rather with the metropole and refused to be governed by Association guidelines.

The central problem, here as elsewhere, lies in the *terms of trade*—in essence, the relation of prices paid in the hinterland for primary raw materials, to the prices of products imported by these same countries from the metropolitan centers.[37] Myriad factors enter into the balance struck, but a time-honored undertow has in every category established ratios radically tilted against the hinterland, in favor of the metropole. It is simply assumed by the global economy that countries such as those of the Caribbean as if by nature deserved, and will be forever content with, the discounted lives they have always lived. Without interventions of the sort Manley envisioned, market forces will never act to correct distortions of this kind in the terms of trade, for there is no motivation whatever on the part of the market-makers to alter a situation at once so satisfactory, and so seemingly God-given.

It is easy to understand the lightning response of the industry to Jamaica's initiative. It was enough that the corporations, quite rightly, perceived here a move toward "socialism," and it was that irritant, rather than any question of the reasonableness of Manley's actual terms, against which they reacted. The corporations struck back, in effect, against Manley's democratic-socialist model with a model of their own, which was the negative image of his. Where he was undertaking to *build* an economy, they set out on a course of destruction which we may call the *destabilization model*. As the negative image of his efforts, each of its elements almost directly matched one of the steps of Manley's model in order to cancel its effect.

Manley's development model would encourage and expand production, and make the aluminum industry a mainstay of a progressive Jamaican economy. Running the model in reverse, the corporations cut back Jamaican production out of proportion to other sources elsewhere, thereby effectively negating Manley's projected earnings and undoing his budget. When, to cover their own losses in an overall market that was declining, they compensated by raising aluminum prices to consumers, they denied Jamaica its proportionate producer's share of this largesse. To rub salt into that wound, they engaged in a public-relations campaign falsely suggesting that the price rise, actually a piece of industry collusion to compensate for reduced volume, was a consequence of the rise in Jamaican taxes.[38] It was suspected that the mining companies may have deliberately provoked strike action and labor unrest in order to create turmoil with which Manley would have to deal within his own ranks. In all of these departments the destabilization model worked very effectively to defeat exactly those elements of the Manley plan which related to the development of bauxite, and managed at the same time to create ill-will for Manley internationally, and unrest at home.

Though we have described the "third path" with respect to Jamaica, Manley was making an attempt to break an overall pattern of dependence in which the interests of Caribbean peoples were collectively joined. Manley was prepared to test the right of Third World nations to exercise sovereignty in defiance of the demand that each identify its policy with one or the other pole of the Cold War power struggle; in the case of the Caribbean nations, the demand was unequivocal that they echo the policies of the United States. The issue came to a head with the requirement that Jamaica join the United States in its denunciation of Cuba's support for Angola. The United States was giving full support, largely covert, to the South African apartheid regime, and in particular to the South African attack on Namibia and Angola. Cuba, despite its own limited resources, was sending volunteers and giving what support it could to the Angolan people, with whom many blacks in Jamaica, as well as in Cuba, had sound reason for feelings of affinity. Manley would not join in the chorus of denunciation of Cuba.[39]

The issue became sufficiently serious in the American view to cause Henry Kissinger to visit Manley in December 1975, to deliver what proved to be a critical ultimatum: a $100,000,000 loan to Jamaica was pending, and Kissinger suggested strongly that the fate of this loan, of crucial importance to Jamaica, might depend on Manley's repudiating his position with respect to Cuba and Angola. This was a test: would Jamaica accept the subservient role the United States demanded and expected? Five days later, to Kissinger's outrage, Manley wrote that Jamaica would continue its relationship with Cuba, and its support for Angola.

It is possible to now recognize this moment as the beginning of the end for Manley. What had been a confrontation with the powers of the aluminum industry now became total engagement with the United States, where the destabilization model, albeit covert, became a primary concern of national policy. In particular, where the Jamaican development model depended fundamentally on the development of domestic *order,* and aimed at the cultivation of a more functional democratic process, the destabilization model sought the reverse: to create both the reality and, even more importantly, the domestic and international impression of *disorder,* and to throw the democratic process into whatever disarray it could by means of disharmony and armed violence—all with the single aim of unseating Manley.

The development plan's economic projection included as one crucial element the cultivation of a growing tourist industry, for which Jamaica's extensive beaches are excellently suited. The tourist industry, however, so dependent on the world's impressions, is particularly sensitive to acts of destabilization. To strike directly at this point, the destabilization plan therefore called for the orchestration of terrorist bombings, which would not only constitute a direct physical threat to tourism, but with professionally managed emphasis in the world press, would create the impression that Jamaica was an altogether unsafe tourist destination.

We must pause to acknowledge that we are dealing here with one of the principal factors on the contemporary global political and economic scene, one which we will need to take into account often in the remainder of this essay—but one which presents at the same time special problems to the historian because of its aspect of stealth and disinformation. This is of course the Central Intelligence Agency of the United States—known throughout the world as the CIA, and in Latin America, without affection, as "La Cia." The full name being too long, and the brief form perhaps too casual for such an entity, let us call it here simply, "the Agency."

"Agency," as Aristotle might remind us, is a term to be predicated relatively: an agent is the agent of something. In this case there is no question whose agent the CIA is, for there is no corner of our constitution in which it can hide except among the powers of the Executive: the president of the United States is ultimately and absolutely responsible for the Agency. Elaborate scaffolding of deniability is routinely constructed around its activities, as if to "protect the president," but this will not do, for if it is the president's responsibility, he is either knowledgeable and thereby responsible, or has chosen to remain ignorant, which is worse. The Agency's activities in destabilizing Jamaica are therefore the work of the presidency—an important question, as they appear to involve terrorism and the introduction of armed violence to disrupt democratic processes. There may surely be times at which in the byzantine obscurities of international affairs, terrorism is to be recommended, though I presume Jamaica is clearly not one of them. To pursue this question of the role of the Agency and the direct responsibility of the American presidency for its regime of horrors would be a matter for another, unpleasant, and very difficult study. Here we shall refer simply, where necessary, to the operations of the Agency.[40]

Edward Seaga unseated Michael Manley to become prime minister of Jamaica from 1980–89.

To destabilize the Manley government, then, it is reported that the Agency dispatched a certain terrorist bombing expert, who was a former secret police officer under the Batista regime in Cuba and a veteran of the Playa Giron invasion of Cuba and, involved as well with the bombing of a Cuban civilian flight out of Trinidad. The bombings occurred as planned, the effect in the press was managed as intended, and the tourist element of Manley's plan—rather than growing as a crucial source of foreign exchange—suffered serious declines—13% in the first year of destabilization (1976), and a further 10% in the following year. Combined with the losses of bauxite income due to industry cutbacks in the same two years, this meant an extremely serious loss of foreign exchange earnings, which translated immediately into an inability to accomplish social goals which were themselves of the essence of the social democratic development program. Many factors were involved in these outcomes, but it is clear that the Agency's efforts contributed significantly to Jamaica's accu-mulating problems.[41]

When Manley found his government in such grave financial crisis, he turned, as most Third World nations eventually must, to the International Monetary Fund (IMF), close partner of the World Bank, whose role in Trinidad we have seen. The IMF plan for Jamaica demanded cutting back government expenditures in virtually all areas, one of which, price supports for essential foodstuffs, immediately affected nutritional levels in Jamaica. Destabilization had helped to force Jamaica to the IMF; the IMF in turn, which is able to dictate standards that must be met in order to qualify for loans, would operate, if only incidentally, to destroy the social purposes at the heart of Manley's plan. Manley's government struggled against the combined forces of these two engines, the destabilization process which remained in full operation, and the IMF conditions and strictures, but it could not prevail. Manley lost an election in 1980 to the conservative Edward Seaga, a friend of Ronald Reagan's. At this point, the "third path" model was lost to view, quite possibly never to be seen again, while a new model began to run in its stead.

This new model is in many respects exactly the inverse of Manley's democratic socialism—privatization replaces nationalization, emphasis on support for social purposes is replaced by measures to curb government functions and expenditures; emphasis on social stability, essential to the security of investments, replaces enlargement of the democratic process. Criteria of fiscal soundness, in general, replace social concerns. The two models concur in the desire to stimulate foreign investment and loans, but the two visions of the means of attractions, and the society which will ensue, are opposites. If we are to identify the neoliberal model which lay behind the World Bank analysis discussed earlier, as chrematistic, we should acknowledge that its advocates argue in effect that sound chrematis-tics is the only possible path to good economics in our Aristotelian sense, and that projects such as Manley's democratic socialism, paying too little attention to the laws of chrematistics, are doomed to failure.

If there were any doubt that political considerations affect investment and production decisions in the aluminum industry, the contrast between the experience of Jamaica during the destabilization era, and the years immediately following the election of Seaga, relieves it. As soon as Seaga took office, everything was done to stimulate bauxite production in Ja-maica.[42] President Reagan personally intervened to insist on massive gov-ernment purchases of bauxite to be added, arbitrarily, to the federal stockpile, violating any number of laws and procedures which stood in the way, including competitive bidding, to ensure that the business go to Ja-maica (as well as, of course, to two major corporations involved). Alto-gether some 3.6 million tons of bauxite, equivalent in total to nearly one-third of a year's normal production, were mined for this account, at a cost estimated at $100,000,000. Later, it was found possible to waive federal insurance limits in order to provide a $50,000,000 guarantee for new indus-try investment in bauxite mining in Jamaica. The floodgates of credit

support were opened as well, and the $100,000,000 loan previously with-
held was released now that Jamaica had elected the government Washington wanted. While total United States support in the final years of the
Manley administration had been throttled back to $56 million, within five
years federal funds totaling $679 million had arrived in support of Seaga.

Endorsement on the part of the United States assured access to other credit
sources which had been sealed to Manley. Historian Clive Thomas writes:

> ...it is common knowledge that the Reagan administration used its influ-
> ence to secure funds for Jamaica through multilateral institutions like the
> IMF, the World Bank and the Inter-American Development Bank.[43]

The enormous leverage applied to this one island during those years
attests to the value Seaga's support would have for American policies in
the Caribbean: it has been computed that on a per-capita basis more aid
was pumped into Jamaica during those years than to any other nation with
the exception of Israel![44] Seaga indeed provided the quid pro quo expected
of him in the sphere of foreign affairs, cutting relations with Cuba, supporting America's Caribbean showpiece, the Caribbean Basin Initiative, and in
domestic policy, rigorously cutting back social programs and adopting
fiscal policies in close compliance with the dictates of the IMF.

From the perspective of the people of Jamaica, the effects of the "adjustments" required to achieve fiscal soundness have been as devastating as
would be expected, but strangely, the immense infusion of international
financial support has failed as well to transform the macroeconomic account. The principal effect of the spectacular financial leverage of the
Reagan era seems to have been the acquisition of a huge and unshakable
foreign debt by the island, which by 1986 had reached $3.5 billion, with a
balance-of-payments problem heavily burdened by the demand for debt
service on those loans. A succession of administrations has passed since
the running of our two models; a chastened Michael Manley was returned
to office, and has since, in 1992, resigned for reasons of health without
having so much as glimpsed the promised land. Meanwhile the levels of
poverty and disease that stand as the doom of Jamaica's citizens are as high
as they have ever been:

> I listened to Manley's resignation speech in the coastal village of Bel-
> mont, along with some women fish-sellers who were cleaning the day's
> catch at a roadside standpipe. They were happy about his successor, P.J.
> Patterson, not only because he is from their neighborhood but also because
> he is the first black prime minister in Jamaica's history. "But P.J. can't
> help we, really," one woman said. "We can't buy food in the shops again.
> Chicken fly so high we only see its shadow. It goin' to banquets else-
> where."[45]

Although it is easy to claim after the fact that Manley's middle road
would be destined to fall between the chairs, satisfying neither capitalists
or socialists, Manley was building on a long European and British tradition

A man selling charcoal in the empty Michael Manley Market in Kingston, Jamaica.

which had been his father's, and which he understood well. There may or may not exist the possibility of a viable third path of development under present conditions. Unfortunately, since his model was soon met by such overwhelming counteracting forces, relentlessly contriving its destruction, Manley's eight years of effort to put the concept to the test do not constitute a valid experiment which would help in resolving this question, one way or the other. If the world continues to mount such devastating and deliberate attacks on all of its social experiments, it is evident that we will never learn anything.[46]

A dialectical alternative
Cuba: Traversing the abyss [47]

We have reviewed a range of efforts at the achievement of good housekeeping in the Caribbean, by no means a complete account, for there have been many of other sorts worthy of similar attention, yet all tending to a single conclusion: the system of constraints under which these experiments have been carried out works strongly against the process of "development." Working compromises can be achieved—indeed, must be, as life is to go on—but no solution appears which could be regarded as a portal to a future of a new kind. A candid look at the history of these efforts of Caribbean nations reads, almost inevitably, as a litany of despair. Restless spirits throughout Latin America have for a long while been reading this same record, and drawing their own conclusions: there is thus a correspondingly long history of revolutionary efforts, most of them merely the *juntas* for which the region is caricatured, changing leadership within unchanged structures—but others deeply grounded in determined efforts to institute lasting reforms and to change the foundations of that system itself. Most such principled revolutions that were attempted have been suppressed, often brutally, but one which survived all initial attacks and succeeded in commanding the world's attention is that which after long struggle achieved power in Cuba in 1959. For over three decades the world has continued to observe Cuba's economic and social revolution.

It is extremely difficult to discuss the case of Cuba objectively in a North American forum. The problem arises in the fact that the Cuban revolution is in some sense *total*: it draws a dialectical line in our moral sands, and it addresses all issues, economic and social, from the other side of that divide. At the same time, American thought has become in recent years increasingly rigid and narrow, so that what lies on the other side of any conceptual alternative, if it is visible at all, tends to be seen as unworthy of consideration and rejected out-of-hand. Yet if we are to understand the Cuban effort at good housekeeping at all, we must be prepared to cross this dialectical abyss, stand for a while on the far side, and examine the Cuban experiment from the Cuban point of view. One suggestion sometimes offered for the meaning of the term "liberal arts" is that they *liberate* by licensing the mind to travel freely, that we know our own position securely only if we have, like Odysseus, traveled far from home. Our earlier ventures in the Caribbean have remained within *Mare Nostrum*. This is to take us over the edge of the world.

Imagine, then, a different world—"different" not necessarily in the sense that we do not, finally, live in it, but certainly that we ordinarily do not *suppose* that we live in it. Across a dialectical bridge, basic terms suffer sea-changes, transform. Our notion of society, for example, and of an individual's relation to it, changes: the center of attention shifts from the isolated, competitive individual to the community of individuals, from the few to the many, from the metropole to the periphery, from the banks to the slums, from the lawyer to the campesino. There is a shift of interest from the merely formal to the concrete, from the written law to the practiced life. The actual welfare of individuals throughout the society is prized more highly; it becomes of first importance to ask what degree of health care, what level of education, what mode of life and work, what sense of dignity, what kind of work the least of the society achieve. In such a society, we are restored to *political* being in a sense Aristotle would understand—belonging fundamentally, and not merely by contract, to the society as a whole, as members in a living body. And yet in a sense which Aristotle could not recognize, each person is an absolute individual, with equal worth, entitled in practice to every equal opportunity to achieve whatever the spirit of human individuality might dictate. It is Marx's contribution to conceive a new order of freedom, in a sense a return to Aristotle, in which the total resources of the whole social body become available to make each individual expression possible in new ways.[48]

The birth of a revolution

How is it that whereas other societies we have examined sought their freedom in more cautious ways, Cuba took a revolutionary path, and one that led to a thoroughgoing commitment to a socialist society? While we cannot hope to find a definitive answer to such a question here, some light may be shed if we seek the chief sources from which the Cuban revolution took shape. Many dedicated Cuban patriots participated in the revolution, and many lost their lives in the course of a desperate and unequal struggle; but it was two gifted leaders, a doctor and a lawyer, Ernesto "Che" Guevara and Fidel Castro, respectively, who guided the evolution of the process. Since neither began with a commitment to armed revolution, or to a socialist form of society, we need, if we can, to track the course that led to these two conclusions—in effect, to discover the underlying logic of the Cuban revolution.

First, what set of circumstances incubated such an outcome? For decades Cuba had been the economic domain of a few American corporations, and

Fidel Castro shown with his staff at a secret base. "[A] group...led by Castro, re-solved on a campaign of armed revolt to restore de-mocracy and establish so-cial justice."

it could be argued that in chrematistic terms, the "economy" had flourished under the rule of these "kings without crowns."[49] The gross national product was cause for satisfaction, while Havana bore an aspect of color, gaiety, and culture to delight the local elite and to lure the foreign visitor. Behind this facade, however, lurked a very different reality, which one source describes in these detailed terms:

> The income from sugar was augmented by vigorous tourism based on hotels, casinos, and brothels... Yet the prosperity... enriched only a few Cubans. For the majority, poverty (especially in the countryside) and lack of public services were appalling: with a national per capita income of $353 in 1958—among the highest in Latin America—unemployment and underemployment were rife, and the average rural worker earned $91 per year. Foreign interests controlled the economy, owning about 75 percent of the arable land, 90 percent of the essential services, and 40 percent of sugar production.[50]

Thus in 1952, at a moment when a youthful Fidel Castro had been chosen as candidate of the opposition "Orthodox" party for a seat in the House of Representatives, a certain hardened political figure, Fulgencio Batista, overthrew the government, suspended the constitution, and canceled the scheduled elections, which had been judged too likely to fall to the opposition.

In direct reaction to this affront to constitutional freedom, a group of young people, led by Castro, resolved on a campaign of armed revolt to restore democracy and establish social justice. The first step was to be the capture of the Moncada barracks in Santiago de Cuba, the capital of Cuba's easternmost Oriente province. The attack was made on July 26, 1953, a date now legendary in the history of the revolution. A few died during the attack, but far more, as prisoners, were tortured and murdered by Batista's troops subsequent to their capture, along with others who had nothing to do with the attack.[51]

In a trial held in secret, in defiance of legal procedures Fidel Castro, as an attorney, undertook his own defense. Though he was summarily convicted and thereafter held in solitary confinement, he contrived to smuggle out of his prison cell a reconstruction of the lengthy argument he had given in his own defense, now famous under a title from its closing words:

> ...I do not fear prison, as I do not fear the fury of the miserable tyrant who took the lives of several of my comrades. Condemn me. It does not matter. *History will absolve me.*[52]

The body of his defense is a reasoned argument in constitutional law. He first accuses the dictatorial government and its trial court of a range of violations of the constitution, but then goes on to assert the ultimate right and obligation to revolution against tyranny, expressly included in the Cuban constitution and articulated in the American Declaration of Independence, which he cites at length—those principles on which, as all

Dictator Fulgencio Batista examines a confiscated shipment of arms and ammunition. The armaments were intended to be used in the revolt against his regime. Batista was deposed in 1959.

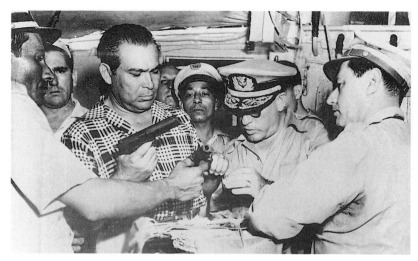

American schoolchildren learn, the legitimacy of the United States government rests today.

In the course of the same statement, Fidel Castro pictures the program which would have been pursued had the revolt been successful. Beginning with the restoration of the Cuban constitution of 1940 and the people's democratic rights, it includes six elements of social reform, which he summarizes in this way:

> The problem of land, the problem of industrialization, the problem of housing, the problem of unemployment, the problem of education, and the problem of the people's health: these are the six problems we would take immediate steps to solve, along with restoration of civil liberties and political democracy.[53]

When in 1959 the revolution did succeed, these were in fact among the first steps it undertook. Meanwhile, Castro remained in prison and his statement to the court was circulated in thousands of copies throughout Cuba. With its vivid description of the plight of Cuba's farmers and workers, its coherent plan of action and its ringing words of patriotism, it became the manifesto of what was later to be known as the "26th of July Movement":

> The nation's future, the solutions to its problems, cannot continue to depend on the selfish interests of a dozen big businessmen nor on the cold calculations of profits that ten or twelve magnates draw up in their air-conditioned offices. The country cannot continue begging on its knees for miracles from a few golden calves, like the biblical one destroyed by the prophet's fury.[54]

Here, then, is one source of the Cuban revolution, thoroughly grounded in a tradition of democratic rights combined with strong social concerns.

The Guatemalan source of the Cuban revolution

It is essential to the logic of the Cuban revolution to take into account a second source as well: a new democratic government with a program strikingly like that of Castro's manifesto, but without its call to revolution, which was taking form during this same period in nearby Guatemala—that of Jacobo Arbenz.[55] It enters our story so decisively because Che Guevara was present as an enthusiastic participant in its rise, and a keen witness to its subsequent ruthless destruction by the United States.

Elected in a triumph of popular democracy, Arbenz emphasized agrarian reform and social reconstruction in a nation suffering from many of the same social ills and structural problems as those of Cuba. In both nations, the interests of the United Fruit Corporation were paramount—in Cuba they owned sugar properties which linked the northern and southern coasts; in Guatemala, they controlled banana production, and held controlling interests in the railroad system, the utilities, and the nation's major port.[56] Arbenz' agrarian reform, as well as the new democratic involvement in the direction of the country, thus ran directly into conflict with United Fruit— which, incidentally, was represented by a New York law firm in which John Foster Dulles, U.S. Secretary of State, and his brother Allen Dulles, new director of the CIA, had been partners.[57]

Che Guevara was in Guatemala as a young Argentinian physician, who upon graduation from medical school had set out to become familiar with other Latin-American countries. The Arbenz program in public health attracted his enthusiastic support, and he later described how he had been ready to dedicate his professional career to it, when he instead watched it destroyed by the United States. He drew his own conclusions, which he was to carry with him when he joined the Cuban revolution:

> However, the aggression came, the aggression unleashed by the United Fruit Company, the State Department, Foster Dulles—in reality, they're all the same thing.... The aggression was successful.... Then I realized one fundamental thing: to be a revolutionary doctor...*there must first be a revolution*. The isolated effort, the individual effort, the purity of ideals...goes for naught if the effort is made alone...A revolution needs...an entire people mobilized...who know what a weapon is worth and what the people's unity is worth.[58]

Che Guevara took refuge in Mexico from the dictatorship installed by the Americans in Guatemala, and there he met an exile from another dictatorship, Fidel Castro; for Castro had been released from prison as a result of huge popular pressure, and was now in Mexico, with a small but dedicated band, planning nothing less than an invasion of Cuba. As these two compared thoughts and experiences, it did not take many hours for Guevara to decide to join the effort and to dedicate his medical skills as physician to the expedition. The group trained and planned together; Guevara, interestingly, earned funds to contribute to the effort as a salesman of encyclopedias.

Havana welcomes the farmers who helped hide Fidel Castro and his troops during the revolution.

In November 1956, the expedition embarked with 82 very seasick revolutionaries crowded into a small yacht still bearing in all innocence its original name in English, the *Granma.* The expedition came under attack immediately upon landing, leaving a band of only twelve to carry on an excruciatingly difficult campaign in the Sierra Maestra mountains of Oriente Province.[59] The campaign was inherently at once military and political, for as the little army grew and gained control of territory, it took on the responsibilities of governance of a peasant citizenry beaten down by Batista's military. Batista had instituted, but then in turn abandoned, a brutal resettlement program of the kind so often used by Central American dictatorships in later years; it was from this suffering that the revolutionary army found the peasants returning. Che Guevara recalls the scene in July 1958, six months before the revolution's final victory:

> Hunger, misery, illness, epidemics, and death decimated the peasants resettled by the tyranny. Children died for lack of medical attention and food, when a few steps away the resources existed which could have saved their lives. The indignant protest of the Cuban people, international scandal...compelled the tyrant to suspend the resettlement program.
>
> Peasants returned with an unbreakable will to struggle until death or victory, as rebels until death or freedom.[60]

Without needing to see, as we have, the fates of the efforts of Muñoz in Puerto Rico, of Eric Williams or Michael Manley in Trinidad and Jamaica, Che Guevara and Fidel Castro had already learned what we may think of as the defining lesson of Guatemala: that there would be no way to gain true independence, or implement real social reform, through any type of social democracy under the aegis of the United States. If democracy means self-rule on the part of the people, then, at least under the conditions which obtain in Latin America, the traditional forms of representative democracy would never achieve it. Thus when the revolution came to power in January 1959, the logic of the experiences out of which it had been born pointed strongly to a new, unified political form, not to the adversarial democracy which would inevitably hand power back to the ruling elite, who had seized it from the people in Guatemala. Che Guevara brought this vivid insight from Guatemala; Fidel Castro brought the political and constitutional convictions born of his experience with Batista; it was the fusion of these two streams that gave the Cuban revolution its shape.

Castro would work over the years to guide the evolution of forms of direct democracy grounded in the workplace and the neighborhood, which would culminate in a constitution that was adopted in 1976 for the new Cuba. His and Che's encounters with the work of the Agency in Guatemala and the brutality of the American-backed Batista dictatorship in Cuba taught them what to expect in response. They would soon see how quickly, and with what inflexible and ruthless determination, Washington would act in an attempt to seize power back in Cuba as well, not only an attempted direct invasion in the Bay of Pigs attack, but in a crippling and unrelenting economic attack by way of a trade embargo as well.[61]

Che Guevara and real economics[62]

As is widely acknowledged, even among his critics, Che Guevara was not only a courageous and principled revolutionary, but a bold and interesting thinker. Remarkably, soon after emerging from the revolutionary struggle in the mountains, Che Guevara found himself appointed Minister of Industry, and president of the National Bank. Still a physician by profession, he approached these new tasks as he did all others with the logic of the medical mind: identify the symptoms, diagnose the problem, and prescribe a rational and appropriate solution. Indeed, there is a striking relation between certain intense discussions which he was soon conducting and the questions we have been raising here, for he saw the central issue in this economic sphere as that of formulating, for the daily practice of efficient socialist accounting, a new structure of real economics as opposed to the market-based methods of the traditional economists.

Guevara had expected that communist economists of the Soviet bloc would have long-since solved this problem; he searched their literature, and he traveled in the fall of 1960 to Russia, Eastern Europe, and China, inspecting their industries and their accounting procedures. He was dismayed to find what he judged on the whole to be poor compromises and inconsistent methods—in effect mixing market methods, infused with profit motivations, with the announced principles of collective socialism. He turned back to the fundamental concepts of Marx and studied carefully Lenin's approach to problems which he found very similar to Cuba's own; but in concrete terms, he saw that Cuba would have to forge its own way. He soon worked out the first sketch of what he termed the *budgetary finance system,* a method of bookkeeping which skipped the marketplace and went straight to the application of economic resources to the production of needed goods and services. In this he found himself opposed by a chorus of technical experts well-trained in conventional economics, among them the French economist Charles Bettleheim, who was among those offering his services to the Revolution. Characteristically, Che Guevara insisted on turning the discussion into a learning experience for the new revolution, forcing the issue into the open in what became an extended debate during 1963–64.[63]

The discussion turned to the *law of value*. (The rule that products in free markets exchange at their values as measured by the investment accumulated in them. Prices would thus be set and exchange conducted according to the law of supply and demand.) Guevara saw this principle, based on the desire of all parties to maximize profits in the marketplace, as challenging the most fundamental concepts of the new society and taking the management of resources out of the control of socialist planning. Would the profit motive with its market pricing rule the distribution of resources in revolutionary Cuba, or would rational judgments of free citizens send available resources where they were wanted and needed? We can recognize in this a direct confrontation between the rule of *chrematism,* and the claims of a true *economics,* now expressed as the contrast between the *law of value,* with its profit motive and market pricing, and a rational *plan*:

> The law of value and the plan are two terms linked by a contradiction and its resolution. We can therefore state that centralized planning is the essence of the socialist society, its defining characteristic, and the point at which man's consciousness is finally able to synthesize and direct the economy toward its goal—the full liberation of the human being in the framework of communist society.[64]

Ernesto "Che" Guevara, minister of industry. "As is widely acknowledged, even among his critics, Che Guevara was not only a courageous and principled revolutionary, but a bold and interesting thinker."

In the budgetary finance system, the many enterprises that made up the Cuban economy were to be regarded a single enterprise; Guevara's paradigm, from which he thought a great deal could be learned, was those very transnational corporations to which the Cuban people and their economy had long served as unwilling hosts—models at the same time, we might remark, of that centralized planning which is the hallmark of capitalist organization.[65]

> We reject the existence of the *commodity* category in relations among state enterprises. We consider all such establishments to be part of the single large enterprise that is the state (although in practice this has not yet happened in our country).[66]

In the reformed system, products would move from enterprise to enterprise within Cuba as from division to division within a transnational corporation, but without the intervention of market exchanges. In addition, materials and labor would be strictly accounted for, but directed to serve the ends of most efficient production.

What was *not* needed, in Guevara's conception, was *competition*, and here we are thrown back to the image of the abyss. What motivates us to do our best work? On the near side of the abyss, it is private gain and advancement for ourselves, our families, and the enterprises we serve, in an environment of intense struggle and competition. No one doubts the efficacy of this eager rivalry in the achievement of great technological advancements, though we know it is also the breeding-ground of vast human and material waste, and war. Such is the world of chrematism, familiar to us all.

On the far side, we have our eyes on, and are motivated primarily by, a higher good which we prize in common. In limited arenas, this sense of personal sacrifice for a higher end is well known, even if regarded as rather special. Certain professions are thought to be devoted to caring; it is the unquestioned rule within our families and within our circles of friendship; a certain human brotherhood is the burden of faith in many of our churches. It is hardly, then, to be despised. Rather, the question becomes a practical one: might an efficiently functioning, free society in the modern world be motivated throughout by such consciousness of participation in a shared human good? In answer to that question, the Cuban revolution committed itself to an unequivocal "yes": it could not succeed by borrowing market methods and private motivations from the paradigm of competition, borrowing from chrematism to solve problems which were intrinsically economic.

This is an issue which is often joined in terms of alternative understandings of our human nature; some assert that it is our destiny to forever seek our own gain, and that we can join effectively in common enterprises only by way of contracts based on demonstrations that we gain privately by working in a public mode. Another view sees our concept of our nature as evolving in the direction of a developing understanding of what it may mean to be human. Marx says "man makes nature," and envisions the unfolding of a new understanding of the human: the individual human being, empowered by participating in the socialized modes of production of the modern era, is liberated from isolation to become a new person, more free and more capable of self-expression and self-fulfillment than earlier separation and self-seeking ever allowed. Che Guevara formulated this insight in terms of the emergence of *el hombre nuevo,* the new man; he sees it in prophetic terms as the successful outcome of a difficult and obscure passage:

In 1959 students at the University of Havana armed themselves to flush out the Batista sympathizers hidden throughout the campus. "[R]evolution is shaping a home for a new kind of liberated citizenry..."

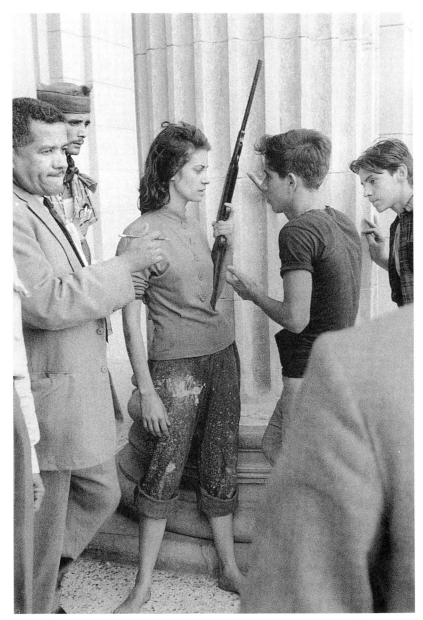

> I would now like to try to define the individual, the actor in this strange
> and moving drama of the building of socialism, in his dual existence as a
> unique being and as a member of society....To build communism it is
> necessary, simultaneous with the new material foundations, to build the
> new man.[67]

Can the question of good housekeeping have arrived in this way at a
fundamental question of the nature, and future, of mankind? Perhaps that
would not be altogether surprising, for a good house must surely be shaped
to the needs and character of the person whose home it is to be; yet also, as
Socrates suggests, we take our own image from the home we have from the
first known and loved.[68] If at the present time, revolution is shaping a home
of a new kind for a liberated citizenry, whose past role has until now been
one of isolation, illiteracy, and poverty—or, for that matter, in the developed world, one of competition, private gain, and strife—we may well
expect when we approach this new house, to have a new form of resident
answer our knock. Good housekeeping, then, and the nature of the good
housekeeper are questions which very properly go hand-in-hand; the design of that house, which will properly be our home, might be regarded as
the project, for example, of Plato's *Republic*.

The central difficulty for those of us on the near side in accepting such
claims for freedom within a unified society on the far side, is that of
believing that diversity can be contained, and flourish, within unity. We are
cynical about this, which we see as authoritarian. Yet those on the far side
see unity as appropriate to freedom, and make the claim that the fullest
freedom is possible *only* within unity. Freedom on the near side is formal,
assuring free speech and the free vote, but lacking implementation in the
absence of a common will; freedom on the far side is substantive, placing
effective power in the hands of the whole body of the people to shape the
society freely for their own purposes and carry through the programs on
which they have agreed. Without unity, Plato, for one, believed such effectiveness in action can never be achieved.[69]

House-building: A revolution in agriculture[70]

Revolutions must be formulated in such broad terms as these if they are
to be sustained by a fiber of principle and conviction that will carry them
through adversity; but revolutions have to find their ways as well in daily
engagement with very specific, concrete tasks. We will learn more about
the Cuban effort, then, by turning, albeit briefly, to an area which lies near
the top of everyone's list of housekeeping goals—the task of providing
food at the family table. After our review of other Caribbean societies, we
will hardly be surprised to find even this most elementary of good intentions entangled in perverse and perplexing ramifications.

The initial intent was clear: to invert the structure of agriculture under
the old regime by taking land which had been in the exclusive possession
of large landholders and the American corporations, and placing it in the

hands of the people. Under an Agrarian Reform Act passed in the first months of the revolution, some 100,000 small farmers who had worked as tenants or sharecroppers on land belonging to others, were given possession of their own farms. However, a much larger number, some 400,000 in all, worked merely as laborers on the great sugar estates, as their counterparts, often migrant laborers, do today on immense factory farms in the United States. Such laborers constitute something closer to a landless rural proletariat. In Cuba, small farmers and these canefield workers alike, lived in very depressed circumstances, without access to health care, sanitation, or education. An agrarian program on the far side is conceived not only in terms of the methods and efficiency of agricultural production, but as rural housekeeping, in terms of the lives and prospects of the workers and their families. Thus the Cuban agrarian program aimed to give the *campesino,* traditionally illiterate, isolated, and oppressed, a new lease on life—a life of dignity, with an altogether new standard of living.

Therefore, it is perhaps not surprising that one of the first acts of the revolution was to defy all sober advice and to launch directly into a nationwide literacy campaign especially focused on the rural population. Yet it was to the astonishment of many, in and out of Cuba, that Fidel Castro made the following announcement, brief but momentous, in the course of his first major speech to the world at the United Nations General Assembly, before the close of the second year of the revolution:

> In the coming year, our country intends to wage its great battle against illiteracy, with the ambitious goal of teaching every single illiterate person in the country to read and write. Toward that end, organizations of teachers, students, and workers—that is, the entire people—are preparing themselves to an intensive campaign. Cuba will be the first country of Latin America that, within the course of a few months, will be able to say it does not have one single illiterate person.[71]

The concept was heroic; everyone who could read would become a teacher; people young and old who had had no contact with rural life found themselves living for a time on farms and in the mountains, sharing forms of life they had never imagined, and introducing fellow human beings to this exciting new instrument, so long denied: the written word. It was a piece of revolutionary romanticism which worked, perhaps because of the power of the word itself to generate an energy sufficient to override all the world's obstacles. Initially, one out of four adults in Cuba could neither read nor write; by the end of the campaign, 700,000 had gained basic literacy, and of these, 500,000 were going on to formal study in a new "campaign for the sixth grade."[72] By 1982, Fidel Castro was able to make the well-founded claim that Cuba had left illiteracy behind.

> Many farmers' children have already become doctors; engineers; economists... It's been a long time since we heard of illiteracy or semi-literacy; we're already speaking of the 6th grade as a minimum level and struggling to make the 9th grade the minimum....[73]

In this common endeavor of the Cuban nation as a whole, the concept of *el pueblo* as one body was taking living form.

Yet deep problems underlay the rural program, for from the outset, the revolution incorporated a nagging contradiction. On the one hand, it was fundamental to the revolution that the Cuban people sense the unity of their own common interest, and act as members of one body—as indeed, they had so effectively done in the literacy campaign. Yet at the same time, by giving land to *campesinos* who had never experienced such a sense of ownership, it focused the attention of these new proprietors on private gain and the welfare of their own separate holdings. These small farmers, who had so newly come into the sense of possession of their own domains—and who had until recently been so unaware of any relation to the city—would have a long journey to make before the more remote goal of the national welfare would overcome the immediate temptation to pick up profits as they could. Just when the greatest social demand arose to consolidate and defend the revolution, which was coming under daily attack even as the agrarian reform was taking effect, it was proving extremely difficult to charm those pigs and onions away from the new small farms and onto the shelves of Havana!

With respect to nutrition itself, the goal was to put an end to widespread hunger by assuring provision of an adequate basic ration of food to every citizen at a fixed price within the reach of all, with special attention to children, nursing mothers, and the elderly. It was evident from the outset that the only means to assure this would be some form of rationing. Americans of the sort likely to be reading this essay are used to thinking of a ration book as a symbol of limitation and wartime deprivation; it is difficult to turn the tables on this thought, and consider what it would mean if it were the poor, as in Cuba, who themselves *issued* the ration book—not as a limitation on purchase, but as a right to obtain. For the poor, the ration book is a passport to food.

At the time of the revolution, Cuba was already producing or importing food enough to provide an adequate diet for all: Cuba's food problem—as it is the world's—is, at least at this point in history, that of distribution.[74] To address this problem, the Cuban revolution initially eliminated the free market in food: a quota of produce from each farm was to be purchased by the state at fixed and reasonable prices, and to be distributed by way of the rationing system. Here was a direct confrontation with the law of value: would the market set prices and rule distribution, or would socialist planning insure a fair ration for all? At one point, in 1982, when the market question was once more the subject of intense discussion, Fidel Castro explained the issue in this way to a convention of farmers:

> If we used prices to regulate distribution, we could put all products on sale on an unrestricted basis tomorrow at predetermined price. We know exactly what prices to set for products placed on unrestricted sale, but we don't want to sell them that way because it would hurt the low-income families. The idea of their being sold freely would make some people

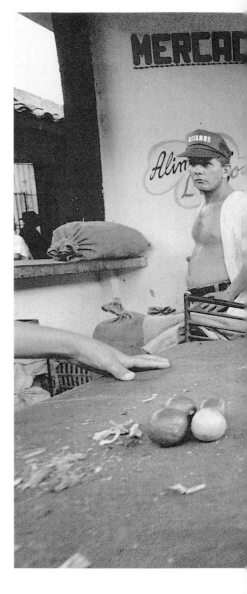

A Cuban farmers' market. The slogan on the back wall (attributed to Raúl Castro, Fidel's brother) reads, "If there is food for the people, the risks are not important."

happy...but what about all the people and families with low incomes? We can't do things that way. Capitalism does it, but capitalism is one thing and socialism is another....There's no doubt that holding prices down makes rationing necessary, and these prices are quite sacred.[75]

Like virtually all other aspects of the Cuban economy, the problem of preserving these principles of food distribution and the maintenance of basic nutrition within the general population has of course become increasingly severe as hunger becomes increasingly the economic weapon of the American blockade against Cuba.

Revolutionary sugar [76]

An ideal plan for Cuban agriculture, it might have seemed, would have been to move by stages toward efficient production of those crops which would serve most directly to feed the Cuban people, with a ready flow of food from countryside to city, and a corresponding flow of the products of Cuban industry from city back to the countryside—a self-contained system. Although critics have argued that Cuba should have followed such a path, this seems never in fact to have been a realistic possibility. The need for foreign exchange, for the purchase of fuel as well as for food the island could not produce in sufficient quantity, would dominate the Revolution for decades. No alternative source of foreign exchange would be as promising as the traditional crop which Cuba was able to grow with the greatest efficiency, sugar. Though sugar had been the symbol of much that was detested in the old order, it did not take much reflection to arrive at this conclusion. Yet shortly after the success of the revolution, the United States first cut its quota for Cuban sugar, and then in a general embargo sealed off all trade with the island; until that moment the United States had not only taken

most of Cuba's sugar crop on favorable terms, but had been by far Cuba's principal trading partner.

The Cuban revolution had not initially been particularly interested in Moscow, and saw nothing to gain by becoming involved in the Cold War. At this point, however, with Cuba left in imminent economic crisis, Moscow made an irresistible offer to replace the United States in the purchase of Cuba's sugar. With this transaction began a relationship of exchange with the Soviet Union and the nations of the Soviet bloc which was to last for nearly thirty years, ending only with the collapse of the Soviet Union itself. The Soviet trade was a mixed blessing. In the first instance, of course, it saved the Revolution, which only by this means was enabled to

Fidel Castro and Mikhail Gorbachev embrace after signing a friendship and cooperation treaty in 1989.

obtain the fuel and food essential to keep going. Thereafter, if the Soviet Union and the supposedly "socialist" nations had in truth achieved genuine socialism, or had even been on a path toward true socialism, Cuba might have found itself in good company and been well-advised. Instead, the new revolution became burdened with residues of inefficient bureaucracy and the spirit of Stalinism, which neither Russia nor its allies had had the strength to shake off.

On a practical level, the Soviet bloc was manufacturing products of distinctly inferior grade, and often felt little compunction in dumping these on recipients of its aid. Cuba thus found itself over the years increasingly locked into a form of barter—Cuban sugar, exchanged for crucial supplies of food and fuel, together with a mixture of bad products and bad ideas. Although Cuba is usually thought of as having become especially favored as a "client state" of the Soviet Union, it is uncertain whether from a strictly material point of view it was Cuba or the Soviet Union which fared better under the arrangement. Though it indeed had important advantages for both sides, for Cuba it brought an era of rigid bureaucracy and a loss of that consciousness Che Guevara had seen as essential to the success of socialism. Fidel Castro had little use for the layers of Soviet managers, and in 1986 guided a "rectification process" in a major attempt to shake off this encrustation and the repression of the human spirit it brought with it.[77] His friend Gabriel Garcia Márquez reports that Castro's own political sense is exactly the opposite:

> He has never been heard to repeat any of the papier maché slogans of communist scholasticism...He is the anti-dogmatist par excellence, whose creative imagination hovers on the edge of heresy's abyss.[78]

With the demise of the Soviet Union and the increasing strictures of the American blockade, Cuba, still heavily committed to the sale of sugar to obtain essential imports, has been forced to trade in the "free market." The United States, in thrusting Cuba into this market, is sometimes thought to have subjected Cuba to a character-building exercise in free-market economics. Actually, there is no real "free market" in sugar. Like other of the world's most important commodities, sugar is normally traded under various forms of long-term special contract at prices agreed between the participants. The tiny "free market," representing on the order of only 10% of the world's sugar trade, is thus a dumping ground for surplus sugar, normally trading there at far less than the true price.[79] Thus Cuba is in truth rather excluded from actual global economics than introduced to it, and is systematically prevented from getting a fair price for the sugar it works extremely hard to produce. At one point, Cuba had achieved the highest level of modern, mechanized sugarcane production—important not only for the level of productivity which could be achieved, but substituting modern labor methods for the backbreaking manual labor which was still traditional throughout much of the Caribbean. Now, having been denied access to normal markets in fuel, machinery, spare parts, or fertilizer by the operation of the U.S. blockade, Cuban agriculture has now been driven literally out of the machine age, forced to have recourse to oxen in place of the farm tractor.

Eccentric ball-bearings and elliptical mill wheels[80]

As we reflect on the Cuban experience in planning a socialist approach to agriculture, it is important to remember not only the vicissitudes of operating in a hostile international environment, but the toll which a covert but unrelenting war on the home front has taken, over the decades. As those who remember the American scene during World War II can readily confirm, an open society is not an option available to a people at war; but if the war is covert, deniable, and hence, invisible to the uninstructed observer, every effort at self-defense may be construed as evidence for the taunt that the exercise of free human rights is being constrained. A scene from the White House following early reports of the Cuban revolution will serve to illustrate the workings of this invisible warfare.

The date is March 1960; the revolution is yet young and American's planning for its destruction has hardly begun. The Agency, however, fresh from its heady and easy success in destroying the fledgling democracy in Guatemala, had begun to do its new homework. Drawing upon the willing expertise of the technical staff from the sugar corporations, experts at the Agency had drawn up a set of interesting options for review by the president. During a meeting with Allen Dulles in the White House, schematic, color drawings of Cuban sugar refineries were presented for Eisenhower's consideration, along with a brilliant and fully deniable scheme for high-tech sabotage. The plan was in all probability the following, as evidenced by events that we later learned in fact transpired. The Cubans, it was known, were planning to renovate the old mills, prudently investing such limited hard-currency as they could gather in the purchase of new machinery from a West German supplier. The Agency was well-positioned, being privy to both sides of the deal; it had a "worm" in the Cuban trade ministry, as well as working contact with German machinery suppliers. The Agency would use its generous funds to bribe the manufacturer to supply nonspherical ball bearings, and to manufacture the huge and expensive gears off-center. The Cubans, neophytes still at the technology they had inherited, would never know the source of the gnawing troubles which would devour their new mill machinery, and curiously, undercut their efforts at efficient

Owing to the American trade embargo and the subsequent lack of fuel and machinery, "Cuban agriculture has now been…forced to have recourse to oxen in place of the farm tractor."

milling of the harvest. Eisenhower was cut from better material; he is reported as responding:

> Allen, this is fine, but if you're going to make any move against Castro, don't just fool around with sugar refineries. Let's get a program that will really do something about Castro.[81]

It would seem that in the long run, both courses were pursued. We know that in time a succession of schemes were devised by the American presidency to murder Castro, and in what became known under Kennedy as the Bay of Pigs invasion, to destroy the revolution by force. But it is reported as well that at the cost of hundreds of thousands of dollars—bad manufacturing ran against the grain and cost West Germany money—manufacturers were indeed bribed into mismanufacturing the sugar mill equipment.[82] Whether the young Cuban technologists ever discovered what would thereafter silently undo their earnest efforts is not reported, but one can easily imagine that they never knew, or would have been mocked and ridiculed mercilessly in the Western press if they had undertaken so much as to whisper the truth.

We need not dwell on this theme, which makes harsh reading for those who grew up in a more innocent era when sabotage was still a hated word. Chemicals were added to lubricating fluids to cause rapid wear of Cuban diesel engines; a French ship was blown up in Havana harbor with the loss of 81 lives; a shipload of new Leyland buses was rammed and dumped into the Thames; a shipload of Cuban sugar was contaminated in a warehouse (though it appears that in fact a great deal of sugar was routinely destroyed in this way); incendiary bombs set sugar fields afire. Through shrouds of disinformation and deniability the truth is emerging concerning the

Agency's biological and chemical warfare campaigns, carried out at least against crops and livestock, if not worse. Powerful illegal transmissions blanket their airwaves with antigovernment propaganda.[83] Currently, a campaign of psychological manipulation in the form of *active civil disobedience* spreads "disorder, fear, pessimism, and defection" by advising absenteeism and calling upon Cubans to "cut the cane badly," to "work at a snail's pace," and to "waste resources" at government offices.[84] It has become clear that in 1976 the Agency planned and supported the terrorist bombing of a Cuban civilian flight, with the loss of 76 civilian lives, including all the members of a Cuban chess team, returning from Caracas with their Olympic gold medals.[85]

Terrorism is not terrorism when carried out by the president's Agency because Cuba and its revolution are perceived as *anathema*; crimes committed by the United States need not trouble us, secured as they are from guilt, encysted in lofty moral armor. It is enough if we keep in mind that Cuba's housekeeping has had to absorb each provocation and somehow contrive to patch its consequences, the worst of which may be the discouragement of generations of Cuban workers as they have seen their honest efforts mysteriously foiled.

Because of the immense financial might it wields in the global economy—farming, in ways we have seen, a large portion of the debt of the entire Third World—the United States has been able to extend its economic embargo, especially since the demise of the socialist bloc, into a near-total blockade. The intent is very simply to seal off as completely as possible Cuban trade in every item, with every nation in the world. Since Cuba is heavily dependent on imports for oil, fertilizers, medicine, and much of its food, this universal blockade has very effectively turned energy, hunger, and disease into potent weapons of war against the revolution. Cuba's prized clinics are without medicines, two million bicycles have filled in for buses which cannot run, its schools, fruits of its literacy campaigns, are without paper and pencils, its mechanized farms are plowed now with oxen. Speaking recently, Fidel Castro summed up the effect of Washington's counter-revolution over the years:

A mute testimonial to the trade embargo: surgical gloves dry on a rack in order to be reused.

> But the blockade is not only that; the blockade is an economic war waged against Cuba...the tenacious, constant persecution of any Cuban economic deal made anywhere in the world. The United States actively operates, through its diplomatic channels...to put pressure on any country that wishes to trade with Cuba, or any business interest wishing to make commercial links with or invest in Cuba, to pressure and punish any boat transporting cargo to Cuba; it is a universal war...
>
> We have also had to endure incessant hostility in the political sphere, from attempts to eliminate the revolution's leaders, through every known form of subversion and destabilization, to direct and perennial sabotage of our economy...[86]

A recent estimate set the cumulative cost of the blockade, life-blood drained from the island's fragile economy, at a staggering $44 billion.[87] One can only wonder how many of the revolution's efforts have been crippled by the necessity of struggling against these immense, often invisible obstacles, set in its path by its mocking neighbor to the north.

It was evidently assumed by the United States, and by most observers as well, that these measures would at last finish off the revolution, and that Cuba would quickly go the way of the Soviet Union and its socialist allies. In any confrontation with the United States, the odds would certainly seem to be against the little island—80:1 in area alone, or nearly 25:1 in population. If, however, as it seems, it is money that counts, the odds on military expenditures are 227:1 in favor of the United States, or for simple gross national product, 285:1. Cuba's immediate proximity to this inflexible enemy, just ninety miles from Key West, makes any thought of successful defense, whatever the heroic determination, implausible: if only Cuba might slip her moorings, and sail off to some new anchorage, to preserve her sovereignty and build her socialist projects in freedom, out of the glare of the enemy! But such a haven, we have seen, if it existed anywhere on the face of the globe, would be nowhere in the Caribbean.

Extremely reluctantly, many of the most prized gains of the revolution have had to be given up, not only in terms of material welfare, but at the level of central principles. In such extremities, the nation has been thrown back to the conceptual struggles with which the revolution began, to recover, if possible, the lessons of Che Guevara.[88] That deceptive balance between socialist principle and capitalist practice, against which Che Guevara issued his warnings, has had to be struck anew. Cuba has gone to the world's banks for loans, always, as a precarious credit risk, at punitive rates of interest. It has had to take that step which it had most avoided, and joined in the queue of the other Caribbean nations in seeking foreign investment—again, however, on the most adverse terms. It has authorized private enterprise, and the ownership of dollars; it has admitted the tourist trade for the sake of the hard currency that would generate, while recognizing that corruption would follow in its train. Worst, perhaps, it has had to acknowledge the advent of serious social inequality on the island, with the corresponding inequalities of individual opportunity which this must entail. One wonders, what could be left of the visions of Che Guevara, and the accomplishments which a few years earlier had reached such impressive heights?

After intense discussions over a period of two months in thousands of workplaces throughout the island, the Cuban organization of labor unions adopted an extensive statement at its Congress in 1996. If we wonder whether the spirit of Che Guevara and *el hombre nuevo* still runs in a new generation of citizens today, we might hear echoes of words we read earlier in certain paragraphs of the laborers' *Theses*. Even that most fundamental confrontation, which we have seen throughout this essay in terms of chrematism and economics, and which Che Guevara met in his battle for mastery over the law of value, is posed here anew in ringing and uncompromising terms:

> Like the other forces of the revolution, the CTC and the unions do not want an alienating market that imposes its blind laws on society. Rather we aim for a market subordinated to our system, that functions within certain limits, and that is an instrument contributing to revitalizing the value of work.

Wrapped in the language of another time and the urgency of a new historic moment, these are nonetheless Aristotle's timeless distinctions with which we began: between means and ends, between the rational and the limitless, and between forces which act blindly and those directed to human goals. They shape into a cry for human freedom:

> We still have enormous problems ahead of us. No one can now doubt, however, that the course we have chosen is the only one possible—faced, as we were, with a perspective of returning to slavery, of ceasing to exist as a nation, and of being incorporated as a bottom-ranked country into a so-called new world order…We continue to confront great difficulties, but Cuba stands today in Latin America as an alternative to the merciless neoliberal policies, to the weakening and destruction of the trade union movement they pursue, and to the enormous social costs they bring on. We also stand as proof that our ideals of independence, solidarity, and justice remain in full force in spite of everything.[89]

So proclaims this beleaguered body of Cuban workers, remembering the revolutionary spirit of Che Guevara and holding their stance, as it seems proudly, on the far shore of the dialectical abyss—and there it is we must leave them, to their fate, as we close this brief exercise in the liberal arts and the exploration of good housekeeping.

Au revoir

Our Caribbean venture has come to an end, and we return to the security of the near shore. Our venture beyond the abyss was for the sake of the mind's perspective; we had loaned credence to the argument, and now we collect it back. The time has come to replace our crumpled note into its bottle, insert the cork firmly, and give it a toss—once more into that sea of all possibilities.

As we do so, we might pause to reflect on its text and acknowledge that we owe a certain special debt to Marx; for it was he who called our attention to the pertinence of Aristotle to the darker issues of our modern times. And of course, to Aristotle himself, for he is always there to remind us that mind has better work to do than we normally assign it—and that there is still room for the light of the good as an option, and a society which takes that good, rather than strife and gain, as its goal.

1. Marx, *Capital,* chap. 4, footnote 2, (*GBWW* I: 50, 72; II: 50, 72); Aristotle, *Politics,* 1256b30–1257a2, (*GBWW* I: 9, 450; II: 8, 450).

2. Marx, ibid.; Aristotle, loc. cit., 1257b33–42 (*GBWW* I: 9, 451–52; II: 8, 451–52).

3. I have discussed this theme in Marx in an earlier article, "Toward a Reading of Marx's *Capital*" (*GIT* 1987, 74) especially pp. 114–17. The author made the voyage suggested here, though with a somewhat different itinerary, on the floating campus of the Institute for Shipboard Education in January 1996. As an American ship, it could not, of course, visit Cuba. Special thanks are due to lecturers on this adventure, Selwyn Ryan and Taimoon Stewart, of the Institute for Social and Economic Research of the University of the West Indies, Trinidad and Tobago, and John Frechione, of the Center for Latin American Studies of the University of Pittsburgh. Many of the insights here stem from their tutelage, though the conclusions here are entirely my own.

4. Only a very limited selection of the available readings on these subjects can be mentioned in these notes. From a very extensive literature on the Caribbean in general, I suggest Gordon K. Lewis, *The Growth of the Modern West Indies* (New York: Modern Reader, 1968); Jan Rogozinski, *A Brief History of the Caribbean* (New York: Meridian Press, 1992); Duncan Green, *Faces of Latin America* (London: Latin American Bureau, 1991); Clive Y. Thomas, *The Poor and the Powerless* (New York: Monthly Review Press, 1988); and Tom Barry, Beth Wood, and Deb Preusch, *The Other Side of Paradise* (New York: Grove Press, 1984) and Hilary Beckles and Verne Shepherd, *Caribbean Freedom* (Kingston, Jamaica, and London: Ian Randle Publishers, 1993). *See,* in general, the *Macropædia* article, "The West Indies," which includes a section on each country (*Encyclopædia Britannica,* vol. 29, pp. 721–89, 1997 ptg., or Britannica Online at http://www.eb.com).

On Puerto Rico in particular, chap. 5 of Thomas, op. cit., and pp. 238 ff of Barry, et al., op. cit. In addition, Americo Badillo-Veiga, *Bread (foreign), Land (wasted), Liberty (denied)* in *NACLA Report on the Americas,* vol. xv, no. 2, March–April 1981, pp. 2 ff.; Emilio Pantojas-Garcia, *Development Strategies as Ideology* (Boulder: Lynne Rienner Publishers, 1990) Richard Weisskoff, *Factories and Food Stamps* (Baltimore: Johns Hopkins Press, 1985) Réné Marques Velasco, *Nuevo Modelo Economico para Puerto Rico* (1993); in Beckles and Shepherd, op. cit., *see especially,* James Dietz, "Operation Bootstrap and Economic Change in Puerto Rico," pp. 421 ff.; and Gordon Lewis, "American Colonial Integration of Puerto Rico," pp. 488 ff.

5. Lilienthaal, David E., *TVA: Democracy on the March* (New York: Harper, 1953).

6. Badillo-Veiga, op. cit., p. 6.

7. Tugwell described his experience in Puerto Rico in *The Stricken Land* (Garden City, N.Y.: Doubleday, 1945). Throughout, I shall use the term "American"—which rightly refers to the whole of what Martí claimed as "Nuestra America"—in order to refer to my fellow-citizens, whom I know no other way to address as I would hope in this essay (lacking as we do the term, "United Statesers"!).

8. On sugar in the Caribbean, *see* in addition to references in note 4 above, in particular, Beckles and Shepherd, op. cit., section 8, passim; and Barry, et al., pp. 31 ff.; William Demas, *Towards West Indian Survival (Black Rock, St. James, Barbados: West Indian Commission Secretariat, 1990).*

9. For the history of the 936 program, *see* Barry, op. cit., p. 243; Dietz, op. cit.,

pp. 424 ff; Velasco, op. cit., pp. 9 ff; Pantojas-Garcia, pp. 9 ff; Pantojas-Garcia, op. cit., pp. 107 ff. The program was, surprisingly, terminated by Congress in 1996; John F. Talbot reviews the program and weighs the significance of its termination in "Puerto Rico in Danger?," *America,* vol. 173, no. 4, Aug. 12–19, 1995, p. 12.

10. On Puerto Rican finances, *see* especially Dietz, op. cit.; Pantojas-Garcia, op. cit.; and essays collected in Carmen Gautier Mayoral et al., Puerto Rico en la Economia Politica del Caribe (Rio Piedrus, Puerto Rico: Ediciones Huracán, 1990). In 1993 the gross public debt was over $14 billion.

11. *1993 Britannica Book of the Year* (Chicago: Encyclopædia Britannica, 1993), p. 696. Figures are approximate: wages are for 1990, but the percentages given are those for 1991.

12. This figure for cumulative federal transfers to Puerto Rico was as of only 1989 (Talbot, op. cit.); but annual flows have continued at very high rates. Total federal transfers in 1994 alone were $8.7 billion (Caspar W. Weinberger, "Puerto Rico," *Forbes,* vol. 155, no. 9, April 24, 1995, p. 33).

13. Pantojas-Garcia op. cit., p. 116. By 1986, direct U.S. investment had reached $24.7 billion (op. cit., p. 167). At one point, in 1974, analysis revealed that a majority of the assets of the isalnd, 55.9%, were foreign-owned (Dietz, op. cit., p. 433).

14. Pantojas-Garcia, op. cit., p. 116. All of the figures have been rounded off here.

15. The characterization as "corporate welfare" appears, for example, in an editorial in *USA TODAY,* cited in Talbot, loc. cit. On the appraisal of the social situation, *see,* for example, Barry, et al., op. cit., pp. 240–42; Pantojas-Garcia, op. cit., p. 89. A chrematistic report, nonetheless, perceives this as a "dynamic" economy, with "...dramatic economic growth over the past 50 years," *1995 Caribbean Basin Commercial Profile* (Cayman Islands: Caribbean Publishing, 1995), p. 239.

16. The correct name for this nation is "Trinidad and Tobago," though here we will often, with apologies, use simply "Trinidad." In addition to appropriate sections in the general readings mentioned in note 4, the following readings on Trinidad may be suggested: Eric Williams, *History of the People of Trinidad and Tobago* (Port-of-Spain, Trinidad: PNM Publishing Co., 1962); and readings in David Lowenthal and Lambros Comitas, eds., *Aftermath of Sovereignty: West Indian Perspectives* (Garden City, N.Y.: Anchor Books, 1973); George Schuyler and Henry Veltmeyer, eds., *Rethinking Caribbean Development* (Halifax, Nova Scotia: International Education Center, 1988), and Basil A. Ince, ed., *Contemporary International Relations of the Caribbean* (St. Augustine, Trinidad/Tobago: Institute of International Relations, 1979, 1987); Selwyn Ryan and Taimoon Stewart, eds., *Entrepreneurship in the Caribbean* (St. Augustine, Trinidad: University of the West Indies, 1994), especially Stewart's Introduction: "Caribbean Entrepreneurship in Historical Capitalism."

17. Eric Williams, *Capitalism and Slavery* (Chapel Hill: University of North Carolina Press, 1994).

18. Williams, op. cit., pp. 210–12. (Italics mine.)

19. This is the theory of Lloyd Best, described by Taimoon Stewart in, "The Aftermath of 1970: Transformation, Reversal or Continuity?," in Selwyn Ryan and Taimoon Stewart, *The Black Power Revolution 1970: a Retrospective* (St. Augustine, Trinidad: Institute for Social and Economic Relations, 1995), pp. 725–27.

20. Eric Williams, "Massa Day Done," in Lowenthal and Comitas, op. cit. *See* Selwyn Ryan, "The Struggle for Black Power in the Caribbean," in Ryan and Stewart, *Black Power,* pp. 25 ff.

21. Overall studies of the international oil industry include Robert Engler, *The Politics of Oil* (Chicago: University of Chicago Press, 1961), and *The Brotherhood of Oil* (Chicago: University of Chicago Press, 1977); Peter R. Odell, *Oil and World Power* (Harmondsworth: Penguin, 1972); Michael Tanzer, *The Political Economy of International Oil* (Boston: Beacon Press, 1969); Neil H. Jacoby, *Mulitnational Oil* (New York: Macmillan, 1974). On petroleum in Trinidad, *see* T. Boopsingh and H. Toney, "Energy: Petroleum" in St. G. C. Cooper and P. R. Bacon, eds., *The Natural Resources of Trinidad and Tobago* (London: Edward Arnold, 1981) pp. 62 ff.

22. Trevor Farrell, "Transnational Corporations and Petroleum Development in the

Third World: Lessons from Trinidad and Tobago: in Schuyler and Veltmeyer, op. cit., p. 89 ff.

23. Selwyn Ryan, "1970: Revolution or Rebellion?" in Ryan and Stewart, *Black Power,* pp. 691 ff. Ryan offers his cautious judgment (p. 694): "...we can argue that 1970 was the culmination of a revolutonary process that began with the struggle of the slaves for emancipation." Lloyd Best, in the same volume, calls it "a revolution in perception...for which we have long been working," p. 709. On its continuing significance, *see* Taimoon Stewart, "The Aftermath of 1970," in this volume, pp. 721 ff.

24. On the bankruptcy of Texaco, and its subsequent recovery: "How Texaco Lost Sight of its Star," *Economist,* April 18, 1987, p. 63; Stratford P. Sherman, "Inside the Texaco-Pennzoil Poker Game," *Fortune,* vol. 113, Feb. 3, 1986, and "The Gambler Who Refused \$2 billion...Fighting Texaco," *Fortune,* vol. 114, May 11, 1987, p. 50; "Catch a Falling Star," *Economist,* Jan. 14, 1989, p. 66; "Texaco: From Takeover Bait to Dynamo," *Business Week,* July 22, 1991, p. 50; Peter J. Bijur, "Operating Successfully in Big Emerging Markets of the World," *Oil and Gas Journal,* vol. 93, no. 32, Aug. 7, 1995, p. 28. (Speech as Senior Vice President of Texaco, Inc. to a U.S. Department of Commerce seminar). On Texaco's return to Trinidad: "Trinidad and Tobago: A Major Returns," *Petroleum Economist,* June 1993, p. 71.

25. World Bank, *Trinidad and Tobago: A Program for Policy Reform and Renewed Growth* (Washington, D.C.: The World Bank, 1988).

26. The thesis of Lloyd Best, note 19, developed fully by Taimoon Stewart in her text cited there.

27. Warren Christopher, "Strengthening the Relationship Between the United States and Trinidad and Tobago," U.S. Department of State Dispatch, vol. 7, no. 10, March 4, 1996, p. 94. (Italics mine.)

28. Stewart, op. cit., p. 737.

29. (Central Intelligence Agency) *Trinidad and Tobago Statistics and Quantitative Analysis, 1996: Executive Summary,* p. 3. *See also,* the World Wide Web.

30. op. cit., p. 2; World Bank, op. cit. p. 60; Stewart, ibid.

31. On Jamaica, in addition to appropriate sections of references in Note 4, I have relied heavily on Michael Manley's own detailed account of his experience as Prime Minister, *Up the Down Escalator* (Washington, D.C.: Howard University Press, 1987); *See also,* Manley, *Jamaica: Struggle in the Periphery* (London: Third World Media Limited, 1982); these may be balanced with the reservations of Clive Thomas, op. cit., 83 ff. *See also,* an interview with Manley by Martha Doggett, "Michael Manley," *NACLA Reporter,* vol. xx, no. 5, December 1986, pp. 27 ff. I regret to note that Michael Manley has died since the preparation of this manuscript.

Anders Danielson, "Economic Reforms in Jamaica," *Journal of Interamerican Studies,* vol. 38, no. 2/3: Summer/Fall 1996, pp. 97 ff; Joanne Koslofsky, "'Going Foreign'—Causes of Jamaican Migration," *NACLA Report,* vol. x, no.1, February 1981, pp. 2 ff; and Kathy McAfee, "Hurricane: IMF, World Bank, U.S. Aid in the Caribbean," *NACLA Report,* vol. xxiii, no. 5: February 1990, pp. 13 ff; George M. Anderson, "The Other Jamaica," *America,* vol. 171, no. 17, Nov. 26–Dec. 3, 1994, p. 10.

32. Laurie Gunst, "'P. J. Can't Help We, Really,' (Jamaican Prime Minister P. J. Patterson)," *The Nation,* vol. 255, no. 2, July 13, 1992), p. 48 ff.

33. Rogozinski, op. cit., p. 138: "...the word *genocide* precisely describes the fate of Africans carried to the sugar islands as field slaves."

34. Robert F. Drinan asks, in the *National Catholic Reporter,* "Why not?" "Jamaica, Entire Third World in Bondage to American Banks," vol. 30, no. 8, Dec. 17, 1993, p. 18.

35. On the bauxite and aluminum industry, *see* Barry, op. cit., pp. 90 ff; many sections in Thomas, op. cit., including pp. 104 ff; and Manley, *Up the Down Escalator,* chap. 1, passim.

36. Manley, op. cit., p. 43.

37. Manley, op. cit., chap. 5, passim and pp. 45–48; Barry, op. cit., pp. 1–12. On terms of trade, *see* Eric Hobsbawm, *The Age of Extremes,* (New York: Pantheon Books, 1994), p. 159. A thoroughly documented study of the issue from the point of view of the underdeveloped nations is *Fidel Castro, the World Economic and Social Crisis: Report to the Seventh Summit Conference of Non-Aligned Countries* (Havana: Publications Office of the Council of State, 1983), *see* especially chaps. 1–3. The concept is dis-

cussed technically in M.A.G. Van Meerhaeghe, "International Commodity Trade," *Encyclopædia Britannica,* vol. 21, pp. 915–17, 1997 ptg., or Britannica Online at http://www.eb.com.

38. Manley suspected that the mining companies may have deliberately provoked strike action and labor unrest in order to create turmoil with which Manley would have to deal within his own ranks. Manley, op. cit., p. 74.

39. William Blum, *The CIA: A Forgotten History* (London: Zed Books, 1986): on Angola, p. 284, and on the issue for Jamaica, pp. 299ff.

40. Blum, loc. cit., and the references there. Joanne Kosiofsky, "Jamaica: Roots of Electoral Violence," *NACLA Report,* vol. xiv, no. 5, October 1980, p. 38; Gunst, op. cit. For literature on the CIA, *see* for example, in addition to Blum, op. cit., John Prados, *Presidents' Secret Wars* (Chicago: Elephant Paperbacks, rev. ed. 1996); Warren Hinckle and William W. Turner, *The Fish is Red* (New York: Harper and Row, 1981; reprinted as *Deadly Secrets*); John Stockwell, *In Search of Enemies* (New York: Norton, 1978).

41. Thomas, op. cit., pp. 221–22.

42. Thomas, op. cit., pp. 232–37; Barry, op. cit., pp. 345ff.; Hans J. Massaquoi, "Interview with Jamaica Prime Minister Michael Manley," *Ebony,* vol. 45, no. 4, February 1990), pp. 110–204.

43. Thomas, op. cit., p. 233.

44. Gunst, op. cit., p. 49.

45. Ibid.

46. For a rigorous study of the dark prospects for the people of the world under the rule of the global free economy, *see* Eric Hobsbawm, op. cit., pp. 579ff.

47. Brief accounts of the recent history of Cuba are to be found at *Encyclopædia Britannica,* vol. 29, pp. 739–40, 1997 ptg., or Britannica Online at http://www.eb.com; Barry, op. cit., pp. 268ff; and Marta Harnecker, *Fidel Castro's Political Strategy,* (New York: Pathfinder Press, 1987). A selection of useful longer works from a variety of sometimes spirited points of view might include James D. Rudolph, ed., *Cuba: A Country Study* (Washington D.C. Headquarters, Dept. of the Army: 1985), and, no less serious for being witty, *Cuba for Beginners* by the cartoonist Ruis (New York: Pathfinder Press, 1970); Edward Boorstein: *The Economic Transformation of Cuba* (New York: Monthly Review Press, 1968), Ernesto Cardenal, *In Cuba* (New York: New Directions, 1974); and José Iglesias, *In the Fist of the Revolution* (New York: Vintage Books, 1968). Marta Harnecker, ed., *Cuba: Dictatorship or Democracy?,* (Westport, Conn.: Lawrence Hill & Co., 1979). Lee Chadwick, *Cuba Today* (Westport, Conn.: Lawrence Hill, 1975); Margaret Randall, *Cuban Women Now* and, twenty years later, *Women in Cuba* respectively (Toronto: Women's Press, 1974; and New York: Smyrna Press, 1981). The developments of recent decades have been chronicled graphically and in remarkable detail in the speeches of Fidel Castro, a number of which will be referred to as we go along; *see also* his *Un Grano de Maíz: Conversación con Tomás Borge* (Havana: Oficina de Publicaciones, 1992).

48. I have suggested this reading of Marx in an earlier essay in *The Great Ideas Today*: "Toward a Reading of *Capital,*" (*GIT* 1987, 114).

49. The characterization is Che Guevara's: "Today there are kings without crowns; they are monopolies, the true masters of entire nations...," in "Political Sovereignty and Economic Independence," David Deutschmann, ed., *Che Guevara and the Cuban Revolution,* (Sydney: Pathfinder/Pacific, 1987), p. 87.

50. *Encyclopædia Britannica,* vol. 29, p. 739, 1997 ptg., or Britannica Online at http://www.eb.com.

51. Castro detailed these charges before the court: "*History Will Absolve Me,* in Harnecker, *Fidel Castro's Political Strategy,* cited above, pp. 120ff.

52. op. cit., p. 152.

53. op. cit., p. 106. Counter-revolutionaires may cite the same passage in defiance of Castro and the revolution.

54. op. cit., p. 109.

55. An excellent overall reference for this section is Richard H. Immerman, *The CIA in Guatemala* (Austin: University of Texas Press, 1982). On the Arbenz government, *see* pp. 68–81.

56. op. cit., p. 106. On "La Frutera" in Guatemala, *see* pp. 68ff.

57. On the Dulles brothers and Sullivan and Cromwell, *see* op. cit., pp. 124–25. The level of refinement of Allen Dulles' grasp of the Arbenz program is well epitomized in this remark: "[The Communists'] stooges took over power…in…Guatemala in 1954, and they were driven out." *The Craft of Intelligence,* (New York: Harper and Row, 1963), p. 221. *See also,* p. 224, where a "a group of Guatemalan patriots" is imagined as having put Arbenz down.

58. *Che Guevara and the Cuban Revolution,* p. 125.

59. The campaign is detailed by Che Guevara in Mary-Alice Waters, ed., *Episodes of the Cuban Revolutionary War,* (New York: Pathfinder Press, 1996).

60. op. cit., p. 259.

61. Blum, op. cit., pp. 206 ff.

62. *See* Mary-Alice Waters, "Ernesto Che Guevara," in *Episodes,* pp. 78ff. Fidel Castro spoke of Guevara and his work in a memorial rally in 1967: "Che's Enduring Contributions to Revolutionary Thought," in *Che Guevara and the Cuban Revolution,* pp. 19ff; Che Guevara was captured with the help of the Agency, and subsequently assassinated, in Bolivia in October 1967.

63. Guevara's dispute with the economists is developed in his articles, "On the Concept of Value: A Reply to Alberto Mora," and "The Meaning of Socialist Planning: A Reply to Charles Bettleheim," in *New International,* no. 8, 1991, pp. 155–75; and "Planning and Consciousness in the Transition to Socialism: On the Budgetary Financer System in *Che Guevara and the Cuban Revolution,* cited earlier, pp. 293ff. On Guevara's economic theories, and Fidel Castro's efforts to recover their spirit in a later period, *see* Carlos Tablada, *Che Guevara: Economics and Politics in the Transition to Socialism,* (Sydney: Pathfinder/Pacific, 1989).

64. "The Meaning of Socialist Planning," cited above, p. 173.

65. Scott Buchanan long ago called attention to the dangerous contrast between our democratic beliefs and our autocratic daily habits, in a 1958 essay, "The Corporation and the Republic," in *So Reason Can Rule,* (New York: Farrar, Strauus, Giroux, 1982), pp. 82ff. As an issue for political action, the same issue is posed by David Schweickart in *Capitalism or Worker Control?,* (New York: Praeger, 1980).

66. Fidel Castro, "A New Type of Election," and his "Speech to the National Assembly of People's Power," on the first meeting of that body following the 1976 elections, in *Fidel Castro Speeches, vol. ii: Our Power is that of the Working People* (New York: Pathfinder, 1983), pp. 242–59. *See also,* Marta Harnecker, *Cuba: Dictatorship or Democracy?,* (Westport, Conn.: Lawrence Hill, 1980). For a constitutional history of Cuba, and the view of the 1976 constitution as simply "authoritarian," *see* Craig H. Robinson, chapter "Government and Politics," in Rudolph, op. cit., 159ff.

67. Guevara, "Socialism and Man in Cuba," in *Che Guevara and the Cuban Revolution,* p. 249–50.

68. The Republic is constructed in thought as such a home on the image of man, and is envisioned in turn as shaping new generations to take this image into their souls. (*GBWW* I: 7, 295–441; II: 6, 295–441).

69. *See* Socrates, in the *Republic*: *GBWW* I: 7, 363; II: 6, 363.

70. On agriculture in Cuba, *see* Medea Benjamin, Joseph Collins, and Michael Scott, *No Free Lunch: Food & Revolution in Cuba Today,* (New York: Grove Press, 1986); Robert S. North, "The Economy," in Rudolph, op. cit., pp. 128 ff; Fidel Castro, speech to the 6th Congress of the ANAP, May 17, 1982, in *Speeches at Three Congresses* (Havana: Editora Politica, 1982), pp. 145ff., excerpted in *Speeches, vol. ii,* above, pp. 351ff.

71. Fidel Castro, Address to the General Assembly, Sept. 15, 1950, in Mary-Alice Waters, ed., *To Speak the Truth,* (New York: Pathfinder, 1992), p. 59. On literacy in Cuba, *see* Jonathan Kozol, *Children of the Revolution,* (New York: Dell Publishing, 1978); chaps. 1–6 describe the literacy campaign. Thirty years later, Fidel Castro reviewed the revolution's accomplishments in literacy and other social programs: "Thirty Years of the Cuban Revolution: in *In Defense of Socialism*, (New York: Pathfinder, 1989), pp. 61ff.

72. Kozol, op. cit., pp. 5, 55–6.

73. Castro, *Speeches at Three Congresses,* p. 163.

74. *See* John W. Warnock, *The Politics of Hunger* (Toronto: Methuen, 1987), passim;

Castro, *The World Economic and Social Crisis,* supra, pp. 95 ff. I discuss distribution in relation to the world food problem in "The New Pythagoreans II: The Scientists of the World and the World Food Problem," in *The Great Ideas Today 1989,* especially 192–96 and 223–26, and references there.

75. Castro, op. cit., p. 180.

76. Gerry Hagelberg and Tony Hannah, "Cuba's International Sugar Trade," in Alistair Hennessy and George Lambie, *The Fractured Blockade* (London: Macmillan Caribbean, 1993), pp. 137 ff. On sugar in Cuba, Benjamin et al., op. cit., pp. 115 ff.

77. *See* a note by Mary-Alice Waters, "Che's Proletarian Policy and Cuba's Rectification Process," in *New International,* no. 8, 1991, p. 15, and two 1986 speeches by Castro: "Renewal or Death," and "Important Problems for the Whole of International Revolutionary Thought": *New International,* no. 6, 1987, 209–53.

78. Gabriel Garcia Márquez, "Plying the Word," *NACLA Report,* vol. 24, no. 7, August 1990, p. 42. Márquez adds that when he asked Fidel at the end of an arduous day "what in the world he would most like to do" he answered "Hang around on some street corner."

79. Benjamin, op. cit., pp. 152–55.

80. Blum, op. cit., pp. 206–16, and references cited there; Hinkle and Turner, *op.cit., passim;* Prados op. cit., 171–17.

81. Prados, op. cit., 177.

82. Blum, op. cit., p. 210.

83. Ann Louise Bardach, "Our Man in Miami," *The New Republic,* vol. 211, no. 14, Oct. 3, 1994, pp. 24 ff; Fidel Castro, *Un Grano de Maíz,* pp. 155–57; Wayne S. Smith, "Pirating Radio Martí," *The Nation,* vol. 264, no. 3, Jan. 27, 1997, pp. 21 ff.

84. Seminar "Una Propuesta de Civilización," sponsored by the group "Hermanos al Rescate," Florida International University, June 15, 1996; from the worldwide web; cf. *Economist,* vol. 336, no. 7931, Sept. 9, 1995, p. 36.

85. Blum, op. cit., p. 213; Hinkle and Turner, op. cit., pp. 384–85.

86. Fidel Castro, speech given no. 25, 1994, to a World Meeting in Solidarity with Cuba, Havana, *Militant,* Jan. 9, 1996, p. 9.

87. "Heroic Illusions," *Economist,* vol. 339, no. 7960 April 6, 1996, p. 14; the article describes, with some satisfaction, "a country of ruins," regarding Fidel Castro as "a slow learner" in an inevitable move to free-market reforms. A different view of the same scene is taken by Mary-Alice Waters: "Defending Cuba, Defending Cuba's Socialist Revolution," *New International,* no. 10, 1994, pp. 21 ff.

88. Castro had spoken in 1987, on the twentieth anniversary of his death, of the importance of a return to Che Guevara's thinking: "Che's Ideas Are Absolutely Relevant Today," in Carlos Tablada, op. cit., pp. 32 ff. *See* a review by Carlos Rafael Rodriguez, "Che's Contribution to the Cuban Economy," *New International,* no. 8, 1991, pp. 33 ff.

89. "Theses for the 17th Congress of the CTC," *Militant,* March 18, 1996, pp. 8–9. The CTC is the Confederation of Cuban Workers (Confederación de Trabajadores de Cuba).

Thomas K. Simpson has written numerous articles for *The Great Ideas Today*. He is a tutor *emeritus* at St. John's College in Annapolis, Maryland, and Santa Fe, New Mexico, where he continues to teach on occasion in the Graduate Institute. His education was at Rensselear Polytechnic Institute, St. John's College, Wesleyan University, and the Johns Hopkins University.

Recently, Mr. Simpson has been engaged in a project with the NEH and the Association of Science-Technology Centers, leading *Great Books* seminars with science museum personnel. Mr. Simpson works with special fascination on the visualization of objects in four-dimensional space. In a new work, *Maxwell on the Electromagnetic Field* (Rutgers University Press), he traces the emergence of the concept of the electromagnetic field through a dramatic succession of three papers by James Clerk Maxwell.

In preparation for the essay which appears this year, Mr. Simpson recently completed a trip to the Caribbean with the *S.S. Universe Explorer,* of the University of Pittsburgh's Institute for Shipboard Education.

3

SPECIAL FEATURES

THE
MERCHANT.
of
VENICE

Shakespeare's Fairy Tales: The Origin of *The Merchant of Venice*

Cynthia L. Rutz

This is the second in what has become a series of essays on Shakespeare and fairy tales. There are several reasons for my interest in this subject. For instance, it is fascinating to see which parts of the plots of the tales Shakespeare kept and which he altered. Sometimes too, the original fairy-tale characters, though much less complex than his, can offer clues by which to interpret Shakespeare's characters. The themes of most fairy tales were universal ones, as these tales had survived by being told in houses all over the world, and only those tales that really hit home (you could say) survived. These themes—the relations between parents and children, dealing with stepparents, picking the right marriage partner, children coming of age, are among those important to Shakespeare as well, and it is instructive to see how he alters the tales to fit his interpretation. There are also fairy tales that are not direct sources of a play, but are referred to within it. Looking closely at these references often provides clues as to how the characters see themselves and each other, just as myths and fairy-tale ideas—about love, for example—still guide many of us, consciously or unconsciously, in our lives.

On the title page of *The Merchant of Venice* dating from 1600, the following appears as a description of the play's contents:

> The most excellent Historie of the *Merchant of Venice*. With the extreme crueltie of *Shylocke* the Iewe towards the sayd Merchant, in cutting a iust pound of his flesh: and the obtayning of *Portia* by the choyse of three chests.[1]

(Overleaf) Frontispiece from an edition of The Merchant of Venice.

Thus Shylock and the casket choice receive equal billing. But that is not how the play has gone down in history. In Shylock, Shakespeare created such a memorable character that many think the Merchant of the title must

Shylock fleeing the trial after Portia's victory.

refer to him. Yet Portia has almost twice as many lines as Shylock, and Bassanio nearly as many. Moreover, after the dramatic trial scene that determines Shylock's fate, Shakespeare chose to end the play by returning to the love story with an entire final act in which Shylock figures not at all. I shall talk most about this half of the play, namely the world of Belmont, in particular the casket story and by extension, the characters of Portia and Bassanio as revealed through the casket test.

I. The source tale: *Il Pecorone*

The main source for *The Merchant of Venice* is a story from a 14th-century collection of Italian tales called *Il Pecorone* (The Dunce).[2] The story is as follows: A Florentine merchant realizes he is near death and decides to divide his property among his three sons. Much to everyone's amazement he gives half to each of his older sons and nothing to the youngest. On his deathbed, however, he calls his youngest son to him and tells him that he can expect the best portion of all. He gives him a letter of introduction to a good friend in Venice and tells the boy that this man, a wealthy and important merchant, will be so delighted to receive him for his friend's sake that the son's fortune and position in Venice will be assured.

After the father dies, the son travels to Venice and indeed finds a second father in his father's friend. Wishing to become involved in his adopted father's business, he asks for a ship fitted out with goods and goes off on a trading voyage to Damascus along with two other friends and their ships. On the way the captain of his ship tells him a story about a harbor they are passing called Belmont. The ruler there is a beautiful widow who has set a test for any man who comes to woo her. They must spend the night with her, and if they succeed in "enjoying her" she and the whole country are his, but if he does not succeed, then all his property is forfeit.

The young man cannot resist attempting the trial, so he has the captain sail into the harbor; he then presents himself as a suitor. The lady seems delighted with him and holds a banquet in his honor that night. After the feast she leads him to her room and asks if he would like a cup of wine before retiring. As you might guess, the wine is drugged, the young man falls into a deep sleep, and in the morning the lady wakes him to say that he has failed the challenge and must forfeit his ship. She gives him a horse and enough money to return to Venice, but when he reaches the city he is so embarrassed that he pretends to have lost everything in a shipwreck.

A year goes by and he still cannot forget the lady, so nothing will do but that his foster father must outfit a second ship and he sets sail again. Events happen just as before. Once again he is welcomed warmly, once again he retires with the lady, and once again he drinks the drugged wine, sleeps through the night, and must forfeit all his goods. Upon returning to Venice he once again claims to have lost all in a shipwreck.

Events in fairy tales often happen in threes, so of course he decides yet again to seek the lady's hand. This time his adopted father bankrupts himself in fitting out another ship and must make a horrible bargain with a moneylender in order to get sufficient funds: if he cannot repay the money he owes by St. John's Day, a pound of his flesh will be forfeit. The young man sets out for the third time to try for the lady's hand, but this time the lady's maid takes pity on him and warns him about the drugged wine. He therefore succeeds in "enjoying" the lady and this time wins her hand. In his elation, however, he forgets all about the pound-of-flesh bargain, and it is not until St. John's Day actually arrives that he remembers his father's friend's predicament. He rushes off at once to try to help him, and the lady follows disguised as a doctor of law.

A trial takes place and the lady in disguise saves the day by insisting that the moneylender must take only flesh and shed no blood, an impossible condition that wins the case for her. In payment for her help, the lady insists on having the ring the young man's wife has given to him. He reluctantly agrees, and when he returns to Belmont, the lady having preceded him there, he is mercilessly teased by her for having parted with her love pledge. She finally reveals her stratagem, and the story ends with the young man marrying off his adopted father to the lady's sympathetic maid.

The similarities between this story and Shakespeare's are too numerous to mention, but there are some significant differences. Shakespeare changes the test to the casket test, about which I will say more later. Also, the young lover in Shakespeare, Bassanio, has no family that we know of, and indeed in a sort of magical transformation, the three brothers and three voyages of this tale become the three suitors and three caskets of Shakespeare's version. Finally, Shakespeare makes Bassanio somewhat less blameworthy in that he is not solely responsible for ruining his friend Antonio, for the latter loses several ships at sea, and when Bassanio has won the lady, he does not entirely forget Antonio's plight.

This source tale contains several fairy-tale motifs that are useful to explore. One is that of voyagers who win the heart of a lady in their travels. Odysseus, Æneas, and Theseus, all of whom are referred to in Shakespeare's play, are examples. The fairy-tale voyager referred to again and again throughout the play, however, is Jason of the Argonauts. From several references it is clear that Bassanio sees himself as that famous hero, as when he compares Portia, Shakespeare's lady of Belmont, to the Golden Fleece:

> For the four winds blow in from every coast
> Renowned suitors, and her sunny locks
> Hang on her temples like a golden fleece,
> Which makes her seat of Belmont Colchos' strand,
> And many Jasons come in quest of her. (*GBWW* I: 26, 408; II: 24, 408)

According to the story, Jason and other famous Greek heroes, among them Nestor and Hercules, set sail in a ship called the *Argo* to capture a famous prize called the Golden Fleece, the pelt of a ram that had been given by the gods. The Fleece belongs to the King of Colchos, and his daughter Medea uses her magic to help Jason to win it. The word "argosy" also appears a several times in Shakespeare's play to refer to Antonio's ships, though the word is not a direct derivative of the name of Jason's ship.

A most menacing reference to the Jason myth occurs during a seemingly romantic exchange between Shylock's daughter Jessica and her lover Lorenzo. It is a beautiful moonlit night and the two lovers are trading accounts of famous romantic pairs using the catchphrase "in such a night as this." The pairs they bring up, however, all came to a bad end—Troilus whose lover Cressida betrayed him; Pyramus and Thisbe, who commit suicide; Dido, abandoned by the wandering Æneas, who also kills herself, and finally Jason's Medea: "In such a night / Medea gather'd the enchanted herbs / That did renew old Æson" (*GBWW* I: 26, 430; II: 24, 430). Here Jessica refers to the story in which Medea uses her magic to restore the youth of Jason's father Æson. One version of this tale is that she had Æson chopped into pieces and thrown into a boiling cauldron. After she added

"Jason...set sail in a ship called the *Argo* to capture a famous prize called the Golden Fleece, the pelt of a ram that had been given by the gods."

some magic potions, he walked out of the cauldron a young man. Another tale is that Medea tricked the daughters of Jason's enemy, Pelias, into trying the same remedy for their father, only she gave them false spells such that in the end they had killed and boiled their own father.[3]

In the context of these fairy-tale exchanges then, Jessica's invocation of Medea is ominous, but the exchange is already an unhappy one, as we can see from the progression of pairs of lovers. Lorenzo begins by bringing up Cressida, unfaithful to Troilus. Jessica counters with Thisbe, who was faithful to her lover unto death. Then Lorenzo brings up Dido, who committed suicide for Aeneas who, unaware, went on to marry someone else. Jessica then "out-myths" Lorenzo with her trump card of Medea, who, like Dido, was abandoned by her lover but whose great powers later gave her the opportunity for revenge. Lorenzo lacks another myth to counter that of Medea, so he reminds Jessica that she betrayed her own father by running off and stealing his possessions, just as Medea did to her father, the King of Colchos. After one more exchange of accusations Jessica gets the final word, "I would out-night you, did no body come" (GBWW I: 26, 431; II: 24, 431). That "out-night" again is ominous in the context of midnight-enchantress Medea. This entire exchange can seem playful, and is probably usually played that way on stage, but the fairy-tale duel here might serve to point out that love founded on falsehood—as in the case of Jessica's and Lorenzo's deception of Shylock—does not flourish.

In still another reference to Jason in the play, Portia obscurely compares herself to the Golden Fleece. Toward the end of the play she is teasing Bassanio for having given up his ring to the doctor of laws (really herself in a man's disguise) and says that she likewise will not deny the young doctor anything:

> No, not my body, nor my husband's bed:
> Know him I shall, I am well sure of it:
> Lie not a night from home; watch me like Argus:
> If you do not, if I be left alone,
> Now, by mine honor, which is yet mine own,
> I'll have that doctor for my bedfellow. (GBWW I: 26, 433; II: 24, 433)

Argus here is not Jason's ship, but rather the hundred-eyed monster sent by the goddess Hera to guard the Golden Fleece. Hera also used Argus to keep guard over Zeus's mistress Io.

Why then should Bassanio be constantly compared to the hero Jason throughout the play? Although in Shakespeare's play he makes no voyages, and may get to Belmont on foot for all we know, he does share many characteristics of the wanderer-hero. He too is an adventurer and a risk-taker, perhaps even in love. He is good-hearted but thoughtless and happy-go-lucky. To convince Antonio, whom he already owes a great deal of money, to fund him again for his wooing of Portia, Bassanio describes the venture as shooting an arrow after one that is lost, hoping to find both. Some might describe this as throwing good money after bad, but Bassanio

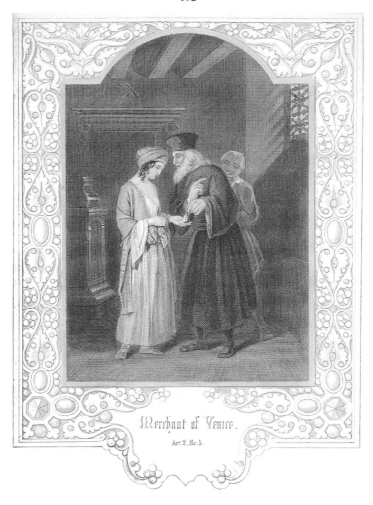

Merchant of Venice.

Act 2, Sc. 5.

shares another characteristic with Jason: namely his charm, which wins him friends who will do anything for him. And so Antonio agrees to the venture.

Another fairy-tale motif present in the source tale is that of the three brothers. It is a fairy-tale staple that wherever there are three brothers, the third and youngest is a good-hearted fool. In many stories of three brothers there is a test to win a princess, and the young, foolish brother triumphs over his elders with simplicity or common sense. In one such story the task is to make cry a princess who has never shed tears. All kinds of ingenious remedies are tried, but then the foolish brother has her peel onions and wins her hand. In Shakespeare's version the two rival suitors stand in for the two brothers, and Portia comments on how they have tripped themselves up with their own wisdom: "O, these deliberate fools! when they do choose, / They have the wisdom by their wit to lose." Her maid Nerissa's response to this remark further shows that the test is not about wisdom: "The ancient saying is no heresy, / Hanging and wiving goes by destiny" (*GBWW* I: 26,

419; II: 24, 419). In the source tale this remark reflects the spirit of the lady's maid, who, when she sees the right man come along for her mistress, gives destiny a helping hand.

The final fairy-tale source I will mention in this connection is *The Arabian Nights.* Tales of merchants as heroes abound in these stories, and indeed that famous sailor Sindbad, is really a merchant.[4] Shakespeare's story also carries from the *Nights* another motif: that of a lady with a test. In the tale of Aziz and Azizah, for example, a lady's test also requires a young man to stay awake, but he is the usual hapless hero of the *Nights* and only passes the test with the help of his childhood sweetheart.[5] Finally, the giving up of a ring is often important in the *Nights.* It is usually demanded by someone who has done one a favor, and refusal is impossible. In *The Merchant of Venice,* too, where it seems Bassanio and his friend must give up their rings to the doctor of laws and his clerk, this principle that one cannot refuse anything to someone who has done one a favor is invoked.

II. The choice of the three caskets

As we have seen, Shakespeare did not get the story of the choice of caskets from *Il Pecorone.* That tale has its sources in the Orient, and in older versions it is not a test for winning a wife but rather a device for testing who will choose show over substance. Versions of the tale appear in two 13th-century collections, the *Speculum Historale* and the *Golden Legend,* and in several medieval collections, including the *Gesta Romanorum* and Bocaccio's *Decameron,* all of which were accessible to Shakespeare.[6] The tale in the *Gesta Romanorum,* translated into English in 1577, is the most like Shakespeare's and I will summarize it here.

A princess sets out for Rome to marry the emperor's son. There is a shipwreck, then she is swallowed by a whale, and finally she is rescued and brought to Rome—bedraggled, grimy, and looking nothing like a princess. The emperor treats her courteously, but insists that she take a test to see if she is worthy to be the bride of his son. Three vessels are brought forth for her to choose from. The first is of pure gold set with precious stones and contains—though the princess cannot see this—dead men's bones. It bears the motto "Whoso chooseth me shall find what he deserves." The second vessel is of fine silver and contains earth and worms. Its motto reads "Whoso chooseth me shall find what his nature desires." The third vessel is of lead and contains precious stones. Its motto: "Whoso chooseth me shall find what God has disposed for him." The girl is told, "If you choose one of these wherein is profit to thee and to others then you shall have my son." Her reasoning about the choice seems to take the form of a catechism: What I deserve is death, what I desire is earthly things, and yet God disposes mercy despite our deserving and desiring. (Note that this bears similarities to Portia's speech to Shylock about the quality of mercy in the courtroom scene.) She asks God for help, and then chooses, of course, the lead casket, and wins the emperor's son.

All of the tales in the *Gesta Romanorum* are provided with a Christian moral that was not a part of the originals. The moral to this tale claims that the first vessel shows how outward pomp and bad deeds deserve hell, the second shows the same fate for the fair-speaker (i.e., the silver-tongued), and the third shows that choosing the simple, poor life is what weds one to Jesus, the precious stones within representing faith and works.

The tale of a test for worthiness to marry has many fairy-tale relatives. The story of "The Princess and the Pea" is one of these, wherein a bedraggled girl arrives at a castle claiming to be a princess. The queen, who has long been searching for a real princess for her son, tests the girl by secretly setting a small pea at the bottom of a pile of mattresses and bidding the girl to spend the night there. In the morning she is black and blue and claims

she did not sleep a wink, thus proving her royal quality. The casket test, however, is less specialized; it tests not for a princess but just for a good and pious girl. Similarly, Bassanio's test is not for a prince but for a good man. In contrast, the test that Penelope sets up for her suitors in *The Odyssey,* that of bending and shooting Odysseus' great bow, is one that only he could pass, though his son Telemachus seems about to.

The moral given to the *Gesta Romanorum* tale reminds us that the fairy-tale maxim is often to choose simplicity. This maxim, however, has religious connotations in this tale, and elsewhere. Consider the choice set forth in the film *Indiana Jones and the Last Crusade.* There, Indiana Jones must choose the real Holy Grail from a table filled with beautiful and costly vessels. He correctly chooses the one earthenware cup, a reminder perhaps of Christ's humble birth in a stable; once again the message is not to choose by outward show.

In Shakespeare's version of the casket choice, the test was set up by Portia's dead father in his will. Though Portia has many suitors, only three, including Bassanio, are willing to try the test, probably because of the forfeit if they fail. Portia mentions the forfeit to one of them in these terms:

> You must take your chance,
> And either not attempt to choose
> at all
> Or swear before you choose, if
> you choose wrong
> Never to speak to lady afterward
> In way of marriage: therefore be
> advised. (*GBWW* I: 26, 411;
> II: 24, 411)

It is not at all clear that this forfeit is seriously meant, for the fool's head in the second casket contains these words: "Take what wife you will to bed, / I will ever be your head." In any case the warning has the effect of scaring off the other suitors so that the choice comes down to our fairy-tale number of three.

The test set by Portia's father here is to choose the casket that has Portia's picture in it. The sayings on the three caskets are quite similar to

Another fairy-tale source is The Arabian Nights. "Tales of merchants as heroes abound in these stories, and indeed that famous sailor Sindbad, is really a merchant."

those of the source tale in Shakespeare. The gold casket's motto is, "Who chooseth me shall gain what many men desire," the silver says, "Who chooseth me shall get as much as he deserves," and the lead says, "Who chooseth me must give and hazard all he hath." Notice that the third motto is the only one substantially changed from the *Gesta Romanorum* tale. If Shakespeare means this test as a catechism, it is not a religious one.

Another difference is that in Shakespeare's version the contents of the caskets are much more complex, as we shall see by looking at the choices. The first to choose is the Prince of Morocco. He sees no advantage to hazarding all for the lead casket, which to him threatens rather than beckons, and feels that silver is too poor a metal to conceal Portia's picture. He settles on the gold casket then as most befitting Portia and also because she must be that which "many men desire." Here are his words when he sees what is inside the golden casket:

> O hell! What have we here?
> A carrion Death, within whose empty eye
> There is a written scroll! I'll read the writing.
> [*Reads*] "All that glisters is not gold;
> Often have you heard that told;
> Many a man his life hath sold
> But my outside to behold:
> Gilded tombs do worms infold.
> Had you been as wise as bold,
> Young in limbs, in judgement old,
> Your answer had not been inscroll'd:
> Fare you well; your suit is cold." (*GBWW* I: 26, 416; II: 24, 416)

Portia's next suitor, the Prince of Aragon, also rejects the lead casket as not fair enough to hazard anything for and rejects the gold because he disdains what "many men," which he interprets as the foolish multitude, would desire. He then chooses the silver casket by its motto—"Who chooseth me shall get as much as he deserves"—assuming that he deserves Portia's hand. Inside he discovers a portrait of a blinking idiot and cannot believe it: "Did I deserve no more than a fool's head?" He then goes on to read the verdict inside:

> What is here?
> [*Reads*] "The fire seven times tried this;
> Seven times tried that judgement is,
> That did never choose amiss.
> Some there be that shadows kiss;
> Such have but a shadow's bliss:
> There be fools alive, I wis,
> Silver'd o'er; and so was this.
> Take what wife you will to bed,
> I will ever be your head.
> So be gone; you are sped." (*GBWW* I: 26, 418; II: 24, 418)

Finally Bassanio makes his choice. He rejects "gaudy gold" as "Hard food for Midas," silver as a "common drudge / Tween man and man," and instead addresses himself to "meager lead, / Which rather threatenest than dost promise aught, / Thy paleness moves me more than eloquence" (*GBWW* I: 26, 421; II: 24, 421). Inside he finds Portia's portrait and this saying:

> [*Reads*] "You that choose not by the view,
> Chance as fair and choose as true!
> Since this fortune falls to you,
> Be content and seek no new.
> If you be well pleased with this
> And hold your fortune for your bliss,
> Turn you where your lady is
> And claim her with a loving kiss." (*GBWW* I: 26, 421; II: 24, 421)

III. Freud's essay

In 1913 Sigmund Freud wrote a short essay about the casket choice.[7] To him, Shakespeare and the Greek tragedies were rich sources for observing the complexities of human psychology. He begins his casket essay with the premise that something rings false in Bassanio's speech on why he prefers lead to the other two caskets. Freud assumes that there must be concealed motives for the choice; motives concealed even from Bassanio himself. In dream interpretation, caskets, or containers of any kind, are always symbolic of women, so Freud reinterprets Bassanio's choice as one among three women. Here he compares the choice to another choice among women, that of King Lear's love test of his daughters. This puts Freud in mind of other mythological and fairy-tale choices among three women: both Paris's choice among the three goddesses Hera, Aphrodite, and Athena, and the Cinderella story are examples. He goes on to note similar qualities among all the chosen women of these triads, primarily dumbness or muteness in some form. Recall for instance that Lear rejects Cordelia because she cannot speak her love. Freud notices the same quality when Bassanio says of the lead casket: "Thy paleness moves me more than eloquence."

Finally, by comparison again to dream analysis, Freud makes the leap that this dumbness is really death, that it is death that is being chosen in all these cases. Moreover, he says that if one woman is the Goddess of Death, then the other two are known; they must be the Fates, the third of whom is called Atropos, the Inexorable. But how, he asks, is the choice of the fairest of women—and recall that Paris chose Aphrodite, Goddess of Love as the fairest—a choosing of death? Freud answers this by pointing to the ancient Mother-goddess who in some early cultures represented both life or fertility and death, goddesses such as Persephone or the tri-form Artemis/ Hecate.

Why is death chosen as preferable in all these cases? Freud's answer is that the choice is what in psychoanalytic terms is called a *reversal*. When it comes to the Fates, there is only necessity, and it is wishful reversal that turns that necessity into a choice we can make, and that choice into a fair woman rather than a terror. Remnants of what is really going on remain in the stories Freud contends, for the choice "must necessarily fall on the third if every kind of evil is not to come about, as it does in King Lear."

We may find Freud's analysis of the casket choice as a choice of death rather extreme, but there are ways in which death as a metaphor for Bas-

A suitor examines the three caskets while Portia and Nerissa await his choice. "Portia...is living in an entirely different atmosphere... her mythical Belmont perhaps lies much closer to Damascus than to Venice. Portia is a lady of the East."

sanio's choice fits very well indeed. Both of the mottos on the other two caskets speak of getting, but Bassanio chooses to "give and hazard all he has." In a sense he chooses real marriage vows, which are about what you need to give, even to give up, for the sake of the beloved. The death of self, or at least of selfishness, may be what is required to give birth to this new union.

The actual death's head (skull) is contained in the gold casket, but note Bassanio's odd description of the picture of Portia he finds in the lead casket:

> Fair Portia's counterfeit! What demi-god
> Hath come so near creation? Move these eyes?
> Or whether, riding on the balls of mine,
> Seem they in motion? Here are sever'd lips,
> Parted with sugar breath: so sweet a bar
> Should sunder such sweet friends. Here in her hairs
> The painter plays the spider and hath woven
> A golden mesh to entrap the hearts of men
> Faster than gnats in cobwebs: but her eyes—
> How could he see to do them? having made one.
> Methinks it should have power to steal both his
> And leave itself unfurnish'd. (*GBWW* I: 26, 421; II: 24, 421)

We could merely call Bassanio a poor poet, but the images he evokes— severed lips, moving eyeballs, a spiderweb with gnats caught in it, a missing eye—are macabre. This is overt praise, but underneath there is a current of morbidity that lends weight to Freud's theory.

Lead itself has some connotations that support Freud's claim. According to the *Dictionary of Mythology, Folklore, & Symbols,* lead can mean firmness, ignorance, stubbornness, torture. It is used in destructive charms with curses written on them; in alchemy it was the metal of Saturn, presiding over death. The leads of Venice were the prison cells in the Doge's Palace.[8] In poetry the metal still carries connotations of death and torture, as in Emily Dickinson's "hour of lead."[9] In this context, Portia and Bassanio's playful exchange right before the casket choice, about Bassanio's being "on the rack," begins to sound ominous.

Yet we must recall the spiritual meaning of the choice in Shakespeare's source for the casket story. There the lead casket—"what God has disposed"—connotes inner spiritual riches. Given the fact that the other two caskets have beauty outside and death within, it makes sense to interpret the lead casket as death outside, with true life within. So perhaps all this symbolism of death really shows that giving and hazarding all only *seems* to be courting "death," which turns out to be new life, whether through marriage or spirituality. Freud might call that a wishful reversal on my part, but we will leave it as an open question whether in some sense Bassanio is choosing death or life.

In discussing the three caskets, Freud speaks of the three Fates, but in folklore and fairy tales there are many other instances of three, including the three Graces, the three seasons (for some of the ancients there was no autumn), the Three Wise Men, three stages, three ages, three wishes, Three Little Pigs, and the Three Bears. The folklore dictionary gives three as a sign of completeness, harmony, perfection.[10] Often in fairy tales, the first two in a group of three are somewhat alike, the third is the exception. Think of the sameness of Cinderella's sisters, or of the first two little pigs. Then too, in many Cinderella variations there are three dresses for the three nights of the ball; the first two are often silver and gold, but the third dress is anything from one as shining as the stars, to a dress made of every kind of flower, or one made of a thousand different furs. Occasionally the three function as thesis, anti-thesis, and synthesis; the simplest case being that of the Three Bears' porridge, which Goldilocks first finds too hot, then too cold, and finally just right. The gold and silver caskets fit this pattern, forming a pair of opposites, symbolic of the Sun and the Moon, male and female. The third casket thus might represent the taking in of these opposites, that is marriage.

IV. Other possible readings

The choice of the lead casket, then, supports many possible meanings besides the one Freud proposes, including not judging by appearances, lack of greed, lack of pride, reconciliation of opposites, and the courage to risk everything. Many of these possibilities bear on the greater themes of *The Merchant of Venice*. How is it that happy-go-lucky Bassanio judges correctly? To begin with, the inscription—"Who chooseth me must give and hazard all he hath"—could have almost been written with Bassanio in mind. He has already risked all he had, even his friend's life, to try to win Portia. Moreover, he has always been a risk-taker, and his recent losses seem not to have changed that. Bassanio loves the things that money will buy, and in describing Portia for the first time to his friend Antonio, he emphasizes that winning her will get him out of debt; indeed his first words about Portia are mercenary, "in Belmont is a lady richly left." Money is not for hoarding for Bassanio, however, as it is for Shylock, so perhaps that is why Bassanio can ignore the immediate lure of the gold and silver caskets. Unlike the pious heroine of the original casket story, he does not make his choice based on the mottoes, but rather the lead itself moves him. In this, Bassanio may be demonstrating the simplicity of the third and youngest brother over and against the first two choosers, who have the wisdom to lose by their wits.

There is yet another possibility as to how Bassanio manages to choose aright, and that is that he has outside help. Adventurous voyagers like Odysseus, Theseus, and Jason all at times receive help from a woman in passing a test or avoiding peril. Theseus and Jason are both set tasks by a father and then aided by the daughter who has fallen in love with them. Theseus conquers the Minotaur and is able to make his way out of the labyrinth by following the golden thread given to him by Minos' daughter

Ariadne. Jason is set certain impossible tasks by the King of Colchos in order to earn the Golden Fleece, and is aided by the King's daughter Medea, who also helps him escape with the Fleece. Each of these heroes abandons his helpful princess later on. It would fit this fairy-tale tradition, then, for love-struck Portia to give Bassanio some help in passing her father's test, and indeed some commentators feel she has done just that.

Before Bassanio is to make his decision, Portia calls for music, and a song is sung and played while he is deliberating. Both the meaning and the rhyme scheme of this song can be construed as giving Bassanio clues to making the right choice. Notice that the first three line endings all rhyme with lead ("nourished" having three syllables):

> Tell me where is fancy bred,
> Or in the heart or in the head?
> How begot, how nourished?
> Reply, reply.
> It is engender'd in the eyes,
> With gazing fed; and fancy dies
> In the cradle where it lies.
> Let us all ring fancy's knell:
> I'll begin it—Ding, dong, bell.
> *All.* Ding, dong, bell. (*GBWW* I: 26, 420; II: 24, 420)

The fancy of the song, which is engendered with the eyes and fed with gazing, means foolish love, so that Portia might also be warning Bassanio not to judge by appearances. Some commentators feel that to suggest that Portia "cheats" here ruins the romantic fairy-tale scenario in which the hero wins the princess on his own. Perhaps these commentators have merely been reading the wrong fairy tales; for in addition to the tales of Jason and Theseus, the various stories from Eastern traditions, from which the casket story comes, particularly *The Arabian Nights,* often show a smart, determined woman helping out her hapless suitor or master. Simple Ali Baba, for instance, would be lost without his clever maid, and Scheherezade's storytelling finally cures her husband of his woman-hating.

Portia herself suggests that Bassanio is less than brilliant, for while he likes to compare himself to adventurers such as Jason, she calls him Hercules, a hero known more for his brawn than his brain. Moreover, she saves him and Antonio again later in the play by cleverly beating Shylock at his own game in the trial scene. But Portia herself suffers from the usual problems that come with cleverness and idleness, namely pride and a taste for the dramatic. By fairy-tale logic she is due for a comeuppance that she never receives here.

When we first meet her, Portia is engaged in what seems to have become a favorite pastime, making fun of her suitors with her maid Nerissa. She has Nerissa name them, and comes up with clever put-downs for them all. Of the Neapolitan prince she says, "Ay, that's a colt indeed, for he doth nothing but talk of his horse...I am much afeared my lady his mother played false with a smith." A French lord gets the cleverest put-down:

"God made him, and therefore let him pass for a man." Asked how she likes a young German duke, she replies, "Very vilely in the morning, when he is sober, and most vilely in the afternoon, when he is drunk: when he is best, he is a little worse than a man, and when he is worst he is little better than a beast" (*GBWW* I: 26, 408–9; II: 24, 408–9).

While her suitors may indeed have many faults, these words seem most ungenerous, and one commentator points out that most of Portia's remarks betray national stereotypes, such as the drunk German, the cowardly Scot, and the uncultured Englishman. While she does not say these things to her suitors' faces, by knowing her attitudes we are privy to her concealed sarcasm, as when the Prince of Morocco asks her not to judge him by his skin color, and she replies that he "stood as fair / As any comer I have look'd on yet / For my affection" (*GBWW* I: 26, 411; II: 24, 411). *We* know that this remark means she does not care for him at all. This might be mere politeness were it not for what she says after Morocco has failed the test and departed, "Let all of his complexion choose me so" (*GBWW* I: 26, 417; II: 24, 417). Portia perhaps would fail her father's own test, then, for she judges by appearances.

When I say that Portia is poised for a comeuppance, I mean that this ridiculing of suitors comes straight from the classic fairy-tale motif of the proud princess humbled. The most familiar Western version of the tale is the Brothers Grimm story "King Thrushbeard." After a beautiful princess has made fun of every suitor who comes to claim her hand, her father, completely out of patience, declares he will marry her to the next beggar who walks through the door. She then is forced to go off and live in poverty with this beggar, undergoing various humiliations. When she is sufficiently chastised, her husband reveals that he is really King Thrushbeard, one of her former suitors, and the two live happily ever after. Shakespeare takes this plot to its completion in *The Taming of the Shrew,* so it is interesting that here he chooses not to complete it.

Portia is prey as well to another defect that often comes with being rich and bored, namely a taste for the dramatic that borders on cruelty.[11] Nerissa, commenting on her mistress' world-weariness, says, "For aught I see, they are as sick that surfeit with too much as they that starve with nothing" (*GBWW* I: 26, 408; II: 24, 408). This weariness with her own life may cause Portia to make fun of her suitors behind their backs, but at the trial her love of drama causes real cruelty. Memorable as is her speech on mercy to Shylock, it is not clear that Portia herself displays much mercy at the trial, drawing her masquerade out for maximum dramatic effect. Thus she even directs Antonio to bare his bosom in anticipation of the knife, calls for a balance to weigh the flesh and a surgeon to stop the blood, and lets Antonio make his farewell speech before she finally stops the proceedings by telling Shylock he dare not shed any blood. Though she wins out in the end, she has meanwhile caused Antonio and Bassanio untold agonies.

Perhaps it is a virtue that Portia at least knows her own faultiness, however, for in an early speech to Nerissa, which can serve as a commentary on her mercy speech and behavior at the trial, she says "I can easier teach twenty what were good to be done, than be one of the twenty to follow mine own teaching" (*GBWW* I: 26, 408; II: 24, 408). She continues this behavior when, still disguised as a lawyer, she will accept no fee but the ring which she had given Bassanio as a love pledge, and with which he was never to part, only so that she can torment him with it later. Such love games are the very stuff of romantic comedies, but Portia so outmatches simple Bassanio and melancholy Antonio that the prolonged teasing over the trial and the rings cannot quite work as innocent fun.

Portia, disguised as a lawyer, appeals to Shylock for mercy at the trial.

In this, too, Portia resembles many of the clever women in *The Arabian Nights,* who tease and often mentally torment their less-than-brilliant husbands and lovers. There is a remnant of such fairy-tale cruelty in the ring story. When Bassanio realizes how angry Portia will be about the loss of his ring, he says, "Why, I were best to cut my left hand off / And swear I lost the ring defending it" (*GBWW* I: 26, 432; II: 24, 432). In *The Arabian Nights,* a hand *is* forfeit for such lapses. In one tale a bridegroom comes to bed with his new wife after the wedding feast and has neglected to wash his hands after eating a particularly pungent dish. When he touches her and she smells the food she immediately calls the servants to chop one of his hands off and has him thrown out in the street.

Portia's disguises and flair for the dramatic are also very much in the mode of Oriental tales. Here she resembles the *Arabian Nights* caliph Haroun al Rashid—as well as Shakespeare's own Cleopatra—both of whom when bored with court life would wander out in disguise with a faithful companion, sometimes conferring great benefits on people, but often playing cruel tricks. It may be Portia's connections to this Eastern fairy-tale world that prevent her from getting the comeuppance often required in Western tales. She is living in an entirely different atmosphere with a different set of rules, and her mythical Belmont perhaps lies much closer to Damascus than to Venice. Portia is a lady of the East.

Belmont itself, which means "beautiful mountain," is a fairy-tale place; and one of the central oppositions in the play is between this idyllic spot, full of music, love, and abundant wealth, and the Venice of Antonio and Shylock, where there is hatred and greed. In fact, one of the most telling lines in the play illustrates the clash of these two worlds. Salerio, a friend of Antonio's, has arrived in Belmont to bring news of Antonio's imprisonment and impending death for his debt to Shylock. Salerio arrives immediately after Bassanio has won the casket contest and Bassanio's friend Gratiano jubilantly says, "We are the Jasons, we have won the fleece." Salerio's response is, "I would you had won the fleece that he hath lost" (*GBWW* I: 26, 422; II: 24, 422). This line brings the dreamers back to earth, reminding them that outside of Belmont real people are suffering nasty consequences. In Shakespeare's source tale, as we have seen, the Bassanio character is more blameworthy, having become so caught up in the dream-world of Belmont that he forgets all about his debt to his friend until it is too late. And even in Shakespeare, some blame still attaches to Bassanio for seeming to forget about Antonio's predicament, however briefly. Such lack of forethought is the dark side of his happy-go-lucky nature—and even though Portia saves the day in typical fairy-tale style, the oppositions set up between the worlds of Venice and Belmont do not go away. The end of the play leaves us uneasy, for we have seen a dark side to the fairy-tale prince and princess, and with Shylock's humiliation and his daughter's betrayal looming on the edges of our consciousness, once again the "happily ever after" here does not quite ring true.

1. Shakespeare, *The Merchant of Venice,* ed. David Bevington, (New York: Bantam Books, 1988), p. 97.

2. Ibid., p. 101.

3. Robert Graves, *The Greek Myths,* (New York: Penguin Books, 1990), vol. 2, pp. 252–53.

4. *The Arabian Nights,* vol. II, trans. Powys Mather, (London: Routledge-Kegan Paul 1989), p. 179.

5. Ibid., vol. I, pp. 488–521.

6. Bevington, p. 103.

7. Freud, *Works,* (London: The Hogarth Press Limited, 1958), vol. XII, p. 289.

8. *Dictionary of Mythology, Folklore, & Symbols,* (New York: Scarecrow Press, 1962) vol. 2, p. 978.

9. Emily Dickinson, "After Great Pain a Formal Feeling Comes." *American Verse,* ed. Oscar Williams (New York: Washington Square Press, Inc., 1955), p. 154.

10. *Dictionary of Folklore,* etc., vol. 2, p. 1563.

The Shakespeare quotes in this essay reflect the *GBWW* edition.

11. For much of what follows in the court scene, I am drawing on Harold Goddard's essay "Portia's Failure."

Cynthia L. Rutz is a lecturer in liberal arts with the Basic Program of the University of Chicago, from which she has an M.A., and where she is writing a dissertation examining the origins of Shakespeare's source tales. A graduate of St. John's College, Santa Fe, New Mexico, she has been an editorial assistant with *The Great Ideas Today* and a coordinator for Mortimer J. Adler of the Paideia Program of Basic Schooling, which she now serves elsewhere as a consultant, administering *Great Books* seminars for elementary and high school students in the city of Chicago.

The essay printed here was originally a Basic Program lecture, one of a number Ms. Rutz has given on the subject of her research. We plan to print more of these in later issues of *GIT*.

Postmodernism:
A Critical
Diagnosis

Alex Callinicos

n the intellectual world, the vogue for postmodernism has now long out-
lasted the usual lifespan of fashions, in, say, rock music or clothes. Not only
is the term itself continually bandied about in cultural debates and everyday conversation, but the broad body of thought of which it is the expression persists, sometimes through transmuting itself into new forms (for
example, postcolonial theory, now well-entrenched in university departments of English and cultural studies throughout the anglophone world).
One possible explanation of postmodernism's apparent vitality is that, if
not exactly true (since it typically involves the denial of the classical
concept of truth as correspondence with reality), postmodernism does accurately capture something distinctive about the world in which we live. If,
on the other hand, one intellectually rejects postmodernism, one must come
up with, not simply philosophical and historical criticism, but also some
account of the social trends, economic, political, and cultural, that have
given birth to it and continue to sustain it. I incline toward the latter view.
In this essay, I try to explain why postmodernism is bad philosophy and
social theory, and to outline the causes of its influence.[1]

What is postmodernism?

It is, however, first necessary to arrive at some view on the nature of
postmodernism. Defining postmodernism is a perplexing affair. This is
partly because the term "postmodern" turns out to be much older than the
contemporary debate surrounding it. Arnold Toynbee suggested in 1934
that Western history after 1875 should be called the "Post-Modern Age."[2]
Usage of the term postmodern may indeed date back even earlier. Perplexity grows when one discovers the sheer diversity—and indeed inconsistency—of the claims associated with postmodernism.[3] There are, as we
shall see, quite deep reasons for the sheer fluidity of the subject matter of
postmodernity.

Nevertheless, some points in the debate surrounding postmodernism
provide something approximating firm anchorage. There is little doubt that
the starting point of this debate was provided by French philosopher Jean-
François Lyotard's 1979 essay *The Postmodern Condition*. Lyotard constructs an opposition between modern and the postmodern in terms of the
concept of "metanarrative." "I define *postmodern* as incredulity towards
metanarratives." And,

> I will use the term *modern* to designate any science which legitimates
> itself with reference to a metadiscourse...making an explicit reference to
> some grand narrative, such as the dialectics of Spirit, the hermeneutics of
> meaning, the emancipation of the rational or working subject, or the
> creation of wealth.[4]

As the examples Lyotard gives indicate, by "metanarrative" he means
primarily the attempts to weave the whole of history into a single, compre-

(Overleaf)
L'Homme au
Chapeau
Melon *by
René Magritte
(1964).*
"Surrealists
sought...
'profane illu-
mination'
from chance
occurrences
in city life."

hensive, and unified account of human development as were made first by Enlightenment *philosophes* such as Turgot, Condorcet, and the Scottish historians, and then by Hegel and Marx. The project of totalizing human historical experience is not merely philosophically mistaken, he believes, in that it ignores the irreducibly heterogeneous character of the events that constitute this experience; it has led to the disastrous political attempts to repress this inherent diversity by totally transforming society with results we know by the names of the Holocaust and the Gulag Archipelago.[5]

These modernist metanarratives have, moreover, Lyotard contends, been rendered obsolete by the advent of "the postindustrial and postmodern age," where science itself, now the driving force of economic progress, has become fragmentary and indeterministic. In this, science shares the fundamental characteristics of Postmodern art, that starts from our inability to experience the world as a coherent and harmonious whole, and draws instead on "the increase of being and the jubilation which result from the invention of new rules of the game, be it pictorial, artistic, or any other."[6]

Lyotard's text contains what have emerged as the three main dimensions of postmodernism. The first is a series of cultural shifts that have occurred since the 1960s and that have in common a reaction against what had become the dominance of high Modernism in the arts around the middle of the century. Perhaps the most obvious example is the rebellion against the International Style in architecture popularized by Robert Venturi in his book *Learning from Las Vegas*.[7] This shift away from the great oblong slabs that came to dominate most downtowns in the postwar era, and in favor of a heterogeneity of styles impregnated with references to the past and to mass culture is often seen as having its counterparts in other artistic media—in a return to figuration in painting, for example; in the fiction of Robert Pynchon and Umberto Eco; and in the films of David Lynch and Peter Greenaway—that collectively represented a Postmodernist break with the great Modernist revolution in the arts at the beginning of the twentieth century.[8]

The second great axis along which postmodernism has developed is the crystallization of a distinctive philosophical current characterized by its development of a comprehensive critique of reason. At its center has been a group of French philosophers, the most important of whom—Gilles Deleuze, Jacques Derrida, and Michel Foucault—all emerged to prominence during the 1960s. Despite the substantial differences between them, all, thanks in large part to the influence of Friedrich Nietzsche, elaborated on certain propositions—that what we call reality is inherently fragmentary, heterogeneous, and plural; that human thought is unable to arrive at an objective account of the nature of this "reality"; and that what modern Western philosophy has conceived as the subject of thought, the individual self, is nothing but an incoherent cluster of drives and desires.[9]

The reception of the work of these philosophers in the English-speaking world, generally packaged under the label of *poststructuralism,* began in the 1970s: Derrida's influence in the area of literary criticism and theory grew rapidly in the United States thanks in large part to the proselytizing activities of his associates and followers among what came to be known as the Yale deconstructionists. Though none of the three major poststructuralist thinkers explicitly associated themselves with the idea of postmodernism (indeed Deleuze explicitly attacked it), their writings helped create the intellectual atmosphere in which the idea could flourish. In particular, they helped undermine belief in the ability of human reason to understand and control the world, thus contributing toward postmodernist "incredulity towards metanarratives." The French theorists more directly associated with postmodernism, Lyotard himself and the cultural commentator Jean Baudrillard, are best seen as pursuing (in a rather minor key) themes most powerfully developed by Deleuze, Derrida, and Foucault.

Postmodernism has taken shape, thirdly, as a social theory that claims to announce and to delineate a new historical epoch, that of postmodernity. This dimension is already present in Lyotard's suggestion that a new "postmodern and postindustrial era" represents the socioeconomic correlate of the philosophical skepticism about reason and the Postmodern art that he seeks to identify and to celebrate. In the background to this thought is the idea of postindustrial society developed somewhat earlier by more conventional theorists such as the American political sociologist Daniel Bell. Bell argues that humankind had been progressing through a series of stages, notably from traditional agricultural society, to the industrial society of the nineteenth and early twentieth centuries, and now on to postindustrial

The Bastille Opera in Paris, France, is an example of the "rebellion against the International Style *in architecture ... [and] the great oblong slabs that came to dominate most downtowns in the postwar era.*"

society, where the production of services prevails over that of material goods. Both Bell and Lyotard conceive postindustrial society as one where the development of theoretical knowledge is the motor of economic progress, a "knowledge society," as Bell puts it, though science for Lyotard is a congeries of incommensurable discourses rather than a means for rationally knowing and controlling the world.[10]

Marxism and postmodernism

16 Jackies *by Andy Warhol (1964). War-hol's* "frag-mentation of the human subject" *illus-trates the* "distinctive features of Postmodern art."

If Lyotard thus gestures toward the idea of postmodernity as a distinctively new historical stage in human history, it is far too redolent of precisely the kind of grand narrative that he is concerned to reject as distinctively modern for him to be entirely comfortable with the concept. Thus he argues that treating the "post" in the term "postmodernist"…in the sense of a simple succession, of a diachrony of periods, each of them clearly identifiable, is "totally modern."[11]

Other theorists, however, have been more willing to seek out social and economic trends which, they argue, represent the historical context in which the cultural and intellectual changes identified with postmodernism have taken shape. Surprisingly enough, given Lyotard's hostility to Marxism as one of the grand narratives we must leave behind us, the best-known attempts to develop a *social* theory of postmodernity have been by Marxists. Probably the most brilliant single piece of writing produced by the great afflatus of discourse on postmodernism is an essay, first published in 1984, by the American Marxist critic Fredric Jameson. In *Postmodernism, or, the Cultural Logic of Late Capitalism,* Jameson uses the work of Andy Warhol in particular to isolate what he argues are the distinctive features of Postmodern art—"a new depthlessness," "the waning of affect," the fragmentation of the human subject, the reduction of the past to a source of endless pas-

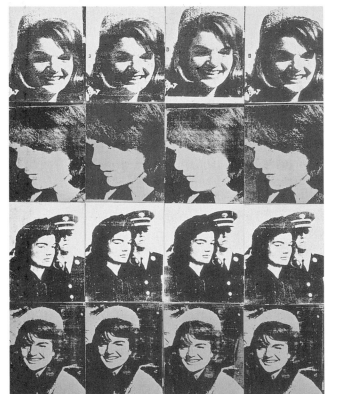

tiches, as in the recurrent vogue for retro-styles and what he calls "nostalgia film," a schizophrenic experience of the world in which "the vivid perception of radical difference" replaces any sense of unifying relationships, "a strange new hallucinatory exhilaration" in the face of "an unparalleled quantum leap in the alienation of daily life in the city."[12]

Jameson argues that this is the art characteristic of a particular phase of capitalist development. Capitalism, he contends, has gone through three major phases since it became the dominant socioeconomic system at the end of the eighteenth century. To each of these stages has corresponded a particular kind of art. The first stage of classical, or competitive capitalism, had as its cultural counterpart the Realism of the great nineteenth-century novelists such as Balzac, Dickens, and Tolstoy (*GBWW* I: 51, II: 52). The second phase, monopoly capitalism, gave rise to the Modernism movement of the early twentieth century—Picasso, Joyce, and Le Corbusier. At the beginning of the 1960s, however, we entered the era of what Jameson calls "late or multinational or consumer capitalism," which is characterized by, among other things, the penetration of the market into every aspect of social life,

> ...the purest form of capital yet to have emerged, a prodigious expansion of capital into hitherto uncommodified areas. This purer capitalism of our own time thus eliminates the enclaves of precapitalist organization it had hitherto tolerated and exploited in a tributary way. One is tempted to speak in this connection of a new and historically original penetration and colonization of Nature and the Unconscious: that is, the destruction of precapitalist Third World agriculture by the Green Revolution, and the rise of the media and advertising industry.[13]

The connection Jameson sees between this new phase of capitalist development and Postmodern art is perhaps best brought out by means of the concept of "critical distance." The art he associates with earlier capitalist stages was undoubtedly part of bourgeois society, but is managed nonetheless to preserve some distance between cultural production and the capitalist system. Thus the Realists sought to penetrate beneath the appearances of everyday life and arrive at some view of society as a whole; the Modernists, on the other hand, made a cult of the work of art itself, prizing its separation from bourgeois normality. Postmodern art, however, is characterized by the fact that "distance in general (including 'critical distance' in particular) has very precisely been abolished," a development which corresponds to the way in which "the prodigious new expansion of multinational capital ends up penetrating and colonizing those very precapitalist enclaves (Nature and the Unconscious) which offered extraterritorial and Archimedian footholds for critical effectivity." Postmodern art, derivative, depthless, and drained of emotion, reflects a social world where everything has become a commodity. Jameson thus finds a "moment of truth" in the concept of postmodernism, since it evokes "this whole extraordinarily demoralizing and depressing original new global space of late capitalism."[14]

Jameson's is not the only attempt to provide a historical explanation for what is seen as the emergence of postmodernism by identifying changes in the pattern of capitalist development. The Marxist urban geographer David Harvey argues that "there is some kind of necessary relation between the rise of postmodernist cultural forms, the emergence of more flexible modes of capital accumulation, and a new round of 'time-space compression' in the organization of capitalism."[15] The sociologists Scott Last and John Urry argue that Postmodern art has arisen against the background of a transition from "organized" to "disorganized" capitalism. Organized capitalism (the phrase was coined by the Austrian Marxist economist Rudolf Hilferding) prevailed in the first half of the twentieth century. It depended on the close cooperation between the state and the big corporations within a national economic framework. The disintegration of this framework in the last decades of the century, driven by the expansion of global trade and investment dominated by vast transnational corporations and volatile financial markets, has unleashed, so Lash and Urry contend, a series of social, economic, and cultural changes to which aesthetic Postmodernism is a response.[16]

Common to all these Marxist or marxisant attempts to contextualize postmodernism, is a tendency to associate it with what has come to be known as economic "globalization." The thought, in other words, is that postmodernism is to be understood as a series of interpretations of and reactions to a fundamentally new experience—that of a globalized capitalism which has somehow broken loose from any sort of national economic anchorage and is able to roam freely throughout the world, abandoning its old industrial sites in Western Europe and North America, and investing wherever it finds it profitable to do so.

The resulting picture of our plight is vividly evoked by the anonymous author of the roman à clef *Primary Colors,* when the author imagines a lightly disguised presidential candidate Bill Clinton telling an audience of laid-off blue-collar workers and their families during the New Hampshire primary:

> No politician can bring these shipyard jobs back. Or make your union strong again. No politician can make it the way it used to be. Because we're living in a new world now, a world without borders—economically, that is. Guy can push a button in New York and move a billion dollars to Tokyo before you can blink an eye. We've got a world market now.[17]

For many, *this* is the postmodern condition—the experience of a globalized, borderless capitalism. A critical assessment of the claims made for "globalization" is thus an essential part of any appraisal of postmodernism. But before going about this, it is necessary to give proper consideration to the aesthetic and philosophical dimensions of postmodernism; and such consideration depends, in turn, on clarification of the meaning of modernity itself.

Modernity and capitalism

The postmodern is typically defined by contrast with that which it succeeds—with, that is, the modern. Though Lyotard is uncomfortable with the idea of the postmodern as simply the chronological successor of the modern, he nevertheless characterizes it in opposition to what he believes to be the characteristically modern reliance on metanarratives of historical development and progress. What is this modernity, however, from which we have supposedly broken? Baudelaire offered a famous definition: "Modernity is that which is ephemeral, fugitive, contingent upon the occasion; it is half of art, whose other half is the eternal and unchangeable."[18]

To direct even one eye toward the momentary and the present represented an enormous cultural shift. Until the seventeenth century, European thought conceived itself as essentially subsuming its contemporary experience under the ancient wisdom inherited from classical antiquity, only somewhat modified by Christianity. "[T]hat which is ephemeral, fugitive, contingent upon the occasion" was either to be interpreted in the light of "the eternal and unchangeable," or to be thrown away as the merest dust. Even great Renaissance figures such as Machiavelli and Montaigne conceive themselves as direct interlocutors with the Greek and Roman ancients, whose accumulated philosophical knowledge and historical experience they seek to apply to their own circumstances.

A decisive break with this devaluation of the present was made possible by the scientific revolution of the seventeenth century: here our understanding of nature was refounded on concepts and principles fundamentally different from those known to Plato and Augustine, Aristotle and Aquinas. The broader implications of this recasting of Western thought, however, were only fully articulated in the eighteenth-century Enlightenment, when the idea of a modern age, radically different from the past and oriented toward the future, took conscious shape. As the German philosopher and social theorist Jürgen Habermas puts it, "the secular concept of modernity expresses the conviction that the future has begun: it is the epoch that lives for the future, that opens itself up to the novelty of the future."[19] Correlatively, an age that self-consciously faces the future can no longer justify itself by appeal to the past. "Modernity can and will no longer borrow the criteria by which it takes its orientation from the models supplied by another epoch," writes Habermas: "*it has to create its own normativity out of itself.*"[20]

What Lyotard calls the grand narratives of modernity, which interpret the whole of human history as a unified process of progressive development, arise precisely from the fact that modernity is an epoch that derives its justification from itself. The German intellectual historian Hans Blumenberg describes "the idea of progress" as "the continuous self-justification of the present, by means of the future that it gives itself, before the past, with which it compares itself."[21] Modernity in other words justifies itself before the ancients, less by the advance it claims to represent over them, but by the indefinite future progress that is makes possible.

We can trace how this conception of modernity and progress takes shape in the Enlightenment. Turgot, a French economist writing in the middle of the eighteenth century, declares that man and therefore his history are inherently progressive:

> Possessor of the treasure-house of signs, which he has had the ability to multiply almost to infinity, he can assure himself of the possession of all his acquired ideas, communicate them to other men, and transmit them to his successors as a heritage which is always being augmented. A continual combination of this progress with the passions, and with the events they have caused, constitutes the history of the human race, in which each man is no more than one part of an immense whole which has, like him, its infancy and its advancement.[22]

The most famous expression of this view of history as a process of gradual, steady, potentially infinite advance is offered by Condorcet in his *Sketch for a Historical Picture of the Progress of the Human Mind* (1795). Even though (as J. B. Bury put it), "prophesying under the shadow of death" (Condorcet wrote the *Sketch* while on the run during the Jacobin Reign of Terror), he "spoke with the verve of a prophet," reducing the "history of civilization" to "the history of enlightenment."[23] The hostages to fortune sometimes given by the *philosophes* often lead to the charge being laid against them, especially by Postmodernists, of naive and facile optimism. They often show, however, an awareness of the ambiguity of progress. Thus Montesquieu has one of his imaginary Persian visitors to France express the fear that the Europeans' very inventiveness and dynamism will lead to destructive consequences: "I am always afraid that they will eventually succeed in discovering some secret which will provide a quicker way making men die, and exterminate whole countries and nations."[24]

It was, in any case, the eighteenth-century appearance of these conceptions of modernity and historical progress that made possible the formulation of the conception of human history as a universal and comprehensive process differentiated into separate stages, each characterized by distinctive principles of social organization. First clearly articulated by leading figures of the Scottish Enlightenment, notably Adam Ferguson, Adam Smith, and John Millar, who saw humankind passing through successive "modes of subsistence" (hunting, pasturage, agriculture, and manufacture), this conception informed some of the main intellectual developments of the nineteenth century: the creation of modern historiography by Bartholl Niebuhr, Leopold von Ranke, and their successors; Marx's development of a materialist conception of history as a series of modes of production; and the foundation of sociology by a variety of theorists—Auguste Comte, Herbert Spencer, Ferdinand Tönnies, Max Weber, and Emile Durkheim—all of whom sought in various ways to conceptualize what made modernity radically different from past forms of society.[25]

It is, however, Marx who provides the single most powerful image of modernity as a dynamic process of development and transformation, a permanent revolution, in these famous lines from the *Communist Manifesto:*

> Constant revolutionizing of production, uninterrupted disturbance of all social conditions, everlasting uncertainty and agitation distinguish the bourgeois epoch from all earlier ones. All fixed, fast-frozen relations, with their train of ancient and venerable prejudices and opinions, are swept away, all new-formed ones become antiquated before they can ossify. All that is solid melts into air, all that is holy is profaned, and man is at last compelled to face with sober senses, his real conditions of life, and his relations with his kind.[26]

The portrait Marx paints here of the modern age has been brilliantly developed by Marshall Berman in his book *All That Is Solid Melts Into Air:*

> There is a mode of vital experience—experience of space and time, of the self and others, of life's possibilities and perils—that is shared by men and women all over the world today. I will call this body of experience "modernity." To be modern is to find ourselves in an environment that promises us adventure, power, joy, growth, transformation of ourselves and the world—and, at the same time, that threatens to destroy everything we have, everything we know, everything we are. Modern environments and experiences cut across all boundaries of geography and ethnicity, of class and nationality, of religion and ideology: in this sense, modernity can be said to unite all mankind. But it is a paradoxical unity, a unity of disunity: it pours us into a maelstrom of perpetual disintegration and renewal, of struggle and contradiction, of ambiguity and anguish. To be modern is to be part of a universe in which, as Marx said, "all that is solid melts into air."[27]

Berman offers a fascinating exploration of how the experience of modernity is articulated primarily by a succession of writers—Goethe, Baudelaire, Gogol, Dostoevsky, and Andrey Bely—but also in Robert Moses's mid-century reconstruction of New York City. Berman's work, however, helps to bring into focus the ambiguity of the concept of modernity. We see that the term "modernity" refers one to both a philosophical idea—the distinctive way in which the Enlightenment came to think of the present relating to both past and future—and to a particular kind of experience of the social world as offering the promise of happiness, and also that of catastrophe. As such, modernity can be seen as a distinct form of society. Durkheim, while not actually using the term "modernity," nevertheless sees it take shape as a result of a process of differentiation in which a division of specialized labor emerges not just in industry, but "in the most diverse sectors of society. Functions, whether political, administrative or judicial, are becoming more and more specialized. The same is true in the arts and sciences."[28] Traditional beliefs and institutions are undermined, thereby requiring the construction of new ones. Essentially the same conception informs the sociology of modernization developed by Talcott Parsons and his followers after World War II.

ВИКТОР ИВАНОЇ

ОТСТРОИМ НА СЛАВУ!

A Communist poster proclaims "Reconstruction will be our glory!" Marx saw modernity as a "dynamic process of development and transformation, a permanent revolution."

These three concepts of modernity—as philosophical idea, historical experience, and form of society—are not equivalent to one another. The "everlasting uncertainty and agitation" evoked by Marx in the *Manifesto,* are conceptualized by him, not as consequences of a process of modernization, but as characteristic of "the bourgeois epoch." In other words, Marx explains what Berman calls "the experience of modernity" by means of his theory of the capitalist mode of production.[29]

Capitalism rests on the employment—and, according to Marx, exploitation—of wage-labor: this makes possible increases in the productivity of labor far outstripping those made in earlier social systems, where the accumulation in the value of his production remained with the laborer himself, who owned it or traded it for apprenticing toward his own mastery. At the same time, rivalries among capitalists—an inherently fragmented class, Marx claims, fighting over the fruits of exploitation—unleash a process of competitive accumulation in which productivity-enhancing investment is not merely possible but mandatory if the individual capital is to survive the perpetual struggle for markets. "The bourgeoisie cannot exist without constantly revolutionizing the instruments of production, and thereby the relations of production, and with them the whole relations of society," and so unleashing Berman's "maelstrom of perpetual disintegration and renewal."[30]

If this explanation were valid, it might help to account, not simply for the distinctive experience of modernity, but also for the emergence of the philosophical conception of the modern age as justifying itself by its movement into the future and away from the past. For capitalism, as conceived by Marx, drives us willy-nilly into the future, as the innovations spewed out by competitive accumulation sweep away traditional relations, institutions, and beliefs. This characteristic of historical progress under capitalism is captured by the German Marxist critic Walter Benjamin:

> This is how one pictures the angel of history. His face is turned toward the past. Where we perceive a chain of events, he sees one single catastrophe which keeps piling wreckage upon wreckage and hurls it in front of his feet. The angel would like to stay, awaken the dead, and make whole what has been smashed. But a storm is blowing from Paradise: it has got caught in his wings with such violence that the angel can no longer close them. This storm irresistibly propels him into the future to which his back is turned, while the pile of debris before him grows skyward. The storm is what we call progress.[31]

Giddens on modernity and postmodernity

Is modernity to be understood thus as a response to and a consequence of capitalism, or is capitalism itself merely one of the dimensions of modernity? The latter answer is given by British sociologist Anthony Giddens in a series of influential texts. Modernity, Giddens argues, has four "institutional dimensions"—capitalism, industrialism, surveillance (of individuals by corporate and state bureaucracies), and war. Each of these dimensions is irreducible to one or more of the other three; there is, therefore, no sense in which capitalism, for example, can be responsible for the general characteristics of modernity.[32]

Giddens's main concern is with the consequences of modernity's tendency toward rapid, destabilizing transformation:

> The dynamism of modernity derives from the *separation of time and space* and their recombination in forms which permit the precise time-space 'zoning' of social life; the *disembedding* of social systems (a phenomenon which connects closely with the factors involved in time-space separation); and the *reflexive ordering and reordering* of social relations in the light of continual inputs of knowledge affecting the actions of individuals and groups.[33]

As a definition of modernity this is less than perspicuous. Nevertheless, it is at least clear that for Giddens modernity involves an intrinsic tendency toward globalization:

> The advent of modernity increasingly tears space away from place by fostering relations between "absent" others, locationally distant from any

given situation of face-to-face interaction. In conditions of modernity, place becomes increasingly *phantasmagoric:* that is to say, locales are thoroughly penetrated by and shaped in terms of social influences quite distant from them. What structures the locale is not simply that which is present on the scene; the "visible form" of the locale conceals the distanci-ated relations which determine its nature.[34]

Thus "disembedding" consists in "the 'lifting out' of social relations from local contexts of interaction and their restructuring across indefinite spans of time-space."[35] This is achieved through one of two kinds of "abstract system," and "symbolic tokens," by which Giddens means essen-tially money and the processes of impersonal market exchanges which sustain it, and "expert systems," where we enter into relationships depen-dent on the expertise and reliability of accredited technical experts—for example, trusting our lives to pilots and surgeons whom we probably will never meet.

Globalization arises from the intrinsic characteristics of modernity, "and can thus be defined as the intensification of worldwide social relations which link distant localities in such a way that local happenings are shaped by events occurring many miles away and vice versa." Giddens thus denies that modernity is being overcome by postmodernity: "Rather than entering a period of postmodernity, we are moving into one in which the conse-quences of modernity are becoming more radicalized and universalized than before."[36]

In this era of what Giddens prefers to call "high modernity" or "radical-ized modernity," the human condition is characterized by a distinctive experience of the self arising from the way in which personal relationships have detached largely themselves from traditional institutions and kinship structures, and come instead to depend on the choices continuously made by the individuals concerned.[37] While Giddens regards this as largely a positive development, allowing individuals to compensate for the disem-bedding of social relations by gaining a degree of control over their own immediate circumstances, he argues that modernity has a "specific risk profile," characterized in particular by *"[g]lobalization of risk."* Thus the number of possible outcomes with absolutely catastrophic consequences for humankind—most obviously nuclear war—increases; moreover, there are more events—for example, economic changes—that can affect very large numbers of people around the world; our attempts to interfere in and control nature can have unforeseen, and disastrous consequences (for ex-ample, the nuclear accident at Chernobyl and the British "mad cow" dis-ease scare); "institutionalized risk environments" (a polite way of referring to organized gambling) such as financial markets come to have growing influence on the life chances of many people; finally, public awareness of these risks and of the limited ability of experts to anticipate and control actual outcomes also grows.[38]

Giddens therefore suggests that we should think of modernity as a jug-gernaut—"a runaway machine of enormous power which, collectively as human beings we can drive to some extent but which also threatens to rush out of our control and which could rend itself asunder."[39] This image of modernity is strikingly similar to Benjamin's memorable and vivid picture of historical progress as a storm from Paradise that drives us complaining into the future.

Suggestive though both these metaphors are, a verbal image is not the same as an explanation. Giddens's account of "high modernity" provides more a stylized and suggestive description of certain trends than an analysis of the processes that have given rise to them. He lays great stress on the tendency for social relations to become drawn into interactions conducted over increasingly long distances. He has, however, remarkably little to say about the causes of this tendency. The metaphor of modernity of a juggernaut invites us to think of the drive to globalization as a force beyond human comprehension and control.

Other theorists have dealt with the same phenomena while confronting more directly the problem of explanation. David Harvey, author of *The Condition of Postmodernity,* focuses on what he calls "time-space compression," "that process of annihilation of space through time that has always lain at the center of capitalism's dynamic":

> As space appears to shrink to a 'global village' of telecommunications and a 'spaceship earth' of economic and ecological interdependencies—to use just two familiar and everyday images—and as time horizons shorten to the point where the present is all there is (the world of the schizophrenic), so we have to learn how to cope with an overwhelming sense of *compression* of our spatial and temporal worlds.[40]

During layovers, passengers at Singapore's Changhi airport can access the Internet on computers provided by the airport. We have indeed become a "global village of telecommunications."

For Harvey, however, time-space compression is less an abstract characteristic of modernity than a consequence of the inherent tendencies of
capitalism as a system of competitive accumulation:

> There is an omnipresent incentive for individual capitalists to accelerate
> their turnover time *vis-á-vis* the social average, and in so doing to promote
> a social trend toward faster average turnover times. Capitalism…has for
> this reason been characterized by continuous efforts to shorten turnover
> times, thereby speeding up social processes while reducing the time hori-
> zons of meaningful decision-making. There are, however, a number of
> barriers to this tendency—barriers in the rigidity of production and labour
> skills, fixed capital that must be amortized, marketing frictions, consump-
> tion lags, bottlenecks to money circulation, and the like. There is a whole
> history of technical and organizational innovation applied to the reduction
> of such barriers—everything from assembly-line production (of cars or
> battery hens), acceleration of physical processes (fermentation, genetic
> engineering), to planned obsolescence in consumption (the mobilization
> of fashion and advertising to accelerate change), the credit system, elec-
> tronic banking, and the like….The general effect, then, is for capitalist
> modernization to be very much about speed-up and acceleration in the
> pace of economic processes and, hence, in social life.[41]

Similarly,

> [T]he incentive to create the world market, to reduce spatial barriers,
> and to annihilate space through time is omnipresent, as is the incentive to
> rationalize spatial organization into efficient configurations of production
> (serial organization of the detail division of labour, factory systems, and
> assembly line, territorial division of labour, and agglomeration in large
> towns), circulation networks (transport and communication systems), and
> consumption (household and domestic layout, community organization,
> and residential differentiation, collective consumption in cities). Innova-
> tions dedicated to the removal of spatial barriers in all of these respects
> have been of immense significance in the history of capitalism, turning
> that history into a very geographical affair—the railroad and the telegraph,
> the automobile, radio and telephone, the jet aircraft and television, and the
> recent telecommunications revolution are cases in point.[42]

From Harvey's perspective, the tentative emergence in the 1970s and
1980s of a new version of capitalism, which he calls "flexible accumulation," represents "a new round of… 'time-space compression' … in the capitalist world—the time horizons of both private and public decision-
making have shrunk, while satellite communication and declining transport
costs have made it increasingly possible to spread those decisions over an
ever wider and variegated space."[43]

I give some critical consideration to Harvey's idea of a new era of
"flexible accumulation" below. Nevertheless, his general approach seems
to me superior to Giddens's in that he offers a relatively concrete and
historically specific account of the processes responsible for the phenomena of time-space compression on which both lay such stress. At the same

time, Giddens's discussions of "high modernity" have the merit that, while focusing on what is new in late-twentieth-century experience (particularly in respect of what he calls "the transformation of intimacy," that is, changes in conceptions of the self and of personal relationships), they do so within a framework that stresses the continuities between these phenomena and features inherent in the project of modernity itself. Such continuities may help to explain why the most influential attempts to provide a social explanation of the postmodern should rely less on some direct contrast between modernity and postmodernity as supposed phases in human history than on the kind of transformation that Jameson and Harvey claim capitalism has undergone.

Does Postmodern art exist?

Before considering such attempts at social explanation, we must consider the assumption they necessarily share, namely that there is something for them to explain. The idea that we are moving into a "postmodern condition" rests, in the first place, on the differences that are claimed to exist between Modern and Postmodern art. Giddens, despite his skepticism about the emergence of a new Postmodern social order, argues: "Postmodernism, if it means anything, is best kept to refer to styles or movements within literature, painting, the plastic arts, and architecture. It concerns aspects of *aesthetic reflection* upon modernity."[44]

What, then, are the characteristic features of this "aesthetic revolution"? Consider this influential statement by the architectural theorist Charles Jencks: "To this day I would define Postmodernism as...*double-coding: the combination of Modern techniques with something else (usually traditional building) in order for architecture to communicate with the public and a concerned minority, usually other architects.*"[45] Though Jencks puts the matter in architectural terms, his definition is intended to be of general significance. One could use the idea of "double-coding" to justify the frequent descriptions of Quentin Tarantino as a Postmodern film director. Fully to experience one of his movies is to operate at two levels: to share the director's evident delight in dialogue and narrative-construction, *and* to pick up the endless references to other films that he makes. (A tacit appeal to a knowing "concerned minority" that shares the artist's cultural dialect is very characteristic of what is thought to be Postmodern art.)

Yet if we take "double-coding" to a necessary condition of a work of art being described as Postmodern, we face an immediate difficulty. For it is by no means peculiar to the art of the late twentieth century. Take one of the great works of the Modernist revolution in the early decades of this century, T. S. Eliot's *The Waste Land*. Peter Ackroyd writes of this poem:

Eliot found his own voice by first reproducing that of others—as if it was only through his reading of, and response to, literature that he could find anything to hold onto, anything 'real.' That is why *Ulysses* struck him

Amanda Plummer and Tim Roth in Quentin Tarantino's Pulp Fiction *(1994). Frequently described as a postmodern film director, Tarantino has* "an evident delight in dialogue and narrative construction."

so forcibly, in a way no other novel ever did. Joyce had created a world which exists only in, and through, the multiple uses of language—through voices, through parodies of style... Joyce had a historical consciousness of language and thus of the relativity of any one 'style.' The whole course of Eliot's development would lead him to share such a consciousness... In the closing sequence of *The Waste Land* itself he creates a montage of lines from Dante, Kyd, Gérard de Nerval, the *Pervigilium Veneris* and Sanskrit... There is no 'truth' to be found, only a number of styles and interpretations—one laid upon another in an endless and apparently meaningless process.[46]

Double coding—"the multiple uses of language"—thus turns out to be a feature of Modernism. The point admits of more general application. Seeking to identify what is common to the art of what is generally accepted to be the high Modernist era of 1890–1930, Eugene Lunn isolates four general characteristics—*"Aesthetic Self-Consciousness or Self-Reflexiveness," "Simultaneity, Juxtaposition, or 'Montage'," "Paradox, Ambiguity, and Uncertainty,"* and *"'Dehumanization' and the Demise of the Integrated Individual Subject or Personality."*[47] These are all features, however, that are frequently claimed for *Post*modern art. To return to the example of Tarantino, "Aesthetic Self-Reflexiveness" is a characteristic feature of his films, which insert themselves by means of a series of references into a space constituted by the interrelations of the various movies that have consciously or unconsciously influenced him.[48]

Postmodernists use various devices in order to overcome this difficulty. One is to assert that Postmodern art implies a different attitude from that typical of Modernism. Another is simply to assimilate Modernism to what is held to be the Enlightenment's crass optimism about historical progress. This is, however, completely to efface the historical specificity of Modernism, whose major practitioners tended in fact to share in the *fin-de-siècle* reaction against Victorian optimism, evincing a profound skepticism about reason's capacity to master the world. Eliot reviewing Joyce's *Ulysses* in 1923, described the novel's use of myth as "simply a way of controlling, of ordering, of giving a shape and a significance to the immense panorama of futility and anarchy which is contemporary history."[49]

A somewhat more sophisticated ploy is to accuse Modernism of elitism. Andreas Huyssen declares that "the most significant trends within postmodernism have challenged modernism's relentless hostility to mass culture."[50] Here the picture is more complex. What Lunn calls Modernism's "Aesthetic Self-Reflexiveness" represents a radicalization of the *l'art pour l'art* movement which gained increasing strength in the latter part of the nineteenth century. Increasingly, the work of art ceases to claim to offer representations of the world, to explore, for example, the relationship between the individual and society as the great Realist novels did, and revolves to focus on itself. Proust's great novel *À la recherche du temps perdu* (a portion of which can be found in *GBWW* II: 59, 281–408) exemplifies this transition, since it offers a fictional reconstruction of the experiences which led to its own writing, at the end of which the narrator suddenly realizes that "all these materials for a work of literature were simply my past life."[51]

In his brilliant study of Proust, *Proust and Signs*, Deleuze describes the cultural condition to which the novel is a response:

> Order has collapsed, as much in the states of the world which were supposed to reproduce it as in the essences or Ideas which were supposed to inspire it. The world has become crumbs and chaos. Precisely because reminiscence proceeds from subjective associations to an originating viewpoint, objectivity can no longer exist except in the work of art: it no longer exists in significant content as states of the world, nor in ideal signification as stable essence, but solely in the signifying formal structure of the work, in its style.[52]

The structure of the work of art thus provides an order that has vanished from the world itself. Art thus serves as a refuge from the "crumbs and chaos" into which the world has disintegrated, from what Eliot calls "the immense panorama of futility and anarchy that is contemporary history." Such a conception of the work of art does easily lend itself to an elitist contempt for popular philistinism. The young Joyce declared in 1901, "No man, said the Nolan [the Renaissance philosopher Giordano Bruno], can be a lover of the true or the good unless he abhors the multitude; and the artist, though he may employ the crowd, is very careful to isolate himself."[53]

In focusing on the work of art, however, rather than anything it can be said to be about, the great Modernists made possible a critique of art itself as a separate institution. In many ways, Cubism marked this turning point. The Cubists sought to display the constructed character of the artwork by producing paintings that were congeries of discrete fragments. More particularly, their collages incorporating bits of the "real world"—scraps of newspaper, for example—undermined the traditional conception of the work of art as a self-contained representation of the world outside it,

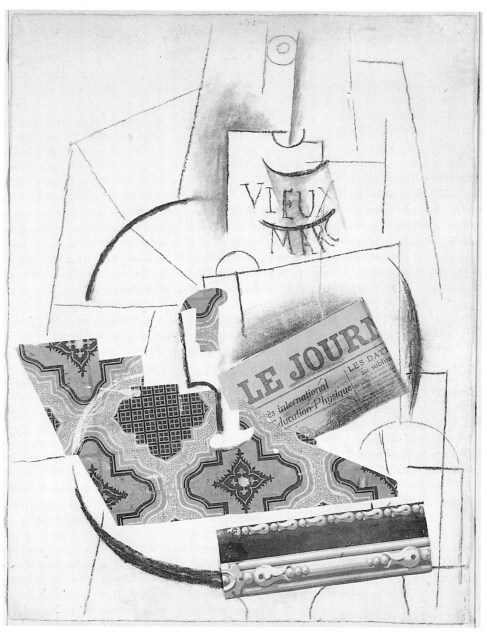

Bottle of Vieux Marc, Glass, and Newspaper Ceret *by Pablo Picasso (1912).* "The Cubists sought to display the constructed character of the artwork by producing paintings that were congeries of discrete fragments."

thereby implicitly breaking down the distinction between art and everyday life. As Peter Bürger puts it,

> The insertion of reality-fragments into the work of art fundamentally transforms that work ... The artist no longer renounces shaping a whole, but gives the painting a different status, since parts of it no longer have the relationship to reality characteristic of the organic work of art. They are no longer signs pointing to reality, they *are* reality.[54]

This transformation of the work of art opened the way to the avant-garde movements of the early twentieth century—Dadaism, early Surrealism, Russian Constructivism after the 1917 Revolution. These launched what Bürger describes as an "attack on the status of art in bourgeois society. What is negated is not an earlier form of art (a style) but art as an institution that is unassociated with the life-praxis of men."[55] The aspiration to break down the distinction between art and everyday life is well-expressed in this pronouncement by the Russian revolutionary poet Vladimir Mayakovsky, a leading figure in the early Soviet literary scene. "We do not need a dead mausoleum of art where dead works are worshipped, but a living factory of the human spirit—in the streets, in the tramways, in the factories, work-shops and workers' home."[56]

The avant-garde critique of art as an autonomous institution implied a revaluation of everyday life. Even the more elitist Modernists such as Eliot and Joyce had in fact drawn on popular culture at the same time as they sought to distance themselves from it. Post-Cubist avant-garde went much further, however. The Surrealists sought what Benjamin called "profane illumination" from chance occurrences in city life.[57] This reflected what Christopher Green describes as "the belief in the essential continuity of life and art, the belief that art and life should become a single undifferentiated search for the marvellous. Only because there was this fundamental sense of continuity did the Surrealists feel the need to act with the ultimate aim of changing society and the day-to-day behaviour of its members."[58] The avant-garde effort to democratize art thus went hand in hand with the aspiration to transform everyday life through social revolution. "'Transform the world,' Marx said; 'change life,' Rimbaud said—these two watch-words are for us one and the same,'" the leading Surrealist André Breton declared in 1935.[59]

The case of Surrealism makes any crude counterposition of Modernist elitism and Postmodernist populism beside the point. Modernism gave rise to movements that explicitly challenged the elitism of *l'art pour l'art* and which sought to marry aesthetic and social revolution. This does not imply any necessary connection between Modernism and political radicalism. If some leading practitioners—Bertolt Brecht and Sergei Eisenstein, for ex-ample—were revolutionary socialists, others—among them Céline and Wyndham Lewis—were fascists. Indeed, in an important essay the Italian critic Franco Moretti has stressed what he suggests is the essential ambigu-ity of Modernism, "an aesthetic-ironic attitude whose best definition still lies in an old formula—'willing suspension of disbelief'—which shows how much of the modernist imagination—where indeed nothing is unbelievable—has its source in romantic irony."[60]

Moretti has in mind Carl Schmitt's account of Romanticism, according to which "the romantic subject treats the world as an occasion and an opportunity for his romantic productivity." Any sense of the world itself and of the subject's transactions with that world being governed by objective causal relationships is lost. "The romantic withdraws from reality....He ironically avoids the constraints of objectivity and guards himself against becoming committed to anything. The reservation of all infinite possibilities lies in irony." Consequently, "everything—society and history, the cosmos and humanity—serves only the productivity of the romantic ego....every event is transformed into a fantastic and dreamlike ambiguity, and every object can become anything."[61]

The ambiguity of Modernism can be seen, not simply in the variety of political stances its practitioners took, but also in the care with which many of its greatest figures sought to maintain a stance of ironic detachment from everyday political and social realities. Leon Edel cites Henry James's remark in a letter of 1873: "I regard the march of history very much as a man placed astride a locomotive, without knowledge or help, would regard the progress of that vehicle. To stick on, somehow, and even enjoy the scenery as we pass, is the sum of aspiration." Edel comments: "James, on his locomotive of history, offers a vision of a comparatively happy observer and artist; the reality in which he had been placed by fate fascinated him to such a degree that the task of observing and recording it from various points of appreciation and ironic judgement proved sufficient for a lifetime."[62] Other great Modernists took essentially a similar stance, though often rather less happily than Edel suggests James rode "the locomotive of history."

Two conclusions emerge from this discussion of Modernism.[63] The first is that the complexity and especially the constitutive ambiguity of Modernism as a cultural phenomenon makes the Postmodernists' effort to associate it with some particular metaphysical or political attitude intrinsically hazardous. Lyotard argues that Modern art is characterized by its nostalgia for a state of affairs—necessarily unattainable—in which we can somehow experience reality as a coherent and harmonious whole.[64] How is this analysis supposed to apply, for example, to the immediate, sensuous exhilaration conveyed by so many of Matisse's paintings, or the subversive sense of fun that the Dadaists brought to their japes?

Second, it is striking how many statements used to identify what is distinctive to Modernism can refer equally to its supposed Postmodernist other. The Romantic irony in which "every event is transformed into a fantastic and dreamlike ambiguity, and every object can become anything," is present in many postmodern artworks. Does this mean that what is called Postmodernism should subsume within the larger domain of Modernism?

Beyond a certain point argument over labels is futile. The habit of calling certain recently produced works of art postmodern is probably too well-entrenched now to do much about it, even if in their basic structural features these works do not radically differ from those which opinion would agree in describing as Modernist. It is more useful to try to understand what it is about the political and cultural climate of the past twenty years that has made the idea of a shift in what Jameson calls the "cultural dominant" toward Postmodernism seem plausible.

Poststructuralism and the critique of reason

The perception of such a shift does not depend only on the apparent emergence of a new, Postmodern art. Indeed, the supposed collapse of Modern art is widely related to the emergence, particularly in poststructuralism, of a philosophical critique of reason. The implied identification of Modernism with the Enlightenment cannot be sustained historically: on the contrary, key figures such as Eliot are more plausibly included in the camp of the Counter-Enlightenment.[65] Nevertheless, the intellectual impact of this critique has been great.

Addressing poststructuralism philosophically in anything like appropriate depth would take me well beyond the boundaries of this essay: there are, in any case, several works already available which do so.[66] All I shall do here is to outline the two main strategies pursued by poststructuralist philosophers, to highlight the potentially fatal difficulty these both involve, and at least to gesture toward the existence of alternative approaches that neither confront the same difficulties nor draw the same apocalyptic conclusions about reason.

Poststructuralism, I have suggested, involves a critique of reason. There are two main respects, both central to the Enlightenment project, in which reason is at stake here. The first is the claim that the forms of scientific inquiry that began to take shape with the emergence of modern physics in the seventeenth century allow us to develop an objective understanding of the physical and social worlds.[67] Second, there is the idea that we can use our reason, not simply to understand the patterns at work in our history, but also, over time, to gain some control over that history.

This second dimension, "[t]he relation of history to reason," Habermas argues, "remains constitutive for the discourse of modernity."[68] It was Hegel who took over and radicalized the concern with this relation in Enlightenment philosophy. He conceived the rationality of finite human subjects as the embodiment of the impersonal Reason of Absolute Spirit: modernity is the epoch in which the Absolute comes fully to self-consciousness through the vehicle of individual minds. Hegel's absolute idealism, in which everything mental, material, and social turns out to be a manifestation of the Absolute, was untenable philosophically, however suggestive his particular arguments or insights might be. The collapse of the Hegelian system, Habermas contends, set the agenda for the debate on modernity to the present day, that has tended to oscillate between three basic positions.

On the revolutionary left, Marx and his followers have argued that capitalism represents only a one-sided and distorted form of rationality: social revolution is necessary to realize the full potential of reason. On the conservative right, many thinkers have argued that, on the contrary, bourgeois society represents the highest attainable social embodiment of reason (Francis Fukuyama's celebrated thesis that the triumph of liberal capitalism in the Cold War marked the "End of History" might be seen as one contemporary version of this view). In the words of Habermas from his work *Philosophical Discourse*:

> Finally, *Nietzsche* wanted to unmask the dramaturgy of the entire stage-piece in which both—revolutionary hope and the reaction to it—enter on the scene. He removed the dialectical thorn from a critique of a reason centred on the subject and shrivelled into purposive rationality; and he related to reason as a whole the way the Young Hegelians related to its sublimations: Reason is *nothing else* than power, than the will to power, which it so radiantly conceals.[69]

Poststructuralism represents a particular set of variations on Nietzschean themes that developed among French philosophers after World War II.[70] The philosophers associated under this label, however, in no sense represent a unified "school:" there are significant differences of approach and of doctrine between them. For present purposes, it is sufficient to note two distinct strategies they pursue whose effect is to place in question both the opposed claims made above for reason.

The first of these strategies is what Richard Rorty calls "textualism."[71] It is summed up by Derrida's famous declaration: *"There is nothing outside of the text."*[72] The significance of this statement derives from a specific conception of language, in which meaning essentially derives from the interrelations of the constituent elements of language rather than from the relationship between language and the world. This conception derives from Ferdinand de Saussure's *Course in General Linguistics* (1915), that exerted a powerful influence on postwar French philosophical and social thought. Saussure, in the first place, drew a crucial distinction between signifier and signified, that is, between the words of which language is composed and the concepts to which they correspond. The effect was, in effect, to bracket the question of reference, that is, of the relationship between linguistic utterances and the items in the real world to which they are used to refer. Saussure never himself doubted the existence of such a relationship, but by focusing on the nature of signification, that is, on the (as he conceived it) intra-linguistic process through which signifiers (words) connect with signified (concepts), he made it possible to conceive language as essentially an autonomous system. Second, he argued that words succeed in signifying, in conveying meaning, by means of the differences between them. It is because words consist in a set of contrasting sounds that they are able to locate concepts which are similarly identified through the differences between them. Language is thus a structure defined by the relations of difference among its constituent items.[73]

Signifier and signified, word and concept, were of co-equal importance to Saussure. They were, as he put it, like two sides of the same piece of paper. In taking over Saussure's structural linguistics in order to use it in his anthropological studies, Claude Lévi-Strauss gave primacy to signifier over signified, so that words through their interrelations somehow autonomously generated meaning.[74] He tended, however, to conceive structure as closed, derived from a finite set of oppositions. Derrida broke with this assumption (it is in this sense that it is valid to call him and philosophers like him *post*structuralists, though the concept of the "structuralism" against which they rebelled is deeply confused and misleading). The process of signification consists in the play of signifiers proliferating to infinity. The signified to which any given signifier corresponds is itself a signifier; *its* signified will turn out to be another signifier; and so on ad infinitum. Nor is this merely a technical claim in the philosophy of language. On the contrary, it serves Derrida's critique of what he calls "the metaphysics of presence"—that is, the idea that our beliefs are ultimately anchored in some sort of direct access enjoyed by the subject to reality. The notion of a "transcendental signified"—of a concept present to consciousness without the mediation of language—let alone that of our utterances having referents in the world to which they allow us access, is a Utopian dream. It is in this sense that "there is nothing outside of the text." We cannot escape from what Jameson calls "the prison-house of language."[75]

One of the most important implications of Derrida's radicalization of the Saussurian conception of language is to undermine the idea—central to Western philosophy since Descartes—of the subject as "self-present," in command not simply of the language it uses but of the thoughts which it uses language to express. The subject is no longer the focal point from which everything must be constructed: as Jacques Lacan insisted in his reinterpretation of Freud (partly inspired by Saussure and Lévi-Strauss), the center of the subject lies "outside itself," in the play of signification, the endless slippage of meaning that is constitutive of language.

Derrida is not interested primarily in dissolving the imaginary self-identity of the subject into an endless sea of difference, however. The metaphysics of presence, he insists, is both impossible and indispensable. In other words, we are compelled to posit a moment of presence—a moment where the play of difference is halted in some kind of final resolution, some kind of direct insight into the nature of reality—even though this moment is never actually attained, is eternally absent. The play constitutive of signification thus necessarily involves both the disruption of presence, that is always posited through a chain of substitutions that transcend it, and the reference to presence, but a presence that can never fully be achieved, is constantly deferred.

Différance is the name Derrida gives to this interplay of presence and absence, in which a *parousia,* a revelation of how things really are, is constantly invoked but never attained. It is, he says, "the obliterated origin of absence and presence."[76] It is thus the source of the endless positing and deferring of presence, but since we only have access to *différance* in and through this process, it is unknowable. From this flows Derrida's practice of deconstruction, the close reading of texts to expose their ambiguities, and through this their dependence on the metaphysics of presence: any positive attempt to give an account of the way in which the world is "outside" textuality, or, say, of how texts are articulated onto "real" institutions and practices would be to collapse into this metaphysics. The role of the critical philosopher is to cultivate an awareness of how our discourse is inhabited by the metaphysics of presence, which we cannot escape.

Derrida's aim in all this is plainly not to encourage any commonplace skepticism about whether or not the tables and chairs and all the other referents of our utterances actually exist independently of our talking about them. The effect of his philosophical *démarche*, however, is undoubtedly to undermine confidence in the ability of human thought to capture any kind of reality except one that is reducible to discourse. Irrespective of Derrida's actual intentions, many scholars have taken the moral of his textualism to be a sort of discursive idealism in which language and the world collapse into each other. Consider, for example, the following remark by British social historian Patrick Joyce: "The major advance of 'post-modernism' needs to be registered by historians: namely, that the events, structures and processes of the past are indistinguishable from the forms of documentary representation, the conceptual and political appropriations, and the historical discourses that construct them."[77]

A critique of knowledge is, however, much more directly the target of the second strategy associated with poststructuralism, that represented particularly by Foucault's writings of the 1970s, but also by the work of Deleuze and his collaborator Félix Guattari. Here the preoccupation with the nature of signification that forms at least one of the starting points of Derrida's deconstruction is largely absent. Foucault declared: "I believe one's point of reference should not be the great model of language and signs, but that of war and battle. The history which bears and determines us has the form of a war rather than a language: relations of power, not relations of meaning."[78]

This explicitly Nietzschean preoccupation with power found fruit in a body of historical writing by Foucault in the mid-1970s concerned with establishing the conditions of existence of particular bodies of discourse. The social body, Foucault argues, is constituted by a historically specific "apparatus" (*dispositif*), "a thoroughly heterogeneous ensemble consisting of discourses, institutions, architectural forms, regulatory decisions, laws, administrative measures, scientific statements, philosophical, moral and philanthropic propositions—in short, the said and the unsaid."[79]

The power that inhabits this apparatus has a number of characteristics. First and most important, it involves a particular kind of *"power-knowledge:"* "There is no power-relation without the correlative constitution of a field of knowledge, nor at the same time any knowledge that does not presuppose and constitute at the same time power-relations."[80] Second, power is not unitary but consists of a multiplicity of microrelationships that inhabit the whole of the social body. Third, power does not proceed primarily through repression, coercively restricting the activities of individuals. It operates more subtly, by constituting individuals, forming them within particular institutions that endow them with certain motives and desires and relations between themselves and others: "The individual is not a pregiven entity which is seized on by the exercise of power. The individual, with his identity and characteristics, is the product of a relation of power exercised over bodies, multiplicities, movements, desires, forces."[81] Finally, power necessarily evokes resistance, albeit as fragmentary and decentralized as the power-relations it contests.[82]

Foucault's theory thus leads from a different starting point to many of the same philosophical conclusions as Derrida's deconstruction. In both, the subject is radically decentered—in Foucault's case because it is an effect of a given apparatus of power-knowledge. Similarly, both are antirealist in the sense that theories are not to be assessed in terms of the degree to which they capture the nature of a world existing independently of discourse. For Foucault, the will to know is merely one form of the will to power. He seeks to avoid a narrowly instrumentalist account of knowledge, in which scientific theories are merely tools, since power presupposes knowledge as much as knowledge power. Nevertheless, in *Discipline and Punish* (1975) Foucault argues that theoretical discourses such as psychiatry originated in the early nineteenth century as part of a new apparatus of power-knowledge, the "disciplinary society," that involved the development of a nexus of institutions (prisons, factories, schools, workhouses) functioning to shape their human raw material into reliable, docile, and productive individuals. Western scientific reason, that claims disinterestedly to pursue the truth, turns out to be inescapably imbricated with relations of domination and subordination.

As a body of philosophical work, poststructuralism undoubtedly offers many rich and suggestive ideas developed by forceful and imaginative thinkers. Deleuze, the least well-known of the three leading figures, left behind at the time of his suicide in 1995 a series of explorations of the Western philosophical tradition (including discussions of thinkers as diverse as the Stoics, Spinoza, Leibniz, Hume, Nietzsche, Lewis Carroll, Bergson, and Proust) that may well last longer than anything else to have emerged from poststructuralism. Nevertheless, inasmuch as Deleuze, Derrida, and Foucault develop a critique of reason, all present the same difficulty.

The difficulty is highlighted by the American philosopher Richard Rorty, who has built up a considerable reputation by effectively acting as a go-between connecting Continental poststructuralism and anglophone intellectual culture, translating the often forbiddingly hermetic pronouncements of Derrida and Foucault into a more accessible Anglo-Saxon idiom. Rorty says that "textualism wants to place literature at the centre, and to treat both science and philosophy as, at best, literary genres."[83]

On this view, great scientists invent descriptions of the world which are useful for purposes of predicting and controlling what happens, just as

poets and political thinkers invent other descriptions of it for other purposes. But there is no sense in which *any* of these descriptions is an
accurate representation of the way in which the world is in itself.[84]

Taking this stand, however, poses, Rorty notes, the problem of its own
status:

> The difficulty faced by a philosopher who, like myself, is sympathetic
> to this suggestion—one who thinks of himself as auxiliary to the poet
> rather than to the physicist—is to avoid hinting that this suggestion gets
> something right, that my sort of philosophy corresponds to the way things
> really are. For this talk of correspondence brings back just the idea my sort
> of philosopher wants to get rid of, the idea that the world or the self has an
> intrinsic nature.... To say that there is no such thing as intrinsic nature is
> not to say that the intrinsic nature of reality has turned out, surprisingly

Prisoners line up at Sing Sing prison in New York. The "disciplinary society... involved the development of... institutions [such as prisons] functioning to shape their human raw material into reliable, docile, and productive individuals."

enough, to be extrinsic. It is to say that the term 'intrinsic nature' is one which it would pay us not to use, an expression which has caused more trouble than it has been worth. To say that we should drop the idea of truth as out there waiting to be discovered is not to say that we have discovered that, out there, there is no truth. It is to say that our purposes are best served by ceasing to see truth as a deep matter, a topic of philosophical interest, or 'true' as a term which repays 'analysis.'[85]

The difficulty that Rorty highlights is essentially that of how the post-structuralist denial that human knowledge can provide us with accurate representations of what the world is, can avoid being interpreted as the claim to offer an accurate representation of what the world is. This is one form of the ancient dilemma: is the skeptic's assertion that there is no such thing as truth itself true? If it is, then it is also false, since there is at least one truth. If, on the other hand, it is false, why should we bother to listen to a skeptic, since by his own admission he is telling us a falsehood, and is therefore a liar?

Habermas argues that there is a sense in which this difficulty is inherent in the Enlightenment project. The Enlightenment started out as the effort to arrive at a thoroughly scientific understanding of both the physical and the social worlds. The more modern social theory developed, however, the more it began to expose the *distortion* of reason—the way, that is, in which apparently objective, rationally founded theories actually conceal, and serve to legitimize sectional social interests. Marx's theory of ideology is the paradigm case of this process of radicalization of the Enlightenment: here the widespread acceptance of certain beliefs is explained not by the existence of good reasons for holding them true but by their role in justifying the position of the economically dominant class.[86]

The final step in this particular process is to turn the critique of ideology onto reason itself. That step is taken by Nietzsche and Foucault, for whom every theory is a particular embodiment of the will to power; in a somewhat different way, the two leading figures of the Frankfurt School, Theodor Adorno and Max Horkheimer, pursue the same course. They therefore find themselves confronting what Habermas calls a "performative contradiction." Habermas writes, "If they do not want to renounce the effect of a final unmasking and still want to *continue with critique,* they will have to leave at least one rational criterion intact for their explanation of the corruption of *all* rational criteria."[87] If every theory is a tool of some exploiting or would-be exploiting interest, what is the status of the theory that purports to point this out?

Rorty offers a pragmatic solution to the problem of using reason to carry out a fundamental critique of reason itself, one in which we should avoid saying that the idea of truth is itself false, but rather should say instead that it is not useful. Theoretical change then becomes, not the development of better (in the sense of more accurate) representations of the world, but of more less-persuasive "redescriptions," that attract us because they are interesting, or aesthetically pleasing, or useful. A new theory should thus be greeted as we would a major new novel, rather than as offering some deeper insight into the way the world is.

The problem with Rorty's suggestion is that it presumes what he needs to establish, namely that science and philosophy can be assimilated into literature. In modern Western culture one of the defining features of literature and the other arts is precisely that art involves the liberation of the imagination, its escape from the constraints imposed on us by the world. (There is then plenty of scope for argument and experiment over what is the best use the imagination should make of its freedom: nevertheless, even the most rigorously Realist novel or painting is still undeniably a work of the imagination.) Scientific theories are, by contrast, distinguished by the respect they pay to these constraints, and by the effort they represent to uncover the underlying structures responsible for them. Rorty urges us to give this contrast up as a distinction without a difference. It is, however, very hard in practice when trying to explain why one theory can be said to be more useful to us than another to avoid at least tacitly appealing to the idea that it captures how things are better than its rival does.

This is as true of poststructuralists as it is of anyone else. Of the key figures Derrida is the most philosophically self-aware, and therefore the most concerned to evade the consequences of the dilemma outlined above. Roughly speaking, his response can be said to take the following form. To say anything definite is to fall into the illusion induced by the metaphysics of presence, namely the belief that we can somehow gain direct access to the real. Any definite utterance must offer some representation or other of the nature of the world, thereby implicitly—and falsely—claiming to have direct access to the world. The practice of deconstruction therefore consists in the avoidance of any determinate claim about the world and the effort instead allusively to indicate that we are compelled to go on as if there is a world to which we gain direct access, even though we cannot.

The nature of what two critics have described as Derrida's *"negative ontology"*—his insistence on alluding indirectly to a real that we cannot directly confront or know—is brought out in a comparatively recent text where he responds to realist criticisms of his textualism.[88] These criticisms typically take him to task for occluding both the referents of utterances and the social and historical context in which they are produced.[89] Derrida's reply involves, on the face of it, an astonishing reversal:

> [T]he emergence of the value of objectivity (and hence of so many others) also belongs to a context. We can call 'context' the entire 'real-history-of-the-world,' if you like, in which this value of objectivity, and, even more broadly, that of truth (etc.) have taken on meaning and imposed themselves. That does not in the slightest discredit them. In the name of what, of which other 'truth,' moreover, would it? One of the definitions of what is called deconstruction would be the effort to take this limitless context into account, to pay the sharpest and broadest attention possible to context, and thus to an incessant movement of recontextualization. The phrase which for some has become a sort of slogan, in general so badly understood, of deconstruction ('there is nothing outside of the text' [*il n'y*

a pas de hors-texte]), means nothing else: here is nothing outside context.[90]

So what Rorty calls textualism turns out actually to be *con*textualism. In a later passage, Derrida appears to go even further before, however, taking back with one hand what he has given with another:

> What I call "text" implies all the structures called "real," "economic," "historical," socio-institutional, in short: all possible referents. Another way of recalling once again that "there is nothing outside the text." That does not mean that all referents are suspended, denied, or enclosed in a book, as people have claimed, or have been naïve enough to believe and to have accused me of believing. But it does mean that every referent, all reality has the structure of a differential trace, and that one cannot refer to this "real" except in an interpretive experience. The latter neither yields meaning nor assumes it except in a movement of differential referring. That's all.[91]

The text is thus continuous with its "real" context. But this real has "the structure of a differential trace," so that to interpret it is to be caught up "in a movement of differential referring." What does this mean? Two other passages provide the basis for an answer. Derrida warns us that "[t]he reconstitution of a context can never be perfect and irreproachable even though it is a regulative idea in the ethics of reading, of interpretation, or of discussion. But," he goes on to tell us, "this ideal is unattainable, for reasons which are essential and to which I shall doubtless return."[92] One reason why to fully contextualize a text is impossible is given a few pages later: "the finiteness of a context is never secured or simple, there is an indefinite opening of every context, an essential nontotalization."[93]

What we have here is a particular instantiation of the general structure of *différance*. The "ethics of reading" requires us to establish as full as possible a context for any text. It is impossible, however, to complete this task. We can never reconstruct a total context. Every context is "indefinitely open." Every context that we establish has its own context, and so on ad infinitum in "an incessant movement of recontextualization." The structure of the problem is identical to that of signification. Just as every signifier has a signified that turns out itself to be a signifier that leads us on in search of a "transcendental signified" contact with which it is indefinitely deferred, so the effort to contextualize a text leads us along a chain of contexts ramifying to infinity. Derrida's declaration that "there is nothing outside context" is an empty concession, since the practice of contextualization turns out to be merely another case of the endless movement of differing and deferring, of absence and presence, constitutive of *différance*. Texts and contexts, words and things, are so much raw material for the deconstructionist's relentless and repetitive demonstration that the world offers us no secure foothold on which to base knowledge and action.[94]

The absence of any such foothold leaves Derrida maintaining a delicate balance between, on the one hand, alluding to the constitutive structure of *différance* and, on the other hand, avoiding any definite account of the real that would trap him into asserting what he insists we must deny, that we can gain direct access to the real. If this position is at least consistent, the work that it generates is, ultimately, not very interesting, since deconstruction revolves around demonstrating again and again the way in which any text (or, as we have just seen, any "real" context) is fatally flawed by a characteristic set of ambiguities that arise from its participation in the movement of *différance*. If Deleuze's and Foucault's work is, in its substance, much more interesting than Derrida's it is, in part, because they ignore the difficulty highlighted by Habermas and Rorty about the status of their own discourse.

This is an easier stand for Deleuze to maintain consistently than Foucault. The former's philosophy amounts to an idiosyncratic form of vitalism, in which life, conceived as an impersonal and indeed (oxymoronic though this may seem) inorganic, structural force throws up ramified layers of objects, bodies, persons, and societies, only to outflank and subvert them.[95] This extravagant *Lebensphilosophie,* exhilarating though the analyses and discussions to which it gives rise often are, takes a lot of swallowing. Foucault, far more philosophically cautious, concentrates on a series of historical interpretations whose shifting epistemological and metaphysical implications are usually only implied, or when made explicit, are stated with epigrammatic brevity. Yet he cannot escape what Habermas calls the "performative contradiction" of pursuing a total critique of reason by rational means.

The particular form this difficulty takes in Foucault's writings of the 1970s arises from his assertion that power is omnipresent: "It seems to me that power is 'always already there,' that one is never 'outside' it, that there are no 'margins' for those who break with the system to gambol in."[96] If power is everywhere, however, how can Foucault provide what purports to be a Nietzschean genealogy of the prevailing form of "power-knowledge," the "disciplinary society" which emerged against the background of the French and Industrial Revolutions, and one, moreover, that is clearly intended to be critical of this "apparatus"? *Discipline and Punish* emerged out of a political experience: Foucault's involvement in radical prison-reform movements in the aftermath of the May 1968 explosion in France.[97] Resistance, he argues, always develops within and often merely promotes

Soldiers cross a Paris bridge during the May 1968 riots in France.

the restructuring of the prevailing power-relations. So oppositional movements do not promote a vantage-point from which critically to confront and to analyze "power-knowledge." This dilemma led Foucault in his last writings, in particular the second and third volumes of the *History of Sexuality* published shortly before his death in 1984, to develop a significantly different conception of the subject, in which it is no longer merely an effect of power, but engages in practices through which it constitutes itself. This "theoretical displacement," as Foucault called it, interesting and potentially fertile though it was, pulled strongly away from the antihumanism so characteristic of poststructuralism.[98]

This return to the subject takes us back to poststructuralism's starting point. Deleuze, Derrida, and Foucault can be seen as participants in a much more extensive rebellion against the basic assumptions of modern Western philosophy. From Descartes onward, the subject was conceived as an essential private and closed entity possessing privileged access to the contents of its consciousness, but separated from the world it sought theoretically to understand and practically to master; language figured here, if at all, as a medium between the self and the world.[99] Poststructuralism dismantled both terms of this relationship. The subject was reduced to a subordinate role, as a cluster of drives and desires brought together in a provisional unity within relations of power; the world vanished amid the ramifying interrelations of texts (or, if you prefer, contexts). What remains are "worlds," as many as there are of us, to whose individualistic pride the thought appeals, though discourse founders on the shoals of private meaning and personal belief.

It is possible to share the poststructuralists' dissatisfaction with the Cartesian conception of the self and its relation to the world without replacing it with their ultimately self-subverting Nietzschean skepticism. Language, for example, can be treated in its own right, as the complex, dense human practice that it is, without it swallowing up the world. The American philosopher Donald Davidson has developed a conception of language that, like Saussure's, is holist, treating meaning as consisting, in the first instance, in the interrelations of sentences while giving the concepts of truth and reference a central role in articulating the structure of language.[100] In the 1920s Russian philosopher and critic Mikhail Bakhtin and his followers (the so-called Vitebsk school), developed a dialogic conception of language that resolutely refused to treat it as the emanation of individual subjectivity, but that at the same time insisted that understanding an utterance depended on grasping the context of social interaction, and indeed often of conflict between real and imagined interlocuters in which it occurred.[101]

These examples are, of course, the merest gestures toward anything that would amount to a proper argument. They nevertheless serve to indicate that a critique of the foundations of modern Western philosophy does not require one to follow the path taken by Deleuze, Derrida, and Foucault. Habermas, their greatest critic, shares their rejection of what he calls "the philosophy of consciousness," but seeks to set in its place a dialogic conception of rationality in which the simplest speech-act commits us to achieving a consensus based on reasoned argument rather than on ideology or coercion.[102] The fact that one particular version of reason and its foundations has been proven wanting does not require us to give up on the very idea of reason itself—particularly since, as we have seen, when criticizing it we turn out to rely on it.

The myth of globalization

The effect of the preceding two sections should have been to cast grave doubt on the idea that there has occurred, over the past few decades, some great cultural break inaugurating a postmodern epoch. On closer examination, the continuities between Modern and Postmodern art turn out to be stronger than the discontinuities, and the philosophical case for dumping the whole Enlightenment project is, to say the least, overstated. What about the more modest claim, advanced particularly by Fredric Jameson and David Harvey, that a change in the character of capitalism is responsible for at least some of the cultural phenomena labelled as postmodernist?

The version of this thesis developed by Jameson has been subjected to a number of cogent criticisms. He has been accused of being inconsistent in his account of when this new epoch of "multinational capitalism" began and of misdescribing its architectural accompaniments.[103] He has also been taken to task for treating the Third World as the West's unitary Other, indeed as Nature to capitalism's Culture.[104] Once these considerations have been stripped away, however, the fundamental question remains: have we entered the "world without borders" evoked in *Primary Colors,* where capital, broken loose from national anchorage, roams free in search of profitable investments?

Since Jameson first advanced his thesis in 1984, the idea of economic globalization has become one of the platitudes of contemporary discourse. A recent example is provided by the following passage which appeared on the front page of German weekly *Die Zeit:*

> [G]lobalization means open frontiers, keener international competition, struggles against extinction. It deprives nation-state politics of their last elbow-room. Those in charge administer, but scarcely govern creatively any more. Regulating, rather than ruling, becomes the name of the game. Leadership fossilizes into impotent gesticulation which can scarcely affect reality. Who can be surprised when a liberal like the French sociologist Alain Touraine laments that public life has [de]generated into a fancy-dress ball...?[105]

Yet this general picture of the world economy has come under increasingly powerful criticism from various quarters.[106] The issues involved are complex, and cannot be dealt with here in the appropriate depth. I concentrate on just two questions. First, to what extent has a genuinely global or "transnational" capital emerged that is able to operate free of national constraints and connections? Second, inasmuch as there has been a move toward globalization over the past generation, does it mark the opening of a new phase of stable capitalist development or not?

The first question is obscured by the tendency of globalization's boosters to plot increases in international trade and investment primarily over the past thirty years.[107] If we take a longer historical time-span, however, the picture changes dramatically. Consider the ratios of merchandise trade to gross domestic product for six major economies (*see* table). Paul Hirst and Grahame Thompson comment:

> Apart from the dramatic difference in the openness to trade of different economies demonstrated by these figures (e.g., compare the US and the Netherlands, the startling feature is that trade to GDP ratios were higher in 1913 than they were in 1973 (with the slight exception of Germany where they were near enough equal), indicating a greater international openness in the earlier year.[108]

Ratio of merchandise trade to GDP at current prices
(exports and imports combined) 1913, 1950, and 1973

	1913	1950	1973
France	35.4	21.2	29.0
Germany	35.1	20.1	35.2
Japan	31.4	16.9	18.3
Netherlands	103.6	70.2	80.1
U.K.	44.7	36.0	39.3
U.S.	11.2	7.0	10.5

Sources: A. Madison, "Growth and Slowdown in Advanced Capitalist Economies," *Journal of Economic Literature,* XXV:2 (1987)
Paul Hirst and G. Thompson, *Globalization in Question* (Cambridge: Polity, 1996)

These dramatic shifts in the degree of international economic integration reflect the changing patterns of economic organization over the course of the twentieth century. The period 1914–45—what the historian Arno Mayer has called "the Thirty Years' War of the general crisis of the twentieth century"—saw the world economy disintegrate under the impact of two total wars and the Great Depression of the 1930s.[109] Nationally organized capitalism, involving a high degree of state regulation and control to protect markets and employment and produce for war, partially supplanted international trade and investment. It was only during the long postwar boom (world gross national product rose three-and-a-half times between 1948 and 1973) that there was a gradual movement back to a more open global economy comparable to that which had existed before the *belle époque* died in August 1914.[110]

This revival of international trade and investment did not, however, mark a simple turn in a very long economic cycle. The main kernel of truth in the globalization thesis lies in the fact that there have been important changes in the organization of production and patterns of economic power. Multinational corporations (MNCs) investing in a number of different countries increasingly dominate industrial production. These firms often rely on internationally integrated production processes in which a facility in one country may be producing parts used by other subsidiaries of the same company elsewhere in the world.

Nevertheless, the emergence of the MNC and of the "global assembly line" has yet to lead to the development of "stateless corporations" operating freely across national borders. Multinationals tend to be tied closely to a particular national base. Hirst and Thompson provide data on the basis of which they "suggest that between 70 and 75 percent of MNC value-added was produced on the home territory." They also point out that the bulk of foreign direct investment (FDI) is concentrated within the developed countries themselves: "Seventy-five percent of the total accumulated stock, and 60 percent of the flow, of FDI was located in just three players at the beginning of the 1990s. North America, Europe, and Japan dominate as both the originators and the destination for international investment."[111]

The idea that capital and jobs are pouring out of the rich countries into cheap labor locations in Latin America and East Asia thus turns out to be greatly exaggerated. So, too, is the belief that productive capital is becoming qualitatively more mobile. MNC investment in foreign countries often takes the form of "glolocalization," where, to evade trade barriers and reach an important market, a firm may establish a foreign subsidiary often creating dense networks reliant on local suppliers and becoming closely identified with the economic policies of the host government (Japanese and South Korean direct investment in Britain to gain access to the European Union market is a case in point). Numerous studies have demonstrated that relative wage-costs are only one factor in decisions about where to site facilities abroad, and are often outweighed by considerations such as the quality of the local infrastructure, availability of a skilled workforce, access to an important market, government subsidies, etc.[112]

The domain of economic activity where the globalization thesis seems strongest is the financial markets. Developments since the 1960s—the emergence of offshore markets in various financial assets, the collapse of the Bretton Woods system of fixed exchange-rates, financial deregulation, the telecommunications and computer revolutions—have created a set of closely connected financial markets capable of moving billions across the globe in microseconds. The power of these markets to bend or break government economic policies has been demonstrated on a number of recent occasions—for example, "Black Wednesday," Sept. 16, 1992, when massive speculation forced the pound sterling out of the Exchange Rate Mechanism of the European Monetary System.[113]

Here, however, the question of whether in its essentials globalization represents anything really new becomes particularly pressing. For international financial crises have been a regular occurrence from the 1820s at the latest. After the 1857 financial and commercial panic, that sped to-and-fro across the Atlantic and Europe, the Elberfeld Chamber of Commerce commented: "The world is a unit; industry and trade have made it so."[114] Governments have long been the victims of financial markets: the interna-

Spectators at a 1953 car show. "It was only during the long post-war boom ... that there was a gradual movement back to a more open global economy ..."

tional banking crisis in the summer of 1931 doomed the United States and Germany to the deepest slumps in their history, thereby helping to bring Franklin Roosevelt and Adolf Hitler to power, and driving Ramsay MacDonald's government out of office and Britain off the gold standard.

It was in the aftermath of this crisis that John Maynard Keynes developed his incisive critique of highly-liquid financial markets where profits derive from anticipating changes in the valuation of assets. They are organized, Keynes stated, like "a game of Snap, of Old Maid, of Musical Chairs—a pastime in which he is victor who says *Snap* neither too often nor too late, who passes the Old Maid to his neighbor before the game is over, who secures a chair for himself when the game is over." He concluded: "When the capital development of a country becomes the by-product of a casino, the job is likely to be ill-done."[115] Today, "casino capitalism" is back in business on the world's financial markets.[116]

These considerations lead directly to the second question, namely whether the trends toward globalization, such as they are, represent the emergence of a new stable phase of capitalist development. Jameson implies that they do, though he fails to develop an analysis to this effect supported by any detailed argument or evidence. It is interesting that Harvey, who argues quite systematically that "there certainly has been a sea-change in the surface appearance of capitalism since 1973," is much more cautious than Jameson, in effect leaving it open:

> ... whether the shifts in surface appearance betoken the birth of a new regime of accumulation, capable of containing the contradictions of capitalism for the next generation, or whether they betoken a series of temporary fixes, thus constituting a transitional moment of grumbling crisis in the configuration of late twentieth-century capitalism.[117]

Harvey observes:

> What does seem special about the period since 1972 is the extraordinary
> efflorescence and transformation of financial markets....the explosion in
> new financial instruments and markets, coupled with the rise of highly
> sophisticated systems of financial co-ordination on a global scale....I am
> therefore tempted to see the flexibility achieved in production, labour
> markets, and consumption more as an outcome of the search for financial
> solutions to the crisis-tendencies of capitalism, rather than the other way
> round. This would imply that the financial system has achieved a degree

of autonomy from real production unprecedented in capitalism's history, carrying capitalism into an era of equally unprecedented financial dangers.[118]

These patterns and the dangers they entail may in fact be less unprecedented than Harvey suggests. The London *Financial Times* recently sought to place in context the economic climate of the late 1990s, where fiscal rectitude, measured by the degree of success achieved in reducing the budget deficit, has become the reigning political orthodoxy in Western Europe, North America, and Japan:

> From the 1970s the developed world has seen persistent structural budget deficits and an associated increase in government debt to levels previously seen only after wars. At the same time bond investors, who were burned by high inflation now punish wayward governments by imposing a big risk premium. This combination has reduced the potency of fiscal policy as a reflationary weapon. Hence the slow recovery from the recession of the early 1990s, which caught many forecasters on the wrong footing.

> In effect we have returned to the pattern of the 19th century, when the public sector was too small to permit active fiscal management and monetary policy was dictated by the requirements of the gold standard. As in the 19th century, cyclical turning points now seem to be dictated by banking crises and market collapses. Recessions are exacerbated by credit contraction and debt deflation.[119]

The brave new world produced by such globalization as has occurred thus turns out to resemble nothing more than the laissez-faire capitalism driven by financial speculation which Keynes sought to reform more than sixty years ago through his writings and public service. It is likely to be no more stable than its earlier variant: indeed, the degree to which production has become integrated internationally could make recessions more rather than less severe than in the past. Jameson may or may not be right to call this state of affairs "extraordinarily demoralizing and depressing," but it is neither "original" nor "new."

The spirit of the age?

Very little thus remains of the elaborate construction called "postmodernism." The philosophical critique of the Enlightenment with which it associates itself is self-defeating. Postmodern art is part of the broader movement of Modernism. The idea that we live in a new social condition of postmodernity or even merely a distinctive phase of globalized capitalism is unsustainable.

Many supporters and critics nonetheless believe that postmodernism carries with it an inherently subversive or radical charge. The neoconservative historian Gertrude Himmelfarb has relentlessly pursued postmodernism as a continuation of the Marxist critique of liberal capitalism, one that seeks to subvert the structure of language and thereby that of society itself.[120] On the other side of the argument, the British literary critic Robert Young sees the poststructuralist decentering of the subject as helping to undermine a Eurocentric view of the world: "Postmodernism can best defined as European culture's awareness that it is no longer the unquestioned and dominant centre of the world."[121]

This association between philosophical postmodernism and political radicalism is denied by some writers. Rorty, for example, distinguishes himself from those Postmodernists "who admire Nietzsche, Heidegger, and Derrida as much as I do," but who "participate in…the 'America Sucks Sweepstakes'":

> By contrast, I see America pretty much as Whitman and Dewey did, as opening a prospect on illimitable democratic vistas. I think that our country—despite its past and present atrocities and vices, and despite its continuing willingness to elect fools and knaves to high office—is an example of the best kind of society so far invented. To think that is, in leftist eyes, about as politically incorrect as you can get.[122]

Rorty's position is at least perfectly clear and consistent. The same cannot, however, be said of other leading postmodernists. Take the case of Jean Baudrillard whose writings came to enjoy a certain vogue in the English-speaking world in the 1980s and 1990s. The particular spin he gave postmodernism was provided by the idea of "hyperreality." According to Baudrillard, "the acceleration of modernity, of technology, events and media, of all exchanges—economic, political and sexual—has propelled us to 'escape velocity,' with the result that we have flown free of the referential sphere of the real and of history."[123] Late capitalism has thus abolished the distinction between the real and its representation. Instead we have the hyperreal: not a world more or less adequately represented in images, but a world *of* images, of hallucinatory evocations of a nonexistent real: "Today, when the real and the imaginary are confused in the same operational totality, the aesthetic fascination is everywhere.… reality itself, entirely impregnated by an aesthetic which is inseparable from its own structure, has been confused with its own image."[124]

Baudrillard's most celebrated—or notorious—application of this thesis came at the time of the Gulf War between the U.S.-led coalition and Iraq. Shortly before the outbreak of this war on Jan. 17, 1991 he wrote a newspaper article declaring that "The Gulf War Will Not Take Place."[125] This was not the kind of prediction liable to refutation by anything so mundane as the coalition's air and missile bombardment of Iraq. Shortly after the war had begun, Baudrillard asked: "Is the Gulf War Taking Place?" His argument depended on what a common-sense view would take to be the mere accompaniments of actual combat—media speculation, diplomatic parleys, the effective censorship of television images of the fighting until it was safely over—for the essence of the war:

We have still not left the virtual war, in other words a sophisticated although often laughable build-up against the backdrop of a global indeterminacy of will to make war, even in Saddam's case. Hence the absence of images--which is neither accidental nor due to censorship but to the impossibility of illustrating this indeterminacy of the war. Promotional, speculative, virtual: this war no longer corresponds to Clausewitz's formula of politics pursued by other means, it rather amounts to *the absence of politics* pursued by other means.[126]

Peter Arnett of CNN reports on the Gulf War. According to Jean Baudrillard, the media represents "not a world ... represented in images, but a world of images, of hallucinatory evocations of a nonexistent real."

These articles caused great anger among Western opponents of the Gulf War, whose chief aim was to break through the media cocoon with which the citizens of the coalition states were surrounded, and to demonstrate that a real war was going on in which tens of thousands of people, many of them civilians, were being killed or injured.[127] Baudrillard eventually acknowledged that the Gulf War had actually happened and that there were casualties, including "two hundred thousand dead." He nevertheless continued to defend his articles: "By making transparent the nonevent of the war, you give it force in the imagination—somewhere other than in the 'real time' of news where it simply peters out. You give force to the illusion of war, rather than become an accessory to its false reality."[128]

The best way of opposing the Gulf War thus consists in denying its reality. No other stance is adequate to "the radical irony of our history ... that things no longer really take place, while nonetheless seeming to." Television has played a major role in bringing about this state of affairs: "The real object is wiped out by the news—not merely alienated, but abolished. All that remains of it are traces on a monitoring screen." This condition of hyperreality, however, constitutes a demystification:

> Television inculcates indifference, distance, scepticism and unconditional apathy. Through the world's becoming-image, it anaesthetizes the imagination, provokes a sickened abreaction, together with a surge of adrenalin which induces total disillusionment. Television and the media would render reality [*le réel*] dissuasive, were it not already so. And this represents an absolute advance in the consciousness—or the cynical unconscious—of our age.[129]

The idea of the couch potato as the true social critic may tickle the fancy of the denizens of the cultural and media studies departments who seem to constitute the main readership of Baudrillard's writings. It is of little use, however, for the innumerable movements and campaigns one of whose main efforts is to break through the media's indifference to their causes. Nor does it help the many worried citizens who, for some reason or other, come to regard media presentations of the world as systematically misleading, and therefore seek out alternative sources of information in order to construct a more adequate account of their situation. For all these, the distinction between reality and its representations remains indispensable (as indeed it does for Baudrillard whenever he has to cross the street or wants to eat a meal that someone has actually cooked for him, as opposed to the enticing images on a TV cooking program).

Despite their differences in philosophical style and surface commitment, both Rorty and Baudrillard embody essentially the same stance, that of the detached, ironic contemplation of the passing show. Rorty calls himself a "liberal ironist" who hopes that people will become kinder to one another, but sees this hope as part of a set of beliefs and desires that can, like all beliefs and desires, never find support from the nature of the world.[130] Irony, with its tendency to relativize all beliefs, is indeed the characteristically postmodernist trope, creating a distance between those who experience it and the world that we cannot avoid attempting to know and to act on.[131] Thus, far from in any way undermining the *status quo,* postmodernism is far more likely to encourage those influenced by it to think that there is nothing to be done about it.[132]

This political mood—accurately described by Baudrillard as one of cynicism and indifference—provides one clue to understanding why postmodernism should have gained such currency in the past two decades. For its disenchanted attitude is not some abstract metaphysical condition, but reflects a particular constellation of historical circumstances.[133]

Two particular features stand out here. First, the late 1960s and early 1970s saw a great wave of political radicalism sweep much of the advanced capitalist world. A combination of mass strikes and student revolts—most famously in France in May–June 1968—led to a brief, but marked intellectual and political revival of Marxism in the developed countries, often in forms (Maoism and Trotskyism) avowedly critical of orthodox Communism. Hundreds of thousands of young people across Western Europe and North America came to believe that social revolution was, if not imminent, certainly a realistic medium-term prospect. By the mid-1970s these hopes were being dashed, as the radical tide receded; by the beginning of the 1980s leading representatives of the New Right such as Ronald Reagan and Margaret Thatcher were pushing the political pendulum throughout the Western world back toward laissez-faire capitalism.[134]

Second, however, the Reagan-Thatcher years did not, as we saw above, mark the return of a period of stable capitalist expansion. Such growth as did occur, particularly in the second half of the 1980s, was erratic and associated in particular with specific sectors, notably those areas which benefited from the speculative surge by newly liberated financial markets—the financial services industry itself, real estate, and the like. This pattern of growth was associated with a sharp growth in inequalities of wealth and income. The beneficiaries included, apart from the already rich and nouveaux riches, the professional and managerial middle class, that saw its size and incomes surge in the 1980s.[135]

This concatenation of events provided a context for the reception of postmodernism. Many of the disillusioned children of the 1960s found themselves experiencing very rapid social mobility as highly-paid professional and managerial positions opened up to able young graduates. Material interest now reinforced political experience in encouraging them to give up a commitment to radical social change. At the same time many

A Vietnam protester challenges military police during a demonstration in front of the Pentagon.

found it hard to buy fully into the system ideologically. The leap from hero-worshipping Che Guevara to supporting the Nicaraguan *contras* was too much for many to make (though some did). Postmodernism provided an ideal halfway house. It gave up on the grand narratives of emancipation and revolution, but refused uncritically to endorse liberal capitalism. Those who accepted it could enjoy the material benefits of the highly inegalitarian boom of the late 1980s while maintaining an ironic, detached stance towards all of what Rorty calls "final vocabularies"—socialism, liberalism, conservatism, or whatever.

Subsequent developments have helped to keep this complex in place. The East European revolutions of 1989 and the subsequent collapse of the Soviet Union seemed to deliver the final quietus to Marxism; moreover, the most influential interpretation of these events, Francis Fukuyama's announcement of "The End of History" had a decidedly postmodern ring about it.[136] At the same time, the global recession which dominated the early 1990s helped to discourage any easy faith in the strength and stability of liberal capitalism. As the decade wore on, postmodernism entrenched itself further in the academy, becoming the orthodoxy in many humanities and social-science departments, and therefore the subject of numerous introductory courses, student textbooks, and doctoral theses. For many the rigorous cultivation of uncertainty hardened into unquestionable dogma.[137]

Longer-term factors may have helped to keep postmodernism in place. French sociologist Pierre Bourdieu has developed a remarkable critique of what he claims are the dominant forms of production and consumption of art:

> The 'eye' is a product of history reproduced by education. This is true of the mode of artistic perception now accepted as legitimate, that is, the aesthetic disposition, the capacity to consider in and for themselves, as form rather than function, not only the works designated for such apprehension, i.e., legitimate works of art, but everything in the world, including cultural objects which are not yet consecrated—such as, at one time, primitive arts, or, nowadays, popular photography or kitsch—and natural objects. The 'pure' gaze is a historical invention linked to the emergence of an autonomous field of artistic production, that is, a field capable of imposing its own norms on both the production and the consumption of its products.[138]

An autonomous artistic producer is likely to create a particular kind of art: "To assert the autonomy of production is to give primacy to that of which the artist is master, i.e., form, manner, style, rather than the 'subject,' the external referent, which involves subordination to functions—even if only the most elementary one, that of representing, signifying, saying something." Correlatively, the pure gaze corresponding to this privileging of form over function "is rooted in an ethic, or rather, an ethos of elective distance from the necessities of the natural and social world" which represents "a social separation."[139] The ability to stylize life, to discover aesthetically pleasing formal properties not simply in works of art, but everywhere, is a mechanism of social discrimination through which the economically and socially privileged, who have developed this ability thanks to their upbringing, and who enjoy the leisure to cultivate it, mark themselves off from the masses who lack the appropriate skills.

If Bourdieu is right, he may have identified one of the forces helping to sustain postmodernism. For the kind of art in which form triumphs over function is, of course, Modernism. What is called Postmodern art is, as we have seen, a continuation of Modernism, employing the same formal devices in a very different social and political context from that of its emergence.[140] One striking contemporary cultural phenomenon is a kind of vulgarization of Modernist themes and motifs that we see about us. This involves not simply the appropriation of Modernist images by the media (an example is the use a few years ago of a famous Constructivist photograph of the revolutionary Russian art-theorist Osip Brik to advertise blue jeans), but also a sort of massification of Modernism's characteristically ironic stance towards reality. Irony has ceased to be the property of a tiny avant-garde, and has become available to a much larger elite of middle-class professionals for whom a knowing, detached attitude seems like the best response to a world neither in whose justice nor in whose transformation can they sincerely believe. This "vulgar-Modernist" attitude allows them to appropriate *any* cultural product—old soap operas, soccer, *The X-Files*—in the right kind of knowing, tongue-in-cheek way. As Bourdieu observes, there is "no area [of life] in which the stylization of life, that is, the primacy of forms over function, of manner over matter, does not produce the same effects."[141]

At any rate, the upshot of this analysis is that what sustains the movement of Postmodernism is not any good reason for holding any of its variants to be true, but rather certain tendencies at work in the social world at large. This does not make the work of intellectual critique I have undertaken unnecessary, but rather it suggests that any real shift in the cultural log-jam of which postmodernism is a prime symptom will depend on larger political and social changes. Since history is not really over, *pace* Fukuyama and Baudrillard, there is every reason to be confident that such changes will take place.

1. See also, Alex Callinicos, *Against Postmodernism* (Cambridge, Mass.: Polity Press, 1989).

2. Arnold J. Toynbee, *A Study of History* (abr. edn., 2 vols., ed. D. C. Somervell, London: Oxford University Press, 1960), p. 39.

3. *See* Callinicos, *Postmodernism,* pp. 16–25.

4. Jean-François Lyotard, *The Postmodern Condition* (Manchester: Manchester University Press, 1984), pp. xxiii–iv.

5. *See* Lyotard, *The Differend* (Manchester: Manchester University Press, 1988), p. 179.

6. Lyotard, *Postmodern Condition,* pp. 5ff, 80. Throughout this essay I follow the convention of capitalizing the names of artistic styles and movements: thus "Modernism" and (artistic) "Postmodernism," but modernity and postmodernity. I also use the term "art" broadly, so that it embraces not just painting and sculpture, but also architecture, music, literature, theater, cinema, etc.

7. Robert Venturi, Denise Scott Brown, and Steven Izenout, *Learning from Las Vegas* (Cambridge, Mass.: MIT Press, 1972).

8. For an influential attempt to group these different trends into a single Postmodern art, *see* Charles Jencks, *What is Postmodernism?* (London: Academy Editions, 1989).

9. The best overviews of poststructuralism are provided by two critical treatments, Jürgen Habermas, *The Philosophical Discourse of Modernity* (Cambridge, Mass.: Polity Press, 1987), and Peter Dews, *Logics of Disintegration* (London: Verso, 1987). The broader philosophical context can be found in Vincent Descombes, *Modern French Philosophy* (Cambridge: Cambridge University Press, 1980). Two recent biographies of Foucault also provide much useful background: Didier Eribon, *Michel Foucault* (Cambridge, Mass.: Harvard University Press, 1991) and David Macey, *The Lives of Michel Foucault* (London: Vintage, 1994).

10. Daniel Bell, *The Coming of Postindustrial Society* (London: Heinemann, 1974).

11. Lyotard, "Defining the Postmodern," *ICA Documents,* 4 (1985), p. 6.

12. Fredric Jameson, *Postmodernism, or, the Cultural Logic of Late Capitalism* (London: Verso, 1991), pp. 3, 10, 31, 33; *see* generally ibid., chap. 1.

13. Ibid., p. 36. Jameson's periodization of capitalist development derives from that formulated by the Belgian Marxist Ernest Mandel in *Late Capitalism* (London: New Left Books, 1975). His interpretation of Realism and Modernism, and his broader critical theory are to be found notably in *The Political Unconscious* (London: Methuen Press, 1981).

14. Jameson, *Postmodernism,* pp. 48–49.

15. David Harvey, *The Condition of Postmodernity* (Oxford: Basil Blackwell, Inc., 1989), p. vii.

16. Scott Lash and John Urry, *The End of Organized Capitalism* (Cambridge, Mass.: Polity Press, 1987).

17. Anonymous, *Primary Colors* (London: Vintage, 1996), pp. 161–62.

18. Charles Baudelaire, *My Heart Laid Bare and Other Prose Writings* (London: Soho Book Company, 1986), p. 37.

19. Habermas, *Philosophical Discourse,* p. 5.

20. Ibid., p. 7.

21. Hans Blumenberg, *The Legitimacy of the Modern Age* (Cambridge, Mass.: MIT Press, 1983), p. 32.

22. Ronald L. Meek, ed., *Turgot on Progress, Sociology and Economics* (Cambridge: Cambridge University Press, 1973), p. 63.

23. J. B. Bury, *The Idea of Progress* (London: Macmillan, 1920), pp. 207, 209.

24. C. L. de Secondat, Baron de Montesquieu, *Persian Letters* (Harmondsworth: Penguin, 1993), p. 192 (Letter 105).

25. *See* Callinicos, *Theories and Narratives* (Durham: Duke University Press, 1995), pp. 54–65.

26. Karl Marx and Frederic Engels, *Collected Works,* VI (50 vols., London: Lawrence and Wishart, 1976), p. 487.

27. Marshall Berman, *All That Is Solid Melts Into Air* (London: Verso, 1983), p. 15.

28. Emile Durkheim, *The Division of Labour* (London: Macmillan, 1984), p. 2.

29. *See* Perry Anderson's critical discussion of Berman in "Modernity and Revolution," reprinted in *A Zone of Engagement* (London: Verso, 1992), where he takes Berman to task for, among other things, in effect eliding the distinction between modernity and capitalism.

30. Marx and Engels, *Collected Works,* VI, p. 487.

31. Walter Benjamin, *Illuminations* (London: Jonathan Cape, 1970), pp. 259–60.

32. Anthony Giddens, *The Consequences of Modernity* (Cambridge, Mass.: Polity Press, 1990), pp. 55–63. *See also,* Giddens, *A Contemporary Critique of Historical Materialism* (London: Macmillan, 1981).

33. Giddens, *Consequences,* pp. 16–17.

34. Ibid., pp. 18–19.

35. Ibid., p. 21.

36. Ibid., pp. 64, 3. *See also,* ibid., pp. 45–53.

37. *See* Giddens, *Modernity and Self-Identity* (Cambridge, Mass.: Polity Press, 1991).

38. Giddens, *Consequences,* pp. 124–25. *See also,* Ulrich Beck, *Risk Society* (Newbury Park, CA: Sage Publications, 1992).

39. Giddens, *Consequences,* p. 139.

40. Harvey, *Condition,* pp. 293, 240.

41. Ibid., pp. 229–30. Harvey's detailed analysis of the relationship between time, space, and capitalism is to be found in the essays collected in *The Urbanization of Capital* (Oxford: Blackwell, 1985) and *Consciousness and the Urban Experience* (Oxford: Blackwell, 1985).

42. Harvey, *Condition,* p. 232.

43. Ibid., p. 147.

44. Giddens, *Consequences,* p. 45.

45. Jencks, *What is Postmodernism?,* p. 14.

46. Peter Ackroyd, *T. S. Eliot* (London: Sphere Books, 1985), pp. 118–19.

47. Eugene Lunn, *Marxism and Modernism* (London: Verso, 1985), pp. 34–7.

48. Interestingly, the critic David Thomson has recently claimed that Howard Hawks's film *The Big Sleep* (1946) "inaugurates a post-modern, camp, satiric view of movies being about other movies that extends to the New Wave and *Pulp Fiction*," *The Tiddler,* no. 20, supp. to *The Observer* (London), Jan. 26, 1997, p. 18. Once again the origins of Postmodernism get pushed back into the past.

49. T. S. Eliot, *Selected Prose* (London: Faber and Faber, 1975), p. 177.

50. Andreas Huyssen, "Mapping the Postmodern," *New German Critique,* 33 (1984), p. 16.

51. Marcel Proust, *Remembrance of Things Past* (3 vols., Harmondsworth: Penguin, 1983), vol. III, p. 956.

52. Gilles Deleuze, *Proust and Signs,* trans. Richard Howard (New York: George Braziller, 1972), pp. 98–99.

53. Quoted in Richard Ellman, *James Joyce* (New York: Oxford University Press, 1982), p. 89.

54. Peter Bürger, *Theory of the Avant Garde* (Manchester: Manchester University Press, 1984), pp. 73–74.

55. Ibid., p. 49.

56. Quoted in Camilla Gray, *The Russian Experiment in Art 1863–1922* (London: Thames & Hudson, 1986), p. 219.

57. Walter Benjamin, "Surrealism," in *One-Way Street and Other Writings* (London: New Left Books, 1979).

58. Christopher Green, *Cubism and its Enemies* (New Haven: Yale University Press, 1987), p. 295.

59. Quoted in Maurice Nadeau, *A History of Surrealism* (Harmondsworth: Penguin, 1973), p. 212 n. 5.

60. Franco Moretti, *Signs Taken for Wonders* (London: Verso, 1988), p. 242.

61. Carl Schmitt, *Political Romanticism* (Cambridge, Mass.: MIT Press, 1986), pp. 17, 71–72, 75–76.

62. Leon Edel, *Henry James* (abr. edn., New York: Harper & Row, 1985), p. 165.

63. For a much more extended discussion, *see* Callinicos, *Against Postmodernism,* chaps. 1 and 2.

64. Lyotard, *Postmodern Condition,* p. 81.

65. Indeed, a strong case can be made for seeing Nietzsche as the philosophical prophet of Modernism, and for regarding the poststructuralists as, among other things, providing a conceptual articulation of themes already explored by Modernist artists: *see* Callinicos, *Against Postmodernism,* pp. 65–72.

66. *See* the books by Habermas and Dews cited in n. 9 above, and also Callinicos, *Against Postmodernism,* chap. 3.

67. Putting the issue like this is not intended to prejudge the question of the extent to which the scientific study of the social world requires different methods from those used in trying to understand the physical world.

68. Habermas, *Philosophical Discourse,* p. 392, n. 4.

69. Ibid., p. 56. Two good recent treatments of Nietzsche in English are Richard Schacht, *Nietzsche* (London: Routledge & Kegan Paul, 1983) and Alexander Nehamas, *Nietzsche: Life as Literature* (Cambridge, Mass.: Harvard University Press, 1985).

70. Heidegger represents another key philosophical reference point for Deleuze, Derrida, and Foucault. An assessment of Heidegger's relevance to the debate on postmodernism, of his own changing and frequently ambiguous relationship to Nietzsche, and of the extent of his actual influence on the poststructuralists would raise issues of such complexity as to fall outside the scope of this essay. For treatments of some of these issues, *see* Luc Ferry and Alain Renaut, *La Pensée 68* (Paris: Gallimard, 1985), esp. ch. IV, Habermas, *Philosophical Discourse,* chap. VI, and Richard Rorty, *Contingency, Irony, and Solidarity* (Cambridge: Cambridge University Press, 1989), chap. 5.

71. Rorty, *The Consequences of Pragmatism* (Brighton: Harvester, 1982), chap. 6.

72. Jacques Derrida, *Of Grammatology* (Baltimore: Johns Hopkins University Press, 1976), p. 158. Derrida's formulation in the French original is somewhat different, and apparently weaker: *"Il n'y a pas de hors-texte,"* *De la Grammatologie* (Paris: Les Editions de Minuit, 1967), p. 227. But the English translation by Gayatri Chakravorty Spivak was prepared in consultation with Derrida, who seems happy to acquiesce in her rendering of his most celebrated saying.

73. Ferdinand de Saussure, *Course in General Linguistics* (New York: McGraw-Hill, 1966).

74. Claude Lévi-Strauss, "Introduction à l'oeuvre de Marcel Mauss," in Marcel Mauss, *Sociologie et anthropologie* (Paris: Presses Universitaires de France, 1950).

75. *See* especially Derrida, "Structure, Sign, and Play in the Discourse of the Human Sciences," in *Writing and Difference* (London: Routeledge & Kegan Paul RKP, 1978). Jameson, *The Prison-House of Language* (Princeton: Princeton University Press, 1972) provides an interesting discussion of the intellectual context in which Saussure's conception of language became one of the chief reference-points of French philosophical discussion.

76. Derrida, *Of Grammatology,* p. 143.

77. Patrick Joyce, "History and Post-Modernism," *Past and Present* 133 (1991), p. 208. *See also,* Joyce, "The End of Social History?," *Social History,* 20 (1995).

78. Michel Foucault, *Power/Knowledge* (Brighton: Harvester Press, 1980), p. 114. In fact, however, both Deleuze's and Foucault's work at the height of the "structuralist" preoccupation with language in the 1960s is much more preoccupied with questions of meaning than they might later be prepared to concede: *see,* in particular, Gilles Deleuze, *Logique du sens* (Paris: Editions de Minuit, 1969), and *Différence et repetition* (Paris: Presses Universitaires de France, 1968), and Michel Foucault, "Nietzsche, Freud, Marx," in *Cahiers de Royaumont: Philosophie VI, Nietzsche* (Paris: Minuit, 1967).

79. Foucault, *Power/Knowledge,* p. 194.

80. Foucault, *Discipline and Punish* (London: Allen Lane, 1977), p. 27.

81. Foucault, *Power/Knowledge,* pp. 73–74.

82. *See* generally, Foucault, *La Volonté de savoir* (Paris: Gallimard, 1976), pp. 123–28.

83. Rorty, *Consequences,* p. 141.

84. Rorty, *Contingency,* p. 4.

85. Ibid., p. 8.

86. For a recent historical and critical survey of the theory of ideology, *see* M. Rosen, *Of Voluntary Servitude* (Cambridge, Mass.: Polity Press, 1996).

87. Habermas, *Philosophical Discourse,* p. 116.

88. Ferry and Renaut, *Pensée 68,* p. 174.

89. *See,* for example, Perry Anderson, *In the Tracks of Historical Materialism* (London: Verso, 1983), and Bryan D. Palmer, *Descent into Discourse* (Philadelphia: Temple University Press, 1990).

90. Derrida, "Afterword: Toward an Ethic of Discussion," in *Limited Inc.* (Evanston: Northwestern University Press, 1988), p. 136.

91. Ibid., p. 148.

92. Ibid., p. 131.

93. Ibid., p. 137.

94. The same text also contains a very unsatisfactory passage where Derrida responds to Habermas's critique in *The Philosophical Discourse of Modernity* with denial and abuse rather than anything resembling an argument: *see* ibid. pp. 156–58, n. 9.

95. The fullest statement of this vitalist metaphysics is Gilles Deleuze and Felix

Guattari, *Mille plateaux* (Paris: Editions de Minuit, 1980). A more accessible version is to be found in Deleuze's little book *Foucault* (Paris: Editions de Minuit, 1986), which, typically, is more an exposition of his own thought than Foucault (Deleuze frequently presents his own views through brilliant and idiosyncratic discussions of other philosophers).

96. Foucault, *Power/Knowledge,* p. 85.

97. *See* Eribon, *Foucault,* chaps. 14–17, and Macey, *Lives,* chap. 12.

98. Foucault, *L'Usage des plaisirs* (Paris: Gallimard, 1984), p. 12. *See also,* Callinicos, "Foucault's Third Theoretical Displacement," *Theory Culture & Society,* 3.3 (1986), and *Against Postmodernism,* pp. 80–91.

99. *See,* for example, A. J. P. Kenney, "Cartesian Privacy," in George Pitcher, ed., *Wittgenstein* (London: Macmillan, 1968).

100. Donald Davidson, *Inquiries into Truth and Interpretation* (Oxford: Oxford University Press, 1984). There is, however, much controversy over whether or not Davidson's philosophy of language admits of a fully realist interpretation: *see,* for example, Ernest LePore, ed., *Truth and Interpretation* (Oxford: Blackwell, 1986), Rorty, *Contingency,* chap. 1, and Donald Davidson, "The Structure and Content of Truth," *Journal of Philosophy,* 87 (1990), pp. 279–328.

101. *See* especially, M. M. Bakhtin, *The Dialogic Imagination* (Austin: University of Texas, 1981) and V. N. Voloshinov, *Marxism and the Philosophy of Language* (Cambridge, Mass.: Harvard University Press, 1986).

102. *See* Habermas, *The Theory of Communicative Action,* I (London: Heinemann, 1984), and II (Cambridge, Mass.: Polity Press, 1987), and the critical discussion in Callinicos, *Against Postmodernism,* chap. 4.

103. Mike Davis, "Urban Renaissance and the Spirit of Postmodernism," *New Left Review,* 151 (1985).

104. Robert Young, *White Mythologies* (London: Routledge, 1990), chap. 6, and Aijaz Ahmad, *In Theory* (London: Verso, 1992), chap. 6.

105. Quoted in N. Ascherson, "Don't be Fooled: Multinationals Do Not Rule the World," *Independent on Sunday* (London), Jan. 12, 1997.

106. Among recent criticism by British writers, moving roughly from the right to the left of the political spectrum are: "The Myth of the Powerless State," *The Economist,* Oct. 7, 1995; Martin Wolf, 'The Global Economy Myth,' *Financial Times,* Feb. 13, 1996; Michael Mann, "As the Twentieth Century Ages," *New Left Review,* 214 (1995); Will Hutton, "Myth that Sets the World to Right," *Guardian,* June 12, 1995; Paul Hirst and Grahame Thompson, *Globalization in Question* (Cambridge: Polity, 1996); Chris Harman, 'Globalization: A Critique of a New Orthodoxy,' *International Socialism,* 2.73 (1996).

107. *See,* for example, one of the first attempts rigorously to argue the thesis of globalization, Nigel Harris, *The End of the Third World* (London: I. B. Tauris, 1986).

108. Hirst and Thompson, *Globalization,* p. 26–27.

109. Arno J. Mayer, *The Persistence of the Old Regime* (New York: Pantheon, 1981), p. 3.

110. *See* Wolf, "The Need to Look to the Long Term," *Financial Times,* Nov. 16, 1987.

111. Hirst and Thompson, *Globalization,* pp. 63, 96.

112. *See* Harman, "Globalization," pp. 9–14.

113. For a mordant and sophisticated insider account of the crisis of the ERM, *see* Bernard Connolly, *The Rotten Heart of Europe* (London: Faber, 1996).

114. Quoted in Charles Poor Kindleberger, *Manias, Panics and Crashes* (London: Macmillan, 1981), p. 130.

115. John Maynard Keynes, *The General Theory of Employment Interest and Money* (London: Macmillan, 1970), pp. 155–56, 159.

116. *See* the discussion of financial markets in Hutton, *The State We're In* (London: Jonathan Cape, 1995), especially chaps. 3–6.

117. Harvey, *Condition,* p. 189.

118. Ibid., pp. 192–94. Harvey's account of post-1973 trends towards 'flexible accumulation' rests on a contrast with an earlier period of 'Fordist' mass production and consumption. The theoretical assumptions and empirical claims implied by analyses of

this kind have been subjected to severe criticism: *see* Robert Brenner and Michael Glick, "The Regulation School," *New Left Review,* 188 (1991).

119. "A Tale of Two Cycles," *Financial Times,* Dec. 23, 1996.

120. Gertrude Himmelfarb, *The De-Moralization of Society* (London: Institute of Economic Affairs, 1995).

121. Young, *White Mythologies,* p. 19.

122. Rorty, "Trotsky and the Wild Orchids," in Mark Edmundson, ed., *Wild Orchids and Trotsky* (New York: Penguin, 1993), pp. 32–33.

123. Jean Baudrillard, *The Illusion of the End* (Oxford: Blackwell, 1994), p. 1. Baudrillard advances this as a "hypothesis," but the two other hypotheses he goes on to outline are elaborations, rather than alternatives, of the first.

124. Baudrillard, *Simulations* (New York: Semiotexte, 1983), pp. 150, 152.

125. Baudrillard, "La Guerre du Golfe n'aura pas lieu," *Libération* (Paris), Jan. 4, 1991.

126. Baudrillard, "La Guerre du Golfe a-t-elle lieu?," ibid., Feb. 6, 1991. Translation from Baudrillard, "The Gulf War Did Not Take Place," trans. Paul Patton (Sydney: Power Publications, 1995) p. 30.

127. *See* especially, Christopher Norris, *Uncritical Theory* (London: Lawrence & Wishart, 1992) which takes Baudrillard's Gulf War articles as the starting point of a more general critique of Postmodernism.

128. Baudrillard, *Illusion,* pp. 63, 64.

129. Ibid., pp. 16, 56, 61.

130. Rorty, *Contingency,* especially, Introduction and chap. 4.

131. *See* Callinicos, *Theories and Narratives,* Conclusion.

132. This is true even of the currently fashionable and apparently more radical variant of Postmodernism known as postcolonial theory. *See* Ahmad, *In Theory,* and Callinicos, "Wonders Taken for Signs: Homi Bhabha's Postcolonialism," *Transformation,* 1 (1995).

133. For a more detailed version of the following analysis, *see* Callinicos, *Against Postmodernism,* pp. 162–71.

134. *See* Harman, *The Fire Last Time* (London: Bookmarks, 1988).

135. *See* Mike Davis, *Prisoners of the American Dream* (London: Verso, 1986).

136. *See* Francis Fukuyama, *The End of History and the Last Man* (New York: Free Press, 1992), and Callinicos, *Theories and Narratives,* chap. 1.

137. *See* Callinicos, "Postmodernism as Normal Science," *British Journal of Sociology,* 46 (1995).

138. Pierre Bourdieu, *Distinction* (London: Routledge & Kegan Paul, 1984), p. 3.

139. Ibid., pp. 3–5.

140. *See,* on the decline of the avant-garde and the more general trajectory of Modernism, Callinicos, *Against Postmodernism,* pp. 60–61, 154–62.

141. Bourdieu, *Distinction,* p. 5.

Alex Callinicos was born in Harare, Zimbabwe in 1950. Having studied at Balliol College, Oxford, and the London School of Economics, he was a junior research fellow at St. Peter's College, Oxford. Since 1981 he has taught at the University of York, England, where he is now a professor of politics.

Professor Callinicos has written extensively on Marxism and social theory. His books include *Marxism and Philosophy* (1983), *The Revolutionary Ideas of Karl Marx* (1983), *Making History* (1987), *Against Postmodernism* (1989), *The Revenge of History* (1991), and most recently, *Theories and Narratives* (1995). He is currently working on a historical and critical introduction to social theory.

ADDITIONS TO

THE GREAT BOOKS LIBRARY

St. Augustine

Aurelius Augustinus (354–430, A.D.), who became bishop of Hippo in the part of the Roman Empire that is now Algeria, and who was subsequently canonized as St. Augustine on the strength of his works and writings, was the greatest expositor of Christian doctrine in antiquity. As his death came nearly at the end of antiquity's dominion, he may also be said to have stood at the beginning of the Middle Ages, which itself ended not long after the death of St. Thomas Aquinas (1224/25–74). In this view, Augustine can be seen as holding one end of a great arch which has Aquinas at the other—the arch of faith, we may call it—and which marks the historic effort of the Western mind to say what God is, endeavoring to reconcile man with that. Others, before and after, contributed to this undertaking, of course, but these two figures stand out, not least because they managed between them to salvage the two most important thinkers of ancient times—Plato, through Augustine, and Aristotle, through Aquinas—who were themselves in this way reconciled, so far as possible, with Christianity, and who thus survived its rejection of pagan philosophy.

Augustine's life is well known from his *Confessions*—the account of his conversion from paganism to Christianity—which may be taken as his first autobiography, and which, though of a spiritual character, gives many personal details: it is not only a soul but a man that we perceive. This indeed is the essence of the story. Paganism, into which Augustine was born, and which was his father's faith, might be said to have served the man; Manichaeism, the faith to which Augustine turned in his youth, rejected this in favor of what may be thought of as the pure soul, ascetic and celibate; neo-Platonism, to which he turned next, found a way to combine these elements—the human and the divine—in a unity which, however, he found unsatisfactory, since it denied the reality of evil and located good in the human spirit, where from his own experience he simply could not believe it. Only Christianity, his mother's faith, to which he was converted at the age of 32, in a dramatic revelation memorably recorded in the seventh book of the *Confessions,* seemed to him able to admit the human—the realities of the flesh—and at the same time offer means for the soul to escape them and find its way to God.

Augustine, who was then living in Milan, where he taught rhetoric (he had received an excellent education of the kind we now call classical in Carthage—an education which enabled him, as he said, to say anything he wanted in any way he wanted to say it), returned to Africa, wishing to lead a quiet, monastic life with a few friends and pupils. But his literary gifts had already manifested themselves in a book about the Church and the Manichaeans, and in 391, he was persuaded to accept induction into the priesthood, whence began his notable career as a defender and apologist of the faith in sermons and other writings devoted to, among other things, the putting down of heresies and the avoidance of schisms. In 395 or 396 he was made bishop of Hippo, a position he held until his death thirty-five years later. As such, he undertook the defense and promotion of the Catholic Church throughout Northern Africa, serving on councils, attending conferences, and preaching, besides conducting an episcopal court and carrying out other duties of his position. Throughout, he maintained his little monastery, members of which went forth to become bishops and saints and spreading the influence of his teachings long after he died.

Although he wrote 230 different works over his lifetime, the books for which Augustine is best known, besides the *Confessions,* are *On the Trinity,* a major doctrinal treatise, *On Christian Doctrine,* and *The City of God.* The latter was written after the sack of Rome by the Visigoths in 410, when the fall of the "eternal city" was blamed upon Christianity, as having undermined imperial authority. Sensitive to this charge, Augustine wrote what is, on one level, a comparison of the Empire and the Church, though in a far more important sense it is a work of exegesis on the Scriptures, an art in which he excelled. For he understood—it was indeed a major article of his belief—that while God has revealed himself in the Scriptures, these are written in human words which cannot be taken literally but must be put through successive stages of interpretation. His capacity for this was his real genius, and no writer of his faith has ever done more to that end. The work here reprinted, *The Teacher,* may be read as an abstract of his method, in which words are seen as possessed of meaning which can only be derived from them by rigorous analysis.

The Teacher

Saint Augustine

Illustrations by Stephen Alcorn

Chapter I

1. *Augustine.* What would you say we are trying to do whenever we speak?

Adeodatus. As it strikes me right now, we want either to teach or to learn.

Aug. I see, and I agree with one of these, but how does this hold for learning?

Ad. How in the world do you suppose we learn, if not by asking questions?

Aug. I think that even then we simply want to teach. Now I am inquiring of you whether you ask a question for any other reason than to teach the person asked what it is you want to know.

Ad. What you say is true.

Aug. So you see that our aim in speaking is simply to teach.

Ad. I do not see this clearly. If speaking is no more than uttering words, I see we do that whenever we sing. And as we often sing when we are alone where no one else is present, I do not think we wish to teach anything.

Aug. For my part, I think there is a form of teaching by way of recalling, and a really important one, which the very subject under discussion will bring to light. But if you do not think that we learn by recalling or that we teach when we bring something to one's mind, I will not oppose you. And I will now take the position that the two reasons for speaking are either to teach or to recall something, whether to others or to ourselves. And this we do even when we are singing. Would you not say so?

Ad. Not entirely, for I very seldom sing to call something to my mind. I do it only for pleasure.

Aug. I see what you mean. But you notice, do you not, that what pleases you in singing is a certain melodious ordering of sound? Since this can be joined to words, or removed from them, is singing not one thing and speaking something else? Melody can be produced by the flute and harp; birds sing too, and there are times when we hum a musical piece without words. This can be called singing, but not speech. Do you have any objection to raise?

Ad. None whatever, really.

2. *Aug.* Do you think then that language has been introduced solely in order to teach or to recall?

Ad. I would were it not for the difficulty that, in praying, we are actually speaking, and yet it is not right to believe that God is taught anything by us, or that we recall something to His mind.

Aug. You do not realize, I think, that the command to pray in the secrecy of our chamber—a term signifying the innermost recesses of the soul—was given only for this reason, that God does not need to be reminded or taught by us in order to give us what we desire. When a person speaks, he gives an outward sign of what he wants by means of an articulated sound. But we must seek and pray to God in the innermost court of the rational soul which is called the "interior man," for it is here that He has wished to make His temple. And have you not read in the Apostle: "Know you not that you are the temple of God and that the Spirit of God dwells in you," and that "Christ dwells in the inner man"? And have you not noted the words of the Prophet: "Speak in your hearts and repent in your chambers; offer the sacrifice of justice and hope in the Lord"? Where do you think the "sacrifice of justice" is to be offered, if not in the "temple" of the soul and in the "chambers" of the heart? Now we have to offer sacrifice there where we are to pray. Hence there is no need, when we pray, for language, that is, for the spoken word, except, perhaps, to express one's thoughts, the way priests do, not so God may hear, but in order that men may hear and, by this verbal reminder, fix their thoughts upon God by a unity of heart and mind. Or do you have another view?

Ad. I am in complete agreement.

Aug. Are you then not concerned by the fact that the greatest Teacher of all taught us certain words to say when He was teaching the disciples how to pray? In so doing, He apparently did nothing else than teach them what they should say when praying.

Ad. That does not trouble me at all, for He did not teach the disciples words, but realities by means of words. In this way they were to call to mind to whom to pray and what to pray for when, as you said, they pray in the inner sanctum of the soul.

Aug. You have the right idea. I believe you notice at the same time that even when a person is trying hard to think, although we utter not a sound, yet because we are thinking of the words themselves, we are speaking inwardly in our minds. So, too, by speaking, we merely call something to mind since, in turning over the words stored therein, memory brings to mind the realities themselves which have words for their signs.

Ad. I understand, and I follow you.

Chapter 2

3. *Aug.* Do we agree then that words are signs?

Ad. We do.

Aug. Well, can there be a sign unless it signifies something?

Ad. No.

Aug. How many words are there in this verse? *Si nihil ex tanta superis placet urbe relinqui* (If it please the gods that nothing remain of so great a city).

Ad. Eight.

Aug. Are there eight signs, then?

Ad. Yes.

Aug. I believe you grasp the meaning of this verse.

Ad. Well enough, I think.

Aug. Tell me what the words mean, one by one.

Ad. I certainly understand what *si* signifies, but I find no other word to explain it.

Aug. Whatever it signifies, do you at least know where it occurs?

Ad. It seems to me that *si* signifies doubt, and where, except in the mind, can doubt exist?

Aug. I will accept that for the time being. Go on to the other words.

Ad. Nihil—what else does it signify except what does not exist?

Aug. Perhaps what you say is true, but I am held back from agreeing by something you granted before, namely, that nothing is a sign unless it signifies something. But what does not exist cannot possibly be something. Therefore, the second word in this verse is not a sign because it does not signify something, and we were wrong in agreeing that all words are signs, or that every sign signifies something.

Ad. I am really hard pressed by what you say. But it is certainly sheer folly for us to utter a word when we have nothing to say. Yet, even as you speak with me now, I do not believe you are making empty sounds, but by every sound coming from your lips you are giving me a sign enabling me to understand something. Consequently, you should not utter those two syllables, when speaking, if you do not signify something by them. But if you see they are necessary to make a meaningful statement and that they teach or call something to our mind when they strike the ear, then you will really see what I want to say, but am unable to explain.

Aug. What, then, are we to do? Instead of saying that *nihil* signifies something which is nothing, shall we say that this word signifies a certain state of mind when, failing to perceive a reality, the mind nevertheless finds, or thinks it finds, that such a reality does not exist?

Ad. Maybe that is the very thing I was trying so hard to explain.

Aug. Be that as it may, let us go on from here so we will not find ourselves in a most absurd situation.

Ad. What in the world is that?

Aug. That "nothing" is holding us back and causing us delay.

Ad. That is certainly ridiculous, and yet I realize that it can happen, I know not how. Yes, I see plainly that it has happened.

4. *Aug.* We shall, God permitting, have a clearer understanding of this sort of contradiction in its proper place. For now, return to that verse and try to explain as well as you can what the rest of the words signify.

Ad. The third word is the preposition *ex,* for which I think we can substitute the preposition *de.*

Aug. I am not asking you to substitute one familiar word for another equally familiar, of the same meaning, if, in fact, it does have the same meaning. But let us grant that for now. To be sure, if the poet had not said *ex tanta urbe,* but *de tanta,* and I were to ask you what *de* means, you would say *ex,* since these are two words, that is, signs, which you suppose mean the same thing. But I am looking for the one thing itself, whatever it is, which is signified by these two signs.

Ad. I think that *ex* signifies a separation of one thing from something in which it had been present and which is now said to be "from" the first; whether this no longer remains, as in that verse where, though the city did not survive, some Trojans were able to depart "from" it, or where it still remains, as when we say there are traders in Africa "from" the city of Rome.

Aug. Granted that this is true, without enumerating many examples that might possibly be cited as exceptions to your rule, nevertheless you will readily notice this one point, at least, namely, that you have been explaining words by words, that is, signs by signs, and what is familiar by what is equally familiar. But I would like you to point out to me, if you can, the realities themselves of which these are signs.

Chapter 3

5. *Ad.* I am astonished that you do not know, or rather, that you pretend not to know, that your request cannot possibly be met by any answer of mine. Actually, we are holding a conversation where we can only reply by means of words. But you are looking for those realities which, whatever else they are, are certainly not words, and yet you are also using words to ask me about them. So you will first have to ask a question without words so I can then reply in the same manner.

Aug. You have a right to do this, I admit. But suppose I should ask you what was signified when these three syllables *paries* [wall] are spoken, could you not point with your finger so I could see clearly the reality itself, of which this three-syllable word is a sign. You would be showing it to me, but without the use of words.

Ad. I grant that this is possible only for names signifying bodily objects, provided these are present.

Aug. Are we going to call color a body? Do we not rather speak of it as a quality of bodies?

Ad. That is right.

Aug. Here again, why can it not be indicated with the finger? Or do you also include with bodies the qualities of bodies, so that these, as well as bodies, can be shown without words, whenever they are present?

Ad. When I said "bodies," I intended that all things corporeal should be understood, namely, everything which the senses perceive in bodies.

Aug. But consider whether even here you should allow for exceptions.

Ad. That is sound advice. For I should not have said all things corporeal, but all things visible. I indeed acknowledge that though sound, odor, taste, weight, heat, and other qualities pertaining to the senses other than sight, cannot be perceived apart from bodies, and are therefore corporeal, yet they cannot be indicated with a finger.

Aug. Have you never noticed how men converse, as it were, with deaf people by gestures and how the deaf themselves in turn use gestures to ask and answer questions, to teach and to make known either all their wishes or, at least, a good many of them? When this is done, visual qualities are not the only ones indicated without the use of words, but also sound, taste, and other such qualities. And there are actors in the theaters who often unfold and act out whole stories by dancing, without the use of words.

Ad. I have no objection, except to note that not only I, but also your dancing actor himself, could not show you what the preposition *ex* signifies without using words.

6. *Aug.* Perhaps what you say is true. But let us suppose that he can. You will have no doubt, I think, that no matter what the bodily movement may be by which he tries to point out for me the reality signified by this word, it will not be the reality itself, but a sign. Therefore, he will be indicating, not indeed one word by another, but still one sign by another so that the monosyllable *ex* and the bodily gesture will signify some one thing which I would like to have pointed out to me without the use of a sign.

Ad. I ask you, how is such a thing possible?

Aug. The same way that it was possible in the case of the wall.

Ad. Even that cannot be indicated without a sign, as the course of our reasoning has shown. For the pointing of the finger is certainly not the wall, but a sign made to indicate the wall. Nothing, therefore, can be made known, as I see it, without the use of signs.

Aug. Suppose I should ask you what walking is, and you were to get up and walk? Would you not be using the reality itself rather than words, or any signs, to teach me?

Ad. I acknowledge that this is so, and I am ashamed that I failed to see something so obvious. From this example, thousands of other things come to mind which can be made known of themselves, and not through signs, such as eating, drinking, sitting, standing, shouting, as well as numberless other cases.

Aug. Well, now, answer me this. Suppose I were completely ignorant of the meaning of this word and were to ask you what walking is while you were walking, how would you teach me?

Ad. I would walk a little faster, so that this new factor, introduced after your question, would bring it to your attention; and all the while, nothing else would be going on except the very thing that had to be made known.

Aug. Do you not realize that walking and hurrying are two different things? A man who walks is not thereby hurrying, and one who hurries is not necessarily walking. For we also speak of hurrying in connection with writing and reading, and for countless other things. Therefore, if you did what you were doing a little more quickly, in response to my question, I might suppose that there is no difference between walking and hurrying. For this acceleration of your pace was the new factor you introduced, and I would be misled on this account.

Ad. I admit that we cannot indicate something without a sign if we are asked about it at the time we happen to be doing it. For if we do not add something to what we are doing, our questioner will take it that we are unwilling to show him and that, having ignored him, we continue what we are doing. But if he asks about things we are able to do, but not at the time we are doing them, then, by performing the act after his question, we can show him what he wants to know by the thing itself, rather than by a sign— unless he chances to ask me what speaking is while I am speaking. For, in that case, no matter what I should say to teach him, I will have to speak. From this point, I shall go on teaching him until I make plain to him what he wants to know, without deviating from the thing itself which he wanted to have shown him, and without looking for signs to indicate it, except for the sign of language itself.

Chapter 4

7. *Aug.* A very keen observation, indeed! See, then, whether we are agreed that those things can be indicated without signs which we are either not doing when asked about them, but can do right away, or those which are perhaps signs themselves while we are making them. When talking, for example, we are making signs, from which the term "signify" is derived.

Ad. We agree.

Aug. When, therefore, a question is asked about certain signs, these can be indicated by means of signs. If, however, the question concerns things that are not signs, these can be indicated either by doing them after being questioned, if this is possible, or by making signs to direct attention to them.

Ad. That is correct.

Aug. Within this three-fold division of signs, let us first consider, if you will, that class in which signs are indicated by signs. Words are not the only signs, are they?

Ad. No.

Aug. I think that in speaking we use words to signify words themselves or other signs, as when we say "gesture," or "letter," for these two words are also signs. Or we use words to signify something else which is not a sign, as when we say "stone." Since it signifies something, this word is a sign, but what it signifies is not in turn a sign. But this kind of sign, namely, that where words signify things that are not signs, does not belong to the class of sign now under discussion. For we proposed to consider the class of signs where signs are indicated by means of signs. We found that this included two sub-divisions, since by means of signs we teach or call to mind either the same signs or different signs. Do you not think so?

Ad. It is perfectly clear.

8. *Aug.* Tell me, then, to which sense those signs pertain which are words?

Ad. To hearing.

Aug. And gestures?

Ad. To sight.

Aug. What about words we find written? Are they words, or are they more properly thought of as signs of words? To be a word, something must be uttered with articulated sound and have some meaning, and sound can be perceived by no other sense than hearing. Consequently, when a word is written, the eyes are given a sign by which something pertaining to hearing is brought to mind.

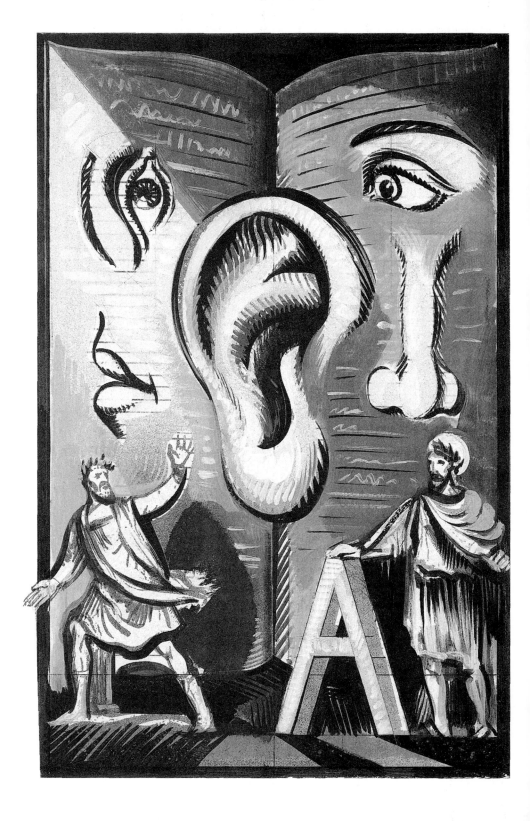

Ad. I fully agree.

Aug. You will also agree, I think, that when we say "noun," we are signifying something.

Ad. That is true.

Aug. Well, what is that?

Ad. That, precisely, which anything is called, as Romulus, Rome, virtue, river, and numberless other things.

Aug. Do these four nouns not signify something?

Ad. They do, indeed.

Aug. And is there any difference between these nouns and the things they signify?

Ad. Yes, there is a big difference.

Aug. I would like to hear from you what that difference is.

Ad. First of all, nouns are signs, things are not signs.

Aug. Would you agree if we call things that can be signified by signs, but are not signs, "signifiables," just as we call things that can be seen "visible"? This will enable us to deal with these matters more easily from here on.

Ad. I would certainly agree.

Aug. Well, what about those four signs you mentioned a short while ago? Can they be signified by any other signs?

Ad. I am surprised that you think I have already forgotten that we found that written words are signs of other spoken signs.

Aug. Tell me the difference between them.

Ad. The former are visible, the latter, audible. Why not allow the term "audible," if we have allowed the term "signifiables"?

Aug. I am quite pleased to allow it. But I ask you again whether those four signs can be signified by any other audible sign, as you recalled was the case for visible signs?

Ad. I recall that this was also mentioned a short while ago. I replied that a noun signifies some thing, and included those four things under its heading. I also realize that both "noun" and those four nouns become audible signs when they are expressed vocally.

Aug. What is the difference then between an audible sign and the audible reality signified, which, again, is a sign?

Ad. I see there is this difference between what is called a noun and those four things included under its meaning. The former is an audible sign of other audible signs, while the latter, though real signs, are nevertheless not signs of signs, but signs of things. Some are visible, such as Romulus and Rome, others are intelligible, such as virtue.

9. *Aug.* I am satisfied to accept this. But are you aware that everything expressed by articulate sound, with meaning, is a word?

Ad. I am.

Aug. Therefore, a noun is also a word, since, as we see, it is expressed by articulate sound, with meaning. And when we say that an eloquent man uses choice words, he is, to be sure, also using nouns. When the slave in Terence's play replied to his old master, "Fair words, I pray you," the master had used many nouns also.

Ad. I agree.

Aug. Then you will grant that when we utter the two syllables *verbum* (word), we are also signifying "noun," and that the former is therefore a sign of the latter.

Ad. That I grant.

Aug. I would like you to answer this question too. You said that "word" is a sign of "noun" and "noun" is a sign of "river" and "river" is the sign of a reality that we can see; also, that there is a difference between the reality and "river," which is its sign, and between this sign and "noun," which is the sign of this sign. Tell me, then, what difference you think there is between the sign of "noun," which was found to be a "word," and "noun" itself, which is its sign.

Ad. I see there is this difference. Things signified by "noun" are also signified by "word," for just as "noun" is a word, so also is "river" a word. On the other hand, not everything signified by "word" can also be signified by "noun." For both the term "if," at the opening of the verse you quoted, and the term "from," are words but not nouns, though they have been occupying our attention for such a long time and have now, with reason as our guide, led us to the present subject. And there are many such cases to be found. Consequently, since all nouns are words but not all words are nouns, I think the difference between "word" and "noun" is plain, namely, the difference between the sign of a sign not signifying other signs, and a sign of a sign which itself signifies other signs.

Aug. Would you grant that while every horse is an animal, not every animal is a horse?

Ad. Who would doubt it?

Aug. Then the difference between "noun" and "word" is the same as that between "horse" and "animal." Perhaps what keeps you from agreeing is the fact that we also use the term *verbum* [word] in another sense to signify verbs that are conjugated throughout the various tenses, such as: I write, I wrote, I read, I have read. Obviously, these are not nouns.

Ad. You have indicated precisely the very thing that made me hesitate.

Aug. Do not let that disturb you. We do, in fact, speak of signs in a general way, to embrace whatever can signify anything, and here, as we see, words are also included. We likewise speak of "military insignia" [*signa militaria*], which are properly called signs, but do not include words. Yet, were I to tell you that just as every horse is an animal but not every animal is a horse, so too, while every word is a sign, not every sign is a word, I think you would not hesitate to agree.

Ad. I now see and fully agree that there is the same difference between "words," taken in a general sense, and "noun," as between "animal" and "horse."

10. *Aug.* Do you likewise see that when we articulate this three-syllable word "animal," the noun is one thing, what it signifies is something else?

Ad. I already granted that before for all signs and things capable of being signified.

Aug. Do you think that all signs signify something other than what they are themselves, in the way that the three-syllable word "animal," when spoken, does not signify the word itself?

Ad. Of course not. For whenever we say "sign," it signifies not only other signs, whatever they are, but also itself, because "sign" is a word, and all words are certainly signs.

Aug. But does not something similar occur when we pronounce the two-syllable word *verbum* [word]? For if it signifies whatever has meaning and is articulated, then it also comes under the heading of "word."

Ad. That is correct.

Aug. But does not the same thing hold true for "noun"? It also signifies nouns of all genders and is itself a noun of neuter gender. If I should ask you what part of speech "noun" is, could you give any other correct answer except a "noun"?

Ad. What you say is true.

Aug. Then there are signs which, among the other thing they signify, also signify themselves.

Ad. There are such signs.

Aug. Do you think the case is similar when we pronounce the four-syllable term *conjunctio* [conjunction]?

Ad. Not at all. For it does not signify nouns, but it is itself a noun.

Chapter 5

11. *Aug.* You have been paying close attention. Consider now whether signs can be found which mutually signify each other in such a way that the first signifies the second, and the second, the first. This mutual relation does not obtain between the four-syllable word *conjunctio* [conjunction] and what it signifies, as when we say, "if," "or," "for," "yet," "unless," "therefore," "since," and the like. For the one word "conjunction" signifies them all, but no one of them signifies that four-syllable word itself.

Ad. I understand, and I am eager to know what those signs are which mutually signify each other.

Aug. Then you fail to see that by saying "noun" and "word," we are expressing two words?

Ad. I see that.

Aug. Why, then, do you fail to see that by saying "noun" and "word," we are expressing two names?

Ad. I see that too.

Aug. Then you know that "noun" is signified by "word" just as "word" is signified by "noun."

Ad. I agree.

Aug. Can you tell me how they differ, apart from the fact that they are spelled and pronounced differently?

Ad. Possibly I can, for it is the same difference I indicated a short time ago. When we say "words," we signify everything expressed by articulate speech and conveying some meaning. Every noun, then, even "noun" itself, is a word, but not every word is a noun, though "word" is itself a noun.

12. *Aug.* What if someone should make this statement, and prove it, namely, that just as every noun is a word, so too, every word is a noun, could you find any difference between them, apart from the different sounds of the letters?

Ad. No, I think there is no difference between them.

Aug. What if all sounds expressed by articulated speech and conveying some meaning are both words and nouns, but are designated words for one reason, and nouns for another—would there be no difference between them?

Ad. I do not see how there could be.

Aug. You will at least understand this, that everything colored is visible and everything visible is colored, though these two words have separate and different meanings.

Ad. I understand.

Aug. What, then, if the same obtains where every word is a noun and every noun is a word, though these same two nouns or words, namely, "noun" and "word," have a different meaning?

Ad. I see now that this can occur, but I am waiting for you to show me how.

Aug. You are, I think, aware that everything expressed by articulate voice and conveying some meaning must both strike the ear to be heard and be committed to the memory to be known.

Ad. I am aware of that.

Aug. So two things happen whenever we give expression to something by means of articulate sound.

Ad. That is correct.

Aug. What if words derive their name from one of the two things, and nouns from the other? Suppose, that is, that words [*verba*] come from "striking" [*verberando*], and nouns [*nomina*] from "knowing" [*noscendo*], so that the former has earned its name because of the ear, the latter, because of the mind.

13. *Aug.* I will grant this when you show me that we are correct in saying that all words are nouns.

Ad. That is easy.

Aug. You learned, I suppose, and still remember, that a pronoun is so called because it can stand for a noun, though it indicates the reality less perfectly than a noun. I think this was the definition you recited to your grammar teacher, namely, that a pronoun is a part of speech which, when substituted for the noun itself, signifies the same thing, though less perfectly.

Ad. I remember the definition and think it is a good one.

Aug. So you see that according to this definition pronouns serve only for nouns and can be substituted for them only. When we say, for example, "this man," "the king himself," "the same woman," "this gold," "that

silver," the terms "this," "himself," "same," "this," and "that," are pronouns; "man," "king," "woman," "gold," "silver," are nouns, which signify
their objects more perfectly than do pronouns.

Ad. I understand this and agree.

Aug. Now, mention some conjunctions—any at all.

Ad. Et [and], *que* [and], *at* [but], *atque* [and].

Aug. Do you think that all these that you have mentioned are nouns?

Ad. By no means.

Aug. Do you think that I was at least speaking correctly when I said: "All
these that you have mentioned"?

Ad. Absolutely. Now I realize how cleverly you made me see that I was
giving expression to nouns, since, otherwise, it would have been incorrect
to say "all *these*." But I still have the fear that you seemed to have spoken
correctly only because there is no denying that these four conjunctions are
also words. Consequently, they could be referred to correctly as "all these,"
because it is correct to say "all these words." But if you ask me what part of
speech is "words," I can only reply that it is a noun. Perhaps, then, it was
the inclusion of the pronoun with this noun that made your expression
correct.

14. *Aug.* You have made an intelligent mistake. But that you may be
mistaken no longer, pay closer attention to what I have to say, if only I can
express it the way I want to. Now dealing with words by means of words is
just as bewildering as intertwining and scratching one's fingers, where it is
almost impossible to tell, except for the person doing it, which fingers are
itching and which are relieving the itch.

Ad. See, I am all attention! That analogy has stirred my curiosity.

Aug. Words, of course, are made up of sounds and letters.

Ad. True.

Aug. Let us first of all make use of that authority so dear to us. When the
Apostle Paul says: "There was not in Christ 'is' and 'is not,' but 'is' was in
Him," I do not think we are to imagine that the three letters used in saying
est [is] were in Christ, but rather what those three letters signify.

Ad. What you say is true.

Aug. So you see that when the Apostle said: "Is [*est*] was in Him," he
said simply that "what was in Him is called 'is' [*est*]." It was as if he had
said, "Power was in Him," which could only mean that what we call
"power" was in Him. We are not to suppose that the two syllables enunci-
ated in saying "power" are what was in Christ, but rather what these two
syllables signify.

Ad. I understand and follow you.

Aug. Do you not also understand that it makes no difference whether
someone says, "it is *called* virtue," or "it is *named* virtue"?

Ad. That is obvious.

Aug. Then it is just as obvious that it makes no difference whether
someone says, "what was in Him is *called* 'is,'" or "is *named* 'is.'"

Ad. I see that here, too, there is no difference.

Aug. Do you also see what I am trying to point out to you?

Ad. I do not, really.

Aug. Then do you likewise fail to see that a noun is that by which a thing is named?

Ad. Clearly, nothing could be more certain.

Aug. So you see that "is" is a noun, since what was in Him is named "is."

Ad. I cannot deny it.

Aug. But if I should ask you what part of speech is "is," I think you would say it is not a noun, but a verb, though our reasoning has shown us that it is also a noun.

Ad. It is just as you say.

Aug. Do you still doubt that the other parts of speech are also nouns in the same way as we have just shown?

Ad. I do not, because I now admit that they signify something. But were you to ask, one by one, what the things they signify are called, that is, what their names are, I could only answer that they are the very parts of speech which are not called "nouns," although our reasoning has, as I now perceive, shown them to be nouns.

15. *Aug.* Are you unconcerned that someone may be found to upset your reasoning by asserting that the Apostle's authority must be allowed where realities are concerned, but not for words, with the result that the basis for this position is not so strong as we think? For, while it is possible that Paul was perfectly correct in his life and teaching, he did, nevertheless, express himself somewhat incorrectly when He said, "'is' was in Him," all the more so, since he admits himself that he is "unskilled in speech." How do you suppose we should refute such a person?

Ad. I could not gainsay such a man. I do entreat you to find someone among those experts in language whose high competence is recognized, whose authority will better enable you to accomplish your purpose.

Aug. So you think that without authorities, reason itself is incapable of proving that all the parts of speech signify something and thereby give it a designation; if it has a designation, it has a name; if it has a name, it certainly gets its name from a noun. This is readily discernible in the various languages. Anyone can see, for example, that if you ask what the Greek word is for "who," the answer is *tis;* for "wish," *thelō;* for "well," *kalōs;* for "something written," *to gegrammenon;* for "and," *kai;* for "from," *apo;* for "alas," *oi.* Now the one who asks such questions concerning all these parts of speech which we enumerated is speaking correctly, which would not be possible unless they were nouns. Accordingly, since we are able to establish that the Apostle Paul spoke correctly according to this line of reasoning, without recourse to all the masters of eloquence, what need is there to look for some person to support our position?

16. But lest there be someone who will not yet yield, because he is too dull or arrogant, but declares that he will not yield at all except to authorities whose function to legislate regarding words is recognized by common consent—then, is there anything more excellent than Cicero to be found in the Latin language? Now, in his finest orations, known as the Verrines, he called the preposition *coram* (before) a noun, though it may be an adverb in this passage. Since I do not quite understand the passage, it is possible that a different explanation may be advanced at another time, either by myself or by someone else. But there is one point, I think, which cannot possibly be gainsaid. The most celebrated masters of argumentation, for example, teach that a complete sentence is made up of a noun and a verb, and may be either affirmative or negative. The same Tullius refers somewhere to this form of discourse as a "proposition." They also teach, and rightly so, that when the verb is in the third person, the case of the noun must be the nominative. If you examine with me such expressions as "the man sits" or "the horse runs," you will, I think, recognize that these are two propositions.

Ad. I do.

Aug. Do you see there is a separate noun in each of the propositions: "man," in the first, "horse," in the other; and also a separate verb: "sits," in the first, "runs," in the other?

Ad. I see that.

Aug. So if I were only to say "sits" or "runs," you would rightly ask me "who?" or "what?", and I would reply "a man," or "a horse," or "an animal," or something else, so that by joining the noun again to the verb, a complete proposition would result, namely, a sentence, whether affirmative or negative.

Ad. I understand.

Aug. Pay attention to what else I have to say. Suppose we are viewing something at a distance and are not sure whether it is an animal or a stone, or something else. If I should say to you, "Because it is a man, it is an animal," would I not be speaking rashly?

Ad. Very much so. But if you should say, "If it is a man, it is an animal," you would certainly not be speaking rashly.

Aug. You are correct. Hence the term "if" in your sentence is acceptable to both of us, while the term "because" in my sentence is unacceptable to both of us.

Ad. I agree.

Aug. See now whether these two sentences are complete propositions: "'If' is acceptable" [*Placet si*]; "'Because' is not acceptable" [*Displicet quia*].

Ad. They are altogether complete.

Aug. Come now, tell me which words are the verbs, and which the nouns.

Ad. I see that the verbs are "is acceptable" [*placet*] and "is not acceptable" [*displicet*], whereas the nouns can only be "if" and "because."

Aug. Then it has been sufficiently established that these two conjunctions are also nouns.

Ad. Quite sufficiently.

Aug. Can you prove by yourself that the same things hold for the other parts of speech in accordance with this same rule?

Ad. I can.

Chapter 6

17. *Aug.* Let us go on from here. Tell me now whether you think that all names are terms [*vocabula*], and all terms are nouns, just as we found that all words are nouns and all nouns are words.

Ad. Except for the different sounds of the syllables, I really see no difference between them.

Aug. I will not object to that for now, although there are those who do make a distinction between them in meaning. But there is no need to examine their opinion just now. It must surely occur to you that we have now come to those signs which signify one another mutually, where the only difference is one of sound, and which signify themselves, together with the other parts of speech.

Ad. I do not understand.

Aug. Then you fail to understand that "noun" is signified by "term" and "term" by "noun" in such a way that, except for the sound of the letters, there is no difference between them so far as the general meaning of "noun" is concerned. For we also speak of "noun" in a particular sense, where it is found among the eight parts of speech and does not include the other seven.

Ad. I understand.

Aug. But that is the very thing I said—terms and nouns signify each other mutually.

18. *Ad.* That I understand, but I am asking what you meant by saying that these signs signify themselves, together with the other parts of speech.

Aug. Did not our reasoning show us before that all the parts of speech can be called both nouns and terms, that is to say, they can be signified both by "noun" and "term"?

Ad. That is right.

Aug. What of "noun" itself, namely, the sound expressed by the two syllables *nomen* [name]? If I ask what you would call it, would you not answer correctly that it is a "noun"?

Ad. That would be correct.

Aug. But does not the four-syllable sign, which is expressed by our saying *conjunctio* [conjunction], signify itself in this way? We cannot include this noun among the things it signifies.

Ad. Now I have it right.

Aug. That is precisely what was said, namely, the "noun" signifies itself together with the other things it signifies, and you can see for yourself that the same things hold for "term."

Ad. Now it is easy. But it occurs to me now that "noun" can be understood both in a general and in a particular sense, whereas "term" is not included among the eight parts of speech. Accordingly, I think they also differ in this respect, over and above the difference in sound.

Aug. What of *nomen* and *onoma*? Do you think there is any difference between them except for the sounds which distinguish the Latin and Greek languages?

Ad. I really see no other difference here.

Aug. We have reached this conclusion, therefore, in our discussion: there are signs which signify themselves; signs that signify each other mutually; signs that have the same extension; signs that differ only in sound. This fourth kind of sign we have just discovered; the first three were understood to apply both to "nouns" and "words."

Ad. That much has been settled.

Chapter 7

19. *Aug.* I would like you to review the results of our conversation.

Ad. I shall do the best I can. I recall, first of all, that we inquired for a time about the purpose of language and discovered that we speak either to teach or to recall. Even when we ask questions, we do nothing more than teach the person interrogated what we wish to learn from him. In the case of singing, what we are apparently doing for pleasure is not the proper function of language. In praying to God, who cannot conceivably be taught or reminded of anything, our words serve either to remind ourselves or to enable us to remind and teach others. Then, after it had been made sufficiently clear that words are merely signs, and that what fails to signify something is not a sign, you recited a verse where I should try to point out the meaning of the words, one by one. The verse was this: "If it please the gods that nothing remain of so great a city." While the second word [nihil] is familiar and perfectly obvious, we failed nevertheless to discover its meaning. And when I was of the opinion that we do not insert it in speaking without some reason, but use it to teach something to one hearing it, you did indeed reply that it possibly indicates a state of mind, whenever the mind has found, or thinks it has found, that something it was looking for does not exist. But you put off clarifying the matter for another time, and avoided probing this unexplored problem by means of a humorous remark. And do not suppose that I have forgotten what you promised.

Then, when I had all I could do to explain the third word of the verse, you kept after me not to explain one word by another of the same meaning, but to point out the reality itself signified by the words. And when I stated that this was not possible in conversation, we went on to consider things that can be indicated by pointing the finger as a reply to those who ask about them. These included, I thought, all corporeal things, but we discovered that only things visible were included. Then, somehow or other, we came to consider the case of deaf people and actors, who, without speaking, use gestures to signify not only things that can be seen, but also many other things besides, in fact, almost everything that we indicated by speech; yet, we found that gestures themselves are signs. After that, we began again to inquire how we might be able, without the use of signs, to indicate the very things signified by signs, seeing that we can indicate the wall, colors, and things visible by pointing the finger, which is also shown to be a sign.

Here, after I had made the mistake of saying that no such thing was possible, we finally agreed that those things can be indicated without signs which we are not doing at the time we are asked about them, but which we are able to do once we are questioned. Speaking, however, is not included in this class, since it was perfectly clear that if we are asked what speaking is, while we are speaking, it is easy to indicate the action by the very thing itself.

20. This enabled us to see that there are signs that manifest signs, and signs that manifest things that are not signs; and again, that those things can be manifested without signs, which we are able to do after being questioned about them. We undertook a more thorough examination and discussion concerning the first of these three. It became clear from our discussion that some signs cannot in turn be signified by those signs which they signify, as is the case when we use the four-syllable word *conjunctio* [conjunction]; also, that there are other signs which can. When we say "sign," for example, we also signify "word," and when we say "word," we also signify "sign," because "sign" and "word" are two signs as well as two words. Within that class of signs, however, which signify one another mutually, we showed that some do not have the same extension, others have the same extension, while others are identical. For example, the two-syllable word expressed when we say *signum* [sign], signifies all the signs by which a thing can be signified at all. But when we say "word," this is not a sign of all signs, but only of those expressed by the articulated voice. It is clear, then, that although *verbum* [word] is signified by *signum* [sign] and vice versa, that is, the first two syllables are signified by the latter two, and the latter by the former, nevertheless, *signum* has a wider extension than *verbum*. That is to say, the first two syllables have a wider extension than the latter two.

But "word" and "noun" have the same extension when used in a general sense. Our line of reasoning has actually shown that all the parts of speech can also be nouns, because pronouns can be used in connection with them. Also, that they name something, and that all of them can form a complete sentence by adding a verb to them. Yet, while "noun" and "word" have the same extension, since every word is also a noun, they do not have the same meaning. We did, in fact, show that it was quite probable that they are designated "words" for one reason, and "nouns" for another. We found that the first of these indicated a "striking" on the ear, and the second a recalling on the part of the mind. This can be seen, for example, from the fact that in speaking, it is perfectly correct to say: "What is the name for this thing?" whenever we want to commit it to our memory; it is not usual for us to say: "What is the word for this thing?"

On the other hand, we found that *nomen* and *onoma* are signs that have not only the same extension, but are also completely the same in meaning, differing only in the sound of their letters. This one point, it is true, did escape me, namely, that in the class of signs which signify mutually, we found none that did not also signify itself among the other things it signified.

I have recalled these points to the best of my ability. I leave it to you to say whether I have arranged them in a good and logical order, for I do not think you said anything in our conversation unless you knew it was certain.

Chapter 8

21. *Aug.* You have done rather well to recall from memory everything that I asked. Furthermore, I must acknowledge to you that these distinctions seem much clearer to me now than they did when we were both bringing them to light from some sort of hidden abode by means of our

inquiry and discussion. But it is hard to say at this point what the objective is that I am trying to reach with you by such roundabout ways. Maybe you think we are being playful and are turning our minds from serious matters by some kind of childish and trifling questions, or that we are only looking for a slight or unimportant result. Or, if you feel that this discussion will result in something important, you want to know right now what it is, or at least to hear what it is. Now I want you to know that I have not injected any worthless comedy into our conversation, though we may perhaps be acting playfully. Yet even this is not to be regarded as child's play, nor are we to suppose that we have only slight or unimportant benefits in mind. And yet, if I assert that there is a happy life, and one that is everlasting, and that I desire that we should be led to it by God, Who is Truth itself, as our Guide, by stages adapted to our faltering steps, I fear I may seem ridiculous for having first embarked upon so long a course with a consideration of signs rather than of the realities they signify. You will pardon me then if I engage in some preliminary play with you, not for the sake of playing, but to exercise and sharpen our mental powers. This will enable us not only to endure, but also to love the warmth and light of that region wherein is found the happy life.

Ad. Do go on as you have begun, for I could never consider as trivial anything which you think is worth saying or doing.

22. *Aug.* Come now, and let us consider the class of signs which signify, not other signs, but the things we call signifiable. And, first of all, tell me whether man is man.

Ad. I cannot tell now whether you are joking.

Aug. Why is that?

Ad. Because you think I have to be asked whether man is anything but man.

Aug. So I suppose you would think I was jesting with you if I were also to ask whether the first syllable of this noun man [*homo*] is other than *ho,* and the second other than *mo.*

Ad. I certainly would.

Aug. But would you deny that these two syllables, taken together, make *homo?*

Ad. Who could deny it?

Aug. I ask you, then, whether *you* are these two connected syllables?

Ad. Not at all. But I do see what you are driving at.

Aug. Well then, tell me, so you will not think I am being offensive.

Ad. You think the conclusion is that I am not a man.

Aug. Why should you not think the same, since you grant as true all the previous points from which this conclusion was drawn?

Ad. I will not tell you what I think until I first hear from you whether, in questioning me as to whether man is man, you are asking about those two syllables, or about the reality itself which they signify.

Aug. You tell me, instead, in what sense you have taken my question. For if it is ambiguous, you should have guarded against this before and should not have answered until you were certain in what sense I proposed the question.

Ad. Why should I be hampered by this ambiguity, when I have replied to both senses of the question? The term *homo* [man] is certainly *homo,* since those two syllables are nothing more than those two syllables, and what they signify is none other than the existing reality.

Aug. An ingenious reply, to be sure. But why have you taken only this term "man" in both senses, and not the others that we also mentioned?

Ad. How can you prove that I did not also take the others in the same way?

Aug. To mention only one, if you had understood my first question entirely from the viewpoint of the sound of the syllables, you would have given me no answer, for you could have thought that I had not even asked a question. But now, when I expressed three words, repeating the one in the middle, and asked *utrum homo homo sit* [whether man is man], you understood the first and last words, not as mere signs, but as realities signified by the signs. This was obvious from the mere fact that you were at once so certain and sure of yourself as to feel that my question should be answered.

Ad. What you say is true.

Aug. Why, then, did you see fit to take only the middle word [*homo*] both with respect to the sound and to the reality it signifies?

Ad. Look here, now I am going to take the whole sentence from the viewpoint of what is signified. For I agree with you that we simply cannot engage in conversation unless the mind is directed by the sound of the words to the realities signified by these signs. Now, then, show me how I was deceived by a line of reasoning that resulted in the conclusion that I am not a man.

Aug. No, but I shall repeat the same questions so that you can find out for yourself where you made your mistake.

Ad. You are right.

23. *Aug.* I will not repeat my first question because you have already answered it. See, now, whether the syllable *ho* is anything other than *ho,* and the syllable *mo* anything other than *mo.*

Ad. Really, I can see no difference here.

Aug. See, likewise, whether man [*homo*] results from the combination of these two syllables.

Ad. I could never grant such a thing. We did agree, and rightly so, that whenever a sign is expressed, our attention should be directed to the reality it signifies, and, once we have considered it, we should either affirm or deny what it expressed. Since, however, those two syllables have no meaning when they are pronounced separately, we agreed that they were only sounds.

Aug. Then you agree, and are firmly convinced, that answers to questions should be made only with reference to the things signified by the words.

Ad. I see no reason to disagree, provided that the sounds are words.

Aug. I would like to see how you would refute the man who concluded that a lion came forth from the mouth of his opponent, as is often told in jest. When asked whether the things we say do come forth from our mouth, the other could not deny it. He had no trouble getting the man to say "lion" while he was speaking. When that happened, he began to make fun of him and to press the point that, good man that he was, he had discharged from his mouth so savage a beast; for he had acknowledged that whatever we say comes forth from our mouth, and he could not deny that he had said "lion."

Ad. Really, it would not be difficult at all to refute such a buffoon, because I would not grant that whatever we say goes out of our mouth. We signify the things we speak of, and what comes forth from the speaker's mouth is not the thing signified, but the sign by which it is signified. We make an exception for signs that signify themselves, but we dealt with this class a short time ago.

24. *Aug.* This would certainly make you a match for him. Just the same, what answer would you give me if asked whether "man" is a noun?

Ad. What else, but a noun?

Aug. Well, then, am I seeing a noun when I look at you?

Ad. No.

Aug. Do you want to say what follows from this?

Ad. Please do not. I can see for myself the inference that I am not a man, since in reply to your question whether man is a noun, I said that it was. We had, in fact, already agreed that when we give or deny assent to what is said, we do so from the side of the reality which is signified.

Aug. But the very fact that you hit upon this reply is, in my opinion, not without significance. For reason's own law, which is implanted in our minds, prevailed over your caution. If I were to ask, for example, what man is, you might answer an "animal." But if I should ask what part of speech is "man," the only correct answer you could give would be a "noun." Consequently, though man is found to be both a noun and an animal, the former designation has to do with signs, the latter, with the thing signified. So when anyone asks whether "man" is a "noun," I can only reply that it is, since he indicates clearly enough that he wants to know what man is precisely as a sign. But if he asks whether man is an animal, I will reply in the affirmative even more promptly. If he does not mention either "noun" or "animal," and merely asks what man [*homo*] is, then, following an approved rule of language, my mind would quickly turn its attention to the reality signified by the two syllables, and answer an "animal"; or I might even state the full definition of man, namely, that he is a mortal rational animal. Do you not think so?

Ad. I do, absolutely. But when we grant that "man" is a noun, how can we escape the highly offensive conclusion that we are not men?

Aug. How do you suppose, if not by showing that this conclusion was not drawn according to the sense of the term agreed upon with the one who asked the question. But if he acknowledges that he drew the conclusion from the other sense of the term, the inference should not frighten us at all.

For why should I fear to admit that I am not "man" [*hominem*], namely, that I am not those three syllables?

Ad. Nothing could be truer. Why, then, does the mind take offense at the inference that you are not "man," since, according to what we have agreed upon, nothing truer could be said?

Aug. Because I cannot help thinking that as soon as the words are expressed, the conclusion has reference to the reality itself signified by these two syllables; and this, by reason of that rule so compelling by nature, namely, that whenever the sounds are heard, our attention is directed towards the things signified.

Ad. I agree.

Chapter 9

25. *Aug.* Now, then, I would have you understand that the realities signified are to be valued more highly than their signs. For whatever exists for the sake of something else must be of less value than that for which it exists. Would you agree?

Ad. I do not think one should assent to this too hastily. When we say "filth" [*coenum*], for example, I think the word far excels the reality it signifies. For that which makes the term offensive to us, whenever we hear it, has nothing to do with the sound of the word. Actually, by changing a single letter, the noun *coenum* [filth] becomes *coelum* [heaven]; and we see how far apart the realities are which these nouns signify. That is why I could never impute to the sign the quality we loathe in the reality which it signifies. I am right, then, in preferring the former to the latter, for we would rather hear the word than experience the reality by any of our senses.

Aug. You are very much on the alert. It is false, then, that all realities are to be valued more highly than their signs?

Ad. It looks that way.

Aug. Tell me, now, what you think those men had in mind when they gave a name to something so foul and revolting as this; also, whether you approve or disapprove what they did.

Ad. For my part, I would not presume to approve or disapprove, nor do I have any idea of what they had in mind.

Aug. Can you at least see what you yourself have in mind when you mention the word?

Ad. I certainly can. My purpose is to use a sign in order to teach or remind the one I am speaking with about this particular reality, because I think that this is something he should know.

Aug. What of the knowledge itself exchanged between you by such teaching and calling to mind, which you aptly express by means of this name? Is it not to be more highly valued than the word itself?

Ad. I grant that the knowledge itself which results from such a sign should be regarded more highly than the sign, but I do think that this is therefore also true of the reality.

26. *Aug.* Although it may be false, in our opinion, that all realities should be valued above their signs, it still remains true that everything that exists for the sake of something else is of less value than that for which it exists. To be sure, the knowledge of filth, for the sake of which the word "filth" has been coined, should be more highly esteemed than the word itself which, in turn, must be preferred, as we have seen, to filth itself. The sole reason why this knowledge has been preferred to the sign now under discussion is that the latter exists for the sake of the former, not the former for the sake of the latter. So it was that a certain glutton, a "worshiper of the belly," to use the words of the Apostle, declared that he lived to eat. Exasperated by what he heard, a certain temperate man replied: "Would it not be much better to eat in order to live?" It was, nevertheless, because of this very same rule that both had so spoken. The glutton was in disfavor simply because he so underestimated the value of his life as to esteem it of less worth than the pleasures of the palate, declaring that he had lived for the sake of feasting. The temperate man deserves to be praised for the single reason that, recognizing which of the two should be done for the sake of the other, subordinate, that is, to the other, he reminded us that we should eat to live rather than live to eat. Again, if some talkative person, with an infatuation for words, should say, "I teach in order to talk," you or any other person capable of discerning the true value of things might well reply: "Dear man, why do you not rather talk in order to teach?"

If all this be true, and you know it is, you must indeed realize how much less value is to be given to words than to the things on account of which we use words. Even our use of words must itself be given priority over words. For words exist to be used, and we make use of them to teach. Teaching, therefore, excels talking just as much as talking excels words. So teaching far excels words. But I am eager to hear any objections that you think might be raised.

27. *Ad.* I certainly agree that teaching is superior to words. But I do not know whether some objection might not be made to that rule which states that everything which exists for the sake of something else is inferior to that for which it exists.

Aug. We shall treat this problem more appropriately and more thoroughly at another time. For the present, the point that you grant is sufficient for what I am trying to prove. You grant, for example, that the knowledge of realities is of greater value than their signs. Consequently, the knowledge of these realities which are signified is to be preferred to the knowledge of their signs. Do you not think so?

Ad. Have I ever granted that the knowledge of realities is superior to a knowledge of their signs, but not superior to the signs themselves? So I am afraid to agree with you on this point. Suppose, for example, that just as the name "filth" is better than what it signifies, so, too, the knowledge of this name is to be preferred to the knowledge of that reality, though the name itself is inferior to this knowledge—then what? We are really dealing with four things here: the name, the reality, knowledge of the name, and knowledge of the reality. Hence, just as the first excels the second, why may the third not excel the fourth? Even if it does not excel, must we also consider it inferior?

28. *Aug.* I see that you have done remarkably well to remember what you have granted, as well as to explain your own views. But you do understand, I suppose, that this three-syllable noun which we express by saying *vitium* [vice] is better than what it signifies, though the knowledge of the noun itself is of far less value than the knowledge of vices. Accordingly, even though you propose those four things and give them your attention—the name, the reality, knowledge of the name, knowledge of the reality—we rightly prefer the first to the second. This name is found, for example, in the poem where Persius says: "This man is stupefied by vice," and not only does it not vitiate the verse, but it even lends embellishment to it. But when the reality signified by the name is found in anyone, it necessarily leaves him vitiated. But then the third thing does not excel the fourth, but the fourth, the third. For the knowledge of this name is of little importance compared to the knowledge of vices.

Ad. Do you think such knowledge is preferable, even when it makes men all the more wretched? For of all the punishments ever devised by cruel tyrants or inflicted by their greed, this same Persius assigns the first place to that which tortures men who are compelled to acknowledge vices which they cannot avoid.

Aug. In the same way, you could also deny that even the knowledge of virtues is preferable to the knowledge of the name "virtue," since to see virtue and not to have it is a torment. And it was the wish of this same satirist that tyrants might be punished this way.

Ad. God save us from such folly! I see now that when the mind is imbued with knowledge by the noblest of all the branches of learning, it is not the knowledge itself that is to be blamed. I see too that they should be deemed the most wretched of all, as I think Persius himself thought, who suffer from a disorder of this kind which cannot even be relieved by so potent a remedy.

Aug. You are right. But what does it matter to us, whatever Persius thought? In matters of this kind we are not subject to the authority of the poets. Then too, the question of which kind of knowledge is preferable to another cannot be easily explained here. I am satisfied with what we have shown so far, namely, that the knowledge of realities which are signified, even if not superior to the knowledge of signs, is nevertheless superior to the signs themselves. So let us examine more and more thoroughly what kind of realities those are which, as we have said, can be indicated without signs, such as speaking, walking, sitting, lying down, and so on.

Ad. I now recall the problem you mention.

Chapter 10

29. *Aug.* Do you think that all those actions which we can perform as soon as we are asked about them, can be indicated without signs, or would you make some exceptions?

Ad. As I consider over and over again this class of signs as a whole, I still find that nothing can be taught without signs, with the possible exception of speaking, and perhaps teaching, if someone should ask just what teaching itself is. For I see that whatever I do to make him learn, in response to his inquiry, he will not be learning from the action itself which he wants to have shown him. Now if someone should ask me what walking is when, as we said, I am not doing anything, or am doing something else, and I should try, without signs, to teach him what he wants to know by starting at once to walk, how shall I keep him from thinking that the distance I walked means the same as walking? He would be mistaken to think so, because he will suppose that someone who walks a longer or shorter distance than I did is not walking. And what I have said about this one word "walking" carries over to all those things which I had agreed could be indicated without signs, apart from the two exceptions we have made.

30. *Aug.* This I accept, of course. But do you not think that speaking is one thing and teaching another?

Ad. It certainly seems so. For if they were the same, no one could teach unless he were speaking. But since we also teach many things by signs other than words, who could doubt that there is a difference?

Aug. What about teaching and signifying? Are they the same, or is there some difference?

Ad. I think they are the same.

Aug. But suppose someone else were to say that we teach in order to use signs? Could he not be easily refuted by applying the rule we mentioned before?

Ad. That is correct.

Aug. So if we use signs to teach, and do not teach in order to use signs, teaching and signifying are not the same thing.

Ad. That is true, and I was wrong when I answered that they were the same.

Aug. Now answer me this: when one is teaching what teaching is, does he do this by using signs, or in some other way?

Ad. I fail to see how he could do it otherwise.

Aug. Then what you said a while ago is untrue, namely, that when one is asked what teaching is, the thing itself can be shown without the use of signs. For we realize now that not even this can be done without signs, seeing that you have granted that using signs and teaching are not the same. If they are different, as it appears they are, and the latter can only be indicated by the former, then teaching is certainly not made known by itself, as you had thought. So nothing has yet been found that can be made known of itself, except for speaking, which, in addition to other things, also signifies itself. But, since even this is also a sign, there is as yet absolutely no evidence to show that anything can be taught without the use of signs.

Ad. I see no reason to disagree.

31. *Aug.* Then it has been established that nothing can be taught without signs, and that we should value knowledge itself more highly than the signs which lead us to it, though it may be that some of the things signified are not superior to their signs.

Ad. It seems so.

Aug. Please bear in mind, will you, what a small result has come from such a roundabout discussion. Now, from the moment we began this fencing with words, which has been going on for so long, we have done our best to find out three things: whether anything can be taught without signs; whether some signs should be preferred to what they signify; and whether the knowledge of realities themselves is better than their signs. But there is a fourth point that I would like to find out from you in a few words, namely, do you think that things we have already discovered are such that you can no longer doubt about them?

Ad. I would certainly like to think that we have arrived at some certainties by so devious and winding a course. But that question of yours unsettles me for some strange reason, and keeps me from giving assent. For I think you would not ask me this unless you had some objection to make. Besides, the very complexity of these questions does not permit me to get a view of the whole problem and give a safe answer. I fear that amidst such complexity some point will pass unnoticed which my mind may not be sharp enough to bring to light.

Aug. I am glad to put up with your hesitation, for it reveals a cautious habit of mind, and this is the surest safeguard to preserve tranquility. It is very difficult indeed not to be perturbed when the things we held with a ready and eager assent are demolished by opposing arguments, and are wrenched, so to speak, from our hands. Accordingly, just as it is reasonable to yield to arguments that have been carefully weighed and examined, so is it hazardous to mistake what is not known for what is known. When conclusions are frequently undermined, which we thought would hold up and endure, there is danger that we may fall into such a hostile and distrustful attitude towards reason as to make it appear that we should not trust even the clearest evidence of truth.

32. But come, let us quickly reconsider now whether you were right to regard these conclusions as doubtful. Suppose now that someone unfamiliar with the business of snaring birds, which is done with reeds and birdlime, should encounter a bird-catcher fitted out with all his equipment, though he is not snaring birds but simply going on his way. At the sight of him, he quickens his pace and, as is usually the case, reflects and, in amazement, asks himself the meaning of the man's paraphernalia. Suppose, too, that the bird-catcher, aware that the other's attention is fixed upon him, and eager to show off his prowess, releases the reeds and, with his rod and hawk, snares a little bird which he sees nearby which he comes up to and captures. Would he not, I ask you, teach that spectator of his what he was so eager to know, not by any sign, but by the reality itself?

Ad. I am afraid we are confronted here with a situation similar to that where I referred to the man who asks what walking is. Neither do I think that everything about bird-catching has been made known even in the present case.

Aug. It is an easy matter to put your mind at ease. I will make the further qualification, that if the spectator were intelligent enough, he could grasp everything there is to know about the art of bird-catching from what he saw. It is sufficient for our purpose that *some* men can be taught *some* things, though not all, without the use of signs.

Ad. I too could further qualify my remarks by saying that if one is really intelligent, he will learn all about walking as soon as someone indicates it to him, by taking a few steps.

Aug. You may make that qualification as far as I am concerned. I not only have no objection, but am even favorable to it. You see, in fact, that we have both reached the conclusion that some things can be taught without the use of signs, and that we were wrong in thinking a little while ago that nothing at all can be taught without signs. Actually, these examples bring to mind, not one or two, but thousands of things, which are made known by themselves without having to resort to signs. Why, I ask, should we have any doubt of this? For, apart from the numerous plays performed in every theater by actors who play their part by enacting the events themselves, without using signs, does not God, as well as nature, exhibit and manifest to the view of all, and just as they are, the sun and the light which covers and clothes all the things around us, the moon and the other stars, the earth and sea, and all the countless things which they bring forth?

33. Now if we examine the matter more carefully, perhaps you will discover that nothing is learned by means of its signs. For when I am shown a sign, it cannot teach me anything if it finds me ignorant of the reality for which the sign stands; but if it finds me acquainted with the reality, what do I learn from the sign? When I read this, for example: "And their saraballae were not changed," the word "saraballae" does not convey to me the thing it signifies. If it is some kind of head-covering that goes by this name, did I, upon hearing the word, come to learn either what "head" or "covering" means? These things I knew before, and I came to know them, not when they were called these names by others, but when I saw them by myself. Indeed, when the sound of the two-syllable word *caput* [head] first struck my ears, I was just as ignorant of what it signified as when I first heard or read the word "saraballae." But, after frequent repetitions of the word "head," I discovered, by paying careful attention at the time it was used, that this was the word for something that was well known to me by sight. Before discovering it, the word was only a sound so far as I was concerned. I came to know it as a sign when I discovered the reality of which it is a sign. And I learned what this reality was, not, as I have said, by any sign, but by looking at it. Hence, it is more of a matter of the sign being learned from the thing we know, than it is of knowing the thing itself from the manifestation of its sign.

34. To grasp this point more clearly, let us pretend that we now hear the word "head" for the first time, and, not knowing whether it is merely a vocal sound or whether it also signifies something, we inquire what "head" is. Remember now, we want to become acquainted, not with the thing signified, but with the sign itself, which we actually do not know as long as we do not know the thing it signifies. But if the reality is pointed out to us while we are inquiring about it, it is by seeing this reality that we learn its sign, which we had heard before but had not understood. But since there are two things about this sign, namely, the sound and its meaning, we certainly do not perceive the sound because it is a sign, but, by the very fact that it strikes the ear, whereas its meaning is perceived by looking at the reality it signifies. For the pointing of the finger can signify nothing else but the reality to which it is pointed, not towards the sign, but towards a member of the body which we call the head. Consequently, by means of this pointing, I learn neither the reality, which I already knew, nor the sign, towards which the finger was not pointed.

But I am not too much concerned about this matter of pointing the finger since, as I see it, this is more of a sign of what indicating is itself than it is of any of the things being indicated. It is like our use of the adverb *ecce* [look!]. Even when we use this adverb, we usually point our finger too, just in case the one sign is not sufficient to indicate the object. The point I am trying most of all to make you see, if I can, is this, that we learn nothing from signs which we call words. For, as I have pointed out, it is rather a question of learning the sense of the word, that is, the meaning hidden in the sound, from a previous knowledge of the reality signified than it is of perceiving that reality from a sign of this kind.

35. And I might also have said the same thing regarding "coverings" and other countless things as I said about the word "head." Yet, though I already know what these are, I still do not know what those *saraballae* are. If someone were to signify them to me by a gesture, or should draw a picture of them or show me something like them, I will not say that he did not teach me what they were, which I could easily prove if I wanted to speak at somewhat greater length. But I do say what is very much to the point, that he did not teach me this by means of words. But if he happens to be looking at them in my presence, and should call my attention to them by saying: "Look, *saraballae*," I will learn something new, not by my words that were spoken, but by looking at the reality. And it was this that also enabled me to become acquainted with the word and to remember its meaning. Certainly, when I learned to know the reality, I did not rely upon the words of another, but upon my own eyes, though I did possibly rely upon words to direct my attention, that is, to see what there was to see by looking.

Chapter 11

36. So far, the most I can say for words is that they merely intimate that we should look for realities; they do not present them to us for our knowledge. But the man who teaches me is one who presents to my eyes or to any bodily sense, or even to the mind itself, something that I wish to know. So by means of words we learn only words, or better, the sound and noise of words. For if something cannot be a word unless it is a sign, I still cannot recognize it as a word until I know what it signifies, even though I have heard the word. Accordingly, it is by knowing the realities that we also come to a knowledge of their words, whereas, by the sound of words, we do not even learn the words. For we cannot learn words we already know, and, as for those which we do not know, we cannot profess to have learned them until we have seen their meaning. And this comes about, not by hearing the sounds they make, but from a knowledge of the realities they signify. It is perfectly logical and true to conclude that whenever words are spoken, we either know what they mean or we do not. If we know, they recall rather than teach something to us; if we do not know, they cannot even recall something, though they may lead us to inquire.

37. You may insist that we cannot really know what those head-coverings are except by seeing them, since the name is only a sound for us, and that we can know no more about the name itself unless we know what the realities are. And yet, we do accept as true the story of those boys: how their faith triumphed over the king and the flames, how they sang a hymn of praise to God and were found worthy to receive honors even from their very enemy. Have we learned all this otherwise than by words? I shall reply by noting that we already knew everything that those words signified. What is meant by "three boys," "furnace," "fire," "king," and, finally, "unharmed by fire," as well as the other things signified by those words, this I already knew. On the other hand, the names Ananias, Azarius, and Misael are just as much unknown to me as the *saraballae*. These names did not help me at all to know them, nor could they possibly do so. But that everything recounted in that story occurred at that time exactly as recorded, that, I admit, is something I "believe" rather than "know," and those same men, whose word we believe, were themselves not ignorant of this distinction. For the Prophet says: "Unless you believe, you shall not understand," which he really could not have said if he thought that there was no difference between the two. Hence, what I understand, that I also believe, although I do not also understand everything I believe. Also, everything I understand, I know, though I do not know everything I believe. Nor do I for that reason fail to see how useful it is also to believe many things which I do not know, including also this account of the three boys. Accordingly, while there are a great many things that I am unable to know, I do nevertheless know how useful it is to believe them.

38. But as for all those things which we "understand," it is not the outward sound of the speaker's words that we consult, but the truth which presides over the mind itself from within, though we may have been led to consult it because of the words. Now He who is consulted and who is said to "dwell in the inner man," He it is who teaches us, namely, Christ, that is to say, "the unchangeable Power of God and everlasting wisdom." This is the Wisdom which every rational soul does indeed consult, but it reveals itself to each according to his capacity to grasp it by reason of the good or evil dispositions of his will. And if the soul is sometimes mistaken, this does not come about because of any defect on the part of the truth it consulted, just as it is not through any defect in the light outside us that our bodily eyes are often deceived. We acknowledge that it is this light which we consult with regard to visible objects so that it may manifest them to us according to our capacity to perceive them.

Chapter 12

39. Now if we consult light for colors, and consult the basic elements of the material world which comprise those bodies known by the senses regarding the other sense qualities, and consult the senses themselves which the mind uses as interpreters to know these things; if, again, we use our reason to consult that inner truth for the things that we understand— then what more could be said by way of proof to show that we learn nothing by means of words, except their sound which strikes the ear? For everything we perceive, we perceive either by the bodily sense or by the mind. We call the former, sense objects, the latter, intelligible objects; or, to appropriate the terminology of our own inspired Writers, we call the first carnal, the second, spiritual. When asked about the former, we can reply if what we perceive is present to us, as when someone asks us about the phase

and position of the new moon while we are looking at it. If my questioner in this instance does not see the moon, he believes my words, though often he does not. In no case, however, does he really learn unless he sees for himself the thing we are talking about. He learns it then, not indeed by the sound of the spoken words, but by the things themselves and his senses. For the words sound the same to one who sees the object as they do to one who does not see it. But when questions are asked, not about things we perceive while they are present to us, but about those which our senses perceived on former occasions, then our words do not refer to the things themselves, but to the images impressed by them upon the senses and stored away in the memory. And, since we are reflecting upon what is unreal, I fail to see how we can possibly speak of them as true, unless it be for the fact that we are recounting, not what we see and perceive at the moment, but what we have already seen and perceived. So it is that we bear these images in the deep recesses of the memory as witnesses, so to speak, of things previously experienced by the senses. When reflecting upon these images in our mind, we can speak of them in good conscience, without lying. But these images are only witnesses for ourselves. If the one who hears what I am recounting has seen these things for himself and was there on the spot, he does not learn them from my words but recognizes them himself by the images he took away with him from these things. But if he has not experienced them with his senses, then it is clearly a matter of his believing my words rather than of learning.

40. But when it is a question of things which we behold with the mind, namely, with our intellect and reason, we give verbal expression to realities which we directly perceive as present in that inner light of truth by which the inner man, as he is called, is enlightened and made happy. But, here again, if the one who hears my words sees those things himself with that clear and inner eye of the soul, he knows the things whereof I speak by contemplating them himself, and not by my words. Therefore, even when I say what is true, and he sees what is true, it is not I who teach him. For he is being taught, not by my words, but by the realities themselves made manifest to him by the enlightening action of God from within. Consequently, he could also answer questions about these things if he were asked. What more absurd than the notion that he is being taught by what I say, when he could explain those very things even before I spoke, if only he had been asked about them?

But as for the case frequently encountered where someone replies to a question in the negative and is led on by other questions to answer in the affirmative, this springs from a weakness in one's mental perception which makes it impossible for him to consult that light regarding the matter in its entirety. He is led on to consider it part by part when questioned about those very same parts comprising the whole, which he was unable to perceive in its entirety. If he is brought around to this by the words of his questioner, the words still do not teach him, but only propose questions in a way suited to his capacity to learn from his inner light. For example, if I should ask you about the very matter now under consideration, namely, whether anything can be taught by means of words, the question might appear to you absurd at first because you are unable to see the whole problem. Consequently, I would have to frame the question in a way suited to your capacity to hear that Teacher who teaches from within. Where, I might ask, have you learned all those things which you admitted were true as I was speaking, and which you think you now know for sure? You might reply that I was the one who had taught them to you. Suppose then, by way of questioning you further, I were to tell you that I had seen a man flying. Would my words give you the same certainty as if you were to hear me say that wise men are better than fools? You would of course deny this, and answer that you do not believe my first statement, or that even if you do believe it, you do not know it, whereas you know the other statement to be absolutely certain. This would surely enable you to see that you had not learned anything by my words, whether, as in the one instance, where you did not know what I was speaking of, or in the other, where you understood perfectly well. As a matter of fact, if you had been asked about those statements separately, you could have even sworn that you did not know the former and that you did know the latter. Then indeed you would admit as true the proposition in its entirety which you had denied, since you would now have a clear and certain grasp of all that it involves. It is this: Whenever we express anything in words, our hearer either does not know whether it is true, or he knows it is untrue, or he knows it is true. In the first of these three, it is a matter of belief or opinion or doubt; in the second, of opposition and denial; in the third, of attesting to what is true. In none of these cases, therefore, does he learn. It follows, therefore, that one who does not grasp the reality after hearing our words, or who knows that what he heard is untrue, or who could have given the same answer, if asked, has learned nothing by any words of mine.

Chapter 13

41. It further follows that where realities discerned by the mind are concerned, it is of no avail for one who does not perceive them to hear the words of one who does, except when it is useful to believe them so long as he lacks knowledge of them. But anyone who is able to perceive them is an inward disciple of the truth and an outward judge of the speaker, or better, a judge of what he is saying. For he very often understands what was said even when the speaker himself does not. Let us suppose, for example, that someone who takes the word of the Epicureans and judges that the soul is mortal, should expound arguments which have been advanced by the wiser philosophers in favor of its immortality. If someone capable of spiritual discernment happens to hear him, he will judge that what this man says is true, whereas the speaker does not know whether such arguments are true; in fact, he even thinks they are completely false. Are we, then, to think of him as teaching what he does not know? Yet he uses the same words which could also be used by one who understood them.

42. Hence, not even the role of expressing what the speaker has in mind is any longer left to words, since it is not certain that he knows what he is saying. There are, in addition, those who lie and deceive, so that you can readily see from them how words not only do not reveal their thoughts, but even conceal them. I have no doubt whatever that the words of truthful men are an attempt and a sort of pledge to reveal the thoughts of the speaker, and that they would succeed in this, as all agree, if only liars were not allowed to speak.

Yet, we have often observed, both in ourselves and in others, that words are spoken which do not express the thoughts in one's mind. I see two ways that this can happen, either some kind of speech, frequently repeated and memorized, flows out of the speaker's mouth while he is thinking of something else, as often happens to us when we are singing a hymn; or, unintentionally, and by a slip of the tongue, some words are blurted out instead of others, so that in this case too, the words which are heard are not signs of what is in our mind. Liars, of course, also think of what they are saying, so that while we may not know whether what they say is true, we know nevertheless that they are saying what is in their mind, provided that neither of the two things I just mentioned happens to them. If someone contends that these things happen only occasionally and that it is obvious whenever they do, I will not object. Yet they often go unrecognized and have frequently deceived me as I listened to them.

43. But in addition to these cases where words do not convey their meaning, there is another kind, quite widespread, to be sure, and the source of endless bickering and disputes. It happens when the speaker actually says what he is thinking, but often does so only to himself and some others, while he does not convey the same meaning to the person spoken to, or to others as well. Suppose, for example, that someone should say in our hearing that man is surpassed in virtue by certain brute animals. We find ourselves at once unable to countenance such a remark and we spare no effort to refute so false and pernicious a view. The speaker, however, may be using the word "virtue" to signify physical strength to express what he has in mind. He is neither lying nor mistaken about the facts themselves. Neither is he spinning out words committed to memory, while he has his mind on something else, or is saying something different from what is on his mind by a slip of the tongue. He is merely indicating his thoughts by a different name than we do. We would agree with him at once on this point if we could read his thoughts, which he has as yet been unable to reveal to us, even though he has already made use of words to set forth his view.

They tell me that definitions can correct errors of this kind. Accordingly, if the speaker in this instance should define what "virtue" is, it would become apparent, so they say, that the dispute is not over the reality, but over the word. Even granting that this is the case, how many can you find who are good at defining? Besides, many points have been urged against the rules of definition, which it is not opportune to consider here, and with which I do not even entirely agree.

44. I pass over the fact that we fail to hear many words distinctly and enter into extended and heated arguments, just as if we had heard them. A short time ago, for instance, when I remarked that a certain word in the Punic tongue meant "mercy," you stated that you had heard from those better acquainted with that language that it meant "piety." But I disagreed, insisting that you had completely forgotten what you had heard. For I thought you had said not "piety" but "faith," even though you were seated close to me and though these two words do not sound so much alike that they would deceive my hearing. Yet I thought for some time that you did not know what had been said to you, when all the while it was I who did not know what you had said. For if I had heard you correctly, I would never have thought it incongruous that "piety" and "mercy" should be expressed by the one word in the Punic language.

Such cases occur quite frequently, but I will, as I said, pass over them so as not to give the impression that I am censuring words unfairly because of carelessness or even deafness on the part of men who hear them. The cases I cited above are more perplexing, where we cannot know the speaker's thoughts, even though we share the same language and the words spoken in Latin are heard very distinctly.

45. See, I am going to yield to a point and grant that when words are heard by one acquainted with them, he can know that the speaker has been thinking about the things they signify. But does he thereby likewise learn that what was said is true, which is the question under discussion?

Chapter 14

Do teachers ever claim that it is their own thoughts that are grasped and retained, rather than the branches of learning themselves which they purport to transmit by their speaking? What foolish curiosity could ever prompt a man to send his child to school in order to have him learn what the teacher thinks? But when teachers have made use of words to explain all those branches of learning which they profess to be teaching, including even those dealing with virtue and wisdom, then those who are known as pupils reflect within themselves whether what has been said is true, contemplating, that is, that inner truth according to their capacity. It is then, therefore, that they learn. And when they discover within themselves that what has been said is true, they praise their teachers, unaware that they are not so much praising the teachers as they are praising those who have been taught, provided, however, that the teachers also know what they are saying. But men make the mistake of calling people "teachers" when they are not that at all, because there is generally no interval of time between the moment of speaking and that of knowing, and because their coming to learn from within follows quickly upon the suggestive force of the speaker's words, they think that they have learned externally from him who spoke those words.

46. We shall, God willing, resume our inquiry on another occasion into the whole question of the usefulness of words, which is one of no small importance if you look into it carefully. For the present, I have cautioned you that we must not ascribe more importance to words than is their due. Accordingly, we should no longer merely believe, but also begin to understand the truth of those words based on divine authority, that we should not call any man on earth a teacher, seeing that "there is One in heaven who is the Teacher of all." What is meant by "in heaven" is something that will be taught us by Him who directs us even through human agencies and external signs to turn inwardly to Him for our instruction. To love Him and to know Him, that is the happy life, which all proclaim they are seeking, but few there are who can rejoice at having really found it. But now I would like you to tell me what you think of this entire discourse of mine. For if you know that what was said is true, then, had you been questioned about each particular point, you would have declared that you know them too. So you can see from Whom it was that you learned these things. It was not from me, for you could have answered to everything I was asking you. But if you did not know that what I said was true, then neither He nor I have taught you. Not I, because I can never teach you; not He, because you are not yet able to learn these things.

Ad. I myself have come to learn through the suggestive power of your words that words merely stimulate a man to learn, and that the words of the speaker seldom reveal his thoughts to any great extent. But as to the truth of what is said, I have also learned that He alone teaches who made use of external words to remind us that He dwells within us. With His help, I shall now love Him all the more ardently as I advance in learning. I am grateful, however, that your remarks have continued without interruption, particularly because they anticipated and answered all the objections I was prepared to raise. You have not neglected a single question that had caused me to doubt, or which has not been answered for me by that inner Oracle exactly as you had expressed it in words.

Margaret Fuller

Celebrated today by feminists, and indeed noted from the beginning for her trenchant writings on behalf of women, Margaret Fuller was and is the figure of a cause she served with brilliance during her relatively short life, the sudden end of which prevented full development of her interests into broader social questions and further ideas of which her writings gave promise. Her talent was that of a revolutionary, and she used it well, but we cannot help wondering what she would have been if she had had the chance to ripen into something more.

Perhaps she would have been the same. There is a sense in which our destinies find us out and it is possible that hers in some way perceived that she would never have been other than she was, even had she had a longer life. Her father raised her to be the equal of a man intellectually, and in time she rebelled, believing that her emotional life had been stunted, though it was not so much feeling that she thought her upbringing lacked as human connection and companionship. But her objection to that came later.

Forced by her father's death in 1835 to look after her many siblings, she somehow managed at the same time with such schools as were available to pursue her education and enlarge her mind, and the sign of her success was that by 1840 she had made her way into the circle of New England Tran-scendentalists which had formed around Emerson and a few others and been appointed editor of *The Dial.* This was a quarterly in which the group sought to express and develop its ideas. Margaret Fuller had, it proved at once, her own ideas, which were more inclined to art than to philosophy, as Emerson's were not, and used the chance to put forth literary and social theories she got from German Romantic writers, in particular Goethe whom she especially admired, writing much of the periodical herself and refusing the contributions of others. In this she was tactless, being wholly without humor, but was allowed to have her way until 1842, when funds ran out and Emerson took over (he was able to make the quarterly last only for another year himself).

In 1844 she came to the attention of Horace Greeley, the editor of the *New York Tribune,* who engaged her to write articles and essays on a variety of subjects. Greeley doubtless knew *The Dial,* but he was more impressed by a book she had published about a summer she spent in the midwest, where among many reflections on frontier life and manners she observed Indians, especially their women, who seemed to her not essentially different in their condition from Negro slaves or—if it came to that— those as white as herself. She had also published some poetry, which has come to be thought interesting.

In New York, where she went to live, she had an unhappy love affair, perhaps her first such experience, which made her not unwilling to leave for England in 1846 with two friends, continuing however, to write for Greeley, only now she wrote travel pieces to support herself. She liked Europe, thinking she might find there "an atmosphere," as she said, "to develop me in ways *I* need." What she did find was the Italian Revolution of 1848, of which the inspiring figure was Manzini, whom she had already met in London. Drawn into Italian politics, she fell in love with an Italian nobleman named Ossoli, whom she regarded in due course as her husband and by whom subsequently she had a child, though she kept her involvement with him secret from friends at home, and it is not clear when, if ever, they were actually married. The Revolution ultimately failed, and Margaret Fuller's dispatches telling of this in June 1849, were printed in *The Tribune.* There was nothing left henceforth for her to do, nor Ossoli either, and the following spring they set sail with their child for America. They never arrived. Their ship ran into a storm off Fire Island in New York harbor, and in the wreck all three of them were lost. So was her account, in manuscript, of the Revolution she had witnessed. She was mourned by, among others, Emerson who said that "I have lost in her my audience." He helped to write a memoir of her life that was for a time its only substantial record.

"Woman in the Nineteenth Century," her longest and most ambitious published work, dates from 1845. Its occasionally inflated rhetoric and wearying erudition take some patience, but its sharp and startling insights and its essential rightness of view—at a time when that view was not otherwise established—make it a valuable and instructive document, deeply moving as the testament of a learned and determined woman who put everything she knew into the argument for justice denied immemorially to half the human race.

Woman in the Nineteenth Century

Margaret Fuller

Illustrations by Jodi Marie Fleischman

done in thought and love,
a baker or weaver solely, than
uld not only corres

"Frailty, thy name is WOMAN."[1]
"The Earth waits for her Queen."

THE connection between these quotations may not be obvious, but it is strict. Yet would any contradict us, if we made them applicable to the other side, and began also,

Frailty, thy name is MAN.
The Earth waits for its King?

Yet Man, if not yet fully installed in his powers, has given much earnest of his claims. Frail he is indeed, how frail! how impure! Yet often has the vein of gold displayed itself amid the baser ores, and Man has appeared before us in princely promise worthy of his future.

If, oftentimes, we see the prodigal son feeding on the husks in the fair field no more his own, anon we raise the eyelids, heavy from bitter tears, to behold in him the radiant apparition of genius and love, demanding not less than the all of goodness, power and beauty. We see that in him the largest claim finds a due foundation. That claim is for no partial sway, no exclusive possession. He cannot be satisfied with any one gift of life, any one department of knowledge or telescopic peep at the heavens. He feels himself called to understand and aid Nature, that she may, through his intelligence, be raised and interpreted; to be a student of, and servant to, the universe-spirit; and king of his planet, that, as an angelic minister, he may bring it into conscious harmony with the law of that spirit.

In clear, triumphant moments, many times, has rung through the spheres the prophecy of his jubilee; and those moments, though past in time, have been translated into eternity by thought; the bright signs they left hang in the heavens, as single stars or constellations, and, already, a thickly sown radiance consoles the wanderer in the darkest night. Other heroes since Hercules have fulfilled the zodiac of beneficent labors, and then given up their mortal part to the fire without a murmur; while no God dared deny that they should have their reward,

> Siquis tamen, Hercule, siquis
> Forte Deo doliturus erit, data præmia, nollet,
> Sed meruise dair sciet, invitus que probabit

Assensere Dei.[2]

(Overleaf)
"[A]nd those moments, though past in time, have been translated into eternity by thought; the bright signs they left hang in the heavens, as single stars or constellations..."

Sages and lawgivers have bent their whole nature to the search for truth, and thought themselves happy if they could buy, with the sacrifice of all temporal ease and pleasure, one seed for the future Eden. Poets and priests have strung the lyre with the heart-strings, poured out their best blood upon the altar, which, reared anew from age to age, shall at last sustain the flame pure enough to rise to highest heaven. Shall we not name with as deep a benediction those who, if not so immediately, or so consciously, in connection with the eternal truth, yet, led and fashioned by a divine instinct, serve no less to develop and interpret the open secret of love passing into life, energy creating for the purpose of happiness; the artist whose hand, drawn by a preexistent harmony to a certain medium, moulds it to forms of life more highly and completely organized than are seen elsewhere, and, by carrying out the intention of nature, reveals her meaning to those who are not yet wise enough to divine it; the philosopher who listens steadily for laws and causes, and from those obvious infers those yet unknown; the historian who, in faith that all events must have their reason and their aim, records them, and thus fills archives from which the youth of prophets may be fed; the man of science dissecting the statements, testing the facts and demonstrating order, even where he cannot its purpose?

Lives, too, which bear none of these names, have yielded tones of no less significance. The candlestick set in a low place has given light as faithfully, where it was needed, as that upon the hill. In close alleys, in dismal nooks, the Word has been read as distinctly, as when shown by angels to holy men in the dark prison. Those who till a spot of earth scarcely larger than is wanted for a grave, have deserved that the sun should shine upon its sod till violets answer.

So great has been, from time to time, the promise, that, in all ages, men have said the gods themselves came down to dwell with them; that the All-Creating wandered on the earth to taste, in a limited nature, the sweetness of virtue; that the All-Sustaining incarnated himself to guard, in space and time, the destinies of this world; that heavenly genius dwelt among the shepherds, to sing to them and teach them how to sing. Indeed,

"Der stets den Hirten gnadig sich bewies."

"He has constantly shown himself favorable to shepherds."

And the dwellers in green pastures and natural students of the stars were selected to hail, first among men, the holy child, whose life and death were to present the type of excellence, which has sustained the heart of so large a portion of mankind in these later generations.

Such marks have been made by the footsteps of *man* (still, alas! to be spoken of as the *ideal* man), wherever he has passed through the wilderness of *men,* and whenever the pigmies stepped in one of those, they felt dilate within the breast somewhat that promised nobler stature and purer blood. They were impelled to forsake their evil ways of decrepit scepticism and covetousness of corruptible possessions. Convictions flowed in upon them. They, too, raised the cry: God is living, now, to-day; and all beings are brothers, for they are his children. Simple words enough, yet which only angelic natures can use or hear in their full, free sense.

These were the triumphant moments; but soon the lower nature took its turn, and the era of a truly human life was postponed.

Thus is man still a stranger to his inheritance, still a pleader, still a pilgrim. Yet his happiness is secure in the end. And now, no more a glimmering consciousness, but assurance begins to be felt and spoken, that the highest ideal Man can form of his own powers is that which he is destined to attain. Whatever the soul knows how to seek, it cannot fail to obtain. This is the Law and the Prophets. Knock and it shall be opened; seek and ye shall find. It is demonstrated; it is a maxim. Man no longer paints his proper nature in some form, and says, "Prometheus had it; it is God-like;" but "Man must have it; it is human." However disputed by many, however ignorantly used, or falsified by those who do receive it, the fact of an universal, unceasing revelation has been too clearly stated in words to be lost sight of in thought; and sermons preached from the text, "Be ye perfect," are the only sermons of a pervasive and deep-searching influence.

But, among those who meditate upon this text, there is a great difference of view as to the way in which perfection shall be sought.

"Through the intellect," say some. "Gather from every growth of life its seed of thought; look behind every symbol for its law; if thou canst *see* clearly, the rest will follow."

"Through the life," say others. "Do the best thou knowest to-day. Shrink not from frequent error in this gradual, fragmentary state. Follow thy light for as much as it will show thee; be faithful as far as thou canst, in hope that faith presently will lead to sight. Help others, without blaming their need of thy help. Love much, and be forgiven."

"It needs not intellect, needs not experience," says a third. "If you took the true way, your destiny would be accomplished in a purer and more natural order. You would not learn through facts of thought or action, but express through them the certainties of wisdom. In quietness yield thy soul to the causal soul. Do not disturb thy apprenticeship by premature effort; neither check the tide of instruction by methods of thy own. Be still; seek not, but wait in obedience. Thy commission will be given."

Could we indeed say what we want, could we give a description of the child that is lost, he would be found. As soon as the soul can affirm clearly that a certain demonstration is wanted, it is at hand. When the Jewish prophet described the Lamb, as the expression of what was required by the coming era, the time drew nigh. But we say not, see not as yet, clearly, what we would. Those who call for a more triumphant expression of love, a love that cannot be crucified, show not a perfect sense of what has already been given. Love has already been expressed, that made all things new, that gave the worm its place and ministry as well as the eagle; a love to which it was alike to descend into the depths of hell, or to sit at the right hand of the Father.

Yet, no doubt, a new manifestation is at hand, a new hour in the day of Man. We cannot expect to see any one sample of completed being, when the mass of men still lie engaged in the sod, or use the freedom of their limbs only with wolfish energy. The tree cannot come to flower till its root be free from the cankering worm, and its whole growth open to air and light. While any one is base, none can be entirely free and noble. Yet something new shall presently be shown of the life of Man, for hearts crave, if minds do not know how to ask it.

Among the strains of prophecy, the following, by an earnest mind of a foreign land, written some thirty years ago, is not yet outgrown; and it has the merit of being a positive appeal from the heart, instead of a critical declaration what Man should *not* do.

"The ministry of Man implies that he must be filled from the divine fountains which are being engendered through all eternity, so that, at the mere name of his master, he may be able to cast all his enemies into the abyss; that he may deliver all parts of nature from the barriers that imprison them; that he may purge the terrestrial atmosphere from the poisons that infect it; that he may preserve the bodies of men from the corrupt influences that surround, and the maladies that afflict them; still more, that he may keep their souls pure from the malignant insinuations which pollute, and the gloomy images that obscure them; that he may restore its serenity to the Word, which false words of men fill with mourning and sadness; that he may satisfy the desires of the angels, who await from him the development of the marvels of nature; that, in fine, his world may be filled with God, as eternity is."[3]

Another attempt we will give, by an obscure observer of our own day and country, to draw some lines of the desired image. It was suggested by seeing the design of Crawford's Orpheus,[4] and connecting with the circum-

"The tree cannot come to flower till its root be free from the cankering worm, and its whole growth open to air and light."

stance of the American, in his garret at Rome, making choice of this subject, that of Americans here at home showing such ambition to represent the character, by calling their prose and verse "Orphic sayings"— "Orphics." We wish we could add that they have shown that musical apprehension of the progress of Nature through her ascending gradations which entitled them so to do, but their attempts are frigid, though sometimes grand; in their strain we are not warmed by the fire which fertilized the soil of Greece.

Orpheus was a lawgiver by theocratic commission. He understood nature, and made her forms move to his music. He told her secrets in the form of hymns, Nature as seen in the mind of God. His soul went forth toward all beings, yet could remain sternly faithful to a chosen type of excellence. Seeking what he loved, he feared not death nor hell; neither could any shape of dread daunt his faith in the power of the celestial harmony that filled his soul.

It seemed significant of the state of things in this country, that the sculptor should have represented the seer at the moment when he was obliged with his hand to shade his eyes.

> Each Orpheus must to the depths descend;
>   For only thus the Poet can be wise;
> Must make the sad Persephone his friend,
>   And buried love to second life arise;
> Again his love must lose through too much love,
>   Must lose his life by living life too true,
> For what he sought below is passed above,
>   Already done is all that he would do;
> Must tune all being with his single lyre,
>   Must melt all rocks free from their primal pain,
> Must search all nature with his one soul's fire,
>   Must bind anew all forms in heavenly chain.
> If he already sees what he must do,
> Well may he shade his eyes from the far-shining view.

A better comment could not be made on what is required to perfect Man, and place him in that superior position for which he was designed, than by the interpretation of Bacon upon the legends of the Syren coast. "When the wise Ulysses passed," says he, "he caused his mariners to stop their ears with wax, knowing there was in them no power to resist the lure of that voluptuous song. But he, the much experienced man, who wished to be experienced in all, and use all to the service of wisdom, desired to hear the song that he might understand its meaning. Yet, distrusting his own power to be firm in his better purpose, he caused himself to be bound to the mast, that he might be kept secure against his own weakness. But Orpheus passed unfettered, so absorbed in singing hymns to the gods that he could not even hear those sounds of degrading enchantment."

Meanwhile, not a few believe, and men themselves have expressed the opinion, that the time is come when Eurydice is to call for an Orpheus, rather than Orpheus for Eurydice; that the idea of Man, however imperfectly brought out, has been far more so than that of Woman; that she, the other half of the same thought, the other chamber of the heart of life, needs now take her turn in the full pulsation, and that improvement in the daughters will best aid in the reformation of the sons of this age.

It should be remarked that, as the principle of liberty is better understood, and more nobly interpreted, a broader protest is made in behalf of Woman. As men become aware that few men have had a fair chance, they are inclined to say that no women have had a fair chance. The French Revolution, that strangely disguised angel, bore witness in favor of Woman, but interpreted her claims no less ignorantly than those of Man. Its idea of happiness did not rise beyond outward enjoyment, unobstructed by the tyranny of others. The title it gave was "citoyen," "citoyenne;" and it is not unimportant to Woman that even this species of equality was awarded her. Before, she could be condemned to perish on the scaffold for treason, not as a citizen, but as a subject. The right with which this title then invested a human being was that of bloodshed and license. The Goddess of Liberty was impure. As we read the poem addressed to her, not long since, by Beranger,[5] we can scarcely refrain from tears as painful as the tears of blood that flowed when "such crimes were committed in her name." Yes! Man, born to purify and animate the unintelligent and the cold, can, in his madness, degrade and pollute no less the fair and the chaste. Yet truth was prophesied in the ravings of that hideous fever, caused by long ignorance and abuse. Europe is conning a valued lesson from the blood-stained page. The same tendencies, further unfolded, will bear good fruit in this country.

Yet, by men in this country, as by the Jews, when Moses was leading them to the promised land, everything has been done that inherited depravity could do, to hinder the promise of Heaven from its fulfilment. The cross, here as elsewhere, has been planted only to be blasphemed by cruelty and fraud. The name of the Prince of Peace has been profaned by all kinds of injustice toward the Gentile whom he said he came to save. But I need not speak of what has been done towards the Red Man, the Black Man. Those deeds are the scoff of the world; and they have been accompanied by such pious words that the gentlest would not dare to intercede with "Father, forgive them, for they know not what they do."

Here, as elsewhere, the gain of creation consists always in the growth of individual minds, which live and aspire, as flowers bloom and birds sing, in the midst of morasses; and in the continual development of that thought, the thought of human destiny, which is given to eternity adequately to express, and which ages of failure only seemingly impede. Only seemingly; and whatever seems to the contrary, this country is as surely destined to elucidate a great moral law, as Europe was to promote the mental culture of Man.

Though the national independence he blurred by the servility of individuals; though freedom and equality have been proclaimed only to leave room for a monstrous display of slave-dealing and slave-keeping; though the free American so often feels himself free, like the Roman, only to pamper his appetites and his indolence through the misery of his fellow-beings; still it is not in vain that the verbal statement has been made, "All men are born free and equal." There it stands, a golden certainty wherewith to encourage the good, to shame the bad. The New World may be called clearly to perceive that it incurs the utmost penalty if it reject or oppress the sorrowful brother. And, if men are deaf, the angels hear. But men cannot be deaf. It is inevitable that an external freedom, an independence of the encroachments of other men, such as has been achieved for the nation, should be so also for every member of it. That which has once been clearly conceived in the intelligence cannot fail, sooner or later, to be acted out. It has become a law as irrevocable as that of the Medes in their ancient dominion; men will privately sin against it, but the law, as expressed by a leading mind of the age,

> "Tutti fatti a sembianza d'un Solo,
> Figli tutti d'un solo riscatto,
> In qual'ora, in qual parte del suolo
> Trascorriamo quest' aura vital,
> Siam fratelli, siam stretti ad un patto:
> Maladetto colui che lo infrange,
> Che s'innalza sul fiacco che piange
> Che contrista uno spirto immortal."
> "All made in the likeness of the One,
>   All children of one ransom,
> In whatever hour, in whatever part of the soil,
>   We draw this vital air,
> We are brothers; we must be bound by one compact;
>   Accursed he who infringes it,
> Who raises himself upon the weak who weep,
>   Who saddens an immortal spirit."[6]

This law cannot fail of universal recognition. Accursed be he who willingly saddens an immortal spirit—doomed to infamy in later, wiser ages, doomed in future stages of his own being to deadly penance, only short of death. Accursed be he who sins in ignorance, if that ignorance be caused by sloth.

We sicken no less at the pomp than the strife of words. We feel that never were lungs so puffed with the wind of declamation, on moral and religious subjects, as now. We are tempted to implore these "word-heroes," these word-Catos, word-Christs, to beware of cant* above all things; to remember that hypocrisy is the most hopeless as well as the meanest of crimes, and that those must surely be polluted by it, who do not reserve a part of their morality and religion for private use. Landor says that he cannot have a great deal of mind who cannot afford to let the larger part of it lie fallow; and what is true of genius is not less so of virtue.[7] The tongue

---

*Dr. Johnson's one piece of advice should be written on every door: "Clear your mind of cant." But Byron, to whom it was so acceptable, in clearing away the noxious vine, shook down the building. Sterling's emendation is worthy of honor:
"Realize your cant, not cast it off."[8]

is a valuable member, but should appropriate but a small part of the vital juices that are needful all over the body. We feel that the mind may "grow black and rancid in the smoke" even "of altars." We start up from the harangue to go into our closet and shut the door. There inquires the spirit, "Is this rhetoric the bloom of healthy blood, or a false pigment artfully laid on?" And yet again we know where is so much smoke, must be some fire; with so much talk about virtue and freedom, must be mingled some desire for them; that it cannot be in vain that such have become the common topics of conversation among men, rather than schemes for tyranny and plunder, that the very newspapers see it best to proclaim themselves "Pilgrims," "Puritans," "Heralds of Holiness." The king that maintains so costly a retinue cannot be a mere boast, or Carabbas fiction. We have waited here long in the dust; we are tired and hungry; but the triumphal procession must appear at last.

Of all its banners, none has been more steadily upheld, and under none have more valor and willingness for real sacrifices been shown, than that of the champions of the enslaved African. And this band it is, which, partly from a natural following out of principles, partly because many women have been prominent in that cause, makes, just now, the warmest appeal in behalf of Woman.

Though there has been a growing liberality on this subject, yet society at large is not so prepared for the demands of this party, but that its members are, and will be for some time, coldly regarded as the Jacobins of their day.

"Is it not enough," cries the irritated trader, "that you have done all you could to break up the national union, and thus destroy the prosperity of our country, but now you must be trying to break up family union, to take my wife away from the cradle and the kitchen-hearth to vote at polls, and preach from a pulpit? Of course, if she does such things, she cannot attend to those of her own sphere. She is happy enough as she is. She has more leisure than I have,—every means of improvement, every indulgence."

"Have you asked her whether she was satisfied with these *indulgences?*"

"No, but I know she is. She is too amiable to desire what would make me unhappy, and too judicious to wish to step beyond the sphere of her sex. I will never consent to have our peace disturbed by any such discussions."

"'Consent—you?' it is not consent from you that is in question—it is assent from your wife."

"Am not I the head of my house?"

"You are not the head of your wife. God has given her a mind of her own."

"I am the head, and she the heart."

"God grant you play true to one another, then! I suppose I am to be grateful that you did not say she was only the hand. If the head represses no natural pulse of the heart, there can be no question as to your giving your consent. Both will be of one accord, and there needs but to present any question to get a full and true answer. There is no need of precaution, of indulgence, nor consent. But our doubt is whether the heart *does* consent with the head, or only obeys its decrees with a passiveness that precludes the exercise of its natural powers, or a repugnance that turns sweet qualities to bitter, or a doubt that lays waste the fair occasions of life. It is to ascertain the truth that we propose some liberating measures."

Thus vaguely are these questions proposed and discussed at present. But their being proposed at all implies much thought, and suggests more. Many women are considering within themselves what they need that they have not, and what they can have if they find they need it. Many men are considering whether women are capable of being and having more than they are and have, *and* whether, if so, it will be best to consent to improvement in their condition.

This morning, I open the Boston "Daily Mail," and find in its "poet's corner" a translation of Schiller's "Dignity of Woman." In the advertisement of a book on America, I see in the table of contents this sequence, "Republican Institutions. American Slavery. American Ladies."

I open the *"Deutsche Schnellpost,"* published in New York, and find at the head of a column, *Judenund Frauen-emancipation in Ungarn*—"Emancipation of Jews and Women in Hungary."

The past year has seen action in the Rhode Island legislature, to secure married women rights over their own property, where men showed that a very little examination of the subject could teach them much; an article in the Democratic Review on the same subject more largely considered, written by a woman, impelled, it is said, by glaring wrong to a distinguished friend, having shown the defects in the existing laws, and the state of opinion from which they spring; and an answer from the revered old man, J. Q. Adams,[9] in some respects the Phocion[10] of his time, to an address made him by some ladies. To this last I shall again advert in another place.

These symptoms of the times have come under my view quite accidentally: one who seeks, may, each month or week, collect more.

The numerous party, whose opinions are already labeled and adjusted too much to their mind to admit of any new light, strive, by lectures on some model-woman of bride-like beauty and gentleness, by writing and lending little treatises, intended to mark out with precision the limits of Woman's sphere, and Woman's mission, to prevent other than the rightful shepherd from climbing the wall, or the flock from using any chance to go astray.

Without enrolling ourselves at once on either side, let us look upon the subject from the best point of view which to-day offers; no better, it is to be feared, than a high house-top. A high hill-top, or at least a cathedral-spire, would be desirable.

It may well be an Anti-Slavery party that pleads for Woman, if we consider merely that she does not hold property on equal terms with men; so that, if a husband dies without making a will, the wife, instead of taking at once his place as head of the family, inherits only a part of his fortune, often brought him by herself, as if she were a child, or ward only, not an equal partner.

We will not speak of the innumerable instances in which profligate and idle men live upon the earnings of industrious wives; or if the wives leave them, and take with them the children, to perform the double duty of mother and father, follow from place to place, and threaten to rob them of the children, if deprived of the rights of a husband, as they call them, planting themselves in their poor lodgings, frightening them into paying tribute by taking from them the children, running into debt at the expense of these otherwise so overtasked helots. Such instances count up by scores within my own memory. I have seen the husband who had stained himself by a long course of low vice, till his wife was wearied from her heroic forgiveness, by finding that his treachery made it useless, and that if she would provide bread for herself and her children, she must be separate from his ill fame—I have known this man come to install himself in the chamber of a woman who loathed him, and say she should never take food without his company. I have known these men steal their children, whom they knew they had no means to maintain, take them into dissolute company, expose them to bodily danger, to frighten the poor woman, to whom, it seems, the fact that she alone had borne the pangs of their birth, and nourished their infancy, does not give an equal right to them. I do believe that this mode of kidnapping—and it is frequent enough in all classes of society—will be by the next age viewed as it is by Heaven now, and that the man who avails himself of the shelter of men's laws to steal from a mother her own children, or arrogate any superior right in them, save that of superior virtue, will bear the stigma he deserves, in common with him who steals grown men from their mother-land, their hopes, and their homes.

I said, we will not speak of this now; yet I *have* spoken, for the subject makes me feel too much. I could give instances that would startle the most vulgar and callous; but I will not, for the public opinion of their own sex is already against such men, and where cases of extreme tyranny are made known, there is private action in the wife's favor. But she ought not to need this, nor, I think, can she long. Men must soon see that as, on their own ground, Woman is the weaker party, she ought to have legal protection, which would make such oppression impossible. But I would not deal with "atrocious instances," except in the way of illustration, neither demand from men a partial redress in some one matter, but go to the root of the whole. If principles could be established, particulars would adjust themselves aright. Ascertain the true destiny of Woman; give her legitimate hopes, and a standard within herself; marriage and all other relations would by degrees be harmonized with these.

But to return to the historical progress of this matter. Knowing that there exists in the minds of men a tone of feeling toward women as toward slaves, such as is expressed in the common phrase, "Tell that to women and children;" that the infinite soul can only work through them in already ascertained limits; that the gift of reason, Man's highest prerogative, is allotted to them in much lower degree; that they must be kept from mischief and melancholy by being constantly engaged in active labor, which is to be furnished and directed by those better able to think, &c., &c.—we need not multiply instances, for who can review the experience of last week without recalling words which imply, whether in jest or

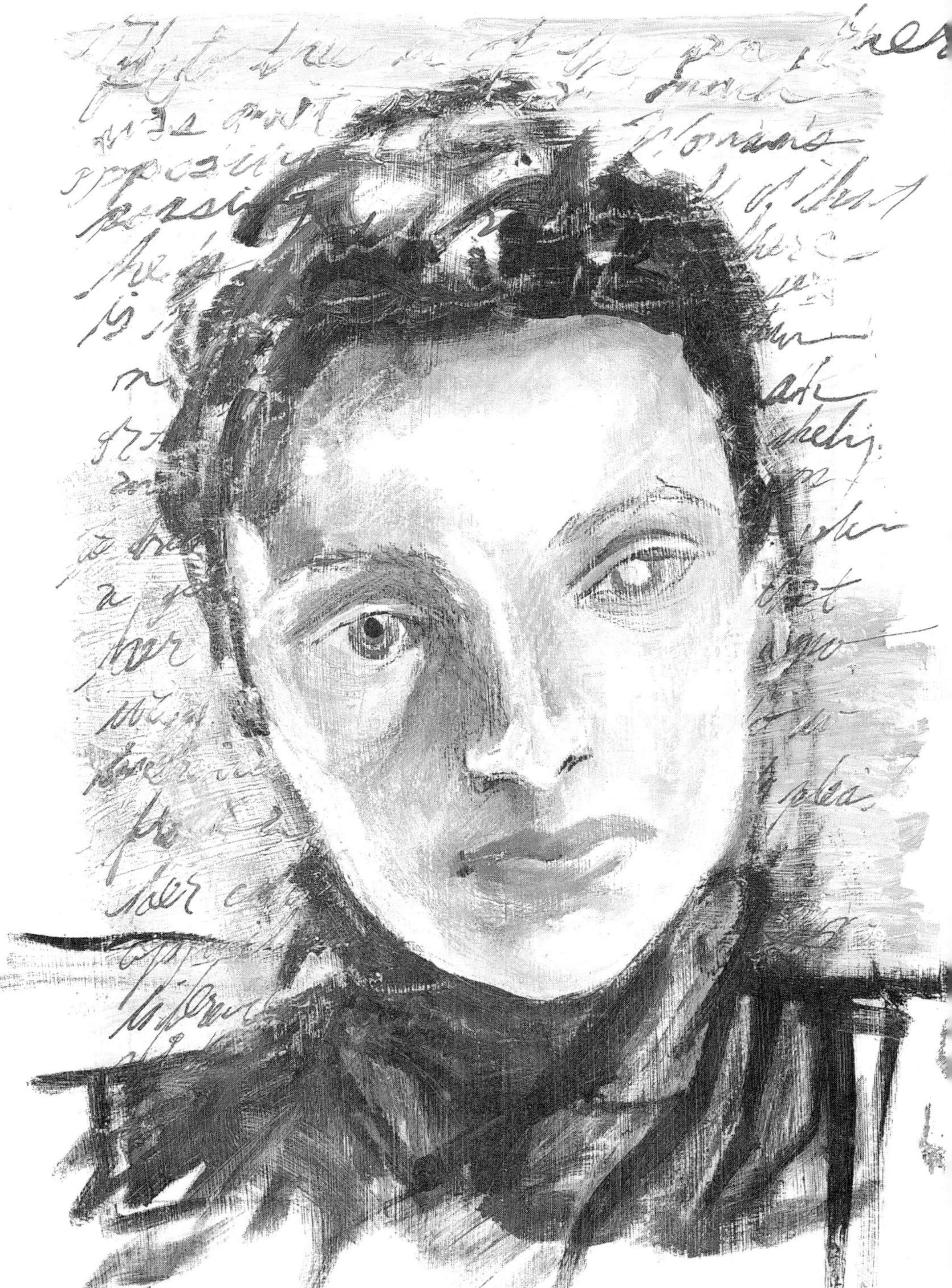

earnest, these views, or views like these—knowing this, can we wonder that many reformers think that measures are not likely to be taken in behalf of women, unless their wishes could be publicly represented by women?

"That can never be necessary," cry the other side. "All men are privately influenced by women; each has his wife, sister, or female friends, and is too much biased by these relations to fail of representing their interests; and, if this is not enough, let them propose and enforce their wishes with the pen. The beauty of home would be destroyed, the delicacy of the sex be violated, the dignity of halls of legislation degraded, by an attempt to introduce them there. Such duties are inconsistent with those of a mother;" and then we have ludicrous pictures of ladies in hysterics at the polls, and senate-chambers filled with cradles.

"Woman can express publicly the fulness of thought and creation, without losing any of the peculiar beauty of her sex."

But if, in reply, we admit as truth that Woman seems destined by nature rather for the inner circle, we must add that the arrangements of civilized life have not been, as yet, such as to secure it to her. Her circle, if the duller, is not the quieter. If kept from "excitement," she is not from drudgery. Not only the Indian squaw carries the burdens of the camp, but the favorites of Louis XIV accompany him in his journeys, and the washerwoman stands at her tub, and carries home her work at all seasons, and in all states of health. Those who think the physical circumstances of Woman would make a part in the affairs of national government unsuitable, are by no means those who think it impossible for negresses to endure field-work, even during pregnancy, or for sempstresses to go through their killing labors.

As to the use of the pen, there was quite as much opposition to Woman's possessing herself of that help to free agency as there is now to her seizing on the rostrum or the desk; and she is likely to draw, from a permission to plead her cause that way, opposite inferences to what might be wished by those who now grant it.

As to the possibility of her filling with grace and dignity any such position, we should think those who had seen the great actresses, and heard the Quaker preachers of modern times, would not doubt that Woman can express publicly the fulness of thought and creation, without losing any of the peculiar beauty of her sex. What can pollute and tarnish is to act thus from any motive except that something needs to be said or done. Woman could take part in the processions, the songs, the dances of old religion; no one fancied her delicacy was impaired by appearing in public for such a cause.

As to her home, she is not likely to leave it more than she now does for balls, theatres, meetings for promoting missions, revival meetings, and others to which she flies, in hope of an animation for her existence commensurate with what she sees enjoyed by men. Governors of ladies'-fairs are no less engrossed by such a charge, than the governor of a state by his; presidents of Washingtonian societies no less away from home than presidents of conventions. If men look straitly to it, they will find that, unless their lives are domestic, those of the women will not be. A house is no home unless it contain food and fire for the mind as well as for the body.

The female Greek, of our day, is as much in the street as the male to cry, "What news?" We doubt not it was the same in Athens of old. The women, shut out from the market-place, made up for it at the religious festivals. For human beings are not so constituted that they can live without expansion. If they do not get it in one way, they must in another, or perish.

As to men's representing women fairly at present, while we hear from men who owe to their wives not only all that is comfortable or graceful, but all that is wise, in the arrangement of their lives, the frequent remark, "You cannot reason with a woman,"—when from those of delicacy, nobleness, and poetic culture, falls the contemptuous phrase "women and children," and that in no light sally of the hour, but in works intended to give a permanent statement of the best experiences,—when not one man, in the million, shall I say? no, not in the hundred million, can rise above the belief that Woman was made *for Man,*—when such traits as these are daily forced upon the attention, can we feel that Man will always do justice to the interests of Woman? Can we think that he takes a sufficiently discerning and religious view of her office and destiny *ever* to do her justice, except when prompted by sentiment,—accidentally or transiently, that is, for the sentiment will vary according to the relations in which he is placed? The lover, the poet, the artist, are likely to view her nobly. The father and the philosopher have some chance of liberality; the man of the world, the legislator for expediency, none.

Under these circumstances, without attaching importance, in themselves, to the changes demanded by the champions of Woman, we hail them as signs of the times. We would have every arbitrary barrier thrown down. We would have every path laid open to Woman as freely as to Man. Were this done, and a slight temporary fermentation allowed to subside, we should see crystallizations more pure and of more various beauty. We believe the divine energy would pervade nature to a degree unknown in the history of former ages, and that no discordant collision, but a ravishing harmony of the spheres, would ensue.

Yet, then and only then will mankind be ripe for this, when inward and outward freedom for Woman as much as for Man shall be acknowledged as a *right,* not yielded as a concession. As the friend of the negro assumes that one man cannot by right hold another in bondage, so should the friend of Woman assume that Man cannot by right lay even well-meant restrictions on Woman. If the negro be a soul, if the woman be a soul, apparelled in flesh, to one Master only are they accountable. There is but one law for souls, and, if there is to be an interpreter of it, he must come not as man, or son of man, but as son of God.

Were thought and feeling once so far elevated that Man should esteem himself the brother and friend, but nowise the lord and tutor, of Woman,— were he really bound with her in equal worship,—arrangements as to function and employment would be of no consequence. What Woman needs is not as a woman to act or rule, but as a nature to grow, as an intellect to discern, as a soul to live freely and unimpeded, to unfold such powers as were given her when we left our common home. If fewer talents were given her, yet if allowed the free and full employment of these, so that she may render back to the giver his own with usury, she will not complain; nay, I dare to say she will bless and rejoice in her earthly birth-place, her earthly lot. Let us consider what obstructions impede this good era, and what signs give reason to hope that it draws near.

I was talking on this subject with Miranda, a woman, who, if any in the world could, might speak without heat and bitterness of the position of her sex. Her father was a man who cherished no sentimental reverence for Woman, but a firm belief in the equality of the sexes. She was his eldest child, and came to him at an age when he needed a companion. From the time she could speak and go alone, he addressed her not as a plaything, but as a living mind. Among the few verses he ever wrote was a copy addressed to this child, when the first locks were cut from her head; and the reverence expressed on this occasion for that cherished head, he never belied. It was to him the temple of immortal intellect. He respected his child, however, too much to be an indulgent parent. He called on her for clear judgment, for courage, for honor and fidelity; in short, for such virtues as he knew. In so far as he possessed the keys to the wonders of this universe, he allowed free use of them to her, and, by the incentive of a high expectation, he forbade, so far as possible, that she should let the privilege lie idle.

Thus this child was early led to feel herself a child of the spirit. She took her place easily, not only in the world of organized being, but in the world of mind. A dignified sense of self-dependence was given as all her portion, and she found it a sure anchor. Herself securely anchored, her relations with others were established with equal security. She was fortunate in a total absence of those charms which might have drawn to her bewildering flatteries, and in a strong electric nature, which repelled those who did not belong to her, and attracted those who did. With men and women her relations were noble,—affectionate without passion, intellectual without coldness. The world was free to her, and she lived freely in it. Outward adversity came, and inward conflict; but that faith and self-respect had early been awakened which must always lead, at last, to an outward serenity and an inward peace.

Of Miranda I had always thought as an example, that the restraints upon the sex were insuperable only to those who think them so, or who noisily strive to break them. She had taken a course of her own, and no man stood in her way. Many of her acts had been unusual, but excited no uproar. Few helped, but none checked her; and the many men who knew her mind and her life, showed to her confidence as to a brother, gentleness as to a sister. And not only refined, but very coarse men approved and aided one in whom they saw resolution and clearness of design. Her mind was often the leading one, always effective.

When I talked with her upon these matters, and had said very much what I have written, she smilingly replied: "And yet we must admit that I have been fortunate, and this should not be. My good father's early trust gave the first bias, and the rest followed, of course. It is true that I have had less outward aid, in after years, than most women; but that is of little consequence. Religion was early awakened in my soul,—a sense that what the soul is capable to ask it must attain, and that, though I might be aided and instructed by others, I must depend on myself as the only constant friend. This self-dependence, which was honored in me, is deprecated as a fault in most women. They are taught to learn their rule from without, not to unfold it from within.

"This is the fault of Man, who is still vain, and wishes to be more important to Woman than, by right, he should be."

"Men have not shown this disposition toward you," I said.

"No; because the position I early was enabled to take was one of self-reliance. And were all women as sure of their wants as I was, the result would be the same. But they are so overloaded with precepts by guardians, who think that nothing is so much to be dreaded for a woman as originality of thought or character, that their minds are impeded by doubts till they lose their chance of fair, free proportions. The difficulty is to get them to the point from which they shall naturally develop self-respect, and learn self-help.

"Once I thought that men would help to forward this state of things more than I do now. I saw so many of them wretched in the connections they had formed in weakness and vanity. They seemed so glad to esteem women whenever they could.

"'The soft arms of affection,' said one of the most discerning spirits, 'will not suffice for me, unless on them I see the steel bracelets of strength.'

"But early I perceived that men never, in any extreme of despair, wished to be women. On the contrary, they were ever ready to taunt one another, at any sign of weakness, with,

"'Art thou not like the women, who,'—

The passage ends various ways, according to the occasion and rhetoric of the speaker. When they admired any woman, they were inclined to speak of her as 'above her sex.' Silently I observed this, and feared it argued a rooted scepticism, which for ages had been fastening on the heart, and which only an age of miracles could eradicate. Ever I have been treated with great sincerity; and I look upon it as a signal instance of this, that an intimate friend of the other sex said, in a fervent moment, that I 'deserved in some star to be a man.' He was much surprised when I disclosed my view of my position and hopes, when I declared my faith that the feminine side, the side of love, of beauty, of holiness, was now to have its full chance, and that, if either were better, it was better now to be a woman; for even the slightest achievement of good was furthering an especial work of our time. He smiled incredulously. 'She makes the best she can of it,' thought he. 'Let Jews believe the pride of Jewry, but I am of the better sort, and know better.'

"Another used as highest praise, in speaking of a character in literature, the words 'a manly woman.'

"So in the noble passage of Ben Jonson:

'I meant the day-star should not brighter ride,
    Nor shed like influence from its lucent seat;
I meant she should be courteous, facile, sweet,
    Free from that solemn vice of greatness, pride;
I meant each softest virtue there should meet,
    Fit in that softer bosom to abide,
Only a learned and a *manly* soul
    I purposed her, that should with even powers
The rock, the spindle, and the shears control
    Of destiny, and spin her own free hours.'"[11]

"Methinks," said I, "you are too fastidious in objecting to this. Jonson, in using the word 'manly,' only meant to heighten the picture of this, the true, the intelligent fate, with one of the deeper colors."

"And yet," said she, "so invariable is the use of this word where a heroic quality is to be described, and I feel so sure that persistence and courage are the most womanly no less than the most manly qualities, that I would exchange these words for others of a larger sense, at the risk of marring the fine tissue of the verse. Read, 'A heavenward and instructed soul,' and I should be satisfied. Let it not be said, wherever there is energy or creative genius, 'She has a masculine mind.'"

This by no means argues a willing want of generosity toward Woman. Man is as generous towards her as he knows how to be.

Wherever she has herself arisen in national or private history, and nobly shone forth in any form of excellence, men have received her, not only willingly, but with triumph. Their encomiums, indeed, are always, in some sense, mortifying; they show too much surprise. "Can this be you?" he cries to the transfigured Cinderella; "well, I should never have thought it, but I am very glad. We will tell every one that you have '*surpassed your sex.*'"

In every-day life, the feelings of the many are stained with vanity. Each wishes to be lord in a little world, to be superior at least over one; and he does not feel strong enough to retain a life-long ascendency over a strong nature. Only a Theseus could conquer before he wed the Amazonian queen. Hercules wished rather to rest with Dejanira, and received the poisoned robe as a fit guerdon. The tale should be interpreted to all those who seek repose with the weak.

But not only is Man vain and fond of power, but the same want of development, which thus affects him morally, prevents his intellectually discerning the destiny of Woman. The boy wants no woman, but only a girl to play ball with him, and mark his pocket handkerchief.

Thus, in Schiller's Dignity of Woman, beautiful as the poem is, there is no "grave and perfect man," but only a great boy to be softened and restrained by the influence of girls.[12] Poets—the elder brothers of their race—have usually seen further; but what can you expect of every-day men, if Schiller was not more prophetic as to what women must be? Even with Richter, one foremost thought about a wife was that she would "cook him something good."[13] But as this is a delicate subject, and we are in constant danger of being accused of slighting what are called "the functions," let me say, in behalf of Miranda and myself, that we have high respect for those who "cook something good," who create and preserve fair order in houses, and prepare therein the shining raiment for worthy inmates, worthy guests. Only these "functions" must not be a drudgery, or enforced necessity, but a part of life. Let Ulysses drive the beeves home, while Penelope there piles up the fragrant loaves; they are both well employed if these be done in thought and love, willingly. But Penelope is no more meant for a baker or weaver solely, than Ulysses for a cattle-herd.

The sexes should not only correspond to and appreciate, but prophesy to one another. In individual instances this happens. Two persons love in one another the future good which they aid one another to unfold. This is imperfectly or rarely done in the general life. Man has gone but little way; now he is waiting to see whether Woman can keep step with him; but, instead of calling out, like a good brother, "You can do it, if you only think so," or impersonally, "Any one can do what he tries to do;" he often discourages with school-boy brag: "Girls can't do that; girls can't play ball." But let any one defy their taunts, break through and be brave and secure, they rend the air with shouts.

This fluctuation was obvious in a narrative I have lately seen, the story of the life of Countess Emily Plater, the heroine of the last revolution in Poland.[14] The dignity, the purity, the concentrated resolve, the calm, deep enthusiasm, which yet could, when occasion called, sparkle up a holy, an indignant fire, make of this young maiden the figure I want for my frontispiece. Her portrait is to be seen in the book, a gentle shadow of her soul. Short was the career. Like the Maid of Orleans, she only did enough to verify her credentials, and then passed from a scene on which she was, probably, a premature apparition.

When the young girl joined the army, where the report of her exploits had preceded her, she was received in a manner that marks the usual state of feeling. Some of the officers were disappointed at her quiet manners; that she had not the air and tone of a stage-heroine. They thought she could not have acted heroically unless in buskins; had no idea that such deeds only showed the habit of her mind. Others talked of the delicacy of her sex, advised her to withdraw from perils and dangers, and had no comprehension of the feelings within her breast that made this impossible. The gentle irony of her reply to these self-constituted tutors (not one of whom showed himself her equal in conduct or reason), is as good as her indignant reproof at a later period to the general, whose perfidy ruined all.

But though, to the mass of these men, she was an embarrassment and a puzzle, the nobler sort viewed her with a tender enthusiasm worthy of her.

"Her name," said her biographer, "is known throughout Europe. I paint her character that she may be as widely loved."

With pride, he shows her freedom from all personal affections; that, though tender and gentle in an uncommon degree, there was no room for a private love in her consecrated life. She inspired those who knew her with a simple energy of feeling like her own. "We have seen," they felt, "a woman worthy the name, capable of all sweet affections, capable of stern virtue."

It is a fact worthy of remark, that all these revolutions in favor of liberty have produced female champions that share the same traits, but Emily alone has found a biographer. Only a near friend could have performed for her this task, for the flower was reared in feminine seclusion, and the few and simple traits of her history before her appearance in the field could only have been known to the domestic circle. Her biographer has gathered them up with a brotherly devotion.

No! Man is not willingly ungenerous. He wants faith and love, because he is not yet himself an elevated being. He cries, with sneering scepticism, "Give us a sign." But if the sign appears, his eyes glisten, and he offers not merely approval, but homage.

The severe nation which taught that the happiness of the race was forfeited through the fault of a Woman, and showed its thought of what sort of regard Man owed her, by making him accuse her on the first question to his God,—who gave her to the patriarch as a handmaid, and, by the Mosaical law, bound her to allegiance like a serf,—even they greeted, with solemn rapture, all great and holy women as heroines, prophetesses, judges in Israel; and, if they made Eve listen to the serpent, gave Mary as a bride to the Holy Spirit. In other nations it has been the same down to our day. To the Woman who could conquer a triumph was awarded. And not only those whose strength was recommended to the heart by association with goodness and beauty, but those who were bad, if they were steadfast and strong, had their claims allowed. In any age a Semiramis, an Elizabeth of England, a Catharine of Russia, makes her place good, whether in a large or small circle. How has a little wit, a little genius, been celebrated in a Woman! What an intellectual triumph was that of the lonely Aspasia, and how heartily acknowledged![15] She, indeed, met a Pericles. But what annalist, the rudest of men, the most plebeian of husbands, will spare from his page one of the few anecdotes of Roman women—Sappho! Eloisa![16] The names are of threadbare celebrity. Indeed, they were not more suitably met in their own time than the Countess Colonel Plater on her first joining the army. They had much to mourn, and their great impulses did not find due scope. But with time enough, space enough, their kindred appear on the scene. Across the ages, forms lean, trying to touch the hem of their retreating robes. The youth here by my side cannot be weary of the fragments from the life of Sappho. He will not believe they are not addressed to himself, or that he to whom they were addressed could be ungrateful. A recluse of high powers devotes himself to understand and explain the thought of Eloisa; he asserts her vast superiority in soul and genius to her master; he curses the fate that casts his lot in another age than hers. He could have understood her; he would have been to her a friend, such as Abelard never could. And this one Woman he could have loved and reverenced, and she, alas! lay cold in her grave hundreds of years ago. His sorrow is truly pathetic. These responses, that come too late to give joy, are as tragic as anything we know, and yet the tears of later ages glitter as they fall on Tasso's prison bars.[17] And we know how elevating to the captive is the security that somewhere an intelligence must answer to his.

The Man habitually most narrow towards Woman will be flushed, as by the worst assault on Christianity, if you say it has made no improvement in her condition. Indeed, those most opposed to new acts in her favor, are jealous of the reputation of those which have been done.

We will not speak of the enthusiasm excited by actresses, improvisatrici, female singers,—for here mingles the charm of beauty and grace,—but female authors, even learned women, if not insufferably ugly and slovenly, from the Italian professor's daughter who taught behind the curtain, down to Mrs. Carter[18] and Madame Dacier,[19] are sure of an admiring audience, and, what is far better; chance to use what they have learned, and to learn more, if they can once get a platform on which to stand.

But how to get this platform, or how to make it of reasonably easy access, is the difficulty. Plants of great vigor will almost always struggle into blossom, despite impediments. But there should be encouragement, and a free genial atmosphere for those of more timid sort, fair play for each in its own kind. Some are like the little, delicate flowers which love to hide in the dripping mosses, by the sides of mountain torrents, or in the shade of tall trees. But others require an open field, a rich and loosened soil, or they never show their proper hues.

It may be said that Man does not have his fair play either; his energies are repressed and distorted by the interposition of artificial obstacles. Ay, but he himself has put them there; they have grown out of his own imperfections. If there *is* a misfortune in Woman's lot, it is in obstacles being interposed by men, which do *not* mark her state; and, if they express her past ignorance, do not her present needs. As every Man is of Woman born, she has slow but sure means of redress; yet the sooner a general justness of thought makes smooth the path, the better.

Man is of Woman born, and her face bends over him in infancy with an expression he can never quite forget. Eminent men have delighted to pay tribute to this image, and it is an hackneyed observation, that most men of genius boast some remarkable development in the mother. The rudest tar brushes off a tear with his coat-sleeve at the hallowed name. The other day, I met a decrepit old man of seventy, on a journey, who challenged the stage company to guess where he was going. They guessed aright, "To see your mother." "Yes," said he, "she is ninety-two, but has good eyesight still, they say. I have not seen her these forty years, and I thought I could not die in peace without." I should have liked his picture painted as a companion-piece to that of a boisterous little boy, whom I saw attempt to declaim at a school exhibition—

"O that those lips had language! Life has passed
With me but roughly since I heard thee last."

He got but very little way before sudden tears shamed him from the stage.

Some gleams of the same expression which shone down upon his infancy, angelically pure and benign, visit Man again with hopes of pure love, of a holy marriage. Or, if not before, in the eyes of the mother of his child they again are seen, and dim fancies pass before his mind, that Woman may not have been born for him alone, but have come from heaven, a commissioned soul, a messenger of truth and love; that she can only make for him a home in which he may lawfully repose, in so far as she is

"True to the kindred points of Heaven and home."

In gleams, in dim fancies, this thought visits the mind of common men. It is soon obscured by the mists of sensuality, the dust of routine, and he thinks it was only some meteor or ignis fatuus that shone. But, as a Rosicrucian lamp, it burns unwearied, though condemned to the solitude of

"Man is of Woman born, and her face bends over him in infancy with an expression he can never quite forget."

tombs; and to its permanent life, as to every truth, each age has in some form borne witness. For the truths, which visit the minds of careless men only in fitful gleams, shine with radiant clearness into those of the poet, the priest, and the artist.

Whatever may have been the domestic manners of the ancients, the idea of Woman was nobly manifested in their mythologies and poems, where she appears as Sita in the Ramayana, a form of tender purity; as the Egyptian Isis, of divine wisdom never yet surpassed.[20] In Egypt, too, the Sphynx, walking the earth with lion tread, looked out upon its marvels in the calm, inscrutable beauty of a virgin's face, and the Greek could only add wings to the great emblem. In Greece, Ceres and Proserpine, significantly termed "the great goddesses," were seen seated side by side. They needed not to rise for any worshipper or any change; they were prepared for all things, as those initiated to their mysteries knew. More obvious is the meaning of these three forms, the Diana, Minerva, and Vesta. Unlike in the expression of their beauty, but alike in this,—that each was self-sufficing. Other forms were only accessories and illustrations, none the complement to one like these. Another might, indeed, be the companion, and the Apollo and Diana set off one another's beauty. Of the Vesta, it is to be observed, that not only deep-eyed, deep-discerning Greece, but ruder Rome, who represents the only form of good man (the always busy warrior) that could be indifferent to Woman, confided the permanence of its glory to a tutelary goddess, and her wisest legislator spoke of meditation as a nymph.

Perhaps in Rome the neglect of Woman was a reaction on the manners of Etruria, where the priestess Queen, warrior Queen, would seem to have been so usual a character.[21]

An instance of the noble Roman marriage, where the stern and calm nobleness of the nation was common to both; we see in the historic page through the little that is told us of Brutus and Portia. Shakespeare has seized on the relation in its native lineaments, harmonizing the particular with the universal; and, while it is conjugal love, and no other, making it unlike the same relation as seen in Cymbeline, or Othello, even as one star differeth from another in glory.

"By that great vow
Which did incorporate and make us one,
Unfold to me, yourself, your other half,
Why you are heavy. * * *

Dwell I but in the suburbs
Of your good pleasure? If it be no more,
Portia is Brutus' harlot, not his wife."[22]

Mark the sad majesty of his tone in answer. Who would not have lent a life-long credence to that voice of honor?

"You are my true and honorable wife;
As dear to me as are the ruddy drops
That visit this sad heart."[23]

It is the same voice that tells the moral of his life in the last words—

   "Countrymen,
My heart doth joy, that, yet in all my life,
I found no man but he was true to me."[24]

It was not wonderful that it should be so.

Shakespeare, however, was not content to let Portia rest her plea for confidence on the essential nature of the marriage bond:

"I grant I am a woman; but withal,
A woman that lord Brutus took to wife.
I grant I am a woman; but withal,
A woman well reputed—Cato's daughter.
Think you I am *no stronger than my sex,*
Being so fathered and so husbanded?"[25]

And afterward in the very scene where Brutus is suffering under that "insupportable and touching loss," the death of his wife, Cassius pleads—

   "Have you not love enough to bear with me,
   When that rash humor which my mother gave me
   Makes me forgetful?
Brutus.—Yes, Cassius, and henceforth,
   When you are over-earnest with your Brutus,
   He'll think your mother chides, and leaves you so."[26]

As indeed it was a frequent belief among the ancients, as with our Indians, that the *body* was inherited from the mother, the *soul* from the father. As in that noble passage of Ovid, already quoted, where Jupiter, as his divine synod are looking down on the funeral pyre of Hercules, thus triumphs—

"Nec nisi *maternâ* Vulcanum parte potentem,
Sentiet. Aeternum est, à me quod traxit, et expers
Atque immune necis, nullaque domabile flamma
Idque ego defunctum terrâ cœlestibus oris
Accipiam, cunctisque meum lætabile factum
Dis fore confido.

"The part alone of gross *maternal* frame
Fire shall devour; while that from me he drew
Shall live immortal and its force renew;
That, when he's dead, I'll raise to realms above;
Let all the powers the righteous act approve."[27]

It is indeed a god speaking of his union with an earthly Woman, but it expresses the common Roman thought as to marriage,—the same which permitted a man to lend his wife to a friend, as if she were a chattel.

"She dwelt but in the suburbs of his good pleasure."

Yet the same city, as I have said, leaned on the worship of Vesta, the Preserver, and in later times was devoted to that of Isis. In Sparta, thought, in this respect as in all others, was expressed in the characters of real life, and the women of Sparta were as much Spartans as the men. The "citoyen, citoyenne" of France was here actualized. Was not the calm equality they enjoyed as honorable as the devotion of chivalry? They intelligently shared the ideal life of their nation.

Like the men they felt

"Honor gone, all's gone:
Better never have been born."

They were the true friends of men. The Spartan, surely, would not think that he received only his body from his mother. The sage, had he lived in that community, could not have thought the souls of "vain and foppish men will be degraded after death to the forms of women; and, if they do not then make great efforts to retrieve themselves, will become birds."

(By the way, it is very expressive of the hard intellectuality of the merely *mannish* mind, to speak thus of birds, chosen always by the *feminine* poet as the symbols of his fairest thoughts.)

We are told of the Greek nations in general, that Woman occupied there an infinitely lower place than Man. It is difficult to believe this, when we see such range and dignity of thought on the subject in the mythologies, and find the poets producing such ideals as Cassandra, Iphigenia, Antigone, Macaria[28]; where Sibylline priestesses told the oracle of the highest god, and he could not be content to reign with a court of fewer than nine muses. Even Victory wore a female form.

But, whatever were the facts of daily life, I cannot complain of the age and nation which represents its thought by such a symbol as I see before me at this moment. It is a zodiac of the busts of gods and goddesses, arranged in pairs. The circle breathes the music of a heavenly order. Male and female heads are distinct in expression, but equal in beauty, strength and calmness. Each male head is that of a brother and a king,—each female of a sister and a queen. Could the thought thus expressed be lived out, there would be nothing more to be desired. There would be unison in variety, congeniality in difference.

Coming nearer our own time, we find religion and poetry no less true in their revelations. The rude man, just disengaged from the sod, the Adam, accuses Woman to his God, and records her disgrace to their posterity. He is not ashamed to write that he could be drawn from heaven by one beneath him,—one made, he says, from but a small part of himself. But in the same nation, educated by time, instructed by a succession of prophets, we find Woman in as high a position as she has ever occupied. No figure that has ever arisen to greet our eyes has been received with more fervent reverence than that of the Madonna. Heine calls her the *Dame du Comptoir* of the Catholic church, and this jeer well expresses a serious truth.[29]

And not only this holy and significant image was worshipped by the pilgrim, and the favorite subject of the artist, but it exercised an immediate influence on the destiny of the sex. The empresses who embraced the cross converted sons and husbands. Whole calendars of female saints, heroic dames of chivalry, binding the emblem of faith on the heart of the best-beloved, and wasting the bloom of youth in separation and loneliness, for the sake of duties they thought it religion to assume, with innumerable forms of poesy, trace their lineage to this one. Nor, however imperfect may be the action, in our day, of the faith thus expressed, and though we can scarcely think it nearer this ideal than that of India or Greece was near their ideal, is it in vain that the truth has been recognized, that Woman is not only a part of Man, bone of his bone, and flesh of his flesh, born that men might not be lonely—but that women are in themselves possessors of and possessed by immortal souls. This truth undoubtedly received a greater outward stability from the belief of the church that the earthly parent of the Saviour of souls was a woman.

The Assumption of the Virgin, as painted by sublime artists, as also Petrarch's Hymn to the Madonna, cannot have spoken to the world wholly without result, yet oftentimes those who had ears heard not.

See upon the nations the influence of this powerful example. In Spain look only at the ballads. Woman in these is "very Woman;" she is the betrothed, the bride, the spouse of Man; there is on her no hue of the philosopher, the heroine, the savante, but she looks great and noble. Why? Because she is also, through her deep devotion, the betrothed of Heaven. Her upturned eyes have drawn down the light that casts a radiance round her. See only such a ballad as that of "Lady Teresa's Bridal," where the Infanta, given to the Moorish bridegroom, calls down the vengeance of Heaven on his unhallowed passion, and thinks it not too much to expiate by a life in the cloister the involuntary stain upon her princely youth. It was this constant sense of claims above those of earthly love or happiness that made the Spanish lady who shared this spirit a guerdon to be won by toils and blood and constant purity, rather than a chattel to be bought for plea-sure and service.

Germany did not need to *learn* a high view of Woman; it was inborn in that race. Woman was to the Teuton warrior his priestess, his friend, his sister,—in truth, a wife. And the Christian statues of noble pairs, as they lie above their graves in stone, expressing the meaning of all the by-gone pilgrimage by hands folded in mutual prayer, yield not a nobler sense of the place and powers of Woman than belonged to the *altvater* day. The holy love of Christ which summoned them, also, to choose "the better part—that which could not be taken from them," refined and hallowed in this nation a native faith; thus showing that it was not the warlike spirit alone that left the Latins so barbarous in this respect.

But the Germans, taking so kindly to this thought, did it the more justice. The idea of Woman in their literature is expressed both to a greater height and depth than elsewhere.

I will give as instances the themes of three ballads:

One is upon a knight who had always the name of the Virgin on his lips. This protected him all his life through, in various and beautiful modes, both from sin and other dangers; and, when he died, a plant sprang from his grave, which so gently whispered the Ave Maria that none could pass it by with an unpurified heart.

Another is one of the legends of the famous Drachenfels.[30] A maiden, one of the earliest converts to Christianity, was carried by the enraged populace to this dread haunt of "the dragon's fabled brood," to be their prey. She was left alone, but undismayed, for she knew in whom she trusted. So, when the dragons came rushing towards her, she showed them a crucifix and they crouched reverently at her feet. Next day the people came, and, seeing these wonders, were all turned to the faith which exalts the lowly.

The third I have in mind is another of the Rhine legends. A youth is sitting with the maid he loves on the shore of an isle, her fairy kingdom, then perfumed by the blossoming grape-vines which draped its bowers. They are happy; all blossoms with them, and life promises its richest wine. A boat approaches on the tide; it pauses at their feet. It brings, perhaps, some joyous message, fresh dew for their flowers, fresh light on the wave. No! it is the usual check on such great happiness. The father of the count departs for the crusade; will his son join him, or remain to rule their domain, and wed her he loves? Neither of the affianced pair hesitates a moment. "I must go with my father,"—"Thou must go with thy father." It was one thought, one word. "I will be here again," he said, "when these blossoms have turned to purple grapes." "I hope so," she sighed, while the prophetic sense said "no."

And there she waited, and the grapes ripened, and were gathered into the vintage, and he came not. Year after year passed thus, and no tidings; yet still she waited.

He, meanwhile, was in a Moslem prison. Long he languished there without hope, till, at last, his patron saint appeared in vision and announced his release, but only on condition of his joining the monastic order for the service of the saint.

And so his release was effected, and a safe voyage home given. And once more he sets sail upon the Rhine. The maiden, still watching beneath the vines, sees at last the object of all this patient love approach—approach, but not to touch the strand to which she, with outstretched arms, has rushed. He dares not trust himself to land, but in low, heart-broken tones, tells her of Heaven's will; and that he, in obedience to his vow, is now on his way to a convent on the river-bank, there to pass the rest of his earthly life in the service of the shrine. And then he turns his boat, and floats away from her and hope of any happiness in this world, but urged, as he believes, by the breath of Heaven.

The maiden stands appalled, but she dares not murmur, and cannot hesitate long. She also bids them prepare her boat. She follows her lost love to the convent gate, requests an interview with the abbot, and devotes her Elysian isle, where vines had ripened their ruby fruit in vain for her, to the service of the monastery where her love was to serve. Then, passing over to the nunnery opposite, she takes the veil, and meets her betrothed at the altar; and for a life-long union, if not the one they had hoped in earlier years.

Is not this sorrowful story of a lofty beauty? Does it not show a sufficiently high view of Woman, of Marriage? This is commonly the chivalric, still more the German view.

Yet, wherever there was a balance in the mind of Man, of sentiment with intellect, such a result was sure. The Greek Xenophon[31] has not only painted us a sweet picture of the domestic Woman, in his Economics, but in the Cyropedia has given, in the picture of Panthea, a view of Woman which no German picture can surpass, whether lonely and quiet with veiled lids, the temple of a vestal loveliness, or with eyes flashing, and hair flowing to the free wind, cheering on the hero to fight for his God, his country, or whatever name his duty might bear at the time. This picture I shall copy by and by. Yet Xenophon grew up in the same age with him who makes Iphigenia say to Achilles,

"Better a thousand women should perish than one man cease to see the light."[32]

This was the vulgar Greek sentiment. Xenophon, aiming at the ideal Man, caught glimpses of the ideal Woman also. From the figure of a Cyrus the Pantheas[33] stand not afar. They do not in thought; they would not in life.

I could swell the catalogue of instances far beyond the reader's patience. But enough have been brought forward to show that, though there has been great disparity betwixt the nations as between individuals in their culture on this point, yet the idea of Woman has always cast some rays and often been forcibly represented.

Far less has Woman to complain that she has not had her share of power. This, in all ranks of society, except the lowest, has been hers to the extent that vanity would crave, far beyond what wisdom would accept. In the very lowest, where Man, pressed by poverty, sees in Woman only the partner of toils and cares, and cannot hope, scarcely has an idea of, a comfortable home, he often maltreats her, and is less influenced by her. In all ranks, those who are gentle and uncomplaining, too candid to intrigue, too delicate to encroach, suffer much. They suffer long, and are kind; verily, they have their reward. But wherever Man is sufficiently raised above extreme poverty, or brutal stupidity, to care for the comforts of the fireside, or the bloom and ornament of life, Woman has always power enough, if she

choose to exert it, and is usually disposed to do so, in proportion to her ignorance and childish vanity. Unacquainted with the importance of life and its purposes, trained to a selfish coquetry and love of petty power, she does not look beyond the pleasure of making herself felt at the moment, and governments are shaken and commerce broken up to gratify the pique of a female favorite. The English shopkeeper's wife does not vote, but it is for her interest that the politician canvasses by the coarsest flattery. France suffers no woman on her throne, but her proud nobles kiss the dust at the feet of Pompadour and Dubarry; for such flare in the lighted foreground where a Roland would modestly aid in the closet.[34] Spain (that same Spain which sang of Ximena and the Lady Teresa) shuts up her women in the care of duennas, and allows them no book but the breviary; but the ruin follows only the more surely from the worthless favorite of a worthless queen. Relying on mean precautions, men indeed cry peace, peace, where there is no peace.

It is not the transient breath of poetic incense that women want; each can receive that from a lover. It is not life-long sway; it needs but to become a coquette, a shrew, or a good cook, to be sure of that. It is not money, nor notoriety, nor the badges of authority which men have appropriated to themselves. If demands, made in their behalf, lay stress on any of these particulars, those who make them have not searched deeply into the need. The want is for that which at once includes these and precludes them; which would not be forbidden power, lest there be temptation to steal and misuse it; which would not have the mind perverted

by flattery from a worthiness of esteem; it is for that which is the birth-right of every being capable of receiving it,—the freedom, the religious, the intelligent freedom of the universe to use its means, to learn its se-cret, as far as Nature has enabled them, with God alone for their guide and their judge.

Ye cannot believe it, men; but the only reason why women ever assume what is more appropriate to you, is because you prevent them from finding out what is fit for themselves. Were they free, were they wise fully to develop the strength and beauty of Woman; they would never wish to be men, or man-like. The well-instructed moon flies not from her orbit to seize on the glories of her partner. No; for she knows that one law rules, one heaven contains, one universe replies to them alike. It is with women as with the slave:

> "Vor dem Sklaven, wenn er die Kette bricht,
> Vor dem freien Menschen erzittert nicht."[35]

Tremble not before the free man, but before the slave who has chains to break.

In slavery, acknowledged slavery, women are on a par with men. Each is a work-tool, an article of property, no more! In perfect freedom, such as is painted in Olympus, in Swedenborg's[35] angelic state, in the heaven where there is no marrying nor giving in marriage, each is a purified intelligence, an enfranchised soul,—no less.

"Jene himmlische Gestalten
Sie fragen nicht nach Mann und Weib,

Und keine kleider, keine Falten
Umgeben den verklarten Leib."[37]

The child who sang this was a prophetic form, expressive of the longing
for a state of perfect freedom, pure love. She could not remain here, but
was translated to another air. And it may be that the air of this earth will
never be so tempered that such can bear it long. But, while they stay, they
must bear testimony to the truth they are constituted to demand.

That an era approaches which shall approximate nearer to such a temper
than any has yet done, there are many tokens; indeed, so many that only a
few of the most prominent can here be enumerated.

The reigns of Elizabeth of England and Isabella of Castile foreboded this
era. They expressed the beginning of the new state, while they forwarded
its progress. These were strong characters, and in harmony with the wants
of their time. One showed that this strength did not unfit a woman for the
duties of a wife and a mother; the other, that it could enable her to live and
die alone, a wide energetic life, a courageous death. Elizabeth is certainly
no pleasing example. In rising above the weakness, she did not lay aside
the foibles ascribed to her sex; but her strength must be respected now, as it
was in her own time.

Mary Stuart and Elizabeth seem types, moulded by the spirit of the time,
and placed upon an elevated platform, to show to the coming ages Woman
such as the conduct and wishes of Man in general is likely to make her. The
first shows Woman lovely even to allurement; quick in apprehension and
weak in judgment; with grace and dignity of sentiment, but no principle;
credulous and indiscreet, yet artful; capable of sudden greatness or of
crime, but not of a steadfast wisdom, nor self-restraining virtue. The second reveals Woman half-emancipated and jealous of her freedom, such as
she has figured before or since in many a combative attitude, mannish, not
equally manly; strong and prudent more than great or wise; able to control
vanity, and the wish to rule through coquetry and passion, but not to resign
these dear deceits from the very foundation, as unworthy a being capable of
truth and nobleness. Elizabeth, taught by adversity, put on her virtues as
armor, more than produced them in a natural order from her soul. The time
and her position called on her to act the wise sovereign, and she was proud
that she could do so, but her tastes and inclinations would have led her to
act the weak woman. She was without magnanimity of any kind.

We may accept as an omen for ourselves that it was Isabella who
furnished Columbus with the means of coming hither. This land must pay
back its debt to Woman, without whose aid it would not have been brought
into alliance with the civilized world.

A graceful and meaning figure is that introduced to us by Mr. Prescott,[38]
in the Conquest of Mexico, in the Indian girl Marina, who accompanied
Cortez, and was his interpreter in all the various difficulties of his career.
She stood at his side, on the walls of the besieged palace, to plead with her

enraged countrymen. By her name he was known in New Spain, and, after the conquest, her gentle intercession was often of avail to the conquered. The poem of the Future may be read in some features of the story of "Malinche."

The influence of Elizabeth on literature was real, though, by sympathy with its finer productions, she was no more entitled to give name to an era than Queen Anne. It was simply that the fact of having a female sovereign on the throne affected the course of a writer's thoughts. In this sense, the presence of a woman on the throne always makes its mark. Life is lived before the eyes of men, by which their imaginations are stimulated as to the possibilities of Woman. "We will die for our king, Maria Theresa," cry the wild warriors, clashing their swords; and the sounds vibrate through the poems of that generation. The range of female character in Spenser[39] alone might content us for one period. Britomart and Belphœbe have as much room on the canvas as Florimel; and, where this is the case, the haughtiest Amazon will not murmur that Una should be felt to be the fairest type.

Unlike as was the English queen to a fairy queen, we may yet conceive that it was the image of *a* queen before the poet's mind that called up this splendid court of women. Shakespeare's range is also great; but he has left out the heroic characters, such as the Macaria of Greece, the Britomart of Spenser. Ford and Massinger have, in this respect, soared to a higher flight of feeling than he.[40] It was the holy and heroic Woman they most loved, and if they could not paint an Imogen, a Desdemona, a Rosalind, yet, in those of a stronger mould, they showed a higher ideal, though with so much less poetic power to embody it, than we see in Portia or Isabella. The simple truth of Cordelia, indeed, is of this sort. The beauty of Cordelia is neither male nor female; it is the beauty of virtue.

The ideal of love and marriage rose high in the mind of all the Christian nations who were capable of grave and deep feeling. We may take as examples of its English aspect the lines,

> "I could not love thee, dear, so much,
>   Loved I not honor more."

Or the address of the Commonwealth's man to his wife, as she looked out from the Tower window to see him, for the last time, on his way to the scaffold. He stood up in the cart, waved his hat, and cried, "To Heaven, my love, to Heaven, and leave you in the storm!"

Such was the love of faith and honor,—a love which stopped, like Colonel Hutchinson's, "on this side idolatry," because it was religious. The meeting of two such souls Donne describes as giving birth to an "abler soul."

Lord Herbert wrote to his love,

> "Were not our souls immortal made,
>   Our equal loves can make them such."[41]

In the "Broken Heart," of Ford, Penthea, a character which engages my admiration even more deeply than the famous one of Calanthe, is made to present to the mind the most beautiful picture of what these relations should be in their purity. Her life cannot sustain the violation of what she so clearly feels.

Shakespeare, too, saw that, in true love, as in fire, the utmost ardor is coincident with the utmost purity. It is a true lover that exclaims in the agony of Othello,

"If thou art false, O then Heaven mocks itself!"

The son, framed, like Hamlet, to appreciate truth in all the beauty of relations, sinks into deep melancholy when he finds his natural expectations disappointed. He has no other. She to whom he gave the name, disgraces from his heart's shrine all the sex.

"Frailty, thy name is Woman."

It is because a Hamlet could find cause to say so, that I have put the line, whose stigma has never been removed, at the head of my work. But, as a lover, surely Hamlet would not have so far mistaken, as to have finished with such a conviction. He would have felt the faith of Othello, and that faith could not, in his more dispassionate mind, have been disturbed by calumny.

In Spain, this thought is arrayed in a sublimity which belongs to the sombre and passionate genius of the nation. Calderon's Justina resists all the temptation of the Demon, and raises her lover, with her, above the sweet lures of mere temporal happiness. Their marriage is vowed at the stake; their souls are liberated together by the martyr flame into "a purer state of sensation and existence."

In Italy, the great poets wove into their lives an ideal love which answered to the highest wants. It included those of the intellect and the affections, for it was a love of spirit for spirit. It was not ascetic, or superhuman, but, interpreting all things, gave their proper beauty to details of the common life, the common day. The poet spoke of his love, not as a flower to place in his bosom, or hold carelessly in his hand, but as a light toward which he must find wings to fly, or "a stair to heaven." He delighted to speak of her, not only as the bride of his heart, but the mother of his soul; for he saw that, in cases where the right direction had been taken, the greater delicacy of her frame and stillness of her life left her more open than is Man to spiritual influx. So he did not look upon her as betwixt him and earth, to serve his temporal needs, but, rather, betwixt him and heaven, to purify his affections and lead him to wisdom through love. He sought, in her, not so much the Eve as the Madonna.

In these minds the thought, which gleams through all the legends of chivalry, shines in broad intellectual effulgence, not to be misinterpreted;

and their thought is reverenced by the world, though it lies far from the practice of the world as yet,—so far that it seems as though a gulf of death yawned between.

Even with such men the practice was, often, widely different from the mental faith. I say mental; for if the heart were thoroughly alive with it, the practice could not be dissonant. Lord Herbert's was a marriage of convention, made for him at fifteen; he was not discontented with it, but looked only to the advantages it brought of perpetuating his family on the basis of a great fortune. He paid, in act, what he considered a dutiful attention to the bond; his thoughts travelled elsewhere; and while forming a high ideal of the companionship of minds in marriage, he seems never to have doubted that its realization must be postponed to some other state of being. Dante, almost immediately after the death of Beatrice, married a lady chosen for him by his friends, and Boccaccio, in describing the miseries that attended, in this case,

"The form of an union where union is none,"

speaks as if these were inevitable to the connection, and as if the scholar and poet, especially, could expect nothing but misery and obstruction in a domestic partnership with Woman.

Centuries have passed since, but civilized Europe is still in a transition state about marriage; not only in practice but in thought. It is idle to speak with contempt of the nations where polygamy is an institution, or seraglios a custom, while practices far more debasing haunt, well-nigh fill, every city and every town, and so far as union of one with one is believed to be the only pure form of marriage, a great majority of societies and individuals are still doubtful whether the earthly bond must be a meeting of souls, or only supposes a contract of convenience and utility. Were Woman established in the rights of an immortal being, this could not be. She would not, in some countries, be given away by her father, with scarcely more respect for her feelings than is shown by the Indian chief, who sells his daughter for a horse, and beats her if she runs away from her new home. Nor, in societies where her choice is left free, would she be perverted, by the current of opinion that seizes her, into the belief that she must marry, if it be only to find a protector, and a home of her own. Neither would Man, if he thought the connection of permanent importance, form it so lightly. He would not deem it a trifle, that he was to enter into the closest relations with another soul, which, if not eternal in themselves, must eternally affect his growth. Neither, did he believe Woman capable of friendship, would he, by rash haste, lose the chance of finding a friend in the person who might, probably, live half a century by his side. Did love, to his mind, stretch forth into infinity, he would not miss his chance of its revelations, that he might the sooner rest from his weariness by a bright fireside, and secure a sweet and graceful attendant "devoted to him alone." Were he a step higher, he would not carelessly enter into a relation where he might not be able to do the duty of a friend, as well as a protector from external ill, to the other party, and have a being in his power pining for sympathy, intelligence and aid, that he could not give.

What deep communion, what real intercourse is implied in sharing the joys and cares of parentage, when any degree of equality is admitted between the parties! It is true that, in a majority of instances, the man looks upon his wife as an adopted child, and places her to the other children in the relation of nurse or governess, rather than that of parent. Her influence with them is sure; but she misses the education which should enlighten that influence, by being thus treated. It is the order of nature that children should complete the education, moral and mental, of parents, by making them think what is needed for the best culture of human beings, and conquer all faults and impulses that interfere with their giving this to these dear objects, who represent the world to them. Father and mother should assist one another to learn what is required for this sublime priesthood of Nature. But, for this, a religious recognition of equality is required.

Where this thought of equality begins to diffuse itself, it is shown in four ways.

First;—The household partnership. In our country, the woman looks for a "smart but kind" husband; the man for a "capable, sweet-tempered" wife. The man furnishes the house; the woman regulates it. Their relation is one of mutual esteem, mutual dependence. Their talk is of business; their affection shows itself by practical kindness. They know that life goes more smoothly and cheerfully to each for the other's aid; they are grateful and content. The wife praises her husband as a "good provider;" the husband, in return, compliments her as a "capital housekeeper." This relation is good so far as it goes.

Next comes a closer tie, which takes the form either of mutual idolatry or of intellectual companionship. The first, we suppose, is to no one a pleasing subject of contemplation. The parties weaken and narrow one another; they lock the gate against all the glories of the universe, that they may live in a cell together. To themselves they seem the only wise; to all others, steeped in infatuation; the gods smile as they look forward to the crisis of cure; to men, the woman seems an unlovely syren; to women, the man an effeminate boy.

The other form, of intellectual companionship, has become more and more frequent. Men engaged in public life, literary men, and artists, have often found in their wives companions and confidants in thought no less than in feeling. And, as the intellectual development of Woman has spread wider and risen higher, they have, not unfrequently, shared the same employment; as in the case of Roland and his wife, who were friends in the household and in the nation's councils, read, regulated home affairs, or prepared public documents together, indifferently. It is very pleasant, in letters begun by Roland and finished by his wife, to see the harmony of mind, and the difference of nature; one thought, but various ways of treating it.

This is one of the best instances of a marriage of friendship. It was only friendship, whose basis was esteem; probably neither party knew love, except by name. Roland was a good man, worthy to esteem, and be esteemed; his wife as deserving of admiration as able to do without it.

Madame Roland[42] is the fairest specimen we yet have of her class; as clear to discern her aim, as valiant to pursue it, as Spenser's Britomart; austerely set apart from all that did not belong to her, whether as Woman or as mind. She is an antetype of a class to which the coming time will afford a field—the Spartan matron, brought by the culture of the age of books to intellectual consciousness and expansion. Self-sufficingness, strength, and clearsightedness were, in her, combined with a power of deep and calm affection. She, too, would have given a son or husband the device for his shield, "Return with it or upon it;" and this, not because she loved little, but much. The page of her life is one of unsullied dignity. Her appeal to posterity is one against the injustice of those who committed such crimes in the name of Liberty. She makes it in behalf of herself and her husband. I would put beside it, on the shelf, a little volume, containing a similar appeal from the verdict of contemporaries to that of mankind, made by Godwin in behalf of his wife, the celebrated, the by most men detested, Mary Wollstonecraft.[43] In his view, it was an appeal from the injustice of those who did such wrong in the name of virtue. Were this little book interesting for no other cause, it would be so for the generous affection evinced under the peculiar circumstances. This man had courage to love and honor this woman in the face of the world's sentence, and of all that was repulsive in her own past history. He believed he saw of what soul she was, and that the impulses she had struggled to act out were noble, though the opinions to which they had led might not be thoroughly weighed. He loved her, and he defended her for the meaning and tendency of her inner life. It was a good fact.

Mary Wollstonecraft, like Madame Dudevant (commonly known as George Sand[44]) in our day, was a woman whose existence better proved the need of some new interpretation of Woman's Rights than anything she wrote. Such beings as these, rich in genius, of most tender sympathies, capable of high virtue and a chastened harmony, ought not to find themselves, by birth, in a place so narrow, that, in breaking bonds, they become outlaws. Were there as much room in the world for such, as in Spenser's poem for Britomart, they would not run their heads so wildly against the walls, but prize their shelter rather. They find their way, at last, to light and air, but the world will not take off the brand it has set upon them. The champion of the Rights of Woman found, in Godwin, one who would plead that cause like a brother. He who delineated with such purity of traits the form of Woman in the Marguerite, of whom the weak St. Leon could never learn to be worthy,—a pearl indeed whose price was above rubies,—was not false in life to the faith by which he had hallowed his romance. He acted, as he wrote, like a brother. This form of appeal rarely fails to touch the basest man:—"Are you acting toward other women in the way you would have men act towards your sister?" George Sand smokes, wears male attire, wishes to be addressed as "Mon frère;"—perhaps, if she found those who were as brothers indeed, she would not care whether she were brother or sister.* We rejoice to see that she, who expresses such a painful contempt for men in most of her works, as shows she must have known great wrong from them, depicts, in "La Roche Mauprat," a man raised by the workings of love from the depths of savage sensualism to a moral and intellectual life. It was love for a pure object, for a steadfast woman, one of those who, the Italian said, could make the "stair to heaven."

This author, beginning like the many in assault upon bad institutions, and external ills, yet deepening the experience through comparative freedom, sees at last that the only efficient remedy must come from individual character. These bad institutions, indeed, it may always be replied, prevent individuals from forming good character, therefore we must remove them. Agreed; yet keep steadily the higher aim in view. Could you clear away all the bad forms of society, it is vain, unless the individual begin to be ready for better. There must be a parallel movement in these two branches of life. And all the rules left by Moses availed less to further the best life than the living example of one Messiah.

Still the mind of the age struggles confusedly with these problems, better discerning as yet the ill it can no longer bear, than the good by which it may supersede it. But women like Sand will speak now and cannot be silenced; their characters and their eloquence alike foretell an era when such as they shall easier learn to lead true lives. But though such forebode, not such shall be parents of it. Those who would reform the world must show that they do not speak in the heat of wild impulse; their lives must be unstained by passionate error; they must be severe lawgivers to themselves. They must be religious students of the divine purpose with regard to man, if they would not confound the fancies of a day with the requisitions of eternal good. Their liberty must be the liberty of law and knowledge. But as to the transgressions against custom which have caused such outcry against those of noble intention, it may be observed that the resolve of Eloisa to be only the mistress of Abelard, was that of one who saw in practice around her the contract of marriage made the seal of degradation. Shelley feared not to be fettered, unless so to be was to be false. Wherever abuses are seen, the timid will suffer; the bold will protest. But society has a right to outlaw them till she has revised her law; and this she must be taught to do, by one who speaks with authority, not in anger or haste.

If Godwin's choice of the calumniated authoress of the "Rights of Woman,"[45] for his honored wife, be a sign of a new era, no less so is an article to which I have alluded some pages back, published five or six years ago in one of the English Reviews, where the writer, in doing full justice to

---

*A note appended by my sister in this place, in the first edition, is here omitted, because it is incorporated in another article in this volume, treating of George Sand more at length.—[ED.]

Eloisa, shows his bitter regret that she lives not now to love him, who might have known better how to prize her love than did the egotistical Abelard.

These marriages, these characters, with all their imperfections, express an onward tendency. They speak of aspiration of soul, of energy of mind, seeking clearness and freedom. Of a like promise are the tracts lately published by Goodwyn Barmby (the European Pariah, as he calls himself) and his wife Catharine.[46] Whatever we may think of their measures, we see in them wedlock; the two minds are wed by the only contract that can permanently avail, that of a common faith and a common purpose.

We might mention instances, nearer home, of minds, partners in work and in life, sharing together, on equal terms, public and private interests, and which wear not, on any side, the aspect of offence shown by those last-named: persons who steer straight onward, yet, in our comparatively free life, have not been obliged to run their heads against any wall. But the principles which guide them might, under petrified and oppressive institutions, have made them warlike, paradoxical, and, in some sense, Pariahs. The phenomena are different, the law is the same, in all these cases. Men and women have been obliged to build up their house anew from the very foundation. If they found stone ready in the quarry, they took it peaceably; otherwise they alarmed the country by pulling down old towers to get materials.

These are all instances of marriage as intellectual companionship. The parties meet mind to mind, and a mutual trust is produced, which can buckler them against a million. They work together for a common purpose, and, in all these instances, with the same implement,—the pen. The pen and the writing-desk furnish forth as naturally the retirement of Woman as of Man.

A pleasing expression, in this kind, is afforded by the union in the names of the Howitts. William and Mary Howitt[47] we heard named together for years, supposing them to be brother and sister; the equality of labors and reputation, even so, was auspicious; more so, now we find them man and wife. In his late work on Germany, Howitt mentions his wife, with pride, as one among the constellation of distinguished English-women, and in a graceful, simple manner. And still we contemplate with pleasure the partnership in literature and affection between the Howitts,—the congenial pursuits and productions—the pedestrian tours wherein the married pair showed that marriage, on a wide enough basis, does not destroy the "inexhaustible" entertainment which lovers find in one another's company.

In naming these instances, I do not mean to imply that community of employment is essential to the union of husband and wife, more than to the union of friends. Harmony exists in difference, no less than in likeness, if only the same key-note govern both parts. Woman the poem, Man the poet! Woman the heart, Man the head! Such divisions are only important when they are never to be transcended. If nature is never bound down, nor the voice of inspiration stifled, that is enough. We are pleased that women should write and speak, if they feel need of it, from having something to

tell; but silence for ages would be no misfortune, if that silence be from divine command, and not from Man's tradition.

While Goetz Von Berlichingen rides to battle, his wife is busy in the kitchen; but difference of occupation does not prevent that community of inward life, that perfect esteem, with which he says,

"Whom God loves, to him gives he such a wife."[48]

"Men and women have been obliged to build up their house anew from the very foundation."

Manzoni thus dedicates his "Adelchi."

"To his beloved and venerated wife, Enrichetta Luigia Blondel, who, with conjugal affection and maternal wisdom, has preserved a virgin mind, the author dedicates this 'Adelchi,' grieving that he could not, by a more splendid and more durable monument, honor the dear name, and the memory of so many virtues."

The relation could not be fairer, nor more equal, if she, too, had written poems. Yet the position of the parties might have been the reverse as well; the Woman might have sung the deeds, given voice to the life of the Man, and beauty would have been the result; as we see, in pictures of Arcadia, the nymph singing to the shepherds, or the shepherd, with his pipe, alluring the nymphs; either makes a good picture. The sounding lyre requires not muscular strength, but energy of soul to animate the hand which would control it. Nature seems to delight in varying the arrangements, as if to show that she will be fettered by no rule; and we must admit the same varieties that she admits.

The fourth and highest grade of marriage union is the religious, which may be expressed as pilgrimage toward a common shrine. This includes the others: home sympathies and household wisdom, for these pilgrims must know how to assist each other along the dusty way; intellectual communion, for how sad it would be on such a journey to have a companion to whom you could not communicate your thoughts and aspirations as they sprang to life; who would have no feeling for the prospects that open, more and more glorious as we advance; who would never see the flowers that may be gathered by the most industrious traveller! It must include all these.

Such a fellow-pilgrim Count Zinzendorf[49] seems to have found in his countess, of whom he thus writes:

"Twenty-five years' experience has shown me that just the help-meet whom I have is the only one that could suit my vocation. Who else could have so carried through my family affairs? Who lived so spotlessly before the world? Who so wisely aided me in my rejection of a dry morality? Who so clearly set aside the Pharisaism which, as years passed, threatened to creep in among us? Who so deeply discerned as to the spirits of delusion which sought to bewilder us? Who would have governed my whole economy so wisely, richly and hospitably, when circumstances commanded? Who have taken indifferently the part of servant or mistress, without, on the one side, affecting an especial spirituality; on the other, being sullied by any worldly pride? Who, in a community where all ranks are eager to be on a level, would, from wise and real causes, have known how to maintain inward and outward distinctions? Who, without a murmur, have seen her husband encounter such dangers by land and sea? Who undertaken with him, and *sustained,* such astonishing pilgrimages? Who, amid such difficulties, would have always held up her head and supported me? Who found such vast sums of money, and acquitted them on her own credit? And, finally, who, of all human beings, could so well understand and interpret to others my inner and outer being as this one, of such nobleness in her way of thinking, such great intellectual capacity, and so free from the theological perplexities that enveloped me!"

Let any one peruse, with all intentness, the lineaments of this portrait, and see if the husband had not reason, with this air of solemn rapture and conviction, to challenge comparison? We are reminded of the majestic cadence of the line whose feet step in the just proportion of Humanity,

"Daughter of God and Man, accomplished Eve!"[50]

An observer* adds this testimony:

"We may, in many marriages, regard it as the best arrangement, if the man has so much advantage over his wife, that she can, without much thought of her own, be led and directed by him as by a father. But it was not so with the count and his consort. She was not made to be a copy; she was an original; and, while she loved and honored him, she thought for herself, on all subjects, with so much intelligence, that he could and did look on her as a sister and friend also."

Compare with this refined specimen of a religiously civilized life the following imperfect sketch of a North American Indian, and we shall see that the same causes will always produce the same results. The Flying Pigeon (Ratchewaine)[51] was the wife of a barbarous chief, who had six others; but she was his only true wife, because the only one of a strong and pure character, and, having this, inspired a veneration, as like as the mind of the man permitted to that inspired by the Countess Zinzendorf. She died when her son was only four years old, yet left on his mind a feeling of reverent love worthy the thought of Christian chivalry. Grown to manhood, he shed tears on seeing her portrait.

The flying pigeon.

"Ratchewaine was chaste, mild, gentle in her disposition, kind, generous, and devoted to her husband. A harsh word was never known to proceed from her mouth; nor was she ever known to be in a passion. Mahaskah used to say of her, after her death, that her hand was shut when those who did not want came into her presence; but when the really poor came in, it was like a strainer full of holes, letting all she held in it pass through. In the exercise of generous feeling she was uniform. It was not

*Spangenberg.

indebted for its exercise to whim, nor caprice, nor partiality. No matter of what nation the applicant for her bounty was, or whether at war or peace with her nation; if he were hungry, she fed him; if naked, she clothed him; and, if houseless, she gave him shelter. The continued exercise of this generous feeling kept her poor. And she has been known to give away her last blanket—all the honey that was in the lodge, the last bladder of bear's oil, and the last piece of dried meat.

"She was scrupulously exact in the observance of all the religious rites which her faith imposed upon her. Her conscience is represented to have been extremely tender. She often feared that her acts were displeasing to the Great Spirit, when she would blacken her face, and retire to some lone place, and fast and pray."

To these traits should be added, but for want of room, anecdotes which show the quick decision and vivacity of her mind. Her face was in harmony with this combination. Her brow is as ideal and the eyes and lids as devout and modest as the Italian picture of the Madonna, while the lower part of the face has the simplicity and childish strength of the Indian race. Her picture presents the finest specimen of Indian beauty we have ever seen. Such a Woman is the sister and friend of all beings, as the worthy Man is their brother and helper.

With like pleasure we survey the pairs wedded on the eve of mission-ary effort. They, indeed, are fellow-pilgrims on the well-made road, and whether or no they accomplish all they hope for the sad Hindoo, or the nearer savage, we feel that in the burning waste their love is like to be a healing dew, in the forlorn jungle a tent of solace to one another. They meet, as children of one Father, to read together one book of instruction.

We must insert in this connection the most beautiful picture presented by ancient literature of wedded love under this noble form.

It is from the romance in which Xenophon, the chivalrous Greek, pre-sents his ideal of what human nature should be.

The generals of Cyrus[52] had taken captive a princess, a woman of un-equalled beauty, and hastened to present her to the prince as that part of the spoil he would think most worthy of his acceptance. Cyrus visits the lady, and is filled with immediate admiration by the modesty and majesty with which she receives him. He finds her name is Panthea, and that she is the wife of Abradatus, a young king whom she entirely loves. He protects her as a sister, in his camp, till he can restore her to her husband.

After the first transports of joy at this reunion, the heart of Panthea is bent on showing her love and gratitude to her magnanimous and delicate protector. And as she has nothing so precious to give as the aid of Abrada-tus, that is what she most wishes to offer. Her husband is of one soul with her in this, as in all things.

The description of her grief and self-destruction, after the death which ensued upon this devotion, I have seen quoted, but never that of their parting when she sends him forth to battle. I shall copy both. If they have been read by any of my readers, they may be so again with profit in this connection, for never were the heroism of a true Woman, and the purity of love in a true marriage, painted in colors more delicate and more lively.

"The chariot of Abradatus, that had four perches and eight horses, was completely adorned for him; and when he was going to put on his linen corslet, which was a sort of armor used by those of his country, Panthea brought him a golden helmet, and arm-pieces, broad bracelets for his wrists, a purple habit that reached down to his feet, and hung in folds at the bottom, and a crest dyed of a violet color. These things she had made, unknown to her husband, and by taking the measure of his armor. He wondered when he saw them, and inquired thus of Panthea: 'And have you made me these arms, woman, by destroying your own ornaments?' 'No, by Jove!' said Panthea, 'not what is the most valuable of them; for it is you, if you appear to others to be what I think you, that will be my greatest ornament.' And, saying that, she put on him the armor, and, though she endeavored to conceal it, the tears poured down her cheeks. When Abradatus, who was before a man of fine appearance, was set out in those arms, he appeared the most beautiful and noble of all, especially being likewise so by nature. Then, taking the reins from the driver, he was just preparing to mount the chariot, when Panthea, after she had desired all that were there to retire, thus said:

"'O Abradatus! if ever there was a woman who had a greater regard to her husband than to her own soul, I believe you know that I am such an one; what need I therefore speak of things in particular? for I reckon that my actions have convinced you more than any words I can now use. And yet, though I stand thus affected toward you, as you know I do, I swear, by this friendship of mine and yours, that I certainly would rather choose to be put under ground jointly with you, approving yourself a brave man, than to live with you in disgrace and shame; so much do I think you and myself worthy of the noblest things. Then I think that we both lie under great obligations to Cyrus, that, when I was a captive, and chosen out for himself, he thought fit to treat me neither as a slave, nor, indeed, as a woman of mean account, but he took and kept me for you, as if I were his brother's wife. Besides, when Araspes, who was my guard, went away from him, I promised him, that, if he would allow me to send for you, you would come to him, and approve yourself a much better and more faithful friend than Araspes.'

"Thus she spoke; and Abradatus, being struck with admiration at her discourse, laying his hand gently on her head, and lifting up his eyes to heaven, made this prayer: 'Do thou, O greatest Jove! grant me to appear a husband worthy of Panthea, and a friend worthy of Cyrus, who has done us so much honor!'

"Having said this, he mounted the chariot by the door of the driver's seat; and, after he had got up, when the driver shut the door, Panthea, who had now no other way to salute him, kissed the seat of the chariot. The chariot then moved, and she, unknown to him, followed, till Abradatus turning about, and seeing her, said: 'Take courage, Panthea! Fare you happily and well, and now go your ways.' On this her women and servants carried her to her conveyance, and, laying her down, concealed her by throwing the covering of a tent over her. The people, though Abradatus and his chariot made a noble spectacle, were not able to look at him till Panthea was gone."

After the battle—

"Cyrus calling to some of his servants, 'Tell me,' said he, 'has any one seen Abradatus? for I admire that he now does not appear.' One replied, 'My sovereign, it is because he is not living, but died in the battle as he broke in with his chariot on the Egyptians. All the rest, except his particular companions, they say, turned off when they saw the Egyptians' compact body. His wife is now said to have taken up his dead body, to have placed it in the carriage that she herself was conveyed in, and to have brought it hither to some place on the river Pactolus, and her servants are digging a grave on a certain elevation. They say that his wife, after setting him out with all the ornaments she has, is sitting on the ground with his head on her knees.' Cyrus, hearing this, gave himself a blow on the thigh, mounted his horse at a leap, and, taking with him a thousand horse, rode away to this scene of affliction; but gave orders to Gadatas and Gobryas to take with them all the rich ornaments proper for a friend and an excellent man deceased, and to follow after him; and whoever had herds of cattle with him, he ordered them to take both oxen, and horses, and sheep in good number, and to bring them away to the place where, by inquiry, they should find him to be, that he might sacrifice these to Abradatus.

"As soon as he saw the woman sitting on the ground, and the dead body there lying, he shed tears at the afflicting sight, and said: 'Alas! thou brave and faithful soul, hast thou left us, and art thou gone?' At the same time he took him by the right hand, and the hand of the deceased came away, for it had been cut off with a sword by the Egyptians. He, at the sight of this, became yet much more concerned than before. The woman shrieked out in a lamentable manner, and, taking the hand from Cyrus, kissed it, fitted it to its proper place again, as well as she could, and said: 'The rest, Cyrus, is in the same condition, but what need you see it? And I know that I was not one of the least concerned in these his sufferings, and, perhaps, you were not less so; for I, fool that I was! frequently exhorted him to behave in such a manner as to appear a friend to you, worthy of notice; and I know he never thought of what he himself should suffer, but of what he should do to please you. He is dead, therefore,' said she, 'without reproach, and I, who urged him on, sit here alive.' Cyrus, shedding tears for some time in silence, then spoke:—'He has died, woman, the noblest death; for he has died victorious! Do you adorn him with these things that I furnish you with.' (Gobryas and Gadatas were then come up, and had brought rich ornaments in great abundance with them.) 'Then,' said he, 'be assured that he shall not want respect and honor in all other things; but, over and above, multitudes shall concur in raising him a monument that shall be worthy of us, and all the sacrifices shall be made him that are proper to be made in honor of a brave man. You shall not be left destitute, but, for the sake of your modesty and every other virtue, I will pay you all other honors, as well as place those about you who will conduct you wherever you please. Do you but make it known to me where it is that you desire to be conveyed to.' And Panthea replied: 'Be confident, Cyrus, I will not conceal from you to whom it is that I desire to go.'

"He, having said this, went away with great pity for her that she should have lost such a husband, and for the man that he should have left such a wife behind him, never to see her more. Panthea then gave orders for her servants to retire, 'till such time,' said she, 'as I shall have lamented my husband as I please.' Her nurse she bid to stay, and gave orders that, when she was dead, she would wrap her and her husband up in one mantle together. The nurse, after having repeatedly begged her not to do this, and meeting with no success, but observing her to grow angry, sat herself down, breaking out into tears. She, being beforehand provided with a sword, killed herself, and, laying her head down on her husband's breast, she died. The nurse set up a lamentable cry, and covered them both, as Panthea had directed.

"Cyrus, as soon as he was informed of what the woman had done, being struck with it, went to help her if he could. The servants, three in number, seeing what had been done, drew their swords and killed themselves, as they stood at the place where she had ordered them. And the monument is now said to have been raised by continuing the mound on to the servants; and on a pillar above, they say, the names of the man and woman were written in Syriac letters.

"Below were three pillars, and they were inscribed thus, 'Of the servants.' Cyrus, when he came to this melancholy scene, was struck with admiration of the woman, and, having lamented over her, went away. He took care, as was proper, that all the funeral rites should be paid them in the noblest manner, and the monument, they say, was raised up to a very great size."

These be the ancients, who, so many assert, had no idea of the dignity of Woman, or of marriage. Such love Xenophon could paint as subsisting between those who after death "would see one another never more." Thousands of years have passed since, and with the reception of the Cross, the nations assume the belief that those who part thus may meet again and forever, if spiritually fitted to one another, as Abradatus and Panthea were, and yet do we see such marriages among them? If at all, how often?

I must quote two more short passages from Xenophon, for he is a writer who pleases me well.

Cyrus, receiving the Armenians whom he had conquered—

"'Tigranes,' said he, 'at what rate would you purchase the regaining of your wife?' Now Tigranes happened to be *but lately married,* and had a very great love for his wife." (That clause perhaps sounds *modern.*)

"'Cyrus,' said he, 'I would ransom her at the expense of my life.'

"'Take then your own to yourself,' said he. * * *

"When they came home, one talked of Cyrus' wisdom, another of his patience and resolution, another of his mildness. One spoke of his beauty and smallness of his person, and, on that, Tigranes asked his wife, 'And do you, Armenian dame, think Cyrus handsome?' 'Truly,' said she, 'I did not look at him.' 'At whom, then, *did* you look?' said Tigranes. 'At him who said that, to save me from servitude, he would ransom me at the expense of his own life.'"

From the Banquet.—

"Socrates, who observed her with pleasure, said, 'This young girl has confirmed me in the opinion I have had, for a long time, that the female sex are nothing inferior to ours, excepting only in strength of body, or, perhaps, in steadiness of judgment.'"

In the Economics[53], the manner in which the husband gives counsel to his young wife presents the model of politeness and refinement. Xenophon is thoroughly the gentleman; gentle in breeding and in soul. All the men he describes are so, while the shades of manner are distinctly marked. There is the serene dignity of Socrates, with gleams of playfulness thrown across its cool, religious shades, the princely mildness of Cyrus, and the more domestic elegance of the husband in the Economics.

There is no way that men sin more against refinement, as well as discretion, than in their conduct toward their wives. Let them look at the men of Xenophon. Such would know how to give counsel, for they would know how to receive it. They would feel that the most intimate relations claimed most, not least, of refined courtesy. They would not suppose that confi-

"Below were three pillars..."

dence justified carelessness, nor the reality of affection want of delicacy in the expression of it.

Such men would be too wise to hide their affairs from the wife, and then expect her to act as if she knew them. They would know that, if she is expected to face calamity with courage, she must be instructed and trusted in prosperity, or, if they had failed in wise confidence, such as the husband shows in the Economics, they would be ashamed of anger or querulous surprise at the results that naturally follow.

Such men would not be exposed to the bad influence of bad wives; for all wives, bad or good, loved or unloved, inevitably influence their husbands, from the power their position not merely gives, but necessitates, of coloring evidence and infusing feelings in hours when the—patient, shall I call him?—is off his guard. Those who understand the wife's mind, and think it worth while to respect her springs of action, know better where they are. But to the bad or thoughtless man, who lives carelessly and irreverently so near another mind, the wrong he does daily back upon himself recoils. A Cyrus, an Abradatus, knows where he stands.

But to return to the thread of my subject.

Another sign of the times is furnished by the triumphs of Female Authorship. These have been great, and are constantly increasing. Women have taken possession of so many provinces for which men had pronounced them unfit, that, though these still declare there are some inaccessible to them, it is difficult to say just *where* they must stop.

The shining names of famous women have cast light upon the path of the sex, and many obstructions have been removed. When a Montague[54] could learn better than her brother, and use her lore afterwards to such purpose as an observer, it seemed amiss to hinder women from preparing themselves to see, or from seeing all they could, when prepared. Since Somerville has achieved so much, will any young girl be prevented from seeking a knowledge of the physical sciences, if she wishes it? De Stael's name was not so clear of offence; she could not forget the Woman in the thought; while she was instructing you as a mind, she wished to be admired as a Woman; sentimental tears often dimmed the eagle glance. Her intellect, too, with all its splendor, trained in a drawing-room, fed on flattery, was tainted and flawed; yet its beams make the obscurest school-house in New England warmer and lighter to the little rugged girls who are gathered together on its wooden bench. They may never through life hear her name, but she is not the less their benefactress.

The influence has been such, that the aim certainly is, now, in arranging school instruction for girls, to give them as fair a field as boys. As yet, indeed, these arrangements are made with little judgment or reflection; just as the tutors of Lady Jane Grey[55], and other distinguished women of her time, taught them Latin and Greek, because they knew nothing else themselves, so now the improvement in the education of girls is to be made by giving them young men as teachers, who only teach what has been taught themselves at college, while methods and topics need revision for these new subjects, which could better be made by those who had experienced the same wants. Women are, often, at the head of these institutions; but they have, as yet, seldom been thinking women, capable of organizing a new whole for the wants of the time, and choosing persons to officiate in the departments. And when some portion of instruction of a good sort is got from the school, the far greater proportion which is infused from the general atmosphere of society contradicts its purport. Yet books and a little elementary instruction are not furnished in vain. Women are better aware how great and rich the universe is, not so easily blinded by narrowness or partial views of a home circle. "Her mother did so before her" is no longer a sufficient excuse. Indeed, it was never received as an excuse to mitigate the severity of censure, but was adduced as a reason, rather, why there should be no effort made for reformation.

Whether much or little has been done, or will be done,—whether women will add to the talent of narration the power of systematizing,—whether they will carve marble, as well as draw and paint,—is not important. But that it should be acknowledged that they have intellect which needs developing—that they should not be considered complete, if beings of affection and habit alone—is important.

Yet even this acknowledgment, rather conquered by Woman than proffered by Man, has been sullied by the usual selfishness. Too much is said of women being better educated, that they may become better companions and mothers *for men*. They should be fit for such companionship, and we have mentioned, with satisfaction, instances where it has been established. Earth knows no fairer, holier relation than that of a mother. It is one which, rightly understood, must both promote and require the highest attainments. But a being of infinite scope must not be treated with an exclusive view to any one relation. Give the soul free course, let the organization, both of body and mind, be freely developed, and the being will be fit for any and every relation to which it may be called. The intellect, no more than the sense of hearing, is to be cultivated merely that Woman may be a more valuable companion to Man, but because the Power who gave a power, by its mere existence signifies that it must be brought out toward perfection.

In this regard of self-dependence, and a greater simplicity and fulness of being, we must hail as a preliminary the increase of the class contemptuously designated as "old maids."

We cannot wonder at the aversion with which old bachelors and old maids have been regarded. Marriage is the natural means of forming a sphere, of taking root in the earth; it requires more strength to do this without such an opening; very many have failed, and their imperfections have been in every one's way. They have been more partial, more harsh, more officious and impertinent, than those compelled by severer friction to render themselves endurable. Those who have a more full experience of the instincts have a distrust as to whether the unmarried can be thoroughly human and humane, such as is hinted in the saying, "Old maids' and bachelors' children are well cared for," which derides at once their ignorance and their presumption.

Yet the business of society has become so complex, that it could now scarcely be carried on without the presence of these despised auxiliaries; and detachments from the army of aunts and uncles are wanted to stop gaps in every hedge. They rove about, mental and moral Ishmaelites, pitching their tents amid the fixed and ornamented homes of men.

In a striking variety of forms, genius of late, both at home and abroad, has paid its tribute to the character of the Aunt and the Uncle, recognizing in these personages the spiritual parents, who have supplied defects in the treatment of the busy or careless actual parents.

They also gain a wider, if not so deep experience. Those who are not intimately and permanently linked with others, are thrown upon themselves; and, if they do not there find peace and incessant life, there is none to flatter them that they are not very poor, and very mean.

A position which so constantly admonishes, may be of inestimable benefit. The person may gain, undistracted by other relationships, a closer communion with the one. Such a use is made of it by saints and sibyls. Or she may be one of the lay sisters of charity, a canoness, bound by an inward vow,—or the useful drudge of all men, the Martha, much sought, little prized,—or the intellectual interpreter of the varied life she sees; the Urania of a half-formed world's twilight.

Or she may combine all these. Not "needing to care that she may please a husband," a frail and limited being, her thoughts may turn to the centre, and she may, by steadfast contemplation entering into the secret of truth and love, use it for the good of all men, instead of a chosen few, and interpret through it all the forms of life. It is possible, perhaps, to be at once a priestly servant and a loving muse.

Saints and geniuses have often chosen a lonely position, in the faith that if, undisturbed by the pressure of near ties, they would give themselves up to the inspiring spirit, it would enable them to understand and reproduce life better than actual experience could.

How many "old maids" take this high stand we cannot say: it is an unhappy fact that too many who have come before the eye are gossips rather, and not always good-natured gossips. But if these abuse, and none make the best of their vocation, yet it has not failed to produce some good results. It has been seen by others, if not by themselves, that beings, likely to be left alone, need to be fortified and furnished within themselves; and education and thought have tended more and more to regard these beings as related to absolute Being, as well as to others. It has been seen that, as the breaking of no bond ought to destroy a man, so ought the missing of none to hinder him from growing. And thus a circumstance of the time, which springs rather from its luxury than its purity, has helped to place women on the true platform.

Perhaps the next generation, looking deeper into this matter, will find that contempt is put upon old maids, or old women, at all, merely because they do not use the elixir which would keep them always young. Under its influence, a gem brightens yearly which is only seen to more advantage through the fissures Time makes in the casket. No one thinks of Michael

Angelo's Persican Sibyl, or St. Theresa, or Tasso's Leonora, or the Greek Electra, as an old maid, more than of Michael Angelo or Canova as old bachelors, though all had reached the period in life's course appointed to take that degree.[56]

See a common woman at forty; scarcely has she the remains of beauty, of any soft poetic grace which gave her attraction as Woman, which kindled the hearts of those who looked on her to sparkling thoughts, or diffused round her a roseate air of gentle love. See her, who was, indeed, a lovely girl, in the coarse, full-blown dahlia flower of what is commonly matron-beauty, "fat, fair, and forty," showily dressed, and with manners as broad and full as her frill or satin cloak. People observe, "How well she is preserved!" "She is a fine woman still," they say. This woman, whether as a duchess in diamonds, or one of our city dames in mosaics, charms the poet's heart no more, and would look much out of place kneeling before the Madonna. She "does well the honors of her house,"—"leads society,"—is, in short, always spoken and thought of upholstery-wise.

Or see that care-worn face, from which every soft line is blotted,—those faded eyes, from which lonely tears have driven the flashes of fancy, the mild white beam of a tender enthusiasm. This woman is not so ornamental to a tea-party; yet she would please better, in picture. Yet surely she, no more than the other, looks as a human being should at the end of forty years. Forty years! have they bound those brows with no garland? shed in the lamp no drop of ambrosial oil?

Not so looked the Iphigenia in Aulis.[57] Her forty years had seen her in anguish, in sacrifice, in utter loneliness. But those pains were borne for her father and her country; the sacrifice she had made pure for herself and those around her. Wandering alone at night in the vestal solitude of her imprisoning grove, she has looked up through its "living summits" to the stars, which shed down into her aspect their own lofty melody. At forty she would not misbecome the marble.

Not so looks the Persica. She is withered; she is faded; the drapery that enfolds her has in its dignity an angularity, too, that tells of age, of sorrow, of a stern resignation to the *must*. But her eye, that torch of the soul, is untamed, and, in the intensity of her reading, we see a soul invincibly young in faith and hope. Her age is her charm, for it is the night of the past that gives this beacon-fire leave to shine. Wither more and more, black Chrysalid! thou dost but give the winged beauty time to mature its splendors!

Not so looked Victoria Colonna, after her life of a great hope, and of true conjugal fidelity.[58] She had been, not merely a bride, but a wife, and each hour had helped to plume the noble bird. A coronet of pearls will not shame her brow; it is white and ample, a worthy altar for love and thought.

Even among the North American Indians, a race of men as completely engaged in mere instinctive life as almost any in the world, and where each chief, keeping many wives as useful servants, of course looks with no kind eye on celibacy in Woman, it was excused in the following instance mentioned by Mrs. Jameson.[59] A woman dreamt in youth that she was betrothed to the Sun. She built her a wigwam apart, filled it with emblems of her alliance, and means of an independent life. There she passed her days, sustained by her own exertions, and true to her supposed engagement.

In any tribe, we believe, a woman, who lived as if she was betrothed to the Sun, would be tolerated, and the rays which made her youth blossom sweetly, would crown her with a halo in age.

There is, on this subject, a nobler view than heretofore, if not the noblest, and improvement here must coincide with that in the view taken of marriage. "We must have units before we can have union," says one of the ripe thinkers of the times.

If larger intellectual resources begin to be deemed needful to Woman, still more is a spiritual dignity in her, or even the mere assumption of it, looked upon with respect. Joanna Southcote and Mother Anne Lee are sure of a band of disciples; Ecstatica, Dolorosa, of enraptured believers who will visit them in their lowly huts, and wait for days to revere them in their trances.[60] The foreign noble traverses land and sea to hear a few words from the lips of the lowly peasant girl, whom he believes especially visited by the Most High. Very beautiful, in this way, was the influence of the invalid of St. Petersburg, as described by De Maistre.[61]

Mysticism, which may be defined as the brooding soul of the world, cannot fail of its oracular promise as to Woman. "The mothers," "The mother of all things," are expressions of thought which lead the mind towards this side of universal growth. Whenever a mystical whisper was heard, from Behmen down to St. Simon[62], sprang up the thought, that, if it be true, as the legend says, that Humanity withers through a fault committed by and a curse laid upon Woman, through her pure child, or influence, shall the new Adam, the redemption, arise. Innocence is to be replaced by virtue, dependence by a willing submission, in the heart of the Virgin-Mother of the new race.

The spiritual tendency is toward the elevation of Woman, but the intellectual by itself is not so. Plato sometimes seems penetrated by that high idea of love, which considers Man and Woman as the two-fold expression of one thought. This the angel of Swedenborg, the angel of the coming age, cannot surpass, but only explain more fully.[63] But then again Plato, the man of intellect, treats Woman in the Republic as property, and, in the Timæus, says that Man, if he misuse the privileges of one life, shall be degraded into the form of Woman; and then, if he do not redeem himself, into that of a bird. This, as I said above, expresses most happily how antipoetical is this state of mind. For the poet, contemplating the world of things, selects various birds as the symbols of his most gracious and ethereal thoughts, just as he calls upon his genius as muse rather than as God. But the intellect, cold, is ever more masculine than feminine; warmed by emotion, it rushes toward mother-earth, and puts on the forms of beauty.

The electrical, the magnetic element in Woman has not been fairly brought out at any period. Everything might be expected from it; she has far more of it than Man. This is commonly expressed by saying that her intuitions are more rapid and more correct. You will often see men of high intellect absolutely stupid in regard to the atmospheric changes, the fine invisible links which connect the forms of life around them, while common women, if pure and modest, so that a vulgar self do not overshadow the mental eye, will seize and delineate these with unerring discrimination.

Women who combine this organization with creative genius are very commonly unhappy at present. They see too much to act in conformity with those around them, and their quick impulses seem folly to those who do not discern the motives. This is an usual effect of the apparition of genius, whether in Man or Woman, but is more frequent with regard to the latter, because a harmony, an obvious order and self-restraining decorum, is most expected from her.

Then women of genius, even more than men, are likely to be enslaved by an impassioned sensibility. The world repels them more rudely, and they are of weaker bodily frame.

Those who seem overladen with electricity frighten those around them. "When she merely enters the room, I am what the French call *herissé*," said a man of petty feelings and worldly character of such a woman, whose depth of eye and powerful motion announced the conductor of the mysterious fluid.

Woe to such a woman who finds herself linked to such a man in bonds too close! It is the cruelest of errors. He will detest her with all the bitterness of wounded self-love. He will take the whole prejudice of manhood upon himself, and, to the utmost of his power, imprison and torture her by its imperious rigors.

Yet, allow room enough, and the electric fluid will be found to invigorate and embellish, not destroy life. Such women are the great actresses, the songsters. Such traits we read in a late searching, though too French, analysis of the character of Mademoiselle Rachel[64], by a modern La Rochefoucault.[65] The Greeks thus represent the muses; they have not the golden serenity of Apollo; they are *over*flowed with thought; there is something tragic in their air. Such are the Sibyls of Guercino[66]; the eye is overfull of expression, dilated and lustrous; it seems to have drawn the whole being into it.

Sickness is the frequent result of this overcharged existence. To this region, however misunderstood, or interpreted with presumptuous carelessness, belong the phenomena of magnetism, or mesmerism, as it is now often called, where the trance of the Ecstatica purports to be produced by the agency of one human being on another, instead of, as in her case, direct from the spirit.

The worldling has his sneer at this as at the services of religion. "The churches can always be filled with women"—"Show me a man in one of your magnetic states, and I will believe."

Women are, indeed, the easy victims both of priest-craft and self-delusion; but this would not be, if the intellect was developed in proportion to the other powers. They would then have a regulator, and be more in equipoise, yet must retain the same nervous susceptibility while their physical structure is such as it is.

It is with just that hope that we welcome everything that tends to
strengthen the fibre and develop the nature on more sides. When the
intellect and affections are in harmony; when intellectual consciousness is calm and deep; inspiration will not be confounded with
fancy.

> Then, "she who advances
>   With rapturous, lyrical glances,
> Singing the song of the earth, singing
>   Its hymn to the Gods,"

will not be pitied as a mad-woman, nor shrunk from as unnatural.

The Greeks, who saw everything in forms, which we are trying to
ascertain as law, and classify as cause, embodied all this in the form of
Cassandra. Cassandra was only unfortunate in receiving her gift too soon.
The remarks, however, that the world still makes in such cases, are well
expressed by the Greek dramatist.

In the Trojan dames there are fine touches of nature with regard to
Cassandra. Hecuba shows that mixture of shame and reverence that prosaic
kindred always do toward the inspired child, the poet, the elected sufferer
for the race.

When the herald announces that Cassandra is chosen to be the mistress
of Agamemnon, Hecuba answers, with indignation, betraying the pride and
faith she involuntarily felt in this daughter.

"Cassandra appears, singing, wildly, her inspired song..."

"*Hec.* The maiden of Phoebus, to whom the golden-haired
    Gave as a privilege a virgin life!
Tal. Love of the inspired maiden hath pierced him.
Hec. Then cast away, my child, the sacred keys, and from thy person
    The consecrated garlands which thou wearest."[67]

Yet, when, a moment after, Cassandra appears, singing, wildly, her inspired song, Hecuba calls her, "My *frantic* child."

Yet how graceful she is in her tragic *raptus,* the chorus shows.

"*Chorus.* How sweetly at thy house's ills thou smil'st,
    Chanting what, haply, thou wilt not show true."[68]

If Hecuba dares not trust her highest instinct about her daughter, still less can the vulgar mind of the herald Talthybius, a man not without feeling, but with no princely, no poetic blood, abide the wild, prophetic mood which insults all his prejudices.

"*Tal.* The venerable, and that accounted wise,
    Is nothing better than that of no repute;
    For the greatest king of all the Greeks,
    The dear son of Atreus, is possessed with the love
    Of this mad-woman. I, indeed, am poor;
    Yet I would not receive her to my bed."[69]

The royal Agamemnon could see the beauty of Cassandra; *he* was not afraid of her prophetic gifts.

The best topic for a chapter on this subject, in the present day, would be the history of the Seeress of Prevorst[70], the best observed subject of magnetism in our present times, and who, like her ancestresses of Delphos[71], was roused to ecstasy or phrensy by the touch of the laurel.

I observe in her case, and in one known to me here, that what might have been a gradual and gentle disclosure of remarkable powers was broken and jarred into disease by an unsuitable marriage. Both these persons were unfortunate in not understanding what was involved in this relation, but acted ignorantly, as their friends desired. They thought that this was the inevitable destiny of Woman. But when engaged in the false position, it was impossible for them to endure its dissonances, as those of less delicate perceptions can; and the fine flow of life was checked and sullied. They grew sick; but, even so, learned and disclosed more than those in health are wont to do.

In such cases, worldlings sneer; but reverent men learn wondrous news, either from the person observed, or by thoughts caused in themselves by the observation. Fenelon learns from Guyon, Kerner from his Seeress, what we fain would know.[72] But to appreciate such disclosures one must be a child; and here the phrase, "women and children," may, perhaps, be interpreted aright, that only little children shall enter into the kingdom of heaven.

All these motions of the time, tides that betoken a waxing moon, overflow upon our land. The world at large is readier to let Woman learn and manifest the capacities of her nature than it ever was before, and here is a less encumbered field and freer air than anywhere else. And it ought to be so; we ought to pay for Isabella's jewels.

The names of nations are feminine—Religion, Virtue and Victory are feminine. To those who have a superstition, as to outward reigns, it is not without significance that the name of the queen of our mother-land should at this crisis be Victoria,—Victoria the First. Perhaps to us it may be given to disclose the era thus outwardly presaged.

Another Isabella too at this time ascends the throne. Might she open a new world to her sex! But, probably, these poor little women are, least of any, educated to serve as examples or inspirers for the rest. The Spanish queen is younger; we know of her that she sprained her foot the other day, dancing in her private apartments; of Victoria, that she reads aloud, in a distinct voice and agreeable manner, her addresses to Parliament on certain solemn days, and, yearly, that she presents to the nation some new prop of royalty. These ladies have, very likely, been trained more completely to the puppet life than any other. The queens, who have been queens indeed, were trained by adverse circumstances to know the world around them and their own powers.

It is moving, while amusing, to read of the Scottish peasant measuring the print left by the queen's foot as she walks, and priding himself on its beauty. It is so natural to wish to find what is fair and precious in high places,—so astonishing to find the Bourbon a glutton, or the Guelph a dullard or gossip.

In our own country, women are, in many respects, better situated than men. Good books are allowed, with more time to read them. They are not so early forced into the bustle of life, nor so weighed down by demands for outward success. The perpetual changes, incident to our society, make the blood circulate freely through the body politic, and, if not favorable at present to the grace and bloom of life, they are so to activity, resource, and would be to reflection, but for a low materialist tendency, from which the women are generally exempt in themselves, though its existence, among the men, has a tendency to repress their impulses and make them doubt their instincts, thus often paralyzing their action during the best years.

But they have time to think, and no traditions chain them, and few conventionalities, compared with what must be met in other nations. There is no reason why they should not discover that the secrets of nature are open, the revelations of the spirit waiting, for whoever will seek them. When the mind is once awakened to this consciousness, it will not be restrained by the habits of the past, but fly to seek the seeds of a heavenly future.

Their employments are more favorable to meditation than those of men.

Woman is not addressed religiously here more than elsewhere. She is told that she should be worthy to be the mother of a Washington, or the companion of some good man. But in many, many instances, she has already learned that all bribes have the same flaw; that truth and good are to be sought solely for their own sakes. And, already, an ideal sweetness floats over many forms, shines in many eyes.

Already deep questions are put by young girls on the great theme: What shall I do to enter upon the eternal life?

Men are very courteous to them. They praise them often, check them seldom. There is chivalry in the feeling toward "the ladies," which gives them the best seats in the stage-coach, frequent admission, not only to lectures of all sorts, but to courts of justice, halls of legislature, reform conventions. The newspaper editor "would be better pleased that the Lady's Book should be filled up exclusively by ladies. It would then, indeed, be a true gem, worthy to be presented by young men to the mistress of their affections." Can gallantry go further?

In this country is venerated, wherever seen, the character which Goethe spoke of as an Ideal, which he saw actualized in his friend and patroness, the Grand Duchess Amelia: "The excellent woman is she, who, if the husband dies, can be a father to the children." And this, if read aright, tells a great deal.

Women who speak in public, if they have a moral power, such as has been felt from Angelina Grimke and Abby Kelly,—that is, if they speak for conscience' sake, to serve a cause which they hold sacred,—invariably subdue the prejudices of their hearers, and excite an interest proportionate to the aversion with which it had been the purpose to regard them.[73]

A passage in a private letter so happily illustrates this, that it must be inserted here.

Abby Kelly in the Town-House of———.

"The scene was not unheroic—to see that woman, true to humanity and her own nature, a centre of rude eyes and tongues, even gentlemen feeling licensed to make part of a species of mob around a female out of her sphere. As she took her seat in the desk amid the great noise, and in the throng, full, like a wave, of something to ensue, I saw her humanity in a gentleness and unpretension, tenderly open to the sphere around her, and, had she not been supported by the power of the will of genuineness and principle, she would have failed. It led her to prayer, which, in Woman especially, is childlike; sensibility and will going to the side of God and looking up to him; and humanity was poured out in aspiration.

"She acted like a gentle hero, with her mild decision and womanly calmness. All heroism is mild, and quiet, and gentle, for it is life and possession; and combativeness and firmness show a want of actualness. She is as earnest, fresh and simple, as when she first entered the crusade. I think she did much good, more than the men in her place could do, for Woman feels more as being and reproducing—this brings the subject more into home relations. Men speak through, and mostly from intellect, and this addresses itself to that in others which is combative."

Not easily shall we find elsewhere, or before this time, any written observations on the same subject, so delicate and profound.

The late Dr. Channing, whose enlarged and tender and religious nature shared every onward impulse of his time, though his thoughts followed his wishes with a deliberative caution which belonged to his habits and temperament, was greatly interested in these expectations for women.[74] His own treatment of them was absolutely and thoroughly religious. He regarded them as souls, each of which had a destiny of its own, incalculable to other minds, and whose leading it must follow, guided by the light of a private conscience. He had sentiment, delicacy, kindness, taste; but they were all pervaded and ruled by this one thought, that all beings had souls, and must vindicate their own inheritance. Thus all beings were treated by him with an equal, and sweet, though solemn, courtesy. The young and unknown, the woman and the child, all felt themselves regarded with an infinite expectation, from which there was no reaction to vulgar prejudice. He demanded of all he met, to use his favorite phrase, "great truths."

His memory, every way dear and reverend, is, by many, especially cherished for this intercourse of unbroken respect.

At one time, when the progress of Harriet Martineau[75] through this country, Angelina Grimke's appearance in public, and the visit of Mrs. Jameson, had turned his thoughts to this subject, he expressed high hopes as to what the coming era would bring to Woman. He had been much pleased with the dignified courage of Mrs. Jameson in taking up the defence of her sex in a way from which women usually shrink, because, if they express themselves on such subjects with sufficient force and clearness to do any good, they are exposed to assaults whose vulgarity makes them painful. In intercourse with such a woman, he had shared her indignation at the base injustice, in many respects, and in many regions, done to the sex; and been led to think of it far more than ever before. He seemed to think that he might some time write upon the subject. That his aid is withdrawn from the cause is a subject of great regret; for, on this question as on others, he would have known how to sum up the evidence, and take, in the noblest spirit, middle ground. He always furnished a platform on which opposing parties could stand and look at one another under the influence of his mildness and enlightened candor.

Two younger thinkers, men both, have uttered noble prophecies, auspicious for Woman. Kinmont, all whose thoughts tended towards the establishment of the reign of love and peace, thought that the inevitable means of this would be an increased predominance given to the idea of Woman. Had he lived longer, to see the growth of the Peace Party, the reforms in life and medical practice which seek to substitute water for wine and drugs, pulse for animal food, he would have been confirmed in his view of the way in which the desired changes are to be effected.

In this connection I must mention Shelley, who, like all men of genius, shared the feminine development, and, unlike many, knew it. His life was one of the first pulse-beats in the present reform-growth. He, too, abhorred blood and heat, and, by his system and his song, tended to reinstate a plant-like gentleness in the development of energy. In harmony with this, his ideas of marriage were lofty, and, of course, no less so of Woman, her nature, and destiny.

For Woman, if, by a sympathy as to outward condition, she is led to aid the enfranchisement of the slave, must be no less so, by inward tendency, to favor measures which promise to bring the world more thoroughly and deeply into harmony with her nature. When the lamb takes place of the lion as the emblem of nations, both women and men will be as children of one spirit, perpetual learners of the word and doers thereof, not hearers only.

A writer in the New York Pathfinder, in two articles headed "Femality," has uttered a still more pregnant word than any we have named. He views Woman truly from the soul, and not from society, and the depth and leading of his thoughts are proportionably remarkable. He views the feminine nature as a harmonizer of the vehement elements, and this has often been hinted elsewhere; but what he expresses most forcibly is the lyrical, the inspiring and inspired apprehensiveness of her being.

This view being identical with what I have before attempted to indicate, as to her superior susceptibility to magnetic or electric influence, I will now try to express myself more fully.

There are two aspects of Woman's nature, represented by the ancients as Muse and Minerva. It is the former to which the writer in the Pathfinder looks. It is the latter which Wordsworth has in mind, when he says,

"With a placid brow,
Which woman ne'er should forfeit, keep thy vow."

The especial genius of Woman I believe to be electrical in movement, intuitive in function, spiritual in tendency. She excels not so easily in classification, or recreation, as in an instinctive seizure of causes, and a simple breathing out of what she receives, that has the singleness of life, rather than the selecting and energizing of art.

More native is it to her to be the living model of the artist than to set apart from herself any one form in objective reality; more native to inspire and receive the poem, than to create it. In so far as soul is in her completely developed, all soul is the same; but in so far as it is modified in her as Woman, it flows, it breathes, it sings, rather than deposits soil, or finishes work; and that which is especially feminine flushes, in blossom, the face of earth, and pervades, like air and water, all this seeming solid globe, daily renewing and purifying its life. Such may be the especially feminine element spoken of as Femality. But it is no more the order of nature that it should be incarnated pure in any form, than that the masculine energy should exist unmingled with it in any form.

Male and female represent the two sides of the great radical dualism. But, in fact, they are perpetually passing into one another. Fluid hardens to solid, solid rushes to fluid. There is no wholly masculine man, no purely feminine woman.

History jeers at the attempts of physiologists to bind great original laws by the forms which flow from them. They make a rule; they say from observation what can and cannot be. In vain! Nature provides exceptions to every rule. She sends women to battle, and sets Hercules spinning; she enables women to bear immense burdens, cold, and frost; she enables the man, who feels maternal love, to nourish his infant like a mother. Of late she plays still gayer pranks. Not only she deprives organizations, but organs, of a necessary end. She enables people to read with the top of the head, and see with the pit of the stomach. Presently she will make a female Newton, and a male Syren.

Man partakes of the feminine in the Apollo, Woman of the masculine as Minerva.

What I mean by the Muse is that unimpeded clearness of the intuitive powers, which a perfectly truthful adherence to every admonition of the higher instincts would bring to a finely organized human being. It may appear as prophecy or as poesy. It enabled Cassandra to foresee the results of actions passing round her; the Seeress to behold the true character of the person through the mask of his customary life. (Sometimes she saw a feminine form behind the man, sometimes the reverse.) It enabled the daughter of Linnaeus[76] to see the soul of the flower exhaling from the flower.* It gave a man, but a poet-man, the power of which he thus speaks: "Often in my contemplation of nature, radiant intimations, and as it were sheaves of light, appear before me as to the facts of cosmogony, in which my mind has, perhaps, taken especial part." He wisely adds, "but it is

---

*The daughter of Linnaeus states, that, while looking steadfastly at the red lily, she saw its spirit hovering above it, as a red flame. It is true, this, like many fair spirit-stories, may be explained away as an optical illusion, but its poetic beauty and meaning would, even then, make it valuable, as an illustration of the spiritual fact.

necessary with earnestness to verify the knowledge we gain by these flashes of light." And none should forget this. Sight must be verified by light before it can deserve the honors of piety and genius. Yet sight comes first, and of this sight of the world of causes, this approximation to the region of primitive motions, women I hold to be especially capable. Even without equal freedom with the other sex, they have already shown themselves so; and should these faculties have free play, I believe they will open new, deeper and purer sources of joyous inspiration than have as yet refreshed the earth.

Let us be wise, and not impede the soul. Let her work as she will. Let us have one creative energy, one incessant revelation. Let it take what form it will, and let us not bind it by the past to man or woman, black or white. Jove sprang from Rhea, Pallas from Jove. So let it be.

If it has been the tendency of these remarks to call Woman rather to the Minerva side,—if I, unlike the more generous writer, have spoken from society no less than the soul,—let it be pardoned! It is love that has caused this,—love for many incarcerated souls, that might be freed, could the idea of religious self-dependence be established in them, could the weakening habit of dependence on others be broken up.

Proclus teaches that every life has, in its sphere, a totality or wholeness of the animating powers of the other spheres; having only, as its own characteristic, a predominance of some one power.[77] Thus Jupiter comprises, within himself, the other twelve powers, which stand thus: The first triad is *demiurgic or fabricative,* that is, Jupiter, Neptune, Vulcan; the second, *defensive,* Vesta, Minerva, Mars; the third, *vivific,* Ceres, Juno, Diana; and the fourth, Mercury, Venus, Apollo, *elevating and harmonic.* In the sphere of Jupiter, energy is predominant—with Venus, beauty; but each comprehends and apprehends all the others.

When the same community of life and consciousness of mind begin among men, humanity will have, positively and finally, subjugated its brute elements and Titanic childhood; criticism will have perished; arbitrary limits and ignorant censure be impossible; all will have entered upon the liberty of law, and the harmony of common growth.

The Apollo will sing to his lyre what Vulcan forges on the anvil, and the Muse weave anew the tapestries of Minerva.

It is, therefore, only in the present crisis that the preference is given to Minerva. The power of continence must establish the legitimacy of freedom, the power of self-poise the perfection of motion.

Every relation, every gradation of nature is incalculably precious, but only to the soul which is poised upon itself, and to whom no loss, no change, can bring dull discord, for it is in harmony with the central soul.

If any individual live too much in relations, so that he becomes a stranger to the resources of his own nature, he falls, after a while, into a distraction, or imbecility, from which he can only be cured by a time of isolation, which gives the renovating fountains time to rise up. With a society it is the same. Many minds, deprived of the traditionary or instinctive means of passing a cheerful existence, must find help in self-impulse, or perish. It is therefore that, while any elevation, in the view of union, is to be hailed with joy, we shall not decline celibacy as the great fact of the time. It is one from which no vow, no arrangement, can at present save a thinking mind. For now the rowers are pausing on their oars; they wait a change before they can pull together. All tends to illustrate the thought of a wise contemporary. Union is only possible to those who are units. To be fit for relations in time, souls, whether of Man or Woman, must be able to do without them in the spirit.

It is therefore that I would have Woman lay aside all thought, such as she habitually cherishes, of being taught and led by men. I would have her, like the Indian girl, dedicate herself to the Sun, the Sun of Truth, and go nowhere if his beams did not make clear the path. I would have her free from compromise, from complaisance, from helplessness, because I would have her good enough and strong enough to love one and all beings, from the fulness, not the poverty of being.

Men, as at present instructed, will not help this work, because they also are under the slavery of habit. I have seen with delight their poetic impulses. A sister is the fairest ideal, and how nobly Wordsworth, and even Byron, have written of a sister!

There is no sweeter sight than to see a father with his little daughter. Very vulgar men become refined to the eye when leading a little girl by the hand. At that moment, the right relation between the sexes seems established, and you feel as if the man would aid in the noblest purpose, if you ask him in behalf of his little daughter. Once, two fine figures stood before me, thus. The father of very intellectual aspect, his falcon eye softened by affection as he looked down on his fair child; she the image of himself, only more graceful and brilliant in expression. I was reminded of Southey's Kehama[78]; when, lo, the dream was rudely broken! They were talking of education, and he said,

"I shall not have Maria brought too forward. If she knows too much, she will never find a husband; superior women hardly ever can."

"Surely," said his wife, with a blush, "you wish Maria to be as good and wise as she can, whether it will help her to marriage or not."

"No," he persisted, "I want her to have a sphere and a home, and some one to protect her when I am gone."

It was a trifling incident, but made a deep impression. I felt that the holiest relations fail to instruct the unprepared and perverted mind. If this man, indeed, could have looked at it on the other side, he was the last that would have been willing to have been taken himself for the home and protection he could give, but would have been much more likely to repeat the tale of Alcibiades with his phials.

But men do *not* look at both sides, and women must leave off asking them and being influenced by them, but retire within themselves, and explore the ground-work of life till they find their peculiar secret. Then, when they come forth again, renovated and baptized, they will know how to turn all dross to gold, and will be rich and free though they live in a hut, tranquil if in a crowd. Then their sweet singing shall not be from passionate impulse, but the lyrical overflow of a divine rapture, and a new music shall be evolved from this many-chorded world.

Grant her, then, for a while, the armor and the javelin. Let her put from her the press of other minds, and meditate in virgin loneliness. The same idea shall reappear in due time as Muse, or Ceres, the all-kindly, patient Earth-Spirit.

Among the throng of symptoms which denote the present tendency to a crisis in the life of Woman,—which resembles the change from girlhood, with its beautiful instincts, but unharmonized thoughts, its blind pupilage and restless seeking, to self-possessed, wise and graceful womanhood,—I have attempted to select a few.

One of prominent interest is the unison upon the subject of three male minds, which, for width of culture, power of self-concentration and dignity of aim, take rank as the prophets of the coming age, while their histories and labors are rooted in the past.

Swedenborg came, he tells us, to interpret the past revelation and unfold a new. He announces the New Church that is to prepare the way for the New Jerusalem, a city built of precious stones, hardened and purified by secret processes in the veins of earth through the ages.

Swedenborg approximated to that harmony between the scientific and poetic lives of mind, which we hope from the perfected man. The links that bind together the realms of nature, the mysteries that accompany her births and growths, were unusually plain to him. He seems a man to whom insight was given at a period when the mental frame was sufficiently matured to retain and express its gifts.

His views of Woman are, in the main, satisfactory. In some details we may object to them, as, in all his system, there are still remains of what is arbitrary and seemingly groundless—fancies that show the marks of old habits, and a nature as yet not thoroughly leavened with the spiritual leaven. At least, so it seems to me now. I speak reverently, for I find such reason to venerate Swedenborg, from an imperfect knowledge of his mind, that I feel one more perfect might explain to me much that does not now secure my sympathy.

His idea of Woman is sufficiently large and noble to interpose no obstacle to her progress. His idea of marriage is consequently sufficient. Man and Woman share an angelic ministry; the union is of one with one, permanent and pure.

As the New Church extends its ranks, the needs of Woman must be more considered.

Quakerism also establishes Woman on a sufficient equality with Man. But, though the original thought of Quakerism is pure, its scope is too narrow, and its influence, having established a certain amount of good and made clear some truth, must, by degrees, be merged in one of wider range.*

---

*In worship at stated periods, in daily expression, whether by word or deed, the Quakers have placed Woman on the same platform with Man. Can any one assert that they have reason to repent this?

The mind of Swedenborg appeals to the various nature of Man, and allows room for aesthetic culture and the free expression of energy.

As apostle of the new order, of the social fabric that is to rise from love, and supersede the old that was based on strife, Charles Fourier comes next, expressing, in an outward order, many facts of which Swedenborg saw the secret springs. The mind of Fourier, though grand and clear, was, in some respects, superficial.[79] He was a stranger to the highest experiences. His eye was fixed on the outward more than the inward needs of Man. Yet he, too, was a seer of the divine order, in its musical expression, if not in its poetic soul. He has filled one department of instruction for the new era, and the harmony in action, and freedom for individual growth, he hopes, shall exist; and, if the methods he proposes should not prove the true ones, yet his fair propositions shall give many hints, and make room for the inspiration needed for such.

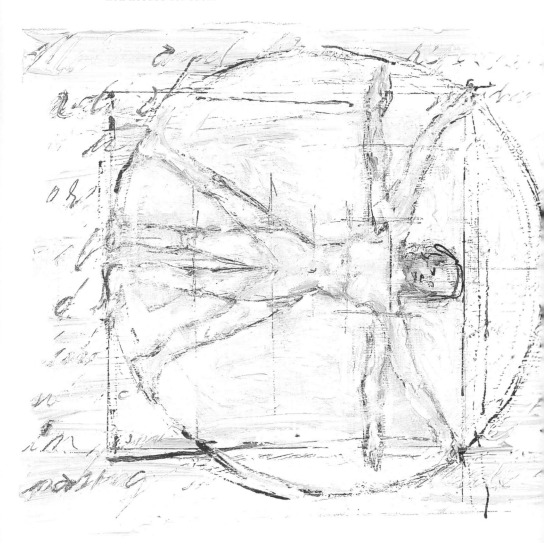

He, too, places Woman on an entire equality with Man, and wishes to give to one as to the other that independence which must result from intellectual and practical development.

Those who will consult him for no other reason, might do so to see how the energies of Woman may be made available in the pecuniary way. The object of Fourier was to give her the needed means of self-help, that she might dignify and unfold her life for her own happiness, and that of society. The many, now, who see their daughters liable to destitution, or vice to escape from it, may be interested to examine the means, if they have not yet soul enough to appreciate the ends he pro-poses.

On the opposite side of the advancing army leads the great apostle of individual culture, Goethe. Swedenborg makes organization and union the necessary results of solitary thought. Fourier, whose nature was, above all, constructive, looked to them too exclusively. Better institutions, he

"He, too, places Woman on an entire equality with Man…"

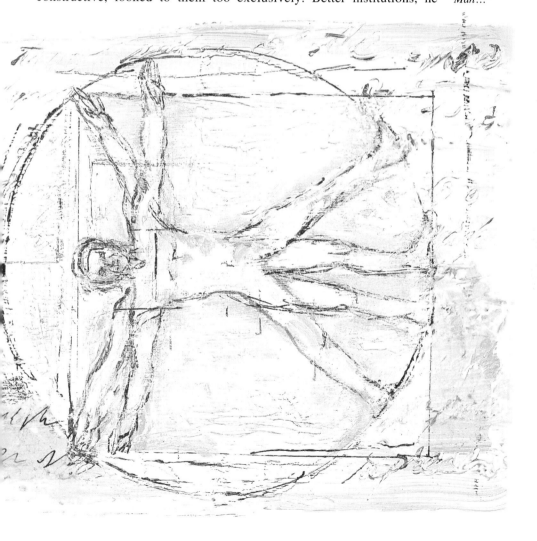

thought, will make better men. Goethe expressed, in every way, the other side. If one man could present better forms, the rest could not use them till ripe for them.

Fourier says, As the institutions, so the men! All follies are excusable and natural under bad institutions.

Goethe thinks, As the man, so the institutions! There is no excuse for ignorance and folly. A man can grow in any place, if he will.

Ay! but, Goethe, bad institutions are prison-walls and impure air, that make him stupid, so that he does not will.

And thou, Fourier, do not expect to change mankind at once, or even "in three generations," by arrangement of groups and series, or flourish of trumpets for attractive industry. If these attempts are made by unready men, they will fail.

Yet we prize the theory of Fourier no less than the profound suggestion of Goethe. Both are educating the age to a clearer consciousness of what Man needs, what Man can be; and better life must ensue.

Goethe, proceeding on his own track, elevating the human being, in the most imperfect states of society, by continual efforts at self-culture, takes as good care of women as of men. His mother, the bold, gay Frau Aja, with such playful freedom of nature; the wise and gentle maiden, known in his youth, over whose sickly solitude "the Holy Ghost brooded as a dove;" his sister, the intellectual woman *par excellence;* the Duchess Amelia; Lili, who combined the character of the woman of the world with the lyrical sweetness of the shepherdess, on whose chaste and noble breast flowers and gems were equally at home; all these had supplied abundant suggestions to his mind, as to the wants and the possible excellences of Woman. And from his poetic soul grew up forms new and more admirable than life has yet produced, for whom his clear eye marked out paths in the future.

In Faust Margaret represents the redeeming power, which, at present, upholds Woman, while waiting for a better day. The lovely little girl, pure in instinct, ignorant in mind, is misled and profaned by man abusing her confidence.* To the Mater *Dolorosa* she appeals for aid. It is given to the soul, if not against outward sorrow; and the maiden, enlightened by her sufferings, refusing to receive temporal salvation by the aid of an evil power, obtains the eternal in its stead.

In the second part, the intellectual man, after all his manifold strivings, owes to the interposition of her whom he had betrayed *his* salvation. She intercedes, this time, herself a glorified spirit, with the Mater *Gloriosa.*

Leonora, too, is Woman, as we see her now, pure, thoughtful, refined by much acquaintance with grief.

Iphigenia he speaks of in his journals as his "daughter," and she is the

---

*As Faust says, her only fault was a "kindly delusion,"—"ein guter wahn."

daughter* whom a man will wish, even if he has chosen his wife from very mean motives. She is the virgin, steadfast soul, to whom falsehood is more dreadful than any other death.

But it is to Wilhelm Meister's Apprenticeship and Wandering Years that I would especially refer, as these volumes contain the sum of the Sage's observations during a long life, as to what Man should do, under present circumstances, to obtain mastery over outward, through an initiation into inward life, and severe discipline of faculty.[80]

As Wilhelm advances into the upward path, he becomes acquainted with better forms of Woman, by knowing how to seek, and how to prize them when found. For the weak and immature man will, often, admire a superior woman, but he will not be able to abide by a feeling which is too severe a tax on his habitual existence. But, with Wilhelm, the gradation is natural, and expresses ascent in the scale of being. At first, he finds charm in Mariana and Philina, very common forms of feminine character, not without redeeming traits, no less than charms, but without wisdom or purity. Soon he is attended by Mignon, the finest expression ever yet given to what I have called the lyrical element in Woman. She is a child, but too full-grown for this man; he loves, but cannot follow her; yet is the association not without an enduring influence. Poesy has been domesticated in his life; and, though he strives to bind down her heavenward impulse, as art or apothegm, these are only the tents, beneath which he may sojourn for a while, but which may be easily struck, and carried on limitless wanderings.

Advancing into the region of thought, he encounters a wise philanthropy in Natalia (instructed, let us observe, by an *uncle*); practical judgment and the outward economy of life in Theresa; pure devotion in the Fair Saint.

Further, and last, he comes to the house of Macaria, the soul of a star; that is, a pure and perfected intelligence embodied in feminine form, and the centre of a world whose members revolve harmoniously around her. She instructs him in the archives of a rich human history, and introduces him to the contemplation of the heavens.

From the hours passed by the side of Mariana to these with Macaria, is a wide distance for human feet to traverse. Nor has Wilhelm travelled so far, seen and suffered so much, in vain. He now begins to study how he may aid the next generation; he sees objects in harmonious arrangement, and from his observations deduces precepts by which to guide his course as a teacher and a master, "help-full, comfort-full."

---

*Goethe was as false to his ideas, in practice, as Lord Herbert. And his punishment was the just and usual one of connections formed beneath the standard of right, from the impulses of the baser self. Iphigenia was the worthy daughter of his mind; but the son, child of his degrading connection in actual life, corresponded with that connection. This son, on whom Goethe vainly lavished so much thought and care, was like his mother, and like Goethe's attachment for his mother. "This young man," says a late well-informed writer (M. Henri Blaze), "Wieland, with good reason, called the son of the servant, *der Sohn der Magd.* He inherited from his father only his name and his *physique.*"

In all these expressions of Woman, the aim of Goethe is satisfactory to me. He aims at a pure self-subsistence, and a free development of any powers with which they may be gifted by nature as much for them as for men. They are units, addressed as souls. Accordingly, the meeting between Man and Woman, as represented by him, is equal and noble; and, if he does not depict marriage, he makes it possible.

In the Macaria, bound with the heavenly bodies in fixed revolutions, the centre of all relations, herself unrelated, he expresses the Minerva side of feminine nature. It was not by chance that Goethe gave her this name. Macaria, the daughter of Hercules, who offered herself as a victim for the good of her country, was canonized by the Greeks, and worshipped as the Goddess of true Felicity. Goethe has embodied this Felicity as the Serenity that arises from Wisdom, a Wisdom such as the Jewish wise man venerated, alike instructed in the designs of heaven, and the methods necessary to carry them into effect upon earth.

Mignon is the electrical, inspired, lyrical nature. And wherever it appears we echo in our aspirations that of the child,

> "So let me seem until I be:—
> Take not the *white robe* away."
> *   *   *   *   *
> "Though I lived without care and toil,
> Yet felt I sharp pain enough:
> Make me again forever young."

All these women, though we see them in relations, we can think of as unrelated. They all are very individual, yet seem nowhere restrained. They satisfy for the present, yet arouse an infinite expectation.

The economist Theresa, the benevolent Natalia, the fair Saint, have chosen a path, but their thoughts are not narrowed to it. The functions of life to them are not ends, but suggestions.

Thus, to them, all things are important, because none is necessary. Their different characters have fair play, and each is beautiful in its minute indications, for nothing is enforced or conventional; but everything, however slight, grows from the essential life of the being.

Mignon and Theresa wear male attire when they like, and it is graceful for them to do so, while Macaria is confined to her arm-chair behind the green curtain, and the Fair Saint could not bear a speck of dust on her robe.

All things are in their places in this little world, because all is natural and free, just as "there is room for everything out of doors." Yet all is rounded in by natural harmony, which will always arise where Truth and Love are sought in the light of Freedom.

Goethe's book bodes an era of freedom like its own of "extraordinary, generous seeking," and new revelations. New individualities shall be developed in the actual world, which shall advance upon it as gently as the figures come out upon his canvas.

I have indicated on this point the coincidence between his hopes and those of Fourier, though his are directed by an infinitely higher and deeper knowledge of human nature. But, for our present purpose, it is sufficient to show how surely these different paths have conducted to the same end two earnest thinkers. In some other place I wish to point out similar coincidences between Goethe's model school and the plans of Fourier, which may cast light upon the page of prophecy.

Many women have observed that the time drew nigh for a better care of the sex, and have thrown out hints that may be useful. Among these may be mentioned—

Miss Edgeworth, who, although restrained by the habits of her age and country, and belonging more to the eighteenth than the nineteenth century, has done excellently as far as she goes.[81] She had a horror of sentimentalism, and of the love of notoriety, and saw how likely women, in the early stages of culture, were to aim at these. Therefore she bent her efforts to recommending domestic life. But the methods she recommends are such as will fit a character for any position to which it may be called. She taught a contempt of falsehood, no less in its most graceful, than in its meanest apparitions; the cultivation of a clear, independent judgment, and adherence to its dictates; habits of various and liberal study and employment, and a capacity for friendship. Her standard of character is the same for both sexes,—Truth, honor, enlightened benevolence, and aspiration after knowledge. Of poetry, she knows nothing, and her religion consists in honor and loyalty to obligations once assumed—in short, in "the great idea of duty which holds us upright." Her whole tendency is practical.

Mrs. Jameson is a sentimentalist, and, therefore, suits us ill in some respects, but she is full of talent, has a just and refined perception of the beautiful, and a genuine courage when she finds it necessary. She does not appear to have thought out, thoroughly, the subject on which we are engaged, and her opinions, expressed as opinions, are sometimes inconsistent with one another. But from the refined perception of character, admirable suggestions are given in her "Women of Shakespeare," and "Loves of the Poets."

But that for which I most respect her is the decision with which she speaks on a subject which refined women are usually afraid to approach, for fear of the insult and scurrile jest they may encounter; but on which she neither can nor will restrain the indignation of a full heart. I refer to the degradation of a large portion of women into the sold and polluted slaves of men, and the daring with which the legislator and man of the world lifts his head beneath the heavens, and says, "This must be; it cannot be helped; it is a necessary accompaniment of *civilization*."

So speaks the *citizen*. Man born of Woman, the father of daughters, declares that he will and must buy the comforts and commercial advantages of his London, Vienna, Paris, New York, by conniving at the moral death, the damnation, so far as the action of society can insure it, of thousands of women for each splendid metropolis.

O men! I speak not to you. It is true that your wickedness (for you must not deny that at least nine thousand out of the ten fall through the vanity you have systematically flattered, or the promises you have treacherously broken); yes, it is true that your wickedness is its own punishment. Your forms degraded and your eyes clouded by secret sin; natural harmony broken and fineness of perception destroyed in your mental and bodily organization; God and love shut out from your hearts by the foul visitants you have permitted there; incapable of pure marriage; incapable of pure parentage; incapable of worship; O wretched men, your sin is its own punishment! You have lost the world in losing yourselves. Who ruins another has admitted the worm to the root of his own tree, and the fuller ye fill the cup of evil, the deeper must be your own bitter draught. But I speak not to you—you need to teach and warn one another. And more than one voice rises in earnestness. And all that *women* say to the heart that has once chosen the evil path is considered prudery, or ignorance, or perhaps a feebleness of nature which exempts from similar temptations.

But to you, women, American women, a few words may not be addressed in vain. One here and there may listen.

You know how it was in the Oriental clime. One man, if wealth permitted, had several wives and many handmaidens. The chastity and equality of genuine marriage, with "the thousand decencies that flow" from its communion, the precious virtues that gradually may be matured within its enclosure, were unknown.

But this man did not wrong according to his light. What he did, he might publish to God and Man; it was not a wicked secret that hid in vile lurking-places and dens, like the banquets of beasts of prey. Those women were not lost, not polluted in their own eyes, nor those of others. If they were not in a state of knowledge and virtue, they were at least in one of comparative innocence.

You know how it was with the natives of this continent. A chief had many wives, whom he maintained and who did his household work; those women were but servants, still they enjoyed the respect of others and their own. They lived together in peace. They knew that a sin against what was in their nation esteemed virtue, would be as strictly punished in Man as in Woman.

Now pass to the countries where marriage is between one and one. I will not speak of the Pagan nations, but come to those which own the Christian rule. We all know what that enjoins; there is a standard to appeal to.

See, now, not the mass of the people, for we all know that it is a proverb and a bitter jest to speak of the "down-trodden million." We know that, down to our own time, a principle never had so fair a chance to pervade the mass of the people, but that we must solicit its illustration from select examples.

Take the Paladin, take the Poet.[82] Did *they* believe purity more impossible to Man than to Woman? Did they wish Woman to believe that Man was less amenable to higher motives,—that pure aspirations would not guard him against bad passions,—that honorable employments and temperate habits would not keep him free from slavery to the body? O no! Love was to them a part of heaven, and they could not even wish to receive its happiness, unless assured of being worthy of it. Its highest happiness to them was that it made them wish to be worthy. They courted probation. They wished not the title of knight till the banner had been upheld in the heats of battle, amid the rout of cowards.

I ask of you, young girls—I do not mean *you* whose heart is that of an old coxcomb, though your locks have not yet lost their sunny tinge. Not of you whose whole character is tainted with vanity, inherited or taught, who have early learned the love of coquettish excitement, and whose eyes rove restlessly in search of a "conquest" or a "beau;" you who are ashamed *not* to be seen by others the mark of the most contemptuous flattery or injurious desire. To such I do not speak. But to thee, maiden, who, if not so fair, art yet of that unpolluted nature which Milton saw when he dreamed of Comus and the Paradise. Thou, child of an unprofaned wedlock, brought up amid the teachings of the woods and fields, kept fancy-free by useful employment and a free flight into the heaven of thought, loving to please only those whom thou wouldst not be ashamed to love; I ask of thee, whose cheek has not forgotten its blush nor thy heart its lark-like hopes, if he whom thou mayest hope the Father will send thee, as the companion of life's toils and joys, is not to thy thought pure? Is not manliness to thy thought purity, *not* lawlessness? Can his lips speak falsely? Can he do, in secret, what he could not avow to the mother that bore him? O say, dost thou not look for a heart free, open as thine own, all whose thoughts may be avowed, incapable of wronging the innocent, or still further degrading the fallen—a man, in short, in whom brute nature is entirely subject to the impulses of his better self?

Yes! it was thus that thou didst hope; for I have many, many times seen the image of a future life, of a destined spouse, painted on the tablets of a virgin heart.

It might be that she was not true to these hopes. She was taken into what is called "the world," froth and scum as it mostly is on the social caldron. There, she saw fair Woman carried in the waltz close to the heart of a being who appeared to her a Satyr. Being warned by a male friend that he was in fact of that class, and not fit for such familiar nearness to a chaste being, the advised replied that "women should know nothing about such things." She saw one fairer given in wedlock to a man of the same class. "Papa and mamma said that 'all men were faulty at some time in their lives; they had a great many temptations.' Frederick would be so happy at home; he would not want to do wrong." She turned to the married women; they, O tenfold horror! laughed at her supposing "men were like women." Sometimes, I say, she was not true, and either sadly accommodated herself to "Woman's lot," or acquired a taste for satyr-society, like some of the Nymphs, and all the Bacchanals of old. But to those who could not and would not accept a mess of pottage, or a Circe cup, in lieu of their birthright, and to these others who have yet their choice to make, I say, Courage! I have some words of cheer for you. A man, himself of unbroken purity, reported to me the words of a foreign artist, that "the world would never be better till men subjected themselves to the same laws they had imposed on women;" that

artist, he added, was true to the thought. The same was true of Canova,[83] the same of Beethoven. "Like each other demi-god, they kept themselves free from stain;" and Michael Angelo, looking over here from the loneliness of his century, might meet some eyes that need not shun his glance.

"Be of pure marble pillars made; Strong to sustain the roof..."

In private life, I am assured by men who are not so sustained and occupied by the worship of pure beauty, that a similar consecration is possible, is practised; that many men feel that no temptation can be too strong for the will of man, if he invokes the aid of the Spirit instead of seeking extenuation from the brute alliances of his nature. In short, what the child fancies is really true, though almost the whole world declares it a lie. Man is a child of God; and if he seeks His guidance to keep the heart with diligence, it will be so given that all the issues of life may be pure. Life will then be a temple.

> The temple round
> Spread green the pleasant ground;
>   The fair colonnade
> Be of pure marble pillars made;
> Strong to sustain the roof,
>   Time and tempest proof;
> Yet, amidst which, the lightest breeze
>   Can play as it please;
>   The audience hall
>   Be free to all
>   Who revere
> The power worshipped here,
>   Sole guide of youth,
>   Unswerving Truth.
>   In the inmost shrine
>   Stands the image divine,
>   Only seen
> By those whose deeds have worthy been—
>   Priestlike clean.
> Those, who initiated are,
>   Declare,
>   As the hours
> Usher in varying hopes and powers;
>   It changes its face,
>   It changes its age,
>   Now a young, beaming grace,
>   Now Nestorian sage:
>   But, to the pure in heart,
>   This shape of primal art
>   In age is fair,
>   In youth seems wise,
>   Beyond compare,
>   Above surprise;
> What it teaches native seems,
>   Its new lore our ancient dreams;
> Incense rises from the ground;
>   Music flows around;
> Firm rest the feet below, clear gaze the eyes above,
> When Truth, to point the way through life, assumes the wand of Love;

> But, if she cast aside the robe of green,
>> Winter's silver sheen,
>> White, pure as light,
> Makes gentle shroud as worthy weed as bridal robe had been.*[84]

We are now in a transition state, and but few steps have yet been taken. From polygamy, Europe passed to the marriage *de convenance*. This was scarcely an improvement. An attempt was then made to substitute genuine marriage (the mutual choice of souls inducing a permanent union), as yet baffled on every side by the haste, the ignorance, or the impurity of Man.

Where Man assumes a high principle to which he is not yet ripened, it will happen, for a long time, that the few will be nobler than before; the many, worse. Thus now. In the country of Sidney[85] and Milton, the metropolis is a den of wickedness, and a sty of sensuality; in the country of Lady Russell,[86] the custom of English peeresses, of selling their daughters to the highest bidder, is made the theme and jest of fashionable novels by unthinking children who would stare at the idea of sending them to a Turkish slave-dealer, though the circumstances of the bargain are there less degrading, as the will and thoughts of the person sold are not so degraded by it, and it is not done in defiance of an acknowledged law of right in the land and the age.

I must here add that I do not believe there ever was put upon record more depravation of Man, and more despicable frivolity of thought and aim in Woman, than in the novels which purport to give the picture of English fashionable life, which are read with such favor in our drawing-rooms, and give the tone to the manners of some circles. Compared with the cold, hard-hearted folly there described, crime is hopeful; for it, at least, shows some power remaining in the mental constitution.

To return:—Attention has been awakened among men to the stains of celibacy, and the profanations of marriage. They begin to write about it and lecture about it. It is the tendency now to endeavor to help the erring by showing them the physical law. This is wise and excellent; but forget not the better half. Cold bathing and exercise will not suffice to keep a life pure, without an inward baptism, and noble, exhilarating employment for the thoughts and the passions. Early marriages are desirable, but if (and the world is now so out of joint that there are a hundred thousand chances to one against it) a man does not early, or at all, find the person to whom he can be united in the marriage of souls, will you give him in the marriage *de convenance?* or, if not married, can you find no way for him to lead a

---

*As described by the historian:—

"The temple of Juno is like what the character of Woman should be.

Columns! graceful decorums, attractive yet sheltering.

Porch! noble, inviting aspect of the life.

Kaos! receives the worshippers. See here the statue of the Divinity.

Ophistodomos! Sanctuary where the most precious possessions were kept safe from the hand of the spoiler and the eye of the world."

virtuous and happy life? Think of it well, ye who think yourselves better than pagans, for many of *them* knew this sure way.*

To you, women of America, it is more especially my business to address myself on this subject, and my advice may be classed under three heads:

Clear your souls from the taint of vanity.

Do not rejoice in conquests, either that your power to allure may be seen by other women, or for the pleasure of rousing passionate feelings that gratify your love of excitement.

It must happen, no doubt, that frank and generous women will excite love they do not reciprocate, but, in nine cases out of ten, the woman has, half consciously, done much to excite. In this case, she shall not be held guiltless, either as to the unhappiness or injury of the lover. Pure love, inspired by a worthy object, must ennoble and bless, whether mutual or not; but that which is excited by coquettish attraction of any grade of refinement, must cause bitterness and doubt, as to the reality of human goodness, so soon as the flush of passion is over. And, that you may avoid all taste for these false pleasures,

> "Steep the soul
> In one pure love, and it will last thee long."

The love of truth, the love of excellence, whether you clothe them in the person of a special object or not, will have power to save you from following Duessa, and lead you in the green glades where Una's feet have trod.

It was on this one subject that a venerable champion of good, the last representative of the spirit which sanctified the Revolution, and gave our country such a sunlight of hope in the eyes of the nations, the same who lately, in Boston, offered anew to the young men the pledge taken by the young men of his day, offered, also, his counsel, on being addressed by the principal of a girl's school, thus:

Reply of Mr. Adams.[87]

Mr. Adams was so deeply affected by the address of Miss Foster, as to be for some time inaudible. When heard, he spoke as follows:

"This is the first instance in which a lady has thus addressed me personally; and I trust that all the ladies present will be able sufficiently to enter into my feelings to know that I am more affected by this honor than by any other I could have received.

---

*The Persian sacred books, the Desatir, describe the great and holy prince Ky Khosrou, as being "an angel, and the son of an angel," one to whom the Supreme says, "Thou art not absent from before me for one twinkling of an eye. I am never out of thy heart. And I am contained in nothing but in thy heart, and in a heart like thy heart. And I am nearer unto thee than thou art to thyself." This prince had in his Golden Seraglio three ladies of surpassing beauty, and all four, in this royal monastery, passed their lives, and left the world as virgins.

The Persian people had no scepticism when the history of such a mind was narrated.

"You have been pleased, madam, to allude to the character of my father, and the history of my family, and their services to the country. It is indeed true that, from the existence of the republic as an independent nation, my father and myself have been in the public service of the country, almost without interruption. I came into the world, as a person having personal responsibilities, with the Declaration of Independence, which constituted us a nation. I was a child at that time, and had then perhaps the greatest of blessings that can be bestowed on man—a mother who was anxious and capable to form her children to be what they ought to be. From that mother I derived whatever instruction—religious especially and moral—has pervaded a long life; I will not say perfectly, and as it ought to be; but I will say, because it is justice only to the memory of her whom I revere, that if, in the course of my life, there has been any imperfection, or deviation from what she taught me, the fault is mine, and not hers.

"With such a mother, and such other relations with the sex, of sister, wife, and daughter, it has been the perpetual instruction of my life to love and revere the female sex. And in order to carry that sentiment of love and reverence to its highest degree of perfection, I know of nothing that exists in human society better adapted to produce that result, than institutions of the character that I have now the honor to address.

"I have been taught, as I have said, through the course of my life, to love and to revere the female sex; but I have been taught, also—and that lesson has perhaps impressed itself on my mind even more strongly, it may be, than the other—I have been taught not to flatter them. It is not unusual, in the intercourse of Man with the other sex—and especially for young men—to think that the way to win the hearts of ladies is by flattery. To love and to revere the sex, is what I think the duty of Man; but *not to flatter them;* and this I would say to the young ladies here—and if they, and others present, will allow me, with all the authority which nearly four score years may have with those who have not yet attained one score—I would say to them what I have no doubt they say to themselves, and are taught here, not to take the flattery of men as proof of perfection.

"I am now, however, I fear, assuming too much of a character that does not exactly belong to me. I therefore conclude, by assuring you, madam, that your reception of me has affected me, as you perceive, more than I can express in words; and that I shall offer my best prayers, till my latest hour, to the Creator of us all, that this institution especially, and all others of a similar kind, designed to form the female mind to wisdom and virtue, may prosper to the end of time."

It will be interesting to add here the character of Mr. Adams' mother, as drawn by her husband, the first John Adams, in a family letter* written just before his death.

"I have reserved for the last the life of Lady Russell. This I have not yet read, because I read it more than forty years ago. On this hangs a tale which you ought to know and communicate it to your children. I bought the Life

*Journal and Correspondence of Miss Adams, vol. I., p. 246.

and Letters of Lady Russell in the year 1775, and sent it to your grandmother, with an express intent and desire that she should consider it a mirror in which to contemplate herself; for, at that time, I thought it extremely probable, from the daring and dangerous career I was determined to run, that she would one day find herself in the situation of Lady Russell, her husband without a head. This lady was more beautiful than Lady Russell, had a brighter genius, more information, a more refined taste, and, at least, her equal in the virtues of the heart; equal fortitude and firmness of character, equal resignation to the will of Heaven, equal in all the virtues and graces of the Christian life. Like Lady Russell, she never, by word or look, discouraged me from running all hazards for the salvation of my country's liberties; she was willing to share with me, and that her children should share with us both, in all the dangerous consequences we had to hazard."

Will a woman who loves flattery or an aimless excitement, who wastes the flower of her mind on transitory sentiments, ever be loved with a love like that, when fifty years' trial have entitled to the privileges of "the golden marriage?"

Such was the love of the iron-handed warrior for her, not his hand-maid, but his help-meet:

"Whom God loves, to him gives he such a wife."

I find the whole of what I want in this relation, in the two epithets by which Milton makes Adam address *his* wife.

In the intercourse of every day he begins:

"Daughter of God and man, *accomplished* Eve."

In a moment of stronger feeling,

"Daughter of God and man, IMMORTAL Eve."

What majesty in the cadence of the line; what dignity, what reverence in the attitude both of giver and receiver!

The woman who permits, in her life, the alloy of vanity; the woman who lives upon flattery, coarse or fine, shall never be thus addressed. She is *not* immortal so far as her will is concerned, and every woman who does so creates miasma, whose spread is indefinite. The hand which casts into the waters of life a stone of offence knows not how far the circles thus caused may spread their agitations.

A little while since I was at one of the most fashionable places of public resort. I saw there many women, dressed without regard to the season or the demands of the place, in apery, or, as it looked, in mockery, of European fashions. I saw their eyes restlessly courting attention. I saw the way in which it was paid; the style of devotion, almost an open sneer, which it pleased those ladies to receive from men whose expression marked their own low position in the moral and intellectual world. Those women went to their pillows with their heads full of folly, their hearts of jealousy, or gratified vanity; those men, with the low opinion they already entertained of Woman confirmed. These were American *ladies;* that is, they were of that class who have wealth and leisure to make full use of the day, and confer benefits on others. They were of that class whom the possession of external advantages makes of pernicious example to many, if these advantages be misused.

Soon after, I met a circle of women, stamped by society as among the most degraded of their sex. "How," it was asked of them, "did you come here?" for by the society that I saw in the former place they were shut up in a prison. The causes were not difficult to trace: love of dress, love of flattery, love of excitement. They had not dresses like the other ladies, so they stole them; they could not pay for flattery by distinctions, and the dower of a worldly marriage, so they paid by the profanation of their persons. In excitement, more and more madly sought from day to day, they drowned the voice of conscience.

"...they were shut up in a prison. The causes were not difficult to trace..."

Now I ask you, my sisters, if the women at the fashionable house be not answerable for those women being in the prison?

As to position in the world of souls, we may suppose the women of the prison stood fairest, both because they had misused less light, and because

loneliness and sorrow had brought some of them to feel the need of better life, nearer truth and good. This was no merit in them, being an effect of circumstance, but it was hopeful. But you, my friends (and some of you I have already met), consecrate yourselves without waiting for reproof, in free love and unbroken energy, to win and to diffuse a better life. Offer beauty, talents, riches, on the altar; thus shall ye keep spotless your own hearts, and be visibly or invisibly the angels to others.

I would urge upon those women who have not yet considered this subject, to do so. Do not forget the unfortunates who dare not cross your guarded way. If it do not suit you to act with those who have organized measures of reform, then hold not yourself excused from acting in private. Seek out these degraded women, give them tender sympathy, counsel, employment. Take the place of mothers, such as might have saved them originally.

If you can do little for those already under the ban of the world,—and the best-considered efforts have often failed, from a want of strength in those unhappy ones to bear up against the sting of shame and the prejudices of the world, which makes them seek oblivion again in their old excitements,—you will at least leave a sense of love and justice in their hearts, that will prevent their becoming utterly embittered and corrupt. And you may learn the means of prevention for those yet uninjured. These will be found in a diffusion of mental culture, simple tastes, best taught by your example, a genuine self-respect, and, above all, what the influence of Man tends to hide from Woman, the love and fear of a divine, in preference to a human tribunal.

But suppose you save many who would have lost their bodily innocence (for as to mental, the loss of that is incalculably more general), through mere vanity and folly; there still remain many, the prey and spoil of the brute passions of Man; for the stories frequent in our newspapers outshame antiquity, and vie with the horrors of war.

As to this, it must be considered that, as the vanity and proneness to seduction of the imprisoned women represented a general degradation in their sex; so do these acts a still more general and worse in the male. Where so many are weak, it is natural there should be many lost; where legislators admit that ten thousand prostitutes are a fair proportion to one city, and husbands tell their wives that it is folly to expect chastity from men, it is inevitable that there should be many monsters of vice.

I must in this place mention, with respect and gratitude, the conduct of Mrs. Child in the case of Amelia Norman.[88] The action and speech of this lady was of straightforward nobleness, undeterred by custom or cavil from duty toward an injured sister. She showed the case and the arguments the counsel against the prisoner had the assurance to use in their true light to the public. She put the case on the only ground of religion and equity. She was successful in arresting the attention of many who had before shrugged their shoulders, and let sin pass as necessarily a part of the company of men. They begin to ask whether virtue is not possible, perhaps necessary, to Man as well as to Woman. They begin to fear that the perdition of a

woman must involve that of a man. This is a crisis. The results of this case
will be important.

In this connection I must mention Eugene Sue, the French novelist,
several of whose works have been lately translated among us, as having the
true spirit of reform as to women.[89] Like every other French writer, he is
still tainted with the transmissions of the old *regime*. Still, falsehood may
be permitted for the sake of advancing truth, evil as the way to good. Even
George Sand, who would trample on every graceful decorum, and every
human law, for the sake of a sincere life, does not see that she violates it by
making her heroines able to tell falsehoods in a good cause. These French
writers need ever to be confronted by the clear perception of the English
and German mind, that the only good man, consequently the only good
reformer, is he

> "Who bases good on good alone, and owes
> To virtue every triumph that he knows."

Still, Sue has the heart of a reformer, and especially towards women; he
sees what they need, and what causes are injuring them. From the histories
of Fleur de Marie and La Louve, from the lovely and independent character
of Rigolette, from the distortion given to Matilda's mind, by the present
views of marriage, and from the truly noble and immortal character of the
"humpbacked Sempstress" in the "Wandering Jew," may be gathered much
that shall elucidate doubt and direct inquiry on this subject. In reform, as in
philosophy, the French are the interpreters to the civilized world. Their
own attainments are not great, but they make clear the past, and break
down barriers to the future.

Observe that the good man of Sue is as pure as Sir Charles Grandison.[90]

Apropos to Sir Charles. Women are accustomed to be told by men that
the reform is to come *from them*. "You," say the men, "must frown upon
vice; you must decline the attentions of the corrupt; you must not submit to
the will of your husband when it seems to you unworthy, but give the laws
in marriage, and redeem it from its present sensual and mental pollutions."

This seems to us hard. Men have, indeed, been, for more than a hundred
years, rating women for countenancing vice. But, at the same time, they
have carefully hid from them its nature, so that the preference often shown
by women for bad men arises rather from a confused idea that they are bold
and adventurous, acquainted with regions which women are forbidden to
explore, and the curiosity that ensues, than a corrupt heart in the woman.
As to marriage, it has been inculcated on women, for centuries, that men
have not only stronger passions than they, but of a sort that it would be
shameful for them to share or even understand; that, therefore, they must
"confide in their husbands," that is, submit implicitly to their will; that the
least appearance of coldness or withdrawal, from whatever cause, in the
wife is wicked, because liable to turn her husband's thoughts to illicit
indulgence; for a man is so constituted that he must indulge his passions or
die!

Accordingly, a great part of women look upon men as a kind of wild beasts, but "suppose they are all alike;" the unmarried are assured by the married that, "if they knew men as they do," that is, by being married to them, "they would not expect continence or self-government from them."

I might accumulate illustrations on this theme, drawn from acquaintance with the histories of women, which would startle and grieve all thinking men, but I forbear. Let Sir Charles Grandison preach to his own sex; or if none there be who feels himself able to speak with authority from a life unspotted in will or deed, let those who are convinced of the practicability and need of a pure life, as the foreign artist was, advise the others, and warn them by their own example, if need be.

The following passage, from a female writer, on female affairs, expresses a prevalent way of thinking on this subject:

"It may be that a young woman, exempt from all motives of vanity, determines to take for a husband a man who does not inspire her with a very decided inclination. Imperious circumstances, the evident interest of her family, or the danger of suffering celibacy, may explain such a resolution. If, however, she were to endeavor to surmount a personal repugnance, we should look upon this as *injudicious.* Such a rebellion of nature marks the limit that the influence of parents, or the self-sacrifice of the young girl, should never pass. *We shall be told that this repugnance is an affair of the imagination.* It may be so; but imagination is a power which it is temerity to brave; and its antipathy is more difficult to conquer than its preference."*

Among ourselves, the exhibition of such a repugnance from a woman who had been given in marriage "by advice of friends," was treated by an eminent physician as sufficient proof of insanity. If he had said sufficient cause for it, he would have been nearer right.

It has been suggested by men who were pained by seeing bad men admitted, freely, to the society of modest women,—thereby encouraged to vice by impunity, and corrupting the atmosphere of homes,—that there should be a senate of the matrons in each city and town, who should decide what candidates were fit for admission to their houses and the society of their daughters.†

Such a plan might have excellent results; but it argues a moral dignity and decision which does not yet exist, and needs to be induced by knowledge and reflection. It has been the tone to keep women ignorant on these subjects, or, when they were not, to command that they should seem so. "It is indelicate," says the father or husband, "to inquire into the private character of such an one. It is sufficient that I do not think him unfit to visit you." And so, this man, who would not tolerate these pages in his house, "unfit for family reading," because they speak plainly, introduces there a man whose shame is written on his brow, as well as the open secret of the

---

*Madame Necker de Saussure.[91]
†*See* Goethe's Tasso. "A synod of good women should decide,"—if the golden age is to be restored.

whole town, and, presently, if *respectable* still, and rich enough, gives him his daughter to wife. The mother affects ignorance, "supposing he is no worse than most men." The daughter *is* ignorant; something in the mind of the new spouse seems strange to her, but she supposes it is "woman's lot" not to be perfectly happy in her affections; she has always heard, "men could not understand women," so she weeps alone, or takes to dress and the duties of the house. The husband, of course, makes no avowal, and dreams of no redemption.

"In the heart of every young woman," says the female writer above quoted, addressing herself to the husband, "depend upon it, there is a fund of exalted ideas; she conceals, represses, without succeeding in smothering them. *So long as these ideas in your wife are directed to YOU, they are, no doubt, innocent,* but take care that they be not accompanied with *too much* pain. In other respects, also, spare her delicacy. Let all the antecedent parts of your life, if there are such, which would give her pain, be concealed from her; *her happiness and her respect for you would suffer from this misplaced confidence.* Allow her to retain that flower of purity, *which should distinguish her, in your eyes, from every other woman.*" We should think so, truly, under this canon. Such a man must esteem purity an exotic that could only be preserved by the greatest care. Of the degree of mental intimacy possible, in such a marriage, let every one judge for himself!

On this subject, let every woman, who has once begun to think, examine herself; see whether she does not suppose virtue possible and necessary to Man, and whether she would not desire for her son a virtue which aimed at a fitness for a divine life, and involved, if not asceticism, that degree of power over the lower self, which shall "not exterminate the passions, but keep them chained at the feet of reason." The passions, like fire, are a bad master; but confine them to the hearth and the altar, and they give life to the social economy, and make each sacrifice meet for heaven.

When many women have thought upon this subject, some will be fit for the senate, and one such senate in operation would affect the morals of the civilized world.

At present I look to the young. As preparatory to the senate, I should like to see a society of novices, such as the world has never yet seen, bound by no oath, wearing no badge. In place of an oath, they should have a religious faith in the capacity of Man for virtue; instead of a badge, should wear in the heart a firm resolve not to stop short of the destiny promised him as a son of God. Their service should be action and conservatism, not of old habits, but of a better nature, enlightened by hopes that daily grow brighter.

If sin was to remain in the world, it should not be by their connivance at its stay, or one moment's concession to its claims.

They should succor the oppressed, and pay to the upright the reverence due in hero-worship by seeking to emulate them. They would not denounce the willingly bad, but they could not be with them, for the two classes could not breathe the same atmosphere.

They would heed no detention from the time-serving, the worldly and the timid.

They could love no pleasures that were not innocent and capable of good fruit.

I saw, in a foreign paper, the title now given to a party abroad, "Los Exaltados." Such would be the title now given these children by the world: Los Exaltados, Las Exaltadas; but the world would not sneer always, for from them would issue a virtue by which it would, at last, be exalted too.

I have in my eye a youth and a maiden whom I look to as the nucleus of such a class. They are both in early youth; both as yet uncontaminated; both aspiring, without rashness; both thoughtful; both capable of deep affection; both of strong nature and sweet feelings; both capable of large mental development. They reside in different regions of earth, but their place in the soul is the same. To them I look, as, perhaps, the harbingers and leaders of a new era, for never yet have I known minds so truly virgin, without narrowness or ignorance.

When men call upon women to redeem them, they mean such maidens. But such are not easily formed under the present influences of society. As there are more such young men to help give a different tone, there will be more such maidens.

The English novelist, D'Israeli, has, in his novel of "The Young Duke," made a man of the most depraved stock be redeemed by a woman who despises him when he has only the brilliant mask of fortune and beauty to cover the poverty of his heart and brain, but knows how to encourage him when he enters on a better course. But this woman was educated by a father who valued character in women.

Still, there will come now and then one who will, as I hope of my young Exaltada, be example and instruction for the rest. It was not the opinion of Woman current among Jewish men that formed the character of the mother of Jesus.

Since the sliding and backsliding men of the world, no less than the mystics, declare that, as through Woman Man was lost, so through Woman must Man be redeemed, the time must be at hand. When she knows herself indeed as "accomplished," still more as "immortal Eve," this may be.

As an immortal, she may also know and inspire immortal love, a happiness not to be dreamed of under the circumstances advised in the last quotation. Where love is based on concealment, it must, of course, disappear when the soul enters the scene of clear vision!

And, without this hope, how worthless every plan, every bond, every power!

"The giants," said the Scandinavian Saga, "had induced Loke (the spirit that hovers between good and ill) to steal for them Iduna (Goddess of Immortality) and her apples of pure gold. He lured her out, by promising to show, on a marvellous tree he had discovered, apples beautiful as her own, if she would only take them with her for a comparison. Thus having lured her beyond the heavenly domain, she was seized and carried away captive by the powers of misrule.

"As now the gods could not find their friend Iduna, they were confused with grief; indeed, they began visibly to grow old and gray. Discords arose,

and love grew cold. Indeed, Odur, spouse of the goddess of love and beauty, wandered away, and returned no more. At last, however, the gods, discovering the treachery of Loke, obliged him to win back Iduna from the prison in which she sat mourning. He changed himself into a falcon, and brought her back as a swallow, fiercely pursued by the Giant King, in the form of an eagle. So she strives to return among us, light and small as a swallow. We must welcome her form as the speck on the sky that assures the glad blue of Summer. Yet one swallow does not make a summer. Let us solicit them in flights and flocks!"

Returning from the future to the present, let us see what forms Iduna takes, as she moves along the declivity of centuries to the valley where the lily flower may concentrate all its fragrance.

It would seem as if this time were not very near to one fresh from books, such as I have of late been—no: *not* reading, but sighing over. A crowd of books having been sent me since my friends knew me to be engaged in this way, on Woman's "Sphere," Woman's "Mission," and Woman's "Destiny," I believe that almost all that is extant of formal precept has come under my eye. Among these I read with refreshment a little one called "The Whole Duty of Woman," "indited by a noble lady at the request of a noble lord," and which has this much of nobleness, that the view it takes is a religious one. It aims to fit Woman for heaven; the main bent of most of the others is to fit her to please, or, at least, not to disturb, a husband.

Among these I select, as a favorable specimen, the book I have already

quoted, "The Study* of the Life of Woman, by Madame Necker de Saussure, of Geneva, translated from the French." This book was published at Philadelphia, and has been read with much favor here. Madame Necker is the cousin of Madame de Stael, and has taken from her works the motto prefixed to this.

"Cette vie n'a quelque prix que si elle sert a' l'education morale de notre cœur."[92]

Mde. Necker is, by nature, capable of entire consistency in the application of this motto, and, therefore, the qualifications she makes, in the instructions given to her own sex, show forcibly the weight which still paralyzes and distorts the energies of that sex.

The book is rich in passages marked by feeling and good suggestions; but, taken in the whole, the impression it leaves is this:

Woman is, and *shall remain,* inferior to Man and subject to his will, and, in endeavoring to aid her, we must anxiously avoid anything that can be misconstrued into expression of the contrary opinion, else the men will be alarmed, and combine to defeat our efforts.

The present is a good time for these efforts, for men are less occupied about women than formerly. Let us, then, seize upon the occasion, and do what we can to make our lot tolerable. But we must sedulously avoid

*This title seems to be incorrectly translated from the French. I have not seen the original.

encroaching on the territory of Man. If we study natural history, our observations may be made useful, by some male naturalist; if we draw well, we may make our services acceptable to the artists. But our names must not be known; and, to bring these labors to any result, we must take some man for our head, and be his hands.

The lot of Woman is sad. She is constituted to expect and need a happiness that cannot exist on earth. She must stifle such aspirations within her secret heart, and fit herself, as well as she can, for a life of resignations and consolations.

She will be very lonely while living with her husband. She must not expect to open her heart to him fully, or that, after marriage, he will be capable of the refined service of love. The man is not born for the woman, only the woman for the man. "Men cannot understand the hearts of women." The life of Woman must be outwardly a well-intentioned, cheerful dissimulation of her real life.

Naturally, the feelings of the mother, at the birth of a female child, resemble those of the Paraguay woman, described by Southey as lamenting in such heart-breaking tones that her mother did not kill her the hour she was born,—"her mother, who knew what the life of a woman must be;"—or of those women seen at the north by Sir A. Mackenzie, who performed this pious duty towards female infants whenever they had an opportunity.[93]

"After the first delight, the young mother experiences feelings a little different, according as the birth of a son or a daughter has been announced.

"Is it a son? A sort of glory swells at this thought the heart of the mother; she seems to feel that she is entitled to gratitude. She has given a citizen, a defender, to her country; to her husband an heir of his name; to herself a protector. And yet the contrast of all these fine titles with this being, so humble, soon strikes her. At the aspect of this frail treasure, opposite feelings agitate her heart; she seems to recognize in him *a nature superior to her own,* but subjected to a low condition, and she honors a future greatness in the object of extreme compassion. Somewhat of that respect and adoration for a feeble child, of which some fine pictures offer the expression in the features of the happy Mary, seem reproduced with the young mother who has given birth to a son.

"Is it a daughter? There is usually a slight degree of regret; so deeply rooted is the idea of the superiority of Man in happiness and dignity; and yet, as she looks upon this child, she is more and more *softened* towards it. A deep sympathy—a sentiment of identity with this delicate being—takes possession of her; an extreme pity for so much weakness, a more pressing need of prayer, stirs her heart. Whatever sorrows she may have felt, she dreads for her daughter; but she will guide her to become much wiser, much better than herself. And then the gayety, the frivolity of the young woman have their turn. This little creature is a flower to cultivate, a doll to decorate."

Similar sadness at the birth of a daughter I have heard mothers express not unfrequently.

As to this living so entirely for men, I should think when it was proposed to women they would feel, at least, some spark of the old spirit of races allied to our own. "If he is to be my bridegroom *and lord,*" cries Brunhilda,* "he must first be able to pass through fire and water." "I will serve at the banquet," says the Walkyrie, "but only him who, in the trial of deadly combat, has shown himself a hero."

If women are to be bond-maids, let it be to men superior to women in fortitude, in aspiration, in moral power, in refined sense of beauty! You who give yourselves "to be supported," or because "one must love something," are they who make the lot of the sex such that mothers are sad when daughters are born.

It marks the state of feeling on this subject that it was mentioned, as a bitter censure on a woman who had influence over those younger than herself,—"She makes those girls want to see heroes?"

"And will that hurt them?"

"Certainly; how *can* you ask? They will find none, and so they will never be married."

"*Get* married" is the usual phrase, and the one that correctly indicates the thought; but the speakers, on this occasion, were persons too outwardly refined to use it. They were ashamed of the word, but not of the thing. Madame Necker, however, sees good possible in celibacy.

Indeed, I know not how the subject could be better illustrated, than by separating the wheat from the chaff in Madame Necker's book; place them in two heaps, and then summon the reader to choose; giving him first a near-sighted glass to examine the two;—it might be a Christian, an astronomical, or an artistic glass,—any kind of good glass to obviate acquired defects in the eye. I would lay any wager on the result.

But time permits not here a prolonged analysis. I have given the clues for fault-finding.

As a specimen of the good take the following passage, on the phenomena of what I have spoken of, as the lyrical or electric element in Woman.

"Women have been seen to show themselves poets in the most pathetic pantomimic scenes, where all the passions were depicted full of beauty; and these poets used a language unknown to themselves, and, the performance once over, their inspiration was a forgotten dream. Without doubt there is an interior development to beings so gifted; but their sole mode of communication with us is their talent. They are, in all besides, the inhabitants of another planet."

Similar observations have been made by those who have seen the women at Irish wakes, or the funeral ceremonies of modern Greece or Brittany, at times when excitement gave the impulse to genius; but, apparently, without a thought that these rare powers belonged to no other planet, but were a high development of the growth of this, and might, by wise and reverent treatment, be made to inform and embellish the scenes of every

*See the Nibelungen Lays.[94]

day. But, when Woman has her fair chance, she will do so, and the poem of the hour will vie with that of the ages.

I come now with satisfaction to my own country, and to a writer, a female writer, whom I have selected as the clearest, wisest, and kindliest, who has, as yet, used pen here on these subjects. This is Miss Sedgwick.[95]

Miss Sedgwick, though she inclines to the private path, and wishes that, by the cultivation of character, might should vindicate right, sets limits nowhere, and her objects and inducements are pure. They are the free and careful cultivation of the powers that have been given, with an aim at moral and intellectual perfection. Her speech is moderate and sane, but never palsied by fear or sceptical caution.

Herself a fine example of the independent and beneficent existence that intellect and character can give to Woman, no less than Man, if she know how to seek and prize it,—also, that the intellect need not absorb or weaken, but rather will refine and invigorate, the affections,—the teachings of her practical good sense come with great force, and cannot fail to avail much. Every way her writings please me both as to the means and the ends. I am pleased at the stress she lays on observance of the physical laws, because the true reason is given. Only in a strong and clean body can the soul do its message fitly.

She shows the meaning of the respect paid to personal neatness, both in the indispensable form of cleanliness, and of that love of order and arrangement, that must issue from a true harmony of feeling.

The praises of cold water seem to me an excellent sign in the age. They denote a tendency to the true life. We are now to have, as a remedy for ills, not orvietan, or opium, or any quack medicine, but plenty of air and water, with due attention to warmth and freedom in dress, and simplicity of diet.

Every day we observe signs that the natural feelings on these subjects are about to be reinstated, and the body to claim care as the abode and organ of the soul; not as the tool of servile labor, or the object of voluptuous indulgence.

A poor woman, who had passed through the lowest grades of ignominy, seemed to think she had never been wholly lost, "for," said she, "I would always have good under-clothes;" and, indeed, who could doubt that this denoted the remains of private self-respect in the mind?

A woman of excellent sense said, "It might seem childish, but to her one of the most favorable signs of the times was that the ladies had been persuaded to give up corsets."

Yes! let us give up all artificial means of distortion. Let life be healthy, pure, all of a piece. Miss Sedgwick, in teaching that domestics must have the means of bathing as much as their mistresses, and time, too, to bathe, has symbolized one of the most important of human rights.

Another interesting sign of the time is the influence exercised by two women, Miss Martineau and Miss Barrett, from their sick-rooms. The lamp of life which, if it had been fed only by the affections, depended on precarious human relations, would scarce have been able to maintain a

feeble glare in the lonely prison, now shines far and wide over the nations, cheering fellow-sufferers and hallowing the joy of the healthful.

These persons need not health or youth, or the charms of personal presence, to make their thoughts available. A few more such, and "old woman" shall not be the synonyme for imbecility, nor "old maid" a term of contempt, nor Woman be spoken of as a reed shaken by the wind.

It is time, indeed, that men and women both should cease to grow old in any other way than as the tree does, full of grace and honor. The hair of the artist turns white, but his eye shines clearer than ever, and we feel that age brings him maturity, not decay. So would it be with all, were the springs of immortal refreshment but unsealed within the soul; then, like these women, they would see, from the lonely chamber window, the glories of the universe; or, shut in darkness, be visited by angels.

I now touch on my own place and day, and, as I write, events are occurring that threaten the fair fabric approached by so long an avenue. Week before last, the Gentile was requested to aid the Jew to return to Palestine; for the Millennium, the reign of the Son of Mary was near. Just now, at high and solemn mass, thanks were returned to the Virgin for having delivered O'Connell from unjust imprisonment, in requital of his

"It is time, indeed, that men and women both should cease to grow old in any other way than as the tree does, full of grace and honor."

having consecrated to her the league formed in behalf of Liberty on Tara's Hill. But last week brought news which threatens that a cause identical with the enfranchisement of Jews, Irish, women, ay, and of Americans in general, too, is in danger, for the choice of the people threatens to rivet the chains of slavery and the leprosy of sin permanently on this nation, through the Annexation of Texas!

Ah! if this should take place, who will dare again to feel the throb of heavenly hope, as to the destiny of this country? The noble thought that gave unity to all our knowledge, harmony to all our designs,—the thought that the progress of history had brought on the era, the tissue of prophecies pointed out the spot, where humanity was, at last, to have a fair chance to know itself, and all men be born free and equal for the eagle's flight,—flutters as if about to leave the breast, which, deprived of it, will have no more a nation, no more a home on earth.

Women of my country!—Exaltadas! if such there be,—women of English, old English nobleness, who understand the courage of Boadicea, the sacrifice of Godiva, the power of Queen Emma to tread the red-hot iron unharmed,—women who share the nature of Mrs. Hutchinson, Lady Russell, and the mothers of our own revolution,—have you nothing to do with this?[96] You see the men, how they are willing to sell shamelessly the happiness of countless generations of fellow-creatures, the honor of their country, and their immortal souls, for a money market and political power. Do you not feel within you that which can reprove them, which can check, which can convince them? You would not speak in vain; whether each in her own home, or banded in unison.

Tell these men that you will not accept the glittering baubles, spacious dwellings, and plentiful service, they mean to offer you through these means. Tell them that the heart of Woman demands nobleness and honor in Man, and that, if they have not purity, have not mercy, they are no longer fathers, lovers, husbands, sons of yours.

This cause is your own, for, as I have before said, there is a reason why the foes of African Slavery seek more freedom for women; but put it not upon that ground, but on the ground of right.

If you have a power, it is a moral power. The films of interest are not so close around you as around the men. If you will but think, you cannot fail to wish to save the country from this disgrace. Let not slip the occasion, but do something to lift off the curse incurred by Eve.

You have heard the women engaged in the Abolition movement accused of boldness, because they lifted the voice in public, and lifted the latch of the stranger. But were these acts, whether performed judiciously or no, *so* bold as to dare before God and Man, to partake the fruits of such offence as this?

You hear much of the modesty of your sex. Preserve it by filling the mind with noble desires that shall ward off the corruptions of vanity and idleness. A profligate woman, who left her accustomed haunts and took service in a New York boarding-house, said "she had never heard talk so vile at the Five Points, as from the ladies at the boarding-house." And why? Because they were idle; because, having nothing worthy to engage them, they dwelt, with unnatural curiosity, on the ill they dared not go to see.

It will not so much injure your modesty to have your name, by the unthinking, coupled with idle blame, as to have upon your soul the weight of not trying to save a whole race of women from the scorn that is put upon *their* modesty.

Think of this well! I entreat, I conjure you, before it is too late. It is my belief that something effectual might be done by women, if they would only consider the subject, and enter upon it in the true spirit,—a spirit gentle, but firm, and which feared the offence of none, save One who is of purer eyes than to behold iniquity.

And now I have designated in outline, if not in fulness, the stream which is ever flowing from the heights of my thought.

In the earlier tract I was told I did not make my meaning sufficiently clear. In this I have consequently tried to illustrate it in various ways, and may have been guilty of much repetition. Yet, as I am anxious to leave no room for doubt, I shall venture to retrace, once more, the scope of my design in points, as was done in old-fashioned sermons.

Man is a being of two-fold relations, to nature beneath, and intelligences above him. The earth is his school, if not his birth-place; God his object; life and thought his means of interpreting nature, and aspiring to God.

Only a fraction of this purpose is accomplished in the life of any one man. Its entire accomplishment is to be hoped only from the sum of the lives of men, or Man considered as a whole.

As this whole has one soul and one body, any injury or obstruction to a part, or to the meanest member, affects the whole. Man can never be perfectly happy or virtuous, till all men are so.

To address Man wisely, you must not forget that his life is partly animal, subject to the same laws with Nature.

But you cannot address him wisely unless you consider him still more as soul, and appreciate the conditions and destiny of soul.

The growth of Man is two-fold, masculine and feminine.

So far as these two methods can be distinguished, they are so as

Energy and Harmony;

Power and Beauty;

Intellect and Love;

or by some such rude classification; for we have not language primitive and pure enough to express such ideas with precision.

These two sides are supposed to be expressed in Man and Woman, that is, as the more and the less, for the faculties have not been given pure to either, but only in preponderance. There are also exceptions in great number, such as men of far more beauty than power, and the reverse. But, as a general rule, it seems to have been the intention to give a preponderance on the one side, that is called masculine, and on the other, one that is called feminine.

There cannot be a doubt that, if these two developments were in perfect harmony, they would correspond to and fulfil one another, like hemispheres, or the tenor and bass in music.

But there is no perfect harmony in human nature; and the two parts answer one another only now and then; or, if there be a persistent consonance, it can only be traced at long intervals, instead of discoursing an obvious melody.

What is the cause of this?

Man, in the order of time, was developed first; as energy comes before harmony; power before beauty.

Woman was therefore under his care as an elder. He might have been her guardian and teacher.

But, as human nature goes not straight forward, but by excessive action and then reaction in an undulated course, he misunderstood and abused his advantages, and became her temporal master instead of her spiritual sire.

On himself came the punishment. He educated Woman more as a servant than a daughter, and found himself a king without a queen.

The children of this unequal union showed unequal natures, and, more and more, men seemed sons of the handmaid, rather than princess.

At last, there were so many Ishmaelites that the rest grew frightened and indignant. They laid the blame on Hagar, and drove her forth into the wilderness.

But there were none the fewer Ishmaelites for that.

At last men became a little wiser, and saw that the infant Moses was, in every case, saved by the pure instincts of Woman's breast. For, as too much adversity is better for the moral nature than too much prosperity, Woman, in this respect, dwindled less than Man, though in other respects still a child in leading-strings.

So Man did her more and more justice, and grew more and more kind.

But yet—his habits and his will corrupted by the past—he did not clearly see that Woman was half himself; that her interests were identical with his; and that, by the law of their common being, he could never reach his true proportions while she remained in any wise shorn of hers.

And so it has gone on to our day; both ideas developing, but more slowly than they would under a clearer recognition of truth and justice, which would have permitted the sexes their due influence on one another, and mutual improvement from more dignified relations.

Wherever there was pure love, the natural influences were, for the time, restored.

Wherever the poet or artist gave free course to his genius, he saw the truth, and expressed it in worthy forms, for these men especially share and need the feminine principle. The divine birds need to be brooded into life and song by mothers.

Wherever religion (I mean the thirst for truth and good, not the love of sect and dogma) had its course, the original design was apprehended in its simplicity, and the dove presaged sweetly from Dodona's oak.

I have aimed to show that no age was left entirely without a witness of the equality of the sexes in function, duty and hope.

Also that, when there was unwillingness or ignorance, which prevented this being acted upon, women had not the less power for their want of light and noble freedom. But it was power which hurt alike them and those against whom they made use of the arms of the servile,—cunning, blandishment, and unreasonable emotion.

That now the time has come when a clearer vision and better action are possible—when Man and Woman may regard one another as brother and sister, the pillars of one porch, the priests of one worship.

I have believed and intimated that this hope would receive an ampler fruition, than ever before, in our own land.

And it will do so if this land carry out the principles from which sprang our national life.

I believe that, at present, women are the best helpers of one another.

Let them think; let them act; till they know what they need.

We only ask of men to remove arbitrary barriers. Some would like to do more. But I believe it needs that Woman show herself in her native dignity, to teach them how to aid her; their minds are so encumbered by tradition.

When Lord Edward Fitzgerald travelled with the Indians, his manly heart obliged him at once to take the packs from the squaws and carry them. But we do not read that the red men followed his example, though they are ready enough to carry the pack of the white woman, because she seems to them a superior being.

Let Woman appear in the mild majesty of Ceres, and rudest churls will be willing to learn from her.

You ask, what use will she make of liberty, when she has so long been sustained and restrained?

I answer; in the first place, this will not be suddenly given. I read yesterday a debate of this year on the subject of enlarging women's rights over property. It was a leaf from the class-book that is preparing for the needed instruction. The men learned visibly as they spoke. The champions of Woman saw the fallacy of arguments on the opposite side, and were startled by their own convictions. With their wives at home, and the readers of the paper, it was the same. And so the stream flows on; thought urging action, and action leading to the evolution of still better thought.

But, were this freedom to come suddenly, I have no fear of the consequences. Individuals might commit excesses, but there is not only in the sex a reverence for decorums and limits inherited and enhanced from generation to generation, which many years of other life could not efface, but a native love, in Woman as Woman, of proportion, of "the simple art of not too much,"—a Greek moderation, which would create immediately a restraining party, the natural legislators and instructors of the rest, and would gradually establish such rules as are needed to guard, without impeding, life.

The Graces would lead the choral dance, and teach the rest to regulate their steps to the measure of beauty.

But if you ask me what offices they may fill, I reply—any. I do not care what case you put; let them be sea-captains, if you will. I do not doubt there are women well fitted for such an office, and, if so, I should be as glad to see them in it, as to welcome the maid of Saragossa, or the maid of Missolonghi, or the Suliote heroine, or Emily Plater.[97]

I think women need, especially at this juncture, a much greater range of occupation than they have, to rouse their latent powers. A party of travellers lately visited a lonely hut on a mountain. There they found an old woman, who told them she and her husband had lived there forty years. "Why," they said, "did you choose so barren a spot?" She "did not know; *it was the man's notion.*"

And, during forty years, she had been content to act, without knowing why, upon "the man's notion." I would not have it so.

In families that I know, some little girls like to saw wood, others to use carpenters' tools. Where these tastes are indulged, cheerfulness and good-humor are promoted. Where they are forbidden, because "such things are not proper for girls," they grow sullen and mischievous.

Fourier had observed these wants of women, as no one can fail to do who watches the desires of little girls, or knows the ennui that haunts grown women, except where they make to themselves a serene little world by art of some kind. He, therefore, in proposing a great variety of employments, in manufactures or the care of plants and animals, allows for one third of women as likely to have a taste for masculine pursuits, one third of men for feminine.

Who does not observe the immediate glow and serenity that is diffused over the life of women, before restless or fretful, by engaging in gardening, building, or the lowest department of art? Here is something that is not routine, something that draws forth life towards the infinite.

I have no doubt, however, that a large proportion of women would give themselves to the same employments as now, because there are circumstances that must lead them. Mothers will delight to make the nest soft and warm. Nature would take care of that; no need to clip the wings of any bird that wants to soar and sing, or finds in itself the strength of pinion for a migratory flight unusual to its kind. The difference would be that *all* need not be constrained to employments for which *some* are unfit.

I have urged upon the sex self-subsistence in its two forms of self-reliance and self-impulse, because I believe them to be the needed means of the present juncture.

I have urged on Woman independence of Man, not that I do not think the sexes mutually needed by one another, but because in Woman this fact has led to an excessive devotion, which has cooled love, degraded marriage, and prevented either sex from being what it should be to itself or the other.

I wish Woman to live, *first* for God's sake. Then she will not make an imperfect man her god, and thus sink to idolatry. Then she will not take what is not fit for her from a sense of weakness and poverty. Then, if she finds what she needs in Man embodied, she will know how to love, and be worthy of being loved.

By being more a soul, she will not be less Woman, for nature is perfected through spirit.

Now there is no woman, only an overgrown child.

That her hand may be given with dignity, she must be able to stand alone. I wish to see men and women capable of such relations as are depicted by Landor in his Pericles and Aspasia, where grace is the natural garb of strength, and the affections are calm, because deep. The softness is that of a firm tissue, as when

"The gods approve
The depth, but not the tumult of the soul,
A fervent, not ungovernable love."

A profound thinker has said, "No married woman can represent the female world, for she belongs to her husband. The idea of Woman must be represented by a virgin."

But that is the very fault of marriage, and of the present relation between the sexes, that the woman *does* belong to the man, instead of forming a whole with him. Were it otherwise, there would be no such limitation to the thought.

Woman, self-centred, would never be absorbed by any relation; it would be only an experience to her as to man. It is a vulgar error that love, *a* love, to Woman is her whole existence; she also is born for Truth and Love in their universal energy. Would she but assume her inheritance, Mary would not be the only virgin mother. Not Manzoni alone would celebrate in his wife the virgin mind with the maternal wisdom and conjugal affections. The soul is ever young, ever virgin.

And will not she soon appear?—the woman who shall vindicate their birthright for all women; who shall teach them what to claim, and how to use what they obtain? Shall not her name be for her era Victoria, for her country and life Virginia? Yet predictions are rash; she herself must teach us to give her the fitting name.

An idea not unknown to ancient times has of late been revived, that, in the metamorphoses of life, the soul assumes the form, first of Man, then of Woman, and takes the chances, and reaps the benefits of either lot. Why then, say some, lay such emphasis on the rights or needs of Woman? What she wins not as Woman will come to her as Man.

That makes no difference. It is not Woman, but the law of right, the law of growth, that speaks in us, and demands the perfection of each being in its kind—apple as apple, Woman as Woman. Without adopting your theory, I know that I, a daughter, live through the life of Man; but what concerns me now is, that my life be a beautiful, powerful, in a word, a complete life in its kind. Had I but one more moment to live I must wish the same. Suppose, at the end of your cycle, your great world-year, all will be completed, whether I exert myself or not (and the supposition is *false*,— but suppose it true), am I to be indifferent about it? Not so! I must beat my

own pulse true in the heart of the world; for *that* is virtue, excellence, health.

Thou, Lord of Day! didst leave us to-night so calmly glorious, not dismayed that cold winter is coming, not postponing thy beneficence to the fruitful summer! Thou didst smile on thy day's work when it was done, and adorn thy down-going as thy up-rising, for thou art loyal, and it is thy nature to give life, if thou canst, and shine at all events!

I stand in the sunny noon of life. Objects no longer glitter in the dews of morning, neither are yet softened by the shadows of evening. Every spot is seen, every chasm revealed. Climbing the dusty hill, some fair effigies that once stood for symbols of human destiny have been broken; those I still have with me show defects in this broad light. Yet enough is left, even by experience, to point distinctly to the glories of that destiny; faint, but not to be mistaken streaks of the future day. I can say with the bard,

"I stand in the sunny noon of life."

"Though many have suffered shipwreck, still beat noble hearts."

Always the soul says to us all, Cherish your best hopes as a faith, and abide by them in action. Such shall be the effectual fervent means to their fulfilment;

For the Power to whom we bow
Has given its pledge that, if not now,
They of pure and steadfast mind,
By faith exalted, truth refined,
Shall hear all music loud and clear,
Whose first notes they ventured here.
Then fear not thou to wind the horn,
Though elf and gnome thy courage scorn;
Ask for the castle's King and Queen;
Though rabble rout may rush between,
Beat thee senseless to the ground,
In the dark beset thee round;
Persist to ask, and it will come;
Seek not for rest in humbler home;
So shalt thou see, what few have seen,
The palace home of King and Queen.

15th November, 1844.[98]

1. *Hamlet* (GBWW I: 27, 33; II: 25, 33).

2. Ovid, *Metamorphoses* 9. "If there is anyone, however, who is likely to be annoyed at Hercules' becoming a god, and grudges him the reward he has been given, even such a one will learn that Hercules has deserved the gift, and will approve it, in spite of private feelings. The gods applauded..." (*GIT* 1966, 386).

3. The quote is ascribed to Louis Claude de Saint-Martin (1743–1803), French philosopher and mystic.

4. "Crawford's Orpheus"—the reference is to F. Marion Crawford (1854–1909).

5. "La Liberté" is the best-known poem of Pierre-Jean de Beranger (1780–1857).

6. Alessandro Manzoni (1785–1873) best known for *I promesi Sposi* (The Betrothed).

7. Walter Savage Landor (1775–1864), author of *Imaginary Conversations* (between historical figures) and other works, and a poet as well.

8. Poet John Sterling.

9. John Quincy Adams (1767–1848), sixth president of the United States (1825–29), who served afterward in the House of Representatives, where he was an outspoken opponent of slavery.

10. Phocion (c. 402 B.C.–318), Athenian statesman who ruled Athens under Macedonia's dominion from 322 B.C. to 318—in youth a student of Plato, a model of personal integrity.

11. From Ben Jonson's (1572–1637) *On Lucy Countess of Bedford.*

12. Fridrich von Schiller's *Dignity of Woman.* Schiller (1759–1805) was the leading German literary figure (with Goethe) of the later 18th century, author of "Wallenstein" and "In Simple and Sentiment Poetry."

13. Jean Paul Richter (1763–1825), German novelist and literary theorist.

14. Countess Emily Plater (1806–31).

15. Aspasia (fl. 440 B.C.), mistress of Pericles who made her house the center of literary and philosophical society. Hence the use of the name to mean any fascinating and cultured courtesan.

16. Eloisa—Heloise.

17. Torquato Tasso (1544–95) was a 16th century Italian poet who wrote an epic called *Jerusalem,* based on the First Crusade. He was thought mad and in 1579 was sent by the Duke of Ferrara to an asylum where he languished for many years despite the protests of Montaigne and the general sympathy of the literary world. This reference is probably to a play by Goethe, "Torquato Tasso" (1790), dealing with Tasso's life.

18. Elizabeth Carter (1717–1806), learned daughter of an English cleric who became a poet and translator of Epictetus.

19. Anne Dacier (1654–1720), classical authority, translator of both the *Iliad* and the *Odyssey* (into French) who with her husband, André Dacier, also edited a famous series of Latin classics.

20. "Ramayana"—ancient Indian epic ascribed to the poet Valmiki and consisting of 24 thousand stanzas in seven books.

21. "manners of Etruria," i.e., of the Etruscans, who inhabited what is now Tuscany until the beginning of the Christian era, and who, unlike the Romans and the Greeks, allowed women both liberty and power. Women participated in public life and were generally given an equal status otherwise unheard of in ancient times.

22. *Julius Caesar: (GBWW* I: 26,577; II: 24, 577).

23. (*GBWW* I: 26, 577; II: 24, 577).

24. (*GBWW* I: 26, 595; II: 24, 595).

25. (*GBWW* I: 26, 577; II: 24, 577).

26. (*GBWW* I: 26, 589; II: 24, 589).

27. Ovid, *The Metamorphoses (GIT* 1966, 385–86).

28. "Macaria"—an idealized soul encountered by Wilhelm Meister in Goethe's novel of that name discussed later in this essay.

29. Heinrich Heine (1797–1856), master ironist and greatest of German lyric poets, a sharp social critic of his age much disliked by some of his contemporaries, partly because he was a Jew.

30. "Drachenfels" refers to an early poem by Fuller.

31. Xenophon (431 B.C.–350), author of the *Anabasis,* which was highly regarded and influenced Latin literature. The *Oeconomicus* was a treatise on estate management, and the *Cyropaedia* was a historical novel that portrayed the ideal education.

32. Euripedes, *Iphigenia in Aulis (GBWW* I: 5, 437; II: 4, 629).

33. Panthea—character in Xenophon's *Oeconomicus.*

34. Jean-Marie Roland (1734–93), French scientist and Girondist (that is, bourgeois) revolutionary, who discovered the King's papers in a safe in the Tuileries in 1792 but omitted to exploit them sufficiently to satisfy the Radical Jacobins.

35. From "Words of Faith" (1798), a poem by Schiller.

36. Emanual Swedenborg (1688–1772), Swedish theologian and scientist who became a mystic, much read and quoted by Fuller and other Transcendentalists. His visions inspired William Blake.

37. Franz Schubert (1797–1828) set these lines to music in his *Lied der Mignon* (1828).

38. William H. Prescott (1796–1859), American historian whose *History of the Conquest of Mexico* (1843) and *History of the Reign of Ferdinand and Isabella the Catholic* (1838), both classics, were well-known to Fuller.

39. Edmund Spenser (1552/53–99), author of *The Fairie Queen* (1590), a chivalric epic modeled on the works of Tasso. Britomart and Belphoebe are characters in Spenser's poem.

40. John Ford (1586–1639?) and Philip Massinger (1583–1639/40), English dramatists, the first known best for his *'Tis Pity She's a Whore,* the second as the possible collaborator with Shakespeare in the writing of *Henry VIII* and *The Two Noble Kinsmen.*

41. Lord Herbert (Edward) of Cherbury (1583–1648), soldier, diplomat, philosopher, and poet, brother of George Herbert (1593–1633), eminent English Metaphysical Poet himself.

42. Jeanne-Marie Roland (1754–93), wife of J-M Roland, *supra,* who greatly influenced the Girondist (moderate) faction during the French Revolution and was as a result imprisoned and eventually executed by the Jacobins.

43. William Godwin (1756–1836), English novelist and political philosopher, expounder of Rousseau, was the husband of the early feminist Mary Wollstonecraft; was also the father of Mary Wollstonecraft Shelley, the author of *Frankenstein.*

44. George Sand (pen name of Amandine Dudevant) [1804–76], French writer famous for her "independence," which extended to wearing men's clothes, and for her love affairs with—among others—Alfred de Musset and Frederic Chopin.

45. Mary Wollstonecraft (1759–97), English author, best known for her work *A Vindication of the Rights of Women* (1792). She was a strong advocate for educational and social equality for women.

46. Goodwyn Barmby (1829–81), Unitarian preacher and Christian socialist.

47. William (1792–1879) and Mary (1799–1888) Howitt—popular English writers and reformers. William studied religion and German culture, while Mary published poetry, fiction, and various translations.

48. Goetz von Berlichingen (1480–1562), German knight and source of Goethe's drama "Goetz von Berlichingen."

49. Count Zinzendorf (N.L., Graf von Zinzendorf) (1700–60) German pietist and leader of the Moravian Church.

50. John Milton, *Paradise Lost* (*GBWW* I: 32, 166; II: 29, 166).

51. Ratchewaine was the wife of an Iowa chief named Mahashah, cited in McKenney and Hall's *History of the Indian Tribes of North America.*

52. In Xenophon's *Anabasis,* Cyrus is a young man, a romantic drawn to danger and excitement.

53. Xenophon, *Oeconomicus,* op. cit.

54. Lady Mary Wortley Montagu (1689–1762), a brilliant woman noted as a patron of Henry Fielding, for her friendship with Alexander Pope, and for her own published letters.

55. Lady Jane Grey (1537–54), proclaimed Queen of England during the Protestant attempt to keep Mary I, daughter of Henry VIII, who was Catholic, from ascending to the throne after the early death of Henry's son, Edward VI.

56. Fuller here mixes literary, artistic, and historical figures indiscriminately, as equally apt.

57. Figure painted by Michelangelo.

58. Victoria (Vittoria) Colonna (1492–1547), Italian poet; friend and correspondent of Michelangelo.

59. Anna Brownell Jameson (1794–1860), recounts this tale of a Chippewa woman in *Winter Studies and Summer Rambles in Canada* (1838).

60. Mother Anne Lee (1736–84), founder of the Shakers. Joanna Southcote (1750–1814), English religious fanatic. *Dolorosa* is a term referring to the Virgin Mary as she grieves over Christ's body.

61. Xavier de Maistre (1763–1852), French Christian philosopher.

62. Jakob Böhme (Behman) 1575–1624, German mystic who influenced the Quakers, Pietists, and the Romantics. Henri de Saint-Simon (1760–1825), was a Christian

socialist, much admired by Friedrich Engles and others, who advocated the enfranchise-ment of women.

63. "Angel of Swedenborg." Swedenborg (*see* above) had visions of Christ.

64. Mademoiselle Rachel (1820–58), French tragic actress.

65. La Rochefoucault (1613–80), French moralist, best known for his *Maximes.*

66. "Guercino,"—Giovanni Francesco Barbieri (1591–1666), "Il Guercino" (the squinter), Italian painter of frescoes noted for their romanticism.

67. Euripedes, *The Trojan Women* (*GBWW* I: 5, 272; II: 4, 366–67).

68. (*GBWW* I: 5, 273; II: 4, 369).

69. (*GBWW* I: 5, 273; II: 4, 369).

70. "Seeress of Prevost"—*see* at Kerner, below.

71. "Delphos"—Delphi.

72. François de Fenelon (1651–1715), French theologian, cleric, and pedagogical theorist, was influenced in later life by Madame Guyon, an exponent of Quietism, whom he defended against charges of heresy. J. A. C. Kerner (1786–1862) was a German poet and physician, interested in spiritualism, who published an extensive study of a clairvoy-ant of the day whom he called The Seerest of Prevost.

73. Angelina (1805–79) and Sarah (1792–1873) Grimké, Quaker sisters who were noted abolitionists although their father owned slaves. Along with Abby Kelly, they protested slavery and also embraced the women's rights movement.

74. William Ellery Channing (1780–1842), the founder of Unitarianism, also an abolitionist, expounded the ideas of self-reliance and spirituality that came to be known as Transcendentalism (a term derived from Kant's *Critique of Practical Reason*). Fuller is associated with this movement, and encouraged it in the *Dial*.

75. Harriet Martineau (1802–76), English Unitarian who wrote on both religious and social subjects. She once visited the United States and wrote an unfavorable report called *Society in America* (1837).

76. Linnaeus—Latinized name of Carl von Linné (1707–78), Swedish botanist, whose classification of plants is the basis of modern botany.

77. Proclus (c. 410 B.C.–485), Greek philosopher identified with Neoplatonism, the doctrine of Plotinus, which envisioned the reconciliation of reason with God by means of an upward journey of the soul—much like Transcendentalism.

78. Robert Southey (1774–1843), published the epic *The Curse of Kehama* in 1818.

79. Charles Fourier (1772–1837), founder of Fourierism, involving the creation of utopian human communities called phalanxes in which private property would not exist. It was the system that guided the establishment of Brook Farm in Massachusetts, where for a time, intellectuals and artists, among them Fuller, labored to maintain themselves.

80. *Wilhelm Meister's Apprenticeship* (1795–96), a novel by Goethe in which a young man grows from excitable youth to responsible manhood—the original *bildung-sroman* ("novel of education"), or work of this type, often imitated since. *Wilhelm Meister's Wandering Years* (1829), a sequel, tells of its protagonist's reconciliation with society. The women mentioned by Fuller in this discussion of Goethe are all characters in these two books.

81. Maria Edgeworth (1767–1849), Irish novelist best known for her *Castle Rackrent* (1800), but more typically a writer of domestic manners in the style of Jane Austen.

82. "Paladin"—a courtier or champion (the name of one of the knights-errant in the books of chivalry studied by Don Quixote) who rescued damsels in distress.

83. Antonio Canova (1757–1822), Italian sculptor, the dominant European figure in that art at the beginning of the nineteenth century. His reputation for "pure" moral character may have been echoic of his artistic achievement, which was often described as sublime.

84. Poem is by Fuller.

85. Sir Philip Sidney (1554–86), poet, scholar, soldier, and courtier, regarded as the type and model of the Renaissance gentleman in Elizabethan times, who wrote "Arca-dia," a pastoral romance, among other works.

86. Lady Rachel Russell (1636–1723), author of *Letters of Rachel, Lady Russell* (1773). She was highly critical of the immorality and corruption of her time.

87. "Mr. Adams"—J.Q. Adams, *ante.*

88. Lydia Maria Child (1802–80), novelist, journalist, abolitionist, and humanitarian. She supported the rights of Native Americans, women, and the poor.

89. Eugène Sue (1804–57), French novelist who wrote *The Mysteries of Paris* (1842–43) and *The Wandering Jew* (1844–45), among other works.

90. *Sir Charles Grandison*—title of a novel (1753) by Samuel Richardson (1689–1761). Its hero had the reputation of an ideal 18th century gentleman.

91. Madame Necker de Saussure (1766–1841), Swiss woman of letters and author of an influential work on the education of women.

92. "This life has no purpose other than to develope the moral education of our hearts."

93. Sir Alexander Mackenzie (1755?–1820), fur trader and explorer whose travels across Canada (1789–93), allowed him to see much Indian life.

94. "Nibelungen Lays"—*The Niedelungenlied,* medieval German epic from the late 12th century in which Brunhilde, Queen of Iceland, vows to marry only a man capable of skillful feats; Valkyrie—mythical armed Norse maidens who served the god Odin and were sent by him to choose those slain in battle who were worthy to live in Valhala, that is, heaven.

95. Catharine Maria Sedgewick (1789–1867), writer and prison reform activist.

96. Boadicea—d. 62, Celtic queen who rebelled against Roman rule of Britain; Godiva—legendary English noblewoman who rode naked through town to save its people from a tax; Anne Hutchinson (1591–1643), Puritan settler in Massachusetts who defied the clergy with sermons devoted to the idea of salvation through intuition as distinct from institutionalized precepts; banished and excommunicated, she moved to Rhode Island, where she and her children and servants were subsequently killed by Indians.

97. Maid of Saragossa, lived in a Spanish city besieged by the French (1808–09) during the Napoleonic Wars; maid of Missolonghi lived in a Greek town twice besieged (1822–23; 1825–26) by the Turks during the Greek War of Independence; the Suliote heroine lived on Suli, a Greek isle that resisted Turkish occupation in 1820.

98. Poem is by Fuller.

Henry David Thoreau

Henry David Thoreau was among those who in the first half of the nineteenth century made New England a center—in some ways the center—of
thought and its expression in the United States. Just what the thought was
has always been hard to say, since it resisted definition; the name by which
it is known, Transcendentalism, implies something above or beyond what
is definable, and most attempts to define it have in fact been unsatisfactory.
We can see its sources in Eastern mysticism, German romanticism and
other writers of the day, but this does not help very much to capture it.
Perhaps we can understand it best in terms of what it was not—what it had
lost—the religious faith of New England's Puritan founders, for which it
substituted an intuition of the infinite in nature and the human soul. Ralph
Waldo Emerson began as a minister but ceased to preach when he ceased
to believe in any God except the one he found, or thought could be discovered, in every human heart.

Of the group—so far as it was a group—Thoreau was the most eccentric,
the least able or willing to come to terms with the world in which he lived.
Yet he is forever associated with the part of it in which he was born and
which he never left for any length of time—the town of Concord, Massachusetts, where Emerson lived himself, and also Nathaniel Hawthorne in
his later years. Born in 1817, Thoreau was sent by his parents to Concord
Academy, where he did well enough to seem worth sending to Harvard
College, from which he graduated in 1837, though without having arrived
at any particular sense of mission. He tried school teaching, business (mak-

ing pencils), and even started a small school, but within five years all these projects had failed, and indeed he was never successful in any line of work—from lack of discipline, some thought, or more likely from indifference. He could write—poems, for one thing, which still take a genuine if minor place in American literature—and there was within him a stubborn self-reliance, a refusal to accept any orthodoxy, or even a received opinion, which Emerson recognized and admired and which Thoreau himself expressed at various times with memorable force. In truth it is impossible to forget some things he said. His credo, if he had one, was the famous exhortation in *Walden:* "If a man does not keep step with his companions, perhaps it is because he hears a different drummer. Let him march to the music that he hears, however measured or far away." But such a sentiment did not put money in his pocket or even bread on his table.

It was not meant to. A familiar figure tramping about the streets and fields of Concord and its neighborhood, never seeming to have much to do, Thoreau wanted little and asked less of the world. His two most famous acts were both in character. In 1846 he was arrested for failing to pay his poll tax, then required by law, which he withheld because he disapproved of the Mexican War. Refusing also to pay the fine, he was put in jail—for one night—until his aunt Maria bailed him out. A famous story is that Emerson, who had protested the war himself, found Thoreau in jail and asked what he was doing in there, and that Thoreau asked what *he* was doing out *there*. Thoreau's own account of the matter was later (1849) set forth in the essay which has become known as "Civil Disobedience," a classic statement that was subsequently cited both by Gandhi and by Martin Luther King, Jr., as formative of their defiance of civil authority.

The other act for which Thoreau has become immortal was his decision about the same time to go and live by himself near Walden Pond, outside Concord, and live as nearly as he could on as little as possible and nothing from another man's hand. In fact, he made do as he could on what he grew for himself near a cabin he built on the pond's edge, where in his spare time he read books, wrote, and contemplated what he called "higher things." Out of this experience came Thoreau's best-known book, *Walden,* a celebration of nature and the simple life, but also an assertion of the presence of the abiding infinite which gives it eminent place, or should, in any list of works that proclaim the human spirit.

"A Plea for John Brown" was written in 1859 after the raid on Harper's Ferry by Brown and his little band in protest at the maintenance of slavery had failed, and Brown was to be hanged. Thoreau was an abolitionist who had helped escaped slaves to make their way to Canada along what was known as the Underground Railroad. Brown's death is said to have shattered Thoreau, and perhaps it did. Still, enough of what he was remained to say, when in 1862 he lay dying of tuberculosis and was asked if he had made his peace with God, that he was not aware that he and God had ever quarreled.

A Plea for John Brown

Henry David Thoreau

Illustrations by Brad Holland

I trust that you will pardon me for being here. I do not wish to force my thoughts upon you, but I feel forced myself. Little as I know of Captain Brown, I would fain do my part to correct the tone and statements of the newspapers, and of my countrymen generally, respecting his character and actions. It costs us nothing to be just. We can at least express our sympathy with, and admiration of, him and his companions, and that is what I now propose to do.

First, as to his history. I will endeavor to omit, as much as possible, what you have already read. I need not describe his person to you, for probably most of you have seen and will not soon forget him. I am told that his grandfather, John Brown, was an officer in the Revolution; that he himself was born in Connecticut about the beginning of this century, but early went with his father to Ohio. I heard him say that his father was a contractor who furnished beef to the army there, in the war of 1812; that he accompanied him to the camp, and assisted him in that employment, seeing a good deal of military life,—more, perhaps, than if he had been a soldier; for he was often present at the councils of the officers. Especially, he learned by experience how armies are supplied and maintained in the field,—a work which, he observed, requires at least as much experience and skill as to lead them in battle. He said that few persons had any conception of the cost, even the pecuniary cost, of firing a single bullet in war. He saw enough, at any rate, to disgust him with a military life; indeed, to excite in him a great abhorrence of it; so much so, that though he was tempted by the offer of some petty office in the army, when he was about eighteen, he not only declined that, but he also refused to train when warned, and was fined for it. He then resolved that he would never have anything to do with any war, unless it were a war for liberty.

When the troubles in Kansas began, he sent several of his sons thither to strengthen the party of the Free State men, fitting them out with such weapons as he had; telling them that if the troubles should increase, and there should be need of him, he would follow, to assist them with his hand and counsel. This, as you all know, he soon after did; and it was through his agency, far more than any other's, that Kansas was made free.

For a part of his life he was a surveyor, and at one time he was engaged in wool-growing, and he went to Europe as an agent about that business. There, as everywhere, he had his eyes about him, and made many original observations. He said, for instance, that he saw why the soil of England was so rich, and that of Germany (I think it was) so poor, and he thought of writing to some of the crowned heads about it. It was because in England the peasantry live on the soil which they cultivate, but in Germany they are gathered into villages at night. It is a pity that he did not make a book of his observations.

I should say that he was an old-fashioned man in his respect for the Constitution, and his faith in the permanence of this Union. Slavery he deemed to be wholly opposed to these, and he was its determined foe.

He was by descent and birth a New England farmer, a man of great common sense, deliberate and practical as that class is, and tenfold more so. He was like the best of those who stood at Concord Bridge once, on Lexington Common, and on Bunker Hill, only he was firmer and higher principled than any that I have chanced to hear of as there. It was no abolition lecturer that converted him. Ethan Allen and Stark, with whom he may in some respects be compared, were rangers in a lower and less important field. They could bravely face their country's foes, but he had the courage to face his country herself when she was in the wrong. A Western writer says, to account for his escape from so many perils, that he was concealed under a "rural exterior;" as if, in that prairie land, a hero should, by good rights, wear a citizen's dress only.

He did not go to the college called Harvard, good old Alma Mater as she is. He was not fed on the pap that is there furnished. As he phrased it, "I know no more of grammar than one of your calves." But he went to the great university of the West, when he sedulously pursued the study of Liberty, for which he had early betrayed a fondness, and having taken many degrees, he finally commenced the public practice of Humanity in Kansas, as you all know. Such were *his humanities,* and not any study of grammar. He would have left a Greek accent slanting the wrong way, and righted up a falling man.

He was one of that class of whom we hear a great deal, but, for the most part, see nothing at all,—the Puritans. It would be in vain to kill him. He died lately in the time of Cromwell, but he reappeared here. Why should he not? Some of the Puritan stock are said to have come over and settled in New England. They were a class that did something else than celebrate their forefathers' day, and eat parched corn in remembrance of that time. They were neither Democrats nor Republicans, but men of simple habits, straightforward, prayerful; not thinking much of rulers who did not fear God, not making many compromises, nor seeking after available candidates.

"In his camp," as one has recently written, and as I have myself heard him state, "he permitted no profanity; no man of loose morals was suffered to remain there, unless, indeed, as a prisoner of war. 'I would rather,' said he, 'have the smallpox, yellow fever, and cholera, all together in my camp, than a man without principle.... It is a mistake, sir, that our people make, when they think that bullies are the best fighters, or that they are the fit men to oppose these Southerners. Give me men of good principles,—God-fearing men,—men who respect themselves, and with a dozen of them I will oppose any hundred such men as these Buford ruffians.'" He said that if one offered himself to be a soldier under him, who was forward to tell what he could or would do if he could only get sight of the enemy, he had but little confidence in him.

He was never able to find more than a score or so of recruits whom he would accept, and only about a dozen, among them his sons, in whom he had perfect faith. When he was here some years ago, he showed to a few a little manuscript book,—his "orderly book" I think he called it,—containing the names of his company in Kansas, and the rules by which they bound themselves; and he stated that several of them had already sealed the contract with their blood. When some one remarked that, with the addition of a chaplain, it would have been a perfect Cromwellian troop, he observed that he would have been glad to add a chaplain to the list, if he could have found one who could fill that office worthily. It is easy enough to find one for the United States army. I believe that he had prayers in his camp morning and evening, nevertheless.

He was a man of Spartan habits, and at sixty was scrupulous about his diet at your table, excusing himself by saying that he must eat sparingly and fare hard, as became a soldier, or one who was fitting himself for difficult enterprises, a life of exposure.

A man of rare common sense and directness of speech, as of action; a transcendentalist above all, a man of ideas and principles,—that was what distinguished him. Not yielding to a whim or transient impulse, but carrying out the purpose of a life. I noticed that he did not overstate anything, but spoke within bounds. I remember, particularly, how, in his speech here, he referred to what his family had suffered in Kansas, without ever giving the least vent to his pent-up fire. It was a volcano with an ordinary chimney-flue. Also referring to the deeds of certain Border Ruffians, he said, rapidly paring away his speech, like an experienced soldier, keeping a reserve of force and meaning, "They had a perfect right to be hung." He was not in the least a rhetorician, was not talking to Buncombe or his constituents anywhere, had no need to invent anything but to tell the simple truth, and communicate his own resolution; therefore he appeared incomparably strong, and eloquence in Congress and elsewhere seemed to me at a discount. It was like the speeches of Cromwell compared with those of an ordinary king.

As for his tact and prudence, I will merely say, that at a time when scarcely a man from the Free States was able to reach Kansas by any direct route, at least without having his arms taken from him, he, carrying what imperfect guns and other weapons he could collect, openly and slowly drove an ox-cart through Missouri, apparently in the capacity of a surveyor, with his surveying compass exposed in it, and so passed unsuspected, and had ample opportunity to learn the designs of the enemy. For some time after his arrival he still followed the same profession. When, for instance, he saw a knot of the ruffians on the prairie, discussing, of course, the single topic which then occupied their minds, he would, perhaps, take his compass and one of his sons, and proceed to run an imaginary line right through the very spot on which that conclave had assembled, and when he came up to them, he would naturally pause and have some talk with them, learning their news, and, at last, all their plans perfectly; and having thus completed his real survey he would resume his imaginary one, and run on his line till he was out of sight.

When I expressed surprise that he could live in Kansas at all, with a price set upon his head, and so large a number, including the authorities, exasperated against him, he accounted for it by saying, "It is perfectly well understood that I will not be taken." Much of the time for some years he has had to skulk in swamps, suffering from poverty and from sickness, which was the consequence of exposure, befriended only by Indians and a few whites. But though it might be known that he was lurking in a particular swamp, his foes commonly did not care to go in after him. He could even come out into a town where there were more Border Ruffians than Free State men, and transact some business, without delaying long, and yet not be molested; for, said he, "no little handful of men were willing to undertake it, and a large body could not be got together in season."

As for his recent failure, we do not know the facts about it. It was evidently far from being a wild and desperate attempt. His enemy, Mr. Vallandigham, is compelled to say that "it was among the best planned and executed conspiracies that ever failed."

Not to mention his other successes, was it a failure, or did it show a want of good management, to deliver from bondage a dozen human beings, and walk off with them by broad daylight, for weeks if not months, at a leisurely pace, through one State after another, for half the length of the North, conspicuous to all parties, with a price set upon his head, going into a court-room on his way and telling what he had done, thus convincing Missouri that it was not profitable to try to hold slaves in his neighborhood?—and this, not because the government menials were lenient, but because they were afraid of him.

Yet he did not attribute his success, foolishly, to "his star," or to any magic. He said, truly, that the reason why such greatly superior numbers quailed before him was, as one of his prisoners confessed, because they *lacked a cause,*—a kind of armor which he and his party never lacked. When the time came, few men were found willing to lay down their lives in defense of what they knew to be wrong; they did not like that this should be their last act in this world.

But to make haste to *his* last act, and its effects.

The newspapers seem to ignore, or perhaps are really ignorant of the fact that there are at least as many as two or three individuals to a town throughout the North who think much as the present speaker does about him and his enterprise. I do not hesitate to say that they are an important and growing party. We aspire to be something more than stupid and timid chattels, pretending to read history and our Bibles, but desecrating every house and every day we breathe in. Perhaps anxious politicians may prove that only seventeen white men and five negroes were concerned in the late enterprise; but their very anxiety to prove this might suggest to themselves that all is not told. Why do they still dodge the truth? They are so anxious because of a dim consciousness of the fact, which they do not distinctly face, that at least a million of the free inhabitants of the United States would have rejoiced if it had succeeded. They at most only criticize the tactics. Though we wear no crape, the thought of that man's position and probable fate is spoiling many a man's day here at the North for other thinking. If any one who has seen him here can pursue successfully any other train of thought, I do not know what he is made of. If there is any such who gets his usual allowance of sleep, I will warrant him to fatten easily under any circumstances which do not touch his body or purse. I put a piece of paper and a pencil under my pillow, and when I could not sleep I wrote in the dark.

On the whole, my respect for my fellow-men, except as one may out-weigh a million, is not being increased these days. I have noticed the cold-blooded way in which newspaper writers and men generally speak of this event, as if an ordinary malefactor, though one of unusual "pluck,"—as the Governor of Virginia is reported to have said, using the language of the cock-pit, "the gamest man he ever saw,"—had been caught, and were about to be hung. He was not dreaming of his foes when the governor thought he looked so brave. It turns what sweetness I have to gall, to hear, or hear of, the remarks of some of my neighbors. When we heard at first that he was dead, one of my townsmen observed that "he died as the fool dieth;" which, pardon me, for an instant suggested a likeness in him dying to my neighbor living. Others, craven-hearted, said disparagingly, that "he threw his life away," because he resisted the government. Which way have they thrown *their* lives, pray?—such as would praise a man for attacking singly an ordinary band of thieves or murderers. I hear another ask, Yankee-like, "What will he gain by it?" as if he expected to fill his pockets by this enterprise. Such a one has no idea of gain but in this worldly sense. If it does not lead to a "surprise" party, if he does not get a new pair of boots, or a vote of thanks, it must be a failure. "But he won't gain anything by it." Well, no, I don't suppose he could get four-and-sixpence a day for being hung, take the year round; but then he stands a chance to save a consider-able part of his soul,—and *such* a soul!—when *you* do not. No doubt you can get more in your market for a quart of milk than for a quart of blood, but that is not the market that heroes carry their blood to.

Such do not know that like the seed is the fruit, and that, in the moral world, when good seed is planted, good fruit is inevitable, and does not depend on our watering and cultivating; that when you plant, or bury, a hero in his field, a crop of heroes is sure to spring up. This is a seed of such force and vitality, that it does not ask our leave to germinate.

The momentary charge at Balaklava, in obedience to a blundering com-mand, proving what a perfect machine the soldier is, has, properly enough, been celebrated by a poet laureate; but the steady, and for the most part successful, charge of this man, for some years, against the legions of Slavery, in obedience to an infinitely higher command, is as much more memorable than that as an intelligent and conscientious man is superior to a machine. Do you think that that will go unsung?

"Served him right,"—"A dangerous man,"—"He is undoubtedly in-sane." So they proceed to live their sane, and wise, and altogether admira-ble lives, reading their Plutarch a little, but chiefly pausing at that feat of Putnam, who was let down into a wolf's den; and in this wise they nourish themselves for brave and patriotic deeds some time or other. The Tract Society could afford to print that story of Putnam. You might open the district schools with the reading of it, for there is nothing about Slavery or the Church in it; unless it occurs to the reader that some pastors are *wolves* in sheep's clothing. "The American Board of Commissioners for Foreign

Missions," even, might dare to protest against *that* wolf. I have heard of boards, and of American boards, but it chances that I never heard of this particular lumber till lately. And yet I hear of Northern men, and women, and children, by families, buying a "life-membership" in such societies as these. A life-membership in the grave! You can get buried cheaper than that.

Our foes are in our midst and all about us. There is hardly a house but is divided against itself, for our foe is the all but universal woodenness of both head and heart, the want of vitality in man, which is the effect of our vice; and hence are begotten fear, superstition, bigotry, persecution, and slavery of all kinds. We are mere figure-heads upon a hulk, with livers in the place of hearts. The curse is the worship of idols, which at length changes the worshipper into a stone image himself; and the New En-glander is just as much an idolater as the Hindoo. This man was an excep-tion, for he did not set up even a political graven image between him and his God.

A church that can never have done with excommunicating Christ while it exists! Away with your broad and flat churches, and your narrow and tall churches! Take a step forward, and invent a new style of out-houses. Invent a salt that will save you, and defend our nostrils.

The modern Christian is a man who has consented to say all the prayers in the liturgy, provided you will let him go straight to bed and sleep quietly afterward. All his prayers begin with "Now I lay me down to sleep," and he is forever looking forward to the time when he shall go to his "*long* rest." He has consented to perform certain old-established charities, too, after a fashion, but he does not wish to hear of any new-fangled ones; he doesn't wish to have any supplementary articles added to the contract, to fit it to the present time. He shows the whites of his eyes on the Sabbath, and the blacks all the rest of the week. The evil is not merely a stagnation of blood, but a stagnation of spirit. Many, no doubt, are well disposed, but sluggish by constitution and by habit, and they cannot conceive of a man who is actuated by higher motives than they are. Accordingly they pronounce this man insane, for they know that *they* could never act as he does, as long as they are themselves.

We dream of foreign countries, of other times and races of men, placing them at a distance in history or space; but let some significant event like the present occur in our midst, and we discover, often, this distance and this strangeness between us and our nearest neighbors. *They* are our Austrias, and Chinas, and South Sea Islands. Our crowded society becomes well spaced all at once, clean and handsome to the eye,—a city of magnificent distances. We discover why it was that we never got beyond compliments and surfaces with them before; we become aware of as many versts be-tween us and them as there are between a wandering Tartar and a Chinese town. The thoughtful man becomes a hermit in the thoroughfares of the market-place. Impassable seas suddenly find their level between us, or dumb steppes stretch themselves out there. It is the difference of constitu-tion, of intelligence, and faith, and not streams and mountains, that make

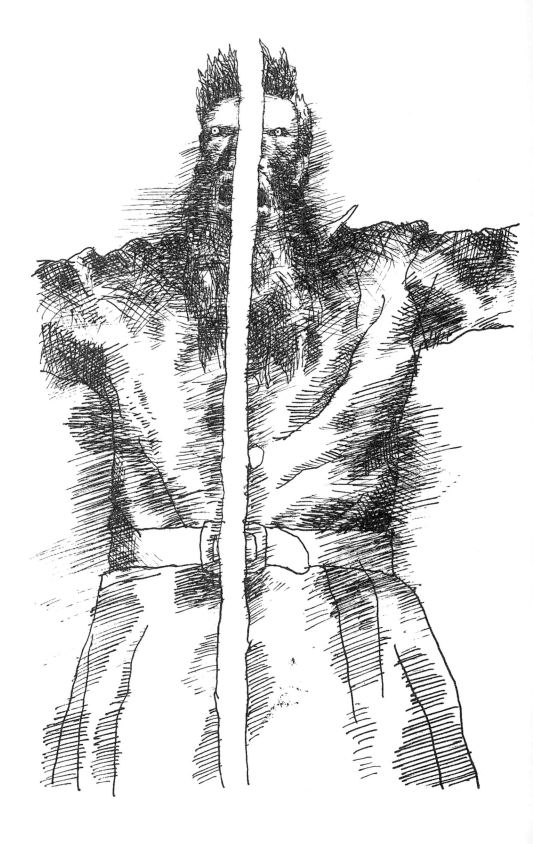

the true and impassable boundaries between individuals and between states. None but the like-minded can come plenipotentiary to our court.

I read all the newspapers I could get within a week after this event, and I do not remember in them a single expression of sympathy for these men. I have since seen one noble statement, in a Boston paper, not editorial. Some voluminous sheets decided not to print the full report of Brown's words to the exclusion of other matter. It was as if a publisher should reject the manuscript of the New Testament, and print Wilson's last speech. The same journal which contained this pregnant news was chiefly filled, in parallel columns, with the reports of the political conventions that were being held. But the descent to them was too steep. They should have been spared this contrast,—been printed in an extra, at least. To turn from the voices and deeds of earnest men to the *cackling* of political conventions! Office-seekers and speech-makers, who do not so much as lay an honest egg, but wear their breasts bare upon an egg of chalk! Their great game is the game of straws, or rather that universal aboriginal game of the platter, at which the Indians cried *hub, bub!* Exclude the reports of religious and political conventions, and publish the words of a living man.

But I object not so much to what they have omitted as to what they have inserted. Even the *Liberator* called it "a misguided, wild, and apparently insane—effort." As for the herd of newspapers and magazines, I do not chance to know an editor in the country who will deliberately print any-thing which he knows will ultimately and permanently reduce the number of his subscribers. They do not believe that it would be expedient. How then can they print truth? If we do not say pleasant things, they argue, nobody will attend to us. And so they do like some traveling auctioneers, who sing an obscene song, in order to draw a crowd around them. Republi-can editors, obliged to get their sentences ready for the morning edition, and accustomed to look at everything by the twilight of politics, express no admiration, nor true sorrow even, but call these men "deluded fanatics,"— "mistaken men,"—"insane," or "crazed." It suggests what a *sane* set of editors we are blessed with, *not* "mistaken men;" who know very well on which side their bread is buttered, at least.

A man does a brave and humane deed, and at once, on all sides, we hear people and parties declaring, "I didn't do it, nor countenance *him* to do it, in any conceivable way. It can't be fairly inferred from my past career." I, for one, am not interested to hear you define your position. I don't know that I ever was or ever shall be. I think it is mere egotism, or impertinent at this time. Ye needn't take so much pains to wash your skirts of him. No intelligent man will ever be convinced that he was any creature of yours. He went and came, as he himself informs us, "under the auspices of John Brown and nobody else." The Republican party does not perceive how many his *failure* will make to vote more correctly than they would have them. They have counted the votes of Pennsylvania & Co., but they have not correctly counted Captain Brown's vote. He has taken the wind out of their sails,—the little wind they had,—and they may as well lie to and repair.

What though he did not belong to your clique! Though you may not approve of his method or his principles, recognize his magnanimity. Would you not like to claim kindredship with him in that, though in no other thing he is like, or likely, to you? Do you think that you would lose your reputation so? What you lost at the spile, you would gain at the bung.

If they do not mean all this, then they do not speak the truth, and say what they mean. They are simply at their old tricks still.

"It was always conceded to him," *says one who calls him crazy,* "that he was a conscientious man, very modest in his demeanor, apparently inoffensive, until the subject of Slavery was introduced, when he would exhibit a feeling of indignation unparalleled."

The slave-ship is on her way, crowded with its dying victims; new cargoes are being added in mid-ocean; a small crew of slaveholders, countenanced by a large body of passengers, is smothering four millions under the hatches, and yet the politician asserts that the only proper way by which deliverance is to be obtained is by "the quiet diffusion of the sentiments of humanity," without any "outbreak." As if the sentiments of humanity were ever found unaccompanied by its deeds, and you could disperse them, all finished to order, the pure article, as easily as water with a watering-pot, and so lay the dust. What is that that I hear cast overboard? The bodies of the dead that have found deliverance. That is the way we are "diffusing" humanity, and its sentiments with it.

Prominent and influential editors, accustomed to deal with politicians, men of an infinitely lower grade, say, in their ignorance, that he acted "on the principle of revenge." They do not know the man. They must enlarge themselves to conceive of him. I have no doubt that the time will come when they will begin to see him as he was. They have got to conceive of a man of faith and of religious principle, and not a politician or an Indian; of a man who did not wait till he was personally interfered with or thwarted in some harmless business before he gave his life to the cause of the oppressed.

If Walker may be considered the representative of the South, I wish I could say that Brown was the representative of the North. He was a superior man. He did not value his bodily life in comparison with ideal things. He did not recognize unjust human laws, but resisted them as he was bid. For once we are lifted out of the trivialness and dust of politics into the region of truth and manhood. No man in America has ever stood up so persistently and effectively for the dignity of human nature, knowing himself for a man, and the equal of any and all governments. In that sense he was the most American of us all. He needed no babbling lawyer, making false issues, to defend him. He was more than a match for all the judges that American voters, or office-holders of whatever grade, can create. He could not have been tried by a jury of his peers, because his peers did not exist. When a man stands up serenely against the condemnation and vengeance of mankind, rising above them literally *by a whole body,*—even though he were of late the vilest murderer, who has settled that matter with himself,—the spectacle is a sublime one,—didn't ye know it, ye *Libera-*

tors, ye *Tribunes,* ye *Republicans?*—and we become criminal in comparison. Do yourselves the honor to recognize him. He needs none of your respect.

As for the Democratic journals, they are not human enough to affect me at all. I do not feel indignation at anything they may say.

I am aware that I anticipate a little,—that he was still, at the last accounts, alive in the hands of his foes; but that being the case, I have all along found myself thinking and speaking of him as physically dead.

I do not believe in erecting statues to those who still live in our hearts, whose bones have not yet crumbled in the earth around us, but I would rather see the statue of Captain Brown in the Massachusetts State-House yard than that of any other man whom I know. I rejoice that I live in this age, that I am his contemporary.

What a contrast, when we turn to that political party which is so anxiously shuffling him and his plot out of its way, and looking around for some available slaveholder, perhaps, to be its candidate, at least for one who will execute the Fugitive Slave Law, and all those other unjust laws which he took up arms to annul!

Insane! A father and six sons, and one son-in-law, and several more men besides,—as many at least as twelve disciples,—all struck with insanity at once; while the sane tyrant holds with a firmer gripe than ever his four millions of slaves, and a thousand sane editors, his abettors, are saving their country and their bacon! Just as insane were his efforts in Kansas. Ask the tyrant who is his most dangerous foe, the sane man or the insane? Do the thousands who know him best, who have rejoiced at his deeds in Kansas, and have afforded him material aid there, think him insane? Such a use of this word is a mere trope with most who persist in using it, and I have no doubt that many of the rest have already in silence retracted their words.

Read his admirable answers to Mason and others. How they are dwarfed and defeated by the contrast! On the one side, half-brutish, half-timid questioning; on the other, truth, clear as lightning, crashing into their obscene temples. They are made to stand with Pilate, and Gessler, and the Inquisition. How ineffectual their speech and action! and what a void their silence! They are but helpless tools in this great work. It was no human power that gathered them about this preacher.

What have Massachusetts and the North sent a few *sane* representatives to Congress for, of late years?—to declare with effect what kind of sentiments? All their speeches put together and boiled down—and probably they themselves will confess it—do not match for manly directness and force, and for simple truth, the few casual remarks of crazy John Brown on the floor of the Harper's Ferry engine-house,—that man whom you are about to hang, to send to the other world, though not to represent *you* there. No, he was not our representative in any sense. He was too fair a specimen of a man to represent the like of us. Who, then, *were* his constituents? If you read his words understandingly you will find out. In his case there is no idle eloquence, no made, nor maiden speech, no compliments to the oppressor. Truth is his inspirer, and earnestness the polisher of his sentences.

He could afford to lose his Sharps rifles, while he retained his faculty of speech,—a Sharps rifle of infinitely surer and longer range.

And the New York *Herald* reports the conversation *verbatim!* It does not know of what undying words it is made the vehicle.

I have no respect for the penetration of any man who can read the report of that conversation and still call the principal in it insane. It has the ring of a saner sanity than an ordinary discipline and habits of life, than an ordinary organization, secure. Take any sentence of it,—"Any questions that I can honorably answer, I will; not otherwise. So far as I am myself concerned, I have told everything truthfully. I value my word, sir." The few who talk about his vindictive spirit, while they really admire his heroism, have no test by which to detect a noble man, no amalgam to combine with his pure gold. They mix their own dross with it.

It is a relief to turn from these slanders to the testimony of his more truthful, but frightened jailers and hangmen. Governor Wise speaks far more justly and appreciatingly of him than any Northern editor, or politician, or public personage, that I chance to have heard from. I know that you can afford to hear him again on this subject. He says: "They are themselves mistaken who take him to be a madman.... He is cool, collected, and indomitable, and it is but just to him to say that he was humane to his prisoners.... And he inspired me with great trust in his integrity as a man of truth. He is a fanatic, vain and garrulous" (I leave that part to Mr. Wise), "but firm, truthful, and intelligent. His men, too, who survive, are like him.... Colonel Washington says that he was the coolest and firmest man he ever saw in defying danger and death. With one son dead by his side, and another shot through, he felt the pulse of his dying son with one hand, and held his rifle with the other, and commanded his men with the utmost composure, encouraging them to be firm, and to sell their lives as dear as they could. Of the three white prisoners, Brown, Stevens, and Coppoc, it was hard to say which was most firm."

Almost the first Northern men whom the slaveholder has learned to respect!

The testimony of Mr. Vallandigham, though less valuable, is of the same purport, that "it is vain to underrate either the man or his conspiracy.... He is the farthest possible removed from the ordinary ruffian, fanatic, or madman."

"All is quiet at Harper's Ferry," say the journals. What is the character of that calm which follows when the law and the slaveholder prevail? I regard this event as a touchstone designed to bring out, with glaring distinctness, the character of this government. We needed to be thus assisted to see it by the light of history. It needed to see itself. When a government puts forth its strength on the side of injustice, as ours to maintain slavery and kill the liberators of the slave, it reveals itself a merely brute force, or worse, a demoniacal force. It is the head of the Plug-Uglies. It is more manifest than ever that tyranny rules. I see this government to be effectually allied with France and Austria in oppressing mankind. There sits a tyrant holding fettered four millions of slaves; here comes their heroic liberator. This most hypocritical and diabolical government looks up from its seat on the gasping four millions, and inquires with an assumption of innocence: "What do you assault me for? Am I not an honest man? Cease agitation on this subject, or I will make a slave of you, too, or else hang you."

We talk about a *representative* government; but what a monster of a government is that where the noblest faculties of the mind, and the *whole* heart, are not *represented*. A semi-human tiger or ox, stalking over the earth, with its heart taken out and the top of its brain shot away. Heroes have fought well on their stumps when their legs were shot off, but I never heard of any good done by such a government as that.

The only government that I recognize—and it matters not how few are at the head of it, or how small its army—is that power that establishes justice in the land, never that which establishes injustice. What shall we think of a government to which all the truly brave and just men in the land are enemies, standing between it and those whom it oppresses? A government that pretends to be Christian and crucifies a million Christs every day!

Treason! Where does such treason take its rise? I cannot help thinking of you as you deserve, ye governments. Can you dry up the fountains of thought? High treason, when it is resistance to tyranny here below, has its origin in, and is first committed by, the power that makes and forever recreates man. When you have caught and hung all these human rebels, you have accomplished nothing but your own guilt, for you have not struck at the fountain-head. You presume to contend with a foe against whom West Point cadets and rifled cannon *point* not. Can all the art of the cannon founder tempt matter to turn against its maker? Is the form in which the founder thinks he casts it more essential than the constitution of it and of himself?

The United States have a coffle of four millions of slaves. They are determined to keep them in this condition; and Massachusetts is one of the confederated overseers to prevent their escape. Such are not all the inhabitants of Massachusetts, but such are they who rule and are obeyed here. It was Massachusetts, as well as Virginia, that put down this insurrection at Harper's Ferry. She sent the marines there, and she will have *to pay the penalty of her sin.*

Suppose that there is a society in this State that out of its own purse and magnanimity saves all the fugitive slaves that run to us, and protects our colored fellow-citizens, and leaves the other work to the government, so called. Is not that government fast losing its occupation, and becoming contemptible to mankind? If private men are obliged to perform the offices of government, to protect the weak and dispense justice, then the government becomes only a hired man, or clerk, to perform menial or indifferent services. Of course, that is but the shadow of a government whose existence necessitates a Vigilant Committee. What should we think of the Oriental Cadi even, behind whom worked in secret a Vigilant Committee? But such is the character of our Northern States generally; each has its Vigilant Committee. And, to a certain extent, these crazy governments recognize and accept this relation. They say, virtually, "We'll be glad to work for you on these terms, only don't make a noise about it." And thus the government, its salary being insured, withdraws into the back shop, taking the Constitution with it, and bestows most of its labor on repairing that. When I hear it at work sometimes, as I go by, it reminds me, at best, of those farmers who in winter contrive to turn a penny by following the coopering business. And what kind of spirit is their barrel made to hold? They speculate in stocks, and bore holes in mountains, but they are not competent to lay out even a decent highway. The only *free* road, the Underground Railroad, is owned and managed by the Vigilant Committee. *They* have tunneled under the whole breadth of the land. Such a government is losing its power and respectability as surely as water runs out of a leaky vessel, and is held by one that can contain it.

I hear many condemn these men because they were so few. When were the good and the brave ever in a majority? Would you have had him wait till that time came?—till you and I came over to him? The very fact that he had no rabble or troop of hirelings about him would alone distinguish him from ordinary heroes. His company was small indeed, because few could be found worthy to pass muster. Each one who there laid down his life for the poor and oppressed was a picked man, culled out of many thousands, if not millions; apparently a man of principle, of rare courage, and devoted humanity; ready to sacrifice his life at any moment for the benefit of his fellow-man. It may be doubted if there were as many more their equals in these respects in all the country,—I speak of his followers only,—for their leader, no doubt, scoured the land far and wide, seeking to swell his troop. These alone were ready to step between the oppressor and the oppressed. Surely they were the very best men you could select to be hung. That was the greatest compliment which this country could pay them. They were ripe for her gallows. She has tried a long time, she has hung a good many, but never found the right one before.

When I think of him, and his six sons, and his son-in-law, not to enumerate the others, enlisted for this fight, proceeding coolly, reverently, humanely to work, for months if not years, sleeping and waking upon it, summering and wintering the thought, without expecting any reward but a good conscience, while almost all America stood ranked on the other side,—I say again that it affects me as a sublime spectacle. If he had had any journal advocating *"his cause,"* any organ, as the phrase is, monotonously and wearisomely playing the same old tune, and then passing round the hat, it would have been fatal to his efficiency. If he had acted in any way so as to be let alone by the government, he might have been suspected. It was the fact that the tyrant must give place to him, or he to the tyrant, that distinguished him from all the reformers of the day that I know.

It was his peculiar doctrine that a man has a perfect right to interfere by force with the slaveholder, in order to rescue the slave. I agree with him. They who are continually shocked by slavery have some right to be shocked by the violent death of the slaveholder, but no others. Such will be more shocked by his life than by his death. I shall not be forward to think him mistaken in his method who quickest succeeds to liberate the slave. I speak for the slave when I say that I prefer the philanthropy of Captain Brown to that philanthropy which neither shoots me not liberates me. At any rate, I do not think it is quite sane for one to spend his whole life in talking or writing about this matter, unless he is continuously inspired, and I have not done so. A man may have other affairs to attend to. I do not wish to kill nor to be killed, but I can foresee circumstances in which both these things would be by me unavoidable. We preserve the so-called peace of our community by deeds of petty violence every day. Look at the policeman's billy and handcuffs! Look at the jail! Look at the gallows! Look at the chaplain of the regiment! We are hoping only to live safely on the outskirts of *this* provisional army. So we defend ourselves and our hen-roosts, and maintain slavery. I know that the mass of my countrymen think that the only righteous use that can be made of Sharps rifles and revolvers is to fight duels with them, when we are insulted by other nations, or to hunt Indians, or shoot fugitive slaves with them, or the like. I think that for once the Sharps rifles and the revolvers were employed in a righteous cause. The tools were in the hands of one who could use them.

The same indignation that is said to have cleared the temple once will clear it again. The question is not about the weapon, but the spirit in which you use it. No man has appeared in America, as yet, who loved his fellow-man so well, and treated him so tenderly. He lived for him. He took up his life and he laid it down for him. What sort of violence is that which is encouraged, not by soldiers, but by peaceable citizens, not so much by laymen as by ministers of the Gospel, not so much by the fighting sects as by the Quakers, and not so much by Quaker men as by Quaker women?

This event advertises me that there is such a fact as death,—the possibility of a man's dying. It seems as if no man had ever died in America before; for in order to die you must first have lived. I don't believe in the hearses, and palls, and funerals that they have had. There was no death in the case, because there had been no life; they merely rotted or sloughed off, pretty much as they had rotted or sloughed along. No temple's veil was rent, only a hole dug somewhere. Let the dead bury their dead. The best of them fairly ran down like a clock. Franklin,—Washington,—they were let off without dying; they were merely missing one day. I hear a good many pretend that they are going to die; or that they have died, for aught that I know. Nonsense! I'll defy them to do it. They haven't got life enough in them. They'll deliquesce like fungi, and keep a hundred eulogists mopping the spot where they left off. Only half a dozen or so have died since the world began. Do you think that you are going to die, sir? No! there's no hope of you. You haven't got your lesson yet. You've got to stay after school. We make a needless ado about capital punishment,—taking lives, when there is no life to take. *Memento mori!* We don't understand that sublime sentence which some worthy got sculptured on his gravestone once. We've interpreted it in a groveling and sniveling sense; we've wholly forgotten how to die.

But be sure you do die nevertheless. Do your work, and finish it. If you know how to begin, you will know when to end.

These men, in teaching us how to die, have at the same time taught us how to live. If this man's acts and words do not create a revival, it will be the severest possible satire on the acts and words that do. It is the best news that America has ever heard. It has already quickened the feeble pulse of the North, and infused more and more generous blood into her veins and heart than any number of years of what is called commercial and political prosperity could. How many a man who was lately contemplating suicide has now something to live for!

One writer says that Brown's peculiar monomania made him to be "dreaded by the Missourians as a supernatural being." Sure enough, a hero in the midst of us cowards is always so dreaded. He is just that thing. He shows himself superior to nature. He has a spark of divinity in him.

"Unless above himself he can Erect himself, how poor a thing is man!"

Newspaper editors argue also that it is a proof of his *insanity* that he thought he was appointed to do this work which he did,—that he did not suspect himself for a moment! They talk as if it were impossible that a man could be "divinely appointed" in these days to do any work whatever; as if vows and religion were out of date as connected with any man's daily work; as if the agent to abolish slavery could only be somebody appointed by the President, or by some political party. They talk as if a man's death were a failure, and his continued life, be it of whatever character, were a success.

When I reflect to what a cause this man devoted himself, and how religiously, and then reflect to what cause his judges and all who condemn him so angrily and fluently devote themselves, I see that they are as far apart as the heavens and earth are asunder.

The amount of it is, our *"leading men"* are a harmless kind of folk, and they know *well enough* that *they* were not divinely appointed, but elected by the votes of their party.

Who is it whose safety requires that Captain Brown be hung? Is it indispensable to any Northern man? Is there no resource but to cast this man also to the Minotaur? If you do not wish it, say so distinctly. While these things are being done, beauty stands veiled and music is a screeching lie. Think of him,—of his rare qualities!—such a man as it takes ages to make, and ages to understand; no mock hero, nor the representative of any party. A man such as the sun may not rise upon again in this benighted land. To whose making went the costliest material, the finest adamant; sent to be the redeemer of those in captivity; and the only use to which you can put him is to hang him at the end of a rope! You who pretend to care for Christ crucified, consider what you are about to do to him who offered himself to be the saviour of four millions of men.

Any man knows when he is justified, and all the wits in the world cannot enlighten him on that point. The murderer always knows that he is justly punished; but when a government takes the life of a man without the

consent of his conscience, it is an audacious government, and is taking a step towards its own dissolution. Is it not possible that an individual may be right and a government wrong? Are laws to be enforced simply because they were made? or declared by any number of men to be good, if they are *not* good? Is there any necessity for a man's being a tool to perform a deed of which his better nature disapproves? Is it the intention of lawmakers that *good* men shall be hung ever? Are judges to interpret the law according to the letter, and not the spirit? What right have *you* to enter into a compact with yourself that you *will* do thus or so, against the light within you? Is it for *you* to *make up* your mind,—to form any resolution whatever,—and not accept the convictions that are forced upon you, and which ever pass your understanding? I do not believe in lawyers, in that mode of attacking or defending a man, because you descend to meet the judge on his own ground, and, in cases of the highest importance, it is of no consequence whether a man breaks a human law or not. Let lawyers decide trivial cases. Business men may arrange that among themselves. If they were the inter-preters of the everlasting laws which rightfully bind man, that would be another thing. A counterfeiting law-factory, standing half in a slave land and half in a free! What kind of laws for free men can you expect from that?

I am here to plead his cause with you. I plead not for his life, but for his character,—his immortal life; and so it becomes your cause wholly, and is not his in the least. Some eighteen hundred years ago Christ was crucified; this morning, perchance, Captain Brown was hung. These are the two ends of a chain which is not without its links. He is not Old Brown any longer; he is an angel of light.

I see now that it was necessary that the bravest and humanest man in all the country should be hung. Perhaps he saw it himself. I *almost fear* that I may yet hear of his deliverance, doubting if a prolonged life, if *any* life, can do as much good as his death.

"Misguided!" "Garrulous!" "Insane!" "Vindictive!" So ye write in your easy-chairs, and thus he wounded responds from the floor of the Armory, clear as a cloudless sky, true as the voice of nature is: "No man sent me here; it was my own prompting and that of my Maker. I acknowledge no master in human form."

And in what a sweet and noble strain he proceeds, addressing his cap-tors, who stand over him: "I think, my friends, you are guilty of a great wrong against God and humanity, and it would be perfectly right for any one to interfere with you so far as to free those you willfully and wickedly hold in bondage."

And, referring to his movement: "It is, in my opinion, the greatest service a man can render to God."

"I pity the poor in bondage that have none to help them; that is why I am here, not to gratify any personal animosity, revenge, or vindictive spirit. It is my sympathy with the oppressed and the wronged, that are as good as you, and as precious in the sight of God."

You don't know your testament when you see it.

"I want you to understand that I respect the rights of the poorest and weakest of colored people, oppressed by the slave power, just as much as I do those of the most wealthy and powerful."

"I wish to say, furthermore, that you had better, all you people at the South, prepare yourselves for a settlement of that question, that must come up for settlement sooner than you are prepared for it. The sooner you are prepared the better. You may dispose of me very easily. I am nearly disposed of now; but this question is still to be settled,—this negro question, I mean; the end of that is not yet."

I foresee the time when the painter will paint that scene, no longer going to Rome for a subject; the poet will sing it; the historian record it; and, with the Landing of the Pilgrims and the Declaration of Independence, it will be the ornament of some future national gallery, when at least the present form of slavery shall be no more here. We shall then be at liberty to weep for Captain Brown. Then, and not till then, we will take our revenge.

Nathaniel Hawthorne

Few writers have survived as Nathaniel Hawthorne has—defying the literary fashions of his own day and surviving those of ours, where he must appear, or can, not so much antique as out of time, like a writer of gothic romances. If it comes to that, he is not without his gothic elements of dark and brooding houses, mysterious figures, and mortal secrets which turn up frequently in his tales. Why, since undoubtedly he lives, has he not been left to do it on the shelves of paperbacks that offer such diversions? No sex, would be an explanation, if his best-known book did not concern adultery.

"A mild, shy, pale, melancholic, not very forcible man," as Hawthorne later described himself, he was born in 1804 in Salem, Massachusetts, where his family had lived since Puritan times—where indeed his ancestor, William Hathorne (as the name was then spelled) had been a magistrate who caused a Quaker woman to be whipped for her refusal to accept New England's orthodoxy, and William's son, John, had been one of the judges in the notorious Salem witch trials of the 1690s. Hawthorne's own father was a ship captain who died at sea, leaving his young widow with two daughters and a son, aged four. She went to live with her relatives, in whose house Hawthorne grew up. He was a reclusive boy who nevertheless attended Bowdoin College in Maine, where he showed no interest in anything except composition, and from which he graduated in 1825 with the determination to become a writer.

It took him a dozen years to accomplish his aim and, after scrapping an early novel, turning out stories of sometimes remarkable power. "Young Goodman Brown," (*GIT* 1979, 444–55), usually described as a story of witchcraft but in fact a very intense depiction of the universality of evil, was an early effort; so was "Roger Malvin's Burial," in which a man who has blamelessly left a friend to die during the Indian wars subsequently kills his own son in a hunting accident on the same spot. So was "My Kinsman, Major Molineux," reprinted here, which dates from 1832. Still, none of them was much regarded—certainly they were not taken as American classics, which they have since become—and Hawthorne regarded himself as more or less a failure, unsuccessful and unknown.

He emerged in 1838 because he fell in love with Sophia Peabody who awakened his passional nature: their letters, which survive, give the lie to notions of Victorian repression. Not that he was yet prosperous, so far as he ever became so. He worked for a time in the Salem Custom House, then went to Brook Farm, near Boston, a utopian experiment in which a number of New England intellectuals lived on socialist terms, which he found unappealing. More exactly, he found the requirement of daily labor in the fields beyond his tolerance: he was a writer, and that sort of life made no sense to him.

He wrote *The Scarlet Letter* in 1849. By common agreement his masterpiece, its tale of a woman of Puritan times taken in adultery, her lover, who is also the village minister, and a physician, her husband, who violates every human decency to discover his betrayer, has never ceased to be read, though its strange power is hard to define. Hawthorne called it a romance, and whatever it was, it made him famous.

Subsequent works, of which *The House of the Seven Gables, The Blithedale Romance* (about Brook Farm) and *The Marble Faun,* written toward the end of his life following a sojourn in Italy, were most ambitious, have had their fame and their admirers, but it may be doubted if any of them would seem important if it were not for *The Scarlet Letter.* In them, Hawthorne produced not romances but novels—more discursive works with social implications—and though he was good at that, he was not great. He did it because he felt more comfortable, or less uncomfortable, in such work, which took less out of him, in which he avoided some moral or psychological strain which he could not sustain.

The truth is, he was a Puritan himself, with a deep sense of the tragic, or of sin—that is, of moral responsibility—and he did not like it. Indeed it had ceased to be taken seriously in his time and place. That it was the thing that mattered in Hawthorne, and is the thing for which we read him, did not reconcile him to it. He wanted to be a free man of democratic, nineteenth century cast, and so he partly was; but the other part, his dark genius, never left him; and in a sense it killed him. The conflict between the two strains in his soul manifested itself toward the end of his life in dark depression and psychological disintegration, and he died in 1864 at the age of 59 after a sharp and quick decline of causes that mystified his friends, though we can think we understand them, or at least their workings in him, now.

My Kinsman,

Major Molineux

Nathaniel Hawthorne

Illustrations by Christophe Vorlet

After the kings of Great Britain had assumed the right of appointing the colonial governors, the measures of the latter seldom met with the ready and general approbation which had been paid to those of their predecessors, under the original charters. The people looked with most jealous scrutiny to the exercise of power which did not emanate from themselves, and they usually rewarded their rulers with slender gratitude for the compliances by which, in softening their instructions from beyond the sea, they had incurred the reprehension of those who gave them. The annals of Massachusetts Bay will inform us, that of six governors in the space of about forty years from the surrender of the old charter, under James II, two were imprisoned by a popular insurrection; a third, as Hutchinson inclines to believe, was driven from the province by the whizzing of a musket-ball; a fourth, in the opinion of the same historian, was hastened to his grave by continual bickerings with the House of Representatives; and the remaining two, as well as their successors, till the Revolution, were favoured with few and brief intervals of peaceful sway. The inferior members of the court party, in times of high political excitement, led scarcely a more desirable life. These remarks may serve as a preface to the following adventures, which chanced upon a summer night, not far from a hundred years ago. The reader, in order to avoid a long and dry detail of colonial affairs, is requested to dispense with an account of the train of circumstances that had caused much temporary inflammation of the popular mind.

It was near nine o'clock of a moonlight evening, when a boat crossed the ferry with a single passenger, who had obtained his conveyance at that unusual hour by the promise of an extra fare. While he stood on the landing-place, searching in either pocket for the means of fulfilling his agreement, the ferryman lifted a lantern, by the aid of which, and the newly risen moon, he took a very accurate survey of the stranger's figure. He was a youth of barely eighteen years, evidently country-bred, and now, as it should seem, upon his first visit to town. He was clad in a coarse grey coat, well worn, but in excellent repair; his under garments were durably constructed of leather, and fitted tight to a pair of serviceable and well-shaped limbs; his stockings of blue yarn were the incontrovertible work of a mother or a sister; and on his head was a three-cornered hat, which in its better days had perhaps sheltered the graver brow of the lad's father. Under his left arm was a heavy cudgel, formed of an oak sapling, and retaining a part of the hardened root; and his equipment was completed by a wallet, not so abundantly stocked as to incommode the vigorous shoulders on which it hung. Brown, curly hair, well-shaped features, and bright, cheerful eyes were nature's gifts, and worth all that art could have done for his adornment.

The youth, one of whose names was Robin, finally drew from his pocket the half of a little province bill of five shillings, which, in the depreciation of that sort of currency, did but satisfy the ferryman's demand, with the surplus of a sexangular piece of parchment, valued at three pence. He then walked forward into the town, with as light a step as if his day's journey had not already exceeded thirty miles, and with as eager an eye as if he were entering London city, instead of the little metropolis of a New England colony. Before Robin had proceeded far, however, it occurred to him that he knew not whither to direct his steps; so he paused, and looked up and down the narrow street, scrutinizing the small and mean wooden buildings that were scattered on either side.

'This low hovel cannot be my kinsman's dwelling,' thought he, 'nor yonder old house, where the moonlight enters at the broken casement; and truly I see none hereabouts that might be worthy of him. It would have been wise to enquire my way of the ferryman, and doubtless he would have gone with me, and earned a shilling from the Major for his pains. But the next man I meet will do as well.'

He resumed his walk, and was glad to perceive that the street now became wider, and the houses more respectable in their appearance. He soon discerned a figure moving on moderately in advance, and hastened his steps to overtake it. As Robin drew nigh, he saw that the passenger was a man in years, with a full periwig of grey hair, a wide-skirted coat of dark cloth, and silk stockings rolled above his knees. He carried a long and polished cane, which he struck down perpendicularly before him, at every step; and at regular intervals he uttered two successive hems, of a peculiarly solemn and sepulchral intonation. Having made these observations, Robin laid hold of the skirt of the old man's coat, just when the light from the open door and windows of a barber's shop fell upon both their figures.

'Good evening to you, honoured sir,' said he, making a low bow, and still retaining his hold of the skirt. 'I pray you tell me whereabouts is the dwelling of my kinsman, Major Molineux.'

The youth's question was uttered very loudly; and one of the barbers, whose razor was descending on a well-soaped chin, and another who was dressing a Ramillies wig, left their occupations, and came to the door. The citizen, in the meantime, turned a long-favoured countenance upon Robin, and answered him in a tone of excessive anger and annoyance. His two sepulchral hems, however, broke into the very centre of his rebuke, with most singular effect, like a thought of the cold grave obtruding among wrathful passions.

'Let go my garment, fellow! I tell you, I know not the man you speak of. What! I have authority, I have—hem, hem—authority; and if this be the respect you show for your betters, your feet shall be brought acquainted with the stocks by daylight, tomorrow morning!'

Robin released the old man's skirt, and hastened away, pursued by an ill-mannered roar of laughter from the barber's shop. He was at first considerably surprised by the result of his question, but, being a shrewd youth, soon thought himself able to account for the mystery.

'This is some country representative,' was his conclusion, 'who has never seen the inside of my kinsman's door, and lacks the breeding to answer a stranger civilly. The man is old, or verily—I might be tempted to turn back and smite him on the nose. Ah, Robin, Robin! even the barber's boys laugh at you for choosing such a guide! You will be wiser in time, friend Robin.'

He now became entangled in a succession of crooked and narrow streets, which crossed each other, and meandered at no great distance from the waterside. The smell of tar was obvious to his nostrils, the masts of vessels pierced the moonlight above the tops of the buildings, and the numerous signs, which Robin paused to read, informed him that he was near the centre of business. But the streets were empty, the shops were closed, and lights were visible only in the second stories of a few dwelling-houses. At length, on the corner of a narrow lane, through which he was passing, he beheld the broad countenance of a British hero swinging before the door of an inn, whence proceeded the voices of many guests. The casement of one of the lower windows was thrown back, and a very thin curtain permitted Robin to distinguish a party at supper, round a well-furnished table. The fragrance of the good cheer steamed forth into the outer air, and the youth could not fail to recollect that the last remnant of his travelling stock of provision had yielded to his morning appetite, and that noon had found and left him dinnerless.

'O, that a parchment three-penny might give me a right to sit at yonder table!' said Robin, with a sigh. 'But the Major will make me welcome to the best of his victuals; so I will even step boldly in, and inquire my way to his dwelling.'

He entered the tavern, and was guided by the murmur of voices and the fumes of tobacco to the public room. It was a long and low apartment, with oaken walls, grown dark in the continual smoke, and a floor which was thickly sanded, but of no immaculate purity. A number of persons—the larger part of whom appeared to be mariners, or in some way connected with the sea—occupied the wooden benches, or leather-bottomed chairs, conversing on various matters, and occasionally lending their attention to some topic of general interest. Three or four little groups were draining as many bowls of punch, which the West India trade had long since made a familiar drink in the colony. Others, who had the appearance of men who lived by regular and laborious handicraft, preferred the insulated bliss of an unshared potation, and became more taciturn under its influence. Nearly all, in short, evinced a predilection for the Good Creature in some of its various shapes, for this is a vice to which, as Fast-day sermons of a hundred years ago will testify, we have a long hereditary claim. The only guests to whom Robin's sympathies inclined him were two or three sheepish countrymen, who were using the inn somewhat after the fashion of a Turkish caravansary; they had gotten themselves into the darkest corner of the room, and, heedless of the Nicotian atmosphere, were supping on the bread of their own ovens, and the bacon cured in their own chimney-smoke. But though Robin felt a sort of brotherhood with these strangers, his eyes were attracted from them to a person who stood near the door, holding whispered conversation with a group of ill-dressed associates. His features were separately striking almost to grotesqueness, and the whole face left a deep impression on the memory. The forehead bulged out into a double prominence, with a vale between; the nose came boldly forth in an irregular curve, and its bridge was of more than a finger's breadth; the eyebrows were deep and shaggy, and the eyes glowed beneath them like fire in a cave.

While Robin deliberated of whom to inquire respecting his kinsman's dwelling, he was accosted by the innkeeper, a little man in a stained white apron, who had come to pay his professional welcome to the stranger. Being in the second generation from a French Protestant, he seemed to have inherited the courtesy of his parent nation; but no variety of circumstances was ever known to change his voice from the one shrill note in which he now addressed Robin.

'From the country, I presume, sir?' said he, with a profound bow. 'Beg leave to congratulate you on your arrival, and trust you intend a long stay with us. Fine town here, sir, beautiful buildings, and much that may interest a stranger. May I hope for the honour of your commands in respect to supper?'

'The man sees a family likeness! the rogue has guessed that I am related to the Major!' thought Robin, who had hitherto experienced little superfluous civility.

All eyes were now turned on the country lad, standing at the door, in his worn three-cornered hat, grey coat, leather breeches, and blue yarn stockings, leaning on an oaken cudgel, and bearing a wallet on his back.

Robin replied to the courteous innkeeper, with such an assumption of confidence as befitted the Major's relative. 'My honest friend,' he said, 'I shall make it a point to patronize your house on some occasion, when'— here he could not help lowering his voice—'when I may have more than a parchment threepence in my pocket. My present business,' continued he, speaking with lofty confidence, 'is merely to inquire my way to the dwelling of my kinsman, Major Molineux.'

There was a sudden and general movement in the room, which Robin interpreted as expressing the eagerness of each individual to become his guide. But the innkeeper turned his eyes to a written paper on the wall, which he read, or seemed to read, with occasional recurrences to the young man's figure.

'What have we here?' said he, breaking his speech into little dry fragments. '"Left the house of the subscriber, bounden servant, Hezekiah Mudge,—had on, when he went away, grey coat, leather breeches, master's third-best hat. One pound currency reward to whosoever shall lodge him in any jail of the province." Better trudge, boy, better trudge!'

Robin had begun to draw his hand towards the lighter end of the oak cudgel, but a strange hostility in every countenance induced him to relinquish his purpose of breaking the courteous innkeeper's head. As he turned to leave the room, he encountered a sneering glance from the bold-featured personage whom he had before noticed; and no sooner was he beyond the door, than he heard a general laugh, in which the innkeeper's voice might be distinguished, like the dropping of small stones into a kettle.

'Now, is it not strange,' thought Robin, with his usual shrewdness,—'is it not strange that the confession of an empty pocket should outweigh the name of my kinsman, Major Molineux? Oh, if I had one of those grinning rascals in the woods, where I and my oak sapling grew up together, I would teach him that my arm is heavy, though my purse is light!'

On turning the corner of the narrow lane, Robin found himself in a spacious street, with an unbroken line of lofty houses on each side, and a steepled building at the upper end, whence the ringing of a bell announced the hour of nine. The light of the moon, and the lamps from the numerous shop-windows, discovered people promenading on the pavement, and amongst them Robin hoped to recognize his hitherto inscrutable relative. The result of his former inquiries made him unwilling to hazard another, in a scene of such publicity, and he determined to walk slowly and silently up the street, thrusting his face close to that of every elderly gentleman, in search of the Major's lineaments. In his progress, Robin encountered many gay and gallant figures. Embroidered garments of showy colours, enormous periwigs, gold-laced hats, and silver-hilted swords glided past him and dazzled his optics. Travelled youths, imitators of the European fine gentlemen of the period, trod jauntily along, half dancing to the fashionable tunes which they hummed, and making poor Robin ashamed of his quiet and natural gait. At length, after many pauses to examine the gorgeous display of goods in the shop-windows, and after suffering some rebukes for the impertinence of his scrutiny into people's faces, the Major's kinsman found himself near the steepled building, still unsuccessful in his search. As yet, however he had seen only one side of the thronged street; so Robin crossed, and continued the same sort of inquisition down the opposite pavement, with stronger hopes than the philosopher seeking an honest man, but with no better fortune. He had arrived about midway towards the lower end, from which his course began, when he overheard the approach of some one who struck down a cane on the flagstones at every step, uttering, at regular intervals, two sepulchral hems.

'Mercy on us!' quoth Robin, recognizing the sound.

Turning a corner, which chanced to be close at his right hand, he hastened to pursue his researches in some other part of the town. His patience now was wearing low, and he seemed to feel more fatigue from his rambles since he crossed the ferry, than from his journey of several days on the other side. Hunger also pleaded loudly within him, and Robin began to balance the propriety of demanding violently, and with lifted cudgel, the necessary guidance from the first solitary passenger whom he should meet. While a resolution to this effect was gaining strength, he entered a street of mean appearance, on either side of which a row of ill-built houses was straggling towards the harbor. The moonlight fell upon no passenger along the whole extent, but in the third domicile which Robin passed there was a half-opened door, and his keen glance detected a woman's garment within.

'My luck may be better here,' said he to himself.

Accordingly, he approached the door, and beheld it shut closer as he did so; yet an open space remained, sufficing for the fair occupant to observe the stranger, without a corresponding display on her part. All that Robin could discern was a strip of scarlet petticoat, and the occasional sparkle of an eye, as if the moonbeams were trembling on some bright thing.

'Pretty mistress,' for I may call her so with a good conscience, thought the shrewd youth, since I know nothing to the contrary,—'my sweet pretty mistress, will you be kind enough to tell me whereabouts I must seek the dwelling of my kinsman, Major Molineux?'

Robin's voice was plaintive and winning, and the female, seeing nothing to be shunned in the handsome country youth, thrust open the door, and came forth into the moonlight. She was a dainty little figure, with a white neck, round arms, and a slender waist, at the extremity of which her scarlet petticoat jutted out over a hoop, as if she were standing in a balloon. Moreover, her face was oval and pretty, her hair dark beneath the little cap, and her bright eyes possessed a sly freedom, which triumphed over those of Robin.

'Major Molineux dwells here,' said this fair woman.

Now, her voice was the sweetest Robin had heard that night, the airy counterpart of a stream of melted silver; yet he could not help doubting whether that sweet voice spoke Gospel truth. He looked up and down the mean street, and then surveyed the house before which they stood. It was a small, dark edifice of two stories, the second of which projected over the lower floor; and the front apartment had the aspect of a shop for petty commodities.

'Now, truly, I am in luck,' replied Robin, cunningly, 'and so indeed is my kinsman, the Major, in having so pretty a housekeeper. But I prithee trouble him to step to the door; I will deliver him a message from his friends in the country, and then go back to my lodgings at the inn.'

'Nay, the Major has been abed this hour or more,' said the lady of the scarlet petticoat; 'and it would be to little purpose to disturb him tonight, seeing his evening draught was of the strongest. But he is a kind-hearted man, and it would be as much as my life's worth to let a kinsman of his turn away from the door. You are the good old gentleman's very picture, and I could swear that was his rainy-weather hat. Also he has garments very much resembling those leather small-clothes. But come in, I pray, for I bid you hearty welcome in his name.'

So saying, the fair and hospitable dame took our hero by the hand; and the touch was light, and the force was gentleness, and though Robin read in her eyes what he did not hear in her words, yet the slender waisted woman in the scarlet petticoat proved stronger than the athletic country youth. She had drawn his half-willing footsteps nearly to the threshold, when the opening of a door in the neighbourhood startled the Major's housekeeper, and, leaving the Major's kinsman, she vanished speedily into her own domicile. A heavy yawn preceded the appearance of a man, who, like the Moonshine of Pyramus and Thisbe, carried a lantern, needlessly aiding his sister luminary in the heavens. As he walked sleepily up the street, he turned his broad, dull face on Robin, and displayed a long staff, spiked at the end.

'Home, vagabond, home!' said the watchman, in accents that seemed to fall asleep as soon as they were uttered. 'Home, or we'll set you in the stocks, by peep of day!'

'This is the second hint of the kind,' thought Robin. 'I wish they would end my difficulties, by setting me there to-night.'

Nevertheless, the youth felt an instinctive antipathy towards the guardian of midnight order, which at first prevented him from asking his usual question. But just when the man was about to vanish behind the corner, Robin resolved not to lose the opportunity, and shouted lustily after him,—

'I say, friend! will you guide me to the house of my kinsman, Major Molineux?'

The watchman made no reply, but turned the corner and was gone; yet Robin seemed to hear the sound of drowsy laughter stealing along the solitary street. At that moment, also, a pleasant titter saluted him from the open window above his head; he looked up, and caught the sparkle of a saucy eye; a round arm beckoned to him, and next he heard light footsteps descending the staircase within. But Robin, being of the household of a New England clergyman, was a good youth, as well as a shrewd one; so he resisted temptation, and fled away.

He now roamed desperately, and at random, through the town, almost ready to believe that a spell was on him, like that by which a wizard of his country had once kept three pursuers wandering, a whole winter night, within twenty paces of the cottage which they sought. The streets lay before him, strange and desolate, and the lights were extinguished in almost every house. Twice, however, little parties of men, among whom Robin distinguished individuals in outlandish attire, came hurrying along; but though on both occasions they paused to address him, such intercourse did not at all enlighten his perplexity. They did but utter a few words in some language of which Robin knew nothing, and perceiving his inability to answer, bestowed a curse upon him in plain English, and hastened away. Finally, the lad determined to knock at the door of every mansion that might appear worthy to be occupied by his kinsman, trusting that perseverance would overcome the fatality that had hitherto thwarted him. Firm in this resolve, he was passing beneath the walls of a church, which formed the corner of two streets, when, as he turned into the shade of its steeple, he encountered a bulky stranger, muffled in a cloak. The man was proceeding with the speed of earnest business, but Robin planted himself full before him, holding the oak cudgel with both hands across his body as a bar to further passage.

'Halt, honest man, and answer me a question,' said he, very resolutely. 'Tell me, this instant, whereabouts is the dwelling of my kinsman, Major Molineux!'

'Keep your tongue between your teeth, fool, and let me pass!' said a deep, gruff voice, which Robin partly remembered. 'Let me pass, I say, or I'll strike you to the earth!'

'No, no, neighbour!' cried Robin, flourishing his cudgel, and then thrusting its larger end close to the man's muffled face. 'No, no, I'm not the fool you take me for, nor do you pass till I have an answer to my question. Whereabouts is the dwelling of my kinsman, Major Molineux?'

The stranger, instead of attempting to force his passage, stepped back into the moonlight, unmuffled his face, and stared full into that of Robin.

'Watch here an hour, and Major Molineux will pass by,' said he.

Robin gazed with dismay and astonishment on the unprecedented physiognomy of the speaker. The forehead with its double prominence, the broad hooked nose, the shaggy eyebrows, and fiery eyes were those which he had noticed at the inn, but the man's complexion had undergone a singular, or, more properly, a twofold change. One side of the face blazed an intense red, while the other was black as midnight, the division line being in the broad bridge of the nose: and a mouth which seemed to extend from ear to ear was black or red, in contrast to the colour of the cheek. The effect was as if two individual devils, a fiend of fire and a fiend of darkness, had united themselves to form this infernal visage. The stranger grinned in Robin's face, muffled his party-coloured features, and was out of sight in a moment.

'Strange things we travellers see!' ejaculated Robin.

He seated himself, however, upon the steps of the church-door, resolving to wait the appointed time for his kinsman. A few moments were consumed in philosophical speculations upon the species of man who had just left him; but having settled this point shrewdly, rationally, and satisfactorily, he was compelled to look elsewhere for his amusement. And first he threw his eyes along the street. It was of more respectable appearance than most of those into which he had wandered, and the moon, creating, like the imaginative power, a beautiful strangeness in familiar objects, gave something of romance to a scene that might not have

possessed it in the light of day. The irregular and often quaint architecture of the houses, some of whose roofs were broken into numerous little peaks, while others ascended, steep and narrow, into a single point, and others again were square; the pure snow-white of some of their complexions, the aged darkness of others, and the thousand sparklings, reflected from bright substances in the walls of many; these matters engaged Robin's attention for a while, and then began to grow wearisome. Next he endeavoured to define the forms of distant objects, starting away, with almost ghostly indistinctness, just as his eye appeared to grasp them; and finally he took a minute survey of an edifice which stood on the opposite side of the street, directly in front of the church-door, where he was stationed. It was a large, square mansion, distinguished from its neighbours by a balcony, which rested on tall pillars, and by an elaborate Gothic window, communicating therewith.

'Perhaps this is the very house I have been seeking,' thought Robin.

Then he strove to speed away the time, by listening to a murmur which swept continually along the street, yet was scarcely audible, except to an unaccustomed ear like his; it was a low, dull, dreamy sound, compounded of many noises, each of which was at too great a distance to be separately heard. Robin marvelled at this snore of a sleeping town, and marvelled more whenever its continuity was broken by now and then a distant shout, apparently loud where it originated. But altogether it was a sleep-inspiring sound, and, to shake off its drowsy influence, Robin arose, and climbed a window-frame, that he might view the interior of the church. There the moonbeams came trembling in, and fell down upon the deserted pews, and extended along the quiet aisles. A fainter yet more awful radiance was hovering around the pulpit, and one solitary ray had dared to rest upon the open page of the great Bible. Had nature, in that deep hour, become a worshipper in the house which man had built? Or was that heavenly light the visible sanctity of the place—visible because no earthly and impure feet were within the walls? The scene made Robin's heart shiver with a sensation of loneliness stronger than he had ever felt in the remotest depths of his native woods; so he turned away and sat down again before the door. There were graves around the church, and now an uneasy thought obtruded into Robin's breast. What if the object of his search, which had been so often and so strangely thwarted, were all the time mouldering in his shroud? What if his kinsman should glide through yonder gate, and nod and smile to him in dimly passing by?

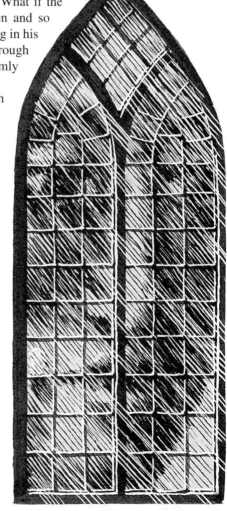

'Oh, that any breathing thing were here with me!' said Robin.

Recalling his thoughts from this uncomfortable track, he sent them over forest, hill, and stream, and attempted to imagine how that evening of ambiguity and weariness had been spent by his father's household. He pictured them assembled at the door, beneath the tree, the great old tree, which had been spared for its huge twisted trunk, and venerable shade, when a thousand leafy brethren fell. There, at the going down of the summer sun, it was his father's custom to perform domestic worship, that the neighbours might come and join with him like brothers of the family, and that the wayfaring man might pause to drink at that fountain, and keep his heart pure by freshening the memory of home. Robin distinguished the seat of every individual of the little audience; he saw the good man in the midst, holding the Scriptures in the golden light that fell from the western clouds; he beheld him close the book and all rise up to pray. He heard the old thanksgivings for daily mercies, the old supplications for their continuance, to which he had so often listened in weariness, but which were now among his dear remembrances. He perceived the slight inequality of his father's voice when he came to speak of the absent one; he noted how his mother turned her face to the broad and knotted trunk; how his elder brother scorned, because the beard was rough upon his upper lip, to permit his features to be moved; how the younger sister drew down a low hanging branch before her eyes; and how the little one of all, whose sports had hitherto broken the decorum of the scene, understood the prayer for her playmate, and burst into clamorous grief. Then he saw them go in at the door; and when Robin would have entered also, the latch tinkled into its place, and he was excluded from his home.

'Am I here, or there?' cried Robin, starting; for all at once, when his thoughts had become visible and audible in a dream, the long, wide, solitary street shone out before him.

He aroused himself, and endeavoured to fix his attention steadily upon the large edifice which he had surveyed before. But still his mind kept vibrating between fancy and reality; by turns, the pillars of the balcony lengthened into the tall, bare stems of pines, dwindled down to human figures, settled again into their true shape and size, and then commenced a new succession of changes. For a single moment, when he deemed himself awake, he could have sworn that a visage—one which he seemed to remember, yet could not absolutely name as his kinsman's—was looking towards him from the Gothic window. A deeper sleep wrestled with and nearly overcame him, but fled at the sound of footsteps along the opposite pavement. Robin rubbed his eyes, discerned a man passing at the foot of the balcony, and addressed him in a loud, peevish, and lamentable cry.

'Hallo, friend! must I wait here all night for my kinsman, Major Molineux?'

The sleeping echoes awoke, and answered the voice; and the passenger, barely able to discern a figure sitting in the oblique shade of the steeple, traversed the street to obtain a nearer view. He was himself a gentleman in his prime, of open, intelligent, cheerful, and altogether prepossessing countenance. Perceiving a country youth, apparently homeless and without friends, he accosted him in a tone of real kindness, which had become strange to Robin's ears.

'Well, my good lad, why are you sitting here?' inquired he. 'Can I be of service to you in any way?'

'I am afraid not, sir,' replied Robin, despondingly; 'yet I shall take it kindly if you'll answer me a single question. I've been searching, half the night, for one Major Molineux; now, sir, is there really such a person in these parts, or am I dreaming?'

'Major Molineux! The name is not altogether strange to me,' said the gentleman, smiling. 'Have you any objection to telling me the nature of your business with him?'

Then Robin briefly related that his father was a clergyman, settled on a small salary, at a long distance back in the country, and that he and Major Molineux were brothers' children. The Major, having inherited riches, and acquired civil and military rank, had visited his cousin, in great pomp, a year or two before; had manifested much interest in Robin and an elder brother, and, being childless himself, had thrown out hints respecting the future establishment of one of them in life. The elder brother was destined to succeed to the farm which his father cultivated in the interval of sacred duties; it was therefore determined that Robin should profit by his kinsman's generous intentions, especially as he seemed to be rather the favourite, and was thought to possess other necessary endowments.

'For I have the name of being a shrewd youth,' observed Robin, in this part of his story.

'I doubt not you deserve it,' replied his new friend, good-naturedly; 'but pray proceed.'

'Well, sir, being nearly eighteen years old, and well grown, as you see,' continued Robin, drawing himself up to his full height, 'I thought it high time to begin the world. So my mother and sister put me in handsome trim, and my father gave me half the remnant of his last year's salary, and five days ago I started for this place, to pay the Major a visit. But, would you believe it, sir! I crossed the ferry a little after dark, and have yet found nobody that would show me the way to his dwelling; only, an hour or two since, I was told to wait here, and Major Molineux would pass by.'

'Can you describe the man who told you this?' inquired the gentleman.

'Oh, he was a very ill-favoured fellow, sir,' replied Robin, 'with two great bumps on his forehead, a hook nose, fiery eyes; and, what struck me as the strangest, his face was of two different colours. Do you happen to know such a man, sir?'

'Not intimately,' answered the stranger, 'but I chanced to meet him a little time previous to your stopping me. I believe you may trust his word, and that the Major will very shortly pass through this street. In the meantime, as I have a singular curiosity to witness your meeting, I will sit down here upon the steps, and bear you company.'

He seated himself accordingly, and soon engaged his companion in animated discourse. It was but of brief continuance, however, for a noise of shouting, which had long been remotely audible, drew so much nearer that Robin inquired its cause.

'What may be the meaning of this uproar?' asked he. 'Truly, if your town be always as noisy, I shall find little sleep while I am an inhabitant.'

'Why, indeed, friend Robin, there do appear to be three or four riotous fellows abroad to-night,' replied the gentleman. 'You must not expect all the stillness of your native woods, here in our streets. But the watch will shortly be at the heels of these lads, and—'

'Aye, and set them in the stocks by peep of day,' interrupted Robin, recollecting his own encounter with the drowsy lantern-bearer. 'But, dear sir, if I may trust my ears, an army of watchmen would never make head against such a multitude of rioters. There were at least a thousand voices went up to make that one shout.'

'May not a man have several voices, Robin, as well as two complexions?' said his friend.

'Perhaps a man may; but Heaven forbid that a woman should!' responded the shrewd youth, thinking of the seductive tones of the Major's housekeeper.

The sounds of a trumpet in some neighbouring street now became so evident and continual, that Robin's curiosity was strongly excited. In addition to the shouts, he heard frequent bursts from many instruments of discord, and a wild and confused laughter filled up the intervals. Robin rose from the steps, and looked wistfully towards a point whither several people seemed to be hastening.

'Surely some prodigious merry-making is going on,' exclaimed he. 'I have laughed very little since I left home, sir, and should be sorry to lose an opportunity. Shall we step round the corner by that darkish house, and take our share of the fun?'

'Sit down again, sit down, good Robin,' replied the gentleman, laying his hand on the skirt of the grey coat. 'You forget that we must wait here for your kinsman; and there is reason to believe that he will pass by, in the course of a very few moments.'

The near approach of the uproar had now disturbed the neighbourhood; windows flew open on all sides; and many heads, in the attire of the pillow,

and confused by sleep suddenly broken, were protruded to the gaze of whoever had leisure to observe them. Eager voices hailed each other from house to house, all demanding the explanation, which not a soul could give. Half-dressed men hurried towards the unknown commotion, stumbling as they went over the stone steps that thrust themselves into the narrow foot-walk. The shouts, the laughter, and the tuneless bray, the antipodes of music, came onwards with increasing din, till scattered individuals, and then denser bodies, began to appear round a corner at the distance of a hundred years.

'Will you recognize your kinsman, if he passes in this crowd?' inquired the gentleman.

'Indeed, I can't warrant it, sir; but I'll take my stand here, and keep a bright lookout,' answered Robin, descending to the outer edge of the pavement.

A mighty stream of people now emptied into the street, and came rolling slowly towards the church. A single horseman wheeled the corner in the midst of them, and close behind him came a band of fearful wind-instruments, sending forth a fresher discord, now that no intervening build-ings kept it from the ear. Then a redder light disturbed the moonbeams, and a dense multitude of torches shone along the street, concealing, by their glare, whatever object they illuminated. The single horseman, clad in a military dress, and bearing a drawn sword, rode onward as the leader, and, by his fierce and variegated countenance, appeared like war personified; the red of one cheek was an emblem of fire and sword; the blackness of the other betokened the mourning that attends them. In his train were wild figures in the Indian dress, and many fantastic shapes without a model, giving the whole march a visionary air, as if a dream had broken forth from some feverish brain, and were seeping visibly through the midnight streets. A mass of people, inactive, except as applauding spectators, hemmed the procession in; and several women ran along the sidewalk, piercing the confusion of heavier sounds with their shrill voices of mirth or terror.

'The double-faced fellow has his eye upon me,' muttered Robin, with an indefinite but an uncomfortable idea that he was himself to bear a part in the pageantry.

The leader turned himself in the saddle, and fixed his glance full upon the country youth, as the steed went slowly by. When Robin had freed his eyes from those fiery ones, the musicians were passing before him, and the torches were close at hand; but the unsteady brightness of the latter formed a veil which he could not penetrate. The rattling of wheels over the stones sometimes found its way to his ears, and confused traces of a human form appeared at intervals, and then melted into the vivid light. A moment more, and the leader thundered a command to halt: the trumpets vomited a horrid breath, and then held their peace; the shouts and laughter of the people died away, and there remained only a universal hum, allied to silence. Right before Robin's eyes was an uncovered cart. There the torches blazed the brightest, there the moon shone out like day, and there, in tar-and-feathery dignity, sat his kinsman, Major Molineux!

He was an elderly man, of large and majestic person, and strong, square features, betokening a steady soul; but steady as it was, his enemies had found means to shake it. His face was pale as death, and far more ghastly; the broad forehead was contracted in his agony, so that his eyebrows formed one grizzled line; his eyes were red and wild, and the foam hung white upon his quivering lip. His whole frame was agitated by a quick and continual tremor, which his pride strove to quell, even in those circumstances of overwhelming humiliation. But perhaps the bitterest pang of all was when his eyes met those of Robin; for he evidently knew him on the instant, as the youth stood witnessing the foul disgrace of a head grown grey in honour. They stared at each other in silence, and Robin's knees shook, and his hair bristled, with a mixture of pity and terror. Soon, however, a bewildering excitement began to seize upon his mind; the preceding adventures of the night, the unexpected appearance of the crowd, the torches, the confused din and the hush that followed, the spectre of his kinsman reviled by that great multitude, all this, and, more than all, a perception of tremendous ridicule in the whole scene, affected him with a sort of mental inebriety. At that moment a voice of sluggish merriment saluted Robin's ears; he turned instinctively, and just behind the corner of the church stood the lantern-bearer, rubbing his eyes, and drowsily enjoying the lad's amazement. Then he heard a peal of laughter like the ringing of silvery bells; a woman twitched his arm, a saucy eye met his, and he saw the lady of the scarlet petticoat. A sharp, dry cachinnation appealed to his memory, and, standing on tiptoe in the crowd, with his white apron over his head, he beheld the courteous little innkeeper. And lastly, there sailed over the heads of the multitude a great, broad laugh, broken in the midst by two sepulchral hems; thus, 'Haw, haw, haw,—hem, hem,—haw, haw, haw, haw!'

The sound proceeded from the balcony of the opposite edifice, and thither Robin turned his eyes. In front of the Gothic window stood the old citizen, wrapped in a wide gown, his grey periwig exchanged for a nightcap, which was thrust back from his forehead, and his silk stockings hanging about his legs. He supported himself on his polished cane in a fit of convulsive merriment, which manifested itself on his solemn old features like a funny inscription on a tombstone. Then Robin seemed to hear the voices of the barbers, of the guests of the inn, and of all who had made sport of him that night. The contagion was spreading among the multitude, when, all at once, it seized upon Robin, and he sent forth a shout of laughter that echoed through the street;—every man shook his sides, every man emptied his lungs, but Robin's shout was the loudest there. The cloud-spirits peeped from their silvery islands, as the congregated mirth went roaring up the sky! The Man in the Moon heard the far bellow. 'Oho,' quoth he, 'the old earth is frolicsome to-night!'

When there was a momentary calm in that tempestuous sea of sound, the leader gave the sign, the procession resumed its march. On they went, like fiends that throng in mockery around some dead potentate, mighty no more, but majestic still in his agony. On they went, in counterfeited pomp,

in senseless uproar, in frenzied merriment, trampling all on an old man's heart. On swept the tumult and left a silent street behind.

*   *   *   *   *

'Well, Robin, are you dreaming?' inquired the gentleman, laying his hand on the youth's shoulder.

Robin started, and withdrew his arm from the stone post to which he had instinctively clung, as the living stream rolled by him. His cheek was somewhat pale, and his eye not quite as lively as in the earlier part of the evening.

'Will you be kind enough to show me the way to the ferry?' said he, after a moment's pause.

'You have, then, adopted a new subject of inquiry?' observed his companion, with a smile.

'Why, yes, sir,' replied Robin, rather dryly. 'Thanks to you, and to my other friends, I have at last met my kinsman, and he will scarce desire to see my face again. I begin to grow weary of a town life, sir. Will you show me the way to the ferry?'

'No, my good friend Robin,—not to-night, at least,' said the gentleman. 'Some few days hence, if you wish it, I will speed you on your journey. Or, if you prefer to remain with us, perhaps, as you are a shrewd youth, you may rise in the world without the help of your kinsman, Major Molineux.'

COMMENTS ON RECENT BOOKS

AS WE INDICATED

LAST YEAR WHEN THIS SECTION OF *THE GREAT IDEAS TODAY* DEVOTED TO BOOK RE-VIEWS FIRST APPEARED, THE BOOKS HERE DISCUSSED ARE AMONG WORKS PUBLISHED IN THE PAST FEW YEARS THAT SEEM LIKELY TO BE OF INTEREST TO SUBSCRIBERS, WHO IF THEY DO NOT KNOW THEM WILL BE GLAD, WE THINK, TO HEAR SOMETHING ABOUT THEM. THEY INDICATE WHAT IDEAS ARE CURRENT THESE DAYS IN SUBJECTS WHICH HAVE NOT BEEN COVERED RECENTLY IN OTHER SECTIONS OF THE BOOK, OR IF THEY HAVE, CAN BE SEEN TO HAVE BEEN CONSIDERED IN OTHER WAYS. WE PLAN TO MAKE A REGULAR FEATURE OF SUCH COMMENTS, ENCOMPASSING ABOUT TEN BOOKS A YEAR — ALL WE HAVE ROOM FOR — TO HELP READERS KEEP ABREAST OF NEW PUBLICATIONS.

*Good Natured: The Origins of Right and Wrong in Humans and
Other Animals*
by Frans de Waal
(Harvard University Press, 1996)
Reviewed by Anthony Quinton

rans de Waal is a leading, perhaps *the* leading, student of the order of primates, which comprises lemurs, tarsiers, monkeys, apes, and of course, ourselves. Although his chief interest is in apes and monkeys, he is concerned in this book to compare aspects of their behavior, its possible motivation and its evolutionary development, with that of the human species. The closest of these primate species to us is that of the chimpanzees and it is with them that de Waal has been most closely concerned; but baboons, macaques, and rhesus monkeys also receive a good deal of attention. He has accumulated a great mass of evidence about primate behavior, most of it observational, but some experimental, in order to answer the question: to what extent, how literally, can morality be ascribed to nonhuman animals?

In the nineteenth century the most impressively audible expounder of the wider implications of the theory of evolution, T. H. Huxley, gave a famous lecture on evolution and ethics. Its main drift was that our evolutionary inheritance predisposed us to ruthless competition, but that we could and should resist this. We should reject the "gladiatorial theory of existence. The ethical progress of society depends, not on imitating the cosmic process, still less in running away from it, but in combating it." Darwin himself, however, convinced, as Huxley was, that morality is a product of evolution, consistently inferred that morality made its contribution to success in "the struggle for existence." Thus "At all times throughout the world tribes have supplanted other tribes; and as morality is one element in their success, the standard of morality and the number of well-endowed men will thus everywhere tend to rise and increase." (I imagine that he was not using "well-endowed" in its vernacular sense, but as meaning something like "well-intentioned.")

It is essential, for clarity of thought, to distinguish two propositions. The first is that morality, as a matter of fact, can be accounted for in evolutionary terms. The second is that the criterion of morally right action can be derived from the way in which the process of evolution has been generally carried on. Consider a parallel case. Our senses of smell and taste have evolved in order for us to be able to distinguish safely edible from poisonous food. That does not in the least imply that fairly high grouse or pheasant are gastronomically inferior to custard and junket. Everyone but a fanatic in the grip of a wild theory agrees that morally right action is directed toward the welfare of others and, therefore, rejects the second proposition that one's own advantage or survival is the criterion of what is morally right. Huxley agreed with that and so does Richard Dawkins or anyone else who contrasts the "selfishness" of genes with the altruism, which they quite rightly, if unthinkingly, take to be the essence of morality.

Is there any conflict, then, between the propositions that morality (i.e., broadly, altruism) is an evolutionary product and that the driving force of evolution is individual self-interest? It might appear so at first glance. If evolution is to go on as it has, or to be speeded up, individuals should be exclusively self-interested. But why should evolution go on or be speeded up? Would it not be preferable to make do with less of it, or even none at all (after all, who wants new, drug-resistant viruses) in return for a bit more decency all round. We, as humans, are naturally well-disposed to the evolutionary process since it culminated in us. But need it go further?

It might be held that the evolutionary process *must* go on, that it is an irresistible necessity, rooted in the nature of things. Well there will, no doubt, always be change and there will always be, whatever happens, evolutionary explanations for it. These would also be available if nothing happened. Does keeping handicapped people alive and in reasonable comfort weaken us in the struggle of our species with rats, disease-bearing insects, and viruses? Not appreciably; we could easily assemble more resources for the struggle without prejudice to the nonhandicapped.

The most satisfactory accommodation of altruism with its evolutionary background of self-interest is the ancient idea that altruism, up to a point at least, *serves* self-interest. The modern, evolutionary form of this is the theory of group selection, intimated in the quotation from Darwin at the end of the second paragraph. Groups do better in the struggle to survive if they are cooperative, if their members can count on each other for assistance. That idea is rather scornfully rejected by gene theorists like Dawkins. A few cheats in a generally altruistic population would do better than everyone else and their genes would thus inevitably come to dominate the population as a whole. That is not altogether persuasive. Cheats are easily detected in ape society, where there are no checks, credit cards, or cash dispensers, and are likely to be very severely punished, even rendered infertile by death or castration, since there are no social workers, counsellors, and so forth to obstruct the workings of rough justice.

Even if group selection does not occur, so that morality is not a genetic acquisition of its possessors, human or simian, it could still be culturally inherited as a learned tradition of behavior. That seems to be the content of Dawkins's theory of "memes," the ideas and beliefs which compete for acceptance and which can spread very much more quickly than genes can. A religion, like Islam, can come to possess a large number of people in a few years; a change in natural hair color or leg length takes millennia.

De Waal is sympathetic to group selection, but it is not his main purpose to reinstate it. His main point is that the rudiments of morality are to be found in the behavior of chimpanzees, particularly, but of other primates as well. His findings are not anecdotal but are the results of protracted and careful observation, aiming to find repeated patterns of conduct. The chief criticism he is concerned to rebut is not that morality is genetically impossible for chimpanzees but that his interpretation of much of their behavior as literally moral is no more than sentimental anthropomorphism.

His technique of exposition is to relieve the more or less abstract matter he has to convey with large and engrossing tracts of description of primate behavior, and also with substantial sections of photography, in which our primate cousins greet each other by shaking each others' genitals, solicit food from each other, give birth in the midst of an interested circle of other females, and so on.

The fields of behavior, and, therefore, of apparent morality, with which he deals are not very clearly or systematically distinguished. The four main chapters cover sympathy toward the injured and handicapped, the maintenance of hierarchical order without despotic excess, the exchange of non-simultaneous services, and the control of aggression within a group. The order seems a little casual. The control of aggression, abstention from doing positive harm to others, is surely the most elementary part of mortality and takes priority over everything else. The maintenance of order without disruptive violence is an aspect of the requirement that others should not be harmed. What the student of animal behavior calls "reciprocal altruism" is a primitive analog of the promissory aspect of human morality, the basis of all nonspontaneous cooperation. Going out of one's way positively to assist those who are suffering is the other side of the coin of not harming them. It would normally be seen as secondary to it, however. Charity has become compulsory only in recent times, by way of redistributive taxation. Restraint of violence, ordinarily in pursuit of the possessions or sexual partners of others, has always been the primary purpose of legal systems, and is more or less definitive of them.

On the control of aggression, de Waal says "Only two realistic alternatives exist in our imperfect world of limited resources: (1) unmitigated competition, or (2) a social order partly shaped and upheld by aggression. Monkeys, apes, humans, and a host of other animals have clearly opted for the second possibility." The first, rejected option is, of course, the scene of nature red in tooth and claw taken as a model for the proper management of human affairs by the rougher kind of social Darwinist. An important form of conflict resolution among chimpanzees is by reconciliation between the warring parties. It is not initiated in an apologetic spirit by the aggressive victor but by the defeated victim. It gives rise to what de Waal calls "reunion euphoria," a relieved display of shouting and jumping about that welcomes the restoration of social peace.

Reciprocal altruism in de Waal's subjects is most evident in food sharing. An ape will give food to a foodless fellow ape who has none if the second has shared food with him in the past, but will not readily do so at all if the second ape has not been open-handed. Whatever may lead it on to such sharing does not seem notably moral. All that is required to explain it is self-interest, memory, and an expectation of favors to come. An interesting point is that chimpanzees share meat in an orderly fashion, but, in a way that explains a common expression, fight wildly over bananas. De Waal's very reasonable explanation of this is that meat is hard to divide, so that if fallen on impetuously it will all go to one of the group, whereas bananas come in convenient individual portions. That is a sensible arrangement but only vestigially moral. What is more to the point is the fact that, as de Waal shows, food sharing is policed; those who cheat are subjected to "moralistic aggression."

The most moral-seeming behavior of primates and other animals is to be found in the field of what de Waal calls, "succorance" as opposed to nurturance. In a species in which mothers were not genetically programmed to provide for and protect their offspring, and the offspring were not able to fend for themselves as soon as they were born, they would soon die out. Giving assistance, however, to unrelated members of the group who are handicapped seems to fly in the face of evolutionary principle. The benefactor gives resources, which might be used to serve her own genes, to assist unrelated genes and thus reduces the competitive position of her own offspring. If the handicap of the beneficiary is inheritable, assistance to it weakens the group. De Waal gives numerous instances of animal succorance, going beyond his own field of the primates to report similar behavior by whales, dolphins, and elephants. The question he poses is how much sympathetic behavior by animals involves "cognitive empathy," the capacity to put oneself imaginatively in the position of another, and is not just learned adjustment combined with the emotional attachment likely to develop between those regularly in each other's company. It is a question he is right to raise. Unless the succorer realizes that the fellow creature she is caring for is in pain or otherwise suffering, she is not knowingly acting to relieve that pain or suffering, is not literally, or, one might say, etymologically, sympathetic. There is an interesting discussion of the role of mirrors in self-awareness. Only chimpanzees and orangutans clearly identify their mirror images with themselves. That, of course, puts them in an advantageous position to compare themselves with others.

De Waal, then, makes a persuasive case for the proposition that some, "higher," animals are moral beings, above all in his treatment of "succorance" where there is neither group pressure nor a self-interested payoff to explain it away. At the same time he is in no doubt that animal morality is a product of evolution. An interesting question is that of whether it is a product of genetic or of cultural evolution. We are left to puzzle over why it does not appear in all creatures. De Waal makes the appealing suggestion that what we and chimpanzees inherit through our genes that is relevant to morality is a capacity to *acquire* a morality; moral attitudes and conduct that is moralized by its motivation by those attitudes. He compares this generalized moral capacity to the generalized linguistic capacity which Chomsky ascribes to all human beings, and which gets filled out concretely in all sorts of different ways through cultural transmission.

The conclusion that (some) animals are moral undermines the idea that there is some deep metaphysical abyss between us and them, as expressed in the idea that we have souls, perhaps infused into us by God. The grossest version of those ideas is Descartes' view that since animals are machines, the cries they emit are no more expressive of pain than the creakings of an unoiled door. Biology once seemed to show that since self-interest is fundamental in our make up, morality must be either disguised self-interest or impossible. Neither inference need be drawn. Morality can be derived from self-interest, can evolve from it, genetically or culturally, without being identical to it. We all know the difference between being moved to help some unfortunate person by a direct concern with their well-being and by an interest in securing a good reputation or in avoiding the anger of the sufferer, if he believes us to be the cause of his suffering. The fact that we quite often confuse the two in practice does not make them one and the same.

Newton's Principia *for the Common Reader*
by Subrahmanyan Chandrasekhar
(Clarendon Press, Oxford, 1995)
Reviewed by George Anastaplo

> Nature and Nature's laws lay hid in night:
> God said, '*Let Newton be!*' and all was light
> —Alexander Pope

his book, by a distinguished theoretical astrophysicist, is dedicated to making Isaac Newton's *Principia* accessible to the modern reader. Subrahmanyan Chandrasekhar (a University of Chicago faculty member from 1937 until his death in 1995) explains (p. xxiii):

> The manner of my study of the *Principia* was to read the enunciations of the different propositions, construct proofs for them independently *ab initio,* and then carefully follow Newton's own demonstrations. In the presentation of the propositions, the proofs that I constructed (which cannot substantially differ from what any other serious student can construct) often precede Newton's proofs arranged in a linear sequence of equations and arguments, avoiding the need to unravel the necessarily convoluted style that Newton had to adopt in writing his geometrical relations and mathematical equations in connected prose. With the impediments of language and of syntax thus eliminated, the physical insight and mathematical craftsmanship that invariably illuminate Newton's proofs come sharply into focus. On occasions, I provide supplementary comments and explanations, sometimes quoting from the masters of earlier centuries.

His primary concern is with how the *Principia* culminates in the formulation of a universal law of gravitation. (*See* pp. xxiii, 353f. All citations in this review are, unless otherwise indicated, to this book, "For the Common Reader.")

The most impressive thing about the Chandrasekhar book, especially for anyone who was privileged to know its eminently self-confident author personally, is how impressive he finds Newton. Chandrasekhar, perhaps the best applied mathematician of our time, may well have been the most, if not even the only, distinguished "practicing scientist" in this century to have attempted such an extended reading of the *Principia*.

The praise lavished upon Newton by him would seem extravagant coming from virtually any other source at this time. Again and again, the arguments of the *Principia* are recognized with a profusion of exclamation points as marvelous, simple, clear, perfect, sparkling, elegant, and ingenious. Chandrasekhar, upon once being asked how he felt upon studying Newton, answered, "I am like a small boy going to the zoo for the first time and seeing a lion." (*See* George Anastaplo, "Thursday Afternoons," in Kameshwer Wali, ed., *S. Chandrasekhar: The Man Behind the Legend* [Imperial College Press, 1997].) The lion's paw is noticed again and again by Chandrasekhar. (*See* pp. 180, 411, 571–73.) Newton is used somewhat the way that Plato uses Socrates: he is the exemplar of a way of life.

The Chandrasekhar book is, in effect, a translation of the *Principia*. It is considered necessary because there has been a movement, among practicing physicists, away from Newton's considerable use of prose and from his reliance, in his mathematics, upon geometric modes of proof. There is far greater reliance today upon algebraic (or in Newton's language, "geometrically rational" [pp. 133, 138]) modes, with little or no reliance upon prose, in scientific exposition. (*Compare* Albert Einstein, *Relativity: The Special and General Theory, GIT* 1961, 421. *See* on the implications of the greater reliance upon algebraic modes, Thomas K. Simpson, "Science as Mystery: A Speculative Reading of Newton's *Principia,*" *GIT* 1992, 118–19, 128, 132. *See also,* Roger Penrose, "Strange Seas of Thought," *The Times Higher Education Supplement,* June 30, 1995.)

One consequence of the shift in mathematical modes is that Newton as physicist was evidently far more accessible to the educated layman of the seventeenth and eighteenth centuries, and remains so to us, than his counterparts have been in the twentieth century. Most of the serious and influential physical scientists of our time can be followed only by specialists. When geometric modes *are* relied upon, as for relativity theory, they are apt to be non-Euclidean and hence not in apparent conformity with ordinary experience.

What does it mean that we have become accustomed to considerable distance between us and our best scientists? (The usefulness of popularizers is generally accepted. The spectacular career of Carl Sagan, whom Chandrasekhar respected as a "serious astronomer," testifies to the need here.) We may wonder about the reliability of any science that is not keyed, or addressed, to the natural understanding. Is nature itself reliably grasped when the natural understanding that may be embedded in everyday language turns out to be virtually useless for scientific discourse? There is something troubling in the determination among contemporary scientists to eliminate the kind of "impediments of language and of syntax" found in Newton.

Of course, the claims of modern science are very much supported, at least rhetorically, by the sustained productivity of the marvelous applications, as in our technology, which scientific discoveries have obviously made possible. Such support is not, strictly speaking, proof—but it does suggest that modern scientists have hold of something significant.

Even for modern science to be as productive as it is—for applications to be so much dependent upon it—is itself a marked departure from pre-modern (or ancient) physics. This emphasis upon applicability, or practicality, may contribute to the tendency of modern science to be "progressive."

The competent physical scientist today is not expected to have studied the work of his great predecessors. Rather, he is able to build upon that work without truly knowing either it or, perhaps even more important, its presuppositions. His predecessors' results are distilled from their work into textbooks and assimilated into a system. The contemporary scientist goes on from there, making, when necessary, adjustments in what had been previously accepted. Certainly, he does not spend much time doing what the ancients did: he does not undertake to learn what it was that his masters had known and how they had come to know it.

One odd feature of this progressivity is something that seems distinctive, in modern scholarship, to the physical sciences: they display an emphasis upon the names of the discoverers of the rules, relations, transformations, quantities, functions, etc., that they make use of. This emphasis upon personal names (as in "the Chandrasekhar limit," "Kepler's law of areas," and "Newton's laws of motion") seems an instinctive attempt at compensation for the radical mathematization of modern science. One does not see this done as much in, say, literary criticism or legal studies, however much the law, for example, may use accidental case names.

I attended in December 1996 a University of Chicago conference of physicists and astrophysicists in honor of Chandrasekhar. It was devoted to the latest thinking about "black holes and relativistic stars." Hovering in the background of all the intricate and ingenious explanations dealt with during the conference was, at least for me, the question of whether black holes in fact exist. If they do, it seems, they are not as exotically different from other celestial phenomena as they had been originally posited to be. If black holes were *sui generis,* would they not be virtually impossible for us to learn much about? A stellar black hole, believed to arise from the "death" of an enormous star, has been said to be an object so massive that nothing, not even light (and hence most information?), can escape its gravitation. The detection of this gravitation may be virtually the only available evidence of its particular existence. In addition, galactic black holes, as well as tiny ones, are conjured up. Strange things are also said about the Big Bang. Should not at least the talk of "infinite density" sometimes heard from cosmologists encounter firm resistance? It is prudent in these matters to determine, with Lucretius, *what cannot be.* (See, e.g., Helmut Fritzsche, "Of Things That Are Not," in John A. Murley, William T. Braithwaite, and Robert L. Stone, eds., *Law and Philosophy: The Practice of Theory* [Ohio University Press, 1992], vol. 1, p. 3.)

I came to appreciate during these two days of high-powered speculation what a medieval conclave of top-flight theologians must have been like. A lot of intelligence and learning was on display, with recognized authorities repeatedly drawn upon and developed. And yet, all the time, the observer on the sidelines could wonder whether the "phenomena" considered to be at the core of the enterprise could truly be known.

This sort of intense activity may also be seen, by the way, in the extensive investigations of biblical data, especially prophecies, to which Newton devoted himself from time to time and, especially, in the last years of his life. It has been estimated that Newton's mostly unpublished writings on theology would produce the equivalent of some seventeen volumes of average size today. This sort of preoccupation, at times obsessive in its complexity, may make Newton seem less astute than Chandrasekhar takes him to have been. Yet a Newton biographer, who did not appreciate how anti-trinitarian his hero was, observed, "If Sir Isaac Newton had not been distinguished as a mathematician and a natural philosopher, he would have enjoyed a high reputation as a theologian." (Sir David Brewster, *Memoirs of Sir Isaac Newton,* II, 313 [1845].) Thomas K. Simpson, who recognizes that Newton held "strong if idiosyncratic views" about the interpretation of scripture, considers Newton's theology to be critical to his physics: "Newton could not have arrived at the *Principia* without a foundation in the faith he brings to it from theology" [*GIT* 1992, 166]. Is this so? Chandrasekhar, however, does not seem to have concerned himself much with this aspect of Newton's thought.

One cannot help but be impressed, upon watching modern scientists in action, by their competence as well as by their limitations—and by the rigorous standards of proof by which they insist upon. This is reflected in the Chandrasekhar book, in which the reader is provided unrelenting criticisms of the errors of various interpreters of Newton, especially Roger Cotes who was relied upon by Newton in the preparation of the second edition of the *Principia*. (*See,* for a more favorable view of Cotes's contributions, Westfall, *The Life of Isaac Newton,* pp. 274–76, 286–91, 298.)

These criticisms make rather curious the abundance of typographical and other errors to be found in the Chandrasekhar book, in turn, perhaps due in part to the haste with which a manuscript had to be prepared for publication by an ailing author in his eighties. Even the very last page of this text displays a careless use of "Ben Johnson" for "Ben Jonson." Other reviewers have noticed mistakes in the mathematical formulations relied upon here and there. (*See,* e.g., 64 *American Journal of Physics* 958 [1996]. But, after all, even Newton makes mistakes. *See,* e.g., pp. 11, 113, 174, 179, 401, 404–5, 407–8, 423, 450, 475–76, 528.)

My own limitations are no doubt exposed when I confess that I have come away from Chandrasekhar's book with little more knowledge about the physical world and the universal law of gravitation than I had when I first opened his book. The "common reader" nominally being ministered to by the book has to have mastered considerably more mathematics and physics than I ever will. (Should the author have "stooped" [pp. 115, 397] more than he did? Does this depend upon whom he really wanted to instruct and guide?) Be that as it may, someone such as Galileo remains much more accessible, even without "translation," for the common reader today. In a way, the Chandrasekhar "translation" of Newton reinforces the worst tendencies of contemporary physics by making the *Principia* seem more "abstract," and less accessible for the layman, than Newton may have intended. (*See* Simpson, pp. 118–19.)

I do know more about Newton—or, at least, about how he is regarded by Chandrasekhar. Perhaps I now know something more as well about how modern scientists work—or, at least, about what they expect of each other. Particularly challenging for them, as it had been for Newton, is the ultimate source of whatever power matter may have to affect or move other matter at a distance. (*See* p. 535: "three hundred years [after Newton], the quest for the 'cause of gravity' still continues.") I find intriguing, if not even reassuring, Curtis Wilson's observation: "The emergence for Newton of the argument that gravitation is universal and therefore mechanically inexplicable must have brought with it a sense of relief…" ("Newton's Path to the *Prinicipia*," *GIT* 1985, 227). But what is the effect of virtually transforming physics into a branch of mathematics? Is the matter that we can personally "relate to" through the animated matter of our own bodies somehow lost sight of? The following observations by Roger Penrose (*The Times Higher Education Supplement,* June 30, 1995) may bear upon this question (emphasis added):

It has often been argued that the geometrical methods used in [Newton's] *Principia* held back the development of mathematical science in England while the "more powerful" analytical approach to the calculus was followed in the work of Leibniz, Euler, Lagrange and others. Undoubtedly it is true that Leibniz's notation, as developed further by Euler, led to the powerful algebraic and analytical techniques of modern-day calculus—techniques that are the common tools of modern mathematical scientific method. Newton's influence on the way in which calculus is used, at least in formal manipulations, is indeed less than that of Leibniz and Euler.

This may be partly due to the fact that Newton did not publish his approach to the calculus until after Leibniz's version had appeared; but also Leibniz developed his tools in a way that allowed formal manipulation to be carried out with greater ease. One advantage of a good notation, such as that of Leibniz, is that calculations can then be performed without the necessity of a continuing understanding of what the symbols actually mean. This can be valuable in freeing the mind from continual reference to the deeper issues involved in what one is doing, but there is a loss, too, in that one may lose sight of the very principles on which the validity of these manipulations is based. This type of dichotomy, between unthinking computation and the alternative of a continual re-examination of basic principles, is especially evident in scientific research today. *The development of modern high-speed computers has enhanced the power of the manipulative approach, to the extent that the importance of the underlying principles is often obscured. Yet a need for continual reference to underlying principles can itself be stultifying.* Newton's geometrical methods might well, in the hands of lesser individuals, have led to little more than a scratching of the surface of the problems of planetary motion. But Newton's supreme combination of geometrical mastery with his profound understanding of the power of perturbational methods, joined with his calculational and experimental abilities and his deep physical insight, enabled him to achieve what no one else could have been able to do using such geometrical methods alone.

The virtual deification of Newton in the Chandrasekhar book includes the repeated suggestion that various discoveries now credited to Newton's successors should have Newton's name included, if not used exclusively, in their nomenclature, recognizing thereby his anticipation of such discoveries. But some of the more important discoveries long attributed to Newton can be understood to have themselves been anticipated by others whose names could plausibly be linked with Newton's in the scientific nomenclature. I do not believe that Chandrasekhar appreciates how often the names not only of scientists such as Kepler, Copernicus, and Galileo but also of investigators such as Aristotle, Archimedes, Pythagoras, Euclid, Apollonius, and even Ptolemy and Descartes might well be linked with Newton's.

Questions remain not only about whether black holes exist and, if they do, in what form. There are questions as well as to what the ultimate "particles" or forces are that modern physics and chemistry presuppose. Consider, for example, how I put these questions for myself in 1974 (reprinted in Anastaplo, *The Artist as Thinker: From Shakespeare to Joyce,* pp. 252–53 [1983]):

Is there any reason to doubt that physicists will, if they continue as they have in the twentieth century, achieve, again and again, "decisive breakthroughs" in dividing subatomic "particles"? But what future, or genuine understanding, is there in *that*? I believe it would be fruitful for physicists—that is, for a few of the more imaginative among them—to consider seriously the nature of what we can call the "ultron." What must this ultimate particle be like (if, indeed, it is a particle and not an idea or a principle)? For is not an "ultron" implied by the endeavors of our physicists, by their recourse to more and more ingenious (and expensive) equipment and experiments? Or are we to assume an infinite regress (sometimes called progress) and no standing place or starting point? Or, to put this question still another way, what is it that permits the Universe *to be* and to be (if it is) intelligible?

Related inquiries, prompted by the elegant Chandrasekhar book, include questions about whether there is anything in the universe at rest—whether, that is, there is a "where" or standing place discernible by the physical scientist and, perhaps related to this, a "when" or starting point as well. Is it possible truly to know anything about the physical world—to have something solid to build upon and with—if fixed and reliable groundings in space and time should never be available to the human mind? Does the constancy of the speed of light substitute for, if it does not contribute to, such groundings? (*See,* Simpson, *GIT* 1992, 114, 123 f, 149 f. Simpson recommends, to "serious students of the *Principia*," Robert S. Bart, *Notes to Accompany the Reading of Newton's "Principia Mathematica"* [St. John's College Press, 1968], a book which I know Chandrasekhar had access to well before he wrote his own book on the *Principia.*) If nature accounts for all that we can observe to happen today, following necessarily upon what happened yesterday, this suggests that cause-and-effect relations may be understood to govern forever both heretofore and hereafter.

Can the solidity requisite for reliable knowledge be somehow identified or at least grasped only if the eternity of the matter/energy of the Universe is understood to be self-evident? That is, should the existence of matter/energy be considered as much an aspect of the very nature of things, and hence *always,* as the existence of numbers? The unexamined tendency of modern physics, as dramatized by the Chandrasekhar "translation" of Newton's *Principia,* may be to make matter/energy and numbering virtually interchangeable—an instructive and challenging development, indeed, especially if infinity is presupposed with respect to time, space, and (somehow or other) matter/energy as well. (But consider the curious notion of the "semi-infinite." *See,* e.g., pp. 318–19.) Perhaps applicable is an observation by Sherlock Holmes, quoted by Chandrasekhar (p. 454), "When you have eliminated the impossible, whatever remains, however improbable, must be the truth." Here, as elsewhere, we may well ponder what Newton meant when he said, "Nor is Nature confined to any bounds" (p. 55).

Nietzsche
by Michael Tanner
(Oxford, 1994)
Reviewed by Seth Benardete

 his very short study of Nietzsche is very long on the opinions of the author without conveying much of the thought of Nietzsche himself. Michael Tanner, who teaches philosophy at Cambridge and writes on opera, speaks of Nietzsche once as a philosopher but then only in inverted commas. For him, Nietzsche is primarily a cultural critic, who diagnosed some of the ailments of the West but suggested no cure that Tanner would swallow. He apparently wants Nietzsche to be edifying and [thus] seems to classify himself, with some self-satisfaction, with Nietzsche's last man, and thereby confirm Nietzsche's characterization of this phenomenon. Perhaps the clearest sign of the confusion in Tanner's negligent approach to Nietzsche is this. In speaking of Nietzsche's advocacy of "life," he puts Nietzsche in the company of "Christ, Blake, Schweitzer, D. H. Lawrence," as if Nietzsche would not have been appalled by the association and dismissed with equal contempt Lawrence and Schweitzer.

The book inserts from time to time bits of Nietzsche's life, from his love for Lou Salomé to his madness, but it is unclear whether these bits are meant to be explanatory or designed to reduce Nietzsche's thought to his nonphilosophical experiences. Although he warns the reader against "the fallacy of origins," Tanner himself seems to be satisfied if such an etiology can be found for Nietzsche. The books and essays Nietzsche wrote during his life determine the plan of Tanner's essay. He grades each work as if Nietzsche were sitting for an examination, but though he prefers *The Genealogy of Morals* to all the rest, Tanner spends less than half the space on it than he does on *Thus Spoke Zarathustra,* which he finds repellent; but in neither case does the reader get any idea of the book's plan and intention, so that it is hard to know why Tanner ranks one much higher than the other. Nietzsche, it is true, is hard to summarize, but Tanner makes no attempt to get past the surface, and even on the surface things are omitted that would make Nietzsche appear incoherent and disjointed to anyone who did not know his writings independently of Tanner's accounts.

After Tanner describes the varied reception of Nietzsche, he turns to *The Birth of Tragedy.* Having set up the opposition between the distinctness of the Apollinian dream and the doubleness of Dionysian intoxication, Tanner does not pursue Nietzsche's development of this opposition into the pairs "individual and community," "family and city," "law-convention and nature," "image and music," "appearance and illusion." He does not mention that Nietzsche works out in the first two-thirds of the book a concealed interpretation of Euripides' *Bacchae:* that play encapsulates the nature of Greek tragedy once its author, with the help of Socrates, has destroyed it. Dionysus, the god of the theater, comes in disguise to make manifest his divinity. In setting out to give a proof of tradition he necessarily fails. Euripides lets loose the god of tragedy onto the tragic stage and has him destroy both it and himself. Tanner, by not grounding Nietzsche's book in its specific subject, cannot see that Nietzsche's account has its basis in both Plato and Aristotle, both of whom observed the monstrous character of tragedy. Nietzsche's stress on music harks back to Socrates' puzzlement about it in the *Republic,* where he cannot match his account of poetic speech to a comparable analysis of music, though, he admits, only music gets to the inside of the soul (*GBWW* I: 7, 333; II: 6, 333). Tanner also does not see that the issue of Christianity lies behind what Nietzsche takes to be the moral of Greek tragedy: "It is best not to be born." How, Nietzsche asks, does this tragic view of life, where suicide becomes the central act, differ from its equally pessimistic understanding in Christianity? Why are the Greeks so cheerful? Nietzsche discerns the tension between the beauty of the Olympian gods and terror, or the two sources of gods in eros and fear, but he takes the terror to be original and ultimately the source of the Apollinian. By failing to get at the core of Nietzsche's thought, Tanner does not see how the Apollinian and the Dionysian get transformed into the opposition between thought and affects, or reason and passion, from which the move that replaces Euripides with Socrates follows as a matter of course. *The Birth of Tragedy* thus contains the germ of much of Nietzsche's later thought, in which the relation between the true and the good becomes the primary problem. It was first raised by Socrates and then by Nietzsche in raising the question whether philosophy is possible.

Tanner touches on this problem but does not go very far with it. An unnecessary obstacle in Tanner's way is his casual identification of happiness and pleasure. Tanner poses Nietzsche's question, "Why science?" but trivializes it. He believes that the issue is why we pursue truth and not rather what is its good, a question that science as we know it cannot answer let alone ask. Nietzsche raised this issue in *The Use and Abuse of History,* but Tanner dismisses it once he has praised it as "great work" because it fails to offer a solution. One would never know from Tanner's single paragraph that Nietzsche is discussing a new phenomenon, "historicism," or the relativity of all horizons and values that follows from the "discoveries" of the historical school. According to Tanner, the issue is how "we can cope with the burden of knowledge, specifically historical knowledge, and still manage to be our own men." It is not a question of coping, however, but of the utter impossibility of living without a closed horizon once "history" has breached all such illusory veils. Tanner does not mention Nietzsche's remark, though it should be crucial for him if Nietzsche were just a cultural critic, that his generation was the first in the history of the world that knew that it did not know. This quasi-Socratic ignorance—for Socrates knew what he did not know—was the consequence of a probity refined out of Christianity into science that had turned around and destroyed its source. Tanner does not take seriously enough Nietzsche's charge of the survival of Christian morality without a Christian god, or that nihilism is a direct outcome of the literal message of Christianity, "God is dead." His dismissal of Heidegger's interpretation of Nietzsche lets him ignore the tracing back on both their parts of modern rationalism to Plato, and their joint appeal to the pre-Socratics, a term that we owe to Nietzsche. Tanner downplays the historical psychology of Nietzsche and thus finds the prophetic Nietzsche of *Thus Spoke Zarathustra* more puzzling than he otherwise would be. Tanner does not realize that Nietzsche's divination of the past is of a piece with his divination of the future.

There is a kind of grumpiness in Tanner that is hard to account for. In praising *Daybreak,* he takes a sideswipe at Kant. It would be worthwhile, he says, to expound *Daybreak* in detail: "It would result in a very large book, but no larger than the ones awarded to such worthless works as Kant's *Critique of Practical Reason.*" This particular bit of petulance is peculiar, since Tanner goes on to quote Nietzsche on contemporary morality—"moral sensibilities are nowadays at such cross-purposes that to one man a morality is proved by its utility, while to another its utility refutes it"—as if Kant had not set up this distinction. In the very chapter in which he criticizes Kant, Tanner validates Nietzsche by quoting at length from G. E. M. Anscombe, whose ignorance of Nietzsche is supposed to show the truth of his arguments. Why a Catholic professor is needed to support Nietzsche is left in the dark; but perhaps a clue is given when Tanner expresses a regret that Chartres and Bach's B-Minor Mass will not be produced by "humanism," as if Nietzsche's *Übermensch* had anything to do with humanism. It seems to point to a nostalgia in Tanner of which there is not a trace in Nietzsche himself.

In the chapter on *The Gay Science,* Tanner believes that he has caught Nietzsche in a difficulty from which there is no way out. The difficulty is presumably this. The recommendation that one should have a "style," or that one should become what one is, does not preclude a Goering, to use Tanner's example, from having a style and yet being wholly reprehensible. If, however, one considers Aristotle's *Nicomachean Ethics,* where the first characterization of man in his specific function, that it is the being-at-work of soul in conformity with reason or not without reason (1098a7; *GBWW* I: 9, 343; II: 8, 343), does not preclude Hitler but certainly does Goering, it is hard to see why Nietzsche should be faulted for not having a way to banish what is base. This is to say nothing of the fact that Goering had a style only in the sense that a fashion magazine might use the term, for, according to Nietzsche, part of "style" is to conceal the ugly that could not be removed. Tanner denies any genuine link among aphorisms; had he admitted that they were not as random as he claims they are, he would have noted that the aphorism on style follows immediately a call on board to philosophers to travel to the moral antipodes. Tanner is very uncomfortable with Nietzsche's nonegalitarian morality. He takes the *Übermensch* as a superior Zarathustra, whereas he seems rather to be his inferior, for he creates the next higher myth for men to live by, and Zarathustra himself is beyond myth. Tanner shares the view of F. R. Leavis that in Swift's *Gulliver's Travels,* though the Houyhnhnms have all the reason, the Yahoos have all the life. The *nostalgie de boue* is always very strong in academics.

When he comes to the central teaching of *Thus Spoke Zarathustra,* the eternal recurrence, Tanner is very unforgiving and colloquial: "I wouldn't give a damn." Rather than measuring Nietzsche by what would fit himself, it would have been more worthwhile to consider why Nietzsche needed some support in nature for his doctrine of perspectivism and historical relativism. It may be a failure, but it shows Nietzsche's awareness of the cosmological problem that philosophy must face. Tanner believes that Nietzsche never noticed a "rending cleavage in his work," between an affirmation of "all of life, or only the noblest, best, strongest kind"; but one would have thought that Nietzsche's constant denial of the separability in genesis of the high from the low, or that freedom has its ground in necessity, is nothing but a reflection on this very issue. Tanner asserts that Nietzsche, in his inability to face the quotidian, could not fit "the nineteenth-century art form *par excellence,* the realistic novel, into any artistic category"; but already in *The Birth of Tragedy* Nietzsche had this to say about it: "Plato has given to all posterity the model of a new art form, the model of the novel—which may be described as an infinitely enhanced Aesopian fable, in which poetry holds the same rank in relation to dialectical philosophy as this same philosophy held for many centuries in relation to theology: namely, the rank of handmaid."

In Tanner's account of *The Genealogy of Morals,* "the last truly original work Nietzsche was to write," there is not a word about justice, punishment, guilt, and conscience, all of which occupy the foreground in the second essay of the book, and are obviously meant to join the first essay on masters and slaves with the last on ascetic ideals. Without such an account the book becomes incoherent and loses its sustained reflection on the noble. In quoting at length from the last section, Tanner omits what is decisive for understanding it, that the ascetic ideal, in bringing fresh suffering, "placed all suffering under the perspective of guilt." If he had merely observed that Freud's interpretation of the super-ego and guilt presupposes Nietzsche's analysis—Western man has kept the Christian morality of intention and killed God—Tanner would not have treated Nietzsche in so impressionistic a manner that, in taking away all of Nietzsche's hardness and sharpness, what was meant to be both a knife and a hammer becomes a feather duster: it brushes but neither cuts nor smashes.

Untitled
by Diane Arbus
(Aperture, 1995)
Reviewed by Paulette Roeske

> When you can assume that your audience holds the same beliefs you do,
> you can relax a little and use more normal means of talking to it; when you
> have to assume that it does not, then you have to make your vision
> apparent by shock—to the hard of hearing you shout, and for the almost-
> blind you draw large and startling figures.
>
> —Flannery O'Connor

n "The Love Song of J. Alfred Prufrock," T. S. Eliot's protagonist is a man who privileges public opinion and consoles himself for his misspent life cautiously "measured out…with coffee spoons" by contradicting a deeper if unarticulated knowledge that time is running out:

> There will be time, there will be time
> To prepare a face to meet the faces that you meet.

Untitled, Diane Arbus's third collection of photographs, all of them published posthumously, offers up in contrast the unprepared faces of a largely adult, white, female population in residences for the mentally retarded photographed on Halloween and other occasions between 1969 and 1971. Her subjects, unlike Prufrock, show no regard for "what they will say." Page after page reveals the frank and unrelenting gaze of the institutionalized, whose very circumstance defines them as, to use current idiom, The Other. At first glance, those too-familiar factions announce themselves: *us* and *them.* At least part of the book's business is to heal that rift.

On July 26, 1971, having already shot the last of the photographs in the project that would become *Untitled,* Diane Arbus slit her wrists in the bathtub of her apartment in Westbeth, the former Bell Telephone Lab turned artists' community, near the Hudson River docks in New York. She was forty-eight years old. The middle child in a wealthy Jewish family, her siblings were Howard Nemerov, three years her senior, to whom Diane referred to as, "my brother the poet," and Renée, five years her junior, a sculptor. David Nemerov, her father, painted with some success, although Russeks, the department store with its several branches that had made the family's fortune, preoccupied him through most of his life. With Allan Arbus, her husband and collaborator, she bore two daughters. She had loved Allan since she was fourteen, but their marriage floundered during her last years. In a creative and advantaged family, Diane spent much of her life battling the depressions that led to her suicide.

A seer in several senses of the word, Arbus's vision was futuristic, anomalous, and passionate. Her rich and inventive metaphors for transformation reflected her own artistic process of discovery and revelation. Yet others did not see as she saw. Magazine editors and art directors regarded her chosen subjects as tastelessly idiosyncratic, if not off-limits, and more often than not her proposals were rejected. Transvestites, transsexuals, drag queens, burlesque queens, a hermaphrodite with his/her dog, nudists in colonies in Pennsylvania and New Jersey, adolescents at a New York camp for overweight girls, a Jewish giant, Russian midgets and a Mexican dwarf, a young man in curlers, a girl with a cigar in Washington Square Park, a portrait of a woman with elephantiasis that Arbus tacked up beside her bed—all those who haunt the periphery captured her interest. Like a poet, Arbus was caught up with the act of looking, and like a poet she refused to avert her eyes. Some of her most challenging photographs are collected in *Diane Arbus: An Aperture Monograph* (1972). Arbus also composed text to accompany many of her published photographs reprinted in the second book, *Diane Arbus: Magazine Work, 1960–71* (1984).

I am not a photographer, although I photograph compulsively; and although I photograph compulsively, I do not look at the pictures I take. For me, the process of framing an otherwise unordered field of vision presses into memory whatever focus I seek in my work as a poet. It is to this extent that I understand photography, but it is as a poet that I respond to the photographs of Diane Arbus. When I came across *Untitled,* my immediate and vigorous attraction, I know, originated in my own long-standing dance with morbidity, with dream images borrowed from history's great wars and persecutions. No real student of psychology, still I recognize the freaks and misfits I encounter on nightmare's reliably twisted terrain as aspects of myself, representing the countless little psychic amputations that constitute daily life. *Yes, I see,* I responded, drawn to her subjects' every imperfection which I read as physical evidence of psychic injury. The more I looked, however, the more convinced I became that the pictures show, above all, the soft and vulnerable underside of the self stripped of the armor of social lies that protects us from each other and ourselves. Having journeyed through the narrative these photographs map, I came to look upon each face with what I can only call love—there is no other word for it—for the part of me coaxed out of hiding.

It is a testament to the power of Arbus's photographs that they raise in us a dis-ease born, perhaps, out of a fear of recognizing our unacculturated selves in the images upon which we gaze: if *They* exist, then *I* could become one of *Them,* we might whisper, employing a brand of magical thinking in which merely looking releases the image from the page. Each of us knows that among the entourage of identities huddled behind the public self resides the unprepared face, the one that tries to lose itself in the crowd but, like all those who are guilty, eventually gives itself away. The unprepared face—the one we confront in dreams and deep imaginings then deny when we gratefully settle back into our comfortable selves, all questions, all fears, on hold. If we recoil, then, it is from what we fear we are beneath the fabrications and dissemblings we have conspired with ourselves to call daily life. Why should we wrestle on Arbus's rocky ground, we may ask, with the numbing threat that someone else's misfortune poses to our hoped-for order? In the story we prefer, we are happy, normal, and we will live forever.

Unlike us, Arbus's subjects are willing. They do not turn away but rather give themselves up to the camera in the head-on confrontation of classic portrait photography. Theirs is the full-frontal-romancing-the-camera presentation of those who take pleasure in the self and whose pleasure is underwritten by a visible confidence: *Look at me,* they say, *I am worthy.* Indeed, the sub-text of every photograph is *looking,* as all of us in the photographer-subject-viewer *ménage à trois* know. Most often it is the photographer we consider empowered: after all, the photographer holds the bright ideas, the photographer is the filter, the photographer presses the shutter. These subjects, however, look back. The camera empowers them and the viewer flinches under their gaze. As for Arbus, *Oh no you don't,* she seems to say if we try to step to her side of the camera, the side we think of as safe only if we have not tried to make art.

To say as I have said that Arbus's subjects are most often adult, white, and female is a useless generalization since these photographs require us to put aside such distinctions to find deeper truths. Arbus's choice of Halloween as an occasion aids us in that process because many of the figures in the fifty-one photographs that comprise *Untitled* are masked. Some masks are as basic as a lion's face crayoned on a brown paper bag, whereas others evoke the intricately designed masks of the Beijing opera. There is the simple black eye mask the Lone Ranger preferred, equally suitable for a Scarlett O'Hara stint at an antebellum ball, the standard-issue rubber witch's mask, and war paint applied directly to the face. The clown, devil, and dunce, the goddess, a lop-eared rabbit, an upside-down harem mask that trails its white veil like poet Walt Whitman's beard—all are gathered here. Because the masked figures are interspersed throughout the collection, it appears neither clear nor important either at a glance or upon further study to identify which figures are masked or costumed and which are not. This is another distinction the viewer stops making just as, at some point, when watching a foreign film we are no longer aware we are reading subtitles. In most of these photographs the subjects sport anklets and sensible shoes, the dress of daily life that plays off against pearls and period hats. One young girl has a shoebox tucked under her arm: "Child Life Shoes," it reads. The viewer, I think, who travels to the collection's end is willing to relinquish the arbitrary and failed distinctions that characterize every false hierarchy, including the one between *us* and *them*. As Arbus remarked to *Newsweek* after the 1967 exhibition of her photographs at the Museum of Modern Art, "It's irrational to be born in a certain place and time and of a certain sex."

Perhaps this is also a reason she photographs her subjects against the blank backdrop of an open field—grass without end, a white and unremitting wall or the repetitions of brick or a night sky; and even these are most often blurred. By eliminating convenient contexts, she features instead her subjects who capture the viewer's gaze in a face-off, for the simple reason that there is nowhere else to look. Partly because the backdrops imply world without end, Arbus is able to feature the vulnerability of anyone who is far from help and home. Sometimes her subjects appear abandoned, set up for an indeterminate wait of an indeterminate nature like Samuel Beckett's roadside tramps in *Waiting for Godot*. (*GBWW* II: 60, 529–82) Perhaps a few steps outside the frame there is an attendant reaching for the reaching hand, or the hand of the mother or a god, a hand attached to the purveyor of our deepest need, a hand that will offer the unconditional embrace or open the door to safety. Perhaps. But the emptiness, the absence, garnered through Arbus's repeated use of blank backgrounds multiplies in the viewer's imagination. In an exercise in endlessness, we extend whatever field or sky beyond the limits of vision. If, in the end, it is our own hand we hold, in the interim, Arbus purchases stock in human connection as her sympathetic portrayals of need suggest. Hand in hand her subjects march across seemingly vast and uninterrupted landscapes moored by and to each other.

Consider the penultimate photograph: two figures, arms interlocked, halted in their progress by the camera's inquisitive eye. Their faces are particularly white against a background so black it conceals the demarcation between the ground and tree line. The foreground figure holds her own hands tight as she clutches her unbuttoned coat against her body. Her companion's white hand, stark against the darker sleeve, fingers curled to mirror her own, could be mistaken for her own third hand, an association the use of dark and light invites us to draw. A nice idea, a third hand—if we can forget what we have been taught—a way to recontextualize as the surrealists have done, to tear down stone by stone the wall we have built around possibility, to remind ourselves that it is, after all, only the familiar human form that Arbus reveals, albeit three-handed.

In the collection's last photograph, nine shockingly illuminated figures trail across a characteristically dark and blurred landscape. We see only the foot of the one who steps out of the frame on the right and of another who steps in on the left—a conga line with no discernible beginning or end, or the long chain of humankind in which everyone is guaranteed a link. I am moved by what I read as trust in progress, by the courage each step demands when you are mapless, when you are without a clear route or destination or guide. Again, the hands present themselves. This time I focus on the two figures whose outstretched right hands are not taken up and held, whose splayed and reaching fingers are replicated in the shadows they cast on themselves or their fellows, multiplying need as two hands become four. Their left hands partner them and hold them in place in the line. Separation. Connection. In a single image, Arbus portrays our worst fear and our greatest hope. No one seems particularly aware of the camera in this photograph, eyes fixed on some point in the distance. They are purposeful, confident in their nightclothes, but somehow small under the vast sky. It is one of those nights when the sky moves, announcing its formidable power. Our little train is also on the move, striding out toward the edge, into the white space that accommodates us all.

Great Books: My Adventures with Homer, Rousseau, Woolf, and Other Indestructible Writers of the Western World
by David Denby
(Simon and Schuster, 1996)
Reviewed by Keith S. Cleveland

n 1991 David Denby, film critic for *New York Magazine,* returned to Columbia College in Columbia University to retake two core curriculum courses he had completed thirty years before as an undergraduate. "Literature Humanities" and "Contemporary Civilization" had undergone modest changes since his first encounter with them, and Denby had undergone significant changes. His own, as he acknowledges, were at least in part the result of his first experience of the courses, though time, an active career as a journalist, marriage, children, and engagement with the political concerns of the day had all worked further transformations in him. Though less resilient than the nineteen-year-olds with whom he shared his studies, his greater experience more than made up for his return to study at age forty-eight.

Denby's skills as a writer are formidable. His book is clear, engaging, often eloquent, always passionate, and never tiresome in spite of recurrent concerns. For example, he returns to the question of "hegemony" again and again: whether the numerous injustices of modern life, actual or alleged, originate in, or are sustained by, the Western canon? He grapples with the issues, at first hesitantly but with increasing confidence, and ultimately writes an intelligent and informed defense of the books he and his fellow students studied.

His book is announced as a series of adventures. In the course of these Denby burrows into many of the greatest texts and structures his story about what he found in certain of them by reflecting upon their structure and concerns in his response. He is a skilled imitator in the sophisticated sense of one who transforms material by subjecting it to a new form. The preoccupations of former ages emerge in Denby's treatment as material to be measured and weighed, tested, and tried, principally against his own experiences, to see how useful they may be to him, his family and friends, and his community.

He absorbs and transforms what he reads by imposing a form on his experience of it that imitates the text he is discussing. *The Iliad* emerges from his pen in battle garb, provoking rebellious feelings and judgments in him (pp. 34–35). *The Odyssey* calls up his own Telemachus-like development during his years at Columbia in the early '60s, and that of his young classmates in the early '90s. Reading the *Bacchae* he discovers a shocking applicability to himself as moviegoer and movie critic, and announces a troubling perception about the deadly essence of audience members as voyeurs, the more startling because of its rise at about the time theater audiences came into being. He finds himself an outsider when he reads the New Testament parables, and is shaken ("Was it possible that I was a victim of 'hegemony' and had simply never admitted it?," p. 180), but recovers his balance after Professor Tayler's suggestions about the fundamental alteration in the idea of time and the irrelevance of dualities that are needed to grasp the working out of God's plan. His reading of *King Lear* calls forth a poignant account of the life and death of his mother, and he returns to these charged memories later in his book as prompted by the course of grief. When discussing Rousseau's revolutionary texts, he tells of his "...Rousseauian act of violence" (p. 289): throwing a tomato at Ronald Reagan, then governor of California. This story follows directly the accounts of "...my Rousseauian sex experience; my Rousseauian drug experience; and my Rousseauian speech" (p. 287).

Writing these accounts, Denby provides his classmates with pseudonyms, but uses the names of his instructors. He describes the faculty candidly, and we gain a pleasing intimacy with the three with whom he spends the most time—Edward Tayler, professor of English, Anders Stephanson, professor of history, and James Shapiro, professor of English and comparative literature. Denby notes their manner as teachers—Professor Tayler, scholarly, intricate, a "devious, devising Kronos" attentive to the details and structure of each text, schooling his students in the "Hermeneutic Circle" (pp. 32, 436); Professor Stephanson, a likeable young faculty member, passionate in his left-wing views and approach to the books, and made usefully vulnerable to the growing knowledge and rigor of his students by his political outlook; and Professor Shapiro, also a younger faculty member, whose classroom risks included allowing Denby to teach a brief, unsuccessful lesson on Jane Austen's *Pride and Prejudice* and choosing to end the year's readings with Conrad's *Heart of Darkness,* a risk that very nearly led to a fistfight in his class. In a "Point of View" article in *The Chronicle of Higher Education* (Sept. 13, 1996, p. A64) Professor Shapiro declares that on his first reading of Denby's book he "felt the rude shock of recognition—and exposure," testimony to Denby's skills.

Near the end of the first century A.D., Plutarch spent a year or more in Rome, teaching and engaging in public business for his native city of Chaeronea and possibly for the province of Greece. A number of Roman notables studied with him and continued as lifelong friends. Denby seems to me someone we can reasonably compare with these Roman nobles. As for them, there are questions of the day which are of urgent concern to every intelligent person involved with the life of his city or country. In the days of Plutarch the principal questions would surely have centered on the rival systems of ethics, the philosophical basis of these systems, its adequacy, and, given the famous practical turn of Romans, all of this centered on the general question: "What should I do?" In Denby's case, the call is less urgent. He is not as close to the actions that make the city as were the Roman nobles two millennia ago; still, he is agitated by the "culture wars" that swirl around him and wishes to form an adequate opinion about the issues of the conflict.

How profound his concern is, or even that of his teachers, we cannot be sure. In his most complete work, the *Parallel Lives,* Plutarch declares:

> It was for the sake of others that I first commenced writing biographies; but I find myself proceeding and attaching myself to it for my own; the virtues of these great men serving me as a sort of looking-glass, in which I may see how to adjust and adorn my own life. Indeed, it can be compared to nothing but daily living and associating together; we receive, as it were, in our inquiry, and entertain each successive guest, view—
> *"Their stature and their qualities,"*
> and select from their actions all that is noblest and worthiest to know.
> (*GBWW* I: 14, 195; II; 13, 195)

Absent from Denby's account is any sense that those from whom he is learning are still learning themselves. Professor Stephanson's struggles with his students' rejection of Marx, and Professor Shapiro's misjudgment as to the reception of *Heart of Darkness,* fail to convey a strong sense that these men are still at work on such authors and their books. In its place is the idea that Denby and his fellow students need to encounter these books at least once in their lives, that they are the historical basis and origin of the culture we live in, that they will be used to form our minds, that we are likely to be unsettled by them but that the experience will be a one-time thing. There is no clear expectation that the younger students will return to any but the Bible, or that the faculty would do so if their teaching responsibilities did not require it. Nor for that matter is it clear that Denby has been encouraged to do so, or that he will.

One result of this missing perception is the sense one derives from *Great Books* that the faculty think they have truly succeeded only when they have "written" their own composite book made from all the separate books examined in the two semesters. This is somehow their principal concern, rather than to allow each book in the two courses to serve as its own teacher, and should. Instead they treat it as if it had to be examined, and even interpreted, like an archaeological find that cannot speak for itself. Denby attempts his own composition of this sort in the form of an epitome near the end of his book (pp. 453–63). In his account, the faculty are the real teachers, though the students participate, and the occasions are the books that make up the reading lists.

It is true that Socrates complains about texts that they cannot answer questions (*Phaedrus, GBWW* I: 7, 139; II: 6, 139), and that he tells the myth of Theuth, who invented the alphabet with the effect of destroying men's memories (*GBWW* I: 7, 138–39; II: 6, 138–39). Plato solved this problem by constructing dialogues that by his own account, are not statements of truth or written versions of philosophy (*Seventh Letter, GBWW* I: 7, 809; II: 6, 809), but works that require the active engagement of discussion to explore their complex meanings. As Denby discovers, all of the works that make up the Columbia core reading lists involve disagreements with other works from the list. An expanded dialogue can be envisioned in the minds of readers of these books that does not require an imposed order, and that both challenges students and leaves them free to discover what the faculty may overlook.

It is difficult to gauge the origin or effects of the interpretive line followed by Denby, much less those by the faculty. It appears that Denby chose wisely in visiting many sections taught by different faculty members to sample alternative approaches. Yet he seems to remain unaware that the approaches faculty take to their teaching are probably subject to repeated discussion in faculty meetings, and consequently may be fluid. His own experience consists of (at most) brief fluidity in his understanding of the book he is reading, followed by the statement of a firm position on at least some of its important aspects. This produces an uncomfortable sense that the books are read in order that they may be put aside.

In connection with Aristotle, as with Plato before him, Denby is particularly dismissive. He reports an initial enjoyment of Aristotle heightened by its coming soon after the "fabulous nonsense" he found in Plato. It is short lived, however:

> So even as I sat reading the *Ethics* and *Poetics,* and enjoying Aristotle's plainness and efficiency, and the well-tended-garden hum of pleasure that he gave, I sensed that order was often something imposed by power—genuine enough, but not intrinsic, not natural. I wanted to unseat Aristotle, or at least to confront him. I was bored by his shrewd, very sane advice in the *Nicomachean Ethics* that we avoid the extremes of behavior and choose the "golden mean" or middle way, a mode of existence practiced by the virtuous man as a way of taming the excesses of appetite. True enough, but so what? All this platitudinous harping on virtue was perhaps the preoccupation of the ancients that was the least invigorating to modern taste. I couldn't even finish Cicero—the philosopher as after-dinner speaker—who came along a little later in the C. C. course, and who also plucked away on the virtue harp (p. 121).

The unintended ironies of this passage are remarkable. Denby's relationship to the books on these reading lists is governed by pleasure, and throughout his own book he indicates, and finally argues for, the primacy of pleasure in our relation to books, and much else as well. He seems not to have noticed that Aristotle himself is urgent in his assertion that moral virtue centers on the relationship to pleasure (*GBWW* I: 9, 350; II: 8, 390). Denby, to be fair, is sturdy and refined in his enjoyments. He is willing to work, works hard, and finds and acknowledges unexpected pleasures, just as he reports unexpected failures of pleasure (as p. 240: "My reading of Dante was a failure, and of the most direct sort: I didn't *enjoy* it"). But he has no way to account for the difference except to state it. Aristotle's insistence that virtue requires action directed to "the right objects..." (*GBWW* I: 9, 352, 54; II: 8, 352, 54) provides a complex and flexible standard for judging the worth of pleasure, particularly in its relation to action, that might have helped get Denby beyond his self-absorption.

Denby confines his discussion to works in philosophy, autobiography, literature, and the Bible, and leaves out any account of books in history, science and mathematics, and the social sciences. He is best on works of literature and autobiography. Particularly intriguing are his presentations of Homer, Sappho, Euripedes, Augustine, Boccaccio, Montaigne, Shakespeare, Austen, Conrad, and Woolf, all of whom Denby enjoyed. He is less successful with Aeschylus, Virgil, and Dante.

His encounter with philosophy produces mixed results. The three chapters on Plato and Aristotle occupy a significant portion of Denby's text, but he finds little of use in these philosophers. Machiavelli is discovered not to be the cynical advocate of murder and cruelty he is popularly believed to be, but he did miss the important issue of legitimacy in government (more Professor Stephanson's idea, it appears, than Denby's). Hume developed a way to ground ethics that avoids the difficulties associated with absolute (metaphysical) standards, but was ill-adapted to the harsh, perverse realities of modern life, in spite of which Denby "...was convinced that Hume had suggested a plausible middle way between the poles of absolutism and relativism" (p. 257). Kant is coldly abstract, sometimes impossible to understand, and the categorical imperative, central to Kant's presentation of the basis of ethics, is irrelevant to the serious matter of "choosing *among* duties" (p. 264). So it goes. Hegel is, like Kant before him, a stiff challenge to Denby's reading skills, but serves to usefully strengthen our adventurer, thus making the later reading of Marx much easier than it would otherwise have been. Nietzsche is a source of profound excitement (as are several other writers Denby discusses), but ultimately unsatisfactory in his judgment that the "...freedom and magnificent health of the few noble spirits matter more than the continued suppression of the many" (p. 372). Beauvoir, who by Professor Stephanson's account "...may have accomplished more in philosophy than Sartre" (p. 388), warns in connection with the coming decline of the patriarchy that "...this change in women's estate...might be painful" (p. 392), and this warning is borne out: "The very success of the women's movement has made their lives more difficult..." (p. 405).

As the adventurer whose path we follow, Denby is appealing, and he meets mostly appealing people along the way. Yet I could not refrain from thinking as I read that Denby needed the University of Chicago's Basic Program of Liberal Education for Adults. In that program Denby would have been spared the stresses of examinations, and he would have engaged with adults every bit as experienced and skilled as he is. The repeated reflection on nineteen-year-old classmates would have dropped out, and the encounter with the books would, I think, ultimately have been more useful to Denby. We might not have this fine book, but its author would have entered upon an experience that need not have ended with a single frenzied year of effort.

The Astonishing Hypothesis
by Francis Crick
(Charles Scribner's Sons, 1994)
Reviewed by Thomas K. Simpson

 rancis Crick, in *The Astonishing Hypothesis,* wants to get on with a piece of scientific work; his immediate aims are strategic rather than metaphysical, and indeed, he does all he can to keep the metaphysics at bay.[1] With James Watson, he once took on and mastered one of the most fundamental problems in biology: the determination of the molecular structure of DNA, the genetic molecule, work for which he shared with Watson the Nobel Prize in 1962. Now at the Salk Institute in California, Crick has embarked on a quest yet more daring: he is looking for strategies for bringing *consciousness* within the domain of scientific investigation and, ultimately, of scientific theory. Although, as I say, he is intent on devising scientific strategies which are carefully disciplined and have the best chance of succeeding in practice, he does not hesitate to raise a banner over the endeavor phrased in the boldest terms. The overall hypothesis which guides his work, one which he rightly terms "astonishing," he phrases in these terms:

> The Astonishing Hypothesis is that "You," your joys and your sorrows, your memories and your ambitions, your sense of personal identity and free will, are in fact no more than the behavior of a vast assembly of nerve cells and their associated molecules.[2]

This might seem a rash and arbitrary plunge into the midst of a long discussion of one of the oldest, and surely most interesting, of the "great questions"—that of the relation of the brain and the mind, or still more largely, of the body and the soul. Everything we most care most about is placed at stake if this terrain is once again to be thrown into question. We will have to go back to the roots of all we thought we knew, to reestablish all we believe. Yet Crick believes that the time may have come to undertake such an effort. If so, it will be what Francis Bacon called a "Work of Time"—Crick asserts that "now is the time to think scientifically about consciousness."[3] Why, we wonder, should this be so?

Western science, and all humanity, has long suffered from a terrible rift: precisely that split between body and soul which we are being asked to reconsider. The question had surely always been a real one, but if we think just of that earlier system of thought—Aristotle's *Organon,* which Francis Bacon's *New Organon* strode forward to replace—there was no rift; soul and body once lived comfortably together. All the terms in all their contexts have shifted their meanings, admittedly, since Aristotle conceived a coherent world, but from the point of view of the term *body,* or *matter,* at least one principle which drove the wedge was the concept of strict obedience on the part of matter to binding mathematical law. Since the body's course was understood after Newton to be inexorable, and *predictable,* after the paradigm of the planets, the only rescue for the free soul seemed to be absolute liberation from entrainment to the body. Newton, at the same time, thought he knew what he meant by the term body.

The body about which Crick is asking us to think is a system of neurons. Each neuron, as the middle section of his book helps us to appreciate, is a highly complex structure, while the system of which he speaks is constructed of immense numbers of these neurons, highly interconnected in intricate and changing ways. Over the pathways of this system travel what he calls the "signals" which constitute, he believes, our perceptive and cognitive mental life. The choice of the term "signals" betrays the elementary paradigm of the transmission line from which we are drawing our initial imagery, but in their subtlety and complexity, these signals become patterns, and might equally be thought of as symbols, significant words or forms. In no simple way will their behavior be predictable, not only because they escape us in their multiplicity but because, as we are now beginning to recognize, the behaviors of systems of this order are not in principle predictable. Perhaps, then, the supposed rift of body and soul is not as absolute as we had imagined.

Initially, there might seem reason to fear that the very concept of the scientific method would be thrown into jeopardy by this kind of effort: can consciousness be fitted into the disciplines of responsible science? There would be greater reason for concern if we were not in the hands of Francis Crick. The speculations above are mine; Crick tends to get to work on the science itself, and in this book designed for the general reader, to show in a few examples how it will be possible to work in a strictly scientific vein on the relation of brain and mind. The basic strategy is to look empirically for evidence of the neural correlates of consciousness. There is, Crick insists, nothing obscure about consciousness: it is exactly that about which we know most, and most directly. Although we cannot observe each other's consciousness, we can report well enough in common terms, and, as Crick insists, science has no need to stop to resolve the problem which he calls that of *qualia*—whether the red you see is the same as the red I see.

In order to consider how this might work in the scientific laboratory, let us look at just one of several experiments which Crick sets out for our consideration—we may refer to it as "Experiment Alpha."[4] His descriptions are succinct, and supported by clear and very helpful descriptions and diagrams of our cortical structures. Here, it will be enough to give a highly schematic account, one that will serve for present purposes as the paradigmatic experiment in the consciousness lab. It may be surprising to discover that we will work with an animal model, but that is exactly what we do in most conventional neural experiments, as we know much more about the brains of our brothers and sisters, the rats, mice, and macaques of this world, than we do about ours—feeling, as we do, freer to poke into theirs in detail rather than into our own.[5] In this matter of consciousness, as in other aspects of psychology, we may take their experiences to be good models of our own in many respects, and in particular, we will feel confident that they experience consciousness as we do—for example, of visual patterns of which they evidence awareness.

Experiment Alpha, then, is based on the useful ability, which it appears that cats have, to sleep with their eyes open. We can thus set them to observing a standardized visual pattern first while in deep sleep, and then again after being wakened. It is exactly the difference between these two states that interests us, for it crosses the gap between the absence and the presence of consciousness. Expert neuroscientists have electrical probes inserted into the visual areas of the cat's cortex and are sampling the signals from selected neurons, in each case first asleep, then awake, in a search for differences. Any such difference will be a clue to the neural correlate of consciousness. Experiment Alpha has been successfully carried out, and does, indeed, reveal such an interesting difference, with more activity in certain deeper cortical layers during consciousness.

Crick is writing as a scientist, though in this fascinating book, a speculative and deliberately provocative one. We, however, in this generous company of the great books, are surely invited to follow the suggestion of this paradigmatic experiment in a spirit of intellectual adventure, to see where it might take us. Let us suppose that many experiments of this and other sorts have proven successful, so that it has indeed been established that cortical activities of certain types in spatial areas or patterns correlate regularly with a corresponding repertory of conscious experiences. We may as well go the whole way, and suppose that in general, all conscious experience is shown, in a series of experiments from Alpha to Omega, to correlate with corresponding states of neural systems. Where will this discovery leave us? How might we best express such an outcome?

Crick has proposed that we *are* our neurons, and now we see what this might come to mean in laboratory terms. Every mode in which we know ourselves has, we envision with Crick, some corresponding state of our neural systems. A proper formulation of this might seem to be that all of my conscious life is a history of states of my particular system of neurons. Crick speaks at times of scientific "explanation," but I think the suggestion of "explanation" is hardly helpful here. Rather, our scientific picture of the world is being filled in. Great progress would be made, nonetheless, in our metaphysics if Crick's hypothesis plays out to such a conclusion, for we will then have a consistent mode of speaking of the relation of body and soul. The interesting "body" in question is the neural system of the cortex, the most intensely energetic focus of the living organism. Certain of the states of activity of this system *are* states of consciousness, and since we would once have called these states of consciousness, states of the *soul*, the soul now has no place to hide. It *is* the underlying, universal state of this special living system; we meet it in prayer or contemplation.

All the apparently reductive aspects of the *Astonishing Hypothesis* have been shaken off, and no longer need worry us; we are now left with something truly interesting. We have long since noticed that, with the happy abandonment of the illusions of earlier centuries concerning something to be called "matter," *form* is a term far more appropriate to the quantum systems which underlie our present concept of the physical world. Plato and the *Timaeus* offer far better clues to our understanding of ourselves and our physical world than do Hobbes and Locke.[6]

The system of my neurons, unified in binding continuity through a lifetime as well, is as we know from Crick's own work, an expression of my DNA, that unbelievably detailed and active living pattern of my being. Thus that neural system which on the *Astonishing Hypothesis* bears my conscious states is but the structure tossed up for my lifetime out of a quasi-timeless system of the DNA—crossing with other such DNA systems by way of the matings through the generations, before and after my own. Each lifetime spelled out by the DNA is, then, bearer of a soul as the unity of all its possible conscious states, and all its states over that lifetime are the history of another individual consciousness. In a way, it seems, Plato had that approximately right, too.[7]

Crick places emphasis perhaps too exclusively on the brain—the soul and consciousness may appear to reside there, but the relation of the brain to the larger body and through it to the world must be essential to our grasp of the meaning of consciousness. It is the world which we are conscious of, the world which has deposited its forms in the forms our neural system takes—our neural system and its states surely model the cosmos, from the human perspective. Crick is very carefully taking only the first steps, but we can see that he is as yet leaving out what must be the most important element of all; he is taking us in our perceptive and cognitive functions, and leaving out love. Our neural systems are activated and modulated in all their functions by that other, no less interesting and indeed inseparable chemical system, the hormonal messengers, transmitters, inhibitors, and activators, each with its sources and targets both in the brain and throughout the body. Yes, consciousness may indeed be a domain of states of the neural system, but as soon as we become interested in life as we know it, the whole immensely integrated organism must be taken into account.[8]

There is another cautionary note to be sounded when we speak of the behavior of systems, neural or otherwise. We have only recently begun to appreciate how richly interesting even the simplest systems may prove to be. Our neural system obviously operates to a large extent in the domain of behaviors we now call "chaotic," and we are beginning to understand that this is by no means a matter of bad news. The chaotic state, seated in a gray area of semi-indeterminacy, is at the same time poised on the edge of restructuring in an island of attraction. I, for one, know too little to speak further about this, but I am prepared as one witness to assert that such mental "drifting" or anticipation feels very familiar to me, and I can see it as the threshold and key to what we think of as learning, mental "restructuring," and creative composition—terrain of the Muses, we might imagine. It is this kind of hint which seems to me to make Crick's *Astonishing Hypothesis* especially interesting. If it turns out that we "are" our neurons, we may have nothing to lose by the discovery!

A great deal of work is being done in the field of research into consciousness, and developments are sure to come rapidly and to move the theory in exciting directions beyond those suggested here. We armchair observers will do well to keep a sharp eye on this unfolding show, and to exercise our special privilege as readers of the great books to speculate largely on the possible meaning of these developments. Francis Crick's book makes a very good platform for launching such an enterprise.

1. Francis Crick, *The Astonishing Hypothesis: The Scientific Search for the Soul* (New York: Charles Scribner's Sons, 1994).

2. op. cit., p. 4

3. op. cit., p. xii.

4. Our "Experiment Alpha" was actually performed by M. S. Livingston and D. H. Hubel: "Effects of sleep and arousal on the processing of visual information in the cat," *Nature,* vol. 291, 1981, pp. 554–61.

5. Not all experiments involve animal models, nor do all involve the measurement of neural signals. Crick describes fascinating examples of simple experiments with human subjects, who need only report what they experience under controlled circumstances.

6. I have suggested this line of thought in a series of articles in past volumes of *The Great Ideas Today,* under the title "The New Pythagoreans." The first essay of the series dealt directly with the *Timaeus* (*GIT* 1988, 162–22) while the third concerned "The Scientists of the Mind" (*GIT* 1990, 174–221 and *GIT* 1991, 142–99). The *Timaeus* is to be found in *GBWW* I: 7, 442–77; II: 6, 442–77.

7. *Compare* the story or the continuity of births and rebirths, as told in Plato's *Republic.*

8. Two works which do tend to point to this larger scope of the problem, and which I have found stimulating, are Jean-Pierre Changeux, *Neuronal Man: The Biology of Mind* (New York: Oxford University Press, 1985); and Richard Bergland, *The Fabric of Mind* (New York: Penguin Books, 1988). Crick rightly remarks of the Changeux volume that it has "rather little to say about consciousness," but I suggest that it serves to remind us of the ultimate scope of the hypothesis Crick is proposing.

PICTURE CREDITS